# The Connoisseurs' Handbook

# of the Wines of California

# and the Pacific Northwest

Symbols used in this book to evaluate wine quality and aging characteristics are as follows:

| | |
|---|---|
| 8̶9̶ | below-average quality, a wine to avoid |
| 93 | a wine of average quality |
| ❀ | a fine example of a given type or style, an above-average wine |
| ❀ ❀ | a very fine wine, likely to be memorable |
| ❀ ❀ ❀ | an exceptional wine, worth a special search |

---

| | |
|---|---|
| **88** | a wine now past its peak |
| **93** | ready to drink now |
| **91** | drinkable now, but will improve with further aging |
| **94** | needs further aging before drinking |

The wine rating system appears mainly in the WINERIES AND WINES chapter, which begins on p. 115.

# The Connoisseurs' Handbook
# of the Wines of California
# and the Pacific Northwest

by Norman S. Roby
and Charles E. Olken

ALFRED A. KNOPF   NEW YORK

1999

THIS IS A BORZOI BOOK
PUBLISHED BY ALFRED A. KNOPF, INC.

Copyright © 1991, 1993, 1995, 1998
by Norman S. Roby and Charles E. Olken
Maps copyright © 1991 by Jean Paul Tremblay

Library of Congress Cataloging-in-Publication Data

Roby, Norman S.
The connoisseurs' handbook of the wines of California and the Pacific
Northwest / by Norman S. Roby and Charles E. Olken. —4th ed.
p.     cm.
Rev. ed. of: The new connoisseurs' handbook of California wines.
3rd ed., 1995.
ISBN 0-375-70329-2 (alk. paper)
1. Wine and wine making—California.   2. Wine and wine making—
Washington (State).   3. Wine and wine making—Oregon.   I. Olken,
Charles E.   II. Roby, Norman S. New connoisseurs' handbook of
California wines.   III. Title.
TP557.R63   1998
641.2′2′0979—dc21          98-6375
CIP

Manufactured in the United States of America

Published December 12, 1991
Fourth Edition, October 1998
Second Printing, March 1999

# Contents

# Introduction to the Fourth Edition

In 1991, when the first edition of this book appeared, the California wine industry had just about reached the lowest point of a down-cycle. Sales were flat, the dreaded phylloxera pest was eating its way through many prime North Coast vineyards, and most winery owners were struggling along just to eke out a living. As this edition goes to press, California's winemakers and their Northwest colleagues are all smiles, happy just to be part of the booming wine business. Overall, sales have been setting records for several years, and the industry is growing as fast as it can to keep pace with the unprecedented demand. The present up-cycle has been an unusually long but enjoyable ride that has positioned the 1990s as one of the most dynamic decades in the history of California wine.

"It is," as winemakers are fond of saying, "a great time to be making wine." They are also well aware that cycles of boom-and-bust are as common to the wine business as they are to other agricultural products. Recent advances in winemaking have enabled vintners to produce soft, user-friendly red wines like Merlot, Zinfandel, and Pinot Noir. More recent technological breakthroughs in grape growing have allowed winemakers to squeeze out exquisite, distinctive flavors from special vineyard sites planted to Cabernet Sauvignon, Chardonnay, and other noble wines.

Still, important as these dramatic quality improvements are, the current boom also owes more than a little to external developments. High on the list are the numerous reports from the medical and scientific community documenting the potential health benefits of moderate consumption of wine in general and red wine in particular. The "it's okay to drink a glass of wine at mealtime" message has undoubtedly brought many new people into the wine-drinking fold. This new understanding came about, moreover, at the same time that adults of all ages were doing much better financially and had more disposable income. With the strong 90s economy providing baby boomers and Gen-Xers the money for discretionary products like wine, the cycle of boom and growth really kicked in with a vengeance.

Spurred on by this strong consumer demand, winemakers have been busily changing the California winescape by replanting old vineyards and developing new ones. Throughout the 90s, both diseased vines and those deemed inappropriate for the given location have been systematically replaced. Applying the latest in viticultural technology, growers have designed vineyards to take full advantage of each specific site to limit crop size and improve grape and wine quality. Among the new tools available to growers are a variety of much-improved rootstocks, a wider-than-ever selection of clones, trellis systems that train the vine to grow upright for improved air circulation, and close vine spacing configurations that limit the crop and concentrate flavors in the grapes.

As they replanted—and to date more than 60% of all North Coast vineyards have been replanted since 1990—growers seized the opportunity to align the varietal mix with the market. In the process, California has added thousands of acres of Chardonnay, Merlot, Cabernet Sauvignon, and Zinfandel, the most in-demand wines of the decade. Before too long, Merlot acreage was rapidly closing in on Zinfandel, which was for many years the most widely planted red grape. Other varieties once labeled esoteric were given a new and fresh look during the replanting stages. The results were impressive, and today Viognier, Sangiovese, and Syrah, once planted only in minuscule amounts, have evolved into established varietals.

Throughout the current decade, vineyards have expanded in both new areas and established ones. In Napa and Sonoma counties, one may get the impression that every available hill and valley has either been planted to vineyards or soon will be. As the dust settles in the Napa Valley after a decade of replanting, this historic district is emerging with a different look. Over half of its vineyards are now planted to Cabernet Sauvignon and Merlot, the prized varieties upon which, above all, the fame of Napa Valley rests. And Chardonnay and Pinot Noir, which were once planted in every corner of the valley, are now concentrated in the Carneros and other cooler southern sites better suited to their needs. Sonoma County has been following a similar pattern, with Pinot Noir and Chardonnay expanded in the Russian River Valley and other cool coastal locations, and Cabernet Sauvignon, Merlot, and Zinfandel increasing their acreage in Sonoma Valley, Dry Creek Valley, and Alexander Valley. As the wine boom continued in the late 90s, growers in Washington State began major vineyard expansion, led by their trump card, Merlot. Though its production is comparatively small, Washington is capable of providing Merlot that can hold its own with California's best.

Along the West Coast, the biggest vineyard makeover of all occurred in Lodi, a warm inland region south of Sacramento. Over the last decade, growers in this historic dessert-wine and brandy-producing region have been ferociously converting vineyards to classic varieties. At present, Lodi is the state's leading supplier of Merlot, Chardonnay, and Zinfandel, most of which is used to produce modestly priced varietals.

To winemakers, the most endearing aspect of this decade is the number of good-to-excellent vintages produced. So far there have been two pairs of back-to-back excellent vintages, 1990 and 1991, and 1994 and 1995. For an industry in the throes of major readjustments in terms of vineyards, regions, and varietals, the timing could not have been better. From the spectacular 1991 vintage for red wines to the incredible 1994 harvest which brought out the best in virtually all varieties, California had the big guns to compete with the world's finest in terms of quality. To win over holdouts from the baby-boomers' heyday, and the untapped, seemingly anti-establishment membership of Generation X, California had at the ready wines from some of the finest vintages in its history. Along the way, as the consumer base increased, California wine began developing a following among a growing number of collectors, and even those with a speculator's bent began looking into California wine for its investment potential.

California wine has definitely become a world-class force. Despite plenty of trade barriers and red tape, the export market has improved dramatically, rising 400% over the years from 1988 to 1997. Today wines from California can be found in retail stores in over 160 countries. The largest single share of these exports goes to the United Kingdom—an accomplishment in which California vintners take great pride, because it is generally agreed that the U.K. is the most competitive wine market in the world. Other highlights of the export scene are healthy recent increases in Japan, Taiwan, and Hong Kong. All indicators suggest that these and other markets are likely to see California wine in greater quantities in the years ahead.

Even when it comes to high-priced wines, California's finest are challenging the French in that arena as well. While Pinot Noir priced at over $30 a bottle and Zinfandel at over $20 are not uncommon today, it is Cabernet Sauvignons, particularly those from the Napa Valley, that have made especially impressive showings. Many of these Cabernets are finding a ready and eager market at prices of $50 a bottle on up to whatever the market will bear. Several small wineries enjoying cult status sell every bottle made even when priced at over $100 a bottle.

Looking back as the 90s draw to a close, we find a scene so transformed that the California wine industry may be said to have practically reinvented itself. To aid readers in understanding all the changes and in enjoying to the full the fine wines of California and the Northwest, this Fourth Edition provides the most up-to-date information about producers, appellations, and vintages. We have expanded the winery section by over 100 enterprises in California, and close to 50 in the Northwest. To help you wend your way through the many new wines from both established and new vintners, we have added hundreds of wine reviews.

June 1998

# Introduction

Compared to the world's other great wine-producing regions, California has a remarkably short history. Time is measured here not by centuries but by decades. Yet it is clear that today California wines can hold their own in company with the world's best, and much of this achievement is relatively recent.

It was not until the 70s that the wines of California began to attract the attention of serious wine lovers. Enjoying the role of underdog, the upstarts from California continued to challenge the old order throughout the 80s. They frequently left their mark, opening eyes and shaking old assumptions, even those of inveterate Francophiles. Now, as the pace of change slows somewhat in the 90s, it is at last possible to get a sense of what has been done—and what may be done in the future.

As will be seen from the size of this book compared to the original *Connoisseurs' Handbook* published in 1980, the sheer number of producers has increased dramatically. Nearly twice as many individuals and companies are making wine now as were a decade ago. The majority of the new names combine limited volume with great ambition. At the other extreme, an important trend of the 80s was the acquisition of California wineries and vineyards by international companies headquartered in the United Kingdom, Japan, Germany, France, Switzerland, and elsewhere.

Changes in wine geography have paralleled to some degree the changes in personalities and ownership. New wine-growing regions such as the Edna Valley and Santa Maria Valley have been developed and many of their wines are now earning accolades alongside those from the better-known valleys in Napa and Sonoma counties. In short, where once the California wine scene was relatively uncomplicated, there is now a maze of names and places capable of challenging the attention and memory of any wine buff.

The quality and character of California wines continue to reflect this dynamic background. At the beginning of the 80s the style of California wine was moving away from the heaviness that characterized many offerings of the 70s. After a brief flirtation with lighter, less ripe "food wines" that often proved to be thin and uninteresting, California's winemakers continued throughout the 80s to experiment, refining their techniques and winemaking procedures. By the end of that decade, it was obvious that overall standards had risen to a point where mediocre wines could no longer be blamed on lack of experience or error.

What we have today, therefore, is a wine scene that demands a balanced critical approach. Some producers have clearly emerged as quality leaders while others are just as clearly mired in inconsistency, or worse. The consumer deserves to know which is which. This book is intended to help him or her to do just that, and to make sense out of the entire business of California and West Coast wines, from grapes to growing areas to production techniques to the finished wines themselves.

We begin with the technology of winemaking, an area in which winemakers from California and the Northwest are rightly regarded as world leaders. The first chapter, BASICS OF WINEMAKING, covers such topics as fermentation, aging, and bottling in a comprehensive way. By detailing the options and choices open to winemakers throughout the entire process, it offers wine drinkers the opportunity to understand some of the behind-the-scenes activities and provides insights into the language of winemaking. The next chapter, Grapes and Wine Types, contains essential information about every grape variety planted, ranging from the long-established Cabernet Sauvignon and Zinfandel to such less familiar names as Viognier and Nebbiolo, increasingly grown in West Coast vineyards. Also included are full explanations of all the wine types and wine names seen on labels.

The third chapter, WINE GEOGRAPHY, examines the increasing importance of California's grape-growing locations, with particular attention given to officially designated Viticultural Areas, the emerging appellations of the West Coast. It is a sign of California's coming of age that so many regions have been carved out and planted to those varieties best suited to the growing conditions. After a period of random plantings in the 70s that led to hit-or-miss results, new vineyard developments have kept quality grape-growing practices in mind. Unfortunately, the White Zinfandel boom and the as-yet-unchecked demand for Chardonnay and Cabernet Sauvignon sometimes led to the planting of these varieties in inappropriate locations. This chapter is a guide to all areas in which grapes are grown, and wherever possible spells out the characteristics and relative merits of the wines from each place name.

The fourth chapter, Vintage Commentary, deals with the effects of weather on the vintages. Each year presents growers with a new set of conditions, and the differences in grape quality from one year to the next add up to qualitative differences in the wine produced. Such differences particularly include the aging characteristics of given wines, so our vintage discussion touches on the relative ageworthiness of those wines likely to benefit from aging—Chardonnay, Cabernet Sauvignon, Merlot, Pinot Noir, and Zinfandel.

Producers and their wines represent the central focus of this book. In the chapter WINERIES AND WINES, each winery receives its own entry and its wines are reviewed in detail. The chapter has two sections. The first, *California*, is a statewide comprehensive listing of producers, special trademarks, and labels. Each entry provides a profile of the winery—its history, its special interests, its goals, and its quality performance—followed by a review of those wines with some sort of track record. The second section, *The Northwest*, presents the same information for that up-and-coming region. Though the annual output of Oregon, Washington, and Idaho together pales in comparison to that of California, each of these states has a nucleus of pioneering and committed wineries.

The sixth chapter, THE PRODUCERS RATED, extends the critiques of individual wines reviewed in the previous chapter. Here will be found comparative ratings of virtually all experienced producers in seven major categories of varietals and sparkling wines. Producers are ranked according to the quality of their Chardonnay, Sauvignon Blanc, Cabernet Sauvignon, Pinot Noir, Merlot, Zinfandel, and sparkling wine output. Best Buys are indicated. This section serves as a quick review and easy reference guide.

Our final chapter deals with wine terms. WINE LANGUAGE presents definitions for all the words and phrases likely to be found on labels, and also covers all of the sensory terms used regularly to describe the appearance, smell, taste, feel, and aftertaste of wine, especially those employed in the hundreds of critical evaluations in this book.

Our intention in *The Connoisseurs' Handbook* is to provide useful information in a comprehensive yet easily accessible form. Each section approaches the California or Northwest wine scene from a specific angle; yet together they comprise a complete guide to the wines of the West. We hope this book leads to a greater understanding of California wines and the wines of the Northwest. Even more, we hope it leads to the greater enjoyment of them.

---

The wine ratings and descriptions in this book are based substantially on evaluations that appear in *Connoisseurs' Guide to California Wine,* a monthly newsletter edited and published by Charles Olken and Earl Singer and distributed only by subscription. A one-year subscription is $50. Each year the *Guide* reviews up to 2,000 wines, mostly vintage-dated varietals. Readers of this *Handbook* interested in learning more about the *Guide* may receive a free copy of the latest issue by writing to *Connoisseurs' Guide to California Wine,* P.O. Box V, Alameda, California 94501.

---

# The Connoisseurs' Handbook
## of the Wines of California
## and the Pacific Northwest

# Basics of

# Winemaking

How a wine is made, especially a fine, priceworthy wine, does influence the way it tastes. However, winemaking techniques are not regarded in the same light in Europe as they are in the United States. In general, the technical side of winemaking takes on far greater importance in the United States among both winemakers and consumers.

In Europe, where most fine wines are identified by the name of the growing region, the internal regulations and traditions of the region often predetermine how the wine must be made. Little latitude is allowed for variation and experimentation. As a result, there is some reasonable expectation that every distinctive Vouvray, Pouilly-Fumé, or Puligny-Montrachet should have a particular taste. Champagne is an extreme case, in which every producer must follow the same specified procedures. Thus the region and the growing conditions during a given year take top billing as the most important variables in European wines.

California winemakers, on the other hand, are not bound by tradition. By using different techniques, producers can radically change the style of wine from one vintage to the next, or else experiment in subtle ways or explore various combinations in hopes of finding something different or better. Sometimes they test what consumers prefer by offering a single varietal made using several different techniques. It is becoming common, for example, for a winery to make a Cabernet Sauvignon aged in American oak barrels and another Cabernet Sauvignon aged entirely in French oak from the same vintage and region. Similarly, a growing number of winemakers are making a Reserve-style Chardonnay that is 100% barrel fermented in new French oak, and an additional Chardonnay from the same vintage and region that is partially barrel-fermented in older, neutral flavored barrels. Therefore, with such latitude given to winemakers, wines from a certain place—Napa Valley or Central Coast—are not required to conform to a regional norm. The consumer has no assurances as to what to expect in terms of taste and style by geographical names alone.

One key indicator of how a given wine will taste is knowledge of how it was made. Who made it, the producer's name, remains the most important information provided on the label, especially if that producer is well established and has been consistent. Otherwise, details of production methods may provide clues.

Winemakers in the United States seem to be quite chatty when they talk about their wines, either in person or in print. Labels often describe the residual sugar or what type of fermentation was employed. Back labels often go on at length about the blending procedures, the yeast strain, and the aging regime.

To help you wend your way through this fascinating aspect of California wines, the following section divides winemaking into its five primary functions, discussing all the related concepts and defining the terminology involved. The sequence is that of winemaking itself: crushing and pressing; fermentation; clarification; aging and blending; and, finally, stabilizing and bottling.

# Crushing

After grapes have been harvested, the first stage in winemaking is extracting their juice. The most common method for obtaining juice from grapes is known as crushing. Pressing is a second method, while the third is the old-fashioned way still practiced in remote parts of the wine world, treading or stomping grapes. When ripe, grapes are plump and their skins so soft that they can be broken easily. Both grapes and juice are vulnerable to deterioration. During crushing, therefore, which is far less brutal than the term suggests, winemakers are careful to avoid any delays. The juice, moreover, must be extracted without breaking the bitter seeds, or "pips," which most wine grapes contain. The stems that hold each grape to the spinelike clusters must normally be detached and discarded because they too may contribute bitterness to wines. With improvements made in modern crushing machinery, the process has become both standardized and continuous as the equipment separates the grapes from the stems, breaks the grape skins without damaging the seeds, and ejects the stems.

In California, the juice for still (nonsparkling) wines is usually obtained through a crushing and pressing combination. A typical large winery prefers high-capacity crushers for the sake of speed, and generally employs at least two sets of crushers for making red and white wines. This avoids color problems in the white wines. The crushing stations usually consist of a receiving hopper with the actual crushing device concealed below. Because grapes are normally delivered in trucks, crush equipment is often located outdoors, near the fermentation areas and connected to the winery through large pipes known as "must lines." The actual crushers consist of paddles and/or nylon rollers through which grapes are pushed, breaking the skins. Inside the crusher, surrounding the paddles is a stainless-steel or nylon-perforated drum, which immediately receives the juice, skins, seeds, and any leaves. The drum rotates so that the juice, seeds, and skins easily fall through the holes to a basin beneath, while the stems and leaves, which are too large to slip through, stay inside. In most crushers, the stems are immediately expelled from the machine and trucked away. The majority of winemakers favor this system, in which the grapes are crushed and de-stemmed in a continuous process.

Visitors to most wineries won't see the actual crushing, which takes place within a covered cylinder. What is visible is the receiving hopper into which the grape clusters are dumped. Inside the hopper, a large rotating auger collects the grapes and feeds them steadily to the crusher. Once the grapes are dumped into the hopper, the process becomes a continuous one. An average-sized winery crusher is capable of receiving and crushing about 40 tons per hour. Large-volume wineries can set up larger units and process as many as 150 tons an hour. A ton of grapes yields somewhere between 60 to 70 cases of wine.

In the 90s, many winemakers began favoring winery designs with extremely gentle crusher/de-stemmer systems for red wines. Though varying from one winery to the next, these new crushers which discard the stems allow a high percentage (50–100%) of the whole berries to remain uncrushed. The reason for doing this is to end up with must and wines with negligible extraction of tannin and bitter compounds from the skins.

While the majority of all wines made in California begin with crushing, noteworthy exceptions exist. Occasionally, a winemaker decides that crushing is not the best method of extracting the juice for a particular wine. In the process of crushing, juice inevitably spends some time in contact with the grape skins. This can contribute both color and possibly some degree of bitter flavor, depending upon the length of exposure and the temperature of the grapes. (Most winemakers prefer handling grapes that are relatively cool, so they harvest in the early morning to avoid the transfer of excessive color from the skins to the juice.) The main reason to avoid crushing, therefore, is to minimize color and bitter components in the juice; these can show up in the finished wine.

## Pressing

The most common alternative to crushing is pressing. The basic mechanics of pressing involve forcing the just-harvested grapes against an immovable object to extract juice through pressure. The pressure applied can be regulated so that the amount of juice extracted is also controllable. To put it simply, the more pressure applied, the more juice extracted. But the juice quality may decline.

Sometimes grapes are so fat and juicy that little external effort is required to start the juice flowing. When grapes are piled high, the weight of the grapes alone may be sufficient to break the skins. In winemaking circles, this juice that flows easily with little or no external pressure is known as free-run juice. As the amount of pressure used in a winepress increases, so does the likelihood that the juice will contain unwanted flavor compounds. Under extreme pressure, grape skins can be so severely pressed that they shred and release harsh, bitter flavors; but with light or only medium pressure, unwanted compounds can be wholly or at least partly avoided. In winemaking, the juice from heavy pressure may be used as some percentage of the blend or not at all. Pressing brings a great range of options to winemakers.

The modern winepress has evolved from the often-depicted wooden slotted basket press, with its ratchet handle, into a highly sophisticated and versatile technological tool. Historically, the press was used to extract as much juice from the grapes as possible. In the early days of winemaking, most white wine grapes went directly into a winepress prior to fermentation. The basket press would exert downward pressure and juice would escape through the slots. The pressure was first limited to human muscle, and later increased by mechanical means. Since all of the activities can be easily visible and therefore monitored, a basket press remains perfectly suited for small-batch efforts and, in fact, is used by some small wineries. It is also well known to many home winemakers for its reliability. Large-capacity basket presses are still used in the French region of Champagne by many famous, well-financed producers who believe that for them the best-quality juice is obtained by means of pressing.

Large-volume producers intent on capturing every possible ounce of juice from the grape, regardless of quality, inspired the development of an efficient winepress known as the continuous screw press. Though widely used for many years, this press is not really suited for high-quality wines. In the screw press, grapes are placed in one end of a cylinder and pushed under pressure to be compressed at the other end. As the grape skins become compacted, potentially good wine is often pushed through potentially harmful skins, seeds, and other solids. As a result, quality is highly variable. The early design of the screw press did not allow for tight control over the degree of pressure, and all wine varieties ended up by being treated the same way. Some fared better than others. Still, with varieties intended for jug-wine quality the screw-type press works well enough even today.

In the late 60s and early 70s many winemakers working for small-volume wineries adopted a relatively new press, the bladder press, in which an inflatable bladder pushes the grapes against a perforated outer drum. Recovered juice slides through the holes and into a pan beneath. This kind of winepress applies pressure evenly, and is programmable, meaning it can be adjusted to suit each grape variety. One major drawback is that it must be carefully cleaned after each batch. Another drawback is that the same perforations which allow juice to escape also allow air to enter, which can possibly oxidize the juice. Nevertheless, bladder presses remain widely used today throughout the West Coast for both red and white varieties.

By the early 80s, another kind of winepress called a tank press was being installed in California wineries. Early versions were designed in Germany by the Wilmes Company. A Swiss firm, Bucher, soon developed a following for its tank presses. This type of press eliminates the problems of the bladder press because it is a single unit that becomes airtight once the only access door is shut. Instead of a bladder, this press uses a membrane that applies very gentle pressure (30 psi maximum) to the grapes. The tank press can handle batches of different sizes and does not need to be full to operate. According to winemakers, juice coming out of a tank press is freer from solids than is juice from the same varieties coming from other types of press. (To winemakers, "grape solids" means all constituents other than juice, such as skins, seeds, and pulp; juice with many solids often ferments rapidly, but not cleanly.)

To those who look to the bottom line, the best feature is that the tank press is capable of extracting a high percentage of wine or juice at much lower pressure levels. As a result, the quality level of the juice is higher overall. With the use of tank presses, the yield per ton is increased, and the quantity is especially higher for white varieties. This obviously makes tank presses even more appealing to winery owners. At first the tank press appealed for use with small batches, but success soon encouraged the installation of large-scale, 45-ton-capacity versions. Smaller tank presses, however, can be portable, and some winemakers enjoy being able to bring the press to the grapes rather than moving the grapes to the press. All of the screw- and most of the bladder-type presses are too heavy to move.

Regardless of their type, all winepresses are capable of performing a variety of functions, and winemakers use them at different stages of the winemaking process. In actual practice, it is important to emphasize that pressing is most often used in conjunction with, not in place of, crushing. However, as noted, the major reason for sometimes preferring pressing over crushing is that it allows greater control over the quality of the juice when bitterness and astringency are to be avoided. With white grapes, pressing the whole fruit allows for quick removal of the juice and thus avoids any skin contact or maceration effect. At warm temperatures this can contribute unwanted components to some of the more delicate and fragile wines, such as Chardonnay, Johannisberg Riesling, and especially sparkling wine made from Pinot Noir and Pinot Blanc grapes.

There are other winemaking situations in which pressing plays a vital role. Besides the initial extraction of juice from grapes, pressing also comes into play when winemakers want to recover finished red wine trapped in solids following fermentation, or to remove red wine from the solids during fermentation. The solids consist of skins, seeds, yeasts, and sometimes stems, and are commonly known as pomace. They contribute color, flavor, and aroma components, along with less desirable bitter notes.

In making red wines, pressing is typically employed when fermentation is completed or nearly so. After the free run has been removed by siphoning it above the sediment level, some remaining wine is trapped within the mass of grape skins. The volume trapped, as much as 15% of the total yield, can represent a significant value to the winery. To separate the usable wine from the skins, the entire remaining mass (pomace) is pumped or shoveled from the fermenters into a press. The wine recovered from the skins is known as press wine. In earlier presses, press wine was coarser and heavier than free-run wine, as well as darker and more tannic. Since the winepresses available today can be both efficient and gentle, the quality of press red wine may be almost indistinguishable from that of free run.

The color of red wines, pink wines, and Blanc de Noirs (blush types) may be readily controlled with the aid of a winepress. The red skins used to make these wines need to be removed immediately after the desired color has been obtained; normally this occurs a few hours after fermentation has begun. Typically, the free-run juice is drained and the rest of the fermenting wine is pumped to a press which separates more—and darker-colored—wine from the skins. Then, with the two lots blended, the properly pink or tinted wine continues to ferment for as long as the winemaker wants it to, or until all of the naturally fermentable sugar is used up.

In the production of sparkling wine, pressing is one of the keys to fine quality. The tiny bubbles of carbon dioxide trapped in Champagne bottles act like amplifiers, broadcasting every little defect in the wine. Therefore, right from the beginning, Champagne makers rely on pressing to give them juice with as little color and the lowest percentage of bitter flavors and grape solids possible. Those adhering to the traditional *méthode champenoise* process harvest grapes from very cool growing regions, when they are physiologically "ripe" but low in sugar, tiny, and thick-skinned. Traditionally, the grapes are harvested in the cool early morning, and then they are not crushed, but rather pressed whole. With most winepresses, Champagne makers can separate the free-run, light-press, medium-press, and heavy-press batches, and use only the desirable components. The portions of juice removed in segments from a press are known in wine talk as fractions. Overall, through selection of the fractions, the initial juice chosen for sparkling wine production is said to be cleaner, meaning freer from bitter and astringent components. Additionally, Champagne makers insist on pressing to avoid excess coloration of the juice. As greater and greater amounts of red varieties such as Pinot Noir become used in sparkling wine production, the winepress is becoming even more valuable for its ability to extract juice while not taking too much color from the skins.

# Fermentation

Wine is the result of fermentation, a natural process in which the sweet juice of grapes is converted into alcohol, carbon dioxide, and another entirely different liquid through the action of yeast and other microflora. Fermentation is a natural biochemical reaction that brings us many delightful edibles, such as bread and cheese, and many potables, including beer and wine. The enzymes in yeast are the crucial ingredients; but when the fermentation is intended to produce alcohol, the other essential is sugar, helped along by inorganic and organic nutrients. Grapes used for wine contain both yeast and sugar, so it is no surprise that wine has been around for a long time. In simplest terms, fermentation occurs when the yeast metabolizes the sugar and in the process converts it into carbon dioxide and ethanol, an alcohol. As soon as all available sugar has been consumed, the yeasts stop working. With a little luck, the liquid that was once grape juice has been converted into flavorful wine.

What we normally refer to as fermentation is known to winemakers technically as the primary fermentation. Actually, this "primary" fermentation is a complex biological and biochemical process, consisting of numerous intermediate reactions. About 55 to 60% of the sugar in grapes, a combination of fructose and dextrose, is converted into alcohol by the yeasts, with the remaining 40 to 45% becoming carbon dioxide that escapes into the air. In addition, many side reactions during the fermentation create aroma compounds known as esters, and flavor compounds known as congeners. At its most active stage, fermentation generates considerable heat.

A typical fermentation starts slowly, as the yeast cells begin to work, and builds to an active tumultuous stage, only to slow down as the amount of available sugar and nutrients diminishes. Before winemakers were able to manipulate temperature and ferment wines cold, a typical fermentation would last from five to seven days from beginning to end. Cold fermentations proceed more slowly and last longer than warm ones, sometimes extending for two to three weeks or more. However, the yeasts don't always cooperate by starting things smoothly and continuing without a hitch. They often refuse to work at temperatures in the mid-90s or higher, and they sometimes stop when the alcohol level created is over 14%. The temperature range best suited to yeast populations is 48° to 65° F. for best growth on a commercial scale. A smooth fermentation is encouraged by a few nonsugar nutrients such as nitrogen and phosphorus, both usually supplied from the uptake of nutrients by the grapevines. Sometimes, however, the yeast will stop working for no apparent reason. Most winemakers speculate that the yeast stops because of either a shortage or an excess of amino acids.

Winemakers pay full attention to both the rate and the temperature of the primary fermentation. In general, the cooler the temperature, the longer the fermentation time. Red wines normally ferment at the warmer ranges (70° to 85° F.), but the trend is to ferment the more complex reds such as Cabernet Sauvignon and Zinfandels in the 80° to 90° range, with an occasional batch of Pinot Noir deliberately fermented at temperatures in the high 80s or low 90s. Winemakers generally prefer longer fermentations (two to three weeks) for white wines, and tend to ferment them in the cool range of 45° to 60° F. White wines destined to be made in a slightly sweet or sweeter style are usually fermented longer at even cooler levels. Cool fermentations are known to retain the grape's fruity characteristics, the esters, which are desirable today. Extreme warmth (above 80° F.) tends to cause the fruitiness to become volatile and escape into the air, leaving more subtle characteristics often desired in red wines. When the juice is extremely high in sugar content, as in late harvest–style wines, the primary fermentation is often a slow, difficult process. In every fermentation, as the grape juice ferments, the carbon dioxide created rises to the surface, tending to protect the wine from excessive air and from premature oxidation. Also, it has been established that the fermentation process creates a small amount of sulfur dioxide, a natural protective by-product that retards oxidation. The two biggest potential problems during the primary fermentation are the development of vinegar and the premature halt of the yeast action before all the sugar has been consumed.

A "stuck fermentation" is the technical description of the latter event. It is always unplanned and usually represents a big problem. The yeast cells simply stop metabolizing the sugar and become inactive, leaving the winemaker with unwanted sugar in the partially fermented wine. Usually, knowing how difficult it is to reactivate the fermentation, winemakers will combine the stuck batch with an actively fermenting batch of the same wine. If that's not possible, they will add vitamins and yeast nutrients in hopes of reactivating the yeast. Fermentation involving extremely sweet juice for a late harvest wine stops or sticks, and the point at which this occurs determines the amount of natural residual sugar in the wine.

## CARBONIC MACERATION

Carbonic maceration is a variation in the primary fermentation that is frequently used to make fruity-style red wines such as French Beaujolais. Nouveau Beaujolais may be the best-known wine made by this fermentation procedure, but it can be used to produce any red table wine. The purpose of making wines by carbonic maceration is to obtain a deep, dark red wine that avoids harsh tannins or bitterness while accentuating youthful fruitiness. The general procedure involves macerating the whole berries in a carbon dioxide atmosphere for several days.

In carbonic maceration, winemakers will dump the just-picked grapes— without crushing or pressing—cluster by cluster into a tank which when full is sealed tight. The weight of the grapes as they pile up automatically crushes those at the tank's bottom, and this in turn leads to a fermentation. The carbon dioxide from this fermentation is trapped within the tank and the remaining grapes are bathed in it. These special conditions result in an intracellular fermentation— in effect, a fermentation within each individual berry. After a few days, the result is deep color, an aroma similar to fresh berries, cherries, and grapes, and low levels of tannin. The objection to wines produced 100% by carbonic maceration is that they are simple, one-dimensional, and fragile. In the mid-70s, a minor trend emerged when over a dozen California producers worked with this type of fermentation to offer Nouveau-style wines. The trend fizzled within a few years, mainly because consumers didn't understand what a Nouveau wine was all about. Today, only two or three California wineries offer wine made entirely by this technique. However, over the last few years several Oregon winemakers have been making Nouveau-style Pinot Noir by carbonic maceration in hopes that the reception will be more favorable.

## WHOLE BERRY FERMENTATION

This is a variation on the carbonic maceration approach, and is now rather widely practiced by winemakers. The purpose is to add lively, berryish character to otherwise heavy-bodied and usually tannic red wines. In this procedure, the winemaker follows the conventional fermentation practice but at certain times he will add clusters of whole, uncrushed berries to the fermentation container. This tends to prolong the fermentation as well as to add desirable components. The chemical reaction involved in whole berry fermentation is such that the uncrushed berries undergo an enzyme breakdown that stretches out the fermentation process without adding alcoholic strength. The resulting wines tend to be intensified in color, fruitiness, and aroma, without being overburdened by tannins and alcohol.

Just about every red wine varietal has been produced at some time by some winemaker with an assist from whole berry fermentation. The wines that winemakers currently believe are definitely improved by it are Pinot Noir and those reds prone to excessive alcohol levels, such as Zinfandel, Petite Sirah, Barbera, and Syrah. Every so often we hear of winemakers adding whole berries to fermenting Cabernet Sauvignon and Merlot.

## MALOLACTIC FERMENTATION

What winemakers call the "secondary" fermentation is a biochemical reaction differing from the primary one in several ways. Also known technically as malolactic fermentation, it is induced by bacteria and does not create alcohol at all. Instead, malolactic fermentation involves a conversion of the acidity in the wine: through bacterial action one kind of acid, called malic acid (which, along with tartaric acid, is a principal acid in grapes), is converted into another kind of acid, lactic acid. Since lactic acid is much softer and smoother than malic, the malolactic fermentation is desirable in some wines under certain circumstances. Winemakers can choose either to allow it to occur or to prevent it from happening.

The bacterium itself is prevalent on the grape skins in all winemaking countries, although it wasn't identified until the 30s. It is known to belong to the large *Lactobacillus* genus. In wineries the bacterium is encouraged by warm conditions, and discouraged and inhibited by cold. Most of the time the bacterium can also be inhibited by sulfur dioxide. One of the more widely used chemicals in winemaking, sulfur dioxide protects wine from damage from air and from bacteria, and at reasonably low levels is regarded as a handy preservative.

The malolactic bacterium, which is generally found in wineries on their walls and storage containers, as well as in all vineyards, cannot be totally eradicated. However, it can be kept in check in the vineyards through application of sulfur dust, which inhibits its activity, and in wineries through filtration, which can remove it from wine. Malolactic fermentation is something that wine is predisposed to undergo, though the process remains capricious and unpredictable. The bacterium itself has been isolated and cultured, and is now available commercially. Rather than waiting around for each batch of wine to decide whether it wants to undergo this secondary fermentation, winemakers can now introduce a malolactic culture to induce it. This is usually done shortly after the primary fermentation is finished, and winemakers working with high-acid wines consider it a natural way to lower the total acidity. One of the beneficial side effects is the creation of a natural compound called diacetyl, akin to butter in aroma and in texture. So, malolactic fermentation contributes a softness through the increase of lactic acid, a buttery-smooth texture through the development of diacetyl, and an aroma that by combining both lactic and diacetyl components at the expense of simple fruitiness is regarded as more complex.

There are, however, drawbacks. One is that malolactic fermentation in process can give off unpleasant aromas along the lines of skunk cabbage and garlic. Also, it is difficult for winemakers to know for certain when a malolactic fermentation is completed. Should it continue after a batch of wine has been bottled, the results are gassy, turbid, and sometimes downright stinky wines. Another problem is that, while it adds a different character, malolactic fermentation can reduce or flatten out a wine's simple fruitiness. Thus, winemakers will choose whether or not to encourage the malolactic fermentation depending on the wine's acidic characteristic after fermentation and on the style of finished wine they believe is best suited to the market. In many instances, winemakers divide a vintage into batches, allowing one portion to experience malolactic fermentation while the remainder does not. The batches are later combined. The point to be emphasized is that for the majority of California wines, the decision to put a wine completely through malolactic fermentation, partially through it, or not at all depends on the style and characteristics the winemaker wants to achieve.

In the Western United States, malolactic fermentation is encouraged in nearly all red wines, and is a frequent option where white wines are concerned. It is particularly common (and often necessary) in dry-style white varietals (Chardonnay and Pinot Gris) from Oregon and Idaho, because the cold climatic conditions there result in extremely high acidity. The same holds true for white wines originating in cool Region I California locations. However, for most California white wines, inducing malolactic fermentation is a matter of personal choice; some winemakers have no real need to lower acidity, but simply like the flavor that results. Chardonnay is the wine most often associated with malolactic fermentation. In the 70s, an increasing number of California Chardonnays were put through the process because the resulting bold flavor dimensions were fashionable. With greater knowledge and experience came a degree of restraint. Winemakers now seem to agree that the desired buttery character will begin to manifest itself when at least 25% of the wine has undergone malolactic fermentation. Today, winemakers in California favoring 100% malolactic fermentation for Chardonnay are in the majority. A few winemakers will encourage a limited percentage of Chardonnay to undergo such fermentation, while preventing it in the rest in order to retain essential fruity characteristics.

### NATIVE YEAST FERMENTATION

Fermenting wine by way of the native or wild yeast rather than by a cultivated variety developed into a major trend in the 90s. After several small-scale producers (Frog's Leap, Franciscan Vineyards, and Chateau Potelle among others) demonstrated positive results with Chardonnay, many others have experienced similar favorable results with other varieties. Because a spontaneous, wild yeast fermentation is known to proceed at a slower rate and thus is a more prolonged fermentation, the wines, most winemakers agree, acquire greater flavor and aroma complexity and a richer texture. Other possible advantages include the development of lower alcohol levels. To date, the most dramatic differences have been achieved with Chardonnay, and in general winemakers are now fermenting more whites than reds on the wild yeast. Zinfandel seems to be the favorite for wild yeast experiments among red wines. A growing number of winemakers are trying their hand at native yeast fermentation as part of a larger movement in California to take a non-interventionist, hands-on approach. However, there remains some debate among winemakers as to whether the native yeast is actually derived from the grapes, which is commonly believed, or from the interior walls and floors of the fermentation areas.

## BARREL FERMENTATION

Wines that undergo the conventional fermentation in a small barrel instead of a vat or tank are said to be barrel-fermented. Today, white wines such as Chardonnay and Sauvignon Blanc are most likely to be made this way. Occasionally, Chenin Blanc, Semillon, Pinot Blanc, or late harvest Sauternes-style white wine will be barrel-fermented. Recently, thanks to the influence of winemakers from Australia and New Zealand, several wineries are now barrel-fermenting red wines such as Syrah, which is also known as Shiraz. We know a few winemakers who like to see what happens when they barrel-ferment Pinot Noir. Fermentation for most red wines begins in a tank before the wine is moved to barrels. Just about all such fermentations take place in oak barrels of 55- to 60-gallon size, though a few wineries use larger oak containers called puncheons, holding about 150 gallons. Winemakers favoring this type of fermentation claim it contributes more subtle oak character, a richer, creamier body, and greater longevity to the wine. Barrel fermentations are expensive because more labor is required to monitor the fermentation and to clean each barrel before and after use.

Barrel fermentations became more common throughout California in the 70s, but they really represent the traditional and classic form of white wine fermentation employed in France for several centuries, primarily in Burgundy and Bordeaux. Not only are they costly, but they also bring greater risks. The temperature can only be regulated externally, so winemakers have less control over the progress of the fermentation. Specially designed barrel-fermentation "cold rooms" are one way now used to protect the wine.

Contrary to a widespread assumption, barrel-fermented wines do not have more oak aroma and flavor than wines that are only oak-aged. But the now-numerous proponents maintain that barrel-fermented wine offers a smoother integration of oak and wine. They also believe that as wines ferment in barrels, they go through a natural kind of filtration which removes overt oak tannins and bitterness along with unwanted sediment.

"Partial" barrel fermentation means that a percentage of the wine is fermented in barrels, and the remainder in another type of container. Before being bottled, the batches are combined. Many skilled winemakers prefer having an option, or several, when it comes down to combining barrel-fermented and stainless-steel-fermented lots into the final blend.

## BOTTLE FERMENTATION

Champagne and all other sparkling wines produced by the traditional *méthode champenoise* are fermented the second time only in a bottle. Sparkling wine made by the modern transfer process also undergoes the second fermentation in the bottle. In both production methods, the bubbles result from bottle fermentation. In either approach, once the base wine blend or cuvée is selected, it is put into each bottle along with a carefully measured amount of sugar and yeast, which activates the second fermentation.

Many yeasts are available, but the preferred ones are known to have an ability to ferment in an alcohol solution, to add a strong yeasty aroma, and to flock and granulate together for easy collection afterwards. Each bottle in this sparkling wine fermentation is closed with a crown cap, fitting tightly over the lip. Typically, producers place the bottles in a cool location, and ideally the fermentation takes place around 55° F. and lasts between 45 to 60 days on average. When it proceeds as desired, the resulting wine acquires numerous tiny bubbles that create a persistent bead and a creamy texture. The pressure that builds up is usually around 90 psi in a standard-style sparkling wine. This second fermentation continues until all sugar has been metabolized. The spent yeasts will later be removed after a specified aging period.

### FERMENTATION CONTAINERS

For centuries most wines were fermented in oak containers, either small barrels or large vats. In the early days, California wine was usually fermented in vats made of redwood, the durable wood that was widely available, then and now. With modernization in the 20th century, wineries were designed for large volume and efficiency, and new types of fermentation containers were introduced. For a time the most popular type was a glass-lined concrete tank and, to a lesser degree, concrete tanks coated with a special epoxy seal. These tanks varied in size, and could be tailored to fit into a winery. In general wine talk, a vat is an open-top container and a tank is a sealed container. In the 50s, wineries began experimenting with tanks made of stainless steel, and soon thereafter a variety of designs and sizes of stainless-steel tanks appeared in both old and new winemaking facilities.

Stainless steel has become the most common fermenting container for several reasons. Stainless-steel containers are easy to clean and to keep free of spoilage organisms. They can be sealed airtight, and once in place last much longer than any wooden container, perhaps indefinitely. Winemakers find that stainless-steel tanks are relatively easy to combine with refrigeration systems, and this ability to control temperature during fermentation sets stainless steel apart from the competition. Being easy to clean, a stainless-steel fermenting tank can also be used as a storage container after fermentation is completed. Furthermore, stainless steel is neutral in flavor to begin with, and, unlike wood, will not develop leaks with age.

Wooden containers are still used to ferment some wines. Small oak barrels are used for white wine fermentations. Redwood was once widely used at a time when most red wine fermentations took place in large open-top vats. However, by 1970 all but a few winemakers had converted to stainless steel. Some of the holdouts were stubborn old-timers, but a few continue to prefer open-top vats for Cabernet Sauvignon fermentations. They are joined by a few underfinanced winemakers who have acquired some of the old redwood vats and sealed them off, and use them as fermentation tanks. Interestingly enough, as part of a general trend in the 1990s returning winemaking to traditional, often literally hands-on procedures, we have been witnessing an increasing preference for open fermentors. Usually of small capacity and made of stainless steel, the new wave open fermentors allow winemakers easy access for monitoring the fermentation. The operative assumption is that the inevitable exposure to air softens young red wines. Open fermentors are now in vogue because they allow winemakers various options for punching down the cap to avoid the abrasive practice of pumping over.

Concrete fermenting tanks have all but disappeared. Only the giant factory-like wineries continue using them just to save money. Every now and then a batch of Pinot Noir from a curious hands-on type of winemaker will have been fermented in concrete tanks as an experiment.

## FERMENTATION YEASTS

Grapes contain yeasts on their surface, and these yeasts are capable of bringing about a fermentation. However, the natural yeasts can't always be relied upon to ferment all of the sugar and to work quickly, cleanly, and smoothly. After World War II California winemakers heeded the advice of university professors at the Davis Campus who advocated selected yeast strains. These selected yeasts were naturally occurring, and the most promising ones were isolated, cultured, and propagated for commercial use. Just about all winemakers now use cultured yeasts, and it is standard practice to inoculate the must (that is, to add pure-culture yeasts to the juice) to start fermentation. A standard practice at most wineries used to be to sprinkle a sulfur dioxide compound on the newly crushed grapes in order to stun or inhibit the wild yeast activity before the cultured yeast could be introduced. In the late 80s many winemakers gave up doing this, instead adding the sulfur dioxide compound later, at the juice stage, or even after fermentation.

Winemakers select each yeast for certain properties. A major way in which yeasts vary is in the amount of foam produced during the fermentation, which is an important consideration for anyone who is barrel-fermenting. Further, yeasts vary in their tolerance of such conditions as cold, warmth, degree of alcohol, viscosity, sugar, and acidity. Yeasts are also capable of contributing a range of aromas and flavors (sometimes distinctly undesirable aromas and flavors). Moreover, they work at different speeds, some being extremely slow and a few others very fast fermenters. In addition, the pure-culture strains are grown specifically for their ability to inhibit the growth of natural but less desirable yeasts. All of these properties must be taken into consideration when yeasts are selected.

Most wineries today simply purchase yeasts from supply houses rather than cultivate their own strains. The commercial yeasts are available in liquid as well as a freeze-dried form, which is now preferred. Winemakers with large-volume brands normally use one strain of yeasts for all red wines and another for all of the whites. We know of some using a single yeast for all wines—red, white, rosé, and sparkling. However, winemakers striving to produce individualized wines believe that the selection of a cultured yeast should be on a grape-variety-by-variety basis. Each vintage provides another chance to try out a different combination. After the 1980 vintage in California produced some wines thought to be flawed by the yeasts used, vintners began to speed up their efforts in the field of yeast selection. What follows is some general assessments of the yeasts most frequently used today.

MONTRACHET yeast has been the most popular among winemakers for many years, and is used for both red and white wines. It is frequently used for Chardonnay in both barrel and stainless-steel fermentations. Montrachet is popular because it tolerates sulfur dioxide better than most other yeasts. However, it is said to be slow and sluggish in its performance, and it does not work well with high-sugar (greater than 23.5%) grapes. Overall, with grapes within normal sugar levels, Montrachet produces some complex whites, especially Chardonnays. In the late 70s (and sometimes even today) this strain was blamed for stuck fermentations and wines with excessive levels of hydrogen sulfide, but it has since been at least partially cleared of these charges by researchers.

CHAMPAGNE yeast is probably the second most popular. It was isolated in the region of Champagne and is technically a mixed-population culture, not a pure single strain. It is favored for sparkling wines because it ferments rapidly and is tolerant of both low temperatures and high alcohol levels—both conditions commonly met with when making sparkling wines.

PASTEUR WHITE, also known by some as French White, is used for a range of white wines. It pairs well with white wines because it works slowly and tolerates cold conditions. Some winemakers like its ability to impart yeasty aromas, and a few believe it helps retain high acidity. Its liability is that it foams considerably, so it is used in stainless-steel fermentations but seldom in barrel fermentations.

STEINBERG is a strain developed in Germany's famous wine school at Geisenheim, and is generally favored for white wines that winemakers prefer to ferment long (two, three weeks or more) and cold. It is said to be the most tolerant of cold of all strains, which makes it a natural for Johannisberg Riesling, Gewurztraminer, Chenin Blanc, and Muscat varieties. This yeast contributes an aroma described as tropical-fruit in nature, which is either a plus or a minus, depending on the winemaker. It is best suited to stainless-steel fermentations.

PASTEUR RED, or French Red, is a mixed-population strain developed from yeasts prevalent in the Bordeaux region of France. Its positive attributes are a tolerance to heat and to sulfur dioxide. It also has a history of working smoothly and of rarely, if ever, being involved in a stuck fermentation. Used for red wines generally, it has recently been matched with Cabernet Sauvignon, Merlot, and Zinfandel.

ASSMANNSHAUSEN is a strain from Germany, where research on yeast strains has been going full-tilt for decades. Advocates for this strain have proclaimed it a wonder yeast for red wines because it seems to intensify the color and impart a strong spicy fragrance. At first it was used for Zinfandel and Pinot Noir exclusively; more recent vintages have witnessed its increased employment with Cabernet Sauvignon. The strain, however, is definitely not well suited for musts with high solid content, such as are characteristically found with several white grape varieties, and so should not be used with these varieties.

PRISE DE MOUSSE is a specific type of Champagne yeast which is best known for being strong-acting and very low-foaming. Both attributes make it a likely partner in barrel fermentations. Winemakers also classify it as a yeast with a strong inclination to ferment to dryness without a hitch. Those who prefer it claim that it intensifies the fruitiness of certain varietals. The only liability, at least to some, may be its strong yeasty aroma. This one attribute, however, makes it highly desirable for the second fermentation in sparkling wine among sparkling-wine producers.

EPERNAY is another specific strain isolated in Champagne that has found some advocates in the U.S. It is frequently used for bottle-fermented sparkling wine because it is an extremely slow fermenter that tolerates cold temperatures. It is also viewed as a moderate-foaming yeast. Winemakers use it for a range of white varietal wines, as well as for the primary fermentation for sparkling-wine stock.

PASTEUR CHAMPAGNE yeast is another that is often employed by winemakers. It is a very active strain, and is a popular choice for sparkling wines because it is unusually tolerant to carbon dioxide. Among those making sparkling wine by the Charmat process this is usually the yeast of choice.

All of the above-mentioned yeast cultures are widely used in California as well as by winemakers in all other states. The Robert Mondavi Winery is one noteworthy producer we are aware of that prepares its own strains of yeasts and has isolated and propagated one or two special strains. At Woodbridge, Mondavi found and later propagated a low-foaming yeast suited for barrel fermentation; it named the yeast Woodbridge. Several of the sparkling-wine producers such as Chandon and Piper Sonoma acquire their yeast strains directly from their respective headquarters in Champagne. Most cultured yeasts are sold by a variety of companies located in and around the major U.S. wine regions.

# Fermentation Techniques

Winemakers can manipulate the wine during fermentation in many ways in order to achieve a certain predetermined style. The winemaker exerts as much influence on the style of a wine as do the climate and the soil conditions. Choices of containers, yeasts, and types of fermentation bear directly on specific wine styles ultimately achieved. During fermentation, winemakers have numerous other technical options before them. Though it is not our intent to chronicle every minute technical possibility, we do want to highlight the major technical areas, which are quite frequently referenced on back labels or in winery-disseminated information.

COLD SOAKING is a technique borrowed from Burgundy and applied in the early days to Pinot Noir. Before fermentation, the must is held in a closed container that is either refrigerated or chilled by dry ice. The duration of cold soaking ranges from several hours to a day or two. The procedure is known to soften harsh tannins and add body to the wine. It is also said to improve a wine's texture. Many winemakers working with hillside and mountain red grapes have discovered cold soaking as a way to help tame the tannins. The downside is that over-long cold soaking can obscure a wine's delicate fruitiness. It is widely used today in Oregon and California with Pinot Noir and for a growing number of other reds.

SKIN-CONTACT TIME involves the juice of white wines between crushing and the beginning of fermentation. White wines generally ferment without the grape skins, but winemakers have learned that these skins contain many aromatic and flavor-contributing compounds that can enhance their wine. To leach out these compounds hidden within the layers of the skins, they allow the white wine juice to remain in contact with the skins in a closed tank for a period of time ranging from a few hours up to a day or two. One risk involved is that the juice may pick up darker-than-desired color from the skins, and another danger is the possibility of added bitterness. Both can be avoided by frequent monitoring of the temperature during the skin-contact process. This procedure of giving white wines time in contact with the skins has certainly helped to improve the overall quality of Gewurztraminer and Chardonnay, and perhaps others.

WHOLE CLUSTER PRESSING emerged in the late 80s as a reaction against giving wine skin-contact time. At first used primarily with Chardonnay, whole cluster pressing has become a widely followed approach for many high-quality wines, whites and a few reds. The process requires equipment that can de-stem with crushing, so that entire whole clusters can be pressed in a gentle membrane press. It involves no crushing or maceration. Whole cluster pressing is slow, hands-on, and better-suited to small batch winemaking. By the mid-90s, the majority of winemakers aiming for high-quality Chardonnay were following this old Burgundian protocol of directly pressing whole clusters.

TEMPERATURE MANAGEMENT While it is true that slow, cool fermentations in stainless-steel tanks are the rule and that most whites ferment at colder levels (45° to 60° F.) and reds somewhat warmer (65° to 75° F.), a number of winemakers employ still warmer fermentations for a few types of wine, mostly reds. Many Cabernets, Merlots, and full-bodied Zinfandels have been fermented in the 80° to 90° F. range, on the assumption that complexity is gained and simple fruitiness avoided. Warmer fermentations are also used by some to diminish the unwanted vegetative notes in reds such as Cabernet Sauvignon and Merlot. Producers of heavy-weight Pinot Noirs are the strongest advocates of warm fermentations. A few winemakers allow Pinot Noir fermentations to reach the low 90s to extract more from the skins and to increase the tannin level. Barrel-fermented white wines are not subject to precise temperature controls, but winemakers usually want to maintain relatively cool (55° to 68° F.) conditions. So, most winemakers place their barrels in specially designed, temperature-controlled rooms, isolated from the rest of the winery. Another precautionary step taken by meticulous winemakers is to pre-chill the juice before running it into the barrels for fermentation.

CAP MANAGEMENT The "cap" is the solid mass, consisting mostly of grape skins and seeds, that rises to the surface during red wine fermentations. This mass of skins needs to be repeatedly pushed down into the fermenting wine because it contributes color and flavors. Left on the surface, it becomes dry and might develop ugly bacterial problems to ruin the wine. In order to manage the cap, the traditional winemaking procedure is to punch it down once or twice a day, submerging it with a long paddle. Among the traditionalists, punching down is performed several times a day throughout the active fermentation. Another way to manage the cap is to "pump over," which means that wine from the bottom of the tank is pumped over to the top, where it moistens the cap and forces it to sink beneath the surface. The modern, labor-free way is to use specially designed tanks. One popular design has a screen fixed inside the tank at around the halfway level that prevents the cap from rising to the surface. This tank requires careful cleaning after use. Another special design, first used by both the Robert Mondavi Winery and Beringer Vineyards, is a roto-tank. This horizontal tank, now used by dozens of producers, is programmed to rotate at intervals and so mix the cap and the fermenting wines enough to keep the cap from staying at the surface for any length of time. Whether reverting to punching down by hand or using roto-tanks, winemakers today are definitely trying to avoid manipulating wine by pumping it from one place to another.

STEM RETENTION This first became a winemaking strategy in California in the mid-70s after many heated discussions about Pinot Noir. By the late 70s the grape stems, removed by the crusher-stemmer, were being returned to the fermenting Pinot Noir on an experimental basis. Stems—usually only a portion of the total—can augment the wine's viscosity, and add richness and aroma. With Pinot Noir, the stems are thought also to help fight off bacterial problems. According to experiments conducted by the Robert Mondavi Winery, wines such as Pinot Noir are likely to benefit when the proportion of stems retained is 30% or higher. How-ever, some winemakers claim differences are noted at 20%, and a few others say the desirable changes require more than 40% stem retention. Just about all agree that the risk involved in stem retention is excessive bitterness. Many winemakers have made wines by stem retention, and most maintain that the stems must be dried somewhat before being included, or else the bitterness can really become a major problem.

EXTENDED MACERATION involves red wines only, which are allowed to remain in con-tact with the skins, seeds, stems, and yeasts after fermentation is complete. The wine rests in sealed containers, usually stainless-steel tanks, for a period of time. The goals in mind are to increase color intensity, to enhance aroma, and to rid the wine of harsh, bitter tannins while retaining only soft tannins. The technical ex-planation is that during this maceration period the small tannin molecules com-bine to form larger molecules. In addition, many of these large (polymeric) molecules are less soluble and therefore will precipitate out of solution. Accord-ing to winemakers, these larger tannin molecules are softer and less bitter than the smaller ones. They are also more complex tannins that provide greater stabil-ity, which allows wine from this procedure to age long.

Extended maceration is widely used in Bordeaux, and Californians began using it for Cabernet and Merlot in the late 70s. French vintners have a special name, *cuvaison,* for the combined time of fermentation and maceration. Advocates claim the beneficial effects occur only after 10 days of maceration, but the time devoted ranges considerably. Quite a few winemakers feel 21 days of maceration is the norm, while others allow the period to extend from 30 on up to 65 days. After maceration the fermented wines are pressed to remove them from the grape skins, racked three or four times, and most likely placed in oak barrels. The one definite liability of maceration is that it ties up fermentation tanks, which at many wineries are needed for other wines during the ongoing harvest.

CHAPTALIZATION is the official French term for adding sugar to wine during the fer-mentation period. Though illegal in California, it is permitted in several states under special circumstances. In extremely cool climates, grapes sometimes fail to develop sufficient sugar to yield balanced wines. Before they are spoiled by harsh late-season weather, the grapes are picked unripe, crushed, and then sugar is in-troduced into the fermentation tanks. In Oregon, where it is sometimes neces-sary, vintners prefer to chaptalize toward the middle or the end of fermentation in order to stretch out the fermentation time. Chaptalizing increases the wine's body because it increases the alcohol. Different states limit the amount of alcohol that can be gained through this technique. Oregon law, for instance, allows "when necessary" the addition of as much as 2% sugar to augment fermentation. This is fairly consistent with the policy in most European wine regions.

ARRESTING FERMENTATION has emerged as the primary way to preserve residual sugar in wine. Of the many methods to stop a fermentation, winemakers prefer chilling the wine when it reaches the desired sugar level. Chilling wine to or slightly below 32° F. will force the yeasts to stop working. At that point the wine has retained the residual sugar and is eventually siphoned or racked away from the yeasts. Send-ing wine that is still fermenting through a centrifuge to remove the yeasts is an-other way to retain the desired degree of sugar. The old technique for stopping the fermentation in order to make a wine with some level of sweetness was to add a large dose of sulfur dioxide when the wine had fermented to the desired stage. The only drawback was that the wines then became so sulfurous they needed to be aged for a time before they were drinkable.

ACIDULATION is a fancy expression for the addition of acidity to wine. In many warm growing regions, wine grapes develop high sugars but at a loss of acidity. In Cal-ifornia, it is legal to add acids to wine so long as the acids are those that occur nat-urally in grapes—tartaric, malic, or citric. Such "acid adjustments" are needed far more often for white varietals than for reds. In California the acid added is usually tartaric, purchased in a dry, powdery form which dissolves in the wine. Winemakers disagree over whether the acid adjustment should be made during or after fermentation. In the late 90s, winemakers have more or less outgrown the need, real or perceived, to add acid to red wines.

# Clarifying Wine

After fermentation, a range of particles, both visible and invisible, remain in wine—among the most common being spent yeast cells, protein particles, tannins, and grape skins. Clarification is the process of removing such particles from newly fermented wines so as to leave the wines bright, clear, and visually acceptable. The process, moreover, is necessary for more than cosmetic reasons—it also serves to remove many potential dangers and prepare the wine for bottling. Today, four clarification procedures are commonly practiced by winemakers throughout the world: racking, fining, filtering, and centrifuging.

### RACKING

Racking is the oldest and, in a way, the only natural system of clarifying wines. Basically, racking is the transfer of wine from one container to another so carefully that only clear wine moves, and sediment along with a small amount of wine is left behind. It is natural primarily because it relies on gravity to pull unwanted particles to the bottom of a container. Just about all wines are racked at least once, most commonly out of the fermentation container. After allowing some time for settling to occur, the winemaker removes the clearer wine from the fermentation lees—mainly yeast cells, skins, and seeds. Normally, a fermentation tank has a racking valve located at about the anticipated sediment level. The clearer wine is pumped or moved by gravity into its next home through a hose attached to the valve. Most wines are racked three or four times over a year, and by the end become quite clear and bright to the eye. Although necessary, frequent rackings are labor-intensive.

Three ways exist to move wines from one container to another. They can be pumped, which is the common way; pushed by pressure of an inert gas (carbon dioxide or nitrogen); or they can flow naturally by gravity. A few winemakers suspect that pumping agitates wine unduly, so these few go the extra yard and rack their wines, usually reds, relying only on gravity in what's known as a barrel-to-barrel racking.

### FINING

Racking removes only those particles that precipitate out from the wine naturally. But not all substances settle to the bottom, and some of those that remain might cause problems later on. Therefore, winemakers often resort to other methods. One of the most widely used procedures is fining by the addition of an outside agent. Fining agents absorb or adsorb (that is, they help collect dissolved substances) particulate matter, and are later removed together with the unwanted substances by racking or filtering. Another property of many fining agents is that they make larger particles out of smaller ones, causing them to settle to the bottom of the container. Basically, fining agents enable winemakers to remove microscopic, dissolved material, and also to improve a wine's color, aroma, and flavor. When used by competent winemakers, fining agents will leave no residue or unpleasant side effects. The agents are either natural or synthetic, though the majority are natural. The most frequently used natural agents are egg whites, bentonite, gelatin, isinglass, and casein. Among the synthetic types, the best known are activated carbon, nylon, and polyvinyl poly-pyrrolidone, known as PVPP. Each agent removes a specific unwanted con-stituent in wine—two of the most common being proteins that cause cloudiness and bitter components known as phenolics. Fining also helps remove unwanted aromas and atypical colors.

Bentonite is a widely used agent, especially for white wines. A powdery clay found in Wyoming, South Dakota, and Germany, it works extremely well in re-moving protein particles. When left in wine, proteins create a hazy, cloudy ap-pearance, especially if the wines experience warmth during shipping or cellaring. Bentonite is otherwise gentle on wine and does not strip away desir-able constituents.

Egg whites—fresh, frozen, or dried—have long been used in fining red wines to reduce tannins and bitter phenolics. In all forms egg whites consist of protein, but their ability to remove excess tannin more than makes up for any trace of protein they may leave behind. Traditionally, egg whites are added to wines such as Cabernet Sauvignon and Merlot during aging in small oak barrels (frequently, they are added after blending in large containers). The number of egg whites added to the barrel is usually four to six, depending on the amount of tannin to be removed. Winemakers are willing to expend the extra labor required because, when used properly, egg whites do not strip away color and are particularly gen-tle on the wine.

A range of other fining agents can be used for both red and white wines. Gelatin is a protein substance derived from collagen and in fining wine is specif-ically used to remove tannins. It is very active, and has sometimes been used by winemakers to lower the limited but nevertheless undesirable tannic astrin-gency in white wines before fermentation. Gelatin can remove color and even strip away fruity flavors, however. So most winemakers, given a choice, would opt for casein when the need is to remove tannic astringency from white wines. Casein, a form of milk protein, removes tannins but with few side effects. An-other fining agent used occasionally for table wines is isinglass. Made from stur-geon bladder, isinglass is a protein scoring high marks from winemakers for tannin reduction and overall clarity. Unfortunately it is expensive, and seems to be used by only a handful of Chardonnay producers. However, in Champagne and in the production of many quality California sparkling wines, isinglass is often preferred for clarification.

Here we should also mention several of the unpublicized treatments used. Though few winemakers would brag about it, activated charcoal is widely used to remove just about anything from wine. With the strong demand for White Zinfandel, many winemakers work with bulk wines which need adjustments in their color. In this context, activated charcoal serves as a great tool. It also helps remove unpleasant aromas, and its "deodorizing" ability is no secret among producers. One widely used synthetic fining agent is PVPP. To date, this relatively new agent has scored well. It is known to help adjust color and aroma without any negative effects. In practice it seems to be called into action frequently to remove brown tones or other unwanted colors in white wines. One of its best attributes is that it is not soluble in wine, and therefore leaves no residual amounts behind.

Usually, after fining in tanks or in barrels, winemakers allow settling to occur. Then typically wines are clarified by racking, filtering, or centrifuging.

## FILTERING

Of all clarifying procedures, filtering is one of the last procedures called upon to remove particles from wine. It also is the one that is potentially dangerous in that, if carried out improperly, filtering can strip away positive constituents. The purpose of filtering wine is to remove yeast cells and other microbes that could create off-character and instability.

Filtering consists of pumping the wine through a series of screens holding pads or special membranes. The pads may be coated with a material such as diatomaceous earth or simply made of cellulose. The pads available to most wineries vary in porosity. Filters using the finest pads are able to capture the smallest suspended particle, even a single yeast cell. (In the latter case, the process is known among winemakers as a "sterile" filtration.) More recently, membrane filters are being used in conjunction with pads because the membranes are finer and tighter in their clarifying ability. They are believed to have no adverse effects on quality. Immediately before bottling, wines often receive a final polishing filtration, with a sterile membrane filter which ensures that they are free from harmful organisms. The winemaking trend of the 90s is to avoid filtration if possible or at least to give wines only a final polishing filtration prior to bottling. Filtration is being avoided because it takes something out of the wine. It has been noted that unfiltered wines do not experience "bottle shock" after being bottled.

## CENTRIFUGING

A centrifuge, even a small one, is a costly piece of equipment. Though many winemakers believe strongly in the merits of centrifuges, others refuse to use them for premium-quality wines. Those swearing by the centrifuge maintain that it works fast and requires little manpower. Because particles of all sizes can be removed through centrifugal force, centrifuging easily replaces several rackings in winery operations and can make clarification simpler. The centrifuge also enables winemakers to combine fining and clarifying in a single step: after the fining agent settles out, the wine can be centrifuged immediately and is then ready for bottling. As for the detractors, they maintain that the centrifuge removes too much from wine, no matter how carefully it is monitored.

In recent years the centrifuge has proven itself an indispensable tool, when used wisely, for moderate-sized (100,000 cases) and larger-sized wineries. It has also been a great boon to those frequently producing late-harvest-style wines.

Two aspects of winemaking that may be considered to belong together are aging and blending. The two often take place within the same time frame. Moreover, both are optional, since not all wines are aged significantly, nor are all wines blended. The processes are also linked in that it is through them especially that winemakers can really assert and distinguish themselves, and thereby set themselves and their wines apart from others. Aging and blending are much more than just stages preparatory to bottling. They are functions in which winemakers have an opportunity to demonstrate their artistry.

# Aging

Many wines age in wooden containers, and the general public usually equates aging with cool cellars full of cobweb-draped oak barrels. The fact is that not all wines are aged substantially before bottling, nor are all aging vessels made of oak. Quite a few wines are bottled just a few weeks or a few months after the harvest. In most instances they will have been stored in stainless-steel tanks, not in oak barrels or even larger wood containers. Though airtight, stainless-steel tanks allow wines to marry and come together as they shed some of their youthful aggressive flavors and harshness. Long aging of wine is rarely performed in stainless-steel tanks, however. On the contrary, wine stored in such tanks may be deliberately held without aging by blanketing the top of each tank with carbon dioxide or an inert gas such as nitrogen. Thus covered, the wine has no contact with air and tends to retain its fruitiness. In actual practice, wines held in stainless steel change very little, and what change there is occurs very slowly.

Most wineries wishing to age wine before bottling will keep the wine in wood. Wines are wood-aged for several reasons. One traditional reason is that the process takes young green wines, rough to the point of being unpleasant, and makes them softer, smoother, and more enjoyable. Red wines are more often in need of aging than whites, because tannins and bitter flavors are more pronounced in young red wines. A few white wines, especially barrel-fermented versions, also benefit from the softening effect of additional wood aging. Wood is porous, and the slow, controlled, but inevitable air contact with the wine results in some degree of evaporation. As evaporation takes place, the wine becomes concentrated, which is another traditional reason for placing wine in wood. As wine ages in wood, the alcohol and tannins leach out flavors from the container, and these wood flavors are usually desirable additions. Many winemakers wood-age white wines naturally low in tannins to enable them to pick up tannins—which at low levels are desirable preservatives—from the wood itself.

Today, the subject of wood aging for wine has been elevated to a science, with major emphasis given to the type of wood, the size of the container, and the origin of the wood and production method of the barrelmaker. The general requirements for a wood container for wine are that it be durable, slightly porous, and pleasantly flavored. Many kinds of wood have been used by winemakers, from chestnut to pine to redwood and white oak. But it is the last two types that are today's favorites on the West Coast. Of course it helps that both white oak and redwood are readily available.

Redwood was preferred by a wide margin in California until the mid-60s. As an aging container, redwood remains as suitable as most other types of wood. However, because it is fairly neutral in flavor, redwood places a distant second to oak when it comes to selecting small barrels intended to contribute flavor to wine. Large vats and storage tanks in California have often been made from redwood. For the early stages of aging and often for the malolactic fermentation, redwood tanks are still used today. The large tanks that stand vertical, known as uprights, are usually made of redwood, which is less expensive than oak, although many wineries may spend money on oak uprights either for the extra measure of character delivered or simply for the prestige. As prices for a winery's product go up, so does the winemaker's propensity to rely exclusively on stainless steel and oak for his wine fermentation and storage vessels.

The shape and storage capacity of an aging container will be determined by its use within the winery. Generally, the smaller the container, the faster the aging process, and vice versa. Most winemakers prefer to start out using large containers for new wine and then complete the aging process with small barrels—a barrel being an oak container with a capacity of between 55 and 60 gallons. This traditional barrel is used for the primary aging period, after the wine has been clarified. Most barrel fermentations occur in this size barrel. Several wineries prefer using a larger oak container known as a puncheon for fermenting their wines. A puncheon has a capacity of 135 to 150 gallons.

In most wineries the larger tanks—oak or redwood—are usually used for the early stages of aging, in which the wines are still in need of clarification. Most fining treatments are conducted in large containers, and the same holds true for malolactic fermentations. It is simply more efficient to employ large tanks when performing these functions. Like their stainless-steel counterparts, redwood tanks range in size from a capacity of a few hundred gallons on up to many thousands. Usually, the largest storage container in a winery will be the blending tank, which is almost always stainless steel. The various batches or lots of wine are eventually combined in blending tanks in order to achieve uniformity before bottling.

In contemporary winemaking, the small oak barrel has emerged as one of the most important factors in achieving wine's ultimate aroma and flavor. The origin of the wood—that is, where the tree grew—has emerged as a primary consideration for winemakers. The most popular kind of oak used in winemaking is white oak, belonging to the species *Quercus sessilis* in Europe and *Quercus alba* in the U.S. White oak is durable, and just porous enough to make it ideal for aging wine. This kind of oak can be found in many states, Kentucky, Tennessee, Ohio, Missouri, and Wisconsin being the leaders. The same oak also thrives in France and Yugoslavia.

In general, the flavors extracted from white oak are the vanillins—flavors obtained from the toasting of the barrel which are believed to be compatible with many wines. There are other subtle oak-provided taste sensations described variously as "spicy," "roasted," "tangy," "creamy," and "lemony." Studies have shown that the flavors and characteristics imparted by white oak barrels vary according to the origin of the oak trees. Manufacturing techniques can also influence the types of characteristics given off by the barrel during the wine-aging process.

Beginning in the 60s and continuing into the 70s California winemakers, both newcomers and veterans, became compulsive students of oak aging. The first stages in the study of oak aging revolved around research into the differences between French oak barrels made from oak trees grown in several locations within France. For example, there are three important French forests supplying white oak barrels. One is the Limousin Forest in south-central France, where the climate is relatively warm and mild. Oak from Limousin develops looser grains, which in turn contribute overt oak flavors and rough, aggressive tannins. Furthermore, Limousin oak contributes a perfumed aroma and a sharp aftertaste. Limousin has been, and still is, used mostly for Cognac. The second important source, known as the Center of France, includes the Nevers and Allier forests, which are found further north, where the climate is cooler and the wood therefore tighter-grained. For wine barrels, this tighter grain creates more subtle oak phenolics, meaning less obvious oak character. The Vosges area in northeastern France is the third important source. While Limousin, the Center of France, and the Vosges supply most of the oak for French barrels, other locations make a contribution. For instance, Allier is a small forest not far from Nevers, but even within Allier is a still smaller area known as Tronçais. Its oak barrels are thought by winemakers to leave a subtle but slightly perfumed character.

The initial obsession of Americans with French oak barrels eventually gave way to a more even-tempered understanding. French winemakers had never engaged in a systematic study of oak barrels, but knew from traditional practice that the methods employed by specific coopers (barrelmakers) were important in some vital way. After added research, California winemakers learned that most subtle differences among oak barrels could actually be attributed to a particular cooper and his techniques rather than to the choice of wood or the superiority of one forest over another.

### COOPERAGE

Quality oak barrels imported from France are hand-crafted in the sense that no two barrels are precisely the same. Furthermore, the ways in which the oak is treated and handled by French coopers differ substantially from the methods originally used in the United States to build barrels. Historically, barrel-building in the U.S. developed to serve the whiskey industry—bourbon and rye primarily—rather than the wine business. Not surprisingly, therefore, American techniques have varied considerably from those in France.

The majority of whiskeys produced in the U.S. acquire most of whatever flavors they end up with primarily from the barrels. Traditionally, the flavors American coopers emphasized in their barrels were woody, along with a strong flavor of char and charcoal. This char or burnt-wood flavor is created automatically when the straight pieces of wood—known as staves—are treated in order to be bent and then set to form a round barrel. In the process of applying high heat, the early American coopers literally charred the inside layers of the staves. The general coopering techniques adopted in the U.S. eventually all worked toward making barrels with a strong char flavor. Even today, American-made distilled spirits display a typical character from American-made barrels.

The traditional coopering techniques followed in the United States involve sawing the timber rather than hand-splitting it, and then drying it in a kiln to expose a coarse rough surface easier to char. The staves selected to be part of a barrel are bent by being steamed, which further opens the grain for the charring to follow. Barrels produced by the American coopering method tend to be more uniform and consistent, and can be produced in volume. But such efficiency comes at a cost of the finer points.

Barrelmaking in France developed along different lines. After the oak trees have been felled, they are split by hand. Then the wood is hand-sawn, and according to tradition, seasoned or weathered for about two years by being air-dried outdoors. Next, the wood is cut by hand into planks destined to become the barrel staves, which ultimately number 30 individual pieces. Only about 20% of an oak tree is suitable for use as barrel staves, by the way. In order to bend each stave, French coopers make the wood pliable by heating it directly over a fire fueled only by oak chips and shavings. Once they are warm enough to bend, the staves are shaped into a barrel. The cooper again applies heat from the fire to set the staves into their final position, where the hoops holding them together are secured in place along with the endpieces, or heads, as they are called. The direct-fire technique used to set the wood actually impregnates the inside with a toasted character. The cooper, however, is careful to avoid burning or charring the barrel by controlling both the temperature of the fire and also the distance between the staves and the fire. It is the firing, or toasting, that imparts a special flavor to French oak barrels, or to barrels made by French techniques.

The most successful French coopering companies add their own individual touches to the barrel, while using standard techniques. Oak barrels for aging wine are usually purchased directly from a builder or cooper, and many American winemakers specify how they want their barrels to be built—the origin of the oak, the thickness of the staves, the hoops used, and the degree of toast built in—in effect ordering them custom-made.

Once the demand was sufficiently strong in the 90s, American coopers began improving their barrelmaking practices, and over the last several years the quality of American oak barrels has improved remarkably. Several manufacturers began by locating better sources of tighter-grained oak in the colder climes of Minnesota, Wisconsin, and Oregon. One winery, Fetzer Vineyards, actually started its own cooperage, the Mendocino Cooperage Co., and obtains oak from a forest it owns in Minnesota. The successes scored by Fetzer's barrelbuilders were not lost on Kentucky Blue Grass Cooperage, one of the nation's largest, whose owner, Brown-Forman, also owns Fetzer. American oak barrels are growing in popularity for aging Zinfandel, Syrah, and Petite Sirah, and it is no longer unusual for a fine-quality Cabernet Sauvignon or Merlot to have been aged at least part of the time, if not entirely, in American oak. That is oak made by barrel-builders willing to follow French coopering techniques. Several French firms still control the lion's share of the market. Following are the leading coopers producing barrels today, with a consensus view from winemakers about their respective products:

DEMPTOS is headquartered in a suburb of Bordeaux. Along with its once-thriving export market, this firm once supplied a significant percentage of barrels used in Bordeaux. The company now buys oak from throughout France, and builds to each buyer's specifications. The Demptos barrel was so much in demand in the United States that in 82 the company established a barrelmaking and -repairing facility in Napa Valley. In mid-89, the main operation in France was sold to François Frères, which now makes Demptos barrels.

FRANÇOIS FRÈRES is a cooper based in Burgundy, where the typical barrel is fat and stocky, usually finished with traditional wood hoops. This cooper is noted for barrels that are strongly flavored and heavily toasted. Many wineries age Pinot Noir in François Frères's barrels.

SÉGUIN MOREAU is a large barrelmaker based in Cognac. It buys oak from all regions of France, but specializes in a sturdy barrel known as the Bordeaux barrel or château barrel, with distinct willow hoops. Séguin Moreau supplies barrels to many of the famous châteaux of Bordeaux, and by the mid-80s this barrel was being widely used in the U.S. for Cabernet Sauvignon, Merlot, and other red wines. Many winemakers refer to Séguin Moreau as "the Cadillac of oak barrels." Its American base of operations is in the Napa Valley. In 95, Seguin Moreau began making about 5,000 American oak barrels a year in its own Napa Valley facility.

SIRUGUE is another well-known cooper from the Burgundy region, but it is a small firm. While the majority of Burgundy coopers favor strong toasty character, Sirugue is an exception. Its light oak, with subtle toastiness, is often used for both Chardonnay and Pinot Noir.

LOUIS LATOUR is another cooper in Burgundy. Latour's barrels are used primarily for barrel-fermented Chardonnay, and winemakers using them point out that they add strong toast flavors and a desirable hazelnut aroma.

TARANSAUD is a name seen on many barrels. This firm is located in the Cognac region and owned by the conglomerate Moët-Hennessey. The oak is air-dried for three years or more, and Taransaud's barrels thus contribute more subtle effects than are usually associated with oak from Limousin. This firm's Limousin barrels are often used with West Coast Chardonnays. In the 80s many producers of Cabernet and Merlot began using Taransaud's barrels made from Center of France oak, and the same barrel is now widely used by many Bordeaux châteaux.

TONNELLERIES DE BOURGOGNE is a Burgundy cooper whose name is quite prominent in California. Actually, it represents a group of small coopers who banded together in 67 to form a co-operative venture. Made by traditional techniques, the barrels are toasted usually in a light to medium range and are said to be extremely spicy in character. In the 80s they enjoyed a slight price advantage over other French producers.

TONNELLERIE FRANCAISE, a partnership between Frenchman Jean Jacques Nadalie and American Duane Wall, was set up in Napa Valley in the early 80s. Today it produces barrels made from either French or American oak, though predominantly the latter (about 75%). Its customers include many leading wineries.

INDEPENDENT STAVE, the largest cooperage in the U.S., is based in Missouri. It still sells most of its barrels to distillers, but in the 90s it has been increasing both the quantity and the quality of its wine barrels. Total annual output is about 450,000 barrels.

CANTON COOPERAGE is a small company in Kentucky that began focusing on the needs of wine producers in the early 90s. Today its American oak barrels are air-dried and the wood is toasted slowly over oak fires. Following all of the traditional French barrel-building techniques, Canton makes oak barrels that appeal to many winemakers. They are also the most expensive American oak on the market.

Just about all of the major French coopering houses have agents on the West Coast. Quite a few of them have established barrel companies in California, either to build new barrels or to repair used ones. Today, some of the firms ship staves from France and then assemble the barrels in California, often under the watchful eye of the local winemaker.

Once built and in place, a well-cared-for wine barrel will last for decades. However, an oak barrel will contribute oak flavors to a wine for only five years on average; thereafter the barrel is close to neutral in flavor. Several companies specialize in breaking barrels down stave by stave, shaving away the inner layers to expose a new layer, and then recombining the parts to make the barrels functional for flavoring again. This procedure remains controversial because the staves are often not toasted at all or, when they are, the flavors are not always acceptable.

Oak-barrel aging adds substantially to the cost of producing premium-level wine. The average price of a French-made oak barrel has ranged from a low of about $225 in the 80s to a high of $650 in 1997. For comparison, the price of an American oak barrel ranged from $125 to $250 in the same time period. Once put into use, oak barrels continue to add to the cost of the final wine. Maintaining wine in oak barrels is more labor-intensive than using large-capacity stainless-steel tanks or larger wood tanks. Furthermore, in an average year about 5% of the wine placed in barrels is lost through evaporation. As a result, winemakers must protect the remaining wine from oxidation by periodically refilling each barrel to the brim, a process known as "topping up." To facilitate this topping procedure, and the required number of rackings, winemakers have devised several systems for storing and stacking their oak barrels. Whatever the system, and regardless of how high they may be stacked, oak barrels take up considerable space. Finally, oak barrels, like all wooden containers, require careful cleaning between vintages or batches, first to avoid bacterial buildup, and second to remove normal tartrate deposits. In most wineries, barrels are rinsed with warm water and sometimes with an alkaline solution of soda ash to both clean and neutralize them. At some wineries the barrels are cleaned by special, expensive machines. In today's world, in sum, aging wine in the traditional oak barrels has become very costly.

## BARREL-AGING PROGRAMS

Winemakers have come to employ wood containers for purposes other than the simple aging of wine. Usually, wines are clarified long before they are placed in small barrels. Yet for those white wines that are fermented in barrels, winemakers sometimes prefer to age the wine in the same barrels because the wine will remain in contact with the lees, which consist mostly of inactive yeast cells.

*Sur lie* is the technical name for this type of barrel aging of wine together with the expired yeast. It is common in cool climates where the high-acid wines need to undergo the malolactic fermentation and deacidification process. Remaining in contact with the yeast lees, the new wine is encouraged by the available nutrients to begin malolactic fermentation. The *sur lie* technique can bring other benefits. Aging wine with the yeast leads to the decomposition of the yeast cells, or autolysis. This reaction will over time release amino acids to enhance the body of the wine, tone down the acid finish, and even imbue the wine with a yeasty, toasty aroma. This process is now used to produce many Chardonnays and Sauvignon Blancs on the West Coast. In the making of Champagne by the classic procedure, the *méthode champenoise,* the same biochemical principle is at work when the Champagne in the bottle ages in contact with the yeast after the second fermentation is completed.

"Barrel rotation" is a winemaker's term for a system in which barrels of different ages are used to age a single vintage. Brand-new barrels may cause rapid aging and hard-to-control oakiness, so winemakers move the wine through a series of barrels of different ages. The frequent pattern for barrel-aged wine like Cabernet Sauvignon is to replace 20% of the barrels with new ones each year—thus, after five years of use, the oldest barrels, which by then have imparted all of the oak character they can give, are phased out. The replenishing is systematic, as winemakers keep close track of how old each barrel is, and where it can best be used in the winemaking process.

One final note about barrel aging relates to the physical storage conditions. In most wine facilities, barrels are stored in areas that are quiet and temperature-controlled. In the early 80s, winery proprietors became intrigued by the concept of barrel-aging wines in cool underground cellars. California has no natural caves, but at the end of the last century a few wineries, notably Beringer, Schramsberg, and Buena Vista, were using caves, dug by hand into the hills by ill-paid immigrants. Today, making a cave simply to age wines in may sound rather extravagant, yet the conditions achieved are ideal—a high humidity, as well as constant temperature and natural air conditioning. A typical cave may have a humidity level around 95% at a temperature around 60° F., conditions in which wines aging in barrels experience little evaporation and age very well. Wineries that have them claim that man-made caves can recover their construction costs within five years through the savings in wine and in energy expense.

# Blending

Blending is a time-honored winemaking process that some winemakers have raised to an art form. It definitely is not synonymous with stretching, though some people do add inferior wine for that purpose. Blending, however, involves much more than just merging or mixing different wines. Winemakers blend by combining wines by region, by vineyard, by vintage, and by type of aging container. Blending to us becomes a noteworthy topic when the purpose behind it is to create a wine whose total quality impression is greater than the sum of its parts.

Combining two or more grape varieties is the most typical example of the act of blending. Many of the standard combinations now produced are classic blends originating in Europe. From Bordeaux we have Cabernet Sauvignon, Cabernet Franc, and Merlot as a standard blend which may also include Malbec and Petit Verdot. The standard white Bordeaux wine blend merges Sauvignon Blanc and Semillon, with a small amount of a Muscat wine (Muscadelle de Bordelaise) as an option. From Champagne, Chardonnay has joined with Pinot Noir and Pinot Meunier to form the classic blending trio for sparkling wine. Originating in the Rhone Valley, another common blend brings together Grenache, Syrah, and Mourvedre.

Trying to follow a classic European blend in the United States is not without its problems. The first is how to label the wine itself. Some California winemakers comply with federal rules regarding varietal labeling, using no more than 25% of other wines in order to retain the varietal name. Others, to achieve a stylistic goal, blend without retaining at least 75% of one variety and forfeit the chance to identify the resulting wine as a varietal. In the 80s, a number of producers began replicating Bordeaux red wine as closely as possible. The result is known as a Bordeaux blend, meaning the wines were made from Cabernet Sauvignon, Merlot, Cabernet Franc, and, if available, Malbec and Petit Verdot. These Bordeaux-style blends became so popular that the name Meritage was coined for them and adopted by many California winemakers, who had formed a voluntary Meritage Association. Most of the Meritage blends, both red and white, are also given proprietary names.

Blending the Bordeaux grape varieties in California has become fairly widespread. But another question raised is when to assemble the blend. The French traditionally assemble the blend before barrel aging, and therefore the components are forced to harmonize early. Californians are divided. Most will hold off on the final blend until the individual components have been aged. The logic in this case is that once a blend is made, winemakers can't change it, so it is better to hold off as long as possible.

Winemakers long ago discovered numerous other ways in which to blend for a better final product. Blending by region involves combining the same type of wine from different growing regions, such as Napa Valley and Santa Barbara County, or the same varietal wine from different Viticultural Areas within one county. In Napa Valley, many varietals are composed of wine from grapes grown in the Carneros or an adjacent area and another, more northerly locale. Some of the original vineyards in California were laid out in what is known as a "field blend." In this blend, the grower has interspersed different varieties within the vineyards and made his blend in the field. This planting system makes it next to impossible for winemakers to change the blend. When two or more varieties in the same field are harvested at the same time, they are bound to become parts of a blend. In Europe, especially in southern France, some of the traditional blends bring together red and white grapes that are harvested separately and then fermented together. The technical term for this is "co-fermenting."

In a similar way, winemakers can use different cooperage to blend wines. More often than not, Chardonnays are a blend of barrel-fermented and stainless-steel-fermented wine. The same Chardonnay can then be blended further by combining wines held in barrels of different ages, barrels made by different coopers, barrels made from different types of wood, or even barrels made of the same oak but from diverse regions and countries.

One of the last ways to blend wines is a method unfairly disparaged in the U.S.: the blending of wines from different vintages. The majority of fine Champagne in the traditional Brut mode represents a blend of several grape varieties and of vintages. Using wines from different years serves as a way to strike a needed balance when winemakers work with grapes grown under extreme conditions of hot or cold weather. Blended sparkling wines often originate in cold climates; blended fortified wines in warm or even hot ones. In California, however, the overwhelming majority of table wines and a surprisingly high percentage of sparkling wines are vintaged. The best explanation for this is that wines with a vintage are easier to market than those without. Chances are that in the future more sparkling wines will be multi-vintage blends because the mixing of old wine with new plays a significant role in the best French sparkling wine.

It is important for consumers to realize that blending has its place, and that 100% of one grape variety does not necessarily always mean better wine. Nevertheless, in the present scheme of things, we can't recall any Chardonnays that have been improved by blending, nor do we believe Pinot Noir benefits by being anything but 100% varietal. Johannisberg Riesling is said to be too delicate to be blended, and many winemakers believe that neither Zinfandel nor Gewurztraminer should be anything but 100% in composition. But a good case has been made in Europe, and is currently being made in the United States, in favor of blending for several other types of wine, notably those modeled after the wines of Bordeaux, the Rhone Valley, and Champagne.

## Stabilizing and Bottling

Putting the wine safely into bottles is the final step in the winemaking process. In recent years bottling facilities have shifted from semi-primitive to clean and efficient to, in some instances, ultra-modern—more sanitary and sterile than many hospital operating rooms. The purpose of these advances is to try to prevent any yeast particle or bacterium from entering the bottle. Indeed, at many modern facilities, wines are bottled in a specially designed bottling room, sealed off from the rest of the winery. Today, at nearly all wine facilities, new and old, when it comes to readying the wines for bottling and actual bottling, the accent falls on cleanliness.

In the last decade it was not uncommon for many new producers on the North Coast to install elaborate bottling lines costing from $200,000 to as much as $750,000. This kind of money brings fully automated bottling lines that can be monitored by one or two workers with push-button control. In a typical contin-uous process, new bottles are loaded onto the conveyor belt, unscrambled and sorted, rinsed, dried, and sterilized. Then each bottle is filled with wine, corked, and dressed in the appropriate garb, which is usually a color-coordinated cap-sule and label. Bottling doesn't require much labor anymore. The fully auto-mated lines only need someone to inspect the bottles for uniformity of fill level, and to spot any defects in the bottles or in the machine's performance. Actually, the most expensive lines now have sensors which can detect any low or high lev-els of fill, and even spot bottles with capsules and no corks, or corks and no cap-sules. Humans are still needed to push the appropriate buttons (start, stop) at the appropriate time.

Not all producers can afford such elaborate bottling equipment, but most reasonably well-financed wineries producing over 50,000 cases will probably have invested in their own automated bottling line. The old adage that it's bet-ter to be safe than sorry applies perfectly to bottling. In the past, more than a few fine wines were ruined at the bottling stage by careless workers or dirty condi-tions. In addition to sterile bottling areas, some wineries now even have equip-ment that blows an inert gas such as nitrogen or carbon dioxide into each bottle to remove dust and lint, and to protect the wine from oxidation. One winery we visit regularly has installed an ozone bottle sterilizer for the absolute in cleanli-ness; and equipment is available to extract oxygen from the bottle neck after the bottles are filled to the required level and before the cork is introduced. Most modern bottling rooms maintain positive air pressure to help keep bacteria and yeast out.

Such extreme attention to cleanliness is not always necessary. Those wines that are likely to be harmed at bottling, and therefore need special protection, are the low (below 10%) alcohol types and all sweet wines; in these, a single yeast cell in a bottle could create a refermentation. Today, when most U.S. wine pro-duction is devoted to white wines, particularly those varying in sweetness, just about all of the small and even the long-established large wineries have up-graded their bottling lines. However, a winemaker producing limited amounts of red wines only, or of red wines and barrel-aged whites, most likely can make do with the bare essentials, even hand-corking equipment, so long as the condi-tions are sanitary.

Speed and efficiency are also important factors behind the preference for high-tech bottling lines. A new and fully automated line equipped with 75 fillers can bottle 350 to 1,000 regular-sized bottles per minute, or over 12,000 cases in a day. That is known as a high-speed line, which it literally is. Most of the very large wineries will have several of these bottling lines running at the same time, making 50,000 cases bottled per day just"a day's work."

Prior to the actual bottling, a number of important cellar activities take place. Most wines on the market are rendered heat and cold stable by the winery. Cold stabilization refers to forcing the wine to form natural tartrate crystals in a stor-age vessel to prevent the harmless but unsightly crystals from showing up in your bottle later on. Wines are cold-stabilized by being chilled below 32° F. for several days. Heat stability, on the other hand, assures that a wine will not develop a protein haze should it be kept under warm storage conditions. This is common among white wines, and the remedy for such harmless haziness is to fine with bentonite prior to bottling. The mid-sized to large-scale producers as a rule prefer to stabilize their wines for both heat and cold.

Wineries of all sizes assemble what is known as the master blend, usually in a large tank just before bottling. Allowing all wines but especially the barrel-aged wines time to be combined and "marry" helps achieve uniformity of the entire bottling. The various batches and lots are combined in the blending tank, where they remain for a day or two. Paddles within the tank mix the fractions and make the entire batch homogeneous. Then the wine is moved from the blending tank to the adjacent bottling room.

## BOTTLE TYPES

Winemakers may or may not go through great mental anguish over which size, shape, and color of bottle they want to use. Sometimes the cheapest available ones are the best. For table wines, producers can choose from among four distinct shapes—the newer California or universal bottle, along with three traditional bottles, the Bordeaux, Burgundy, and Hock. The Burgundy and Bordeaux bottles can be either flat-bottom or the slightly more expensive push-up style. The indentation at the bottom, common in Champagne bottles, is also known as a kick-up or a punt. Its function has aroused some debate. We are content to believe the push-up makes it difficult for any sediment formed during aging to cling to the bottom, and it originally helped to strengthen the bottle so that it could withstand the pressure. We also sense that producers know the push-up bottle makes for a more handsome package, for which they can charge more money. Hock bottles came our way via Germany, and the name originates from the wine village of Hochheim. In Great Britain, German wines, particularly Rhine wines, are known as Hock. The long, cylindrical bottle shape is more traditional than functional. Winemakers select the Hock shape because the wines placed into it are Germanic in type, such as Riesling and Gewurztraminer, or Germanic in style, sweet wines such as Chenin Blanc.

A mention of Hock bottles, though, leads naturally into a discussion of color. Hock is either dark green or dark brown, better known as amber. Dark glass was first used long ago to keep harmful ultraviolet light away from low-alcohol, sweet-finished table wines. Along Germany's Mosel River, producers preferred the green color, but along the meandering Rhine River the favorite color was brown. The Bordeaux bottle is traditionally made in either of two colors, dark green and clear: dark green for red Bordeaux and clear glass for white. Such traditions are more or less followed as well in California. Cabernet Sauvignon and Merlot, the two red grapes of Bordeaux, usually appear in a Bordeaux bottle. But many Zinfandels also come in the same bottle, because at times winemakers like to think Zinfandel resembles a Cabernet Sauvignon.

The use of the clear Bordeaux bottle for Sauvignon Blanc follows the strict tradition only when the wine contains Semillon in some proportion, or else when the winemaker has assembled a proprietary blend of Sauvignon Blanc and Semillon. Similarly, a naturally sweet white wine fashioned along the lines of

Sauternes, a Bordeaux region, is frequently placed in the clear Bordeaux bottle. But now, of course, many White Zinfandels, which have nothing to do with Bordeaux or its wines, appear in a Bordeaux clear bottle. Otherwise, Bordeaux-shaped bottles with a dark brown color are traditional in some parts of Italy, primarily Piedmont, but the bottle is rarely used by any California winery. Also in Italy, Chianti producers use either a brown or, more typically, a dark green Bordeaux bottle.

The Burgundy bottle bears a resemblance to a Champagne bottle and is widely used for a variety of wines, red and white, dry and sweet. The color of the popular Burgundy bottle is a dark green known as "champagne green." Pinot Noir and Chardonnay, the traditional grapes of Champagne and Burgundy, are at home in this bottle. Some of the older Burgundy bottles used for white wines, such as Montrachet, were made of a thicker glass with a special tint of green known as "dead-leaf green." Many Californians associated this shade with prestige and began adopting it for their Chardonnays. Here, as in many other instances, traditions associated with wine bottles have been distorted for the purpose of promoting and packaging the product.

The different bottle sizes, however, are often of great interest to wine lovers. Bottle size influences the rate of aging: in general, the smaller the bottle, the more quickly the wine will reach maturity, and vice versa. In practice, however, wine in a magnum bottle (twice the regular 750-ml bottle) does not age twice as slowly; nor does the imperial (the largest bottle made commercially for wine and equal to eight bottles) reduce the aging speed by anything like eight times. Any bottles larger than the imperial will have been made by hand for some special occasion such as a wine auction, and the contents may have been poured in from smaller containers a short time before the special occasion takes place. The 187 ml, the bottle known as a "split" and sold primarily on airplanes, is now making a comeback as a container for serious wine, even Champagne.

## CORKS

The use of a cork to seal a bottle is surrounded with even more murky mythology than the evolution of bottles. In fact, the cork is often unnecessary and purely ornamental for wines that won't improve if aged in bottle—which covers most of the wines made. A cork became associated with quality years back when screw caps first appeared and were scoffed at. Corks offer many advantages for protecting and aging wines, but they also cause problems because of their tendency to leak, to harbor bacteria, and to dry out when not kept moist. The best features about a cork are that it is compressible and adheres well to glass. Corks are thus well suited to bottled wine, and particularly those wines one intends to keep for some time.

Cork is actually the inner layer of bark from a type of oak tree that is found today mostly in Portugal and Spain. The variety is known as *Quercus suber*, and the tree must be at least 20 years old before it can yield its cork commercially. Stripping it does not kill the tree, and cork can subsequently be harvested at nine-year intervals. The bark is first removed and cut into strips, then corks are stamped out of the strips, washed, bleached, dried, and ranked into quality levels. In Portugal, there are six grading categories for corks, with "extra superior" ranking above "superfine," which is right above "extra first," which is above "first quality" in a system amusing for its silly superlatives. "First quality" is usually good enough for most wines.

Cork suppliers try to make sure that their product is free of defects. Typically, a cork is dusted in a special vacuum system, rendered relatively sterile, and finally coated with paraffin and/or silicone for ease of insertion. Some wineries purchase corks in quantities of 1,000, packaged in sealed bags containing a blanket of sulfur dioxide for further protection. Despite all of these efforts, an average of 3 out of every 100 corks is said to contain some defect. The primary problem associated with a "corky" or "corked" wine is caused when a mold indigenous to cork reacts to the cleaning agent used.

The three top grades of cork are offered by manufacturers in three standard sizes. For most wines with a cork as an ornament, the small 1 1/4-inch cork is adequate. The more common size is 1 3/4 inches, the next size up being a 2-inch cork. Longer corks are made, but usually are purchased through special order by the winery. Ordered in quantities of 1,000, corks range in price from a low, in 95, of 8 cents each to a high of 40 cents for the 2-inch versions. For wines likely to be cellared for 10 years or more, the longest cork available is the one that we like to discover when we remove it from our corkscrew.

### DRESSING

The next step in the bottling process is the dressing, which includes capsules and labels. Usually the capsule goes on right after the cork has been inserted. All wine is required by federal law to have something covering the closure or cork. The most common materials for capsules are plastic, tin foil, a poly-aluminum, various laminated types and, on occasion, wax. Image-conscious producers favor tin foil by a great margin, primarily because the foil can be fitted smoothly and tightly, and so helps give the bottle an upscale appearance. Plastic, because it is plastic, lacks the association with fine wine. But it serves the purpose. The lead capsule has been phased out in response to consumer concerns. It has been replaced by the pure tin capsule, which is very expensive, or by a heat-shrink plastic capsule, cheaper but less pretty. By the mid-90s, Robert Mondavi Winery and Kendall-Jackson Vineyards had introduced a new type of closure known as the B-Cap. Using a custom-made flange-tip bottle, Mondavi found a way to avoid a capsule entirely and sealed the bottle with a splash of beeswax on top of the cork. Kendall-Jackson also designed a special bottle, but uses paraffin to cover the top of its corks. The bottles stand out because this B-Cap seal eliminates the need for a foil of any type. Despite the different outward appearance of these bottles, the cork is extracted by conventional means. Dozens of producers have expressed an interest and will be adopting the B-Cap by the end of the decade.

### LABELING

Labeling completes the activity on the bottling line. Present laws require only a front label; though popular, side or back labels are optional. Mandatory information in the U.S. includes the type of wine, the alcohol content, the fluid contents, the brand name, the address of the brand, and the area supplying the grapes. All wine labels must be approved by the federal government prior to their use. The particular federal agency overseeing wine labels is the Bureau of Alcohol, Tobacco and Firearms, a division of the U.S. Treasury Department. The watchful eye of our federal government looks out for misleading statements or implications, and guards against nudity, obscenity, and any suggestion that wine could be the least bit healthful. The government also watches for trademark infringements and look-alike logos.

Designing labels that can catch the eye of a potential consumer is now a big part of wine marketing. The label designers in California have become numerous, and many rather prosperous, in a short time. Sometimes a colorful or artsy label is the only reason a wine will sell at all. In any event, though France's Château Mouton-Rothschild was the first to use specially designed artistic labels, hundreds of California wineries have entered the competition, with no end in sight. As a result, collecting wine labels has become something of a fad. Since a few winery owners prefer to be sure their labels will not become unglued when placed in a refrigerator or ice bucket, they use a water-resistant super-glue to affix labels. However, most labels can be removed by soaking.

### BOTTLE AGING

The next step following bottling and labeling is one of the more important ones: bottle aging. Most wine will experience a reaction known as "bottle shock" immediately after being bottled. There are several reasons for this, among them the fact that a wine picks up excessive oxygen during bottling, which flattens its aroma and leaves a chemical stink. Within one to three weeks, the wine will show signs of recovering and regaining its appeal. Bottle shock also has to do with levels of sulfur dioxide in the wine and how much was added during the bottling procedure.

Bottle aging by the winery is well worth the extra time and effort. Winemakers universally agree that with a wine like Chardonnay, the bottle-aging minimum should be 3 months and the ideal is from 9 to 12 months. It takes some time for the wine to begin to reveal its full potential. Since the average barrelaging time for most serious Chardonnay is from 6 to 9 months, consumers can begin to understand why Chardonnays from one vintage trickle into the market over a two-year period. Red wines such as Cabernet and Merlot are bottle-aged by the more quality-minded winemakers for about a full year, and some even longer. To hold back wines in order to bottle-age them indicates a general interest in quality, a most admirable trait.

# Grapes
# and Wine Types

There is a tendency among people who write about wine from California and the Pacific Northwest to talk as if the vinous millennium has arrived. They, and we, are probably encouraged in this because of the extraordinary quality now being exhibited by the best wines produced from the local wineries, and because of the continuing series of tastings in Europe at which California wines have frequently been rated higher than their European counterparts by experienced and objective tasters.

Here in the West, of course, wineries designate almost all of their leading wines by the grape from which the wine was made, whereas most leading European wines carry the name of the vineyard or commune where the grapes were grown. Grape names are employed here for reasons of history—or perhaps the lack of history. The French, with their centuries of experimentation, have arrived at a system of grape and wine laws under which only certain varieties may be used in the production of given vineyard-designated wines. Vouvray, for example, can be made only from Chenin Blanc; Clos Vougeot, only from Pinot Noir. West Coast grape growers and winemakers have not had this opportunity to learn from centuries of experience; and even though the producers have proven capable of making world-class wine, California and the West are still in their formative years when it comes to the knowledge of exactly where best to grow specific varieties. If the truth be known, California winemakers have not fully resolved the question of *which* varieties they should be growing, let alone *where* those varieties should be grown.

In this chapter, we take a look at grapes from the standpoint of what they have meant to California winemakers up to the present, and we also examine the roles they may play over time.

ALICANTE BOUSCHET   Here is a grape that the French use only to add color to their thinnest, most meager red *vin ordinaire,* but which in California has enjoyed a modest success beyond its value as a tinting agent. It gained this standing with home winemakers and commercial wineries because it yields a full-bodied, deeply colored wine with a noticeable tannic edge to toughen its otherwise soft structure. Even at best, however, it has never been much of a commercial hit as a varietal wine. It is now losing its popularity with the do-it-yourself crowd, and has been gradually disappearing from California vineyards. From a peak of 30,000 acres at the end of Prohibition, it now occupies only 1,600 acres, almost all of them in the hot Central Valley. It has only occasionally been offered as a varietal within the last decade.

BARBERA    Not more than two decades ago, Barbera was probably the fourth-leading red varietal in California. But its early history as a source of fuller-bodied, tannic, fairly high-acid red wines grown in California's coastal areas is now substantially behind it—the limited offerings from Martini and Sebastiani notwithstanding. Rather, Barbera has blossomed into the darling of the Central Valley jug-wine producers, who rely on its high-acid propensities to balance their otherwise soft red plonk. Interestingly, Barbera's fall from grace in California has been paralleled in its native Italy, where it is disappearing from the famous Piedmont grape-growing area while at the same time becoming that country's most widely planted red wine grape, especially in the hotter regions. By 95, Barbera had made a very modest comeback as a coastal-grown grape—but with little critical acclaim to date.

In California there are now over 11,100 acres planted and, with the exception of some 300 acres along the coast or in the Sierra Foothills, the grape is entirely restricted to the Central Valley. Recent plantings in Texas and New Mexico parallel the California jug-wine experience. Although some two dozen wineries around the country report making Barbera (most of them in California), it is rare to find more than one or two labels in even the most handsomely stocked wine shop.

BLANC    Literally "white," the term *Blanc*, in any of its forms, is used to denote a white wine. Names like Zinfandel Blanc, Cabernet Blanc, Gamay Blanc, and others that combine "Blanc" with the names of red wine grapes mean that a white wine has been made from the identified grape. The designations of "White" Zinfandel, "White" Cabernet, and their related brethren in name calling have exactly the same meaning. A few producers label their generic whites as "Chablis Blanc," perhaps on the theory that one good white wine name deserves another.

BLANC DE BLANCS    Literally "white from whites," this term applies both to sparkling wines and to still wines made from white grapes, often but not always a blend of varieties. Many champagnes called Blanc de Blancs typically contain substantial fractions of Chardonnay in their makeup.

BLANC DE NOIRS    Literally applied, the term denotes white wine made from black-skinned (red wine) grapes and applies to either champagne or still wines. Although employed most visibly on sparkling wines, it has been seen increasingly on California table wines. In theory, the color ranges from the palest hint of pink to light onionskin. However, in actual practice, wines labeled Blanc de Noirs, especially table wines but now even including some champagnes, are often outright pink or even light red in color. So, for some wineries, the name has become a marketing gambit under which rosés have become more easily salable.

BLUSH    Another alternative name for white or pink wines made from red wine grapes, this trademarked term belongs to Mill Creek Vineyards, which collects a fee from anyone else who uses it on a wine label. The term has also gained wide recognition as the generic category under which the industry lumps its so-called "White" or "Blanc" offerings made from red wine grapes.

BURGER    Back in the days when jug wines were the rule rather than the exception in California's North Coast, this white vinifera grape was more plentiful than all major white varieties combined. Its bountiful crop (about two to three times that of Chardonnay) of neutral, pleasant stuff was just fine for the gallon-bottle crowd and there was no point in planting better-tasting but less generous grapes for which no market existed. When the American wine palate changed for the better, Burger's fortunes changed for the worse, and the total acreage devoted to it fell off from the 3,000 acres extant just after Prohibition to about 1,500 acres by the mid-80s. (For comparison, Chardonnay zoomed from less than 100 acres to over 66,000 in the

80s and 89,000 now.) A minor rebound of sorts has occurred in recent years, with a few hundred acres of new vines being planted in the North Coast reportedly to go into the production of sparkling wine as an inexpensive extender, and for wine coolers, with the result that total acreage now has come back as high as 2,600 before dropping back to 1,900 acres.

BURGUNDY    This term, borrowed from the famous wine district of France in which some of the world's best and most expensive table wines are produced, in California wine parlance invariably refers to inexpensive wines of indeterminate parentage—generally red unless otherwise specified (for instance, White Burgundy or Sparkling Burgundy). A few wineries have recently dropped this generic moniker in favor of "Red Table Wine." California burgundies are usually soft, often slightly to medium sweet, and aimed at a broad market. Needless to say, they have absolutely nothing in common with French Burgundies.

CABERNET FRANC    Ignored in California until the 80s and still treated as something of a mystery, this red wine variety has enjoyed a much happier and more clearly defined set of roles in its native France, where it is used variously to make light, fruity red wines in the Loire Valley, to blend with Merlot in the cool-climate vineyard areas of Bordeaux, and to blend with and perhaps add a slight raspberryish or violetty perfume to Cabernet Sauvignon in the Médoc area of Bordeaux. It is this latter role, as a complexing and prettifying agent for Cabernet Sauvignon, that has brought about the recent California interest in Cabernet Franc (see also the discussion of Cabernet Sauvignon).

In the late 80s and early 90s, up to two dozen wineries vinified Cabernet Franc on its own, but only a few of those wines enjoyed widespread critical acclaim. Some of the early efforts were pushed too much toward overripeness, while others, possibly because of the grape's tendency to overcrop, seem to have been dilute and unfocused. All were more coarsely astringent than their fruit character could comfortably balance.

While it is possible that Cabernet Franc may one day make a name for itself as a separate and distinct wine, it has today settled down into a blending grape. Several wineries have made very fine Bordeaux blends with substantial portions of Cabernet Franc in their makeups. Among them are Viader and Dalla Valle. Important plantings (by county) include: Monterey (200), Napa (800), Santa Barbara (100), and Sonoma (500).

CABERNET SAUVIGNON    For most of the world, Cabernet Sauvignon is the undisputed king of red wine grapes. With the exception of some limited patches of Pinot Noir in France, Nebbiolo in Italy, and local favorites in lesser locations, it is Cabernet Sauvignon that is planted and admired as the quality leader in the majority of wine-growing and wine-drinking places around the globe. This is true in California, where Cabernet is planted in the most precious soils and its wines are valued more highly than any other red produced. The only grapes that exceed Cabernet in acreage, either in California or around the world, are planted for their copious production of inexpensive table wines.

Grown here for more than a century, and producing award-winning wines in international competitions for most of that time, California Cabernet Sauvignon has come into its own only in the last three decades as a widely planted, widely successful grape. Back in 1961, just before the dawn of the current era for California premium winemaking, Cabernet Sauvignon plantings totaled 606 acres, or about 1/2 of 1% of all wine grapes in the state. Now there are some 45,000 acres of Cabernet, and they represent 11% of all wine grapes here.

More important for devotees of premium wine, Cabernet is grown almost exclusively in the cooler coastal vineyards, where it has a chance to produce wines worthy of its regal reputation. In Napa County alone, 10,600 acres of Cabernet produce a wealth of world-class wines from makers as venerable as Beaulieu and Beringer, as 60s-ground-breaking as Robert Mondavi and Heitz, as newly matured as Stag's Leap Wine Cellars, Caymus, and Diamond Creek, as upstart as Dunn,

Spottswoode, and Girard. Before 1970, there were barely two dozen Cabernet Sauvignon bottlings available. Today, that number is closing in on 600.

Not only does Napa lead the way in Cabernet acreage, it also sets the California standard for quality, and does so with deeply fruity, rich wines whose variations in style are typically focused on flavors and structure of world-class depth and beauty. In the area of the Napa Valley lying at the western edge of the valley floor, from Yountville northward through Oakville and Rutherford, extending to St. Helena, Cabernet reaches optimal ripeness and fruitiness with a black-currant richness and firm but not imposing tannins. Referred to as the West Rutherford Bench (or more simply as the Rutherford Bench), this 10-mile stretch of well-drained, slightly elevated alluvial soils, being substantially within the Oakville and Rutherford viticultural areas, is home to some of the world's most famous Cabernet Sauvignons, including Beaulieu Private Reserve, Robert Mondavi, Opus One, Heitz (both Martha's Vineyard and the Bella Oaks Vineyard are located here), as well as Niebaum-Coppola, Dominus, Grgich Hills, Spottswoode, Staglin, Freemark Abbey's Bosché, and others of great fame and beauty.

On the opposite side of the Napa Valley is the smaller but rightfully famous Stags Leap District, whose wines, while a little less bold than those of the West Rutherford Bench, contain an equal measure of fruit and typically a rich, elusive hint of earth and truffles. Wineries of note in this area are Stag's Leap Wine Cellars, Clos du Val, Pine Ridge, Shafer, and Silverado.

The hillsides of coastal valleys, most notably those of the Napa (Diamond Creek, Dunn) and Sonoma (Carmenet, Laurel Glen) valleys, but also including some fairly prominent vineyards in the Santa Cruz Mountains (Ridge, Mount Eden) and a sprinkling of locations in Mendocino, Lake, and Monterey counties, also contribute their share of award-winning, exemplary Cabernets.

Finally, one dare not leave this subject without a mention of the many fine Cabernets that come directly from valley floor locations. Whether it is Caymus sitting beside the Napa River in Rutherford, or the Robert Pecota wine from Kara's Vineyard in Calistoga, proof is available that good Cabernet is not the sole province of benchland or hillside soils.

Nevertheless, all that's Cabernet does not glitter. In a great vintage, 12% to 15% of the labels on the market (but not so high a percentage of the total Cabernet gallonage) will rise into the most praiseworthy classes. Another 25% to 30% of the labels will front very sound, highly enjoyable wines of above-average quality, often selling at more reasonable prices and providing the world with a large supply of very good, representative wines worthy of almost any table. The remainder runs the gamut from acceptably average/eminently drinkable to lousy—and "lousy" is not necessarily limited to wines of low price.

But, whether full-bodied and rich or underfilled and uninteresting, the majority of California Cabernets share the grape's tendencies toward curranty, or sometimes cherryish, fruit, fairly firm structure, and noticeable tannins and astringency. Other frequently used analogies to Cabernet's varietal character include herbs, green olives, truffles, loam, briar, tobacco leaf, raspberry, violet, mint, tea, cedar, bell pepper, tar, and black cherry. Wineries seeking to make more accessible, early-drinking bottlings employ a variety of winemaking techniques, such as reducing the amount of hard-pressed wine in the final blend, cutting back on skin-contact time during fermentation, and fining and filtration to ease the grape's propensity for producing hard wine.

Another technique for altering and, at least theoretically, improving the character of Cabernet Sauvignon wines is the blending in of other varieties. The practice has existed in France for decades, but was rarely followed in California except by those few wineries that were looking for ways to stretch their Cabernets and, in some instances, to make them less expensive to market. However, it is only since the early 70s that California has possessed the so-called "classic" blending varieties used in Bordeaux.

The most popular among them is Merlot, employed both because its herbal and cherry character fits so well with Cabernet and also because its softer, more open structure helps mitigate Cabernet's coarseness. In theory, such a Cabernet-dominated blending with Merlot will maintain its strong varietal focus, gain some added complexity, and become a little more approachable in its youth.

The second most likely grape to appear in what might be called "classic" Cabernet Sauvignon blends is its upcountry relative, Cabernet Franc. This latter grape is a minor player in French wines dominated by Cabernet Sauvignon, but has found the beginnings of a home in California, where major wineries like Robert Mondavi and Joseph Phelps employ it generously in their leading Cabernet Sauvignon–based wines. While the structure of Cabernet Franc does little to soften or round out Cabernet Sauvignon, its fragrant, herb-laced, strawberry/raspberry-ish fruit seems to its fans to extend and enhance the tighter, somewhat brooding nature of the best young Cabernet Sauvignons.

Whether blended or not, however, it is the aromas and flavors, the depth and ageability of Cabernet Sauvignon that are prized above all else. Winemakers fill it with hard tannins or soften it by blending and fining, grow it on hillsides or valley floors, sell it for $100 or $10. But, whatever its blend, whatever its structure, whatever its assigned place in the market, Cabernet Sauvignon reigns as the king of red wine grapes in California. Important plantings (by county) include: Mendocino (1,500), Monterey (3,800), Napa (10,600), San Joaquin (7,400), San Luis Obispo (3,700), and Sonoma (7,500).

CARIGNANE   This workhorse of a grape, the most widely planted red variety in France and for many years the most often seen variety in California, formed the basis for an ocean of *vin ordinaire*. From the early 1900 s through the Prohibition years, Carignane was one of the major grapes of choice because of its extraordinarily high yields when grown in warm and fertile areas such as California's Central Valley and in the warmer, more protected areas of the North Coast. The wine rarely appeared as a varietal; and even now, producers who attempt varietals from the remaining older Carignane vines throughout the state generally end up with lighter ordinary wines. From a peak production during Prohibition approaching 50,000 acres, Carignane has dropped to somewhere in the neighborhood of 7,800 acres today, and will, one presumes, continue to diminish as other grapes, which seem to produce sturdier, better-balanced wines, come into greater favor for the production of jug wines. A half dozen wineries report producing Carignanes, although they are rarely seen beyond the wineries' tasting rooms. The attention being paid to Rhone varieties has brought a minor, limited resurgence for Carignane but has done little to reverse its continuing decline.

CARNELIAN   This University of California–created grape comes from a cross of Cabernet Sauvignon and Carignane crossed again with Grenache. The purpose was to create a grape that would grow in the relatively hotter climates of California's Central Valley, produce high yields, and still carry some of the class and flavor interest of Cabernet Sauvignon. The attempt seems only to have produced vines which overcrop without yielding wines that are more interesting than those from most other grapes grown in intense heat. Carnelian's future thus seems clouded. Unless some new form of vineyard management comes to the rescue, it seems likely to remain among the list of also-rans when it comes to the production of California jug wine. Its release in 1972 was followed by plantings of several thousand acres, but very little new planting has been done since, and the amount standing has slowly dropped to some 1,500.

CHABLIS   In California, this is the most broadly used generic name for white table wines. Although a few wineries continue to use the name for dry, crisp offerings that follow the style of wines from France's Chablis region in some modest way, most of the wines under the name Chablis are inexpensive, sweet, and blended primarily to sell in the least demanding white wine markets. Indeed, the name Chablis has been further diluted by the trend lately for North Coast wineries to call their drier generic blends White Table Wine, and to relegate Chablis to even coarser and sweeter offerings. The best of the jug-wine Chablis will use Chenin Blanc and French Colombard in their mix; the lesser will use whatever is on hand, occasionally including such lowly grapes as Thompson Seedless.

CHAMPAGNE   Named after the location in France whose sparkling wines are the most famous in the world and synonymous with sparkling wine in the U.S. This description is used less and less by makers of expensive bubbly but can apply to any wine whose carbonation is derived naturally during a second fermentation in a closed container. There are three ways to produce sparkling wine: the *méthode champenoise,* the transfer method, and the bulk (Charmat) process (see the chapter BASICS OF WINEMAKING).

CHARBONO   If it were not for the 50 acres or so of this otherwise unknown variety now growing in certain Napa and Mendocino vineyards, it is likely that the world would be without Charbono. It tends to produce wines that are high in tannin, thick but stolid in body, acidic, dark in color, and generally lacking in definable or interesting flavors. It is the rare California winery that continues to report production of Charbono, perhaps for the fun of trying to make something out of nothing.

CHARDONNAY (once known as Pinot Chardonnay)   This white vinifera grape produces superb dry wines all over the globe, ranging from its premier role in France's Burgundy region and its importance as the white grape of real Champagnes, to its dominant position as California's best dry white and major force in the locally produced sparkling wines. In the U.S., beyond California's borders Chardonnay is the most widely planted vinifera varietal, and is made into wine by some 200 wineries from Massachusetts to Ohio to Washington and Oregon. In recent years, Australian Chardonnays have become somewhat popular in this country, and Italian Chardonnays, although thinner and simpler than those mentioned above, have also sold well.

California Chardonnays are widely regarded as among the best in the world and have been winning tasting competitions on both sides of the Atlantic for more than a decade. Those wines most prized by connoisseurs tend to be fairly fruity, yet carry plenty of balancing acidity and an array of attractive flavor characteristics. These include apple, pineapple, mildly tropical, and sweet or tart citrus among the fruits, while buttery, smoky, spicy, nutty, grassy, or dried-leafy suggestions will often be present in combination with the primary fruit character. In Chardonnay, more than in other white wines, the aromas and flavors derived from oak-barrel fermentation and aging assume a leading role. Indeed, most of the world's great Chardonnays (French Chablis usually being a major exception) sport the toasty, sometimes creamy or spicy character derived from the use of oak barrels in the winemaking process.

Chardonnay seems to produce well in almost all coastal locations, but not so well in warmer inland locales such as Lodi and Fresno. Nevertheless, it has proven itself at home in a wide range of settings, although showing important character variations from one site to another. Many wines are specifically delimited to small geographic areas and carry the stamp of that location. Others, whether identified simply as California in appellation (Kendall-Jackson among the higher-priced wines; Glen Ellen as an example of the lower-priced offerings), or labeled with a countywide appellation such as Sonoma or Napa, are blends of several areas. Such blends frequently are intended to suit the winemaker's sense of style and complexity; but, as often as not, they are reflections also of economic reality. Most large producers simply cannot limit themselves to one tight geographic area because the grapes are not available in sufficient quantities and at suitable prices for the styles and market niches they have chosen.

In the Napa Valley, where Chardonnay is far and away the leading white wine grape, with 9,300 acres representing some 75% of the white vines in production, the variety produces exceptional white wines full of flavor and capable of achieving superb balance and aging potential. At the valley's southernmost (and coolest) location, in the Carneros District where much of Napa's Chardonnay is grown, the grapes ripen with a high degree of natural acidity. Much of the Carneros harvest is left to hang to full maturity on the vines, and displays the broad spectrum of rich varietal character; but some grapes retain more of the narrow, pineapple-like, and grassy side of Chardonnay. Among the wineries making sparkling wine from Napa Valley grapes, the Chardonnay of Carneros is widely sought because when picked at the desirably low (16–19° Brix) sugar levels, the grapes are perfectly understated in character while very high in the natural acidity that makes sparkling wine such a refreshing beverage.

As Chardonnay plantings move further north in the valley, they tend to yield rounder and richer wines. Some of the best-balanced Napa Chardonnays come from places like the Big Ranch Road area between the city of Napa and Yountville (Chateau Montelena and Trefethen), and in cooler locations, often in proximity to the Napa River, as one moves further up-valley. Hillside-grown Chardonnays in Napa (Sterling's Diamond Mountain bottling, for example) tend to have harder, more angular compositions, but can compensate with deep, often rich character, and good balance.

In Sonoma County (13,300 acres, 80% of white-grape acreage, 33% of total grape acreage) the range of sites and soils makes Chardonnay even more widely varied in its character. The cooler locations are much like Napa in the character they deliver to Chardonnay, and so are the hillside sites. But flatland-grown Chardonnays throughout Sonoma, especially in the Alexander and Russian River valleys, tend to have more effusive fruitiness, which can border on the tropical and make the wine both extremely easy to like on its own and harder to place with food. Even wines like De Loach and Ferrari-Carano, which are extraordinary wine-making accomplishments by any standard, seem to require service with sweeter fish and shellfish like sole and crab, or with rich or fruit-flavored poultry dishes. The westernmost Chardonnays grown in Sonoma County are usually high in natural acidity and thus tend to a crisper style as finished wines. Chardonnays from these cool-climate areas are also popular in sparkling wine production.

Just to the north of Sonoma, the vineyards of Mendocino County are rapidly becoming a home for Chardonnay. The 4,600 acres planted represent over two-thirds of all white grapes there and produce wines much in the fashion of Sonoma. The cool-area grapes (such as those from the Anderson Valley) are high in acidity, and many are picked early for sparkling wine production, while those grown further inland tend to produce fatter, riper-styled wines.

In the last 20 years, as grape growing has moved south of San Francisco in a serious way, Chardonnay has found a happy new home in the Central Coast counties of Monterey (15,100), San Luis Obispo (3,600), and Santa Barbara (6,900). At their best, wines from those areas have exemplary balance and brightly fruit-oriented flavors, often with a slightly floral touch. Within those counties, the districts of Arroyo Seco, Chalone, Edna Valley, Santa Maria Valley, and Santa Ynez Valley have been the names most likely to appear on highly regarded Chardonnays. Standard producers include Byron, Cambria, Edna Valley Vineyards, Meridian, Ojai, and Talley. As is true for all cool regions of California, some Chardonnay grown in the Central Coast is sought for sparkling wine production.

The small but important production of Chardonnay undertaken in the Pacific Northwest varies from Oregon's high-acid, piquant wines to Washington's often floral-tinged bottlings, to Idaho's full-bodied, rich, but sometimes underfruited offerings. Adding up to less than 7% (4,500 acres in Washington and 1,500 in Oregon) of California's outpouring of Chardonnay on a statistical basis, the Northwest wines nonetheless stand shoulder to shoulder with their California brethren for seriousness of intent and adherence to the search for the best the grape can deliver. Total Chardonnay acreage in California continues to increase and now covers some 89,000 acres, up from 56,000 in 91, 29,000 in 85, 17,000 in 81, 11,000 in 76, 2,500 in 69, and 295 in 61. Important plantings (by county) include: Mendocino (4,600), Monterey (15,000), Napa (9,300), San Joaquin (11,000), San Luis Obispo (4,000), Santa Barbara (6,900), and Sonoma (14,400).

CHENIN BLANC    A native of France, prized in California for its ability to produce clean, balanced wines in hotter climates, this early-budding but late-maturing variety can be marked by delicate, floral, and melonlike characteristics when grown in cooler areas. Chenin Blanc reaches its qualitative peak in France's Loire region, where in the districts of Vouvray, Saumur, and Savennières its pert fruit and bright acids are employed happily to make a variety of wines, ranging from perfumed sparkling wines (Saumur), to dry and zesty (Savennières), to medium sweet (Vouvray and Mont-Louis), and even to the occasional late harvest wine (Côteaux du Layon) of substantial sweetness.

In Chile, South Africa, and the U.S., there is more Chenin Blanc standing than in France. But in each of those locales, the wines produced tend to be neutral and decidedly ordinary. Almost 88% of the 21,600 acres in California are concentrated in the hot Central Valley, and are given over primarily to the production of jug wines. Even a large portion of the 2,600 acres grown in California's cooler locations finds its way into less expensive bottlings because the higher acidities and more attractive aromas are useful when blended into duller wines.

Coastal wineries also produce Chenin Blanc as part of their varietal lines and, like their French counterparts, offer wines ranging from dry to medium sweet. Of the few who offer dry wines, some (notably Chalone) also give extended oak aging to their wines to both deepen and enrich them. The majority, however, favor sweetness ranging from less than 1.0% (barely above threshold—especially if the acidity is slightly elevated) to soda-pop sugars in the 3% to 4% area. On rare occasions, a late harvest version will appear. Fewer than 100 wineries make Chenin Blanc, down from 120 in the mid-80s.

CHIANTI    In California, the name Chianti has appeared on generic red wines that have been fairly full-bodied and that have, at least in the early usage of the name, suggested wine to go with Italian foods. Lately the term has pretty much fallen out of use and those Chiantis that remain on the market are, with very few exceptions, the cheapest of the red generic wines, often the sweetest, and usually the dullest. In its current California usage, Chianti shares precious little in common with the Italian Chiantis, grown in the central part of Italy (Tuscany, just south of Florence), which have become so deservedly popular over the last several decades in Italian restaurants.

CLARET    In international usage, particularly British, "Claret" refers to the red wines of Bordeaux, and there are those in California who have agitated for limiting its use to wines made in the same style—that is to say, wines based on Cabernet Sauvignon, Merlot, and Cabernet Franc. Unfortunately, the few California wineries that have attempted to upgrade the name Claret have not always found a willing and accepting market. Thus, for the most part, the term continues to mean lower-priced generic red wines of no particular origin, and in that sense is fairly well synonymous with the term "Burgundy." In the late 80s, the term "Meritage" was invented by a group of California vintners to refer to wines made from the traditional Bordeaux grapes.

DURIF    A minor variety from the southeastern part of France, where it is now all but abandoned, Durif has found a home in the U.S. under the name Petite Sirah. And, nomenclature aside, the grape performs better in this country than it ever did in its homeland.

EMERALD RIESLING    Like so many other University of California–bred grapes, this cross of Johannisberg Riesling and the lightly regarded Muscadelle was intended to produce wines of interesting quality when grown in hot areas. Up to now, Emerald Riesling grown in California's hot Central Valley has certainly provided acidity, but has never made anybody smile about the quality. The few attempts to grow the grape in coastal areas have met with intermittent success, but its failure to measure up to Johannisberg Riesling has dimmed its prospects. There are some 600 acres in

California, down from 3,000 just a few years ago, most of which are in the Central Valley.

FINO    Fino sherries in Spain are the driest, usually the youngest, wines made in the Jerez area. They derive their unique, sharp and yeasty character from the natural development of a crusty yeast called *flor.* In the U.S., by contrast, Fino sherries derive their character in almost all instances from flor yeast cultures that are artificially introduced into the wine rather than, as in Spain, from naturally occurring surface growths. As a result, U.S. Finos tend to be a little less sharp and at the same time to lack some of the Spanish wines' unique tangy perfume and underlying fruit. Nevertheless, California Finos, like Spanish Finos, are dry and can be very handsomely used with food, especially slightly spicy appetizers. Fino is often served chilled without ice. If the still small interest in the U.S. in Spanish appetizers *(tapas)* should grow, one may eventually see an increased following among the wine-drinking public for both Spanish and American Fino sherries.

FLORA    This white wine–grape cross of Gewurztraminer and Semillon yields, not surprisingly, soft floral wines with an intriguing, somewhat spicy perfume. But it has never fully taken hold in California, because Flora wines have generally proven of less interest than wines produced from the progenitors of the cross. There are fewer than 50 acres currently standing in California, down from 350 acres in the mid-80s. Flora is offered by less than a half dozen wineries, often in slightly sweet to fairly sweet styles, is featured in Schramsberg's sweet sparkling wine "Cremant," and occasionally has raised a good deal of interest when grown in cooler North Coast vineyards.

FOLLE BLANCHE    This unheralded grape produces thin, tart wines of little distinctive character when vinified on its own and has attracted little interest in California. Yet its tendency toward acidity has made it useful to some producers of sparkling wine. Its historical role in the production of French brandies from the Cognac and Armagnac regions also suggests that it may appeal to California brandy producers—although we have seen little evidence of that to date. The few acres of Folle Blanche in California are located in Napa and Sonoma counties.

FRENCH COLOMBARD (also known as Colombard to the French)    This white variety's long and unheralded career in France for the production of dull white table wines and brandy is now coming to an end. But it has found in California a new and happy home, where it has become the second most widely planted wine grape. Its approximately 46,000 acres are concentrated primarily in the Central Valley and, given its high-yielding propensities in warmer climates, French Colombard accounts for about 40% of all the white wine produced in California in any given year.

Colombard has been propelled into its present popularity by its ability to yield wines of simple but clean, slightly floral fruitiness combined with good acidity in warmer areas. A few coastal wineries also produce French Colombard, generally in a dry style, but frequently with a little sugar left in it, to make softer, more palatable wines which have met with moderate success. There were even attempts to make Colombard in a ripe, barrel-aged style along the lines of Chardonnay. But, given the wine's inability to improve with age and its fairly narrow and limited flavor range, these efforts at a poor man's white did not meet with great public acceptance and have been discontinued.

Not surprisingly, French Colombard is also showing up in the newly planted, hot-area vineyards of Texas, as well as other experimental vineyards around the U.S. Indeed, California's handling techniques for French Colombard have led some vineyardists in the warmer parts of France to plant the variety and attempt to follow the California regime of cool fermentations. Initial positive results suggest that Colombard may one day return to France in a more elevated status than when it left.

## Grapes and Wine Types

FUMÉ BLANC   Not a grape variety, Fumé Blanc is, rather, a marketing name for Sauvignon Blanc. It was popularized in the late 60s and early 70s by the Robert Mondavi Winery as a new way of differentiating its Sauvignon Blancs vinified in a dry and oak-aged style from the sweet-finished versions then dominating the marketplace. The success of Mondavi Fumé Blanc has led to the grape's becoming the second most popular dry white table wine in California, after Chardonnay, and the adoption of the name Fumé Blanc by a variety of wineries. In the last half a dozen years, however, we've seen the Fumé Blanc cognomen lose some of its standing—especially as the suggestion of sweetness previously associated with Sauvignon Blanc has been forgotten. Government labeling rules now require all wines called Fumé Blanc to show the subtitle "Dry Sauvignon Blanc" directly below in small print.

GAMAY   There have been grapes in California called Gamay (or more specifically Napa Gamay and Gamay Beaujolais) for as long as anybody can remember. But it now appears that both of those names have been applied to grapes which have no relationship to the Gamay Noir à Jus Blanc variety, the Gamay that grows in the Beaujolais region of France. Nevertheless, wines called Gamay here in California have usually been made in the Beaujolais style. Indeed, from time to time, some producers have succeeded handsomely in making wines which are light, fruity, and enjoyable in their youth in the manner of French Beaujolais. It now appears that very little of the true Beaujolais grape exists in California vineyards. Usage of the Gamay/Beaujolais moniker will expire in 2007.

GAMAY BEAUJOLAIS   Until the 70s, the red vinifera grape variety traditionally identified as Gamay Beaujolais was thought by California vineyardists to be the true grape of France's Beaujolais region. Then, it was reidentified as one of the many versions (or clones) of Pinot Noir. It is a productive vine that requires cool growing conditions and can yield either a light or medium-bodied red wine, depending on vineyard management and winemaking choices. Because of historical usage, the vines planted as Gamay Beaujolais have been allowed to retain the name if the proprietor prefers. Another grape, the Napa Gamay, which is also not truly from Beaujolais, took on the standing of the true Beaujolais grape when that which we call Gamay Beaujolais turned out to be Pinot Noir. The wines now made from Napa Gamay may also be called Gamay Beaujolais even though it, like the Gamay Beaujolais, is not from Beaujolais.

   In the midst of all this confusion over grape names, and owing perhaps to the fact that wines identified as Pinot Noir can sell for more money than wines identified as Gamay Beaujolais, the number of wines carrying the Gamay moniker has been steadily decreasing in recent years. Given the fact that almost nothing grown in California is true Gamay, the Bureau of Alcohol, Tobacco and Firearms (BATF) has ruled that the name will no longer be allowed on wine labels starting in 2007. Nomenclature and science notwithstanding, California vineyardists still report some 800 acres of Gamay Beaujolais standing.

GEWURZTRAMINER   Grown in most European countries and having found a home in Australia and New Zealand as well, this highly perfumed white wine grape with the difficult name has succeeded well in California, Washington, and Oregon. Although a native of Italy, but not widely grown there now, its best showing is in the Alsace region of France, where it ripens to near-perfection with somewhat high alcohols and just the right amount of natural acidity. Elsewhere in the world, California included, the grape presents a bit of a trial. Grown too cold, it never gains the intense aromatics that mark it when fully ripe. When grown too warm, it loses acidity in the vineyard before it ripens and also shows a distinct bitter edge. The cooler parts of California (the Anderson Valley in Mendocino County, the Carneros District, and Monterey and Santa Barbara counties), as well as appropriate sites in the Pacific Northwest, have yielded the best-balanced Gewurztraminers grown in the country.

In spite of—or perhaps because of—its incredibly full and heady perfume that can be reminiscent of roses, cloves, nutmeg, lychee, and wildflowers, the wine has not grown in popularity and instead remains as one of the also-ran "sweet whites" amidst the Chardonnay and Sauvignon Blanc booms. More's the pity, because in addition to having deep and pretty characteristics, the wine, in its just slightly sweet configuration, goes exceptionally well with most pork-based sausages, with chicken prepared with a touch of sweetness or fruitiness, and with most Oriental foods. Though rarely produced to good effect as a dry wine in California or the Northwest, Gewurztraminer in that style, when successful, is absolutely smashing with fresh trout or cracked crab. The medium-sweet, quaffing style is well suited to the wines from middle-warmth vineyards, and allows California wineries to retain some of the grapes' natural sugars as a way of keeping the alcohol lower and at the same time using the retained sugar to buffer any tendency toward bitterness.

In the last few years, the California acreage devoted to Gewurztraminer has steadied at 1,700 (down from 3,900 in 85) and the number of wineries producing it has fallen. But it has retained its place of favor elsewhere in the West and, indeed, in most of the northern states with wine-producing industries. Important plantings (by county): Mendocino (300 acres), Monterey (600), Napa (100), Santa Barbara (200), Sonoma (300). There are also 300 acres in Washington and 200 acres in Oregon.

GRAY RIESLING   This popular, modestly priced, simple-tasting white vinifera wine is produced from the grape known as *Trousseau* or *Chauche Gris* in France, and is not, in fact, a member of the Riesling family. The widest-selling Gray Rieslings are offered in a mild, medium-acid style, with light, fruity flavors and no oak-barrel aging. They seem well suited for meals, especially seafood, and have become mainstays on some wine lists. Since the grape has very muted flavors on its own, the better Gray Rieslings on the market are usually blended with a little Sylvaner or Chenin Blanc to uplift their character. A few slightly sweet or medium-sweet versions are offered by the dozen or so California wineries that still put this variety on the market. The 100 acres of Gray Riesling standing in California represent a reduction of 95% in the last 15 years.

GRENACHE   The second most widely planted variety in the world, Grenache has never really made a home for itself in this country. Here, we use it for blending some fruit into jug wines, for rosés, and now, even for a so-called White Grenache. Until recently, Grenache was almost never used in the production of cork-finished red table wines, either on its own or as a major blending component. Perhaps one of the reasons is that 98% of all Grenache growing in California is in the Central Valley or in the almost abandoned vineyards of the Cucamonga area. Of late, a few enthusiasts of Rhone-type wines have begun searching out the coastal acreage (about 200 of some 11,700) for blending into their experimental and often successful flirtations with Rhone wines influenced by Grenache.

GRIGNOLINO   A grape of minor moment in its native Italy, where it produces light, simple red wines that barely hold their own with the most unchallenging foods, frothy reds, and base wines for red bubbly, Grignolino is, in California, used only by a tiny handful of wineries. The best-known Grignolino is the Rosé produced by Heitz Wine Cellars. Total plantings are less than 100 acres.

ICE WINE   Called *Eiswein* in Germany, it is produced from grapes whose juice has been frozen while they are still hanging on the vine (or occasionally nowadays in cold storage). When the frozen grapes are pressed, the resulting juice has a very high concentration of sugar; accordingly, the wines tend to be very sweet, and, one hopes, also carry concentrated aromas and flavors. These wines are a treasured rarity in Germany. We know of only a handful of American Ice Wines that have been produced naturally on the vine, although Bonny Doon Vineyards has been experimenting with Ice Wine from artificially frozen grapes—in refrigerators.

JOHANNISBERG RIESLING (also known as White Riesling in the U.S. and simply as Riesling in Germany)   Producing white wines with a distinctively fruity, floral, sometimes peachy, typically delicate varietal character, Johannisberg Riesling is made in every style from bone dry to very sweet, concentrated dessert wine. It has enjoyed great popularity in California but has lately fallen out of favor. In the 60s most California wineries produced this white vinifera in a dry, relatively austere, high-alcohol style, sometimes with a hint of oak, usually at the expense of the grape's subtle charms. The trend beginning in the 70s, spurred by consumer demand and improved technology, has been to stress the grape's more delicate qualities and to finish the wine in a slightly sweet to medium-sweet style. Another recent trend has been to allow the grapes to be attacked by *Botrytis cinerea*, the result being a luscious sweet wine. Rapid expansion of Johannisberg Riesling plantings pushed the 1980 acreage over 10,000; but now the total has dropped back to about 2,500 acres, over half of which is in Monterey County. Important plantings (by county): Mendocino (100 acres), Monterey (1,500), Napa (200), Santa Barbara (300), Sonoma (200).

MALBEC   Aside from its modest standing (200 acres total) as a potential blending grape for Cabernet Sauvignon, Malbec has no following in California. In its own right, it does produce decent, somewhat sturdy wine in some parts of the South of France and in Chile and Argentina. But in California, it has yet to prove itself either on its own or as a blender for Cabernet. Attempts to experiment with Malbec here have been discouraging because of the grape's tendency to yield little or no crop.

MALVASIA BIANCA   Something of an alternative to Muscat, the white wines made from this varietal are typically fragrant, sweet, and low in acidity. Most often, Malvasia wines are fortified to keep them from oxidizing quickly and to take advantage of the grape's ability to produce pleasing sweet after-dinner sips. Some 2,400 acres of the grape stand in California, of which the significant majority is in the hot Central Valley. Malvasia's 2,000-year presence in Mediterranean winemaking makes it more interesting as an historical footnote than as a wine.

MARSANNE   One of three dominant white grapes in the northern Rhone, Marsanne (along with Roussanne, with which it is sometimes blended, and Viognier) has enjoyed the most popularity because it is the easiest of the three to cultivate. Almost all wines identified as White Hermitage are made with Marsanne exclusively. In this country, Marsanne is an experiment, albeit one that has initially produced wines with a perfumed raciness not typical of the French version.

MATARO   This red vinifera variety, long out of favor in California but once planted substantially in the vineyards around Cucamonga, which have been disappearing in the last three decades under housing subdivisions, is in fact the Rhone-variety Mourvedre. In that guise and in the face of an awakening interest in Rhone-type wines, Matero or Mourvedre has begun to show the first signs of a comeback via new plantings in the North Coast. Small, forward-looking wineries like Bonny Doon, Cline, Qupe, and Edmunds St. John have recently used Mataro/Mourvedre in wines of interesting character. After a brief flirtation with Mataro as its own stand-alone varietal bottling, the grape has become more of a blending component. Of the 400 acres currently standing, 200 are in Contra Costa County.

MELON   Once a white grape of Burgundy, Melon became the major varietal in the Loire-Atlantique district of France in the 18th century and remains so today, under the more familiar name Muscadet. In California, many of the wines we called Pinot Blanc are, in fact, Melon (or Muscadet).

MERLOT   Long a variety of major importance in Bordeaux, where it is used for blending with Cabernet Sauvignon–based wines in the Médoc and Graves areas and as the primary grape in the red wines of Pomerol and St. Emilion, Merlot is also widely planted in other regions of France, as well as in Italy, in Hungary, and (to a lesser extent) in the Southern Hemisphere. In California, Merlot has come into fashion during the last two decades. Indeed, it was during the Cabernet planting boom of the early 70s that Merlot was first sought and planted as a blending grape to round out, soften, and add some complexity to Cabernet. But, just as some parts of Bordeaux are able to produce better wines based on Merlot than on Cabernet, so the vineyardists and wineries have found the same to be true here. As the vines matured, Merlot proved itself capable of yielding a wine that could stand on its own, and by the latter 70s California wineries had added a new name to their list of offerings.

The most critically acclaimed wines are medium-deep red to dark in color and have openly fruity aromas and flavors, often tinged with herbaceous, tealike, orange-rindy, currant, and/or cherryish notes. Merlot wines are almost always softer, rounder, and more supple than Cabernet in their youth, yet retain much of the latter variety's tendencies toward richness and complexity. While it is too early to know volumes about their long-range aging potential in California, current indications are that most mature earlier than Cabernet (which can last 15 to 30 years), but that the best have appeared to be holding well as they edge into their second decade. Moreover, there is an increasing tendency to add some Cabernet Sauvignon or some Cabernet Franc to Merlot to stiffen its constitution and add complexity, in hopes of pushing the wine into a longer and deeper aging cycle. As a result, Merlot easily challenges Pinot Noir as the second most expensive red varietal wine from California.

Merlot is also grown in the Pacific Northwest and has shown better in the warmer, eastern-lying vineyards of Washington than in Oregon's chilly and often damp settings. The wines of Leonetti, Chateau Ste. Michelle, and L'Ecole No. 41 have been frequent standouts. The standing acreage of Merlot in California hovered around the 3,500-acre mark until the mid-80s, but has grown rapidly to 38,500 acres in the last 15 years, with a marked decrease in acreage south of San Francisco and increasing concentration in the North Coast. Important plantings (by county) include: Mendocino (2,100), Monterey (3,200), Napa (5,900), San Joaquin (4,700), and Sonoma (5,500). In Washington, Merlot is the leading red varietal with some 3,900 acres in the ground, 50% of all red wine vines in the state.

MOSCATO    In its many variations, *Moscato* is nothing more than an artistic play on the name Muscat, based on the Italian spelling of the word, also spelled *Muscato* in Italy. The two Muscat grapes used primarily in California winemaking are Muscat Blanc and the Muscat of Alexandria.

MOURVEDRE    Also known in California as Mataro, this grape is a major player in the Rhone area of France; now, because there is a burgeoning interest among California vintners in trying to emulate Rhone wines, Mourvedre is making a comeback here. A few hundred acres of old vines remain standing and there is evidence that new plantings, albeit in small lots, are going in. In the hands of a new generation of experimenters, the old thin, tart style of wine has given way to a much riper and softer style. Yet even this style has not taken hold, and much of what is grown now goes into Rhone-type blends.

MUSCAT BLANC    One of the two Muscat grapes used extensively for winemaking in California, the Muscat Blanc is the finer and thus tends to be the predominant grape in most Muscat and Moscato bottlings. Its fragrant perfume of flowers and slight grapiness is best captured by modern, cold-fermentation techniques that also allow the winemaker to retain some of the grape sugars in the finished wine and to maintain a bit of a lively sparkle that further adds to the pretty, happy, highly quaffable nature of a well-made Muscat Blanc. Of the 1,300 acres currently planted in California, one-third are in cooler, coastal vineyards and two-thirds in the hotter Central Valley locations. The names Muscat Canelli and Muscat Frontignan are also used for wines made from this variety.

MUSCAT CANELLI   Another name for white, usually sweet-finished table wines made from the Muscat Blanc grape.

MUSCAT FRONTIGNAN   A synonym for the Muscat Blanc grape, it is typically reserved in California for wines that have been fortified by the addition of alcohol to produce after-dinner products. Beaulieu Vineyard makes an especially attractive fortified Muscat de Frontignan that captures the grape's fragrant charms.

MUSCAT OF ALEXANDRIA   A white wine grape in Mediterranean vineyards, it has historically been grown primarily as a raisin grape in California's Central Valley, where it has increasingly found its way into sweet-edged quaffing wines of little distinction. It is not unfair to report that a dollop of this wine is added to other inexpensive quaffers in order to boost and prettify aromas. Of the 5,200 standing acres (down from 11,500 in 76), only a portion is converted into wine.

NAPA GAMAY (also known as Gamay)   Once thought to be the grape of the Beaujolais region, this heavy-footed red varietal now turns out to be the lackluster Valdiguié, one of the workhorse grapes in the hot French Midi. As the truth of its heritage has become known in California, and with the Gamay Beaujolais strain of Pinot Noir producing more attractive wines, this mislabeled variety has slowly lost its place. The current 1,100 planted acres (down from 6,000 in 76) appear to be just a way station on this grape's journey to oblivion. The Gamay name will be phased out by 2007.

NEBBIOLO   Without question, Nebbiolo is one of the great red wine grapes of the world. In Italy's Piedmont region, Nebbiolo yields wines of depth, complexity, and, with aging, great finesse. The best of Italy's wines from Nebbiolo are called Barolo, Spanna, and Barbaresco. Here in California, Nebbiolo sits near the top of our wish list. We wish it grew here; we wish the few experiments with it had proven to be more successful; we wish more vineyardists would try it in hopes of finding a suitable site that would capture the grape's inherent charms. Once totaling over 500 acres, mostly in the Central Valley, it now covers about 200 and, aside from an occasional offering having little in common with Nebbiolo-based wines from Italy, has not yet earned a place as a separate varietal wine in California.

PETIT VERDOT   A minor grape in Bordeaux, it is used primarily (and not very extensively) to add color and tannin to red wines that otherwise lack those qualities. In California, a few producers of Cabernet Sauvignon/Merlot blends have planted Petit Verdot in the search for the quintessential locally grown combination of Bordeaux grapes. Only about 300 acres exist here, however, and little has come out of the early experiments with Petit Verdot to create a rush for new plantings.

PETITE SIRAH   During the early 70s, when the world discovered California wine and California winemakers discovered the world, grapes like Petite Sirah, which were capable of producing big, inky, tannic wines, came into vogue. It was California's way of saying, "We have arrived and we can make wines that live as long as any grown anywhere in the world." At the same time, the Central Valley growers of grapes for jug wine began to think that Petite Sirah would perform marvelously in their locales, and thus, thousands of acres were planted in California's warmest vineyards during that time. As a result of this unprecedented wave of new Petite Sirah plantings all over the state, the grape boasted some 13,000 acres by the end of that decade. Now, more than a decade later, Petite Sirah has fallen out of favor and shows but 2,700 acres still standing. Tastes changed away from big, tannic wines; whites replaced reds as the wines of choice; and Petite Sirah did not perform as well as expected in the Central Valley. Acreage in Napa County fell from 1,300 to 350, while acreage in Fresno County fell from 1,200 to 0!

Intriguingly, the vines left standing are producing better wine now than ever before, in part because the winemakers have adjusted to a somewhat more accessible style of wine and in part because those who still work with the grape are the ones who enjoyed the most critical success in the previous decades. Today's wines are still firm and robust, with more than a little tannin, and they match best with sturdy beef and lamb dishes and the occasional piece of cheese. But they are no longer confused by vineyardists with the true Syrah grape of France's Rhone region. Petite Sirah is now widely believed to be the common, and minor, French variety Durif; if so, it performs substantially better in California than it has ever done in France. Important plantings (by county): Mendocino (300 acres), Monterey (400), Napa (350), Sonoma (300).

PINOT BLANC    This white vinifera grape developed in France as a natural variant of Pinot Noir and is planted primarily in the Alsace region there. Both in France and in California, Pinot Blanc usually produces simple, moderately fruity, somewhat steely and narrow wines, although a few producers seem able to coax something richer and riper from the grape. Coupled with its modest flavors, the typical low yield in the vineyard has kept it from gaining popularity, in spite of attempts to cast it as another poor man's Chardonnay. Only a few outstanding examples coming from the dedicated efforts of small wineries achieve even that modest status. A number of wineries are turning to Pinot Blanc as a component in their better sparkling wines because of its brisk natural acidity and clean, almost neutral flavor. There are 1,000 acres planted in California, about 60% in Monterey County, but the number of producers offering it as a varietal wine has dropped from 24 to 10 or less in just the last few years. A good deal of Pinot Blanc's changing fortunes seems to be explained by recent research reports that claim much of what is planted here to be Melon rather than true Pinot Blanc.

PINOT CHARDONNAY    Not so long ago, the Chardonnay grape was thought to be one of the many variants (or clones) of the Pinot family—hence the Pinot prefix. That usage has all but disappeared on California wine labels, consistent with the evidence that Chardonnay is its own variety. Only a few wineries keep "Pinot" Chardonnay around for historical (albeit inaccurate) reasons.

PINOT GRIS    A red, sometimes pink-grey, variant of Pinot Noir, it is planted widely in Europe yet rarely produces memorable wines. Its most widely noted accomplishments have been in Italy, where the grape is called Pinot Grigio and yields simple, clean, inoffensive white wines. It has found a small but growing home in Oregon, where it is offered by about 50 producers. Among recent offerings, we have favored the King Estate Pinot Gris for its bright, open fruitiness. Recent plantings in California have increased its acreage here to 600. Oregon boasts almost 1,200 acres making Pinot Gris the number three grape there.

PINOT NOIR    The great red Burgundies of France, made from this grape, rate among the finest wines in the world. In vineyards like Romanée-Conti, Richebourg, Bonnes Mares, and Chambertin, Pinot Noir produces rich, lush, complex wines that age into even richer, lusher, and more complex wines having almost no rivals for range and drama. The natural comparisons with wines from Cabernet Sauvignon and its Bordelais associates show the Pinot Noirs as more inviting and more complex, often better suited to richer foods, and given to a much wider range of flavors and levels of performance. By contrast, the better Bordeaux reds, especially those influenced substantially by Cabernet Sauvignon, tend to be sturdier, longer-lived, more direct and more predictable wines.

But not all Pinot Noir is so well favored as the most famous names. And it is sadly true that when Pinot Noir wines are not rich and round, they tend, even in Burgundy, to become thin, mean, and uninviting. There is not much room for a middle ground in Burgundy and almost no middle ground for Pinot Noir outside of Burgundy. It is, some vineyardists and winemakers will tell you, the single greatest challenge of their careers to learn the secrets of this enigmatic grape and to find a way to tap its full potential. After all, even in Europe, there is a good deal of Pinot Noir planted outside Burgundy, but none of it makes red wines of real note.

Pinot Noir does, however, play an important role in the making of French Champagnes. For those wines, Pinot Noir is picked at somewhat low sugar levels and with high acids. It is combined with Chardonnay, also picked at lower sugars and higher acids, to make up the base cuvées for sparkling wine. Interestingly, for a grape capable of such dramatic range and complexity as a red wine, its usefulness in Champagnes is based on its ability to show almost no character in that setting, bringing only—but importantly—body and ageability rather than flavor.

In the New World, Pinot Noir displays all of the problems experienced by European producers. That has not stopped vineyardists from growing it and winemakers from trying to coax the best of red Burgundy out of it. If failure occurs more often than success, there is an increasing number of growers and producers in California and Oregon who are proving that the cause is not lost. Indeed, for most of California's vinous history, Pinot Noir was the number-two red wine at the quality end of the scale. Those early wines, while in no way resembling their French counterparts, always managed to convey a sense of depth and weight as a substitute for the more subtle and complex phrasings that are Pinot Noir's claim to nobility. Then, in the early 70s, first Zinfandel and then Merlot seemed to push Pinot Noir from center stage; as a result, the number of labels offered in California shrank dramatically.

The true Pinot Noir aficionados, however, never gave up on the grape, and even as its market popularity was slipping, its fortunes in the hands of the true believers were rising. For more than a decade now, a dedicated band of wineries has been conducting a wide variety of experiments. Trials with clones, stems in the fermentation, open versus closed fermenters, crop levels in the vineyard, soil types, trellising systems for the vines, and leaf stripping have produced a variety of positive but not always replicable results. So, even today, just as a decade ago and a decade before that, consistently and reliably great Pinot Noir from West Coast vineyards remains as much hope as reality.

Some things have been learned. It is now almost universally recognized that Pinot must not be allowed to get too ripe lest it lose its fruit and its potential for grandeur. This single discovery in itself means that Pinot Noir is a more enjoyable wine now than it was in the past. Another recent finding that produces more fruit in Pinot Noir is to plant it in cooler areas, rather than the mid-valley hotlands where it once grew side by side with Cabernet Sauvignon and other medium-warmth varietals. The Carneros District in southern Napa and Sonoma counties, the near-coastal Russian River Valley, and cool areas south of San Francisco in Monterey, San Luis Obispo, and Santa Barbara counties have all proven to be rewarding places to plant Pinot Noir. To these cool-climate California locations must be added the majority of Oregon locations. Indeed, Oregon Pinots seem to develop color and flavor at excessively low levels of ripeness and, as a result, only in an unusual year will Oregon produce richness to go along with balance and fruit.

Even with all the obstacles, there is plenty to like about locally grown Pinot Noir wines. Smaller producers such as Dehlinger, Talley, Ojai, and Drouhin have shown the ability to find fruit, balance, and richness in the grape. To their number must be added another two to three dozen small and dedicated establishments that have raised the stakes in the Pinot game. They have brought the grape back to the point where it now challenges the number-two red position in California again, and is already clearly number one among reds in Oregon.

The use of Pinot Noir in French Champagne is paralleled in California. In recent years, the best California bubblies have contained anywhere from 60% to 100% Pinot Noir. By some estimates, in fact, as much as one-third of all the Pinot Noir grown in California goes into the production of sparkling wine. It plays a more important role here than in France, however; the locally grown fruit has more flavor and contributes a positive fresh, bright quality.

Plantings of Pinot Noir in California have remained more or less static for the last decade and now total some 11,200 acres. Important plantings (by county) include: Mendocino (700 acres), Monterey (1,800), Napa (2,400), Santa Barbara (1,200), and Sonoma (4,100). There are 3,000 acres of Pinot Noir planted in Oregon and about 200 in Washington.

PORT   In the United States, this term is applied to sweet, fortified, usually red wines made in the style of the Port produced in the Douro region of Portugal. A few U.S. producers (Quady, St. Amant, Ficklin, Masson, among others) attempt to employ the same or similar grapes as used in Portugal and, at their best, achieve a reasonable semblance of the real thing—that is to say that their ports can combine richness, depth, fruit (as opposed to raisins), and aging potential. Those examples notwithstanding, most local ports are simple, cheap, quickly made, and have little in common with their Portuguese namesakes.

RED TABLE WINE   This title is gaining increased usage for generic wines, usually blended and inexpensive, in substitution for the borrowed handles Burgundy, Claret, and Chianti. In current practice, the coastal-oriented wineries have been more likely to adopt this term than the big jug-wine producers, for whom Burgundy remains the generic name of choice (and marketplace acceptance).

RHINE   Borrowed from one of the premier wine-growing regions of Germany, this title is often used by American wineries as a generic name for ordinary white wines with lots of sweetness.

RIESLING   Used as a shortened version for any of the grapes (Johannisberg, Grey, Sylvaner) whose last name is Riesling, the term is most often applied to those wines deriving their identity from one of the lesser varieties, since Johannisberg Riesling on the label would seem to carry more prestige than the Riesling title by itself. "Rieslings" usually carry slight to medium sweetness.

ROSÉ   This is the artsy term for pink wine made for early consumption. The best achieve a fresh, fruity taste and carry enough acid to balance the sweetness that most rosés have. Many rosés also possess varietal names (Zinfandel Rosé, Gamay Rosé, for example) but rosés made from blends of grapes are not necessarily less attractive. The wine's color is achieved either by blending red wine into white or by keeping the juice of red wine grapes (which starts out white and acquires color during fermentation) from extensive contact with the grape skins. Either way, the trick is to acquire a pleasing pinkish hue that suggests a lighter body and taste than red wine. Use with food depends on the degree of sweetness.

ROUSSANNE   One of three white wine grapes usually associated with the northern Rhone area (along with Marsanne, with which it has often been blended, and Viognier), Roussanne yields wines of great perfume and a certain delicacy. Its presence in California is strictly on an experimental basis, and it has been seriously pursued mainly by just a handful of producers. Only 80 acres are planted in California, mostly in the last five years.

RUBY CABERNET   In theory, Ruby Cabernet should have been the answer. After all, it is a man-created grape that was said to combine the wonderful intensity and beauty of Cabernet Sauvignon with the high yield and heat-withstanding abilities of Carignane. Plant it, the professors said, in the hot Central Valley and we'll be awash in the best low-priced red wine ever to gladden the palate of mankind. Its meteoric rise in the grape-planting extravagances of the early 70s (2,000 acres added in 71; 7,000 in 72; 4,000 in 73) accounted for the greater part of its 18,000 standing acres by 76. But the wines turned out to be dull, soft, and not at all like Cabernet Sauvignon, and that sad result, together with the ensuing white wine boom, has led to the elimination of two-thirds of the Ruby Cabernet in just over 10 years. By the 90s, the grape can claim just 7,500 acres remaining. Fewer than 10 wineries offer it as a separate varietal wine, and half of those are fledgling efforts in Texas or New Mexico.

SANGIOVESE   The dominant grape in the Chianti wines of Italy's Tuscany region has been almost totally ignored throughout California's vinous history. Since 90, 2,500 acres have been planted, almost half in Napa and Sonoma but with sprinklings everywhere from Monterey to Lodi to Amador County. Among the successful practitioners to date are Shafer and Swanson in the Napa Valley and Vino Noceto in Amador. Ferrari-Carano makes an impressive Sangiovese-Cabernet Sauvignon blend called Siena, which is somewhat sturdier and long-aging than the typical easy-drinking California Sangiovese. Important plantings include: Napa (500) and Sonoma (300).

SAUTERNE  Bearing no resemblance to the stunning wines from France's Sauternes region, the few cheap white wine blends that appear under this generic moniker are most often overly sweet, dull, and uninviting.

SAUVIGNON BLANC  This very popular white grape is second only to Chardonnay for the production of quality dry white table wines in California (many of which are identified by the name Fumé Blanc). The grape produces wines with a distinctive grassy, herbal quality, usually with a bounty of natural grape acidity. This combination has made Sauvignon Blanc very useful and exceptionally popular for service with fish and shellfish, as well as with herb-seasoned poultry dishes. Its typical price is one-half to two-thirds that of the same producers' Chardonnays, which may also account for its continuing rise in popularity.

Much of the California inspiration for Sauvignon Blanc has come from France, where the grape is planted in the Loire region and produces, especially in Sancerre and Pouilly-Fumé, wines of a refreshingly fruity, sometimes green character. As in California, the Loire's best Sauvignon Blancs can age to gain an added measure of complexity and a certain supple richness they never had when young. Sauvignon Blanc is also grown in Bordeaux, although only a few châteaux try to make truly great wine from it. Rather, Sauvignon is usually consigned to vineyards in which red grapes cannot produce miracles, and that, for the majority of white Bordeaux wines, means areas like Entre-Deux-Mers and other Bordelais regions of less than "classified" standing. In the Sauternes region of Bordeaux, however, Sauvignon Blanc is a minor but important player in the luscious sweet wines of the area.

The predominant style for California's Sauvignon Blanc wines has undergone a change in recent years. The once-sought-after extremes of varietal character, which gave the wine a pungent, almost dandelion-greens quality, have been tempered. Most producers are now trying to make wines that are a bit more subtle in their grassy, weedy aspects. To accomplish this, wineries employ a variety of techniques, including warmer fermentations, more sun exposure for the grapes in the vineyard, and reduced skin contact with the grape skins prior to the initial phases of fermentation.

The inclusion of Semillon in some Sauvignon Blancs has also had a salutary effect in producing less varietally overbearing versions. Winemakers have found that Semillon helps flesh out the somewhat narrow flavors of Sauvignon Blanc, without detracting from its essentially tight-knit structure on the palate. At the same time, it can bring along a note of floral prettiness that fits comfortably with the Sauvignon Blanc personality.

The most noteworthy producer of the variety remains the Robert Mondavi Winery, with names like Matanzas Creek, Kenwood, Duckhorn, and Simi having important places in the sweepstakes and often winning the highest-quality awards, if not the volume title. After a brief surge in attention during the 80s, this variety has remained more or less static in planted acreage even while Chardonnay has grown at an astronomical rate. The existing 11,200 acres include the following important plantings (by county): Lake (900), Mendocino (700), Monterey (1,100), Napa (1,900), San Joaquin (1,600), and Sonoma (1,700).

SAUVIGNON VERT  This grape variety can still be found in California, but its 30 acres, down from 1,000 two decades earlier in the face of the trebling of planted grape acreage, is dramatic proof of its low standing. Long thought to be a cousin of Sauvignon Blanc and eclipsed by that variety in every regard, Sauvignon Vert is now believed to be, in fact, Muscadelle—a minor and vanishing variety from the

Sauternes region of France. The grape has rarely shown up in varietally designated bottlings in the last decade.

SCHEUREBE   One of many German crossbreeds, this one came into being in 1916 when the botanist Georg Scheu crossed Johannisberg Riesling with Sylvaner. The result was a grape with both higher yields and higher natural sugars when grown on the same sites as Riesling. Nonetheless, Riesling has remained king in the high-quality regions (Rheingau and Moselle) of Germany, while the Scheurebe and Müller-Thurgau have found success only in regions where volumes of wine sold at lesser prices (i.e., Liebfraumilch) are produced. It is occasionally made into wine in this country and has its Riesling parent's ability to develop late harvest characteristics.

SEMILLON   Semillon seems to be all over the globe—but where there is Semillon, there is not necessarily exciting wine. Indeed, everywhere it is planted in France, except for Sauternes, as well as in Chile, Argentina, Australia, and South Africa, Semillon almost always seems to produce wines of mediocre character, at best. Yet, attempts to make dry Semillons into something better are now succeeding in California, Australia, and France. The wine's natural sense of weight has allowed it to accept a substantial amount of oak aging with grace, while at the same time those wines grown in cooler climates and fermented at relatively lowered temperatures have shown an attractive floral streak. Whether these directions will take hold and lead to a new generation of Semillons throughout the world and an increase in acreage in California remains to be seen. Certainly, Semillon is at present a minor player on the West Coast. Its acreage, now 1,400, planted all around the state in both moderate and overheated locations, has been dropping slowly in spite of the continued increase in acreage of varieties like Chardonnay and Sauvignon Blanc. And while some wineries in the Pacific Northwest have produced very fine Semillons, the wine remains on the second team there as well.

Semillon does enjoy a role as a blending agent for dry-styled Sauvignon Blanc in some parts of the world, including Bordeaux and the U.S., where Semillon may constitute anywhere from 10% to 25% of the Sauvignon Blancs of Joseph Phelps and Duckhorn to 50% of wines like Haut-Brion Blanc. California, however, has not yet found the key to the sweet, late harvest wines made from Semillon-dominated blendings with Sauvignon Blanc which are so successful in the Sauternes region of France (Château d'Yquem being the most famous example). Important plantings (by county): Alameda (100 acres), Monterey (100), Napa (200), Sonoma (200).

SHERRY   In California, and indeed throughout the U.S., the term "Sherry" is used generically for fortified wines, usually sweet, which have been baked, aged, or artificially infused with yeasts, all of which are intended to create a product similar to Spanish Sherry. The dry versions rarely measure up, although occasionally a wine in the rich, sweet style of Cream Sherry can challenge the popular Spanish blends.

SOUZAO   This Portuguese grape is more highly thought of for port production in the U.S. than it is in its native land. It adds a ripe, slightly raisiny, concentrated quality to California port and, in the hands of the Masson Winery, has been made successfully into one-varietal port.

SPARKLING WINE   Any wine with noticeable bubbles (beyond the mild spritz that occasionally remains behind in still table wines) is probably a sparkling wine. In technical terms, it must contain at least two atmospheres of pressure. In layman's terms, this means that it pops and fizzes when opened and has lots of bubbles rising exuberantly in the glass. The gas, carbon dioxide, is the same as that which puts the bubbles into your Pepsi or Perrier, but the method for getting it into sparkling wine is usually a little more complicated than that used with soft drinks and bottled waters. For, while it is legally permissible to inject the fizz into wine, almost no one does it, even for low-end products. The techniques used in this country for putting the bubbles into bubbly, ranging from most complex (expensive) to least, are: *méthode Champenoise,* transfer process, and bulk (Charmat) process. Each is explained in the chapter WINE LANGUAGE. In the U.S., the term "champagne" is a legal alternative, but it has become the custom for the best bubblies to avoid it and instead to be sold as sparkling wines.

SYLVANER (also called Sylvaner Riesling and Franken Riesling)   Heading for the endangered species list here in California, this once famous white variety has held on tenaciously although not entirely successfully in Germany, where it has been substantially replaced by the ubiquitous Müller-Thurgau. Never the hit in California that it was for German vineyardists, Sylvaner has now been abandoned by most West Coast producers and growers. Standing acreage has dropped to about 50 and no new acreage has been reported in any location for over a decade. Twenty years ago there was as much Sylvaner as there was Chardonnay or Sauvignon Blanc in California.

SYMPHONY   This new grape variety, produced from a cross of Muscat of Alexandria and Grenache Gris, was released for commercial planting in 81. Today, some 400 acres are in production, and one winery, the now defunct Chateau de Baun, gave the grape full opportunity to show its mettle by using it for everything from sparkling wine to dry table wine to sweet dessert wine. Symphony's character varies from mild spiciness at average ripeness for table wine to intense peach-and-apricot qualities at higher levels of ripeness. However, Symphony has not made much of a home for itself in a wine setting that has seen sharp acreage decreases in all of the coastal-grown "sweet whites."

SYRAH   California vineyardists have long grown a grape they call Petite Sirah which, until the last decade, they believed to be the Syrah grape of France's Rhone district. Now it turns out that Petite Sirah is almost certainly Durif, and California has had to plant Syrah (4,200 acres almost all in the 90s). From this somewhat meager resource, a handful of enterprising vintners are trying, with increasing levels of success, to produce Rhone-like red wines. The growing number of triumphs capture Syrah's deep, almost dense quality, reminiscent of wild blackberries cast in a slightly drier, less effusively fruity mold than Zinfandel's berryish fruit, and adding in hints of black pepper, tar, saddle leather, cassis, and other vinous exotica. That kind of complexity, taken together with the richness, depth, and sturdiness found in the near 100%-Syrah northern Rhone wines, has allowed French appellations like Hermitage and Côte Rotie to challenge the leading Bordeaux and Burgundies in price and attractiveness. Elsewhere in the Rhone, especially in the southern Rhone, Syrah tends to be blended with other grapes, and in many areas is submerged to the point of losing its identifiable character. Châteauneuf-du-Pape, the most famous southern Rhone red, can legally contain 13 separate varieties; and, while Syrah and Grenache may dominate some wines, others are fully integrated blends.

Now with a decade of experimenting coming to a close, Syrah has established a small but increasingly important foothold in the New World. When successful, it is giving us wines of depth, intensity, mass, and aging potential. And while it often comes blended with such lesser grapes as Mourvedre and Grenache, Syrah is the base even in most of the Rhone blends. On its own, Syrah has shown spectacularly of late in many parts of California, including the Central Coast (Ojai and Eberle), Napa (Phelps and Swanson), Sonoma County (Geyser Peak and Hamel), and the Sierra Foothills (Domaine de la Terre Rouge and Sierra Vista). Important plantings include: Mendocino (200), Monterey (200), Napa (200), San Joaquin (700), San Luis Obispo (400), Santa Barbara (200), and Sonoma (400).

THOMPSON SEEDLESS   Not so long ago, this popular table and raisin grape, which represents almost 35% of all grapes of every type planted in California, was also California's most widely used wine grape. Although no winery in recent memory has called attention to the inclusion of Thompson in its inexpensive jug blends and cheap sparkling wine, many producers still do rely on this low-acid, low-flavor grape for their generic products. Thompson Seedless's number-one position as a wine grape was surpassed in 83 when immense waves of new French Colombard acreage surged into production. One hopes that the ready availability of Colombard, and Chenin Blanc as well, taken together with the demand for raisins, will continue to diminish Thompson's role in winemaking. Much of the current Thompson Seedless crush goes into brandy or into grape concentrate.

TINTA MADEIRA   Claimed as, but not proven to be, a true Portuguese variety, this red grape is grown almost exclusively in the Central Valley for use in the production of port. Its near-total drop in acreage over the last decade (to less than 50 acres) evidences its fall from grace.

VIN GRIS   Following the custom of a few small regions of France, a winery will occasionally offer a bottle of dry, lightly colored rosé or Blanc de Noirs that carries the name Vin Gris (literally, "Gray Wine") in an attempt to separate its bottling from the mounds of sweeter versions. Many wines labeled Vin Gris are made from Pinot Noir grapes, following the traditional Burgundy practice.

VIOGNIER   Once one of the rarest varieties in the world, this white grape measured but 49 acres in its native France in the late 70s. Then along came the Californian contingent, which planted a few acres as an experiment and immediately began to make wines of uncommon depth and prettiness. Highlighted by a fresh, floral quality that is not found in the French versions of the variety, Viognier has begun to catch on in California. And, based on the success shown here, it has begun to expand its place in France as well. The best of the French versions still come from the Northern Rhone around Condrieu, while California's leaders are spread across the state, from Phelps and Graham in the North Coast to Calera and Alban in the Central Coast. Plantings of Viognier now total 1,100 acres and are centered in: Mendocino (100), Napa (100), San Benito (100), and Sonoma (150).

WHITE   Except for the White Riesling, all the so-called "white varietals" (White Zinfandel being most prominent among them) are nothing more than white (or light pink) wines made from the free-run juice of red-skinned (and thus, red wine) grapes. This term, in conjunction with the varietal name of a red wine grape, is synonymous with Blanc de Noirs.

WHITE RIESLING   Some wineries and at least one state (Oregon) have opted to use this name on wines made from the grape more commonly called Johannisberg Riesling in the U.S. or simply Riesling in its native Germany.

WHITE TABLE WINE   Generic white wine blends, often from coastal wineries wishing to find an upscale term as an alternative to the ubiquitous Chablis-labeled jug-wine offerings, are found under this name.

WHITE ZINFANDEL   Not a grape variety, but rather a white wine (usually with a distinct pink "blush") made from the Zinfandel grape, it has been around in limited production for most of the century. Only in the last decade, however, has the popularity of White Zinfandel skyrocketed. The Sutter Home Winery, whose brawny Amador County Zinfandels gained prominence in the early 70s, is generally given the credit for initiating the White Zinfandel boom sometime in the latter 70s. And while it is true that Sutter Home White Zinfandel was the first to gain widespread fame and remains today one of the best-selling White Zinfandels, the wine was first made in California by other wineries, including David Bruce.

   The dominant style of White Zinfandel intends to be high in freshness and fruitiness, with 1% to 3% residual sugar, and enough acidity and occasionally a slight spritziness to be light and lively on the palate. At its best, the wine is a fine quaff and can, in its less sweet styles, accompany most picnic foods. It should be consumed in the bloom of youth and well chilled.

The White Zinfandel phenomenon appears to be a combination of several converging trends, including the white wine boom, the aging of the "Coca-Cola" crowd, and the search for something better by wine cooler aficionados. It has occurred concurrently with a decrease in the popularity of every other sweet white variety, especially including Chenin Blanc, and is probably partly responsible for the latter's current lack of favor.

ZINFANDEL    Its origins cloaked in mystery for most of its 130-year history in California winemaking, this red grape, now thought to be related to southern Italy's Primativo, and possibly Yugoslavia's Mali Plavac, is used in everything from the production of the trendy White Zinfandel (and its derivative, sparkling White Zinfandel) to hearty, robust red wines filled with fruit, tannin, depth, and semblances of complexity and longevity. It is in this latter guise that Zinfandel came to popularity in the early 70s through the interest shown in stands of old vines by wineries like Sutter Home (now known more for its tidal wave of White Zinfandel) and Ridge. Within a few years, the modern-era boom in California wine took Zinfandel along for the ride; using the enormous standing acreage as a base, this now noble grape was elevated from jug-wine obscurity into something approaching the adored status of Cabernet Sauvignon. By the late 70s, hundreds of wineries were producing Zinfandel (the red version) in a full-bodied, fairly sturdy style, and aging the wine in barrels heretofore reserved for the likes of Cabernet and Pinot Noir. Of course, the price escalated as well, and when the backlash came against red wines in general and California reds more specifically, the expensive versions of Zinfandel took it on the chin.

Along came White Zinfandel to take up the overflow in grape production, and, for a period of time lasting through most of the 80s, wineries found they could often make as much or more money selling the "white" product within months of harvest rather than the barrel-aged, red version two to three years after picking the grapes. During that time, the number of red wines from Zinfandel fell by over 50%. It is only in the 90s that robust, red Zinfandel has come back into favor, boosted, in large measure, by the renewed focus on California Cabernet and the resulting price escalation in that variety, which has made the $8–12 Zins of the early 90s seem like relative bargains.

In medium-warmth coastal locations, especially sheltered hillsides, Zinfandel yields medium-full-bodied, intensely flavored wines with substantial tannin. The best wines of this type show Zinfandel's vigorous, berrylike, sometimes spicy varietal character. Late-harvest Zinfandels (a style more associated with the 70s than the 80s) are high in alcohol and frequently contain residual sugar. When well made, they are a fruity alternative to port; but when made poorly or from poor grapes, they take on cooked, desiccated flavors often running in the direction of "pruniness." Lately, the overripe style of Zinfandel has made a comeback with a few aficionados for its out-and-out power and intensity. Favorites of the "more is better" crowd are Turley, Martinelli, DeLoach, and Lava Cap.

Parts of Sonoma County—notably the Dry Creek Valley, the Sonoma Valley, and the Lytton Springs and Geyserville areas—as well as Amador and Napa counties have yielded most of the exceptional Zinfandels of the last decade and a half. The Paso Robles area also produces its share of ripe, fleshy, somewhat early-maturing Zins in the hands of such worthies as Peachy Canyon and Saucelito Canyon. The grape is also widely grown in the Central Valley, including the Lodi area, which contains almost 40% of the state's total plantings. Lodi Zinfandels often display the variety's berrylike nature, but tend toward flatter, earthier qualities at the expense of the lively, vigorous character found in other regions. Jug-wine Zinfandels exhibit the same lack of virtue found in most wines of the type.

Zinfandel is a versatile grape, and has proven successful in a variety of other styles, including light fruity red wine, rosé, and Nouveau. Over 400 producers and a substantial number of private bottlers produce Zinfandel from the state's 50,500 standing acres, a number that has grown in the last few years after holding steady for several decades even as the grape's fortunes as a wine grape have changed with some regularity. Important plantings (by county) include: Amador (1,700 acres), Mendocino (700), Monterey (1,900), Napa (2,000), San Joaquin (17,300), San Luis Obispo (1,700), and Sonoma (4,300).

# Wine Geography

Every bottle of wine identifies the source of its grapes—its "appellation"—prominently on its label. For wines of the United States, the appellation shown can be as broad as "American," meaning that the grapes could have come from anywhere in the 50 states, or as limited as "Sonoma Mountain," meaning that the source could only have been those few hundred acres of vines grown on that one particular hill southeast of Santa Rosa, California.

The rules governing the use of appellations in this country are established by the U.S. Bureau of Alcohol, Tobacco and Firearms. Under BATF regulations, any wine produced from grapes grown here can carry the appellations American or United States. Similarly, any wine is entitled to bear the name of the state or states (up to three contiguous), or the county or counties (up to three within the same state), where the grapes were grown. Wine labels may also bear the appellation of a specified delimited area, officially called an "American Viticultural Area" (AVA), which distinguishes itself from surrounding areas by geographic features (including soil, elevation, topography, and climate).

When one county is named as the appellation, only 75% of the grapes used in its production need come from that county; if two or three counties are specified, all grapes must come from the named counties. Wines from Viticultural Areas are required to have 85% of their contents from the named appellation. Wines labeled with one or more states as their appellations must be made 100% from the named state(s).

To establish such a delimited American Viticultural Area, which may range in size from a few hundred acres to several million (total acreage—not grape acreage), interested parties (usually growers and/or wineries) petition the Bureau of Alcohol, Tobacco and Firearms for recognition by providing evidence that the proposed area is worthy of special consideration by virtue of its unique character for grape growing. BATF holds public hearings and receives evidence from anyone with an opinion on the proposed Viticultural Area, then accepts, rejects, or amends the boundaries as it sees fit. The process moves slowly and often with great difficulty when conflicting views are presented by the various vested interests.

Some of the defined Viticultural Area appellations (for example, Howell

Mountain or Shenandoah Valley) are small enough and possessed of such uniform soil and weather that their names on the label offer a clear indication of the conditions under which the grapes were grown. Others are either so large (North Coast) or so remote and undeveloped (Willow Creek) that no inference can confidently be drawn or, indeed, needs to be. The one thing that can be said about any approved AVA appellation on a label is that it defines the source of the grapes. By contrast, most appellation systems in Europe, particularly those used in the most famous wine-growing areas, specify the grape varieties which may be grown within an appellation, the maximum production allowed, the degree of ripeness the grapes must attain in order to be considered representative of the area, and for a few appellations, a minimum level of quality.

In this chapter, we discuss each of the identified American Viticultural Areas in California and in the Pacific Northwest, with an eye toward giving the reader a sense of the importance each enjoys and why. Other place names are also referenced, either because they are destined to become Viticultural Areas in the future or because they appear frequently on wine labels or crop up in discussions about wine.

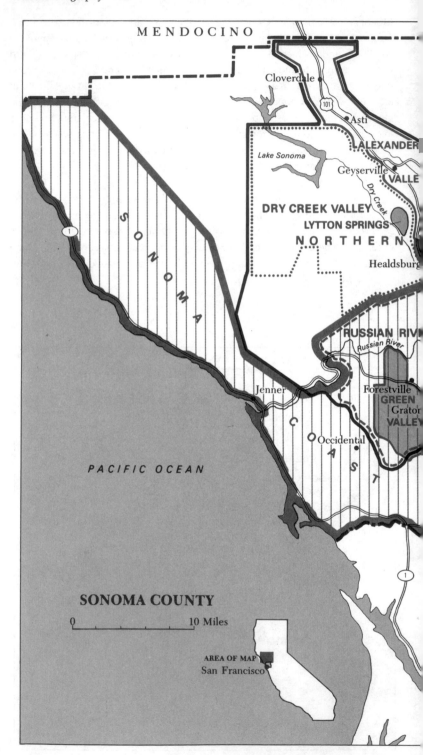

MENDOCINO

Cloverdale

101

Asti

LALEXANDER

Lake Sonoma

Geyserville

VALLE

DRY CREEK VALLEY

LYTTON SPRINGS

NORTHERN

Healdsburg

Dry Creek

S O N O M A

RUSSIAN RIV

Russian River

Jenner

Forestville

GREEN

Grator

VALLEY

C O A S T

Occidental

1

PACIFIC OCEAN

**SONOMA COUNTY**

0         10 Miles

**AREA OF MAP**

San Francisco

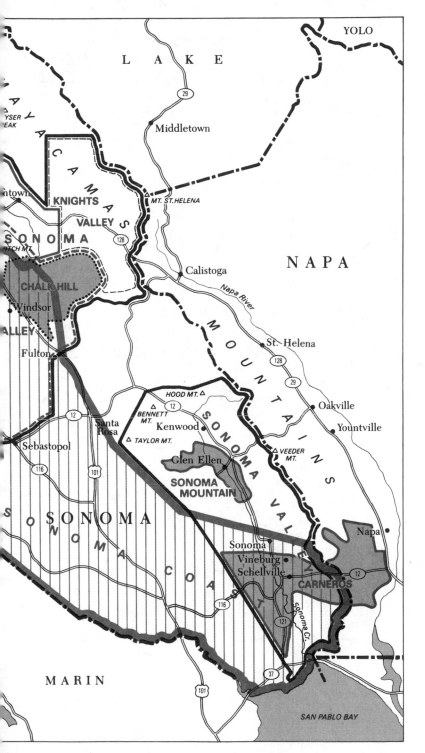

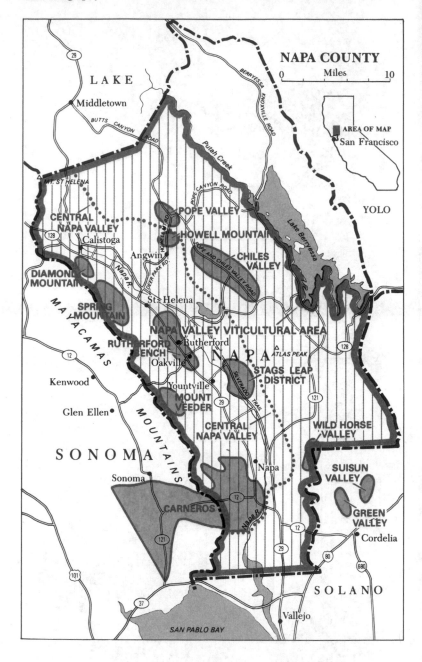

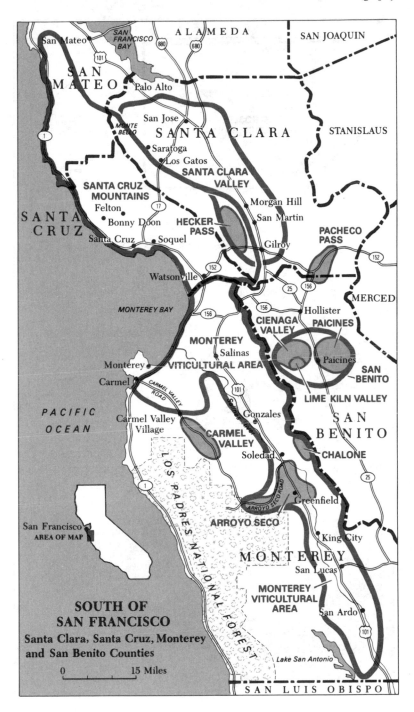

SOUTH OF
SAN FRANCISCO

Santa Clara, Santa Cruz, Monterey
and San Benito Counties

0        15 Miles

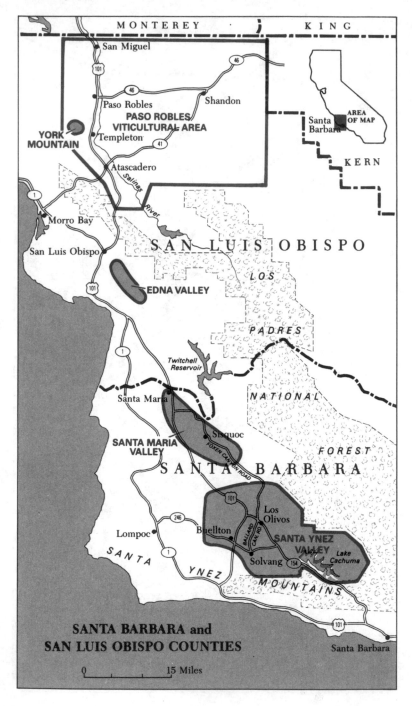

**SANTA BARBARA and
SAN LUIS OBISPO COUNTIES**

0     15 Miles

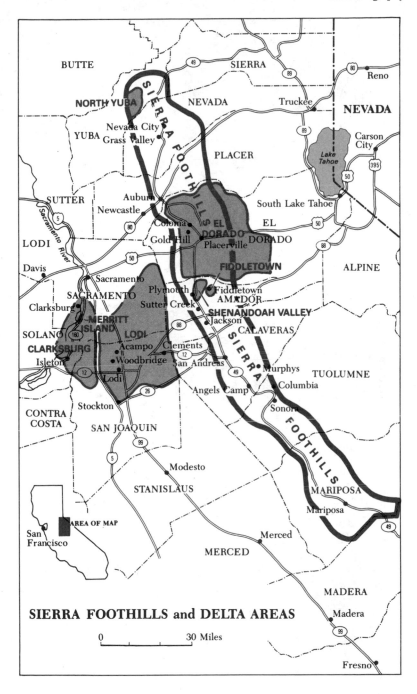

# SIERRA FOOTHILLS and DELTA AREAS

0            30 Miles

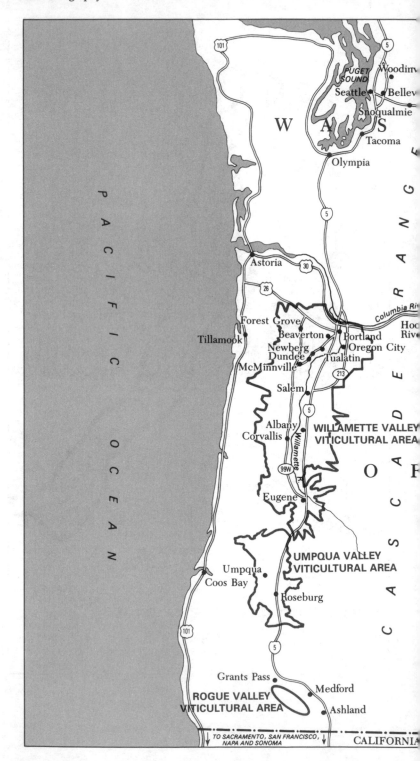

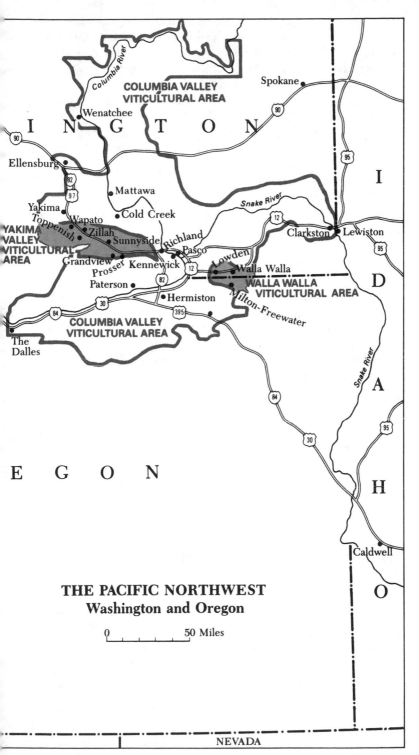

**THE PACIFIC NORTHWEST**
Washington and Oregon

0       50 Miles

In California, a principal distinguishing characteristic of a place where grapes are grown is the amount of heat to which the grapes are subjected during a typical growing year. The conventional measure employed is "degree days," which is the average temperature in excess of 50° F. for each given day during the growing season (i.e., a day that averages 66° is said to have 16 "degree days"). The total of the degree days during the growing season is used as a measure of the warmth of a particular growing area. Cool areas, those with fewer than 2,500 degree days, are referred to as Region I, and are considered to be most suited to grapes like Johannisberg Riesling and Pinot Noir and grapes for sparkling wine. Areas that have accumulations of 2,500–3,000 degree days are called Region II, and are regarded as appropriate for Cabernet Sauvignon, Chardonnay, Sauvignon Blanc, and Merlot.

Region III growing areas, with heat totals in the range of 3,000–3,500 degree days, are on the borderline between temperatures suitable for growing the better (and more difficult) grapes and temperatures best for growing high-volume, jug-wine grapes and inexpensive varietals. Nevertheless, Region III can be hospitable to Zinfandel, Petite Sirah, Syrah, and Chenin Blanc, and is not totally inappropriate for the varieties that thrive in Region II growing conditions. Regions IV and V, with degree days ranging up to and beyond 4,000, are relatively warm for grapes and rarely produce wines of significance from a collector's viewpoint, but do yield the greatest part of the wines produced in California.

Acreage figures for each of the listed counties are derived from reports of the various state departments and are funded by the U.S. Department of Agriculture. Figures quoted for counties are dated May, 1998.

ALAMEDA COUNTY   Located directly across the Bay from San Francisco, Alameda County contains 1,600 acres devoted to grapes today, down from 2,000 a decade ago. Almost all of the acreage is found in the Livermore Valley, and about 75% of the total is used to grow white varieties. The Livermore Valley was famous for white wines long before Prohibition. Today, the leading grapes are Chardonnay (700 acres), Cabernet Sauvignon (300), Merlot (150), and Sauvignon Blanc (100). Wente and Concannon, two of the oldest wineries in Livermore, own most of the vineyards. Both worked hard in the 80s to restore the reputation of Livermore Valley. Of the 20 other producers in the county, many can be found in the Oakland-Berkeley area, and the majority tend to be part-time winemakers. Though their production is often only a few hundred cases per year, their performances can surpass many big, well-financed competitors. Rosenblum Cellars, on the basis of its great success with Zinfandel, and Edmunds St. John, renowned for its Rhone-type wines, are two of the best-known and most successful of the urban producers.

ALEXANDER VALLEY (Sonoma)   This 12-mile-long inland American Viticultural Area follows the course of the Russian River from north of Cloverdale until it flows past Healdsburg in the south. The northern boundary of the area is defined by the Mendocino County border, and its southern boundary, shared with the Chalk Hill Viticultural Area, is found northeast of Windsor. As a landlocked piece of topography, the Alexander Valley is a warm part of the county, with the river offering the primary tempering influence. Summertime fog is an infrequent guest that rarely stays long. The northern pockets from Cloverdale to just south of Geyserville tend to satisfy heat-loving varieties like Zinfandel. For other locales, especially those near the river or along the benchlands, earlier-ripening grapes (Chardonnay, Riesling, Gewurztraminer) fare surprisingly well. Such well-known Chardonnay suppliers as Robert Young Vineyards, Belle Terre, and the Gauer Ranch are located on upper benchlands. In general, the valley's gravelly, sandy loam soils are quite fertile, and vines tend to be vigorous and productive. This vigorous tendency helps to account for the strong, often pungent character of Alexander Valley–grown Sauvignon Blanc.

Of the close to 8,000 acres under vine, the leading varieties are Cabernet Sauvignon and Chardonnay. The Cabernets range widely in style. The best capture a berry, cherry fruit, with herbal notes that avoid a strong bell pepper character and overripeness. Napa's Silver Oak—along with Clos du Bois and Simi—has coaxed the most depth and charm out of Alexander Valley Cabernet, in our experience. Noteworthy Alexander Valley Chardonnay is more plentiful, and at its best presents ripe apple and spice aromas, fat, ripe fruit flavors that are deep and lush, and typically strong. At their finest, these Chardonnays reach °°° levels. Chardonnay from local growers is much in demand, and many wineries outside the region regularly bottle an Alexander Valley Chardonnay.

Close to two dozen producers are located within the Alexander Valley. Among the best known are larger ones such as Geyser Peak, Chateau Souverain, and Clos du Bois, and smaller ones like Jordan and Simi. Gallo has a large vineyard in the Alexander Valley from which it has successfully produced copious quantities of moderately priced varietal and limited quantities of expensive bottlings.

AMADOR COUNTY    Smack in the middle of the Sierra Foothills grape-growing district, Amador County shares the rich heritage of Gold Rush era winemaking with counties both north and south of it. And, as with its neighbors, the times passed it by, except for the legacy of a few hundred acres of vineyard that remained in production from those halcyon days. Then, in the late 60s, with most of its grapes being sold to the makers of jug wines, Amador got a boost when the notion of making Zinfandel from old vines, including those in Amador County, developed among home winemakers and quickly passed to the commercial wineries. At that point only 450 acres remained in production, mostly Zinfandel, and only one winery of longevity existed.

The first widely recognized wine of the new era for Amador came from Sutter Home, and its first vintages were quickly followed by a rush of coastal wineries that found superb, if somewhat overripe, grapes in the Shenandoah Valley and Fiddletown area. Almost at the same time came a small but significant rush of new wineries to the area and a tripling of grape production. Now, acreage reaches 2,400, and Zinfandel still reigns supreme with 1,700 acres. Sangiovere, Syrah and Barbera have the next greatest importance at close to 100 acres each. Led by the efforts of Domaine du la Teure Rouge, Syrah began showing well in Amador County (°°° in each of the 94 and 95 vintages).

ANDERSON VALLEY (Mendocino)    Tucked away into a 25-mile-long, 2-mile-wide valley halfway between Ukiah and the Pacific, the Anderson Valley is an isolated Viticultural Area. Enclosed by steep mountains on three sides, this cool Region I and Region II area experienced wholesale expansion in the 80s. Most of the dozen or so producers and 1,000 acres of vineyards are located between Philo and Navarro, where vineyards are situated along a series of elevated river terraces. The valley's reputation improved once the area was planted to compatible varieties such as Chardonnay, Pinot Noir, and Gewurztraminer, now representing about 70–75% of the total acreage. In the early 80s, the French firm of Louis Roederer purchased close to 600 acres and has developed 400 acres to vineyards used exclusively for sparkling wine. A few winemakers cling to the belief that along the high-elevation ridges there is less fog and enough warmth to ripen Cabernet Sauvignon, Merlot, and even Zinfandel. One of the oldest vineyards in the state, the DuPratt Vineyard, noted for its Zinfandel, is located along the Greenwood Ridge.

In 1964, the Edmeades family planted 11 acres to become the valley's first modern-day grape grower. Husch, Lazy Creek, and Navarro soon appeared as wine producers to steadily improve the valley's reputation. All three producers contribute to the belief that Gewurztraminer may be the most successful wine made in the Anderson Valley. Roederer Estate and Scharffenberger Cellars (Pacific

Echo) settled in the Anderson Valley in the 80s to establish the region's credentials for sparkling wine production. Lately, the Greenwood Ridge winery has produced some of the best wines coming from this area.

ARROYO GRANDE VALLEY *(San Luis Obispo)* Lying south of the City of San Luis Obispo, near the quaint town of Arroyo Grando, this Viticultural Area starts in the flat plains the lie along Highway 101 and then twists its way inland through a narrow east-west valley the lies due south of the Edna Valley. Very cool growing conditions predominate in the western end of this area, and things warm increasingly as the valley heads up into the hills. The Laetitia Winery, which until recently was the sparkling wine producer known as Maison Deutz, occupies the cool area near the highway, and specializes in Pinot Noir and Chardonnay. A few miles inland, in a somewhat warmer zone, Talley Vineyards ripens Pinot Noir and Chardonnay to seeming perfection, and its grapes have produced superb results both under it own label and in the hands of such worthies as Au Bon Climat and Ojai. At the valley's hotter eastern end, Saucelito Canyon grows Zinfandel that reaches high levels of ripeness.

ARROYO SECO *(Monterey)* Most of this Viticultural Area falls within a protected area nestled against the foothills of the coastal range. It begins due south of Soledad and extends about a mile south of Greenfield. Shaped somewhat like a triangle, it fans out west from Greenfield and crosses the Arroyo Seco Road, covering a low-lying, gently sloped benchland. Over its first two decades, Arroyo Seco has been the identified source of several late harvest Rieslings and many vintages of superb Chardonnays grown at Ventana Vineyards. Wente is the major grower within the area, along with Jekel, J. Lohr, Hess, and Ventana. Chardonnay and Riesling are the leading varieties here.

CALAVERAS COUNTY Despite the efforts of its one major winery, Stevenot, Calaveras has not made much progress as a wine-growing location in the last two decades. Chardonnay, Sauvignon Blanc, and Zinfandel are the leading varieties, with less than 100 acres each. All told, Calaveras contains some 300 planted acres and has not generally shared in the return to prominence of the Gold Rush counties that brought Amador and El Dorado counties back into the vinous limelight.

CALIFORNIA The number-one state in population, cars per capita, wine and beer consumption, and natural beauty, California is also number one in vineyard acreage, with over 407,000 acres of wine grapes in 46 of the state's 58 counties. Some 80% to 85% of all wine produced in the U.S. is grown in California and, by some estimates, up to 95% of this country's premium wine production is Californian by origin. The approximately 4 million tons of grapes crushed for wine produce over 500 million gallons, making viticulture the third most important agricultural activity in the state.

On wine labels, the appellation California typically means that the grapes came from a combination of areas and thus the wine is not entitled to a more specific appellation. On inexpensive wines labeled with a California appellation, the grapes most often will have their origins in the hot Central Valley, home for 80% of the total California crush. The majority of California's wineries, however, are located in the coastal counties and are producers of varietal wines, typically using more narrowly defined appellations than California.

CALISTOGA *(Napa)* The northernmost community in the Napa Valley has become its most densely packed tourist center. Calistoga boasts hotels, restaurants, wine bars, glider rides over the vineyards, hot springs, geysers, mud baths, and just about anything else the weary tourist could want at the end of a long day of trekking through vineyards and production facilities. Surrounded by mountains on three sides and vineyards on all four, Calistoga provides a warmer climate for grape-growing than its down-valley neighbors; its best-known products are the fat, rich Cabernets of Chateau Montelena and Robert Pecota, as well as the highly regarded Eisele Vineyard (now Araujo). Sauvignon Blanc and Zinfandel also often grow well in the Calistoga area. Among the important wineries located near Calistoga, in addition to Montelena and Pecota, are Sterling, Cuvaison, and Clos Pegase. The area is generally rated medium-warm Region III in heat accumulation, with high daytime temperatures often moderated by cooling winds that blow in at night through the narrow, twisting gap that connects the upper Napa Valley to Knights Valley.

CARMEL VALLEY *(Monterey)*    Inland and beginning a few miles southwest of the famous resort town of Carmel, the Carmel Valley Viticultural Area runs parallel to the Salinas Valley, which in turn is several miles further inland. The Carmel Valley is situated at higher elevation than its neighbor and receives considerably more rainfall. The climate within this protected valley is generally warmer and better suited to red varieties than the Salinas Valley. The Cabernet Sauvignons of Galante are among the top wines produced here.

CARNEROS (also known as Los Carneros) *(Napa and Sonoma)*    As an appellation, Carneros falls within the counties of Sonoma and Napa where they meet at the northern edge of San Francisco Bay. From a wine-identification standpoint, they are also part of the Sonoma and Napa valleys and are the southernmost appellations of origin within each. Most of the land is low-lying or rolling terrain, almost all within sight of the Bay and moderated climatically by its cooling influence. Heat accumulations are generally thought to be cool Region II, although some of the protected locations and upper hillsides can be somewhat warmer. Most of the total Carneros acreage (some 8,500 acres planted to grapes) lies within Napa County, while the rest (about 25–30%) occupies a narrow strip that juts out into and across the bottom of the Sonoma Valley Viticultural Area.

On the Napa side of this justifiably famous area are located vineyards that have yielded the Carneros-identified Pinot Noirs and Chardonnays of Acacia, Bouchaine, Beaulieu, Carneros Creek, and Saintsbury, as well as the highly esteemed Winery Lake Vineyard founded by the iconoclastic art collector and wine lover Rene Di Rosa, and now owned by Sterling Vineyards. Sparkling wine producer Domaine Carneros is located there, and Domaine Chandon also draws heavily on grapes from Carneros. On the Sonoma end, Buena Vista has substantial holdings—now reaching toward 900 acres—in which it grows the usual "cool-area" varieties as well as an often-successful Cabernet Sauvignon. Several Sebastiani vineyards are dotted throughout Sonoma Valley–Carneros, and the Sangiacomo Vineyard, whose name appears on numerous Chardonnays, is also here. Tucked in the southwest corner of Carneros are the champagne cellars of Gloria Ferrer, among the first wineries one sees when coming to Sonoma on the Golden Gate Bridge/Marin County approach to the wine country from San Francisco. Chardonnay (4,200) and Pinot Noir (2,500) dominate, with Cabernet Sauvignon (400) and Merlot (800) coming next in acreage.

CENTRAL COAST    Covering an immense span of territory south of San Francisco, this Viticultural Area includes the following counties: Alameda, Monterey, San Benito, San Luis Obispo, Santa Barbara, Santa Clara, and Santa Cruz. Despite seeming to include every vine between San Francisco and Los Angeles, the Central Coast appellation is frequently used to identify wine produced from grapes grown in two neighboring counties. The combined acreage in the Central Coast adds up to 62,000 acres, oriented to whites more than reds by 36,000 to 26,000. Chardonnay, at 28,000 acres, outdistances the pack with Cabernet Sauvignon (7,900), Merlot (4,600), Pinot Noir (3,700) and Zinfandel (3,300) making up the better part of the remainder.

CENTRAL VALLEY    California's Central Valley, the most productive agricultural area in the state and one of the most important in the world, dominates Californian grape growing from a quantitative standpoint. In actual fact, the Central Valley consists of two major portions: a northern section, often referred to as the Sacramento Valley, and a southern portion, which is the more important agriculturally and viticulturally, called the San Joaquin Valley. Between the two is the Delta area, whose wetlands contribute to a slight lowering of the otherwise scorching midsummer temperatures experienced throughout the valley. Except for some 9,000 acres of grapes in the northern portion, including about 6,000 acres in or near the Delta, the bulk of the Central Valley's 190,000 acres of grapes (about 56% of California's total planted grape acreage) lie within the San Joaquin Valley. There, spread across some eight valley floor counties, are grown the grapes for the vast quantities of jug wines and inexpensive varietals, including the majority of White Zinfandel, that make up the greatest part of the California wine output.

Until the last decade or so, Central Valley wines were very often bad: low in acid, oversweetened to hide a multitude of faults, and possessing a cooked quality in aroma and flavors. The bad days are not totally past, but things have certainly changed. Varieties with higher natural acidity (French Colombard, Barbera, and Chenin Blanc) have been planted where once Carignane, Mission, and Grenache ruled. Grapes are picked with more care so that balance and ripeness are more nearly achieved. And the modern technology of temperature-controlled, stainless-steel fermentation keeps the fruit cleaner and retains whatever freshness is brought into the winery from the vineyard. Notwithstanding the few failed attempts to make long-aging, pricey (or even mid-priced) wines from the Central Valley, the best wines in their youth are clean, flavorful, and among the highest-quality everyday drinking wines in the world. Of course, at their worst, they remain as unpalatable as before.

---

CHALK HILL *(Sonoma)*    Located southwest of Knights Valley, and south of the Alexander Valley, Chalk Hill is a small Viticultural Area that is also a subappellation contained within the western corner of the Russian River Valley. With some 1,000 acres under vine, Chalk Hill covers the hilly terrain due east of the town of Windsor, most of which (but not all) is characterized by white soils. The color actually derives from volcanic ash, not from chalk as was once mistakenly assumed. Chardonnay is the primary variety planted in this almost exclusively white wine region. The terrain consists of gentle hills, which help distinguish it from the rest of the Russian River Valley. These hills discourage the intrusion of fog and cooling marine air, so the climate of Chalk Hill is slightly warmer than the rest of the Russian River Valley. Chalk Hill Winery and Rodney Strong Vineyards are among the best-known vineyard owners in the area.

---

CHALONE *(Monterey)*    Home to one winery of the same name, Chalone is a vast span of land located high in the steep hills to the east of Salinas. The area covers a total of 8,600 acres, but only a few hundred are planted to vines, most of which are owned by Chalone Vineyards. As a Viticultural Area, Chalone enjoys one of the highest elevations in California, averaging 1,650 feet above sea level. The soils are volcanic, with generally rocky topsoil that contains heavy limestone deposits. The cool but extremely dry climate contributes further to generally stressful conditions for the vine. Chardonnay and Pinot Noir are the dominant varieties planted. Both varieties produce small crops of usually intensely flavored grapes. The David Bruce Winery has recently produced very good Pinot Noir from the Chalone area. The name Chalone is taken from the North and South Chalone Peaks, which flank the area but are not included within it.

---

CHILES VALLEY *(Napa)*    Located in the hills east of the main body of the Napa Valley and at higher altitude, this small valley has been allowed to call its grapes Napa Valley because of historical precedent. In point of fact, the growing season is shorter, hotter, and seemingly less hospitable than the real valley. Very few wines of significance are grown here aside from the occasional Zinfandel from Green and Red.

---

CIENEGA *(San Benito)*    Located at the base of the Gabilan Mountain Range, the Cienega Valley separates Monterey County from San Benito County. It is a pretty, hilly region with a moderately warm climate. Almadén Vineyard developed and owned most of the vineyards. After Almadén was sold in 87 and moved its winemaking facilities to the Central Valley, it harvested only a portion of its Cienega holdings. It was in Cienega that Almadén cultivated most of the Grenache used for its once popular rosé wines. One minor distinction is that an active section of the San Andreas Fault line runs across the northeast border of Cienega.

CLARKSBURG *(Sacramento, Solano, and Yolo counties)*   Lying almost immediately southwest of the city of Sacramento, the Clarksburg Viticultural Area extends southward through the Sacramento River Delta for some 16 miles and is up to 8 miles wide at its broadest point. In spite of its size, the area contains only a couple of wineries and a handful of vineyards. The water and the occasional cooling breezes blowing up the river from the San Francisco Bay moderate the Clarksburg climate, and allow it to produce grapes with better balance and depth than in the hotter places of the Central Valley. With few exceptions, however, the best wines produced here are marketed as low-priced varietals. Chenin Blanc and Petite Sirah have been the most successful to date.

CLEAR LAKE *(Lake County)*   Covering an enormous expanse of land measuring approximately 250 square miles, the Clear Lake AVA incorporates all agricultural land in and around Clear Lake, and with the exception of the Guenoc Valley, accounts for 90% of the grapes in the rest of Lake County.

COLE RANCH *(Mendocino)*   This mountainous area located midway between Ukiah and Boonville became a Viticultural Area in the early 80s, even though it was defined and controlled by a single grape grower.

COLUMBIA VALLEY   By far the largest Viticultural Area in the Northwest, this one covers some 18,000 square miles and as an appellation is practically synonymous with Washington State. Located in south-central Washington, it encompasses both the Yakima Valley and the Walla Walla region, the two other major Viticultural Areas of the state. It also includes a big slice of land in northern Oregon facing the Columbia River. The Columbia Valley is a semi-arid valley protected from Pacific marine intrusion by the Cascade Mountains to the west, but its climate overall is quite likely the warmest of any wine region in the Northwest. As a result, there is a range of growing conditions from Region I through III, enabling growers to succeed both with cool-climate Riesling and with warm-weather grapes such as Merlot and, in some sites, with Cabernet Sauvignon. Over three dozen winemaking premises are found within this region. Wine quality has improved continuously and now rivals California's and the world's best for Merlot, Cabernet Sauvignon, and Chardonnay. Most of Washington's 17,000 acres of vines are found here.

DAVIS *(Yolo)*   Ninety miles northeast of San Francisco, on the doorstep of Sacramento, sits the pretty university town of Davis, home of the University of California, Davis. Its Viticulture and Enology Department, the best in the country, has trained winemakers from more than half of the premium wineries in the state and has contributed substantially to the high-tech orientation of most California winemaking. The university is a world leader in studies of grapevine diseases, vineyard problems, and grape clones.

DELTA *(Sacramento, Yolo, and Solano)*   The watery lowlands lying in the triangle formed by the confluence of the San Joaquin and Sacramento rivers is known as the Delta. On some of the many islands, especially those in the eastern Delta, and on the adjoining terra firma to the immediate east, there is a small but increasing winegrowing industry. The Delta is warm (high Region III to Region IV) but more temperate than its Central Valley neighbors to the south because of the San Francisco Bay marine influences. The Clarksburg and Merritt Island Viticultural Areas lie within the Delta, and the Lodi appellation lies immediately to the east.

DIAMOND MOUNTAIN   Part of the Mayacamas Range that separates the Napa Valley from the Sonoma Valley, Diamond Mountain forms a portion of the Napa Valley's western hills between St. Helena and Calistoga. Its sunny slopes and rich soils are planted primarily to Cabernet Sauvignon, with some Chardonnay and Merlot also present. The most notable players on Diamond Mountain are Sterling, Von Strasser, and Diamond Creek, all of which have produced exceptional wines from grapes grown there. The Cabernets are firm, deep in tannin, and somewhat closed-in, but are capable of extraordinary depth and beauty when aged. The steep vineyards of Diamond Mountain are not always deep in soil, making them difficult to farm and frequently stingy yielders.

DRY CREEK VALLEY *(Sonoma)*   This northwest-to-southeast-running appellation practically parallels the Alexander Valley. The eastern border stretches from Geyserville down to Healdsburg, while the Warm Springs and Dry Creek intersection defines its northwest boundary. The climate is both wetter and warmer than that of the Russian River Valley, and the growing season tends to be longer. The red soils of Dry Creek are more common in the benchlands and hills in the north, and these sites seem just about perfect for Zinfandel and close to that for Sauvignon Blanc. Zinfandels from the Dry Creek Valley appellation are ripe, rich, with berrylike fruit and peppery nuances. The area's Sauvignon Blanc can often be too exuberant in a pungent, weedy-grassy manner, needing some calming influence from barrel fermentations or from blending with Semillon. The finer Cabernet Sauvignons are very expressive, with a strong bell pepper, green olive, earthy nature. As one moves south toward the Russian River, the plantings begin to favor Chardonnay and Riesling. Vineyards have steadily expanded through the 80s to bring the current total acreage beyond 6,000. About a dozen producers are located within Dry Creek, including Dry Creek Vineyards, Preston, Ferrari-Carano, Meeker, A. Rafanelli, Quivira, and the North Coast outpost of Gallo.

EDNA VALLEY *(San Luis Obispo)*   Beginning a little southeast of the town of San Luis Obispo, the Edna Valley is a Region I wine-growing valley, granted Viticultural Area status in 1982. Cool marine air from Morro Bay is partially deflected by a low string of hills along the valley's western boundary. Edna Valley is bordered on the northeast by the Santa Lucia Mountains and on the southwest by the San Luis Range. Chamisal Vineyards was the first producer in the area, establishing the first commercial vineyard in the late 70s; it now has 52 acres of Chardonnay. Paragon Vineyards, co-owner of the Edna Valley Vineyards, developed 400 acres in the Edna Valley, planted to Chardonnay and Pinot Noir. With close to 100 acres under vine, the MacGregor Vineyard is the best-known independently owned vineyard, whose Chardonnay grapes have been sold to Leeward, Morgan, Karly, Windemere, and Mount Eden Vineyards. Corbett Canyon is the largest producer in the Edna Valley. The majority of the 3,000-plus total acres planted are Chardonnay, with Pinot Noir a distant second. Without question, Chardonnays from the Edna Valley can be successful. The best versions have a somewhat distinctive butterscotch character and are deeply fruited and viscous. Alban Vineyards is enjoying success with Viognier.

EL DORADO *(El Dorado)*   Grape growing in El Dorado County is limited to the area of the county lying between 1,200 and 3,500 feet elevation; accordingly, this Viticultural Area is also so delimited.

EL DORADO COUNTY   During the 19th-century Gold Rush days, El Dorado County is reputed to have contained 5,000 acres of vineyards. While the current count of 800 acres is not much by comparison, most of it has been planted since the mid-70s and every year seems to see a small but steady growth in the total. El Dorado County's dozen or so wineries also date from the same period. The most plentiful grapes, and the most successful, are Zinfandel (usually made in a ripe, medium-full style) and Sauvignon Blanc. Recent Syrahs have also shown great promise. The recognized Viticultural Area of El Dorado encompasses all of the county lying between the 1,200-foot and 3,500-foot levels of the Sierra Nevada Range's western slope. The eight-county Sierra Foothills appellation includes El Dorado County within its boundaries. Zinfandel is the leading variety with some 200 acres planted while Cabernet Sauvignon, Merlot and Chardonnay each come in above 100 acres.

FIDDLETOWN *(Amador)* Lying just to the east across the ridge from the Shenandoah Valley, this area yields typical ripe, concentrated Zinfandels in the Amador County style, but possibly a little less forceful in flavor and alcohol than those of the Shenandoah Valley, apparently because of Fiddletown's slightly higher elevations and cooler nighttime temperatures. The Eschen Vineyard is Fiddletown's most notable grape-growing property and is referenced on several wineries' products. Fiddletown was granted Viticultural Area status in 1983. About 100 acres of grapes are planted in the area.

GEYSERVILLE *(Sonoma)* Surrounded by vineyards, Geyserville is a small town located just a few miles north of Healdsburg in the northwest corner of the Alexander Valley. It is the home address of many wineries, including Geyser Peak, Chateau Souverain, Clos du Bois, and Murphy Goode Estate. However, what also makes it noteworthy is its association with excellent, ripe-style Zinfandels, especially those bottled by Ridge and identified as "Geyserville." The vineyards in this warm region also contribute ripe, full-bodied Cabernet Sauvignons.

GLEN ELLEN *(Sonoma)* Jack London once had the good sense to live in this enchanting rustic village, and his name adorns many local points of interest. The original vineyard developed by Jack London is now leased by Kenwood Vineyards. Located halfway between the towns of Sonoma and Kenwood, Glen Ellen is home today to several wineries, notably Grand Cru Vineyards, Valley of the Moon, B. R. Cohn, Kistler, Laurel Glen, and Glen Ellen Winery.

GREEN VALLEY–SOLANO *(Solano)* One of two Green Valley appellations in California, this is the lesser of the two and is rarely seen on labels. It lies one valley east of Napa County and several valleys east of the true Napa Valley and, accordingly, has hotter, drier, and shorter-season growing conditions.

GREEN VALLEY–SONOMA *(Sonoma)* This subdivision of the Russian River Valley can be found in its southwest corner. The tiny town of Sebastopol fixes its southeastern border, and the area extends a few miles north of Forestville. Located 10 miles inland from the Pacific, Green Valley experiences less intense heat during the growing season than the rest of the Russian River Valley. Therefore, it is planted to cool-climate varieties, primarily Chardonnay and Pinot Noir, which are used for both table and sparkling wines. The most distinctive wines are the medium-bodied Chardonnays, with a typical lively, green apple character. Iron Horse Vineyards produces its attractive sparkling wines from grapes grown here. Dehlinger, Laurier Vineyard, and Iron Horse Vineyards are strong supporters as well as residents of this appellation, which is labeled Green Valley–Sonoma County to distinguish it from another Green Valley in Solano County. Total acreage approaches 1,000 today, led by Chardonnay with close to 500.

GREENFIELD *(Monterey)* Hometown to Jekel Vineyards and to the vineyards owned by J. Lohr, Greenfield falls at the midpoint of the Salinas Valley. The climate, however, is cool and extremely breezy on summer afternoons, best suited, it seems, for early-maturing white varieties. The early leader was Riesling, which remains consistent, but Chardonnay is now more important. Arroyo Seco is located west of Greenfield.

GUENOC VALLEY *(Lake and Napa counties)* Located 15 miles north of Calistoga, the Guenoc Valley extends from the upper part of Napa Valley into Lake County. Granted Viticultural Area status in 81, the Guenoc Valley is home to one winery, Guenoc Winery. Encompassing some 23,000 total acres, this valley is currently planted to 385 acres of vines, with about 1,400 acres suitable for planting in the future. The vineyard sites are located at the 1,000–1,400-foot-elevation levels. With widely fluctuating warm days and cool nights during the growing season, the region is categorized as a cool Region III. Spring frosts have turned out to be a serious problem, so all vineyards have frost-protection systems. The leading varieties are Cabernet Sauvignon and Chardonnay, with Sauvignon Blanc a distant third.

HEALDSBURG (*Sonoma*)   If there can be a hub to Sonoma County's dispersed winemaking activities, then the town of Healdsburg is emerging as the logical candidate. This small city's borders touch three important Viticultural Areas: Alexander Valley, Russian River Valley, and Chalk Hill. Immediately to the west of Healdsburg is the Dry Creek Valley. Over 50 wineries call Healdsburg their home, with several—among them Clos du Bois, Alderbrook, and Seghesio—operating wineries and tasting rooms within city limits.

HECKER PASS (*Santa Clara*)   The Coast Range Mountains to the west of Gilroy gradually open up to the coastal plain. In this low-lying area, known as the Hecker Pass, about a dozen wineries can be found. Most of them are family-owned, and their wines generally harken back to the old days when heavy but often pleasing generic jug wines were purchased by local folks. The Hecker Pass wineries are popular among the weekend picnic crowd. Sarah's Vineyard has loftier ambitions and targets its efforts outside of the area.

HOWELL MOUNTAIN (*Napa*)   In the hills northeast of St. Helena, this Viticultural Area is found amidst a rolling hillside of vineyards, forest, and brush, at elevations between 1,600 and 2,200 feet. The soils in this near–Region III growing area are volcanic in origin and have a rusty, terra-cotta appearance. The location and moderately warm temperatures make it a hospitable place for grapes like Zinfandel and the Rhone varieties, yet it is the Cabernet Sauvignon, grown here by Dunn Vineyards and La Jota, that has given a special standing to the few hundred acres of vines on Howell Mountain. The area has a long and successful vinous history dating back to the late 1800s, when its four producers, relying on the 600 acres then planted, were winning gold medals for their wines.

IDAHO   The main Idaho wine region is located across the Snake River from Oregon, in the southwestern corner between Boise and Caldwell. Situated at the far western end of the Snake River Valley, most of the vineyards are planted along its slopes above the 2,000-foot level. About 1,000 acres of vineyards have been developed in an area referred to as the Sunny Slope district, where the summer weather is dry and moderate but the growing season is quite short. As a result, most red varieties have difficulties developing full maturity, and some of the whites are tart and overly acidic. Ste. Chapelle is the oldest brand, having established vines in 76 and a winery in 79. It is also the largest, producing over 80,000 cases from 400 acres it either owns outright or leases. A half dozen other wineries perform pioneering work in the state. Early vintages suggest Chenin Blanc and Riesling can be consistently successful. The Chardonnay has yet to come across with the ripe varietal fruitiness needed to complement its otherwise pleasing acidity and body.

KENWOOD (*Sonoma*)   A whistle-stop town located at the midpoint of the Sonoma Valley, Kenwood can also be found on nonwine maps by stopping midway between the city of Santa Rosa to the north and the town of Sonoma to the south. All of this suggests there isn't much there when you find Kenwood, except for three noteworthy wineries—Kenwood, Chateau St. Jean, and St. Francis. Each cultivates vineyards within the town's borders, but only St. Francis relies substantially on home-grown grapes.

KNIGHTS VALLEY (*Sonoma*)   Flanked by Alexander Valley on the north and the Napa Valley on the south, Knights Valley shares warm growing conditions with the Alexander Valley. Most of the approximately 1,000 acres planted belong to Beringer Vineyards. To date the region's most consistent wines are Cabernet Sauvignon and Sauvignon Blanc, both showing ripe fruitiness and modest varietal intensity. Limited amounts of Merlot made by Whitehall Lane Winery have been the most exciting red wine from this region so far. However, several wineries—Peter McCoy Vineyards, Johnson Turnbull, and Peter Michael Winery—have emerged as prominent Knights Valley Chardonnay producers. Completed in 89, the Peter Michael Winery became the first new winery to settle in Knights Valley since Prohibition.

LAKE COUNTY   Located due north of Napa County and directly east of Mendocino County, Lake County is home to a large lake—Clear Lake—and about 3,400 acres of vineyards. Approximately 52% of the total now consists of red varieties, 48% of whites. In 70, only 100 acres contained vines, but tremendous plantings in 73 and 74 brought the total quickly to 2,500. After a lull, expansion resumed in the mid-80s. However, the current total of 3,900 still remains below the 5,000-plus acres that existed during the county's heyday in the 1880s.

Though part of the North Coast appellation, Lake County touches no coasts, and is generally warmer in midsummer than its neighbors to the south and west. It is visited by cooling summer fog only on rare occasions. Many of the vineyards are situated along upper elevations on the mountainous terrain, which allows for a needed cooling evening effect during the summer. The majority of today's vineyards consist of Sauvignon Blanc (900 acres), Chardonnay (700), Cabernet Sauvignon (900), Merlot (500), and Zinfandel (400), which together represent 87% of the total. So far the most distinctive white varietal has been Sauvignon Blanc. Kendall-Jackson, Guenoc, and Steele are the major forces among local wineries, but many grapes are sold to wineries outside of the region—often to be blended and sold as North Coast wines. Fetzer buys high percentages of grapes and wines from independent growers in this appellation.

Napa Valley's Louis Martini Winery is developing several hundred acres in Lake County, primarily to Cabernet Sauvignon and other red varieties. Beringer, Sutter Home Winery, Geyser Peak, and Parducci all purchased considerable acreage in the late 80s and have developed vineyards in the county. Geyser Peak has about 300 acres planted in a subregion known as the Benmore Valley, located midway between Lakeport and Hopland.

LIME KILN VALLEY (San Benito)   A subregion of the Cienega Valley Viticultural Area, Lime Kiln Valley contains fewer than 100 acres of grapes today. The only producer using it to identify wines at all had been the Enz Winery, which helped define the region.

LIVERMORE VALLEY (Alameda)   Southeast of San Francisco, and lying in its own enclosed pocket, is the 15-mile-long, 10-mile-wide Livermore Valley. Settled in the 1880s, this once-famous region has been whittled down by urban expansion until today only about 1,600 acres of vineyards remain. Of the dozen local wineries, Wente and Concannon are the oldest and best-known. The Bonny Doon Winery is moving production into the old Ruby Hill facility. Marked by a warm (low Region III) climate and rocky soil, Livermore Valley fares best with Sauvignon Blanc and Semillon.

LODI (San Joaquin and Sacramento counties)   Lying between the cities of Stockton and Sacramento, this diverse growing region and designated Viticultural Area starts near the watery Delta area (which forms its western boundary for all intents and purposes) and runs eastward into the hills until it abuts the lower edge of the Sierra Foothills Viticultural Area. For years this has been primarily Zinfandel country, but recent plantings have increased the percentage of whites grown here as well, especially Chardonnay . Although part of the Central Valley, those parts of the Lodi appellation lying nearest the Delta are cooled by its marine-influenced breezes, which can lower the average temperature by as much as 10 degrees in midsummer in comparison to the immediately adjoining areas. In addition to being a recognized source of grapes on labels, Lodi is home to a number of wineries. The best known is Robert Mondavi, which makes its generic and inexpensive table wines in Lodi. Lodi is also referred to as the center of California brandy production, which relies substantially on the crush of locally grown Flame Tokay table grapes as the base for the distillation process. By the mid-90s, Lodi led the state in total tonnage for Sauvignon Blanc, Cabernet Sauvignon, Merlot, and Zinfandel (over half of all Zinfandel crushed in California). Important plantings include: Zinfandel (17,300), Chardonnay (10,600), Cabernet Sauvignon (7,500, Merlot (5,300) and Sauvignon Blanc (1,700).

**LYTTON SPRINGS** *(Sonoma)* Just north of the town of Healdsburg is a small pocket in the low-lying hills that has been the source of many brawny Zinfandels. This region became famous through the superb Zinfandels made by Ridge Vineyards and by the Lytton Springs Winery. This subregion technically belongs to the Alexander Valley Viticultural Area.

**MADERA** *(Madera and Fresno)* An appellation in search of a purpose, this 700-square-mile Viticultural Area contains some 38,000 acres of vines, mostly in Madera County, but also some that lie in the northern end of Fresno County. In spite of being given its own special name and the fact that it grows over 10% of the grapevines in California, the Madera appellation is rarely seen on wine labels.

**MADERA COUNTY** Its 44,000 acres of wine grapes make Madera County the second most heavily planted county in California. Its mid-Central Valley location marks it mostly as jug-wine country, but several noteworthy ports and dessert wines from the likes of Quady and Ficklin are grown here as well. The major plantings in the county consist of French Colombard (14,000 acres), Chenin Blanc (5,100), Chardonnay (2,100), Grenache (3,700), Merlot (3,100), Carignane (2,700), and Barbera (1,900). The government-recognized Madera (note the absence of "county") Viticultural Area is located here, as well as in the northern end of adjoining Fresno County. Madera County is now the home of Almadén Vineyards.

**MCDOWELL VALLEY** *(Mendocino)* This one-winery Viticultural Area lies in southeastern Mendocino County just east of Hopland. All of the grapes are grown by four independent growers, and by the McDowell Valley Winery, which owns or controls over 600 acres. About 50 acres are planted to Syrah, with the oldest parcel established in 1919. In general, the region is slightly cooler than the Redwood Valley, and is categorized as a Region II. Total acreage now stands at 750, the leading varieties being Chardonnay, Cabernet Sauvignon, and Sauvignon Blanc.

**MENDOCINO COUNTY** The northernmost of the coastal regions, Mendocino County established a wine identity of its own by the late 70s. Best known for its rugged, majestic coastline and rough timberlands with giant redwood forests, Mendocino reserves a series of isolated valleys and canyons cut into the hills by the Russian River for vine cultivation. Its primary growing regions are the marine-influenced Anderson Valley, running southeast to northwest in the direction of the Pacific, and the inland Redwood Valley, running south to north with its heaviest concentration of vines around Ukiah. Three small Viticultural Areas in the county—Cole Ranch in the middle, McDowell Valley in the southeast, and Potter Valley in the northeast—help push the total acreage to over 13,500. The majority of the county's wine regions are a warm Region III climate. However, the Anderson Valley directly experiences cooling coastal influences and offers an unusually long growing season. Over 1,000 acres are planted in the Anderson Valley, mostly to cool-climate varieties.

Historically, the vast majority of grapes in Mendocino were Carignane and Colombard, grown in the Redwood Valley and intended for jug wines. By the mid-70s the county's reputation began to improve with the success of ripe, brawny Zinfandels, powerful Cabernets, and muscular Petite Sirahs. Today, Chardonnay has assumed preeminence with 4,600 acres planted, and Sauvignon Blanc at almost 700 is more popular than Colombard. Among red varieties, Zinfandel (1,900 acres), Cabernet Sauvignon (1,500) and Merlot (1,400) have edged out Carignane (800).

The number of producers within the county now tops three dozen. Among the best known are Fetzer, Parducci, and McDowell Valley Vineyards. A relative new-comer that quickly made its presence felt, Roederer Estate, owned by Louis Roed-erer Champagne, is located in the Anderson Valley. Most of the other producers are small, family-owned enterprises opened for business since 1970.

MERRITT ISLAND *(Yolo)*  A part of the much larger Clarksburg Viticultural Area, Merritt Island is located just south of the city of Clarksburg and west of the Sacramento River. The northernmost of the Delta islands, it is cooled by the marine breezes which come up the river from San Francisco Bay but is rarely affected by fog. Its loamy soil separates it from the peaty and claylike soils that are found elsewhere in the Delta. A very warm but not hot growing climate allows Merritt Island to pro-duce passable Chenin Blancs and Petite Sirahs.

MONTEREY *(Monterey County)*  In the Monterey Viticultural Area (formerly the Monterey County Viticultural Area) the primary grape-growing district is an inland valley called the Salinas Valley. Several smaller appellations—Arroyo Seco, Chalone, Santa Lucia Highlands, and the Carmel Valley—are also included within the offi-cial boundaries of the Monterey Viticultural Area. In the early 60s the Salinas Val-ley contained no vines, but university studies identified it as an ideal site for premium wine varieties because of its cool climate and dry summer weather. From less than 5 acres in 1966, the area experienced vineyard expansion to 2,000 acres by 1970. Then a full-scale planting boom got under way, and acreage rose to a peak of 35,000 in 1975. Today, it stands near 32,500.

Over the next few vintages, wines began to appear under the Monterey County appellation. At least some of them, however, were marred by an excessively vege-tative character. The most unsuccessful varietal of all was Cabernet Sauvignon, which unfortunately was widely planted; but other red grapes also suffered from an overly aggressive vegetative note.

The problem was eventually traced to highly abnormal growing conditions. The region is extremely dry, with a scant 6 to 8 inches of rainfall per year. Irrigation is a must, and the Salinas Valley was the first wine region in the West to depend en-tirely on irrigation. The Salinas Valley is also subject to high winds in the summer afternoons, which retard vine maturity. Some vines often had difficulties develop-ing mature grapes with balanced fruit flavors and acids. Growers developed new trellising and vine management techniques to cope with such conditions, or else planted more suitable varieties.

Cabernet Sauvignon, which once covered over 5,000 acres, has been whittled down to 3,800. Today, the Monterey appellation is a region focused on white wine grapes and a more sensible sprinkling of reds in the warmer, southern locations or in a few isolated hillside sites in the north. White varieties represent close to 68% of the total plantings, with Chardonnay topping the list at about 15,000 acres. Chenin Blanc, Johannisberg Riesling and Sauvignon Blanc each hover in the 1,000 to 1,500 acre range. Pinot Blanc, with about 600 acres, claims 56% of California's total; the Riesling acreage represents 60% of all plantings in the state.

Some of the state's most intensely fragrant Johannisberg Rieslings are grown in Monterey. Though less consistent, Monterey Chardonnays have ranked among the finest and, in the hands of several winemakers, display tremendous varietal inten-sity and balance. A handful of wineries have demonstrated that Cabernet Sauvi-gnon from a few choice sites can result in wines of °°caliber, but such results are very few and very far between. Galante is capable of such results from its Carmel Valley site.

Today, the number of wineries located in the area remains over a dozen, ranging in size from The Monterey Vineyard to smaller ones such as Jekel, Morgan, Lock-wood, Ventana, and Talbott. Wente, Mirassou, and J. Lohr are all pioneers who own substantial acreage in Monterey and identify many of their wines as Monterey in origin. However, Delicato Vineyards, located in the Central Valley, owns 8,000 acres (most of which is not in vines), which makes it the largest holder of Monterey wine turf. A high percentage of the grape crop still leaves the valley, often destined to be blended.

ChaloneVineyards, though located within the general area, formed the Chalone appellation to separate itself from the Monterey place name.

MONTEREY COUNTY    With some 33,000 acres planted to wine varieties, Monterey County contains several Viticultural Areas. The largest appellation is Monterey, which also includes the Arroyo Seco appellation and contains all but several hundred acres of the county's total wine-grape lands. Chalone in the northeast and Santa Lucia Highlands and the Carmel Valley on the western edge are the other noteworthy appellations within the county. In the southern area of the county is San Lucas, a Viticultural Area that has rarely, if ever, appeared on the label of any wine bottle.

MOUNT VEEDER *(Napa)*    West ofYountville, near the southern extremity of the Mayacamas Mountains, Mount Veeder rises some 2,500 feet above the Napa Valley floor. As a Viticultural Area, MountVeeder encompasses a territory ranging from 400 feet to 2,400 in elevation and boasts 1,000 acres in grapes, a dozen wineries, and a few more than two dozen producers. Dotting its flanks are numerous small vineyards and a few wineries, the best known of which are the Mayacamas Vineyards, long famous for their full-bodied Cabernets and Chardonnays, and the Mount Veeder Winery, whose wines are substantially of the same stripe. Chateau Potelle and Hess Collection are also important producers on Mount Veeder. Cabernet Sauvignon and Chardonnay account, in equal measure, for 80% of current plantings. Noteworthy vineyards include Brandlin Ranch and Hendry.

NAPA COUNTY    For all intents and purposes, the Napa County name means Napa Valley when one speaks of grape-growing and winemaking. Virtually every vine standing in the county is, in fact, included within the recognized Napa Valley appellation. Only a small portion of the county, in the upper northeast quadrant, miles removed from the valley itself in distance, climate, and soil type, is not included in this appellation. However, it is the county which is the category employed in measuring such important statistics as grape acreage, number of wineries extant, tonnage crushed, and grape price levels. In addition, some wineries choose to use the Napa County appellation on their labels for a variety of reasons, including philosophical opposition to the use of a "valley" designation for mountain-grown grapes. Within the county, there are about 200 wineries (the most in any county in the U.S.) and some 36,100 acres of wine grapes (fifth highest in California but second among coastal counties). The most widely planted varieties here are Cabernet Sauvignon (10,600), Chardonnay (9,300 acres), Merlot (5,900), Pinot Noir (2,400), and Sauvignon Blanc (1,900). Napa County is the leader in number of wineries and in planted acreage of Cabernet Sauvignon, Sauvignon Blanc, and Merlot; it ranks fourth in Chardonnay and second in Pinot Noir acreage.

NAPA VALLEY *(Napa)*    The most famous wine-growing area in the U.S., this land lives up to its Indian moniker as the "Valley of Plenty." As a geographic mass, it begins at the base of Mount St. Helena in the north, dissolving some 30 miles to the south into a floodplain as the Napa River enters San Francisco Bay. From Mount St. Helena to the city of Napa, the valley is defined by two north-south ridgelines of the Coast Range Mountains. The valley floor varies from 3 to 4 miles in width in the south to 1 mile or less in the north. The hills to the west of the valley floor are part of the Mayacamas Range; they contain peaks and watersheds that start with MountVeeder to the west ofYountville and include Mont St. John, Spring Mountain, and Diamond Mountain as the hills progress up-valley. The hills on the eastern side of the valley are not nearly so important on a winemaking basis or so well known, although Howell Mountain, Pope Valley, and Chiles Valley are all part of that area, and the productive but relatively unknown Gordon and Wooden valleys lie further east again. The bulk of grape growing takes place on the valley floor, and in the gentle slopes adjoining the floor. Indeed, the Napa Valley floor is almost totally committed to vineyards; just as in the developed vineyard areas of Europe, there is little land left that can now be converted into new space for grapes.

From its earliest days, the Napa Valley has been the home of some of California's most famous wine estates, including such well-known producers as Charles Krug, Beringer Brothers, Schramsberg, and Inglenook. Today, the valley boasts upward of 36,000 acres planted to wine grapes and some 250 wineries, most of which offer high-caliber, often expensive wines.

With some notable exceptions, the best California Chardonnays, Cabernet Sauvignons, and Merlots come from the Napa Valley, and the greater part of the valley's worldwide reputation is based on the success of those varietals, which account for two-thirds of its planted acreage. But the valley is large and filled with varied growing conditions that support many varieties with great success. The cool Los Carneros region by San Francisco Bay yields good Chardonnay and Pinot Noir but less frequently produces well-ripened Cabernet Sauvignon. At the other end of the valley, the warm Calistoga area can produce nicely ripe Zinfandel and Petite Sirah as well as near-blockbuster Cabernets, but overcooks Pinot Noir and the other heat-sensitive varieties.

On wine labels, the term "Napa Valley" has historically included all areas within Napa County and now, as a defined Viticultural Area, continues to include all but the most outlying and inhospitable lands of Napa County. Over 20 major sub-areas have been identified within the Napa Valley; 15 have already gained prominence as viticulturally important political subdivisions or recognizable microclimates, and are described in the adjoining pages (see Atlas Peak, Calistoga, Chiles Valley, Diamond Mountain, Howell Mountain, Los Carneros, Mount Veeder, Oakville, Pope Valley, Rutherford, Rutherford Bench, St. Helena, Spring Mountain, Stags Leap, and Yountville).

NORTH COAST   Given its somewhat tortured history, once including almost every grape north of Bakersfield, the government-recognized North Coast appellation as now constituted actually makes a good deal of sense. Today it is limited to those coastal and near-coastal counties north of San Francisco which are actually thought of as being north and coastal by the people who live there. Included in this catchall Viticultural Area are the counties of Mendocino, Napa, Sonoma, Lake, Solano, and Marin. While the North Coast's 96,000 acres of grapes form about 24% of the statewide total, they include about 35% of the state's Merlot, 45% of the Cabernet Sauvignon, and 30% of the Chardonnay.

NORTH YUBA *(Yuba)*   Thirty square miles of appellation in the low foothills of the Sierra Nevada Range west of Grass Valley and Nevada City contain a few hundred acres of vines. In granting Viticultural Area status to North Yuba, the government was moved to observe that boundaries define "a region well-suited to viticulture." To date, however, the small acreage of Cabernet Sauvignon, Johannisberg Riesling, and Sauvignon Blanc planted there has yet to prove out that statement.

NORTHERN SONOMA *(Sonoma)*   This infrequently used appellation yokes together under one name six Viticultural Areas: Alexander Valley, Dry Creek Valley, Knight's Valley, the Russian River Valley, and its subregions, Chalk Hill and Green Valley. It excludes Sonoma Valley and Los Carneros, along with a series of smaller places within the county. When the appellation was being proposed, the Gallo Winery argued strongly in its favor. Now Gallo join Rodney Strong and others in identifying some wines as Northern Sonoma.

OAKVILLE *(Napa)*   Situated in the southern half of the Napa Valley, midway between Yountville and Rutherford, this way station is the home of several wineries (foremost among them the Robert Mondavi Winery) and adjoins some of the Napa Valley's best Cabernet-growing turf. The superb Martha's Vineyard produced by Heitz Cellars and a substantial portion of the Robert Mondavi and Beaulieu Vineyard vines are in Oakville, along the western edge of the valley floor right in the middle of the justifiably famous Rutherford Bench. Other wineries in the area include De Moor and Far Niente on the bench, and Girard, Silver Oaks, and Villa Mount Eden across the valley floor. The Oakville AVA cuts across the valley following political rather than grape-growing lines.

OREGON    From modest beginnings in the mid-60s, the Oregon wine industry came of age in the 80s to earn international praise by the end of its first quarter century. With 100 wineries in operation, and some 400 separate vineyards located in the state's five small growing regions, Oregon now produces about 2,500,000 gallons of vinifera from 7,800 acres of grapes. The primary growing regions—the Willamette Valley and the Umpqua Valley—are located 60 miles inland from the Pacific. As a river valley/watershed, the Willamette Valley begins a little northwest of Portland in the Tualatin Valley and extends south through Eugene. The smaller Umpqua Valley is located in the south and is carved out by the Umpqua River. A smaller, warmer region known as the Rogue River Valley is emerging in the south. The Willamette and Umpqua Valley regions in western Oregon are situated on hills overlooking small valleys which form a north-south corridor, and they struggle to ripen fruit in a climate that is cool and wet by California standards. Yet the climate is drier during the growing season than France's Burgundy region. The typical Oregon growing season lasts from April through the end of October. The last three weeks of October often run the risk of early fall rainstorms.

The prime variety is Pinot Noir, which now covers more than 3,000 acres. Pinot Noir, Pinot Gris (400 acres), and Chardonnay (1,500 acres), the three top varieties, account for 75% of the 7,800 acres under vine by 98. Riesling remains popular within Oregon, where 90% of its output is sold as opposed to 80% for Chardonnay and 55% for Pinot Noir, Oregon's major vinous export. However, a few producers have ignored Riesling in favor of Pinot Gris, a white variety widely believed by some growers to be the third best variety for Oregon after Pinot Noir and Chardonnay. About 700 acres of Pinot Gris have been established to date. Oregon's finest Pinot Noirs tend toward the cherry-berry side of the varietal spectrum, with a sometimes wiry, medium-bodied feel, and relatively high acidity. Most others, even in fine vintages, seem to have a somewhat narrow flavor profile, though the aromas are often beautifully complex. Chardonnays as a rule tend to be austere and hard, though exceptions are frequent enough to hold our attention. Minor initial interest in producing sparkling wine surfaced in the late 80s. At around the same time, several wine companies from both Europe and California were beginning to invest in Oregon vineyards, spurred on by the state's reputation for Pinot Noir and by the relatively low cost of vineyard land.

In the mid-70s, Oregon winemakers imposed a few special regulations governing their labeling. First, learning from California's mistakes, Oregon banned the use of generic names derived from European types—Chablis, Burgundy, Champagne. Second, to carry a varietal name, an Oregon wine must contain at least 90% of the designated variety; Cabernet Sauvignon is an exception and follows the federal varietal minimum of 75%. To warrant an appellation of origin, Oregon law requires that 100% of the wine originate in the region named on the label.

PACHECO PASS (San Benito and Santa Clara)    Flanked east and west by the hills of the Diablo Mountain Range, Pacheco Pass is a small Viticultural Area—5 miles long, 1 mile wide—where several modest wineries are located. The winemaking emphasis falls upon everyday table wine, sold mostly to locals and to tourists wandering through on their way elsewhere.

PACIFIC NORTHWEST    Linked geographically, the burgeoning wine states of Washington, Oregon, and later Idaho banded together in the 70s in order to focus national attention on the area and gain respect for the vinifera wines produced. Climatically, the Pacific Northwest wine regions are generally cooler overall and unlike most of California's growing areas. Therefore, the growers and winemakers are confronted by different problems and situations. However, most of the pioneering winemakers and the current new generation learned their trade in California and are much closer philosophically to California than to Europe or elsewhere. We sense more of a kinship between the Northwest and California vintners than any rivalry, friendly or otherwise. Besides, most of the wines from the Northwest are available in many important wine markets today. Over the last two decades the Northwest has produced much more white wine than red. About two-thirds of the total 25,000 acres is in Washington.

PAICINES *(San Benito)*  Located in the relatively warm plains 12 miles south of Hollister, Paicines was once an important growing region for Almadén Vineyards. It is a Region III growing area in terms of climate because during the summer days ocean breezes and an occasional fog roll in, to make it cooler than Fresno, which is located to the southeast. After Almadén was sold in 87, the 2,000 acres under vine remained.

PASO ROBLES *(San Luis Obispo)*  With over a century of grape-growing history, the Viticultural Area of Paso Robles is in the northern part of the county, the town of Paso Robles comprising its focal point. It is a large area (over 600,000 acres), consisting mostly of the low-lying land and the foothills, bordered on the west by the Santa Lucia Mountains and extending east to the foothills known as the Cholame Hills. Along the modest elevations the climate is generally Region III, which makes many of its sites well suited to Cabernet Sauvignon and Zinfandel. By the 90s, vineyard acreage approached 7,000 total, with red varieties enjoying a slight lead. The primary whites grown are Sauvignon Blanc, Chardonnay, and Chenin Blanc. Zinfandel and Cabernet lead the red contingent handily in terms of total acreage, and also in terms of overall quality. However, some success has been achieved by the Syrah variety from the large planting established by Estrella River Winery. After a few wineries experienced financial difficulties in the 70s, renewed interest in the following decade brought the number of wine producers to the two-dozen mark. Most are small and family-owned; Arciero and Meridian are the two largest by a substantial margin.

POPE VALLEY  Nestled in the hills east of the main portion of the Napa Valley, this hot and dry depression hosts a few hundred acres of vines that suffer a shorter, hotter growing season than the main valley but are, for financial and historical reasons, still entitled to use its prestigious appellation. Wines from this subsection have generally proven to be as rustic as the setting, but St. Supéry Vineyards, using grapes from the Dollarhide Ranch in Pope Valley, has produced tamer wines.

POTTER VALLEY *(Mendocino)*  The most northerly region in the North Coast, Potter Valley now contains approximately 1,000 acres of wine varieties. Chardonnay, Sauvignon Blanc, and Johannisberg Riesling have historically been the major varieties planted. Pinot Noir was increasing in acreage in the late 80s. Generally, Potter Valley contains deep, rich soils. The climate is characterized by extremely warm days and cool nights, and by early rains which when not excessive often encourage *Botrytis* to occur on Riesling and Semillon. Most grapes are sold to producers outside the region who mix them as part of a Mendocino County appellation. In the late 80s several producers, including La Crema and Hidden Cellars, made successful Pinot Noir from this region. To meet the demand, growers have added Pinot Noir along the higher-elevation sites. Most of the white varieties are grown on the valley floor.

REDWOOD VALLEY *(Mendocino)*  Following the northern meanderings of the Russian River, this Viticultural Area begins 15 miles north of Ukiah and continues south until it ends about a mile below Ukiah. North of Ukiah, the region fans out to encompass Lake Mendocino and includes the major grape-growing territory in and around Ukiah—Talmage, the Sanel Valley, and Hopland. More than 8,000 acres are located within the Redwood Valley, a name used primarily by Lolonis Winery and by several others. In the 70s many dry-farmed hillside vineyards in the Redwood Valley produced excellent Zinfandels and Petite Sirahs to help launch Mendocino as a wine region.

ROGUE VALLEY   Located in southwest Oregon not far from the California border, this area enjoys a warmer climate than other parts of Oregon. The main metropolis is the Medford-Jacksonville area on the eastern edge. Most vineyards are located at elevations above the 1,000-foot level or higher which look down on those towns. The limited amounts of wines produced from this region over the first decade offer some encouragement for Chardonnay and Cabernet Sauvignon. Chardonnay, Pinot Noir, and Cabernet Sauvignon are the leading varieties. Valley View Winery and Foris Vineyards are the best-known producers in this area.

RUSSIAN RIVER VALLEY *(Sonoma)*   The Russian River ranks among the longest rivers in Northern California and helps define quite a few wine regions within Sonoma County as it meanders through. As a Viticultural Area, the Russian River Valley consists of the low-lying flat plains between Healdsburg and Sebastopol which extend westward as the river heads toward the Pacific. At Guerneville, the coastal hills close off the area and mark its western boundary. The Russian River Valley includes the western half of Chalk Hill and all of Green Valley–Sonoma. Its total vineyard acreage now approaches 10,000. The soil types are widely varied, with most of the vines planted on benchlands or bottom lands. The region's climate is quite uniform in that it is cooled by fog intrusion and by proximity to the river. In the southwest sector, fog is a frequent intruder in July and August, which makes that portion well suited to Chardonnay, Gewurztraminer, and Pinot Noir. Also, the same conditions make the lower Russian River Valley hospitable to Pinot Noir and Chardonnay grown especially for sparkling wines. Some success has even been achieved in making dry-styled Gewurztraminers and Johannisberg Rieslings from Russian River Valley grapes. However, the crowning achievements of the entire region go to Chardonnay and Pinot Noir.

Over 50 wineries reside within this appellation. Those that use it regularly and that also help define its capabilities include Sonoma-Cutrer, Dehlinger, De Loach, J. Rochioli, Hop Kiln, and Gary Farrell.

RUTHERFORD *(Napa)*   If Napa Valley is the name most likely to be associated with exceptional California wine, then Rutherford must stand next in line, especially for Cabernet Sauvignon. To be sure, Rutherford town as a place is not much. As a political subdivision and American Viticultural Area, it is a swath cut across the Napa Valley from side to side rather than one identifiable and cohesive source of grapes. But Rutherford has lent its name to the western benchland that encompasses areas both north and south of the town and grows Cabernet Sauvignon known round the world. And it is Rutherford that grows some of the best valley floor Cabernet for Caymus, Silver Oak, and Raymond. For years, insiders have referred to the special character of wines from the area as "Rutherford Dust." For us, it is closer to a rich, loamy, near-spicy/rooty quality that fits perfectly with the deep, curranty, and sometimes black-cherry fruit of Rutherford Cabernets. In some wines—especially those grown on the Rutherford Bench—this added seasoning can head in the direction of tea leaves, mint, and allspice. The Rutherford Viticultural Area contains some 3,500 acres of vines oriented very substantially to the red grapes of the Bordeaux region. Important plantings include: Cabernet Sauvignon (2,000), Merlot (600), and Cabernet Franc (100). The 300 acres of Chardonnay and 200 acres of Sauvignon Blanc are often planted in cooler or lower-lying areas. Not surprisingly, 26 of Rutherford's 30 wineries offer Cabernet Sauvignon. And while 24 wineries offer Chardonnay as well, they are obviously obtaining the grapes elsewhere in the Napa Valley.

RUTHERFORD BENCH   By now the wine world knows that the benchland of warm alluvial soils lying along the western edge of the Napa Valley floor from Yountville to

St. Helena yields much of the best Cabernet Sauvignon in California. It has been doing so for the entire half century since the end of Prohibition and was doing so another half century before that. Whether it was good luck or good thinking that landed Napa Valley pioneers like Captain Gustave Niebaum of Inglenook there around 1880 and Georges de Latour in 1900, their early successes along the Rutherford Bench have led inexorably to the great California Cabernets of today. The Rutherford Bench, however, is not its own AVA, but does lie along the western edge of the Oakville and Rutherford AVAs.

Research aimed at establishing the Bench as an official Viticultural Area showed that two adjoining alluvial fans—one near Rutherford and the other near Oakville—extend from just north of Yountville some 6 miles until they run out just south of St. Helena somewhere in the Zinfandel Lane area. With the exception of the area between Rutherford and Oakville, in which the alluvial soils cross the highway by some half-mile or so, all of the land of the Rutherford Bench lies west of Highway 29. This revered expanse of well-drained, gently sloping vineyards is home to grapes that appear in a veritable *Who's Who* of Cabernet Sauvignon. Among the producers who draw grapes from the Bench are Robert Mondavi, Joseph Phelps, Beaulieu, Heitz Wine Cellars (both its Martha's Vineyard and its Bella Oaks bottlings are from the Rutherford Bench), Inglenook, Grgich Hills, Opus One, Far Niente, Sequoia Grove, Cakebread, and Freemark Abbey (Bosche)—to name a few.

Today, there are more than 2,500 acres of grapes planted on the Bench, of which Cabernet Sauvignon and its blending partners comprise an estimated 80%, a substantial change in the last 15 years brought about mainly by the increased recognition of the area as a site for high-quality Cabernet and the resulting increase in the value of Cabernet grown there. A smaller amount of Chardonnay also appears, especially in the lower, colder, creekside locations. We favored recognizing this special area as a separate appellation, but, after a decade of debate, only the broad Oakville and Rutherford AVAs were proposed and accepted.

SACRAMENTO COUNTY    While not famous for its viticultural achievements or even very often noted on wine labels, Sacramento County has slowly increased its standing as a wine-producing area because the fertile soils south and southeast of the city of Sacramento receive cooling breezes off the nearby water-oriented Delta area. All of this territory is included in the recognized Viticultural Area of Lodi, which also includes portions of northern San Joaquin County. Merlot (2,400), Cabernet Sauvignon (1,700 acres) and Chardonnay (4,000) are the leading grape varieties among the county's 10,800 acres planted.

ST. HELENA (*Napa*)    This picturesque town and its environs are host to several dozen wineries, including such historically important producers as Beringer, Charles Krug, and Louis Martini. Among important newer properties, St. Helena can boast Heitz Cellars, Joseph Phelps, Duckhorn, Spottswoods and St. Clement. The vineyards surrounding St. Helena range in climate from Region II just west of town to warmer Region III conditions elsewhere. The low-lying, creekside soils often produce above-average to superb Chardonnays, while the hillside slopes along the western edge of the valley floor are earning a reputation for Cabernet. Here, in what seems like an extension of the Rutherford Bench in soil type and exposure, have been grown grapes for such notable producers as Spottswoode, Duckhorn, and Merryvale. Across the valley, the eastern hillsides get the hot late-afternoon sun and are agreeable hosts to Zinfandel and Syrah. Now a defined Viticultural Area of this name runs from Zinfandel Lane south of town to Bale Lane to the north and includes the foothills on both sides of the valley floor.

SAN BENITO (*San Benito*)    Just about every vine within San Benito County is part of this Viticultural Area. As such, the appellation begins 2 miles south of Hollister and follows the San Benito River for several miles. Though the landmass encompasses 45,000 acres, only 1,700 are vineyards. Four of the county's other Viticultural

Areas—Mount Harlan, Paicines, Cienega, and Lime Kiln Valley—are within the borders of San Benito.

SAN BENITO COUNTY    For years anything involving grape growing and winemaking within San Benito County could be traced directly to Almadén Vineyards. The winery owned most of the acreage, and during peak production periods its acreage exceeded 4,500. As Almadén's sales slipped in the 80s, the county's acreage diminished accordingly. The county contains four Viticultural Areas. Almadén was also directly responsible for defining two of them—Paicines and Cienega—where its production facilities were located. Lime Kiln Valley and San Benito are the others. Over the years Almadén offered a range of varietals from San Benito County that rose above average in quality only on rare occasions. Before the 80s ended, Almadén had new owners who immediately closed both facilities in the county and moved all operations to Madera in the Central Valley. Only a portion of Almadén's holdings in San Benito County were harvested after the move. Vineyards here cover 3,500 acres, about two-thirds of which was planted in 96 and 97.

SAN JOAQUIN COUNTY    Near the northern end of the grape-growing area within the Central Valley, the very warm vineyards of San Joaquin (especially in the Lodi and Delta areas) benefit from their proximity to the Delta by receiving the cooling marine breezes that flow across it from San Francisco Bay. This may account for the somewhat higher reputation enjoyed by San Joaquin County's wines in comparison to its even hotter neighbors to the south. The plantings in the 55,300 acres of vineyards located here are a mix of rapidly disappearing old-fashioned varieties (Alicante Bouschet, Mission, Palomino), coastal grapes hoping to benefit from the occasional fog, and the typical high-acid choices for new Central Valley plantings. The 19,500 acres of Zinfandel in the county represent about 40% of the statewide plantings and an even greater percentage of the total tonnage. Reportedly, they are the basis for much of the White Zinfandel selling at low prices. Other grapes include: Chardonnay (11,000 acres), Cabernet Sauvignon (7,400), Merlot (4,700) and Sauvignon Blanc (1,500).

SAN JOAQUIN VALLEY    The southern portion of the Central Valley running south from the Stockton-Sacramento area to Bakersfield is often referred to as the San Joaquin Valley (to distinguish it from the Sacramento Valley, which runs north from Sacramento). The San Joaquin Valley is one of the world's most fertile agricultural regions and offers hospitable conditions to all but the most tender plants (leafy greens and some citrus fruits, for instance). As a grape-growing area, it tends to be too hot for the prime varieties but suitably productive for grapes that tolerate heat well, and as a result is the source of most of the jug wine produced in California. Within the counties that make up the San Joaquin Valley (San Joaquin, Stanislaus, Merced, Madera, Fresno, Tulare, Kings, and Kern), some 150,000 acres of wine grapes stand in production (about 46% of the statewide total); and because of the higher yields gained from the grape varieties planted, new viticultural techniques, and extra heat, the San Joaquin Valley crush constitutes almost 80% of all wine grapes crushed in California. By contrast, Napa County holds 10% of the state's wine grapevines but crushes just 3% of the statewide total.

Except for the medium-warm area of the San Joaquin Valley, which abuts the Delta and is high Region III in heat accumulation during the growing season, most of the valley is rated as hot Region IV and V and rarely produces noteworthy wine. Nevertheless, most San Joaquin Valley wine, like other California jug wine, is clean, vinous, and made to be palatable when young. As such, it makes up the greatest part of the wine consumed in this country and is beginning to make inroads in the rest of the world.

SAN LUIS OBISPO COUNTY    This county is a part of the Central Coast region and, in terms of wine activity, really began to come alive in the early 80s. The total acreage now exceeds 13,500, with red varieties accounting for slightly more than whites. The majority of the vineyards can be found in its two principal growing regions, the

Viticultural Areas of Paso Robles and the Edna Valley. (Both regions appear as separate entries.)

Over 20 wineries are located within the county. Overall, the leading varieties are Cabernet Sauvignon (3,700), Chardonnay (3,600 acres), Zinfandel (1,700), Merlot (2,000), and Sauvignon Blanc (600). Other Viticultural Areas are found within its borders—York Mountain, Arroyo Grande Valley, and a small portion of the Santa Maria Valley.

SANTA BARBARA COUNTY    Some of the most picturesque vineyards in the entire state can be found in this Central Coast county, along the coast north of Los Angeles. The modern era of winemaking started relatively late here, but grew surprisingly fast. From 11 acres in 69, the county expanded to over 7,000 acres a decade later. Today's total approaches the 11,000 mark, pushed along by the about three dozen local wineries. The majority of the plantings are found in two Viticultural Areas north of the city of Santa Barbara: the Santa Ynez Valley and Santa Maria Valley.

White wine varieties cover over 75% of the vineyarded areas, the leaders being Chardonnay (6,900), Johannisberg Riesling (300), Sauvignon Blanc (300), and Chenin Blanc (200). Cabernet Sauvignon and Pinot Noir, at 500 and 1,200 acres respectively, top the red varieties. The most successful wines have been Chardonnay and Riesling. Among the reds, Pinot Noir, though erratic, has greatly outdistanced Cabernet Sauvignon, which is usually hindered by a strong herbaceous character.

Firestone, Byron, Sanford, and Zaca Mesa were among the first-recognized nationally known brands from the county. In the 80s, however, a nucleus of small, highly experimental wineries and brands appeared and prospered, such as Au Bon Climat and Qupe, to add excitement and draw attention to Santa Barbara as a wine region.

SANTA CLARA COUNTY    Once among the leaders for both volume produced and wine quality, this fast-urbanizing area has managed to preserve only small pieces of its immense wine heritage. The once abundant vineyards to the north and east of San Jose have been replaced by homes and malls. Of the 1,200 remaining acres, the majority is concentrated in the south, in and around Gilroy. Though the number of wineries within the county approaches 30, only Mirassou and J. Lohr are left in San Jose. These two, however, are the county's largest producers. Chardonnay is the leading variety, with 400 acres while Cabernet Sauvignon and Merlot boast 200 each. All but the smallest producers rely on grapes from outside the county. Hecker Pass and Santa Clara Valley are Viticultural Areas within this county. Both the Santa Cruz Mountains and Pacheco Pass Viticultural Areas lie partly within it.

SANTA CLARA VALLEY *(Santa Clara)*    Most of the still-standing vineyards in Santa Clara County are found within the Santa Clara Valley. As a Viticultural Area, this valley encompasses the present acreage (under 100) in southern Alameda County, from Pleasanton on south through the Sunol Valley. Its western border is shared with the eastern boundary of the Santa Cruz Mountains Viticultural Area. However, most of the vineyards that once existed in the north are history, except for a few mountain vineyards to the north and west of San Jose. Otherwise, grape-growing is largely confined today to the lower part of the valley, south of San Jose. Fewer than 1,100 acres remain, scattered among such quaint areas as Morgan Hill, Hecker Pass, and Gilroy. Chardonnay and Cabernet Sauvignon are the leading varieties in acreage.

SANTA CRUZ COUNTY    A cool coastal county located between Monterey and San Mateo County, Santa Cruz is home to quite a few wineries (over 20) for a region with a total of only 185 acres, over half in Chardonnay, planted. However, many of the winemakers are part-time and work in either San Jose or other parts of Silicon Valley within commuting distance. The region has a cool Region I climate, and the leading varieties planted are Pinot Noir, Cabernet Sauvignon, and Chardonnay. Most wine producers regularly purchase grapes from outside the region, often from the Central Coast, to supplement the local supply. But even those wines made exclusively from county-grown acreage are usually identified as originating in the Santa Cruz Mountains appellation.

SANTA CRUZ MOUNTAINS   This Viticultural Area begins in the coastal mountain range rising south of San Francisco and extends south well beyond San Jose. Since the early 19 th century, it has been collectively referred to as the Santa Cruz Mountains. It officially includes part of southern San Mateo County, and the mountainous area on the Santa Cruz side of the ridge, as well as the entire ridgeline through Santa Cruz County. The predominant varieties planted in this generally mountainous region are Chardonnay, Pinot Noir, and Cabernet Sauvignon. The region's two dozen wineries are generally small in output but boundless in ambition. The best known include Ridge Vineyards, David Bruce, Mount Eden, Thomas Fograty, and Bonny Doon.

SANTA MARIA VALLEY *(Santa Barbara)*   Except for a tiny bit of its northern boundary which slips over into San Luis Obispo County, this Viticultural Area is located within Santa Barbara County. It is a pretty valley, lying south and east of Santa Maria and extending south toward Los Alamos. The climate is regarded as a cool Region II, but a few isolated pockets in the west are cooled directly by ocean breezes and are a Region I. The soil tends to be sandy loam, but it becomes light sand in those vineyards close to the ocean. Such sandy soil heats up quickly and holds heat for a long time to compensate for cool weather. Of the present 7,000 acres under vines, the best and most consistent results have been achieved with Chardonnay. Some exciting though erratic results have come from Pinot Noir. In the late 70s–early 80s, many vintners from both the Central Coast and North Coast regions purchased grapes from Santa Maria. Several outsiders like Beringer, Robert Mondavi Winery, ZD, and Kendall-Jackson were among the first major buyers of Santa Maria white varieties, mainly Chardonnay.

By the late 80s, many producers both within and outside of the area, fearing a shortage of Chardonnay, became interested in purchasing well-regarded, independently owned vineyards and vineyard sites within Santa Maria. Robert Mondavi and Kendall-Jackson joined forces to purchase the large (1,400 acres) Tepusquet Vineyard. Jackson acquired 1,000 acres; Robert Mondavi took possession of 340 acres. Beringer acquired several vineyards in the area, including the 2,000-acre Rancho San Antonio, planted predominantly to Chardonnay. Two other prominent vineyards whose grapes are highly regarded are the Sierra Madre Vineyards and Bien Nacido Vineyards. Both names have appeared on many noteworthy Pinot Noir bottlings. Founded in 84, Byron Vineyards was the region's first major winery and now ranks third in volume (50,000 cases) behind Cambria (100,000) and Firestone (85,000).

SANTA YNEZ VALLEY *(Santa Barbara)*   Having its western border defined by the ocean front, the Santa Ynez Valley enjoys the cooling influence dictated by the flow of fog and offshore breezes. The valley itself surrounds the Santa Ynez River and extends east until it meets the Los Padres National Forest. The climate is a cool Region II. Most of the county's wineries are clustered within the Santa Ynez Valley, which also is home to the colorful Danish community of Solvang. In the early 70s, the Firestone Vineyard was among the first to establish extensive acreage and it has, ever since, assumed the pioneering role. Zaca Mesa and Au Bon Climat have also helped bring national recognition to this area. Overall, the consensus is that white varietals led by Chardonnay and Riesling enjoy success and consistency among white wines. Chardonnay has risen above ° ranking on a regular basis. Though recent vintages of Cabernet Sauvignon show improvements over their predecessors, Cabernet Sauvignon continues to vary widely in styles but usually contains vegetal notes. However, by the mid-80s the number of attractive Pinot Noirs began to increase, and on some occasions, Pinot Noir has achieved standout status in the hands of Babcock Vineyards.

SHENANDOAH VALLEY *(Amador)* Despite its grape-growing history dating from the 1880s, the Shenandoah Valley is in some ways a discovery of modern times. Until the late 1960s, the grapes grown there, mostly Zinfandel, were sold under contract to jug-wine producers or in the smallest of lots to home winemakers. Then, building on the reputation being garnered by the intrepid amateurs, the Sutter Home winery gave Shenandoah Valley Zinfandel a try and put the region back on California's wine map. Soon, a dozen Zinfandel makers were making the trek to the Sierras and offering Shenandoah, and other foothill, wines. Plantings were expanded (now in excess of 2,000 acres), still mostly Zinfandel, and new wineries were founded. In the early 80s, when Zinfandel—especially the heavy, jammy style prevalent in the Shenandoah Valley—went temporarily out of fashion, most of the coastal-based winemakers abandoned the area. Now most of the grapes grown in the area are vinified there as well. In the past few years, Syrah has become important and successful, especially through the °°° Syrahs from Domaine de la Terre Rouge. Formal Viticultural Area status was granted in 1983.

SIERRA FOOTHILLS *(Amador, Calaveras, El Dorado, Mariposa, Nevada, Placer, Tuolomne, and Yuba)* East of Sacramento and Stockton, which lie on the floor of the Central Valley, rise the majestic Sierra Nevada Mountains. Partway up this 10,000-foot-high range, about an hour's drive from the lowlands, runs a belt of foothills at 1,000- to 3,000-foot elevations that have a long, if uneven, history for winemaking. During the Gold Rush era, places like El Dorado, Placer, Calaveras, and Amador counties were reported to have contained up to 10,000 acres of grapes. By 1970, when the area was rediscovered by makers of varietal wines, there were fewer than 1,000 acres standing. Most of that was in Amador County and was purchased by jug-wine makers. In the ensuing two decades, acreage has grown to approximately 3,200. Some two dozen wineries have established themselves throughout the 160-mile-long swath of the recognized Sierra Foothills Viticultural Area, which extends from Yuba County in the north to Mariposa County in the south. Amador County with 2,400 acres and El Dorado County with 300 acres are the most active regions within the Sierra Foothills area, and Zinfandel remains the favored variety.

SOLANO COUNTY Though its 2,000 acres of grapes do not make much of a splash in the California wine pool, and the places where grapes are grown lie mostly at the fringes of the county rather than at its heart, Solano County nonetheless can claim three separate and distinct Viticultural Areas within its borders. Solano's Green Valley and Suisun Valley areas lie on the western edge of the county, near the eastern borders of Napa County, while the Clarksburg appellation sits astride the Delta area at Solano County's easternmost boundaries, where it runs into Yolo and San Joaquin counties. There are about 700 acres of Chardonnay and 350 acres each of Cabernet Sauvignon and Merlot.

SONOMA COAST *(Sonoma)* This large (750-square-mile) Viticultural Area was created to include only those sections of the county categorized as a Region I or cool (under 2,800 degree days) Region II. It excludes the Alexander Valley, the Dry Creek Valley, and the western, hilly portion of Chalk Hill. Sonoma Coast does overlap other Viticultural Areas such as Green Valley–Sonoma, Los Carneros, Sonoma Valley (but only from the south to the town of Sonoma), and the lower end of the Russian River Valley known as the Santa Rosa plain. The coast serves as its western border beginning a few miles north of Bodega Bay and Fort Ross. To the southwest, Sonoma Coast ends at the Sonoma-Marin border. As a result, potential vineyard areas in and around Penngrove, Petaluma, Lakeville, Cotati, and all along the coastal ridgetops which had been excluded from other Viticultural Areas became part of this place name. All told, over 12,000 acres of vineyards are included.

SONOMA COUNTY Prior to 1970 Sonoma County was a rural, tranquil wine region, best known for its generally pleasing, modestly priced red jug wines. In fact, except for a brief period in the mid-1800s when Sonoma Valley was the hub of winemaking activity in Northern California, Sonoma County had always run a distant second to its neighbor, Napa County. But within the last two decades, Sonoma County has emerged as home to many fine wines, to numerous high-energy, well-financed producers, and to several significant Viticultural Areas. Today, the county has closed the gap, and is regularly well represented among the highest-ranked wines, especially Zinfandels, Pinot Noirs, Sauvignon Blancs, and Chardonnays.

Sonoma County awakened to the wine boom a few years after Napa Valley had come alive. Despite the late start, it eventually experienced dramatic growth and change. Before 1970, most of the planted grape acreage consisted of the hearty red jug-wine varieties—Petite Sirah, Carignane, and Zinfandel. The primary white grape at the time was French Colombard. Of the 33 wineries within Sonoma at that time, the majority were longtime family-owned producers turning out a range of wines, sometimes under their own brands, but more often selling them as bulk wines to neighbors in Napa Valley. In the vineyards the emphasis fell generally on tonnage, as growers favored high-yielding varieties and methods.

Today, however, Sonoma County is a far different place on the wine map. In areas where the primary crops were once walnuts, pears, peaches, almonds, and prunes, grapevines now predominate. The total acreage has shot up to 40,500, which moves it past Napa County and makes it the most heavily planted coastal county. The major change within Sonoma is in the mix of varieties cultivated. The county experienced such a rapid conversion to premium wine varieties that, at the start of the 90s, over 70% of its plantings consisted of Chardonnay, Cabernet Sauvignon, Zinfandel, Pinot Noir, and Sauvignon Blanc. More significantly, the breakdown of grapes grown in this one-time red jug-wine county shows whites nearly as plentiful as reds. Today, the primary white varieties planted in terms of acreage are Chardonnay (13,300), Sauvignon Blanc (1,700), and Gewurztraminer (300). The leading reds are Cabernet Sauvignon (7,500), Zinfandel (4,300), Pinot Noir (4,100), and Merlot (5,500). By 90, Sonoma County had become the leading county for both Chardonnay and Pinot Noir cultivation, and it is the leader in the North Coast for Zinfandel.

The county of Sonoma covers more territory than Napa County and contains a wide range of climatic zones. As a result, the growers and winemakers agreed to define those places and push for their recognition as federally approved Viticultural Areas. By the mid-80s over a dozen such Viticultural Areas had been identified. Among the first to be defined were the county's cooler zones, such as Los Carneros, Sonoma Valley, and the Russian River Valley, as well as warmer inland regions such as Alexander Valley, Dry Creek Valley, and Knight's Valley. A number of other Viticultural Areas have been delineated since 1983, such as Chalk Hill, Green Valley, Northern Sonoma, Sonoma Mountain, and Sonoma Coast.

Sonoma County has built a strong reputation for Chardonnay, Sauvignon Blanc, and Gewurztraminer among white varietals. Top-rated Chardonnays have originated in the Alexander Valley, Dry Creek Valley, and Russian River Valley. Among red wines, Zinfandels from Dry Creek Valley, Alexander Valley, and Sonoma Valley are some of the most flavorful and distinctive. Both Merlot and Pinot Noir from the cooler regions are showing steady improvement and the best Pinot Noirs from the Russian River Valley are quality leaders statewide. Cabernet Sauvignon can be excellent, but as yet has not equaled the consistency of Napa Valley Cabernet Sauvignons. However, some fine Cabernets have emanated from the Alexander Valley, Sonoma Mountain, and the Sonoma Valley in particular. Sparkling wines have started to come on strong through a cluster of producers relying on Russian River Valley grapes for their cuvées. Sonoma County's leading red wine producers include Gary Farrell, J. Rochioli, Dehlinger, Geyser Peak, Matanzas Creek and Ferrari-Carano.

The number of wineries and vineyards within Sonoma County is likely to continue growing. Two of the oldest wineries in Sonoma County, Sebastiani Vineyards and Korbel, are its two leaders in terms of volume.

SONOMA MOUNTAIN (*Sonoma*)  This Viticultural Area, a subregion of the Sonoma Valley, is located along the mountain range just to the west of Glen Ellen. It includes east-facing vineyards at the 400- to 600-foot elevation, and west-facing land located at the 1,200- to 1,600-foot elevation. These slopes share similar soils identified as Spreckles-Felta. By virtue of being above the fog line this appellation enjoys a climate that is warmer than the valley floor, but also it is an unusual climate because the daily temperature does not fluctuate widely during the growing season. The total acres planted now stand at close to 700, the majority being Cabernet Sauvignon and Zinfandel. Laurel Glen Vineyards is the best-known winery within this appellation.

SONOMA VALLEY *(Sonoma)* Nestled between the gentle Sonoma Mountain Range on the west and the towering Mayacamas Mountains on the east, the Sonoma Valley is a picturesque wine valley with a rich history. It was in this valley, also known as the Valley of the Moon, that North Coast winemaking began back in 1825 when the missionary fathers established Mission Sonoma. By the 1850s, thanks to the dealings and accomplishments of Agoston Haraszthy, who started the valley's first winery, Buena Vista, Sonoma Valley had evolved into a winemaking center, better known to the world than Napa Valley. However, by the end of the 19 th century the Sonoma Valley was eclipsed by its neighbor to the east. As an appellation, it did not call attention to itself until the early 1970s.

Today the Sonoma Valley, with more than 7,000 acres planted to wine grapes, actually stretches for some 40 miles as one traces it from the San Pablo Bay in the south to just below Santa Rosa in the north. The generally welcomed summer fog enters the valley from points both north and south. But the cooler regions by far are located toward the south, primarily in the Los Carneros District. In the valley's midsection between Glen Ellen and Kenwood, the climate along the valley floor warms. However, Sonoma Valley's grape acreage, though quite compact, covers such a wide array of soil types, elevations, and topography that the viticultural conditions probably vary as much in this small space as in other larger wine regions of California.

Some general patterns have emerged. In the southern Sonoma Valley from Los Carneros on up to the town of Sonoma, the best wines come from early-maturing varieties: Chardonnay, Gewurztraminer, Pinot Noir, and, from some producers, Merlot. On the hillsides and along the hilltops both eastern and western, so long as the elevation is above the frost line, Cabernet and Zinfandel usually fare the best. The two most widely cultivated grapes in the valley, Chardonnay and Pinot Noir, perform better than average along the benchlands between Sonoma and Kenwood. Cabernet and Zinfandel are the next two popular varieties.

Most of the 30 wineries in the valley were founded after 1970, except for Sebastiani and Buena Vista, the two oldest. Most of the producers remain small to midsized. Sebastiani is larger than any of them by a wide margin.

SOUTH COAST Similar in concept to North Coast and Central Coast, South Coast is a multi-county Viticultural Area bringing together a portion of southwestern Riverside County, the west coastal region of San Diego County, and a tiny grape-growing parcel in Orange County. Included in the South Coast are two primary subdistricts, Temecula and San Pasqual. As the first new winery to settle here, Callaway focused attention on this area in the mid-70s and eventually set the tone by specializing in white varietals. The climate varies slightly, but for the most part is categorized as a warm Region III, despite the cooling assist from frequent fog intrusion. Today, close to two dozen wineries and 3,000 acres are within this Viticultural Area. Together, Sauvignon Blanc and Chardonnay account for over 50% of the total acreage, with Johannisberg Riesling a distant third in popularity. Fewer than 500 acres are planted to red grapes.

SPRING MOUNTAIN DISTRICT *(Napa)* A distinctly identifiable watershed area known as Spring Mountain lies west of St. Helena and forms part of the Mayacamas Mountain Range, the boundary between the Napa and Sonoma valleys. This picturesque stretch of hillside has a long and fabled history of grape growing that dates back to the 19th century. It maintained itself fitfully after Prohibition, but many of Spring Mountain's great estates have only been put back into winemaking in the last two decades. Soils and exposures vary considerably on Spring Mountain, with most vineyards seemingly favoring later-maturing red grapes like Cabernet Sauvignon. The York Creek Vineyard, which has been providing grapes to the Ridge winery (among others) for almost two decades, has earned a reputation for its gutsy Cabernets, Zinfandels, and Petite Sirahs. In some vineyards, however, it is the early-ripening varieties such as Chardonnay and Pinot Noir which have earned the better reputations. Among important wineries on Spring Mountain are Keenan, Cain, Newton, and Stony Hill. Viticultural Area status was granted in 1993.

STAGS LEAP DISTRICT *(Napa)*   About a mile east of Yountville is the picturesque Stags Leap area. Known primarily for its rich, supple, balanced, often mouth-filling, usually expensive Cabernet Sauvignon, this superb viticultural pocket has distinctly red soil and gets its name from a prominent knoll of red rocks that marks its eastern boundary. According to legend, the promontory is the home of the cavorting antlered quadruped. In recent history, the name has been applied to the limited area of land near the eastern hills thought to be influenced by reflected sunlight and warmth from the rocks. However, wineries from as far south as the Chimney Rock area to as far north as S. Anderson on the Yountville Cross Road have managed to slip within the shadow of the stag and the borders of the defined Viticultural Area. The early leader in the revival of this area was Warren Winiarski's Stag's Leap Wine Cellars. Important followers include Clos du Val, Stags' Leap Winery, Pine Ridge Winery, and Steltzner Vineyard. All told, about a dozen wineries and 1,500 acres of grapes are found in the Stags Leap area.

SUISUN VALLEY *(Solano)*   Like its neighboring appellation to the immediate west, Green Valley–Solano, this little-heard name is of almost no vinous consequence in spite of having 24 square miles within its government-recognized boundaries. The few grapes that grow here suffer through a relatively hot and dry summer and are nobody's prize when it comes to reputation.

TALMAGE *(Mendocino)*   Extending east and south of Ukiah and occupying the foothills is a region referred to by local growers as Talmage. About half of the Redwood Valley's grape acreage is located here, and most of the plantings were established in the early 70s. The primary varieties are Zinfandel, Cabernet Sauvignon, and Chardonnay.

TEMPLETON *(San Luis Obispo)*   Located 8 miles south of Paso Robles, Templeton is a small town included within the Paso Robles appellation. The York Mountain Viticultural Area, 9 miles due west of Templeton, is home to several wineries, including old-timers such as York Mountain, Las Tables, and Pesenti, as well as newcomers such as Wild Horse Winery. Most of the 400 acres within Templeton are planted today to red varieties. Zinfandel and Petite Sirah dominate the old plantings, but Cabernet, Merlot, and Chardonnay are definitely on the increase.

UKIAH *(Mendocino)*   Ukiah is the urban center of the county and home to three of the county's oldest and largest producers: Parducci, Cresta Blanca (now Dunnewood Vineyards), and Weibel. Most of the vineyards within sight of Ukiah are located directly to the north.

UMPQUA VALLEY   In the early 60s the Umpqua Valley was the location for Oregon's wine awakening when the state's oldest winery, Hillcrest Vineyards, opened its doors. Located due south of the Willamette Valley, Umpqua extends south for another 70 miles and ends at the Klamath Mountains. Sharing a similar Region I climate with its northern neighbor, the Umpqua Valley has more frost threats but less rainfall than the Willamette Valley. About 600 acres of vines are located both along the hillsides and on the valley floors. The leading varieties are Pinot Noir and Chardonnay. Hillcrest is the oldest, and, along with Bjellend, the best known of the six establishments within this Viticultural Area.

WALLA WALLA    Like the larger Columbia Valley which contains it, this Viticultural Area falls chiefly within Washington State but also takes in a tiny portion of northern Oregon. It can be found west of the city of Walla Walla along the river of the same name. About a half dozen producers are located in the region. In the past decade, Merlots from producers such as Leonetti, L'Ecole No. 41, Woodward Canyon, and Waterbrook have achieved near-superstar status for their rich, supple, deeply fruited character.

WASHINGTON STATE    With some 17,000 acres of vinifera grapes, Washington has become the second-largest premium wine–producing state. The total amount of wine produced annually exceeds 9 million gallons. Washington ranks fourth in the U.S. in terms of per capita wine consumption and is the ninth-largest wine market. The primary growing regions are located east of the Cascade Mountains and they consist of three Viticultural Areas—the Yakima Valley (Yakima and Benton counties), the Walla Walla Valley, and the Columbia Valley area to the east, where the Columbia, Snake, and Yakima rivers converge. These regions are semi-arid, with long, dry, moderately warm summer days and cold winters. Vineyardists rely on irrigation throughout the growing season. Located at the northerly 47° latitude, these wine regions are characterized by a growing season that is generally longer than in California, but with somewhat lower heat totals. However, the summer days experience longer daylight hours, and most varieties with the possible exception of Cabernet Sauvignon have adapted well and ripen more than adequately in most years. We should note that in western Washington, some vineyard activity and small-scale winemaking take place in and around Puget Sound. Most of the state's wine activities, however, are centered in eastern Washington.

Washington's first serious vinifera vineyards were planted in the Yakima Valley in the 60s. Because there was no history of *Phylloxera* in the region, all of the vines are planted on their own root systems. The region soon proved to be unusual in several ways. On the positive side, over the first two decades vinifera vines have carried more quality fruit per acre than many of their counterparts around the world. The one risk encountered is that winter weather can be too tough on the sensitive vinifera vines, and fall frosts have on occasion also taken their toll. When damage has occurred, it has usually been the newly planted vines that suffer.

Gewurztraminer, Riesling, and Grenache were among the first varietals made by pioneers in the late 60s, and those wines were judged good enough to encourage expansion. Since 75 the vinifera acreage has increased sixfold. White varieties once enjoyed the lion's share and represented 80% of the total as late as 1988. Now whites, led by Chardonnay (4,500 acres) and Johannisberg Riesling (2,000) are about 53%, and reds, almost totally oriented to Merlot (3,900) and Cabernet Sauvignon (2,600), have increased to 48%. Labrusca varieties, primarily Concord, have been grown for decades in Washington to supply producers of grape juice and sacramental wines.

The number of producers is over 100 and the industry continues to expand. Chateau Ste. Michelle remains the largest in terms of volume and the most visible in terms of national availability. Its special bottlings of Chardonnay, Cabernet, and Merlot are often among the best on the West Coast.

Over recent vintages Hogue Cellars has emerged as a quality leader as well as a volume leader. Columbia Crest joins Ste. Michelle and Hogue as wineries making more than 100,000 cases a year. Leonetti and Quilceda Creek have been among the best-regarded small producers and are lately joined by a host of others, including DeLille, Chinook, L'Ecole No. 41, and McCrea.

Washington Chardonnays are often pleasingly fruity and often exhibit the depth and intensity found in California's finest. The most successful varietals to date have been Riesling, Chenin Blanc, and Semillon—all with pert, lively fruitiness. Merlot, however, may with greater maturity achieve consistently high marks. Over the first two decades it has proven to be far more exciting here than Cabernet Sauvignon or any other red grape.

WILD HORSE VALLEY *(Napa and Solano)*   100 acres of grapes reside in this little-known Viticultural Area on the border between Napa and Solano counties.

WILLAMETTE VALLEY   Beginning just north of Portland, the Willamette Valley traverses the state from north to south for 170 miles until it ends near Eugene. Classified as a Region I, it is Oregon's principal wine region and home to a majority of the wineries and vineyards. Most of the plantings are in the hills on the west side of the Willamette River, and as a rule the vineyards are located at elevations between 300 and 1,000 feet. The most extensive plantings fall within the central section from Salem to the Chehalem Mountains. In the foothills along the eastern side, the newly emerging Eola Hills region (a row of low hills stretching from just north of Amity 15 miles south to the Bethel gap) was the site of modest expansion in the 80s. At the north end of the Eola Hills, just west of Amity, William Hill Winery purchased 200 acres in 89. In the late 80s the southern part of the Willamette near the town of Monroe was being viewed as yet another location suitable for establishing Pinot Noir acreage. Napa Valley's Steve Girard acquired land in this region in 88 for the purpose of making Pinot Noir.

From the mid-70s onward, Pinot Noir has been the leading variety in terms of acreage and performance. Chardonnay and Riesling are also widely planted. The Viticultural Area could undergo considerable expansion, with potential sites estimated to be in the neighborhood of 20,000 total acres, if demand continues to grow. Throughout the rough formative days and in the early glory era, Eyrie Vineyard has been recognized as the pioneer and the most influential local winery. Eyrie's Pinot Noirs were the first to win international recognition. Three producers noted for Pinot Noir—Eyrie, Sokol Blosser, and Knudsen Erath—own vineyards in the Dundee Hills, a subregion noted for its red soils and steep hillsides. Australian winemaker Brian Croser founded his Dundee Wine Co. in 86 to produce sparkling wines under the Argyle label. In 87, the influential Burgundy producer Robert Drouhin bought land in Dundee. Drouhin purchased additional land since then and now owns 180 acres. In 89, Laurent-Perrier of Champagne acquired 80 acres in the Willamette Valley's Dundee Hills area for the purpose of making sparkling wine.

Overall, about 80% of Oregon's vineyard lands lie within the Willamette Valley. The current total of 6,300 acres planted there covers all of the varieties for which Oregon has become known, and while other areas are also expanding, it is the grapes and the wineries of the Willamette Valley to which the state's wine fame is chiefly due. Important plantings in this multi-county appellation include: Pinot Noir (2,800), Pinot Gris (1,000), Johannisberg (White) Riesling (600), Chardonnay (900), Cabernet Sauvignon (100), and Gewurztraminer (100).

WILLOW CREEK *(Humboldt and Trinity)*   This Viticultural Area is located east of Eureka, near the confluence of the Trinity River with its south fork. Since fewer than 10 acres of grapes grow in both counties combined, Willow Creek is more name than reality.

YAKIMA VALLEY   The first officially recognized Viticultural Area in the Northwest, the Yakima Valley is 75 miles long and 22 miles wide, and is heavily planted to both labrusca and vinifera grapes. Though semi-arid, this region was among the nation's first to become a prosperous agricultural center with total reliance on modern irrigation systems. It grows over 18,000 acres of Concord and related labrusca varieties for grape juice, some of the country's most desirable hops, and has yielded some of the Northwest's most distinctive vinifera wines, especially Riesling, Chenin Blanc, Semillon, and Grenache. It experiences the coolest weather in the Columbia Valley and the coldest, most dangerous winter temperatures. Ste. Michelle, Hogue, and Covey Run are among the leading producers within the area.

According to estimates, the potential vinifera acreage could grow to 20,000 if and when demand warrants expansion.

YAMHILL COUNTY   This county contains the midsection of the Willamette Valley, including the vinous triangle with apexes at Newberg, Salem, and McMinnville. Still responsible for growing about one-third of Oregon grapes, Yamhill County contains about 2,400 acres of grapes, with Pinot Noir (1,200), Chardonnay (500) and Pinot Gris (350) leading the way.

YOLO COUNTY   Lying west of Sacramento in an area that is technically part of the warm Central Valley, Yolo County vineyards (6,000 acres) experience slightly cooler growing conditions because of the coastal marine influences that push up from San Francisco Bay across the Sacramento River Delta. The majority of vineyards are planted in the eastern part of the county, within the Clarksburg and Merritt Island Viticultural Areas. A newly developing grape-growing area lies in the county's western hills near Dunnigan. Chardonnay is the most widely planted variety (3,100 acres), with Chenin Blanc (300) and Sauvignon Blanc (300) coming next among white grapes. Cabernet Sauvignon and Merlot, with 300 acres each, and Syrah, at 200 acres, are the leading reds.

YORK MOUNTAIN *(San Luis Obispo)*   Situated on the eastern side of the Santa Lucia Mountains and west of Paso Robles, this Viticultural Area is one of the smallest on the West Coast. The average elevation is about 1,500 feet, and the area contains 23 acres of vineyards and one producer, York Mountain Winery. Compared to its neighboring Viticultural Areas, York Mountain is cooler, but also receives more rainfall, especially during the late summer. The varieties planted are a mix of reds, led by Pinot Noir and Zinfandel.

YOUNTVILLE *(Napa)*   Lying just 6 miles north of the city of Napa, the little but no longer sleepy, increasingly tourism-oriented town of Yountville is the first true wine community one encounters when entering the Napa Valley. Surrounding Yountville are a variety of important growing areas and wineries. To the south, in relatively cool growing conditions, are Chardonnay vineyards that supply Chateau Montelena, Trefethen, Beringer, Rutherford Hill, and others. To the west, in the midst of what might be considered prime Cabernet country, sits the dramatic home of Domaine Chandon, while the eastern side of the valley contains the Stags Leap area, renowned for its rich, generally elegant Cabernet and Merlot from such vinous stars as Stag's Leap Wine Cellars, Clos du Val, Pine Ridge, Shafer, and Chimney Rock.

# Vintage Commentary

As vines, regions, and winemakers have all continued to mature quickly through-out the last decade, it has become increasingly obvious that vintages indeed play a role in California wines. One year may not vary as much from the next as is often the case in Europe, but there are differences, and those differences can be significant. A solid knowledge of California vintages can—and should—affect buying decisions.

Climatic differences are primarily responsible for defining vintage differences. The amount of rainfall, frosts, hail, heatwaves, cold spells, droughts, floods, and what-have-you are all part of the general climate. So far in the 90s, California has experienced just about every extreme and possibility. Untimely rain—or the lack of it—certainly influences the quality of grapes a vine yields. But certain climatic variables are also important. A cold spell, heavy rains, or hail during the period of bloom and set (usually in May, when flower blossoms convert into fruit) may hin-der both quantity and quality. A cold spell during the harvest, on the other hand, often provides welcome relief because it slows the ripening process, which in turn slows the pace of harvesting.

The sum total of climatic conditions during one growing season, usually April 1 through the end of September, constitutes the vintage conditions and helps de-fine the wines made that year in two ways. The first is the most obvious, and the one most people associate with the word "vintage." That refers to the overall *quality* of a specific wine from a specific region, categorizing it as excellent, above av-erage, average, weak, or poor.

The second relates to the character or the general *style* of a particular wine from a given year. For instance, Cabernet Sauvignons grown in Napa Valley in 94 and in 95 are both categorized as good to excellent, but the wines are definitely not of the same style. They vary in varietal intensity, depth of flavor, and aging potential. A similar important distinction will be made between California Chardonnays from 96 and 97—they differ slightly in overall quality and in the general vintage style. The vintage assessments that follow highlight, when ap-propriate, both the qualitative and the stylistic distinctions.

Our assessments are derived from two sources. First, we observe the climatic drama from the day it begins to unfold with budbreak to the time it ends with the last grape of the season being crushed. We do not base our judgments of vintages solely on what happens in the vineyards, however. Many Europeans rely almost exclusively on the climatic conditions and patterns, which is why you may have heard or read someone declaring "a vintage of the century" in Europe as early as October or November when the wines are still fermenting.

We, on the contrary, perform "blind" (meaning objective) tastings of all the wines we are able to locate before passing final judgment on a vintage or, for that matter, on a producer. Neither the winemaking process nor the winemaker can be relied on to follow a predictable and infallible path once the grapes have been harvested. Thus over the last 20 years, no two vintages have yet to be carbon copies in our experience. Producers and winemakers have to prove themselves each and every year.

In this chapter, we concentrate on five varietals: Cabernet Sauvignon, Merlot, Pinot Noir, Zinfandel, and Chardonnay. These five are the most sought after by consumers and collectors, and they also are the five most likely to reward cellaring. The data presented here range from specific climatic information to generalized stylistic commentary. They relate only to vintages. For well-informed buying decisions, we urge you to consider this chapter together with Wine Geography, and of course the guide to individual producers and brands.

# Cabernet Sauvignon

Exceptional earlier, ageworthy vintages: 1947, 1949, 1951, 1954, 1958, 1966

1968   A copious vintage that surprised many with full-flavored, tannin-laden wines that developed slowly. The most exceptional wines produced were Napa Valley in origin. With aging the finest wines began to display a classic, ripe style. The majority peaked by the early 80s. However, a few show some signs of surviving well into the late 90s. Beaulieu's Private Reserve and Heitz Martha's Vineyard will make it into the next century alive.

1969   Starting out from an underrated vintage, the wines were viewed as short-lived because they lacked the ripeness of 68. Those that were properly cellared responded well and evolved into soft, likable wines with straightforward character. Those made from hillside plantings were often the pick of the bunch. Most are past prime.

1970   This was a vintage that eventually aroused national excitement and became the best of the 70s. It began with a mild, wet winter, followed by severe spring frosts that reduced the crop by close to half. Ideally warm late-summer weather brought the grapes to full, intense ripeness. The wines ranged from ripe and balanced to overripe, slightly raisined, and heady. With aging, many became less balanced and barely survived their 10 th year. Others made with some restraint developed normally—and by the mid-80s were magnificent. A vintage with many great to excellent wines, but not quite a classic style.

1971   A year that began with a cool spring, and a long, cool growing season that lacked real warmth and distinction. Most of the wines, mirroring the weather, possess a thin, simple character. The major exceptions came from low-yielding mountain vineyards, such as Ridge Monte Bello. Beaulieu's Reserve stood out. Most were over the hill by the early 80s.

1972   A much-troubled vintage. Heatwaves in July reduced the crop. Persistent late-season rains created mold problems and diluted flavors. Most versions were soft in body and often light in varietal character. Overall quality was average to below average. Few wines lived very long.

1973   The winter began wet and cold and finally gave way late in the spring to warm, lovely weather that remained through most of the growing season. This one was classified as a cool year. The crop turned out to be bountiful, and early reports on quality were cautious and doubt-ridden. After some aging, many wines began to blossom and display fine character, balance, and harmony. A tannic undercurrent provided structure that aided long-term aging. Above-average to excellent quality overall.

1974   A cool spring, moderate summer weather, and a warm harvest made this year seem textbook perfect. The crop was large, and the grapes ripened steadily and well. The best wines were dark, concentrated, tannic in their youth, and seemed long-lived. A few of the tannic versions turned out to be fat and ponderous. But the other big wines were developing inner beauty and complexity within a decade. Many of the medium-priced, moderately tannic wines matured nicely and peaked around their 10 th year, with good holding ability. A few of the better-structured Reserve bottlings are just beginning to shed their tannins and may last well into the next century. Ridge Monte Bello and Heitz Martha's Vineyard, both stellar, will outlive all others. Some disappointments mar this vintage. Still, it is an excellent one.

1975   Early frosts and early rains were followed by a cool, unusually long growing season. This was a difficult and unusual vintage, leading to a wide array of styles. By a thin margin, the majority were short on fruit and underfilled, though occasionally elegant. Some superb examples emerged with forthright character, moderate intensity, and balance. Only a few, aged beyond a decade. Both Caymus and Hertz Martha's Vineyard, tasted recently, are superb.

1976   The first drought year caught producers ill-prepared. After prolonged dry, warm weather throughout the summer, the only consolation was periodic harvest rains. The grapes were tiny, with high sugar, low acidity, and thick skins. As a result, most wines were dark, dense, high in alcohol, and lacking balance or the structure to bring them into balance. The best of an odd year peaked by 1986; the majority were uninteresting, ugly, or dead long before then.

1977   The second drought year was handled by better-prepared winemakers who, with the help of dry but relatively cool summer weather, achieved better-balanced wines. Sporadic harvest rains provided a little lift to the vine and enabled the grapes to avoid dehydration. Overall, the vintage was average in quality, with good varietal character and short-term aging.

1978   This banner warm year produced many ripe, occasionally overripe, wines. A heatwave arrived at the beginning of the harvest and remained to the end, necessitating round-the-clock picking. The crop was larger than normal, but many wines were fat, tannic, and high in alcohol. The finest were well stuffed with varietal fruit, with an ability to age beyond one decade. A few—Mondavi Reserve, Silver Oak, Caymus, and Stag's Leap Cask 23—are alive and well today. Those less well balanced have faded. Well above average quality.

1979   A difficult vintage. Frequent late-season heatwaves sent sugar levels soaring and acidity readings falling, sometimes out of control. Then the hot spells were followed by heavy rains that tended to dilute flavor and lower tannins of the remaining grapes. Some wines turned out flavorful and balanced, often those made from grapes picked before the rains. Most wines turned out to be on the austere and tight side. Most peaked within a decade. The primary long-agers were the Reserve bottlings. An average-quality year.

1980    Heavy winter rains persisted into early spring. A cool early season led to warm conditions as the harvest neared. The grapes developed an unusual combination of high sugar content and high acidity which created widespread anticipation of high quality during the harvest. But the harvest was over quickly, indicating grape maturity was achieved too rapidly. Most wines, as a result, never lived up to their early promise of long aging. However, many wines offer generous fruit, moderate tannins, some depth, and high alcohol levels. Similar in style to 78, yet with accessible fruit and depth, this vintage produced many °° and a few °°° bottlings. Well above average.

1981    An intense early heatwave reduced the crop and resulted in an extremely early harvest in the North Coast. Both varietal intensity and aging potential were question marks at first. Most wines appealed early on, with an open, fleshy style that invited near-term consumption. However, they have an inner balance that responds well to aging, and are turning out to be moderately complex. From the beginning, this underappreciated vintage offered numerous fine values and gave us a reasonable share of ° and even a few °° wines. Slightly above average, and most wines are now fully mature.

1982    A wet winter, a mild summer, and a rainy harvest season yielded a mixed bag of wines. The successes offered plummy, jammy fruit, with moderate tannins. Generous, solid, and substantial, the best of the 82 s, Dunn and Spottswoode, were among the biggest critical hits. Most °° bottlings were along Reserve lines. Average overall.

1983    Moderate weather during the growing season was followed by persistent harvest rains, causing numerous difficulties. Harvesting was slowed by the rains, which led to diluted, out-of-balance grapes. The number of °° wines was small, primarily restricted to Reserve types. Dunn's Howell Mountain was exceptional. Newcomer Forman Winery debuts with °°° results. Most of the ° wines offer modest varietal character and moderate aging potential. The majority of others are on the heavy, muscular side and lack integration of fruit and tannin. Average quality. Most are way over the hill by now.

1984    Early budbreak, and a virtually rain-free, persistently warm growing season, resulted in a relatively early harvest. Though similar to the conditions of 74 and 78, the hot weather during the vintage forced many wineries to harvest quickly to avoid overripeness and high alcohols in their wines. Despite these precautions, the majority of the wines are big, ripe, and tannic. The style tends toward ripe, well-stuffed fruit, with ample tannins for support and for long-term cellaring. Many Reserves and a few regular bottlings are likely to age for 20 years or more, but most are now at or near their peaks. Overall, the best vintage since 78. Well above average to excellent. Many wines are fully mature at this point.

1985    This year began with early budbreak. A warm early spring was followed by a cool late spring. Then pleasant warm weather in June and July set the stage for one of the most incredible years, even for California Cabernet Sauvignon. The steady warm weather led up to a cool August, resulting in one of the longest growing seasons ever. Dry September weather allowed for an evenly paced crush. The grapes matured with full flavors and good acidity at somewhat lower than normal Brix. The resulting wines were often ripe, yet many managed to possess an inner balance without being heavy. The 85s are compressed and compact, their varietal personality and balancing acidity giving them great aging potential. In style they are the most likely Cabernets in recent memory to invite comparison with the finest from Bordeaux. An excellent vintage, said by some to be the best since Prohibition, it is opening up in the better wines but may never find generosity in others.

1986    The year began with winter floods. Then heavy warm February rains once again encouraged early budbreak. The spring weather was hot, but turned cool in late July to slow down maturity and enhance flavor development. Warm weather returned in September to increase sugar and occasionally to contribute less than desirable acid balance. Light rainfall in September caused few problems. The best of the vintage combine the fatness of 84 with the fragrant, inviting, deep fruitiness of 85. With ample tannins, the successes should age for a decade or two. But while the majority have evolved nicely until their tenth birthday, only a few will be alive at the end of their second decade. Many °° and °°° wines. Above average to excellent.

1987    The winter was extremely dry; the North Coast received only 60% of normal rainfall. Cool early spring weather was followed by a brief heatwave in May that occurred during bloom and caused a crop reduction of about 15%. The summer weeks were mild but dry, which resulted in small berries with intense flavors. A brief harvest-time heatwave forced wineries to pick rapidly to avoid overripeness. Only a few wines (Caymus Special Selection, Montelena, the Terraces) display extraordinary depth and richness. The other successes are moderately intense.

1988    Another dry winter, with rainfall again only 50% of normal. The dry weather encouraged early budbreak. A short hot spell in mid-May caused significant crop reduction due to berry shatter. The spring and early summer weeks were warm. A cooling trend in July started what turned out to be a cooler-than-normal summer. The berries were small, but maturation of the fruit was slow and even, boding well for quality. The Cabernet harvest began in mid-September and was completed prior to October 14, when heavy rains arrived. Too many wines lack intensity and balance. Most are simple and fruity, and range from dull to above average. Few rise above *. Most are peaking early, but the Dunns will age for another decade, and the Beringer Private Reserve is not far behind.

1989    Favorable springtime weather extended through the bloom and set period, resulting in a potential bumper-sized crop. From June through August the weather was mild and ideal, and grape development was slow and even. By mid-September, when the first rains arrived, few producers had harvested any Cabernet. In the North Coast another storm dumped more rain a week later, setting the sugar levels back. Warm days, cool nights over the last three weeks of October allowed the remaining Cabernet to recover and to reach maturity. Generally, the wines offer likeable fruit, but often lack vitality and end up being short or thin in flavors. Average to below average. Never real keepers, even the better ones should be drunk up.

1990    Heavy rains in late May arrived during the bloom period in the North Coast and reduced the crop by 20% to 30% overall. June and July provided mild summer weather that extended into the fall. Most grapes ripened evenly, and because of general drought conditions and the low crop yield, Cabernet often developed intense, rich character and considerably high tannins. Most vineyards were picked before the light rains arrived in late September. This vintage will be noted for wines of intensity and complex, deep flavors. Even allowing for some degree of unchecked tannins, many producers came up with one of their better Cabernets; those winemakers able to rein in the tannins made the superstars. The best vintage since 85. Excellent.

1991    A vintage noted for its cold, dry winter, miracle March rains, and a long growing season extending into late October or early November. A big crop requiring thinning for quality. In cooler growing regions, Cabernet did not always ripen fully, and impatient growers in many regions picked by the calendar, not by grape maturity, contributing a green, unripe note to the wine. The best wines show deep color and forward fruit; a few Cabernets are betrayed by high alcohol and high pH. The overall quality is mixed, with hillside-grown wines leading the way. Above average, with many excellent bottlings, but not as uniformly good as 90. Napa Valley Cabernets stood head and shoulders above the crowd.

1992    The year began with adequate rainfall and early budbreak. Cool weather early in the season delayed the bloom period. Light rains in June proved to be harmless. After a warm period in mid-August, September turned out to be ideal for Cabernet. A pattern of cool nights and warm days prevailed throughout the Cabernet harvest in the North Coast. Most wines are intense in color and flavor with better balance and pHs than in 91. However, in Napa and other North Coast regions, the tannin levels were high. Overall the crop was slightly bigger than normal. Above-average quality, but not as well structured as 90 or 91.

1993    Winter rains broke the drought and restored nutritional balance to the badly depleted soils. The growing season alternated between cool spells and heat spikes, but ripening was behind schedule until late-August heat waves sent sugar levels soaring. Although some producers delayed, most others panicked and picked long before mid-September cooling arrived. Those who waited were rewarded. As a rule, most wines have plenty of tannin, sometimes too much, and they do not always have the required fruit and balance to age gracefully. Most lack classic concentration. Thus, an average to slightly above average vintage. Sonoma was slightly better than Napa Valley.

1994    A relatively cool growing season culminated in a late harvest that stretched into early November. Mid-May rains hindered flowering and berry set, and both berry and cluster sizes were small throughout the North Coast. Rains in September caused slight problems in the Central Coast and in Mendocino. Napa and Sonoma escaped relatively unscathed, and the fruit developed excellent color, good to excellent flavor concentration, and moderate tannins. Napa and Alexander Valley wines are exceptionally good; the quality was variable and less dramatic elsewhere. Above average to excellent most places, with many standouts from Napa and Sonoma. Rivals 85 as the best vintage in the last 25 years.

1995    After such an uneventful, smooth-sailing 1994 vintage, winemakers were on edge throughout most of this year. But the end result was another good vintage. A wet winter moved right into a cool, wet spring. Under these wet and windy conditions, the fruit set was below normal, and the berries were on the small side. The growing season was long and cool, and harvest in the North Coast was late. A series of late-season warm spells pushed the fruit to maturity and required vintners to harvest quickly. Despite the difficult conditions along the way, the wines have good depth, balance, and structure. Unlike 94, which gave ripe, supple, precocious wines with gobs of fruit, this vintage yielded firmer wines with more muscle and sturdy tannins. Though the tannins are soft, their presence is felt, and the wines should age well and long. The best are very good.

1996    A pleasant spring led to early budbreak, but the critical period of flowering and berry set was interrupted by persistent rains beginning in May and extending into June. The remainder of the summer was warm, with several heat spikes sending sugar levels high and upsetting balance. September's brief cooling trend may have saved the vintage. A burst of intense heat in early October quickly ripened all remaining Cabernet in what turned out to be an early harvest and a small one. Those making a rigorous selection in the vineyards and later in the cellars made good wines. But overall quality ranges from average to slightly above in this difficult year.

In Washington, the damage done by an evil week-long winter freeze reduced the crop by at least half. The fruit, however, developed great flavor concentration during ideal weather throughout July and August, and the Cabernets are dark, rich, and powerful. Well above average.

1997    A warm spring with a quick period of bloom and set created a situation that eventually led to unusual uniformity of maturity. The vines were heavy with a big crop, but the summer weather was one great smooth stretch of moderate temperature. Rain in mid-August created some fear. Despite mid-September rain and thoughts of a repeat of 1989, the fruit ripened uniformly from cluster to cluster. The crop was so unexpectedly large, wineries had trouble finding the tank space needed to process the fruit. Definitely well-above-average quality overall, but not everyone succeeded.

    Rebounding nicely from the freeze of 96, Washington returned to a normal-size crop. Warm weather in July and August pushed maturation along until cool spells around the harvest allowed for good acid retention. Dark, ripe, but softer in style than 96, this vintage is another above-average year.

# Merlot

Exceptional earlier California vintages: 1978, 1981

Exceptional earlier Washington vintages: 1979

1982    The abundant winter rains gave way to a cool, damp spring, and the result was later than normal budbreak in the North Coast. The growing season was mild and grapes matured very slowly, but most of the Merlot was picked before the rains arrived. The crop from Napa Valley was large. Keenan and Gundlach Bundschu were among the early standouts. A dozen others entered the expanding competitive arena. The number of °° bottlings increased dramatically. Well-focused varietal character and generally restrained tannins characterize this vintage. Excellent.

1983    Overall, an uneventful, mild growing season from the beginning until a warm spell arrived in September. Indian summer weather prevailed during the Merlot harvest, and the resulting wines were opulently fruity and rich. With numerous ripe and racy versions made, this was a classic vintage, made doubly important in the way Merlot had outperformed Cabernet for depth, extract, and appeal. Aging potential was also good, with quite a few aging well for close to a decade. Excellent.

1984    Wet winter months were followed by unusually warm spring weather. The grapes ripened fast, and Merlot was harvested about two to three weeks early as September remained hot for close to three weeks. Rather variable quality, with some Merlots overripe and raisined; most lean more toward power than finesse. The finest, such as Cuvaison and Whitehall Lane, offered a voluptuous ripeness. Not quite as well balanced overall as the 84 Cabernets. Above average.

1985    A warm early spring, consistently cool, even summertime temperatures, and just slightly warm harvest weather all added up to a classic vintage for Merlot. The wines are not as universally successful as Cabernets, and a few have not quite lived up to their promises at the crushers'. Markham, Ravenswood, Dehlinger, and Inglenook bid for top honors of the vintage. Hogue and Ste. Michelle demonstrate Washington State's competency with Merlot. Well above average.

1986    The winter floods were forgotten by the time of early budbreak for Merlot. The summer was mild, with numerous foggy mornings and warm afternoons. Most Merlot was picked by mid-September. The wines are often wonderfully concentrated, well stuffed with fruit and buttressed by tannins, but there is a wide range in quality. The successes are intense, with deep, ripe fruit in a plump style. A few others are light and simple. Above average, but variable.

1987    Low rainfall in the winter tended to stress the Merlot vine. Then two weeks of un-seasonably warm May weather played havoc with berry development, and the shattered berries reduced the crop by 30% to 40%. The remainder of the summer was temperate and stretched out the growing season. The slow maturation re-sulted in rich, focused, and in some cases incredibly fruity wines. The crush in the North Coast was uneventful for Merlot. A small crop. Above-average quality in general, with several wines achieving greatness.

1988    The dry winter conditions led to a difficult bloom period, which stretched out over three weeks. Merlot emerged with heavy berry shatter and a resulting light crop. With relatively warm weather during the summer, the reduced crop (in parts of Napa Valley by as much as 40% to 50%) reached maturity early. On their own, most Merlots have good color and good balancing fruit. Those producers who had the resources available blended more than usual amounts of Cabernet Sauvi-gnon and Cabernet Franc for depth. Most wines generally lack the depth of 87, but offer well-knit structure and balance. Slightly above average.

1989    An almost textbook-perfect spring led to an excellent set period, followed by cool weather in the early summer, which resulted in an overly large crop. Large crops ripen slowly, and mid-September rains caused numerous problems. *Botrytis* was evident in many vineyards. In general, many big names fell short of the mark. The majority of Merlots lack lively fruit and are coarse and simple. The vintage yielded a scarcity of ° performers, and even they are not destined for a long life. Average at best. However, 89 turned out to be a blockbuster vintage for Washington Mer-lots. Made in a big, concentrated, layered style, they have aged well, and a few are still holding on.

1990    Slightly colder than normal winter led to late budbreak. Any tendency toward a big crop was checked by May rains during the bloom period, which reduced the crop size. Moderately warm weather prevailed, bringing the Merlot fruit to a rel-atively quick and easy harvest. Yields were down by 10% to 15% in Napa and Sonoma. Overall, the vintage displays pert fruit and better flavor concentration than either 88 or 89. The best producers return to form in this vintage, with wines of well-ripened fruit and soft, supple flavors. A good number of °° performers show good aging potential. Well above average overall. Most reached a very pleasant peak by 98, with only a few holding on.

1991    The heavy March rains revived the water-starved vines, and Merlot went on to enjoy the long, cool summer. Cluster thinning was essential to avoid overcrop-ping. Harvesting was 3 to 4 weeks late, but most grapes were picked before the last heatwaves. The crop was slightly larger than in 90. In cooler sites and in older vineyards in most locales, Merlot experienced difficulties in ripening. In warmer sites, especially those with young vines, Merlot yielded rich, focused, concen-trated wine. Above average, with several superstars. The real keepers are from Washington, where the crop was small, but the wines were immense, with po-tential to last 10–15 years.

1992    Normal winter rainfall was followed by excellent spring growing conditions. Vines experienced normal budbreak, and then warm weather set in and became the norm for most of the summer. Hot temperatures during late summer pushed fruit maturity, making this one of the earliest harvests of Merlot in the North Coast since 1981. In most medium-warm vineyard sites, the fruit developed typ-ical berry and black cherry character. Tannins were more developed and thus softer than in 91. Average crop size. Numerous °° and several °°° performances make this an above-average to excellent vintage.

1993   Spring rain and early June heat spikes combined to reduced the crop by 20% or more. In Napa the remaining ripe, clean fruit reached maturity early and was harvested smoothly. From an early stage, the wines displayed forthright varietal character, but are not as intense in aroma and color as are wines from previous three vintages. However, this vintage experienced few problems with *botrytis* or other molds, and is therefore reliable. Most wines are for near-term enjoyment. Average to slightly above average quality.

1994   Owing to light rains and winds during flowering and set, the vines set a small crop in the spring, which proved a blessing as growers struggled to ripen the fruit during this long, cool vintage. Yields were down 10–15%. Older vines reached maturity much later than newer ones. In Napa and other North Coast areas, the wines are dark, concentrated, and better than average overall. Excellent in the Carneros. Central Coast Merlot was low in quantity and average in quality. Highly variable but many excellent versions from North Coast names. Also Washington fields a star-studded Merlot team. The best from the West will reach a very high plateau around 1999–2000 and hold for several years thereafter.

1995   Proving again that 1994 is a tough act to follow, the 1995 vintage yielded Merlots that range from pert and nominally ripened to ripe, lush, and opulent. A hot spell in early spring and hail in June reduced the crop. As the growing season unfolded, the stressed vines could handle only small berries. However, the long, cool season delayed maturation, and with warm weather arriving in September, the ripening process was completed. Though quantities were well below normal, the quality ended up above average, with the standouts displaying tanning and structure to age moderately well. Washington went from a wet summer to a cool, late-ripening vintage that provided mid-sized Merlots of average to slightly above-average quality.

1996   Because the period of flowering and berry set was interrupted by persistent rains beginning in May and extending into June, Merlot experienced considerable berry shatter. With their crop load greatly reduced, the vines went into the remainder of the summer, which was warmer than normal. Several heat spikes caused sugar levels to increase too fast and dehydrated some of the berries. Quality varies widely.
       The winter freeze in Washington damaged more than half the crop and wiped out Merlot vineyards in marginal sites. What precious little Merlot was made turned out to be pure blockbuster material, the stuff of dreams.

1997   Merlot, which has a tendency to set a big crop under normal conditions, went over the top after the wonderful spring weather. The mild, sunny conditions during the growing season had vines on a course to ripen the crop, but the August rains prompted some growers to thin the clusters before the grapes rotted. With harvesting beginning in early September in the North Coast, the crop began filling up tanks reserved for late-ripening varieties. In Lodi growers experienced the first rush of many new acres coming into production. Overall tonnage increased by 89% over 96. No longer a North Coast exclusive, Merlot turned out to be a mixed bag ranging from ordinary red wine to spectacular stuff made from special sites. Generally above average.
       Bouncing back from the previous year's disaster, Washington Merlot was back to normal in yields and the quality was solid, with many wines destined to return to the form of 1994. Well above average.

# Chardonnay

Exceptional earlier vintages: 1972, 1975, 1977, 1981, 1984

1986   A cold winter; late rains continued and developed into flood conditions in the North Coast. The early spring weather was warm and it prevailed through June.

By July the fog's return restored slow, normal development of the fruit, and cool conditions continued into September, creating one of the longest growing seasons for Chardonnay. Generally, the pleasantly intense character without the high acidity of 85 gives 86 an accessible, pretty, deeply fruited personality. The best were forward, concentrated, and balanced. The majority reached their peak by 1995. Excellent.

1987    A tough vintage on the nervous system that began with a wet spring in which April brought 2 inches of rain. Budbreak was early, but was followed by many cool, dry summer weeks that finally ended with a hot spell in late August. Chardonnay began to ripen quickly, competing for attention with Merlot in the North Coast. The crop size was a little below expectations. The medium-intensity wines offered pretty, blossomy aromas, and deeply fruited, well-focused flavors. As a rule, the wines were more accessible in their youth than the 85 s because of tamer acid levels. Wines from the Central Coast have shown especially well in this vintage. Well above average quality.

1988    This second year of drought conditions caused vintners to be concerned about vine stress, particularly among the new plantings. Chardonnay in both the North and Central Coasts withstood the relatively wet conditions during bloom to set a relatively good-sized crop. The warm spring and mild summer weather matured the fruit evenly. The crush began in late August in the North Coast, and then because of regular foggy mornings was stretched over the following three weeks. For quantity, this year turned out to be normal. Most will have reached their peak by 1996. The quality for this fruity, forthright, medium-intense vintage was generally above average.

1989    Because the crop was big and the growing season cool, the harvest was behind schedule when rain arrived in mid-September. It left 2 inches of rain in most coastal regions, with the Russian River area in Sonoma County receiving twice as much. Another rainstorm a week later left its mark on the North Coast to create genuine problems in the form of mold and *Botrytis*. Growers aiming for a big crop with vineyards in fog-prone regions never fully recovered. Though 10% to 33% of the Chardonnay (depending upon region and exposure) was picked before the rains, the remainder was picked over the following four to five weeks. The Carneros region suffered crop loss to mold and rot. Parts of the Russian River Valley were hard hit. In the Central Coast, the quality was more consistent. Most wines lacked intensity and tended to be dull. Below-average to average quality overall.

1990    Most coastal-grown Chardonnay had gone through bloom and set before the May rains, and thus the quantity was average. Cool summer weather and warm mid-August days enabled most grapes to develop intense flavor and balance. Harvested under cool, mild conditions, most North Coast Chardonnay was in the cellars by the third week of September. The Central Coast fared just as well for quality. The style of this vintage tends toward the exuberant, with lush fruity aroma and with deep, well-defined flavors. The best are able to stand up to a good dose of oak and are complete, well-integrated wines. A host of good bottlings, and many outstanding ones as well. An outstanding vintage.

1991    The cold winter and miracle March rains resulted in a big crop that hung on the vine through the cool summer. Warm October weather brought the fruit to adequate maturity in most regions. Some *Botrytis* developed on grapes picked late. Late-season rains caused minor problems in the Central Coast. Overall, a large crop with quality better than 89 but below that of 90. Most wines displayed forward, youthful aromatics but lacked the depth of 90. Generally, a vintage that takes oak-aging less well than most others. Slightly above average to good.

1992    Early budbreak was followed by an uninterrupted process of bloom and set. The June rains disrupted the ripening process in Napa and Sonoma, and there were scattered problems with *Botrytis*. Fruit maturation was speeded up by the heat wave in August. Many vineyards continued to ripen fast, and the harvest was earlier than normal. In most regions, the Chardonnay fruit was mature, with some problems of balance. In parts of Sonoma and Napa many winemakers reported higher than normal levels of malic acid along with good tartaric readings, and thus tended to put a greater percentage of their Chardonnay through malo-lactic fermentation than they otherwise would have. Quick ripening fruit in September also created higher than desirable alcohol levels. Generally, an above-average year.

1993   In most regions, rain during flowering and set reduced the crop by 10%–15% on average. A warm spell in August came along in the North Coast to ripen the fruit quickly, reduce the acid levels a little, and make this a vintage of mixed quality, particularly in the Napa Valley. A few vineyards in Northern Sonoma and Mendocino never recovered from late rains and encountered unwanted *Botrytis*. In the Central Coast, which enjoyed an early harvest and abundant yields, the wines were intensely fruity. Overall, a spotty vintage with a majority of pleasing if unexciting wines. Average to slightly above-average quality.

1994   The growing season was long and cool but vineyards with large crops had difficulties achieving desirable ripeness. Rains in September were light in the North Coast. In the Carneros district, picking continued into October, but quality there and in other North Coast regions ranged from average to well above. In the Central Coast, Monterey fared the best, followed by Santa Barbara, which was above average, and San Luis Obispo, which was hurt by late rains and rot. Crop size was below expectations. Overall quality was above average, with Napa Valley being excellent.

1995   In the North Coast spring rains and cool weather got the Chardonnay season off to a slow start. Because of some shattered berries, the crop was slightly below normal and the clusters were abnormally small. As the harvest approached, the temperature turned warm enough to move maturity along. Early September heat quickly ripened North Coast Chardonnay. In the Central Coast a poor set led to a really short crop, but the fruit developed deep flavors and good balance. The Central Coast wines are more concentrated and show less of the typical tropical fruit character. With many °° wines this vintage is well above average but is lacking in depth to be in the same class as 94.

1996   The spring brought rains in April, and after a period of warm weather, bloom started early. A rainstorm in mid-May damaged blooming clusters and reduced yields in the North Coast by 20% or more, and then a 10-day heat wave in July increased sugars a little too fast. The quality was enhanced by a series of warm days followed by cool ones, which brought the small berries to really high sugar levels. September was cooler, but overall 1996 was one of the warmest years in the Carneros, and throughout most of the North Coast. Central Coast wineries were happy to have a normal-size crop, and the quality there, as elsewhere, ranges from good to above average.

1997   An early warm spell in the spring was followed by great weather, resulting in incredible bloom and set. Not only were vines carrying a large crop, but also many new plantings were coming into production along with redeveloped vineyards. Following the mid-August rain, the weather was dry enough to stop botrytis from getting out of control. Three weeks of sun in late September helped ripen a record-setting crop. Overall, viewed as a warm vintage in the North Coast, 1997 is similar to 86 and 92. Quality is above average.

# Pinot Noir

Exceptional earlier vintages: 1969, 1977, 1980

1982    The weather was mild well through August, which is ideal for maturing Pinot Noir. Though it rained, the better versions were made from grapes harvested prior to the September rains. In this vintage, however, a big increase in tonnage went into sparkling wine production. The rest went into what turned out to be an exciting, above-average vintage for Pinot Noir. Quite a few ° and several °° efforts emerged from the Carneros and Russian River as overall quality was above average. The Central Coast region and its producers began to make a mark. Calera, however, was the vintage standout. Above average.

1983    After a difficult harvest bothered by late rains, this turned out to be a watershed year for the varietal. The old, brawny style finally gave ground to a new one favoring medium-depth varietal fruitiness and finesse. The total of ° wines again showed a dramatic increase in a ripe, open, but under-control style. The Carneros region enjoyed the greatest success in this above-average vintage. Several wines from Russian River Valley were among ° bottlings. In Oregon, mild dry weather throughout the harvest helped make 83 one of that state's finest years. Well above average.

1984    A generally warm, dry growing season. Two dozen or more wineries, however, managed to make well-stuffed wines with depth but also with focused varietal intensity. As more and more marginal brands dropped out of this division, the overall quality again improved as many °° and a few °°° versions came along. Exciting efforts from newcomers—Au Bon Climat, Wild Horse, and Byron—joined Calera to improve the Central Coast's reputation. Well above average.

1985    This cool, long, problem-free vintage was kind to Pinot Noir just about everywhere in the West, with good wines from Oregon as well as from Carneros, Russian River, and the Central Coast. The style favored well-ripened, pretty fruit, with often fleshy but balanced flavors. The standouts were numerous and included newcomers like Byron, Etude, Caymus, and La Crema. Above-average vintage. In Oregon, the weather was both pleasantly warm for most of the growing season and dry during the harvesting. The result was an unusual vintage with many successes.

1986    The rainy winter and warm spring returned Pinot Noir vintners to reality. However, the growing season was cool enough and also long enough to allow the grapes to develop cherry-spicy flavors, deep color, and moderate aging abilities. Wines from the Carneros and other cool locales are often deeper in color and more intense in flavor than the 85 s. Above-average.

1987    The hot, dry summer months put Pinot Noir vines under stress. An intense heatwave in August caused grapes to ripen quickly and early. The crop size was down in quantity, and the quality was average. Generally, the wines have average color, and a light, simple, fruity character. Limited aging ability. In Oregon, many Pinot Noirs showed good aromas, but extremely hard acidity and insufficient flavors made for a generally disappointing year.

1988    Poor berry set in late May reduced the crop by 10% to 20% in most regions. Temperatures were moderate during the season, with a slightly warm July and cool August. The drought condition contributed to small berries, which combined with the shot berries intensified color. The harvest began early in the Carneros and Russian River Valley, but proceeded smoothly. The character of the vintage is slanted toward jammy fruit of medium-full intensity. Many of the North Coast wines were relatively rich but soft, owing to low acidity. Most wines offered early appeal and accessibility. Above average overall. Best to drink up soon.

1989   Planted more selectively than Chardonnay, Pinot Noir by its nature also tends to carry a smaller crop. Thus it enjoyed the long, relatively cool growing season; but because the crop was smaller, the majority of its vines were picked before the mid-September rains, more than 75% in the Carneros region and in the Russian River Valley. In most of the Central Coast, Pinot Noir went unscathed and was picked at normal sugar and acidity. However, many North Coast vintners harvested the remaining crop right after the rains. Most wines are simple and lackluster. Most of the ° exceptions come from Carneros, and some from Santa Barbara. Oregon enjoyed warm harvest weather, leading to an above-average year.

1990   In the North Coast, the May rains reduced the crop by 20% to 30%, but a cool August following two warm months led to a harvest in full swing by mid-September. The Central Coast harvest was late and interrupted by rains. Overall, the cool weather and reduced crop led to well-focused wines that offer pert fruit, charm, and medium intensity. Above average in both the Central Coast and North Coast regions.

1991   Revived by March rains, Pinot Noir vines carried a normal-sized crop through the long, cool growing season. Unusually small berries concentrated flavors, and the cool weather helped sustain balancing acidity. Generally dark-colored and moderately intense wines, with the front runners from Carneros and Santa Barbara. Excellent overall. The best will age to 2001 and beyond.

1992   Generally, a smooth growing season early on, disrupted by brief showers in June. There were many foggy mornings in June in both the Carneros District and Russian River Valley. The remainder of the season was warm. The harvest was early, but clear skies made it progress smoothly. Although the crop size was down in Napa, the demand for Pinot Noir was weak, because many sparkling wine producers, suffering from slow sales, were not crushing as much Pinot Noir as in past years. Average to slightly above average.

1993   The crop was down by as much as 15%. Late June heat wave created some sunburn problems, but a cool September led to a late, evenly paced harvest. Above-average quality in the Carneros and in the Russian River Valley and good to excellent in the Central Coast. With wines of deep color and good fruit, the Central Coast experienced its best Pinot Noir vintage of the 90s. Several Oregon Pinot Noirs possessed great depth and balance to earn °° and °°° . For Oregon with new leaders such as Drouhin, Fiddlehead, Beaux Freres, and Benton Lane, 93 is the best vintage since 1985, likely the best ever. In California, the quality is above to well above average.

1994   Rains in May resulted in erratic flowering and set, and the yields were down by 10 to 20% in major districts. The growing season was relatively smooth and cool. Most North Coast vineyards had been harvested before rains arrived in October. The majority of Central Coast Pinot Noir was also safely in the wineries. The yields were light in the Central Coast, but the wine quality is high, particularly in Santa Barbara. In the North Coast, the wines have good flavor, color, and balance, with Carneros being especially good with great depth. The wines have turned out to be as good as they can get, making 94 the best vintage in memory for California Pinot Noir. Oregon experienced an unusually warm summer season, and though the crop was small, the wines are concentrated, with jammy fruitiness and some power. Many °° from Oregon with good aging potential. A well-above-average vintage.

1995   Early-season rain and drizzly weather caused problems with berry set, and the crop was small and the set often irregular within clusters. In the Central Coast the spring was more troubling, and the crop size was greatly reduced. Despite the small crop, the overall quality is neither as high nor as uniform as 1994. With average intensity, most wines lack the focused fruit and depth of 94. Fewer ° and °° wines appeared, and few producers equaled their success in 94. Signorello confirmed its dynamic progress with a °°° effort. Otherwise, an average to slightly above average vintage best for near-term consumption. The same rating applies to Oregon, where vintners grappled with a series of harvest rains. Those either picking early or selectively ended up with delicate-style wines to drink in their youth.

1996    The unseasonably warm winter encouraged early budbreak. Turning cool, the spring season also experienced light rain, which caused some shattered berries. Several heat waves in July and August forced the fruit to color early and speeded up the ripening process. A much-anticipated cooling trend in late August along with the absence of rain brought the fruit into balance. From a small crop in a longer-than-normal growing season, the wines range widely in quality. Most North Coast wines display fine aromatics and are also more tannic, riper, and powerful than the 95s but in too many cases lack depth of fruit. Quality was higher in the Central Coast, where the crop was of normal size. A vintage to buy selectively.

Oregon was in the midst of a late ripening vintage when outstanding weather during early October provided the last great push needed to ripen vines supporting a light or normal crop. Some overcropped vineyards were hurt by rains in mid-month. Oregon ends up with well-above-average quality.

1997    An odd year made more interesting as new and unproven acreage from densely planted vineyards containing new clones came on-line. Early conditions encouraged a big crop in the North Coast. A modest heat wave hit Russian River Valley in early August, and a few days later a tropical storm added a lot of rain throughout the North Coast. Fortunately dry windy conditions followed, and the fruit matured. For most wineries this was a split harvest, with about half the crop picked before the mid-September rains, and the quality of that portion was super. Grapes picked later were not on the same level. New vineyards in Carneros yielded wines of deep color and flavor, and the vintage turned out above average in Russian River Valley.

In Oregon there was an early bloom period, generally dry summer, and then the deluge began in mid-September just before the harvest was to kick in. Rain continued intermittently and vintners worked hard in-between storms. Those producers who regularly practice cluster thinning ended up making good Pinots. Others made Rosé from Pinot Noir.

# Zinfandel

Exceptional earlier vintages: 1970, 1973, 1974, 1976, 1977

1982    As many contenders dropped out of the competition, the remaining Zinfandel producers tried to redesign and/or revive the varietal. Rains forced early harvesting, which encouraged many streamlined, fruity, slightly tannic versions. Burgess and Grgich Hills excelled. Newcomer Storybook Mountain captured ripe fruit and power. Slightly above average.

1983    Uneven ripening and late-season rains again imposed limits and encouraged better-integrated, accessible, ripe-berry style. Many °° wines were made, with Sonoma County rapidly building a strong reputation as the leader. Quivira, Lytton Springs, and Ravenswood earn high praise. Ridge completed its return to top form, and Kendall-Jackson entered the competition with attractive Mendocino bottlings. The best have aged well. Well above average.

1984    A warm year, free from harvesting difficulties, enabled Zinfandel to complete its comeback as a bona fide, quality red wine. The favorites are rich, ripe, and hearty without being overripe or overly coarse. Sonoma, led by bottlings from Dry Creek Valley, became unchallenged leader, but Napa's microclimate Howell Mountain emerged in this vintage. Several °°° wines, led by Ridge, Quivira, Haywood, and Rosenblum. Quality well above average to excellent.

1985    The all-but-perfect vintage helped advance Zinfandel's fortunes by accentuating the variety's deep, ripe-berryish fruit. Many producers earned ° or more by capturing a dense fruity core without any unpleasant excesses. Clos du Val joined Ridge and Ravenswood as °°° leaders in what turned out to be a star-studded vintage. Most reached their peak around 94–95, but more than a few will still be drinking well in 2001.

1986    A long-drawn-out growing season saw a high proportion of the crop go into White Zinfandel. The red versions possess amicable fruit, variable depth and flavor interest, and many are suited for near-term drinking. However, some superb Zins emanated from old, dry-farmed vineyards in the Dry Creek Valley, northern Napa Valley, and Mendocino. Storybook Mountain in Napa and Mazzocco in Sonoma County were true °°° standouts. The Ridge "Geyserville" bottling returned to form to lead a pack of °° wines. In this year the Dry Creek Valley is validated as a leading source of distinctive Zinfandels. Well above average.

1987    With limited water available because of the drought, the vines were under stress early in the season. Then the heat wave in May further reduced the crop. By harvest time, the berries remained tiny. They yielded intense varietal fruit and high-extract wines in Sonoma, Napa, and Amador. The style is on the coarse side, but similar otherwise to 84. The Russian River Valley joined Dry Creek Valley as a source of distinctive Zinfandels. The best versions of Sonoma County and Napa aged well for a decade, but drink any remaining bottles. Average to slightly above average.

1988    Beginning with abnormally warm weather in January and February, which encouraged early budbreak, this year remained unusual in most respects, including a disastrous bloom period. By mid-June, the Zinfandel crop was reduced by 25% to 50%. The rest of the growing season was cooler than normal. From mid-September to harvest, foggy mornings and cool evenings stretched out the growing season in the North Coast and in the Sierra Foothills. As a result, the sugar levels were kept under control and the acidity often remained ideal. With much of the marginal plantings picked to produce White Zinfandel, what remained by late September/early October was often spectacular. Dry Creek Valley, Sonoma Valley, Howell Mountain in Napa, and Amador generally yielded Zinfandels in a ripe, lush fruit style with balance. Though riper, this year is similar to 85. Excellent overall quality, possibly the best of the 80s.

1989    This year began as ideal for Zinfandel. Berry set was outstanding and the crop was large. The early summer weather seemed just right to bring the large crop to full maturity. By early August unusual cool weather set in, and grape development slowed. Only a few vintners in Sonoma and warmer parts of Napa and Mendocino had picked any Zinfandel before the September rains. With its full, compact clusters and relatively thin skins, Zinfandel began to disintegrate in some North Coast vineyards after the rains. In the Sierra Foothills, only 5% of the Zin was in before the rains came. Growers waited and ended by picking in October. Amador County Zins are moderately fruity, without being high in alcohol and tannins. Overall a mixed bag, with few notable high spots. Average quality.

1990    Following the big crop of 89, Zinfandel yields were down, which is typical for this grape. The quality was up everywhere, as the fruit ripened easily and relatively early. The best wines capture generously fruited aromas and ripe, vibrant flavors, avoiding a tendency to be too jammy or too alcoholic. Dry Creek Valley was exceptional, but other parts of Sonoma County as well as Napa Valley yielded a number of successes. Rich with highly inviting fruit overall, this vintage gave us scores of wines ranking well above average to excellent. Certainly the best vintage since 85; possibly the finest ever.

1991  Always one of the last grapes harvested, Zinfandel hung on the vines for an extremely long time this year. Some vineyards experienced more than usual irregular ripening, partly due to the good-size crop level. Because of the extended growing season, most berries developed plenty of ripe fruit flavors, and the tannins tended to become soft. In Dry Creek Valley, Napa, and Amador County, small berries were common, and the wines have deep color. Lacking the forthright fruit of 90, and being slightly more supple, with softer tannins, the finer Zinfandels are more subtle, less forceful, but still immensely appealing. Less consistent than 90, the 91 Zinfandels range from good to excellent, with a few rivaling the 90s. Well above average to excellent.

1992  Springtime rains helped nourish many of the hillside and old non-irrigated vineyards. The summer season was mild until a hot spell in August, which caused sugars to soar. Mild weather throughout September brought better balance to the fruit. Overall, the wines' acidity levels remained slightly low and pH readings slightly high. A mixed vintage with better wines made from normally low-yielding, dry-farmed vineyards. Most Zinfandels are lighter in body and in fruit than either the 90s or 91s, but still medium-intense. All told, a good vintage. Average to slightly above average quality.

1993  With demand for Zinfandel at an all-time high, growers in the North Coast did not hold back in quantity and lucked out as most vines ripened the fruit adequately. The wines show moderate intensity, though some wines ended up over 14% alcohol. The general character of the vintage reflects lively berry-fruit and early maturation. However, more than a few heavily cropped vineyards in parts of Sonoma and Mendocino were caught by late-season rains, and either were not harvested or yielded unbalanced wines. Given better conditions in the Sierra Foothills, Zinfandel escaped late rains and the overall quality in the Foothills ranges from average to excellent. Average to slightly above average elsewhere.

1994  The harvest story everywhere was low yields, with a few key areas reporting harvesting less than 50% of expectations. Vines trying to support large crops suffered some rot problems after late season rains. Old vines with their meager crops fared better for quality, and yielded the vintage's best wines. But the crush was down in quantity in the Dry Creek Valley and Mendocino's Redwood Valley. Yields were so low that a number of wineries harvested second crop for White Zinfandel. Quality ranges from above average to excellent.

1995  By this vintage Zinfandel is again a hot wine, and the number of single-vineyard and Old Vine bottlings has greatly expanded. A move toward riper, high-alcohol Zinfandel also began to develop into a trend in this vintage. The wet spring kept yields down considerably in the North Coast. In Paso Robles the growing season began late but fell into the typical hot days, cool nights pattern. In both Dry Creek and Russian River the crop was light, but the weather was ideal for ripening the fruit. In Amador the cool and wet spring was made more unusual by hail in early June, all of which reduced the crop significantly. In all major regions the fruit maturity moved along slowly and the harvest was a few weeks later than normal. However, the long, long season combined with the small crop contributed to the best vintage in Amador and Paso Robles in some time, and generally well above average in Sonoma County.

1996  The number of Old Vine and single-vineyard bottles continue to increase as demand for Zinfandel reaches an all-time high. A late-ripening variety with a tendency to ripen irregularly, Zinfandel is at risk to harvest rains. In the 1990s winemakers have learned the importance of sorting out the unripe, raisined or damaged fruit at the crushers. It paid off in this vintage as the heat waves in September ripened the fruit quickly. The yields in Sonoma and Amador were down by 20% on average. Tending to be full-bodied with high alcohol, the best wines display deep, ripe fruit. One of the better performers of the vintage, Zinfandel is nonetheless only above average and has shown some limits in intensity.

1997   Typical of the vintage, Zinfandel set a huge crop in the spring and ripened smoothly throughout the growing season. The mid-August rains sent many North Coast vintners into the vineyards to thin the crop. After light rains in September, dry weather helped bring Zinfandel to full maturing as harvesting proceeded at a fast pace. Unfortunately, not all vineyards were picked, since wineries were overflowing with wine. Overall quality is good to excellent, with Dry Creek Zinfandels showing lush berry flavors and medium weight. Excellent crop in Paso Robles, and good to excellent in Amador. Many Old Vine versions are powerful but also display plush texture and good balance. Big crop of big wine. Quality ranged from good to excellent.

# Wineries and Wines

Great—or good—wines are not merely grown, they are made. One need only look at the differences in quality and style that result when two wineries make wines from the same vineyard to realize the importance of the winery's hand in the production process. In this section we consider, both descriptively and critically, the wineries and labels most likely to appear on the shelves of wine merchants and on restaurant wine lists. Some are second labels for front-line wineries and some are the products of individuals or organizations acting as buyers/blenders/packagers of readymade wine. They are an ever-changing, ever-increasing group whose number has more than doubled in the last decade.

The winery entries follow a standard format. We first focus on ownership, intent, acreage controlled, varietal wines produced, and wine quality. In addition, for those producers with intelligible track records, we offer vintage-by-vintage evaluations of their leading varietals. Each of the wines reviewed is rated for quality and for current drinkability. Overall, some 18,000 individual bottlings of Chardonnay, Cabernet Sauvignon, Merlot, Pinot Noir, and Zinfandel are assessed in this manner.

---

The wine ratings and descriptions in this book are based substantially on evaluations that appear in *Connoisseurs' Guide to California Wine,* a monthly newsletter edited and published by Charles Olken and Earl Singer and distributed only by subscription. A one-year subscription is $50. Each year the *Guide* reviews up to 2,000 wines, mostly vintage-dated varietals. Readers of this *Handbook* interested in learning more about the *Guide* may receive a free copy of the latest issue by writing to *Connoisseurs' Guide to California Wine,* P.O. Box V, Alameda, California 94501.

Symbols used here are as follows:

| | |
|---|---|
| 8̶9̶ | below-average quality, a wine to avoid |
| 93 | a wine of average quality |
| ° | a fine example of a given type or style, an above-average wine |
| °° | a very fine wine, likely to be memorable |
| °°° | an exceptional wine, worth a special search |
| | |
| 88 | a wine now past its peak |
| 93 | ready to drink now |
| **91** | drinkable now, but will improve with further aging |
| 94 | needs further aging before drinking |

*Examples:*

| | |
|---|---|
| 93 | an average-quality wine, drinkable now |
| 92° | an above-average wine, drinkable now |
| **95°°** | a very fine wine that can be drunk now, but will improve even more with age |
| 94°°° | an exceptional wine that should be held before drinking |

# California

ABUNDANCE   *Sonoma 1995*   A partnership headed by Bruce Rector, former winemaker for Glen Ellen Winery and Benziger Family, this company makes mid-priced Sangiovese and Chardonnay. From the Santa Maria Valley, its Chardonnay is barrel-fermented and oak-aged. With Sangiovese Rector aims for a soft, fruity style, and to achieve that end he adds a splash of Pinot Noir. Given their mid-level prices, both wines are unlikely to disappoint.

ACACIA WINERY   *Napa 1979*   Founder Mike Richmond put together a group of investors including vineyardists Paul Perret, Robert Sinskey, and Ira Lee. The partnership developed the 50-acre Marina Vineyard to supply Chardonnay. Acacia purchased fruit from its partners and other growers, most of whom own vineyards in Carneros. Its focus fell on vineyard-designated Pinot Noirs and multiple Chardonnay bottlings.

Acacia's wines in the early 80s were often exceptional in quality, and just about always provided lessons in the effect of different microclimates. Of the two varietals, Chardonnay was much more consistent, and on occasion the Winery Lake, Marina Vineyard, and Carneros bottlings soared to °°° levels. However, with Pinot Noir, Acacia often offered six vineyard-designated bottlings—Carneros, Madonna Vineyard, Winery Lake Vineyard, St. Clair, Lee Vineyard, and Iund Vineyard—and in the process generated more excitement for that varietal than anyone else.

With its own acreage and neighboring vineyards suffering from phylloxera in the 1990s, Acacia pared down the number of single vineyard wines and emphasized its Reserve Chardonnay and Reserve Pinot Noir. It continued offering a St. Clair Pinot Noir, and in 1995 added Pinot Noir from Beckstoffer Vineyards. The 91 vintage was the last Marina Vineyard Chardonnay offered, and since then the vineyard has been replanted to 60 acres of Pinot Noir. Plans call for gradually bringing back single-vineyard bottlings, but the present focus is on a Carneros Chardonnay and Carneros Pinot Noir, which account for 75% of the winery's 60,000 cases annual output. Wines with limited availability include Old Vine Zinfandel, Viognier, and a Brut sparkling wine aged 5 years prior to being sold at the winery.

### Chardonnay

(Carneros)　86°°°　87°°　88°　89°　90°　91°　92°　93　94°
95°　**96°**

(Carneros Reserve)　92°　93°　94°

*Both wines are crisp, appley, toasty, and somewhat lean in character, and both have been consistently good, if never exceptional*

### Pinot Noir

(St. Clair)　80°　81°°　82　83°°　84°°　85°°　**86°°°**　87°°
88°　89°　90°　91°　92°°

(Carneros)　84　85°　86°　87　88°　89°　90°　91°　**92°**　93
**94°　95°**

*All of the Acacia Pinot Noirs (including those which are no longer offered—Iund, Lee, and Winery Lake) have steered a fairly consistent line toward cherryish, moderately bright fruit, restrained tannins, and a shorter rather than longer ageability; the St. Clair is often the deepest and frequently shows a roasted herb, dried-bark note*

---

ADELAIDA CELLARS　*San Luis Obispo 1983*　Owner-winemaker John Munch worked in the cellars of Estrella Winery before starting his own line of wine. Leasing space in the Estrella facility, Munch began making Cabernet Sauvignon and Chardonnay. In 1990 Munch became partners with the Van Steenwyk family, which owned acreage in Paso Robles and expanded its holdings by later acquiring the 60-acre Hoffman Mountain Ranch in 1994. Shortly thereafter a winery was built. Cabernet and Chardonnay remain the flagship wines, but Adelaida has expanded its production of Pinot Noir, Zinfandel, and Sangiovese. Its experiments with Syrah might eventually lead to a varietal bottling. As it gradually replants acreage, Adelaida will grow from 10,000 cases to its capacity of 25,000 cases a year.

---

ADLER FELS　*Sonoma 1980*　Precariously situated on the northwestern slope of the Mayacamas Mountains in Sonoma Valley, Adler Fels makes 15,000 cases of wines a year. The volume leader is Fumé Blanc, followed by Chardonnay and Gewurztraminer. The winery also makes Pinot Noir and Reserve Chardonnay. The Fumé Blancs tend to be on a strong, bold scale, with assertive herbal character. When balanced, they can be of ° quality. The winery's Gewurztraminer in a slightly sweet style is also effusively varietal and on occasion has merited °° ratings. Sangiovese has recently been added to the line. Owner David Coleman is a graphic artist who became familiar with the wine business when he began designing labels. Adler Fels has no vineyards.

### Chardonnay

(Sonoma County)　86°　87　89　90́　91°　93　94　96°

(Reserve)　91°　92　95　96

*An inconsistent performer, showing toasty oak, ripe but somewhat restrained fruit in both bottlings*

---

AHLGREN VINEYARD　*Santa Cruz 1976*　Though still tiny, this family-run winery finally outgrew the Ahlgren family basement where it began and now makes 1,500 cases a year. Doing all of the winemaking by hand, the Ahlgrens have made a range of varietals from purchased grapes. What they do best most of the time are red wines. Their Cabernets from the Santa Cruz Mountains are usually ripe and highly extracted, and designed for long aging. Chardonnays from the Santa Cruz Mountains and some of the more prestigious vineyards in Santa Barbara and Monterey County (Ventana Vineyards is a regular offering) have yet to rise above average. Barrel-fermented Semillons from Santa Cruz appellations are among the richest made by anyone, and the most consistent of the winery's whites. Most wines are made in quantities ranging from 80 to 600 cases.

ALBAN VINEYARDS   *San Luis Obispo 1991*   John Alban fell in love with Rhone wines at an early age, and after working in the cellars of Leeward for a few vintages he started his own vineyard in 1989. On his 250-acre ranch in the cool-climate Edna Valley, Alban planted 50 acres to Viognier, Roussanne, and Syrah, and another 30 acres are plantable. He buys the heat-loving Rhone varieties Grenache and Mourvedre from vineyards in the Paso Robles area. Alban's inaugural vintage (91) was made in leased space. His own winery was operational the following year, and he is currently producing Viognier, Roussanne, Marsanne, and a red Rhone proprietary blend. The winery's annual output will gradually grow to 9,000. The first several vintages have placed Alban among the Viognier leaders, and its Roussanne, regular, and Reserve bottlings have impressed.

### Viognier

(San Luis Obispo/Estate)   91   92   94   95°°   **96°**   **97°°**

*Ripe, deep wines, occasionally a bit thin on fruit relative to their full-bodied stance.*

ALBINI FAMILY VINEYARDS   *Sonoma 1991*   Don Albini, long-time home winemaker, is a building contractor by day and a winemaker specializing in Merlot the rest of the time. He purchases grapes from two low-yielding hillside vineyards in the Russian River Valley, and blends those wines with his own Merlot grown in the Chalk Hill appellation. Albini ferments by the native yeast and bottles his wines without filtration. The annual output is steady at 500 cases, and the quality has hit the ° mark in the early goings.

ALDERBROOK VINEYARDS   *Sonoma 1982*   In the early 80s partners John Grace, Phil Staley, and Mark Rafanelli converted an old ranch and prune orchard located in the southernmost corner of the Dry Creek Valley into a winery and 55-acre vineyard. They believe that their vineyard site has a microclimate best suited to a few white varieties, Sauvignon Blanc, Semillon, Chardonnay, and Muscat Blanc. Alderbrook's Chardonnays are attractively priced, and have enormous youthful appeal. In some vintages, the winery offers a Reserve Chardonnay aged longer in small oak. Its Sauvignon Blancs are made in a light style, Alderbrook makes a Gewurztraminer from the Russian River Valley. In 1990 it made its first-ever red wines, purchasing Zinfandel and Syrah from an old vineyard in the Dry Creek Valley. In 94 Alderbrook was sold to George Gillemot, an investor who acquired the 55-acre vineyard in 1991. He has added Merlot, Pinot Noir, and Viognier to the roster. Emerging as the house specialty, Zinfandel now consists of several bottlings. The Old Vine–Old Clone Zinfandel is the volume leader, and two single-vineyard Zinfandels—Gamba Vineyard from Russian River Valley and George's Vineyard from Dry Creek Valley—are usually made in 400–500 case lots each year. Current vineyard holdings are 68 acres. With Chardonnay at 20,000 cases and Zinfandel in its many guises accounting for 10,000, the winery's annual output has leveled off at 50,000.

### Chardonnay

86°   87°   88°   89   90°   91   93   94   95   **96°**

*Lots of pretty fruit in a fresh, appley, almost blossomy vein, supported by creamy, quietly stated oak, medium-full body*

### Zinfandel

(Old Vines)   91   **92**   93   **94**   **95°**   96

*Ripe, medium-full-bodied, moderately fruity, fairly rich and moderately tannic*

ALEXANDER VALLEY VINEYARDS   *Sonoma 1975*   This well-manicured 128-acre estate vineyard in the midsection of the Alexander Valley is the pride of the Wetzel family, which purchased the site in 63. Harry Wetzel, the patriarch, also is a major partner in a 500-acre vineyard adjacent to the winery. The winery was expanded in 86, and produces seven varietals, with Chardonnay, Merlot, and Cabernet

Sauvignon the major emphasis. Annual production is level at 40,000 cases. This winery has at one time or another performed well with each wine, but at best has lacked consistency and real distinction. Its prices, however, have remained on the modest side. The winery started off well with Chardonnay, but it experienced some disappointing vintages. Occasionally its Pinot Noir earns ° status when it avoids a tendency toward overripeness. A dry (under 1% residual sugar) Chenin Blanc enjoys popularity in restaurants, a segment of the market to which the Wetzels devote considerable attention. Overall, the winery's most reliable wine has been Cabernet Sauvignon, blended with Merlot. After significant vineyard replanting in the 1990s, the winery has added Cabernet Franc and Syrah to its roster, with the Syrah showing outstanding promise. An old 5-acre block of Zinfandel continues to be used for a popular, hearty-style wine named "Sin-Zin."

### Cabernet Sauvignon
80   81°   82°   83°   84°   86   87   **88°**   89   91   **92**   **95**

*Usually high in ripeness with black-cherry fruitiness, sometimes a touch of herbs or brush, sweet oak*

### Chardonnay
86   87   90   91   92°   93   96

*Blossomy fruit in best years, drier and less pretty in others*

### Pinot Noir
81°   82   84°   85   86   **87**   **89**   **91**   92

*Ripish, usually fairly deep, sometimes muddled*

ALMADÉN VINEYARDS   *Madera 1852*   Almadén Vineyards occupies a special place in the history of California winemaking and, until the early 80s, Almadén wines were a real force in the wine market. At that time, Almadén was selling over 13 million cases a year and had three large facilities producing an assortment of table, sparkling, and dessert wines. Almadén was left with an image as a jug-wine producer, and all efforts in the 80s to change that image failed. Sales slipped badly, and Almadén was sold to Heublein in 87. ° To consolidate production, Heublein closed the former facilities, sold most of the vineyards, and moved Almadén to its own vast all-purpose facility in Madera in the Central Valley. Almadén brought to Heublein its established "Le Domaine" sparkling wine label, as well as its ill-fated upscale brand, "Charles Lefranc." Almadén is now one of several labels produced and bottled in the Heublein-owned facility.

ALTAMURA VINEYARDS *Napa 1985*   After working in the cellars of Caymus Vineyards for five years, Frank Altamura decided to produce estate-bottled wines from his own vineyard. In 80 his family purchased a 70-acre vineyard on the Silverado Trail, just north of the town of Napa. For several vintages Chardonnay was made at this facility, but in the late 1980s Frank departed to start his own vineyard and winery in the Wooden Valley, a small, isolated bowl in the distant southeastern foothills of Napa Valley. Planted to Cabernet Sauvignon and Sangiovese, the 35-acre, non-irrigated vineyard was ready in time for the 1992 harvest. Since then Altamura has produced only Cabernet Sauvignon and Sangiovese, and has proven to be a success at both as production moves toward 3,000 cases annually.

### Cabernet Sauvignon
**90°°**   **91**   **92°**   **93°**   **94°°**

*Ripe, fairly solid, deep wines with black cherry fruit and occasional spicy notes; expect them to age well*

AMADOR FOOTHILL WINERY   *Amador 1980*   Located east of Plymouth, Amador Foothill specializes in Zinfandel, Red and White. The red is made from older vineyards, frequently from the Eschen, Esola, Ferrero or Clockspring vineyards. The winery has bottled each under vineyard designations. By 1990 10 1/2 acres were planted to Sangiovese, Sauvignon Blanc, and Semillon. Owners Ben Zeitman and Katie Quinn, the winemaker, decided there was enough Zinfandel available within Amador. The winery enjoyed sales success with its first vintages of White Zinfandel. Oak-aged and blended with Semillon, the Fumé Blanc offers fresh fruitiness in a lean, tart style. Having reduced its production of White Zinfandel, the winery has added Semillon, Carignane, and Sangiovese Rosato (Rose) to its roster. Annual production is 9,000 cases.

AMBERHILL *(Raymond Vineyards)* Growing rapidly in the 1990s, Amberhill is Raymond's line of competitively priced varietals. Blends of fruit from Monterey, Napa, and other regions, the three major wines are Chardonnay, Cabernet Sauvignon, and Merlot. All wines show a modest degree of oak barrel aging and represent decent wines for the money. The annual production is about 100,000 cases, with Chardonnay representing 70% of the total.

ANAPAMU *(Gallo Winery)* Anapamu is a brand created by the Gallo family for Central Coast wines that to date consists of Chardonnay. Introduced in 1997, along with a half-dozen other new brands with flashy labels developed by the historically conservative winery, Anapamu represents niche marketing at its best as the Chardonnay offered the typical tropical fruit character of the Central Coast at a competitive price level.

S. ANDERSON VINEYARD *Napa 1979* Dentist Stanley Anderson and his wife, Carol, a dental hygienist, purchased a vineyard site in 71 located in the Stags Leap District, planting it in 73–74 to Chardonnay. By 79, the Andersons had constructed a small winery near their home and produced about 1,000 cases combined of Chardonnay and *méthode champenoise* Brut. In 84 they decided to expand the winery operation and built underground aging facilities. Their 7,000-square-foot caves are used for aging 250,000 bottles of sparkling wine and for the barrel aging of their estate Chardonnay. The sparkling wine line now consists of Brut, the mainstay, along with limited amounts of Blanc de Noirs, Blanc de Blancs, Rosé, and a Reserve. Production continued to grow in the 80s, and topped 15,000 cases in 90. "Tivoli" is the name given to a Brut sparkler made from press juice. The estate vineyard contains 32 acres of Chardonnay. The Andersons also own 70 acres in the Carneros, which they began developing in the late 80s. In 89 S. Anderson debuted a Cabernet Sauvignon from the Stags Leap area, blended with Merlot and Cabernet Franc, which demonstrated high quality. In the 1990s the varietal wine roster expanded further to include three Chardonnays (Carneros District, Stags Leap District, and Reserve), a Merlot Reserve from Stags Leap, and a Carneros Pinot Noir.

**Cabernet Sauvignon**

(Chambers Vineyard)  **90°°  91°  92°°  93  94°**

*Ripe and rich flavors well buttressed by oak are firmed by noticeable tannins*

**Chardonnay**

(Carneros)  86  87°°  88°  89  90  91°  92  93  94  95  96

*Typically well balanced between rich, toasty oak and focused varietal fruit directly suggestive of apples and less so of fresh, citrusy influences; 89 was typical of vintage, but 90 was disappointing*

ANDERSON'S CONN VALLEY VINEYARDS *Napa 1987* From vineyards developed in 83, founder Gus Anderson, a retired orthodontist, produced his first 500 cases of Cabernet Sauvignon in 87. With maturity, his 26-acre vineyard, planted predominantly to Cabernet Sauvignon and its blending cousins, will yield 7,000 cases of Cabernet a year. The Andersons also own 2 acres of Pinot Noir near the town of Napa which contribute 200 to 300 cases a year. The quality of their Cabernets began on a high level and has continued on that pace.

## Cabernet Sauvignon
88°° 89 90°° 91°° 92° 93° 94

*Ripe, fairly concentrated cherryish fruit sweetened by creamy oak comes in a long-aging package*

ANGELINE  *(Codera Wine Co.)*  Old Vine Cuvee Zinfandel is the only wine marketed under this negociant label. Vintages to date have been blends of Zinfandel from Paso Robles and Amador County. The first bottlings have been lively and attractive in a medium-deep fruited style.

ARAUJO ESTATE WINES  *Napa 1991*  Bart Araujo, a San Francisco businessman, purchased the well-known Eisele Vineyard in mid-1990. This vineyard enjoyed a long and noble association with Joseph Phelps Vineyards, which for close to two decades bottled an "Eisele Vineyard" Cabernet Sauvignon. After Araujo acquired the 35-acre vineyard nestled at the foot of the Palisades near Calistoga, he replanted 20 acres to Cabernet and its blending varieties. The remaining 15 acres contain the oldest block of Cabernet Sauvignon, along with new plantings of Syrah, Sauvignon Blanc and Viognier. The goal is to offer three wines from the Eisele vineyard. Cabernet Sauvignon (blended with a dollop of Syrah) is the flagship, and eventually Araujo will make 3,000 cases per year. The estate white, a Sauvignon Blanc blended with Viognier, is made in a fruity, no-oak style. The third wine is a Syrah. Production of the Sauvignon Blanc will grow to 1,500 cases, and the Syrah will be limited to 500 cases per year. Tony Soter of Etude is the winemaker. A small winery with aging caves has been built on the property.

ARCIERO WINERY  *San Luis Obispo 1986*  Frank and Phil Arciero operate a construction and development company in Southern California, and together with their families run this winery located 6 miles east of Paso Robles. Starting their vineyard in 83, they now have close to 500 acres planted. The leading varieties are Chardonnay (200 acres), Cabernet Sauvignon (100 acres), and Zinfandel (99 acres). Experiments with Nebbiolo encouraged the planting of 5 acres. Arciero's winery and tasting-room complex is the largest wine facility in San Luis Obispo County, and at its peak capacity the winery will be able to turn out 500,000 cases a year. At the end of 90, Arciero was making about 100,000 cases, with Chardonnay and Cabernet Sauvignon combining for half of the total. Today the holdings have grown to 700 acres of vines, and the roster has expanded to include Sangiovese and a red Meritage named "Arpeggio." With annual production closing in on 200,000 cases, the winery is best at making honestly priced varietals, with the Estate Chardonnay and Zinfandel often representing good value. Early vintages of Sangiovese show promise.

ARGONAUT WINERY  *Amador 1976*  This winery started small and stayed small. Its owners are all engineers on a full-time basis and winery owners on a more casual basis. Zinfandel and Barbera are made every year, with the Barbera from the 2-acre estate vineyard. The only white produced on occasion has been a Sauvignon Blanc. Total annual production is just under 2,000 cases.

ARMIDA WINERY  *Sonoma 1989*  Over its first decade Armida hit a bump or two along the way with vineyard changes and winemaker turnover. New owners came along in the late 90s to settle things down. Perched on a knoll in the northern end of Russian River Valley, the winery has made Chardonnay and Merlot in each vintage and has recently added Pinot Noir and Zinfandel. The latter is from the Dry Creek Valley, and all other varietals are from Russian River Valley. So far it has a solid track record for Chardonnay, with Merlot showing potential in recent vintages.

## Chardonnay
90  91°  92  94

*Fruity, citrusy, well-balanced wines, they have so far been offered at reasonable prices*

ARMSTRONG RIDGE  *(Korbel Champagne Cellars)*  Reacting to slow sales of sparkling wines in the 90s, Korbel created this brand for lower-priced Brut and other sparklers made by the *méthode champenoise.*

ARNS WINERY  *Napa Valley 1994* John Arns manages vineyards in Napa Valley and also oversees the family's seven acres of Cabernet Sauvignon adjacent to his home in the hills east of St. Helena. Arns sells most of the crop, saving enough to produce 500–700 cases of 100% Cabernet Sauvignon per year. Annual production is likely to grow slowly to 2,000 cases. The first vintages sold out quickly.

ARROWOOD WINERY  *Sonoma 1988*  Dick Arrowood, one of the best-known wine-makers in the state, started construction of his own winery in 86, while continuing work at Chateau St. Jean (which he joined in 74) until 90. Located in the Sonoma Valley and perched on a knoll, Arrowood Winery emphasizes Chardonnay and Cabernet Sauvignon. Arrowood's barrel-fermented Chardonnays are blends from three Sonoma County appellations—Russian River Valley, Alexander Valley, and Carneros. The Cabernets are made from vineyards in Knight's Valley, Alexander Valley, and the home acreage. In the first offering, the winery's production was close to 10,000 cases. By 95 the winery was at its full capacity of 30,000 cases, with Cabernet Sauvignon representing 30% of the total. Chardonnay production is steady at 6,000 cases a year. Though once viewed as a minor player, Arrowood's Merlot has grown to 3,000 cases, and has risen to ° levels. In addition to a limited bottling of Late Harvest Riesling, Arrowood started making Viognier in 91, and plans to take production of that varietal to 1,000 cases. Arrowood also makes small quantities of full-flavored Pinot Blanc, Malbec, Syrah, and Réserve Spéciale bottlings of Cabernet, Merlot, and Chardonnay. The winery owns 25 acres of vineyards and purchases about 75% of the grapes crushed under long-term contract.

### Cabernet Sauvignon

85°  86°°°  87°  88°  89°°  90°  91°  92°  93°  94°°

*Ripe, rich style, deep in curranty and black-cherry fruit; good aging potential*

### Chardonnay

86°  87°  88°  89°  90°  91°  92  93  **94°**  95°

*Nicely focused, appley fruit, with sweeter pearlike overtones well supported by oak*

### Merlot

88°°°  89°  90°°  91°  92°  93  94

*Often containing up to 15% Cabernet Franc, the wine has been fragrant, fairly deep, and inviting in its first vintages*

### Viognier

(Saralee's Vineyard)  91°  92  93°  94  95°  **96°°**

*Attractive Viognier fruit in occasionally lean wines*

VINCENT ARROYO WINERY  *Napa 1984*  Seeking an alternative to the electronics business, Vincent Arroyo bought an old vineyard in Calistoga. At the time, the mature 37-acre vineyard contained Petite Sirah, Gamay, and Cabernet Sauvignon. During the first few years Arroyo sold most of the fruit to the large Co-op Winery in St. Helena. Encouraged by Bob Pecota, a neighbor and longtime advocate of Petite Sirah, Arroyo began making wine in 84, and the mainstay has been Petite Sirah, aged for one and a half years in French oak. Having purchased another vineyard in the area containing 22 acres, Arroyo still sells most of his fruit to other producers. As his production grows to the 3,000-case-a-year target, he is offering Cabernet Sauvignon and Chardonnay, along with Petite Sirah.

DAVID ARTHUR VINEYARDS  *Napa 1985*  After running a restaurant in Colorado, David Arthur Long returned to his family's 920-acre ranch in the eastern hills of Napa

Valley. In the same general area as Chappellet, 40 acres of vineyards were planted there in the early 80s. The winery's name avoids the family's last name in deference to Long Vineyard, a neighboring winery owned by Bob Long. Chardonnay and Cabernet Sauvignon are the leading varieties grown, plus a few acres of Cabernet Franc, Merlot, Petit Verdot, and Sangiovese. After gradual growth the winery will level off at 3,000 cases a year, with Chardonnay representing two-thirds of the total. Quality has been spotty to date.

ATLAS PEAK VINEYARDS    *Napa 1989*    This wine company was created by Whitbread, one of the largest British brewers, in partnership with two prestigious wine firms—Antinori of Italy and Bollinger of Champagne. Buying land, vineyards, and a winery facility from William Hill, the owners spent considerable time and money developing vineyards on Atlas Peak in the southeastern hills of Napa Valley, ending with 460 acres planted. The vineyards' first crush was in 89, and the roster was headed by Cabernet, Chardonnay, Semillon, Sauvignon Blanc, and Sangiovese. With more than 150 acres planted to Sangiovese, the largest single planting of that red grape, Atlas Peak seemed likely to be closely followed. However, before the next crush was under way, Whitbread's interest was bought out by an even larger British corporation, Allied-Lyons, the owners of Hiram Walker, which in turn owns Callaway, Clos du Bois, and William Hill. In 1993 Antinori acquired all of the vineyards and formed a partnership with the Wine Alliance, which owns the trademark and company. To date Atlas Peak has produced Sangiovese and a Reserve Sangiovese. It is also using Sangiovese in its proprietary blend, "Consenso," which contains varying amounts of Cabernet Sauvignon and Cabernet Franc. Production plans call for a maximum of 30,000 cases annually of Sangiovese, and no more than 1,000 cases of the Reserve. "Consenso" will remain around 7,500 cases. In the mid-90s Atlas Peak offered Chardonnay and Cabernet Sauvignon, blended with all four Bordeaux varieties. Recent vintages indicate the winery is settling into a groove, as both Sangiovese bottlings have displayed charm and richness enough to reach ° levels. Production of Chardonnay and Cabernet Sauvignon have grown to 6,000 and 5,000 cases, respectively, and recent vintages of Cabernet have risen above average.

**Sangiovese**

| 89 | **90°°** | **91** | **92°°** | 93 | 94 | 95 | **96°** |
|----|----------|--------|----------|-----|-----|-----|---------|
| (Reserve) | **92°°** | 93 | **94°** | **95°** | | | |

*Full-bodied, fruity, noticeably tannic wines, they have lacked brightness in some vintages*

AU BON CLIMAT    *Santa Barbara 1982*    While working for the Zaca Mesa Winery, Adam Tolmach and Jim Clendenen decided to form a small company dedicated to producing Chardonnay and Pinot Noir. Au Bon Climat began life in a corner of the now defunct Los Alamos Winery, where they made wines from the adjacent vineyards. In 89 they moved into a larger facility on the Bien Nacido Ranch, which is a primary source of Chardonnay and Pinot Noir. Clendenen has since become the sole owner. For each varietal, he prefers making vineyard-designated bottlings, and over the first several vintages he worked with a number of vineyards in the Central Coast and even one in Oregon. In recent vintages he has settled on Chardonnay bottlings from Talley Vineyard, Alban, Sanford & Benedict, La Nuits Blanches Bien Nacido, Central Coast, and the estate vineyard known as Le Bouge D'a-Cote. The Estate Pinot Noir is known as La Bauge Au-Dessus, and it is joined by other Pinot Noir from Sanford & Benedict Vineyard, Talley's Rosemary's Vineyard, Ici/La Bas from Oregon, and Isabelle, a blend of the best barrels in a given vintage. Pinot Blanc is offered in two forms, a regular bottling made from the Melon clone and a Reserve produced from the true Pinot Blanc clone. Fairly consistent high praise has been bestowed on the Chardonnays, especially the Reserve, fermented entirely in new French oak. The Pinot Noirs are often among the most highly extracted versions offered, but are sometimes over the top. Chardonnay accounts for 75% of the annual output, Pinot Noir and Pinot Blanc the remainder. Steady expansion has taken the brand close to its goal of 10,000 cases per year. Nebbiolo and small lots of other Italianate wines are bottled under the "Il Podere dell'Olivos" label. Clendenen is also co-owner of the Vita Nova (see entry) label, and Tolmach owns the Ojai Winery (see entry) outright.

### Chardonnay

(Reserve/Bien Nacido/La Bauge)     85°°     86°°     87°     89°°     **90°°**
**91°**     **92°°**     93     94     95

*Fruit is the key here; when there is enough, the wine shows all the balance needed to carry its heavily oaked, rich style*

### Pinot Noir

(Benedict Vineyard/Sanford & Benedict)     **87°**     88     **89°**     **93**     **94**

(Reserve/Bien Nacido/La Bauge)     **89**     **90°**     **91°**     92     **93°**     **94°**
**95°**

(Los Alamos Vineyards)     83     **84°°**     **86°**     87

(Rancho Viñedo)     **87°**     88     **89°**     92
**93°**

*Always deep, always complex, not always able to keep its herbal and tobacco characteristics in check*

---

AZALEA SPRINGS WINE CO.     *Napa 1991*     Norman Stone purchased a 6.5-acre Merlot vineyard along with a 100-year-old farmhouse, both located at the base of Diamond Mountain. With Kent Rasmussen supervising winemaking, the first several vintages of this Merlot-only brand have been made in a rented facility. Initial annual output of 400 cases is expected to grow to a maximum of 1,200 cases once the vines are fully productive.

---

BABCOCK VINEYARDS     *Santa Barbara 1983*     The Babcock family became interested in wines by way of the restaurant business. Along the western edge of the Santa Ynez Valley, they developed 50 acres to five varieties—Chardonnay, Johannisberg Riesling, Gewurztraminer, Sauvignon Blanc, and Pinot Noir. The first few vintages were on the erratic side as the production team apparently learned on the job. With experience the winery emerged as one to watch for Gewurztraminer, made both in a bold, barrel-fermented, bone-dry style and in a slightly sweet style. In the best years, the opulent, varietally intense dry Gewurztraminer reaches °°° performance. Babcock is also becoming reliable for Johannisberg Riesling in a light, lively, slightly sweet style. In more recent vintages, the winery's Eleven Oaks Ranch Sauvignon Blanc has stood out in a rich, brisk style. In the 1990s Babcock came on strong with Pinot Noir from both the Estate Vineyard and Mt. Carmel, and its Chardonnay roster consists of bottlings from Mt. Carmel, Bien Nacido Vineyards, and the winery's showcase Chardonnay, Grand Cuvee. Forced by phylloxera to replant the estate vineyard, Babcock has added Pinot Gris and Syrah, which in the early vintages showed tremendous promise. A line of limited production wines such as Syrah and Sangiovese are offered along with Chardonnay under the Cuvée Lestat label, which Babcock produces in partnership with author Anne Rice. Annual production is steady at 15,000 cases.

### Chardonnay

86     87°     88°     89     90     91     93     **94°**     95

*Decently fruity and crisp in balance with oak for richness*

### Chardonnay (Reserve/Grand Cuvée)

86     87°°°     88°°     90     92°     **95°**     96°

*More oak and richness than the regular bottling and lots of fruit in top years, when it reaches near-classic dimensions, but too oaky when the fruit doesn't measure up*

### Pinot Noir

(Estate as of 92)     88     89     90     91°     **92°**     **93°°**     **94°°**     **96°**

BALLENTINE WINE  *Napa 1992*  The Ballentine family was making wines in Napa Valley from the 1930 s until the early 1950 s. Until recently, the current generation of Ballentines devoted full attention to their 110 acres of vineyards in Napa Valley, and today most of their grapes are sold to well-established neighboring wineries. However, the Ballentines now operate a small winery north of St. Helena and to date have focused on red wines. Zinfandel heads the list, followed by Merlot and Cabernet Franc. The annual production currently stands at 3,000 cases.

BANDIERA WINERY  *Sonoma 1977*  This was one of Sonoma County's old jug-wine producers (founded in 37), revived and reopened in 77 to bottle decent-quality jug wines. Chris Bilbro operated it for a few years, then it changed hands again in 80. Its current owner, known as the California Wine Company, modernized the rapidly decaying old plant. Drawing from 200 acres of vineyard in Sonoma and in Napa Valley, it offered a range of table wines under several labels until settling on Bandiera. By the end of the 80s Bandiera was focusing on four varietals: White Zinfandel, Chardonnay, Cabernet Sauvignon, and Fumé Blanc. Owning 57 acres of Cabernet Sauvignon, Bandiera produces 30,000 cases of Cabernet from the Napa Valley. Chardonnay from the Carneros, where the winery has 42 acres, is the second significant wine in terms of volume, at 32,000 cases. Overall production has leveled off at 100,000 cases a year, with White Zinfandel remaining a popular item. Headquartered in England, the California Wine Company has been successful in marketing Bandiera wines in Europe and Asia. In the 1990s Bandiera's Napa Valley Cabernet Sauvignon has regularly earned "Best Value" citations and continues to be a runaway best-seller.

BANNISTER WINERY  *Sonoma 1990*  Marty Bannister is co-owner of VinQuiry, an independent wine laboratory providing services to dozens of wineries in the North Coast. With her wine chemistry background, she decided to venture into winemaking. Chardonnay and Zinfandel from the Russian River Valley and Dry Creek Valley are the primary wines produced by Bannister. Both wines have earned critical praise. Recently she has been trying her hand at Pinot Noir from the Russian River Valley and Anderson Valley. Total production is close to 1,000 cases, most of which is barrel-fermented Chardonnay.

### Chardonnay

89*  90  91**  92**  93  94  95

*Firm, fairly rich, appley Chardonnays with better than average ageworthiness*

### Zinfandel

**90*  91  92*  94**  95**

*Ripe berry fruit and full-bodied palatal impressions*

BARGETTO WINERY  *Santa Cruz 1933*  One of the oldest wineries in the area, Bargetto has made a graceful shift from old-style wines to those with contemporary appeal. Located on the main street in Soquel, it developed a reputation years ago through its tasting room for its fruit and berry wines and a specialty wine named "Chaucer's Mead." In the late 70s, under the direction of the third generation, it began shifting to the classical varietals and purchasing grapes from better vineyards in the Central Coast and in Napa Valley. In its 35,000-case-a-year line, it places major emphasis on Chardonnay (12,000), Cabernet Sauvignon (6,500), White Zinfandel (5,000), and Gewurztraminer (3,000). Lower-priced Chardonnay and Cabernet Sauvignon intended for early enjoyment have been produced from varying appellations, but are united under the "Cypress" designation. The least expensive bottlings are its Red and White Table Wine. Purchasing most of its grapes, mainly now from the Central Coast and Santa Cruz Mountain appellations, Bargetto is developing its 20-acre Regan Vineyard in the Santa Cruz Mountain appellation. Chardonnay, Pinot Noir, and Merlot are the main varieties planted, but trial plots of Nebbiolo, Dolcetto, and Barbera are being closely monitored with an eye toward expansion. Best success has been enjoyed with

Chardonnay and Gewurztraminer, with both the low-end Cypress Chardonnay and the regular bottling offering good value in better vintages.

**Chardonnay**

(regular bottling)   84   85°   86   87°   88   89   90   92

*Medium-bodied wines with direct fruit, sometimes floral and tropical in tone, and moderate oak*

BARNETT VINEYARDS   *Napa 1989*   A family-owned winery and vineyard located near the top of Spring Mountain, Barnett produces estate-grown Cabernet Sauvignon, Merlot, and Chardonnay. Covering 14 acres, the steeply terraced vineyards were planted in 84 to Cabernet, and then Chardonnay was added; Cabernet Franc and Merlot are also grown, for blending into the winery's Cabernet. With Cabernet Sauvignon expected to represent two-thirds of total production, the winery is heading toward a goal of 3,000 cases a year. From time to time, it produces Pinot Noir from Santa Lucia Highlands in Monterey, and also bottles a few hundred cases of a highly concentrated Cabernet from a parcel on the estate known as Rattlesnake Hill.

**Cabernet Sauvignon**

89°   91°°   92   93°   94°

*Tight, tannic, ripe fruit with somewhat loamy and spicy notes*

BAYVIEW CELLARS   *Napa 1992*   Longtime Inglenook winemaker John Richburg launched this brand in partnership with vineyard owner Ken Laird. Using a custom winemaking facility, they have been making Chardonnay from Laird's Carneros acreage and Cabernet Sauvignon, Merlot and Gewurztraminer from other Napa Valley sources. Initial annual output of 1,000 cases will level off at 2,000 cases.

BEAULIEU VINEYARDS   *Napa 1900*   The pride of Napa Valley for several decades, Beaulieu contributed mightily to the recognition of Napa Valley Cabernet Sauvignon, which in turn had a dramatic impact on the emergence of Napa Valley and the reputation of the entire California wine industry. In 1900 founder Georges de Latour, a man of meticulous standards, planted the winery's original vineyards on the western edge of Rutherford, a region recognized by others decades later as prime Cabernet turf. Beaulieu was the leading Cabernet producer, along with Inglenook, prior to Prohibition, and Latour kept his vineyards so well maintained that Beaulieu easily resumed winemaking in 34, the first vintage after Repeal.

In 38, Latour succeeded in convincing the Russian-born, French-taught André Tchelistcheff to become winemaker at Beaulieu. Though Latour died in 40, Tchelistcheff proved to be a wise choice, successfully guiding Beaulieu until early 73. One special lot of 36 Cabernet Sauvignon made from the two oldest vineyards was separately bottled and dedicated to Georges de Latour. That wine began a fabled series of Private Reserve Cabernets that came to be the most prestigious and sought-after California wine in many vintages from 36 through the early 70s. In 69, the heirs of Latour sold Beaulieu to Heublein; over the following years the product line was expanded, along with production. Heublein added a low-end Beau Tour Cabernet bottling and a line of generic wines in magnums, and doubled production within a decade.

In the 90s Beaulieu is holding steady at the 450,000-case annual output level, focusing on four varietals—Cabernet Sauvignon (50% of total production), Chardonnay, Pinot Noir, and Sauvignon Blanc. From its 300 acres in the Carneros District, Beaulieu offers a regular and Reserve of both Chardonnay and Pinot Noir. In Napa Valley, the winery owns or controls 385 acres of Cabernet Sauvignon, apportioned among three bottlings—Private Reserve, Napa Valley–Rutherford, and Coastal. After 1970 its Private Reserves registered more than their share of disappointments: 1972 (a disaster), 74 (short-lived), 83 (a lightweight), and 84 (an average wine from a superb Cabernet vintage). Tchelistcheff returned to

Beaulieu in 1991 to oversee production. From then until his death in 1994 at the age of 90, Tchelistcheff worked hard to bring French oak barrels into the red wine programs, and to use Merlot in the Private Reserve Cabernets. He also encouraged Heublein to secure long-term contracts with local vineyards. In 1990, Beaulieu added "Tapestry," a Meritage blend of Cabernet Sauvignon, Merlot, and Cabernet Franc. This was the beginning of a Signet Collection Series of unusual, limited production wines. With the 91 vintage, Beaulieu began to recapture the old magic and started to put its Private Reserve Cabernet Sauvignons back in center stage. Once again it is regularly earning °°, and Tapestry has also developed a good track record. The entire line seems to have been upgraded by the mid-90s as the Rutherford Cabernet along with Carneros Pinot Noir and Carneros Chardonnay began earning ° ratings. Though its roster changes with each vintage, the Signet Collection has also been impressive overall, with Zinfandel and Viognier as standouts. A line of Coastal varietals introduced in 98 replaced the former Beau Tour Cabernet and other modestly priced wines.

### Cabernet Sauvignon

(Private Reserve)  68°°°  69°°  70°°°  71°  72  73°  74 °
75°  76°  77°  78°°  79°  80°  81  82°°  83  84°  **85°**
**86  87°  88°  89°  90°  91  92°°  93°°  94°°**

*Once the holiest name in California Cabernet, this wine endured a decade of less-than-outstanding performance throughout the 80s; medium-intensity currant, tea leaf, and vaguely dusty and peppery character that too often has lacked intensity relative to the wine's usually firm structure and its bold oakiness; recent vintages have returned to form*

### Cabernet Sauvignon

(Rutherford)  80  81°  82°  83  84  85  86  87  88  89  90
91  92  **93°  94°  95°**

*Generally clean, unchallenging wines of medium weight, moderately intense cherry and vaguely curranty flavors, and light tannins; 93 was a watershed vintage and elevated the wine into one of the good values among early drinking Cabernets*

### Chardonnay

(Carneros Reserve)  86°  87°  88  89°  91°  **92°**  93  **94°°**
**95°**

(Carneros/Napa Valley)  86°  87  88  89  90  91  92  93  94
95°

*Though offering comparable records of success, these wines differ in character. The Carneros Reserve is the oakier and crisper of the two, while the Napa Valley bottling is a bit more open, in a clean, uncomplicated, well-balanced style*

### Pinot Noir

(Carneros Reserve)  84°  85°  86°  **87°**  88°  **89  90  91°°**
92°  93  **94°°**  95

(Carneros/Napa Valley)  84  85  86  87  88  89  90  91  92
93  94°  **95°**

*The Reserve, the most consistently likable wine from Beaulieu in the last several years, generally focuses on direct, ripe bright cherrylike fruit, with a dollop of toasty oak for enrichment; even the lighter-styled 88, somewhat strawberryish in tone, turned out well. The Beaumont is a lightweight wine intended for early consumption*

### Zinfandel
94°  95°  **96°**

---

**BECKMEN VINEYARD**  *Santa Barbara 1994*  Tom and Steve Beckmen acquired the former Houtz Winery in Los Olivos and the 23-acre vineyard belonging to it in the Santa Ynez Valley. That vineyard contains Chardonnay, Sauvignon Blanc, Cabernet, Merlot, and Syrah. In 1996 the Beckmens bought a 365-acre mountain property in Santa Ynez Valley. This Purisima Mountain Vineyard will eventually be planted to 200 acres of Rhone varieties, primarily Syrah, but also Grenache and Viognier. The winery is currently making Syrah, Cabernet, Chardonnay, and Sauvignon Blanc.

BEDFORD THOMPSON WINERY   *Santa Barbara 1993*   Partner Dave Thompson brings 25 acres of estate vines in the Los Alamos district, and Steve Bedford provides the winemaking know-how. Syrah fermented in small-batch, open-top fermenters has been the early quality leader of this 3,000-case winery. Also offered from the estate vineyard are Chardonnay, Pinot Blanc, and Cabernet Franc.

BEL ARBORS VINEYARDS   *(Fetzer Vineyards)*   Fetzer's original winery is located on Bel Arbres Road in Hopland, and for many years the Fetzers used the name for a second label. The product line under Bel Arbres changed with the fads. In the mid-70s it was led by three low-priced generic table wines: Blanc de Blancs, Red Table Wine, and White Table Wine. Although the output under this label grew as it was targeted for supermarkets and chain stores, it was not until the blush wine blitz, when Fetzer decided to label all of its blush wines as Bel Arbres, that this line took on great importance to the owners. By 87, in order to keep pace with the demand for low-priced Chardonnay, the Fetzers began buying grapes and wines from Washington to blend with California wine. By law, the appellation then had to be "American." With the addition of a large volume of American wines to Bel Arbres, Fetzer decided to simplify the line and rechristened it "Bel Arbors," the way most consumers were said to pronounce it. The leading wines so labeled are White Zinfandel, Chardonnay, Cabernet Sauvignon, Merlot, and Sauvignon Blanc. When demand for low-priced wine exceeded the local supply, Bel Arbors was among the first California labels to bottle Chardonnay, Merlot, and Cabernet made in Chile. Bel Arbors was selling over 500,000 cases in 90. The long-term goal is 3 million cases a year. Brown-Forman acquired this brand when it bought Fetzer in 1992.

BELLA LUNA WINERY   *Napa 1994*   The Charles Shaw Winery had been closed for a few years until John Benish purchased the winery and its surrounding 35-acre vineyard. Benish immediately began replanting the vineyard to focus on red varietals, primarily Cabernet Sauvignon and Merlot. Until the new vines are mature, he will be producing a few hundred cases of Cabernet Sauvignon from bought-in grapes.

BEHRENS & HITCHCOCK   *Napa 1993*   Restaurateur Les Behrens teamed up with wine-maker Bob Hitchcock for the purpose of producing small-volume wines to offer to upscale restaurants. Cabernet Sauvignon from several Napa Valley vineyards and Petite Sirah were among the initial offerings.

BELL WINE CELLARS   *Napa 1992*   Anthony (Tony) Bell was born in South Africa and came to California to study winemaking. By the mid-1980s he was head wine-maker for Beaulieu Vineyard, and he departed to form Rutherford Benchmarks, a company that owns Quail Ridge, Monterey Peninsula Winery, Van der Kamp Champagne Cellars, and his own brand. Bell Cellars currently offers Cabernet Sauvignon from Baritelle Vineyard in the heart of Rutherford. Central Coast Viognier blended with Marsanne is made in eye-dropper quantity to date. Although pricey (up to $50), the Cabernet has been inconsistent, earning ●● in 91 but nothing since.

BELLEROSE VINEYARD   *Sonoma 1979*   In 1978 Charles Richards bought 35 acres of vines in the southern part of Dry Creek Valley. Richards, the winemaker, was among the first in California to specialize in a Bordeaux-style Cabernet blend. He labels his version "Cuvée Bellerose," a blend of Cabernet Sauvignon, Merlot, Cabernet Franc, and, in most years, Petit Verdot and Malbec. Production gradually decreased in the early 1990s, and by 1997 the winery and a few remaining acres were sold. The current owners are retaining the Bellerose name for Zinfandel and a blend named Workhorse Red.

**Cuvée Bellerose/Reserve Cuvée**
**83   84   85°   87   88**

*Complex, herbal, sometimes slightly earthy, smoky, usually fairly tannic and in need of long aging*

**Merlot**
**83**   84   **85°**   86   **87°**   88

*Much like the above wine in range and toughness, and, for that reason, taking a different road from most Merlots*

BELVEDERE WINERY   *Sonoma 1979*   Peter Friedman, co-founder of Sonoma Vineyards/Rodney Strong Vineyards, went on to found Belvedere, which he co-owned until 1989. Today, Belvedere is in the hands of Bill Hambrecht, a venture capitalist and broker who helped finance Belvedere among his many winery investments. Until Hambrecht acquired the controlling interest, Belvedere produced its top wines from purchased grapes and bottled many wines under vineyard designations. Between 82 and 86, Hambrecht acquired 400 acres of vineyards in Sonoma County and a 220-acre ranch in Mendocino's Anderson Valley, which is under vineyard development. Beginning with the 89 vintage, all of Belvedere's wines have been produced from Hambrecht's own grapes. Under the new regime, the roster consists of Sonoma County Chardonnay, Alexander Valley Chardonnay, Russian River Valley Chardonnay, Dry Creek Valley Zinfandel, Sonoma Merlot, and a Cabernet Sauvignon from the Dry Creek Valley. The three primary Chardonnays, modestly priced and styled to be direct and immediately approachable, have received plaudits for good value in the early rounds. By the end of the 90s, Chardonnay production will represent 90% of the winery's expected yearly maximum of 70,000 cases. In certain vintages, Belvedere makes "Preferred Stock" Chardonnay and Cabernet Sauvignon, both in small quantities.

**Chardonnay**
(Alexander Valley/Sonoma County)   86°   87°   88   89   90   92
93°   **94°**   95   96
(Preferred Stock)   90°°   91°   92°°   **94**

**Zinfandel**
89   **90**   **91**   **93°**   **94°**   95°

*Riper, berryish, but occasionally lacking in the depth to stand up to their noticeable tannins*

BENESSERE VINEYARDS   *Napa Valley 1995*   Specializing in Sangiovese and Zinfandel, Benessere has developed a 50-acre vineyard and built a small winery south of St. Helena. Its Sangiovese, blended with 10–15% Cabernet remains faithful to the variety's lively bing cherry, boysenberry character with more flavor interest than is usually encountered.

BENZIGER WINERY & VINEYARDS   *Sonoma 1988*   By 88 the family-owned Glen Ellen Winery had become so successful (sales topped 3.2 million cases) with its low-priced, highly visible line that its owners, the Benziger family, decided to use the family name for a line of upscale varietals. The Benzigers sold Glen Ellen Winery in 1994 to Heublein. Benziger wines are all made in part from grapes grown in their adjacent 85-acre vineyard, planted to Cabernet Sauvignon, Merlot, Chardonnay, and Sauvignon Blanc. The quantities average about 2,000 cases for each primary Sonoma Valley bottling. In addition to these home-grown wines, Benziger produces a line of Sonoma County varietals from grapes purchased throughout the county. Made in 10,000–40,000-case lots, the wines, offered are Cabernet Sauvignon, Chardonnay (partially barrel-fermented), and oak-aged Fumé Blanc. Generally, the estate-grown Sonoma Valley varietals offer more intensity, and the quality leaders have been Merlot, Cabernet Sauvignon, Zinfandel, and Chardonnay. Meritage wines, both a red and a white, are labeled Tribute. Benziger has recently added an Old Vine Zinfandel and is developing a series of single-vineyard Chardonnays from Carneros. The family also makes a separate line of wines under the Imagery Series (see entry) label. Seeming to be always starting something new, the Benzigers are now operating a small brewery and growing hops in Glen Ellen. The family will also soon be producing wines from their Oregon holdings. Annual output of California wines is 180,000 cases.

### Cabernet Sauvignon

(Sonoma County)   85   86   87   88   89   **90°**   91   **92°**   93°
**94°**   **95°**

*Fruity, moderately tannic, accessible wines*

### Chardonnay

(Sonoma County)   86   87°   88   89   90   91°   92   94

*Simple, clean, direct in approach, the wine has shown moderate fruit and quiet oak*

### Merlot

(Sonoma Valley)   86   87°°   88°   89   **90°°**   91°°   **92°**   93°
**94°**   **95°**

*Round and rich with good fruit, good depth*

### Tribute Red

**87°**   **88**   **89**   **91°**   **93°**   **94°**

*A Merlot-dominated blend, with Cabernet Sauvignon and Cabernet Franc, it has been rich and moderately tannic in its first releases*

### Zinfandel

88°   89   90   **91**   **92°°°**   **93°°**   **94°°**   **95°°**

*After four vintages of average results, 92 turned out deep, fruity, and perfectly focused and subsequent years have followed in step*

---

BERINGER VINEYARDS   *Napa 1876*   Jacob and Frederick Beringer, the brothers who founded this winery, would have little trouble identifying their estate, their home (the Rhine House), and the old stone winery behind it carved into the hillside. However, everything else has changed. Operated by the Beringer family until 71, this grand old name had run into serious problems by the 60s. The winery was making a range of dull, nonvintaged wines that undermined the reputation gained by the better vintaged versions bottled through the 40 s. In 71, the winery and its old, worn-out cooperage (mostly redwood tanks and large German oak ovals) and equipment along with some 800 acres were bought by Wine World, Inc., a division of the Swiss-based conglomerate Nestlé. The new owner invested millions of dollars in renovating the Rhine House and the old aging caves, turning them into a popular visitors center. Construction of a large production facility across the road was finished in 74, and the winery acquired and developed prime vineyard lands in Napa and Sonoma counties. Winemaking was turned over to Myron Nightingale, who was later succeeded by his apprentice, Ed Sbragia.

Signs of quality improvements were first noticed with the release of the 73 Napa Valley Chardonnay and Cabernet Sauvignon. Gradually but persistently, Beringer worked to remove the tarnish left from the 50s and to counter the corporate image. In 77, Beringer made a Private Reserve Cabernet Sauvignon from the Lemmon Ranch (renamed Chabot Vineyard) that caught our attention. Building upon that Private Reserve Cabernet base, Beringer toiled away to improve its overall track record and image. Today, Beringer draws from the 3,100 acres it owns, 2,300 in Napa Valley and the rest in Knight's Valley. Beringer has substantial Napa Valley Chardonnay vineyards in Napa, Yountville, and Oakville, adding up to 620 acres, while 520 acres in both Napa and Sonoma counties are devoted to Cabernet Sauvignon. Chenin Blanc remains an important grape for the winery, with 260 acres, followed by Sauvignon Blanc at 240 acres.

To fill out its large line of table wines, Beringer still purchases grapes from growers in the Napa Valley or other North Coast regions. The current volume leaders are White Zinfandel (over 750,000 cases), Chardonnay (150,000 cases) and Chenin Blanc (100,000 cases). In terms of prestige, Cabernet Sauvignon is Beringer's leader, represented by three bottlings—Private Reserve, Chabot Vineyard, and Knights Valley. Second is Chardonnay (Private Reserve and Proprietor Grown). Other noteworthy offerings include its Napa Valley Fumé Blanc; its oak-aged Knights Valley Meritage white blend, a richly fruity, intense, lively combination of Semillon and Sauvignon Blanc; and its remarkably attractive Gewurztraminer, a well-kept secret. A Zinfandel partially made by carbonic maceration and a late harvest Semillon/Sauvignon Blanc blend bottled as "Nightingale" are also worthy of attention. In the late 80s Beringer added Merlot from Howell Mountain. Today, the winery bottles about 1.3 million cases a year. Nestlé sold its winery and vineyard interest to a limited partnership named Silverado Partners. They renamed the wine company Beringer Estates, which includes Beringer, Chateau Souverain, Meridian, Napa Ridge, Chateau St. Jean and Stags Leap Winery. In 1997 the company went public.

### Cabernet Sauvignon

(Private Reserve—Lemmon Ranch)   **77°**   **78°**   **80°°**

(Private Reserve)   81°   83°°   **84°°**   **85°**   **86°°**   **87°**   **88°°**
**89°**   **90°**   **91°**   **92°**   93

(Lemmon–Chabot; Chabot Vineyard)   81°°   83   **84°°**   **85°**

*This group of wines, under their varied and changing nomenclature, represents the evolution of Beringer into a producer of top-quality Cabernet; the wines have been medium-full-bodied and fairly tannic, usually with enough ripe, curranty fruit to achieve satisfactory balance for medium- to long-term aging*

### Cabernet Sauvignon

(Knights Valley)   82°   83°   84   86   87   88   89   **90°**   **91°**
**92°**   93   **94°°**   **95°**

*A medium to medium-full-bodied wine, with direct, moderately ripe, accessible cherry and quietly herbal flavors supported by light-medium tannins*

### Chardonnay

(Private Reserve)   86°°   87   88   89°   **90°°**   **91°°**   **92°°°**   93
94°   **95°°°**   **96°°**

(Proprietor Grown—Napa Valley)   86°   88°   89   90°   91°   92
93°   **94°**   **95°**   **96**

*Generally well-made wines, showing appley and sometimes citrusy fruit with toasty oak, especially in the Private Reserve, and good acid balance*

### Merlot

(Bancroft Ranch)   **87°°°**   **89**   **90°°°**   **91°**   **92°°**   **93°**   **94°°°**

*Grown on Howell Mountain, this wine has generally been flavorful, slightly coarse, and full of aging potential*

---

BERNARDUS WINERY   *Monterey 1992*   Owner Ben (Bernardus) Pon was born and raised in Holland, where he ran his family's wine distributorship. An avid wine collector and former race driver for Porsche, Pon regularly vacationed in Monterey and Carmel. In 1989 he bought a 220-acre ranch in the Carmel Valley from the owners of Talbott Winery. Now planted to 50 acres of Bordeaux red varieties, the vineyards—which lie on a 1500-foot-high plateau—yielded their first full harvest in 93. The Estate red Meritage named Marinus is the flagship wine. Chardonnay and Sauvignon Blanc from Ventana Vineyards and Pinot Noir from Bien Nacido Vineyards in Santa Maria Valley round out the line. Total production will level off at 40,000 cases.

---

BETTINELLI VINEYARDS   *Napa 1995*   Vineyard owners with 37 acres in Rutherford and another 12 acres at the base of Spring Mountain District in St. Helena, Bettinelli sells most of its tonnage to its Napa Valley neighbors. On its own, this family winery makes Chardonnay, Cabernet Sauvignon, and Merlot. Each to date is made in small (300–700) case lots. Greg Graham of Rombauer Cellars oversees the wine production. 95 Cabernet was more rugged than fruity.

BIALE VINEYARDS   *Napa 1991*   After selling grapes for close to five decades, the Biale family is venturing slowly into winemaking. From "Aldo's Vineyard," the family vineyard planted in 1937, the Biales make about 500 cases of Zinfandel from the home vineyard. Buying grapes from some of their neighbors, they have also made Refosco and Cabernet Sauvignon. Preferring Zinfandel, the owners have added bottlings from Old Crane Ranch in Napa Valley and Monte Rosso Vineyard in Sonoma Valley. A Sangiovese appeared as of the 95 vintage.

**Zinfandel**

**91°   92   93°°   94   95   96°**

*Compact, concentrated, slightly closed-in wines; inconsistent results*

BLACK SHEEP VINTNERS   *Calaveras 1987*   Formerly known as Chispa Cellars, this old winery was acquired in 86 by its present owner, Dave Olson, onetime winemaker for Stevenot. He promptly changed the name to Black Sheep. Chispa had produced limited amounts of often tanky, old-style Zinfandel. Black Sheep's current production consists of Zinfandel and Cabernet Sauvignon from Amador County and Sauvignon Blanc from Calaveras County. Zinfandel is the major wine in the annual output of 1,000 cases.

**Zinfandel**

91   92   94   96

BLACKSTONE VINEYARDS   *(Codera Wine Co.)*   This label is devoted primarily to Merlot, which is bottled under three appellations—Napa Valley, Sonoma County, and California. A limited amount of Chardonnay brings this label's total annual output close to 70,000 cases.

BLOSSOM HILL WINERY   *(Almadén Vineyards)*   In early 89, two years after Heublein acquired Almadén Vineyards, this spin-off brand of table wines was introduced. Blossom Hill offers low-priced varietals and generics in magnums only as an upscale jug-wine line. Bottled at Heublein's main production facility in Madera, Blossom Hill wines consist of two reds, Cabernet Sauvignon and Merlot, along with Chardonnay, Sauvignon Blanc, and White Zinfandel, the volume leader. Red Table and White Table bottlings complete the line. All are vintaged and display the California appellation.

BLUE HERON LAKE WINERY & VINEYARD   *Napa 1985*   In the early 80s, owner/winemaker Dave Mahaffey developed 24 acres in the Wild Horse Valley and worked hard to see that the valley was approved as a Viticultural Area. To date he has been selling most of his grapes, retaining enough to produce 500 cases each of Chardonnay and Pinot Noir. Using space in the White Rock Winery, he makes a barrel-fermented, full-blown style of Chardonnay, and a more restrained style of Pinot Noir.

BOEGER WINERY   *El Dorado 1973*   As the first winery established in El Dorado County after Prohibition, Boeger quickly became the best known and also the biggest in the county. This family-owned producer has led the way for others in El Dorado through its many experiments with numerous varietals. In 73 the Boegers established a 35-acre vineyard on an old, pre-Prohibition winery site. They planted Cabernet Sauvignon, Chardonnay, and Sauvignon Blanc in significant acreage along with parcels of Semillon, Zinfandel, and Merlot. This estate vineyard is a series of beautiful terraces situated at the 2,000- to 3,000-foot elevation. The Boegers also lease a nearby 20-acre vineyard, the Peek Vineyard, which they planted to Johannisberg Riesling, Flora, Symphony, Cabernet Franc, and Petit Verdot.

The neighboring Walker Ranch supplies Boeger with Zinfandel. In most vintages the winery offers estate-bottled Cabernet Sauvignon, Chardonnay, and Merlot, and each has risen to ° level on occasion. Boeger makes a light, refreshing, slightly sweet Johannisberg Riesling and a sweet-tasting Sauvignon Blanc. Now that its plantings of Cabernet Franc and Petit Verdot are full-bearing, Boeger is combining them with Cabernet and Merlot to produce a red Meritage, in an annual output of under 1,000 cases. The winery has now reached its maximum level of 15,000 cases a year. The volume leaders are Chardonnay, Cabernet Sauvignon, Merlot, and Sauvignon Blanc. In their typical quiet way, the Boegers have added three pioneering blends to accompany their Meritage. "Migliore" is the name of an Italian-style blend of Barbera, Zinfandel, Rofosco, and Sangiovese, and the Spanish blend is "Milagro," made from Tempranillo, Graciano, and Garnacha. "Majeure" is the proprietary Rhone Valley blend of Syrah, Grenache, and Mourvedre. The Boegers have also revived the Nichelini Winery (see entry) brand.

### Cabernet Sauvignon

75° 76° 77° 78° 79 80 81° 82 83 84 85 86 87 89 **90** 91 94

*Usually made in a ripe, not overblown style, with curranty, sometimes jammy or tarry notes, moderate tannins, all adding up to good value when it succeeds*

### Chardonnay

86 88 89 90 91

*Round but underfruited wines*

### Merlot

82° 83° 84° 85 86 87 88 89 **90** **91** 92 **93** 94 95

*Seemingly deeper wine in its first vintages, now showing enjoyable ripish, briary character and good oak richness, but less distinctive fruitiness*

### Zinfandel

86 87° 88 89 90 91 **92°** 93 94° **95**

*Ripe, moderately intense, somewhat stiff wines*

BOGLE VINEYARDS   *Yolo 1979*   In the Delta region of Clarksburg, the Bogle family has long been involved in agriculture. Although they have entered grape growing in a big way with more than 600 acres under vine, the Bogles remain diversified farmers, and continue to sell many crops as well as a major portion of their grape crop. In the mid-80s, like many other growers, they removed several varieties such as Chenin Blanc and Gray Riesling in favor of Chardonnay and more Chardonnay. Cabernet Sauvignon is the second most widely planted variety. Under their own brand, they are making about 100,000 cases. Most of their output consists of low-priced varietals, the top-selling wines being Chardonnay. Bogle also makes Zinfandel, Petite Sirah, Merlot, and Semillon, all of which are moderately priced. A cut above in price and quality are a big, brawny Old Vine Zinfandel and a lush, fruity Petite Sirah.

BONNY DOON VINEYARD   *Santa Cruz 1981*   A former philosophy instructor, Randall Grahm purchased land on Bonny Doon Road in 81. He planted Pinot Noir and Chardonnay, and proclaimed himself a Burgundian. His first wine to appear was a Vin Gris from Pinot Noir that met with a mixed reception. Then in 84, turning to Rhone Valley wines, he created a proprietary wine, "Le Cigare Volant," to replicate a red Châteauneuf-du-Pape. (The wine's name, French slang for a flying saucer, was an inside joke poking fun at a proclamation in the 50s prohibiting UFOs from landing in the region of Châteauneuf-du-Pape.) That wine, made from Grenache and Syrah, was of high quality. Not long afterwards, Grahm made a Nouveau-style wine from Grenache grown in Gilroy, known as the garlic capital of the world, and bottled it under the name of "Clos de Gilroy."

By the end of 86, Grahm was marketing a range of wines, from Syrah originating in Paso Robles, to Chardonnay from Monterey County, to Pinot Noir grown in Oregon. At about this time, Grahm determined that wines with Mediterranean origins, initially from France's Rhone Valley and Provence but later extended to include Italy and Spain, were better suited to California's climate. Gradually the Bonny Doon label was restricted to wines from Mediterranean types. Heading the roster are Le Cigar Volant (a red Rhone blend), Old Telegram (Mourvedre), Le Sophiste (blend of Roussanne & Marsanne), Vin Gris de Cigare (light pink blend), Roussanne, Muscat, and Zinfandel, nicknamed "Cardinal Zinfandel." A major portion of Syrah and Roussanne come from a Paso Robles vineyard selling exclusively to Bonny Doon. In the early 1990s he began developing vineyards in Northern Monterey, near the town of Soledad. Planted to a range of Rhone and Italian varieties, this vineyard now covers 64 acres. Major varieties are Barbera (10 acres), Dolcetto (10 acres), and Orange Muscat (10 acres). As this vineyard was maturing Grahm was also becoming fascinated with distillation. Using the Santa Cruz facility, he now makes Eau-de-vie from apricots, cherries, and plums, and produces Marc de Cigare and Grappa from Muscat.

The wines from Italian varieties evolved into a separate category and are sold under the Ca' del Solo (see entry) label. Always fond of neglected varieties, Grahm created Pacific Rim as a label grouping Riesling and Gewurztraminer, which he usually makes, and for Chenin Blanc and Sauvignon Blanc made on occasion. He has been known to buy Grenache and Riesling from Washington State, and he has also used Riesling from Germany and Grenache grown in Spain. With total annual wine production at about 80,000 cases, Randall Grahm's expansion plans call for adding to his Soledad acreage and developing 80 acres in the Livermore Valley, where he has refurbished the historic Ruby Hill Winery. Purchased in 1997, this winery site will eventually handle most of his production needs. The land will be planted to "an eclectic field blend of Mediterranean types yet to be determined, working title Succotash."

BONTERRA VINEYARDS  (Fetzer Vineyards)  Fetzer's line of Mendocino County wines from organically grown grapes, Bonterra enjoyed immediate success. Most of its 100,000-case annual output is Chardonnay and Cabernet Sauvignon, both of which offer straightforward varietal character. The limited-volume wines to date—Syrah, Viognier, and Sangiovese—have been richer in character, higher in price, but more erratic in quality.

BONVERRE VINEYARDS  Napa 1992  Part of the St. Supery Vineyard & Winery organization, Bonverre (French for "good tipple") is a modestly priced line of varietals headed by Chardonnay and Merlot. Most of the wines have been made from the winery's own acreage, and in the case of Zinfandel, have been made from the winery's new plantings. However, in the late 1990s the company's French owner brought in Viognier and Merlot from the South of France and bottled it as Bonverre.  Volume is about 15,000 cases per year, and the quality has been average.

BORRA'S CELLAR  San Joaquin 1975  South of Lodi on property farmed by his grandfather in the early 1900 s, Steve Borra has been busy replanting the old vineyard and reviving winemaking. The 35-acre vineyard contains 12 acres of Barbera, the rest consisting of Zinfandel and Flame Tokay, the pride of Lodi. From a first crush that yielded under 200 cases, the winery focused on Barbera in the 80s, making both a red and a blush version. With the offering of Zinfandel, production has edged to the 1,000-case level. However, Borra began removing some of the Barbera in favor of Cabernet Sauvignon, which he will emphasize in the 90s. To date, the quality has been variable.

BOUCHAINE VINEYARDS   *Napa 1980*   When it started, this winery seemed to have everything going for it: financial backing (the owners were an heir of the DuPont dynasty and a member of the Kiplinger family) and its location in Carneros. After renovating the old Garetto Winery (founded in 1899), Bouchaine made its initial vintage in 81, and also started a strong custom-crush business. The early vintages of Pinot Noir and Chardonnay consisted of a variety of vineyard-designated bottlings. The quality often seemed to lag behind the reputation of the vineyard and the competition. In 82 Jerry Luper, formerly of Chateau Montelena, was brought in as winemaker, staying until 86. Since then, the winery has placed emphasis on its estate-bottled Chardonnay, and on the Pinot Noir from its own 31-acre vineyard in Carneros. On average it makes 10,000 cases of Chardonnay, 5,000 cases of Pinot Noir. Additional grapes from Carneros or the Yountville area have been purchased. The Chardonnays, including an occasional Reserve, are 100% barrel-fermented and undergo partial malolactic fermentation. The roster is rounded off by Gewurztraminer and Cabernet Franc. By the mid-90s the winery had been completely renovated and modernized. In the years ahead, Bouchaine intends to focus most of its production efforts on Pinot Noir.

### Chardonnay

(Napa Valley)   86°   89   90

(Carneros)   86°   87°°   88°   91   92   93°   94   95°   96

(Estate Reserve)   86°   87   88   90   91   93°   94°   95

*Throughout its twists and turns, Bouchaine has produced Chardonnays that are crisp, oaky, well fruited, and moderately rich*

### Pinot Noir

(Carneros)   82°   83°   84   85   86   87°   88   89   **90°**   **91°** **92°**   **93°**   95

(Reserve)   86   **87°**   **88°**   **90**   **91°**

*Direct, sometimes thinly fruited, cherrylike qualities come with moderate oak enrichment, hints of herbs, and mild tannins*

BOYER WINES   *Monterey 1985*   Like several other full-time winemakers, Rick Boyer branched out to start his own limited-production specialty wine company. In the beginning he traded services for goods as he made Chardonnay from Ventana Vineyards. Since then, he has developed an 8-acre Chardonnay vineyard. With vineyard maturity, Boyer will switch sources from Ventana to his own grapes. In any event, Boyer's Chardonnays are barrel-fermented and aged *sur lie*. His production has been steady at 1,500 cases per year. Already showing well, this winery seems poised to grab the brass ring with upcoming Chardonnay vintages. In 1994 Boyer became the winemaker for Jekel, but continues making wines under his own label. Syrah and Pinot Noir have joined the roster recently.

### Chardonnay

(Ventana Vineyard)   86°   87°   88°   89   **90°°**   91°   92°   93 **95°**

*Fairly bright fruit and creamy oak are combined in well-balanced, medium-depth wines; 93 was an aberration in an otherwise solid record*

BRANDBORG CELLARS   *Marin 1986*   A longshoreman in San Francisco, Terry Brandborg lives in the quaint town of Fairfax in the middle of Marin County. At first, he only wanted to produce a few hundred cases to sell locally. However, as he experimented with small batches of varietals from different microclimates, he found himself making 1,200 cases a year, the facility's maximum capacity. By 93, Brandborg moved operations to a bigger facility in Richmond, enabling him to expand production to 3,000 cases a year. We have found his Pinot Noirs to be among his best. The varietals he enjoys producing are Zinfandel, Charbono, Pinot Noir, and Sauvignon Blanc. He has come to prefer Zinfandel from Mount Veeder and from

El Dorado, Charbono from Napa Valley, and Pinot Noir from many sources, including Anderson Valley, Sonoma Valley, and Santa Barbara.

---

**BRANDER VINEYARD** *Santa Barbara 1980* Fred Brander, owner and winemaker, came to Santa Barbara County to work initially for the Santa Ynez Winery. After three vintages he left to make wines under his own brand and from his own vineyard. From 79 through the 84 vintage, Brander specialized in Sauvignon Blanc (blended with Semillon) from his vineyard. Other wines were made from his vines, such as several blush wines, but they were marketed under St. Carl, his second label. In 85 he added Chardonnay and upgraded the Cabernet Blanc (blush Cabernet Sauvignon) to the Brander line. The Cabernet Blanc from 85 ranks as one of the finest, most flavorful of the blush type. Though it was produced in limited volume, a Cabernet Franc from Brander's vineyard was among the first California wines sold with that varietal identity. Then from the 84 vintage, Brander released another new wine in 86 called "Bouchet," a blend of Cabernet Franc, Merlot, and Cabernet Sauvignon.

So far, Brander Chardonnays have been erratic and unimpressive. Its mainstay is Sauvignon Blanc, which in its best vintages captures bold, varietal character in a crisp, slightly fruity, lean style. We peg it as a ° performer. With annual production at 8,000 cases, Brander is at its optimum. The Sauvignon Blanc represents about 50% of the total.

---

**BRAREN PAULI WINERY** *Sonoma 1979* Partners Bill Pauli and Larry Braren are long-time friends who decided to combine their talents in this small company. Pauli is a vineyardist who owns part of the Richetti Vineyard in Mendocino County, which has supplied Fetzer with its Richetti Vineyard Zinfandel for many years. Braren oversees the red wine winery, located in Petaluma. The two owners are also partners in a vineyard in the Potter Valley that grows Chardonnay. Cabernet Sauvignon and Merlot are made from vineyards they lease under long-term contract. The style of wine has leaned a little toward the heavy-handed, excessively wood-aged for the two reds. The white roster includes Sauvignon Blanc and Semillon, and the winery white wine style is one of forthright fruitiness. Occasionally the Sauvignon Blanc stands out.

---

**BRINDIAMO** *(Thornton Winery)* Though the name is Italian, Brindiamo has so far been used to label a variety of wines that are either Italian or new to the winery as of the 1990s. Chardonnay, Cabernet Sauvignon, and Pinot Noir are joined by several Italianate wines. Among them are Nebbiolo and two proprietary blends, Gioveto (Sangiovese and Cabernet Sauvignon) and Rosso Vecchio, a blend of several reds.

---

**DAVID BRUCE WINERY** *Santa Cruz 1964* In his first decade of winemaking, David Bruce accomplished enough to deserve a special place in the history of post-Prohibition wine. While he was earning his medical degree at Stanford, Bruce became acquainted with Martin Ray and volunteered to work with him. He shared Ray's enthusiasm for the Santa Cruz Mountains appellation and for mountainside vineyards. Setting up a dermatology practice in San Jose in 60, Bruce began making wines at home. In 61, he built a winery and planted 25 acres on terraces high in the hills of Los Gatos. In contrast to his quiet demeanor, Bruce made wines that were bold, sometimes bizarre, and often highly experimental. Among his many curious wines, he made a White Zinfandel in 64, forerunner of the blush wines of the 80s. He also made a range of late harvest wines, including both dry and sweet late harvest Zinfandels, and a late harvest Grenache. Bruce expressed an interest in making Petite Syrah and Grenache long before the Rhone Valley trend arrived in the 80s.

But it is the Chardonnays that elevated Bruce to special status. Believing in extremely ripe grapes, barrel fermentation, high extraction, plenty of new oak, and in the complexity achieved by malolactic fermentation, Bruce began cranking out

Chardonnays in 67, 68, and 69 that were big, powerful, sometimes overwhelming—and unlike any others of the era. His 72 and 73 Chardonnays added to his reputation for big, controversial, and unusual wines. In 73, half of the Chardonnay harvested was labeled "Late Harvest." With Zinfandels made into a variety of styles, often big and portlike, and with Pinot Noirs made with the minimal handling approach, David Bruce wines from 67 to 77 were the center of attention.

By 82, Bruce's wines had turned toward a more conventional style, and he yielded the chores to his staff. Today, Bruce maintains that his winemaking style has not changed, but rather that other winemakers have adopted it and made it seem more conventional. The estate vineyard, located at the 2,000-foot level in a Region I climate, contains 16 acres of Pinot Noir, 12 of Chardonnay. Production is steady at 30,000 cases a year. The flagship wines are the estate-bottled Chardonnay and Pinot Noir. Recently Bruce has expanded his Pinot Noir arsenal to include a first-rate version from the Chalone District and impressive Pinots from Russian River Valley and Anderson Valley. In the late 1990s David Bruce Pinot Noirs are again playing to rave reviews, with several wines earning °° in their early appearances.

## Chardonnay

(Santa Cruz Mountains)   87   8̶8̶   91   92   93   94

*More ripe than fruity, yet always with plenty of acid and oak, these wines have seemed short of richness and center in most years*

## Pinot Noir

(Vintner's Select)   82   83   84   85   86   88°   89°   90   91°
92   **93°**   94

*Herbal, dried-leaf qualities are the predominating characteristics, with somewhat thin, cherrylike fruit in quiet support*

---

BRYANT FAMILY VINEYARDS   *Napa 1992*   Don and Barbara Bryant grow only Cabernet Sauvignon on the north-facing slopes of Pritchard Hill in the eastern hills of Napa County. Their 10-acre vineyard is managed by David Abreu. As of 1993 consulting winemaker, Helen Turley, has been making Bryant's Cabernet in leased space. Early annual output was 900 cases, but production has been reduced to 500 cases for the remainder of the 90s because of a program of vineyard replanting. Bryant Family began on a high quality level.

---

BUEHLER VINEYARDS   *Napa 1978*   Starting with a vineyard site purchased in 72, the Buehlers have nurtured 61 acres of vines. Both vineyard and winery are in the remote mountainous terrain along the eastern edge of Napa Valley near Lake Hennessey. John Buehler, Sr., is an engineer who retired as vice president from the Bechtel Corporation in 72. John Buehler, Jr., developed the vineyard and now oversees the entire operation. The vineyard was planted to 27 acres of Zinfandel, 26 acres of Cabernet Sauvignon, and 8 acres of Pinot Blanc. The winery has earned plaudits for its robust Zinfandels and its rich, highly distinctive, but sometimes controversial Cabernet Sauvignons. Aged in French oak for 18 months, Buehler Cabernets display to some degree an earthy, tarry component, and their success depends on how well that characteristic is controlled. Buehler's Zinfandels are ripe in style, with a deep blackberry fruitiness. With regard to Pinot Blanc, however, the Buehlers, after a valiant struggle to convince consumers of its merits, threw in the towel after the 88 vintage. This defeat was made less painful by the success enjoyed by White Zinfandel. After testing the market for Zinfandel Rose, Buehler consolidated its pink wine efforts into White Zinfandel. The highly successful White Zinfandel brings Buehler's annual production to the 35,000-case level. For an everyday style of Chardonnay, Buehler bottles a bright, moderately oaky Russian River Valley version. A relatively new Reserve program consists of a Reserve Estate Zinfandel made in the 300–400-case range and a Reserve Chardonnay of similar quantity. Each is worthy of a special search.

### Cabernet Sauvignon

(Napa Valley)　80　81　82°°　83°　84°　**85°**　**86°°°**　**87°**　89
**90°°**　**91°**　**92**　**93°**　**94°**　**95**

(Estate)　**95°°**

*Opulent, deep, curranty, leathery, sometimes earthy and tarry, and always loaded with character and tannin, this series of wines possesses all the stuffing for long aging, but sometimes seems a little too heavy and ripe to stay on course*

### Zinfandel

82°　83　85°°　86°　**87**　**88**　89　**90**　**92°**　**93°**　94　95
96

*Not unlike the Cabernet in its emphasis on full-blown character, this wine is usually ripe and tannic, with suggestions of tar thrown in*

BUENA VISTA WINERY　*Sonoma 1857*　This old, historically significant winery was established by the flamboyant Count Agoston Haraszthy and is now owned by the West German firm of A. Racke. It was acquired in 79 from Young's Market of Los Angeles, and under the Racke regime the winery has been given a new and more vigorous direction. The original stone winery (Haraszthy Cellars) in the Sonoma Valley has been restored, caves and all, and serves as a visitors center and picnic grounds. The modern working winery sits amidst a 1,700-acre estate in the Carneros, where the owners have planted 900 acres of vines. With the annual production of table wines in excess of 200,000 cases, the owners use the Buena Vista name for the top varietals. Most varietals are from the Carneros appellation, with the exception of Sauvignon Blanc, which generally hails from Lake County.

Throughout the 80s the winery worked hard to develop a small line of Private Reserve wines, which are now labeled Carneros Grand Reserve. We often like the Reserves of Chardonnay, Pinot Noir, and Cabernet. The winery also enjoys critical success with Sauvignon Blanc and Chardonnay. Lively and loaded with melony-grassy fruit, the Lake County Sauvignon Blanc is a perennial best value. A new sparkling wine program began on a good quality level with an easy-to-like Brut. Working in a region not hospitable to Cabernet, the winery is making close to 20,000 cases of friendly, fruity Cabernet Sauvignon and a bold, highly laudable, but not always successful Reserve. Overall, the winery has had few continuing winners.

### Cabernet Sauvignon

78　79°　80°　81　82　83　84　85　**86**　87　88　90　91
92　93　**94**　95

*Balanced, low-key, cherryish, medium-bodied, often herbal*

### Cabernet Sauvignon

(Special Selection/Grand Reserve)　78°°　79°°　80°　81°　83　**86**
**88**　**90**　**93°**　**94°**

*Balanced, ripe, aromatic, cherry and currant fruitiness*

### Chardonnay

(Carneros)　86　87°　88　89　90　91　92　94°　95
(Reserve)　86°°　87°　88　91　**94°**　95

*Fruity, lean, simple, brisk acidity; the Reserve is riper and richer, with oak filling out appley fruit, but acidity remains ample*

### Merlot

89　90　91　93　94　95

### Pinot Noir

(regular bottling)　90　91　92　94　95
(Reserve)　**90°**　**91**　**92°**　**94**　**95°**

*There is not much to like in the thin, underfilled regular bottling but the Reserve often captures riper, deeper fruit*

BURGESS CELLARS  *Napa 1972*  Occupying a site used for winemaking since 1880, Burgess Cellars is located along the steep hillsides on the western edge of Howell Mountain. Former Air Force and private corporation pilot Tom Burgess purchased the property originally known as Souverain Cellars, founded by the legendary winemaker Lee Stewart. After selling the winery, Stewart retained the Souverain name, which eventually was bought by Pillsbury. Burgess began replanting the hillside vineyard to Cabernet Sauvignon and Cabernet Franc. Over the first several vintages Burgess purchased grapes from hillside locations, and before long his winery had developed a good reputation for Zinfandel, Cabernet Sauvignon, and a dry, oak-aged Chenin Blanc. Though it ranked among the finest in most vintages, the Chenin Blanc was discontinued in 84. From 72 to 76, Burgess also made some incredibly rich Petite Sirahs, before removing the old vines near the winery. In 79, he acquired a 50-acre vineyard in Yountville and planted it to Chardonnay. From 83 on, he has produced Chardonnay entirely from his Trière Vineyard. Until 81, a Napa Valley Cabernet Sauvignon from purchased grapes was offered in addition to a Reserve bottling.

Beginning with the 82 vintage, Burgess has produced only one Cabernet Sauvignon, labeled "Vintage Selection." Made entirely from nonirrigated, low-yielding hillside grapes, and blended with Merlot and Cabernet Franc, the Vintage Selection Cabernet is aged for two years in French oak. The Zinfandel, also made from hillside grapes partly from the Burgess vineyard, has long been a favorite of ours, and over recent years has become more refined and polished without sacrificing any of its lovely ripe-berryish flavors and tannic backbone. Burgess Chardonnays are barrel-fermented in small oak vessels made exclusively by the Damy cooperage in Meursault.

Burgess had reached his optimum production of 30,000 cases a year. Over half consists of Chardonnay, with his Vintage Selection Cabernet Sauvignon falling in the 6,500- to 7,000-case range. From time to time, the second label, "Bell Canyon," appears on wines that did not make the primary label.

### Cabernet Sauvignon

(Vintage Selection)  73**  74***  75*  76*  77*  78*  79*
**80**°° 81 **82**°° 83* **84**°°° **85**°° 86* 87 88* 89 **90**°
**91  92  93  94**°

*Typically tight and closed-in when young, yet full of promise, these curranty and well-oaked wines seem to age slowly and with a certain firmly structured refinement; they are among the top tier of California Cabernets*

### Chardonnay

86**  87*  88  89**  **90**°  91  92  93  94  95

*Sophisticated aromas of toasty oak and crisp apples remind some of French Burgundies, and the ample acidity that adds firmness to the wine's backbone follows suit, while also making it a little on the hard, unyielding side in some vintages*

### Zinfandel

81**  82***  83**  84  85**  **86**°°  87  **88**°  89  **90**°  91
**93  94**°  **95**°

*Tight in the Burgess mold, these slowly unfolding, berryish, and richly oaked wines are among the firmest and best-aging Zinfandels; recent vintages have needed more fruit*

RAYMOND BURR VINEYARDS  *(J. Pedroncelli Winery)*  A well-known actor best remembered for his role as lawyer Perry Mason, Raymond Burr was living part-time in the Dry Creek Valley, where he had developed a small vineyard with partner Robert Benevides. Burr's favorite varieties, Cabernet Sauvignon and Cabernet Franc, take up most of the vineyard, but a small sector was given over to classic Port varieties. Burr, who passed away before his first wines from the 1990 vintage were ready for the market, had arranged to have his wines produced by his neighbor Jim Pedroncelli. The wines include 1,000 cases of Cabernet Sauvignon and a few hundred cases of Vintage Port. The Cabernet, blended with Cabernet Franc, was aged for two years in oak, two years in the bottle before leaving the winery. Future vintages of Cabernet will consist of about 1,500 cases.

BUTTONWOOD FARM WINERY   *Santa Barbara 1989*   Converting a portion of their cattle and horse ranch into organic gardens and vineyards, the Williams family planted 40 acres to Sauvignon Blanc and Cabernet Sauvignon along with lesser amounts of Merlot, Cabernet Franc, Semillon, and Marsanne. Moving cautiously into winemaking, the owners built a small hilltop winery in 1989. The winemaking focus is on Sauvignon Blanc, Marsanne, Merlot, and Cabernet Franc. Total production has yet to top 2,000 cases. Both Merlot and Sauvignon Blanc have rated.

BYINGTON WINERY & VINEYARD   *Santa Cruz 1989*   On hillside property between Los Gatos and Boulder Creek, William Byington, owner of Byington Steel, has developed a chateaulike winery and visitors complex. The facility was completed in time for the 90 harvest, but from 87 through 89 Byington made wines from purchased grapes in rented space. The first vintages consisted of Chardonnay, Cabernet, Pinot Noir from Napa Valley, and Fumé Blanc from Monterey. In the mid-1990s Byington decided to emphasize Estate Bottled Chardonnay and Pinot Noir, along with Cabernet Sauvignon from a neighbor's vineyard in the Santa Cruz Mountains. Merlot from Sonoma and other varietals from the Central Coast region round out the line. To date, quality record has been erratic. Steve Devitt, who helped place Signorello on the wine map, was hired in 1998 to oversee winemaking. Annual production remains at 10,000 cases.

DAVIS BYNUM WINERY   *Sonoma 1975*   After operating a storefront winery in Berkeley for a decade, Bynum moved to his present location in the Russian River Valley area, where he expanded production. The line has steadied at 23,000 cases a year and consists primarily of Pinot Noir, Chardonnay, and Fumé Blanc. Today, most of the wines are made from Sonoma County vineyards owned by shareholders in the winery. In its early history the winery enjoyed success with Zinfandel and Fumé Blanc. In recent years it has achieved some distinction with Pinot Noir. Bynum's Chardonnay has been consistently average, except for the occasional higher rankings earned by the Reserve-type bottlings. After many years of erratic performances, the winery hired Gary Farrell as winemaker in 86, and he brought stability to the brand. Today, Bynum's top-of-the-line wines carry either the Reserve or Limited Release designations and account for 20% of the total output. To produce Pinot Noir, the winery uses relatively small, 1/2-ton capacity fermenters, which are said to facilitate punching down and extraction during fermentation. Cabernet Sauvignon, Merlot, Gewurztraminer, Zinfandel, and "Eclipse," a red meritage-style wine round out the roster.

**Pinot Noir**

(Limited Reserve)   83°   84°   85   86°   87°   **88°**   89°   **90**   91   92   **93**   **94**

*Light cherry fruit, moderate oak, medium body, and herbal-toned in some years*

BYRON VINEYARD & WINERY   *Santa Barbara 1984*   Byron Ken Brown, better known as Ken Brown, was the first winemaker at Zaca Mesa. After six crushes, he formed a small corporation and moved a few miles north in the Santa Maria Valley to establish this winery. The winery grew quickly to the 15,000-case level, with Chardonnay, Sauvignon Blanc, and Pinot Noir representing over 80% of the total. Small amounts of Cabernet Sauvignon and Pinot Noir Blanc were added to the line. However, the partnership began to weaken, and in early 90 the winery was sold to the Robert Mondavi family, with Brown remaining in charge. Byron currently owns 125 acres of vineyards, with Chardonnay (65) and Cabernet (24) predominating.

Mondavi inherited a winery with an interesting, if uneven, track record. In recent vintages Byron's Reserve Chardonnays have ranked among the best from the Central Coast, and on occasion the Reserve Pinot Noir rises above average. One of the most consistent of all Byron wines is the Sauvignon Blanc, which tends to be soft and round, yet can be perfectly balanced with layered flavors and brisk acidity. At its finest, Byron's Sauvignon Blancs are ° gems. Annual production is moving closely toward the 50,000 case level, with Chardonnay representing 40% of the total. Byron's long-term prospects for Pinot Noir and Chardonnay are looking really bright with the Mondavi acquisition of the 670-acre Sierra Madre Vineyard, once the source of many outstanding wines from a half-dozen other wineries within the area. A red Rhone blend (Syrah, Grenache) is in the works, and a crisp, highly promising Pinot Gris is off to a great start.

### Chardonnay

(regular bottling)  86  87  88  89°  90°  91°°  93°  94  **95°** **96°**

(Reserve)  86°°  87°°  88  89°°  **90°°°**  **92°°°**  **93°°°**  **94°°** **95°**

*Oaky, appley, fully expressed but not always pretty; the Reserve has been bigger, richer, fruitier and even more successful*

### Pinot Noir

(regular bottling)  **84°°**  85  86  **88°°**  **89**  90°  9ʹ4  92  9ʹ3 94  9ʹ3  **96°**

(Reserve)  **86°**  87  **88°**  89  90  **91°°**  **92°**  **93°°**  **94°**

*Sometimes rich, supple, complex, balanced, sometimes less so; the Reserve exhibits admirable fruit, range, depth, and velvety texture*

---

CA' DEL SOLO  *(Bonny Doon Vineyard)*  This label is being used by Randall Grahm for a line of Italian-type wines. In the early goings he was bottling two reds, Barbera and a blend called "Big House Red." Also in the lineup are several white wines, including a bone-dry Malvasia Bianca. Currently rounding out the line is a high-priced eclectic white blend called "Il Pescatore" intended, as the name implies, to accompany seafood. Sales of Big House Red (predominantly Barbera and Carignane) have exceeded 25,000 cases a year, and Il Pescatore is holding steady at 6,000 cases. Labeled "Il Fiasco," newcomer Sangiovese is beginning to attract a following. New to the team are Dolcetto and Freisa.

---

CAFARO CELLARS  *Napa 1988*  Well-known winemaker and consulting enologist Joe Cafaro added his own label to his impressive résumé in 86. Cabernet Sauvignon and Merlot are the primary wines offered by Cafaro, who has made wines for Chappellet Vineyards, Keenan Winery, Acacia Winery, and Sinskey, as well as working with numerous other brands on a part-time basis. Cafaro's Cabernets and Merlots are made in part from grapes grown by Hess Collection and Spottswoode. Using only Nevers oak barrels, Cafaro ages both reds for about 18 months. To date, an average production consists of 1,000 cases of Cabernet Sauvignon and 1,000 cases of Merlot. A Reserve Cabernet Sauvignon (300 cases) has recently been added. In the late 1990s Cafaro also began developing his own 14-acre vineyard in the southern sector of Stags Leap District.

### Cabernet Sauvignon

**86°°°**  **87°°**  **88°°**  89  **90°°°**  91°  92°  93°  94  95°

*Keen focus, round and deep fruit, handsome oak all contribute to this superb wine*

### Merlot

**86°°**  **87°°°**  **88°°**  **89°°**  **90°°°**  91°  **92°°**  **93°°**  94  95°

*An unqualified success in the deep, ageworthy style exhibited by Cafaro's Cabernet Sauvignon.*

CAIN VINEYARDS *Napa 1983* After selling his electronics business, Jerry Cain purchased a 540-acre parcel along the Mayacamas Mountain Range in 80. Over the next few years the terraced vineyards were planted with 84 acres of the five Bordeaux red varieties. The stunning winemaking facility and home, located close to a ridgetop overlooking St. Helena, were completed in 85. Forced to make wines in the first vintages entirely from purchased grapes, Cain Cellars was a little slow out of the gate, but when it tapped its own vineyards in 85, making both a Cabernet Sauvignon and a proprietary blend, "Cain Five," the winery made heads turn. In 86, Cain turned out attractively styled Merlot. Usually blended with 10% Cabernet Sauvignon and 5% Cabernet Franc, Cain Merlot captures the grape's sought-after aroma and suppleness in most vintages.

In 91 Jim Meadlock, founder of the computer company Intergraph and until that year Cain's silent partner, became the winery's sole owner. He decided to revamp the line and emphasize "Cain Five." The winery soon dropped Cabernet Sauvignon and the often-praised Merlot from its line. Chardonnay from the Carneros region was dropped, but an attractive wine called "Sauvignon Musque" is holding steady at 1,200 cases. Its primary wines are "Cain Five," which will peak at 6,000 cases a year, and "Cain Cuvée," blended from the same varieties but made in a lighter style, which is heading for a maximum of 8,500 cases per year.

### Cabernet Sauvignon

(Cain Cuvée) 82 **83°** **84°** **85°°°** **86°** **87°** **88°** 89 91 92 **93** 94 **95**

*An attractive mix of curranty fruit and sweet oak is seasoned with background notes of herbs and mint in a wine that is generally medium in depth and moderately tannic; in strong vintages, it seems capable of aging for five years or so*

### Cain Five

**85°°** **86°°** **87°** 90 **91°°** **93°** 94

*Seemingly a little richer and a bit stiffer-structured than the Cabernet Sauvignon, this blended wine combines currants and hints of berries with creamy oak, in a style that appears to promise substantial improvement with extended bottle age; 88 and 89 were not made*

CAKEBREAD CELLARS *Napa 1973* In the late 60s Jack Cakebread was operating the family auto-repair business in Oakland, studying photography with Ansel Adams, and working as a professional photographer himself. In 71, on a two-week assignment in the Napa Valley to illustrate a wine book, he suddenly decided to buy 60 acres and a house in the Rutherford area. A 22-acre vineyard was planted with Cabernet Sauvignon, Sauvignon Blanc, and Chardonnay. Though he made wines in 73, Cakebread had intended to sell most of his grapes, but the general slump in grape prices in 75–76 pushed him further into winemaking. By 78, the winemaking facility was enlarged, and Cakebread Cellars began growing to its present 45,000-case-a-year capacity. Vineyard holdings were expanded to 75 acres, including the major planting of Cabernet Sauvignon on their Hill Ranch on the western edge of the valley. The Chardonnays, made in part from Carneros District grapes, are barrel-fermented. In the early 90s, Cakebread began a four-year program to totally replant its phylloxera-ridden 75-acre vineyard and, as a result now has enough Sauvignon Blanc and Cabernet to supply its own needs.

Cakebread was among the first to produce barrel-fermented Sauvignon Blancs aged *sur lie* and imbued with French oak character. The better-balanced Sauvignon Blancs merit **°°** , but overall Cakebread's Sauvignon Blancs have earned fairly consistent **°** rankings. In the mid-80s, Cakebread added a Rutherford Reserve Cabernet Sauvignon to accompany its regular Napa Valley Cabernet Sauvignon, Chardonnay, and Sauvignon Blanc. Zinfandel made from the Howell Mountain appellation has returned to the roster after being dropped in 83. With its Oakville vineyard entirely replanted and with new vineyards in the Carneros District in production, Cakebread had added Merlot, Pinot Noir, and Syrah to its lineup.

### Cabernet Sauvignon

(Napa Valley)　76°　77　78°　79　80°　81°　82　83°　**84°**
**85°°**　86°　**87°**　**88**　**89°**　**90°**　**91°**　92　**93°**　**94**　**95°**

(Reserve)　**84°°**　**85°**　**86°**　**87**　**88°**　**89°**　**93°**　**94**

*Ripe cherries and hints of currants, lots of sweet oak, and plenty of tannin; sometimes tar and herbs are evident as well*

### Chardonnay

(regular bottling)　86　87　88°　89　90　91°　92　93　94　95
96

(Reserve)　86　87°　89°°　90　91°

*Always ripe and oaky, but frequently lacking adequate fruit for the wine's size*

---

CALE CELLARS *Sonoma 1991* Michael Cale earned fairly decent marks for his first vintages of Chardonnay from the Sangiacomo Vineyard in the Carneros District. He has recently expanded his roster by adding three wines from the Kunde Estate—Chardonnay, Barbera, and Zinfandel. Erich Russell of Rabbit Ridge serves as Cale's consulting winemaker. Carneros Pinot Noir is a recent addition

---

CALERA WINE COMPANY *San Benito 1976* Owner Josh Jensen came to winemaking by the unlikely route of Yale and Oxford. Fascinated by French wines, he spent two years working the harvests in Burgundy and the Rhone Valley. In 72, determined to specialize in California Pinot Noir, he began searching for a site whose soil was thin and overlying limestone, like that of the Côte d'Or, and in 74 he ended up in the hills of the Gavilan Mountains near Hollister. A lime kiln had been built there around 1900 (*calera* is Spanish for lime kiln). The nature of the soil justified planting 24 acres to Pinot Noir. Three microclimates near the peak were identified, and have since always been treated individually. They are the Jensen Vineyard (14 acres), Reed Vineyard (5 acres), and Selleck Vineyard (5 acres). A rock-crushing facility on the property was converted into a gravity-feed winery, and in 78 Jensen made 700 cases total, all in half bottles.

Serving as his own winemaker for the early vintages, Jensen established a traditional regime. Using small open-top fermenters, he ferments with the natural, native airborne yeast, including a high percentage of stems and, during the fermentation, whole uncrushed berries. After a long, warm fermentation, the wines are clarified by racking and egg-white fining. In 84, Jensen planted a fourth Pinot Noir vineyard, the 14-acre Mills Vineyard. Jensen also buys Santa Barbara grapes and produces Pinot Noir labeled "Central Coast."

Always barrel-fermented and almost always an adventure to taste, Calera Chardonnays originate in two appellations. The estate or Mount Harlan Vineyard contains 6 acres planted in 84. The first vintage offered was 87. A second bottling is from the Central Coast area. Viognier, also first made in 87, is the third varietal offered. With 2 acres planted to Viognier in 83, Calera was among the first wineries to succeed with this difficult-to-grow Rhone variety. The vineyard has since been expanded to 5 acres. When his 47-acre estate vineyard reaches full maturity, Jensen envisions leveling off production at 20,000 cases a year. Based on its performance to date, Calera deserves a place as one of the genuine leaders in the emergence of Pinot Noir.

### Chardonnay

(Central Coast)　84　85°　86　87　88°　90°°　91°　92°　93°
94°　**95°**　**96**

(Mount Harlan)　87°°°　89°°　**91°**　92°　93　94　95

*Both wines are marked by extensive reliance on rich oak, but the greater depth of the estate wine handles its heavier oak better than the less complete fruit of Calera's high-volume wine*

### Pinot Noir

(Reed) 79•• 81• 82• 84• **85••** **86•** **87•** **88••** 8̶9̶
**90•** 91 **92•** 93

(Selleck) 79•• 8̶0̶ 81• 82••• **84•••** **85••** **86•••** **89•**
92 **93••**

(Jensen) 79• 8̶0̶ 81• 82•• 83 85••• 86••• 87•• 88•
90• 91 92 **93•** **94•**

(Mills) 86• 87• 88• 90• 91 **93** **94**

*From the mid-8os onward, this group of ripe, rich, complex, supple wines has set the standard for California Pinot Noir; their balance and underlying tannins help contribute to their considerable aging potential*

### Viognier

90•• 91• 92••• 93•• 94•• **95•••** 96• 97•

*Arguably California's finest Viognier, these wines are full of fruit and carry complexing notes suggestive of hardwoods and dried flowers*

CALLAWAY VINEYARD & WINERY *Riverside 1974* The long-departed founder, Ely Callaway, one-time president of Burlington Industries, might not recognize his old Temecula winery and vineyards today. Hiram Walker bought the property in 82 and set the winery on a fast-paced expansion course, quickly abandoning all attempts to produce red wines over the next several years and concentrating instead on whites. Today, one proprietary wine, the "Calla-Lees" Chardonnay, represents half of the winery's total production. Made without any oak aging and instead aged *sur lie*, Calla-Lees quickly became a sales success. Other wines made today are Sauvignon Blanc (slightly sweet), Fumé Blanc (dry-finished, oak-aged), Chenin Blanc, Pinot Gris, Viognier, and Mourvedre. Land controlled by the winery now totals 720 acres, with 500 planted to Chardonnay alone. Cabernet Sauvignon returned to the lineup in 89, made in a simple fruity style. Close to 15,000 cases of Cabernet are bottled. Callaway is moving toward a maximum annual output of 250,000 cases.

### Chardonnay

85• 86 87 88 89 90 9̶1̶ 94

*Tropical and floral qualities on the simple and fruity side even when successful*

### Viognier

93 94• 95 96

*Smaller, floral toned wines*

CAMBRIA WINERY *Santa Barbara 1988* Jess Jackson, owner of Kendall-Jackson, bought Chardonnay grapes from several vineyards in order to keep pace with the demand for his Chardonnay in the 80s. One of his major suppliers was the Tepusquet Vineyard, a 2,000-acre ranch in the Santa Maria Valley. In 88 Jackson bought the lion's share (the Robert Mondavi Winery bought the rest) of Tepusquet, and now has 1,200 acres planted, 1,000 to Chardonnay and 200 to Pinot Noir. Having built a winery on the property, Jackson is using Cambria as the primary brand for Santa Barbara–grown Chardonnay and Pinot Noir. He also has retained the rights to the Tepusquet name. Located 12 miles southwest of Santa Maria, the 84,000-square-foot winemaking facility was operating by late 90. It has a capacity of 100,000 cases a year. Cambria's Reserve Chardonnays show lots of depth. In addition to Pinot Noir from "Julia's Vineyard," Cambria has been making limited quantities of Syrah, Sangiovese, Reserve Chardonnay and Reserve Pinot.

### Chardonnay

(Katherine's Vineyard) 86• 88• 89• 90 91• 93•• 94 95
(Reserve) 88••• 89•• 91• 92•• 93•• 94 **95••**

*Appley, somewhat citrusy from ample balancing acidity, toasty oak, a bit obvious in
style but pleasing; the Reserve is uncommonly rich*

**Pinot Noir**

(Julia's Vineyard)    88    **89°**    91    9̶2̶    94°    95    **96°**

(Reserve)    **92°**    **93°**    94

*Ripe, sometimes herbal, full-bodied and generally soft-textured*

---

CAMELOT VINEYARDS    *Santa Barbara 1993*    Another member of the Kendall Jackson
family of wineries, Camelot is based in the Santa Maria Valley but draws from
vineyards throughout the Central Coast region. Initial vintages of attractive, partially barrel-fermented Chardonnay were from Santa Barbara County. Made predominantly from vineyards located in San Luis Obispo, Camelot's Cabernet
Sauvignon is styled to emphasize fruit and youthful approachability. The first several vintages of Camelot have been produced at Cambria Winery, a sister winery
which also bottles its own Chardonnay from Camelot Vineyards. Production is
growing toward 25,000 cases.

---

CANEPA VINEYARD    *Sonoma 1991*    The Canepa family, owners of a popular gourmet
food and wine shop in Mill Valley, have owned a 16-acre vineyard in the Alexander Valley since the mid-70s. For many years they sold their grapes to several producers, including the Robert Pecota Winery, which bottled their Chardonnay as a
vineyard-designated wine for several vintages. In 91 Helen Turley was hired as
winemaker and produced about 400 cases of Canepa Chardonnay. Phylloxera
devastated Canepas's vineyard and wine production was interrupted after the 93
vintage, but wine was made from Gauer Vineyard grapes in 94 and 95.

**Chardonnay**

91°    92    93    94°    95

*Regardless of winemaker, the vineyard has offered mixed blessings from year to year;
better vintages balance fruit with oak and firm acid*

---

CANYON ROAD CELLARS    *Sonoma 1990*    A secondary line of varietals produced by
Geyser Peak, Canyon Road wines are generally priced lower than those of Geyser
Peak. Made partly from vineyards belonging to the Trione family, former owners
of Geyser Peak, the line consists of Chardonnay, Sauvignon Blanc, Semillon,
Cabernet Sauvignon, and Merlot. The Chardonnay is aged entirely in stainless
steel and bottled a few months after the harvest. The Cabernet is blended with
Cabernet Franc and aged briefly in small oak barrels. Total output is 200,000
cases, 50% being Chardonnay.

---

CARDINALE    *(Kendall-Jackson Winery)*    When first made in the mid-1980s, Cardinale
represented Kendall-Jackson's one and only proprietary red Meritage. By 1990
Cardinale was elevated to the status of a stand-alone label. Charles Thomas, ex-
Robert Mondavi Winery enologist, was brought in to take charge. Made from hillside vineyards in Napa and Sonoma, Cadinale is usually aged for two years in new
French oak chateau barrels. Production of Cardinale is likely to increase now that
it has a home in Oakville, where Mr. Jackson built a 50,000-case-capacity winery
on the site originally known as Robert Pepi Winery.

**Cardinale**

83    84°    **85°**    **86°**    **87°°**    **88°**    89    **90°°**    **91°**    **92°**    **93°**
**95°°**

*This mix of Cabernet Sauvignon (50% to 70% depending on vintage), Merlot and
Cabernet France is ripe, full-bodied, supple underneath and tannic at the front; it
should age well for up to 10–12 years.*

---

CARMENET VINEYARD    *Sonoma 1982*    Owned and managed by Chalone, Inc.,
Carmenet is a picturesque winery perched high in the eastern hills above the

Sonoma Valley. It was intended to produce Bordeaux-style red and white wine blends. Along steep terraced hillsides, 66 acres are planted to Cabernet Sauvignon, Cabernet Franc, and Merlot. With vineyard maturity, Carmenet grows all of the red varieties needed for its 10,000-case production goal. The winery was designed to replicate the winemaking conditions and to encourage the same winemaking practices traditional in Bordeaux. During the crush, the red wines from 15 separate blocks are handled separately. In the spring the master blend is composed, and the blend is then barrel-aged for two years. Racking is the primary clarification method and is strictly handled barrel to barrel. Carmenet was one of the first companies to dig into the hillsides and create aging caves.

Carmenet's red wine roster now features four bottlings. "Moon Mountain Estate Meritage" (mostly Cabernet Sauvignon and Cabernet Franc) is viewed as the winery's signature wine. It is joined by another Meritage red named "Vin de Garde," meaning a wine for aging, which this firm, tannic mountain wine certainly has been. At the opposite style is "Dynamite Cabernet," made in a relatively early-maturing style and aimed toward the restaurant trade. The fourth is a limited-bottling of Estate Cabernet Franc, which has much more depth and flavor than one usually encounters in this varietal. A White Meritage from Paragon Vineyard in the Edna Valley and a barrel-fermented Carneros Chardonnay from Sangiacomo Vineyard lead the white wine list. Old Vine Zinfandel was added in the late 90s. With these wines Carmenet's total production has reached 30,000 cases a year.

### Cabernet Sauvignon

(Estate)  82°°  83°°°  84°°  85°  86°  87°  88°  89  90°  91°  93°

*Capable of offering deep and broad fruit, suggestive of currants and cherries always enriched by obvious oak, the wine has become exceptionally tannic and unyielding in recent vintages, sometimes at the expense of fruit*

(Dynamite)  91  92°  93  94  95

*Lighter than the Estate but still tough, it has lacked sufficient fruit in some vintages*

CARNEROS CREEK WINERY  *Napa 1972*  This winery has made a major contribution to the improved quality of California Pinot Noir and has played a vital role in the development of the Carneros appellation. Native San Franciscan Francis Mahoney became interested in wine, and particularly Pinot Noir, while working as a clerk in a wine retail shop. In the late 60s he studied enology at U.C. Davis and in 73, with his former employer Balfour Gibson joining him as a partner, Mahoney purchased 30 acres in the Carneros and planted 10 of them to Pinot Noir. Over the next several vintages Carneros Creek made a variety of wines from purchased grapes, including Amador County Zinfandels in a late harvest style. It was not until the 76 Pinot Noir was released that the winery signaled its commitment to that varietal.

A fascinating and potentially far-reaching viticultural experiment is being conducted jointly by Carneros Creek Winery and U.C. Davis. Beginning in 74, they selected 20 different clones of Pinot Noir, and planted a few vines to each on 9 acres at the winery. In 80 they began harvesting each clone, making wines under identical conditions, and monitoring the quality level achieved. Beginning in 87, the winery added a "Signature Reserve" limited-edition Pinot Noir, and this top-of-the-line bottling is now offered along with a mid-level Carneros version and a light-bodied, early-maturing Pinot Noir labeled "Fleur de Carneros." Today production of the three Pinot Noirs approaches 30,000 cases a year. When a new 110-acre Carneros vineyards planted to a variety of clones reaches full production, Carneros Creek expects to increase its Pinot Noir output to 75,000 cases. The winery still has 12 acres of Chardonnay, which yields an Estate Chardonnay that is 100% barrel-fermented and Fleur de Carneros Chardonnay in a fruit-driven style.

**Chardonnay**

86  87°  88  89°  90°°  **91°**  92°  95

*Tending toward the lean, wiry side of the spectrum, the wine succeeds when it man-
ages enough fruit to fill out its frame and balance its oaky, buttery aspects*

**Pinot Noir**

(Carneros)  83°°  84°  **85°°**  86°  87°°  88°  **89°**  **90°**
**91°°**  92°  **93°**  **95°**

(Signature Reserve)  **88°°**  89°  **91°°**  **93°°**  **94°°°**

*Usually moderately rich in oak, and filled with ripe, cherryish fruit, backed by suf-
ficient tannins for backbone and mid-term aging potential; the Reserve is ripe, supple, high in rich oak*

CARTLIDGE & BROWNE  *(Stratford)*  In 81 Tony Cartlidge, a wine broker in Napa Valley,
with financial help from Glen Browne, a friend and neighbor, ventured into winemaking and produced 1,000 cases of Napa Valley Chardonnay. The next year, they
teamed up with others to develop the Stratford label (see entry) with the stipula-
tion that Cartlidge & Browne would continue to be used for Chardonnay. Over
recent vintages, Cartlidge & Browne Chardonnays have become less exciting than
some of the early vintages, but remain acceptable for the price.

CASA NUESTRA VINEYARDS  *Napa 1979*  In the early 70s, San Francisco attorney Gene
Kirkham and his wife, Cody, purchased an old farm and 8 acres of vineyards south
of Calistoga. After renovating the house on weekends, the family moved to Napa
Valley. By 79 they had opened a winery and begun specializing in Chenin Blanc,
made from the 10-acre estate vineyard. Over the years, the Chenin Blanc has always been kept in stainless-steel tanks and the residual sugar has been below 1%.
Occasionally, a *Botrytis*-affected Chenin Blanc is made and marketed as "Dorado."
In 86 the Kirkhams bought 4 acres of Cabernet Franc located next door to their
vineyard and began making a varietal Cabernet Franc. In an average vintage, Casa
Nuestra makes 800 cases of Chenin Blanc and 400 cases of Cabernet Franc. Just
about all of the wine is sold direct by the owners, either at the tasting room or via
a mailing list.

CASTALIA WINERY  *Sonoma 1993*  Owner Terry Bering is the winemaker for Rochioli
Vineyards, one of our favorite Pinot Noir producers whose grapes are much in demand. In 1993, using a corner of Rochioli's winery, he launched his own brand,
which has always featured only one wine, Pinot Noir from Rochioli Vineyard.
Bering makes 200–300 cases a year. Quality can be very high.

CASTLE VINEYARDS  *Sonoma Valley 1994*  Renaissance man Vic McWilliams is a phar-
macist who was a successful home winemaker for years. He was growing grapes
for more than a decade before founding his small winery. To date he has regularly
offered small batches of Chardonnay, Zinfandel, Merlot, and Pinot Noir. Experiments with Cinsault encouraged McWilliams to plant other Rhone varieties in his
50-acre vineyard located east of the town of Sonoma. He sees 2,000 cases a year
as the winery's optimum level.

CASTELLETTO  *(Mount Palomar Winery)*  In the Temecula district, Mount Palomar developed 5 acres to Sangiovese in the late 1980s and created Castelletto as its label
for a modest quantity of wines from Italian varieties. To date a few hundred cases
of Sangiovese and Cortese, a rare white variety, have been bottled. The Sangiovese shows good potential.

CASTORO CELLARS  *San Luis Obispo 1983*  Having worked in the cellars for several
wineries, Niels Udsen branched out to start his own brand in 83. All of his wines
originate either in the Paso Robles appellation or other regions in San Luis

Obispo County. Now at the 15,000-case level, the winery is emphasizing three varietals—Zinfandel, both White and Red, Chardonnay, and Cabernet Sauvignon. Limited amounts of Sauvignon Blanc and Pinot Noir are occasionally produced. Overall, the wines have been more than acceptable, but the winery is capable of turning out an excellent value from time to time. The winery's ultimate production goal is 25,000 cases per year.

CAYMUS VINEYARDS   *Napa Valley 1972*   Longtime Napa Valley grape-grower Charlie Wagner had been selling most of his grapes before venturing into winemaking in 72. At the time, the family simply converted an old barn into a functioning winery. Produced from their 65-acre vineyard situated in Rutherford, Caymus's estate-bottled Cabernets from 73 to 86 established themselves as benchmarks of Napa Valley Cabernet. The estate vineyard contains 40 acres of Cabernet Sauvignon, but its annual production averages only about 4,000 cases. In the 75 vintage, Caymus offered its first Special Selection Cabernet, a pick-of-the-bunch bottling given extended wood aging. It averaged 500 to 600 cases a year until in the late 80s it grew to about 1,000. Randy Dunn served as winemaker for Caymus from 75 to 82, developing a sufficiently outstanding reputation to form his own winery. However, Chuck Wagner, the owners' son, has performed well as winemaker since Dunn's departure, and now supervises the operation.

In 84, blessed with an excellent reputation and a growing demand for Cabernet, Caymus added a Napa Valley bottling made from grapes purchased within Napa Valley, labeled "Napa Valley Cuvée." Beginning with the 87 vintage, Caymus has been combining its estate-grown Cabernet with its Napa Valley Cuvée, and the result is a single "Napa Valley" bottling. Caymus was among the first to produce a blush wine; named "Oeil de Perdrix," its debut vintage, made in a lively, dry style, was 75. Its last vintage was 92.

Even though they are growers, the Wagners preferred buying Zinfandel from old hillside vineyards to produce Zinfandels that were ° performers. Other Caymus wines produced today include Sauvignon Blanc and a proprietary white blend, "Conundrum." As growers, the Wagners were proud of the plaudits earned by their home-grown Pinot Noir Special Selection, made from grapes planted in a region assumed to be inhospitably warm. In the 1990s, Caymus established Mer & Soleil (see entry) for big-time Central Coast Chardonnay and is developing property in Russian River Valley for Pinot Noir and southern Monterey County for Syrah. Annual production for all Caymus wines is steady at 55,000 cases. In recent years both Pinot Noir and Zinfandel have disappeared from the line.

### Cabernet Sauvignon

(Special Selection)   78°°   79°°°   **80**°°°   81°°   82°°   **83**°°
**84**°°°   **85**°°°   **86**°°°   **87**°°°   **88**°   89°   **90**°°   **91**°°°   **92**°°
**94**°

*Almost universally ranked among the top few Cabernets made in California, the wine is consistently ripe, broad, deep, supple, intense, loaded with rich, creamy oak, and backed up by a decade's worth of tannin. If too weighty and viscous ever to achieve much refinement or elegance, it still manages to remain well balanced and highly inviting*

### Cabernet Sauvignon

(Estate)   72°°   73°°°   **74**°°°   75°°   76°°   77°   78°   79°°
**80**°°°   81°°   **82**°°   **83**°°   **84**°°°   **85**°°   **86**°°   **87**°°   **88**°
**89**°   **90**°   91°   **92**°   **93**°   **94**°   **95**°°

*Only slightly less rich and broad than the Special Selection, although decidedly less oaky, this set of wines, selling at near-average prices for Napa Valley Cabernets, has consistently been among the best values. Its curranty, spicy, and rich character is firmed up by noticeable but never harsh tannin, and the wine tends to age exceptionally well*

## Pinot Noir

(Special Selection)    81°°    82°°    **83°°**    **84°°**    **85°°**    **86°°**    **87°°**
**88°**    **89°**    90

*Ripe black-cherry character is enriched by pushy oak in this fairly deep and velvety-textured wine; like the upscale Cabernet, this one holds little in check and turns out to be almost as good*

## Zinfandel

80    81    82°    83°    84°    **86°**    **87°**    **88**    **89°°**    **90°**    **91**
**92°°**

*Usually medium-full-bodied, with medium-depth berryish fruit and moderate oak richness; it has tannin for several years of bottle aging*

CECCHETTI–SEBASTIANI CELLAR    *Sonoma 1985*    Don Sebastiani decided to return to the wine business and eventually started this brand with his brother-in-law, Roy Cecchetti. Cecchetti-Sebastiani began by having Cabernet Sauvignon, Sauvignon Blanc, and Pinot Noir custom-made from purchased grapes, adding Chardonnay to the line in the second vintage. As production levels off at 6,000 cases a year, they are making Cabernet from Sonoma County, the two white varietals from Napa Valley, and Pinot Noir from Santa Barbara County. Don Sebastiani is now involved with the larger family winery, but Roy Cecchetti remains at the helm. In 88, the brand was extended to imported extra-virgin olive oil; sales of olive oil grew quickly to 2,000 cases a year. To market a much larger line of low-priced varietals that would not be confused with Sebastiani Vineyard, the partners created the "Pepperwood Grove" brand. Initial output of this line of wines was 20,000 cases.

CEDAR BROOK CELLARS    *(Codera Wine Co.)*    Over its first several years this negociant label was used for a line of Napa Valley wines, primarily Cabernet Sauvignon and Chardonnay. In recent years Pinot Noir with a California appellation has been added.

CEDAR MOUNTAIN WINERY    *Alameda 1990*    Owner and winemaker Earl Ault purchased a small Livermore Valley vineyard in 1988 and replanted it to Cabernet Sauvignon and Chardonnay. By 1991 Ault was producing estate-grown Cabernet Sauvignon and Chardonnay and was purchasing grapes from Amador County for the production of vintage port. The annual output of 1,200 cases will level off at 2,000 cases.

CHALK HILL WINERY    *Sonoma 1980*    In 74, attorney Fred Furth bought a 650-acre ranch and began developing 260 of those acres to vineyards. The vineyards fall within the Chalk Hill Viticultural Area. The winery itself used the name Donna Maria Vineyards for its primary wines, and Chalk Hill for its second-label wines until 86, when Chalk Hill became the only name used. The production grew quickly to the present 60,000-case level, all grown on the estate. Chardonnay accounts for over 50% of the total output, with the other half equally divided between Sauvignon Blanc and Cabernet Sauvignon. On those occasions when climatic conditions encourage it, the winery makes a late harvest, *Botrytis*-affected Sauvignon Blanc. Merlot and Pinot Gris have recently been bottled. Given the financial commitment of its owner and the location of its vineyards, in our opinion Chalk Hill was a great underachiever of the 80s, offering a decade of not terribly interesting wines. In early 90, Fred Furth hired David Ramey, formerly of Matanzas Creek, as the winemaker. After four vintages, Bill Knuttel replaced Ramey, who is now at Rudd Estate.

## Cabernet Sauvignon

**88**    **89**    **90°**    9⁄    **92**    **93**

*Although mixed in result, the winemaking intent heads toward ripe, solid, and long-aging*

### Chardonnay

| 83 | 84 | 85 | 86 | 87 | 88 | 89 | **90°°** | 91° | 92 | **93°°** | 94 | 95 |

*Under winemaker Ramey, this wine has become deeper, rounder and toastier in both oak and roasted grain lees characteristics*

CHALONE VINEYARD   *Monterey 1960*   Located on a ridge in the hills east of Salinas, with the Pinnacales National Monument as a dramatic backdrop, this much-revered winery has contributed mightily to the present reputation of California wine. The site and the old winery saw several owners come and go until Richard Graff and partner Phil Woodward took over in 69. The vineyard by then covered 32 acres, consisting of Pinot Noir, Chardonnay, Pinot Blanc, and Chenin Blanc. In 72, after making noteworthy vintages of powerful barrel-fermented Chardonnay and rich, often exotic Pinot Noir (the 69 and 71 still rank among the greatest ever), the owners added 50 acres of Chardonnay and 25 acres of Pinot Noir. To cultivate and tend the vines, workers at Chalone have had to truck water in from the valley for irrigation, and it was not until the mid-80s that the facility had electricity. As production grew gradually, Graff and Woodward formed a management company and eventually had 150 private investors involved in Chalone.

In 82, a new facility got under way, aiming to handle a production increase to 12,000 cases in 85. Today, with close to 200 acres planted, the winery is moving toward a goal of 25,000 cases per year. Made from the 125 acres planted, Chardonnay is the mainstay and is produced in a full-blown style—barrel-fermented, and aged in new oak barrels. From its 30 acres of Pinot Noir, Chalone has been making an estate bottling from the newer vines and a Reserve from the old block. Pinot Blanc is barrel-fermented and oak-aged, and Chenin Blanc is barrel-fermented and full-bodied. From 2 1/2 acres planted in the early 80s, Chalone has been making 500 cases of estate Cabernet Sauvignon a year. Gavilan Vineyards (see entry) is a second label used in random fashion for years. Now incorporated, Chalone offers most of its Reserve Pinot Noir bottlings to its stockholders. Chalone, Inc., also owns Carmenet, Acacia and Canoe Ridge Vineyard, and co-owns Edna Valley Vineyards.

### Chardonnay

| 84°°° | 85° | 86 | 88 | 89°° | **90°** | 91 | 92° | 93 | 94 | **95°** |

*Immensely toasty in its combination of charry oak and sur lie yeast-aged character, this wine can be among the best Chardonnays when its fruit measures up to the rest of its personality, but tends to be overdone and overwhelmed when the fruit fails to bring it into balance*

### Pinot Noir

| 73°°° | **78°°°** | 79°° | **80°°°** | 81° | 82° | **83°°** | **84** | **85** | **86°** |
| **88** | 89 | **90** | 91 | **93°** | | | | | |

*Ripe and dense wines of effusive black-cherry and cassis character in the best vintages, they also can turn out poorly in years when the fruit is not as bold as the wine's structure; some of the older wines, including the stunning 73 and the still-strapping 78, continue to show extremely well*

CHAMISAL VINEYARD   *San Luis Obispo 1980*   The 60-acre Chamisal Vineyard owned by the Goss family is the oldest in the Edna Valley. At present, it consists of 52 acres of Chardonnay; the other few acres are planted to Cabernet Sauvignon and Pinot Noir. Beginning with its first vintage of Chardonnay made in 79, the winery was highly erratic until the 86 vintage, when the winemaking team changed. Since then, the quality has steadied. Most of the 3,000 cases made each year consist of its big, ripe, oak-influenced style of Chardonnay.

CHANDON   *Napa 1973*   This beautiful winery, restaurant, and tourist complex, situated in Yountville, opened in 77 after four years of construction. Chandon was the first French-owned sparkling wine company in California. Its parent Moët-Hennessy owns and operates three producers of Champagne—Moët & Chandon, Ruinart, and Mercier—and when it merged in 87 with Louis Vuitton, its sparkling family was extended to include Veuve Clicquot, Canard Duchêne, and Henriot. The same company also owns Hennessy and Hine Cognac, Christian Dior perfume, Scharffenberger Cellars, and Simi Winery. Napa's Chandon outpost concentrates primarily on three sparkling wines—Brut, Blanc de Noirs, and Reserve. Using the *méthode champenoise,* Chandon prefers multi-vintage blends, adds 20% to 30% of aged Reserve wines from previous harvests, and relies heavily on traditional Champagne varieties, Chardonnay, Pinot Noir, and, to lesser degrees, Pinot Blanc and Pinot Meunier.

From a modest beginning in 77 of 20,000 cases, Chandon quickly exceeded its original target of 100,000 cases. Its vineyard holdings have been augmented considerably and the winery owns 1,600 acres of land with over 1,000 in vineyards. Its biggest vineyard site consists of close to 500 acres in the Carneros. Chandon believes in using hillside-grown grapes in all cuvées and developed 150 acres on Mount Veeder for that purpose. Within sight of the winery west of Yountville, Chandon established 220 acres. In its sparkling wine production, Chandon generally relies on Pinot Noir as a key component. Chandon's Brut, its best-seller, blends Pinot Noir, Chardonnay, and Pinot Blanc in proportions that usually are 65%–25%–10%, respectively. The Blanc de Noirs cuvée is 100% Pinot Noir and has always displayed a reddish hue despite its cool-climate origins. Made in marketable quantity since 88, the Reserve is a Brut cuvée aged for about four years *en tirage,* or twice as long as its two others. "Etoile" represents its long-aged deluxe cuvée. The latest addition is the "Club Cuvée, a long-aged bubbly made from Chardonnay grown on hillside sites.

Overall, for sparkling wine, quality has been admirably well maintained. Chandon's Blanc de Noirs has reached °° levels at times, and its Brut is a frequent ° performer. Occasionally, the Brut in magnum has hit °°° level, with the Reserve often earning °°° reviews. Chandon's annual output is close to 500,000 cases. Future growth is limited to availability of grapes from the Napa Valley appellation. Chandon also owns Shadow Creek, another brand of sparkling wine, made from non-Napa Valley–grown grapes.

CHANSA WINERY    *Santa Barbara 1989*    Owner Kim McPherson was born into a wine-making family. His older brother is Culbertson's winemaker and his father owns Teysha Cellars in Lubbock, Texas. Chansa wines are made from Central Coast appellation grapes and are crushed and fermented in leased space. The winemaking is traditional and typical of a small-scale, one-man operation. The Chardonnay is fermented in oak puncheons and then given extended *sur lie* aging. The Pinot Noir is whole cluster–fermented and punched down by hand. Total production of 1,000 cases is evenly split between Chardonnay and Pinot Noir.

CHAPPELLET VINEYARD    *Napa 1969*    In a rustic setting, this beautiful winery with its unique pyramid design remains something of an enigma to us. In 67, when he was in his early 30s, Donn Chappellet left a highly successful career in the industrial food-vending business to become a vintner in the eastern hills of the Napa Valley. His terraced vineyards cover 110 acres and cling to the steep hillsides up to the 1,700-foot level. The puzzling aspect is that after making such a successful first-ever Cabernet Sauvignon in 69, the winery has rarely fulfilled that early promise. Instead, its Cabernets have been surprisingly erratic, ranging in quality from one of the finest 73s to one of the weakest 74s. On average the winery produces 7,000 cases of Cabernet, which is usually blended with Merlot from its 35 acres.

Chappellet now makes two styles of Cabernets. The Reserve-type is labeled "Signature Selection," and the more readily available, approachable version carries the Pritchard Hill name. Early on Chappellet began making a bone-dry, oak-aged Chenin Blanc, and despite the general decline in that varietal's popularity, the winery continues to enjoy success with its version, producing 5,000–6,000 cases a year. It has also been making Old Vine cuvée from Chenin Blanc grown in the old 15-acre block; this wine is 100% barrel fermented and put through malolactic fermentation. It too has proven popular in the 90s. Chardonnay has been extremely consistent; Chappellet makes it in a barrel-fermented ripe fruit style, but puts only 50% of the wine through malolactic fermentation. A once-delightful Riesling was dropped from the roster after 1988. On rare occasions, Chappellet bottles a Merlot, but only in 500-case quantities when it does. Sangiovese has been planted and Chappellet makes a few hundred cases of a varietal Sangiovese. The winery is functioning at its full capacity of 25,000 cases annually. Recent releases have jumped dramatically in quality.

### Cabernet Sauvignon

69°°°   70°°°   73°°   74   75°   76°   77°   78°   79°   80°
81°   82°   **83°°**   **84°°**   85°   **86**   **87**   **88**   **89**   **90**   **91°**   **92**
**93°**   **94°°**

*After the first several vintages, in which vibrant fruit accompanied the firm, tight structure, this series of wines began to show less intensity from the mid-70s to the present, leaving it more tannic than fruity, and demanding long aging that seems likely to prove unrewarding in weaker years; 94 may be a watershed vintage*

### Chardonnay

86   87   88   89   90°   91°   92°   **94**   **95°**   **96°°**

*Firm, tight wines, lacking fruit intensity and roundness, have turned out low on overall appeal; 95 and 96 look like this wine has a new lease on life*

### Merlot

86   87°   **88**   90   **91**   92°   93   **94**   **95°**

*Often lacking depth to its cherryish fruit, this one succeeds in a few ripe years*

---

CHASSEUR   *Sonoma 1995*   Winemaker Bill Hunter (English for Chasseur) gained experience at Bonny Doon Vineyards, Rombauer, and Chauffe Eau (French for "hot water") before branching out on his own. His specialty is full-bodied, barrel-fermented Chardonnay and stylish Pinot Noir from Russian River Valley. Chasseur wines are aged entirely in new French oak before being bottled without benefit of fining or filtering. Production remains about 500 cases a year. Quality is high.

---

CHATEAU CHEVRE   *Napa 1979*   Former airline pilot Gerry Hazen bought 21 acres in Napa Valley in 73, about a mile south of Yountville along the western edge of the valley. The place was once a goat farm. Hazen contracted with the owner of Franciscan Vineyard to plant 8.5 acres of Merlot under a 25-year agreement to sell his grapes to that winery. When Franciscan was sold, Hazen found himself on his own, and decided to make wine himself. Still, most of his grapes are now sold to Havens Wine Cellers.

It is Merlot that places the winery on the map. The 80 bordered on the spectacular for intensity and richness, only excess tannins holding it back. Blended with Cabernet Franc, the 84 and the 85 showed more restraint and suppleness. The typical aging regime for Merlot is close to two years in French oak and six months in bottle. The winery has produced limited amounts of varietal Cabernet Franc on an experimental basis. Its production of Merlot is close to 600 cases. It disappeared from view for a few years but has remained small and in business.

### Merlot

80°°°   81   82°   **83°**   **85°°**   **86°**   **94°**

*More supple now than in its first vintages, the wine remains ripe in character, with oak and tannins as major elements in its makeup*

---

CHATEAU JULIEN   *Monterey 1982*   Five miles inland from the Monterey Peninsula, Chateau Julien stands next to the main road taking you through the Carmel Valley. Named after and modeled upon châteaux in the St. Julien district of Bordeaux, Chateau Julien has from the start emphasized Merlot and Cabernet Sauvignon, but Chardonnay has always been important. Originally buying grapes from other parts of the Central Coast, it has relied more and more on Monterey County for Chardonnay (both the regular and Reserve are barrel-fermented), as well as for Merlot, Cabernet Sauvignon, and Semillon and Sauvignon Blanc. The latter two go into a proprietary blend called "Platinum." Riesling and Gewurztraminer remain as minor players on the roster. Aged longer than usual in barrel and bottle, a Reserve Cabernet Sauvignon was made in 86 and in 89, turning out to be the most noteworthy versions ever from the Monterey appellation. Great American Wineries, Inc., is the owner of Chateau Julien, and also produces two other brands of wine, Emerald Bay and Garland Ranch (see entries). All told, the facility with its three labels is producing 70,000 cases a year. Chateau Julien itself accounts for an average of 10,000 cases a year. Cabernet Sauvignon/Private Reserve has been successful from time to time.

CHATEAU MONTELENA   *Napa 1972*   Built in 1882, the medieval-looking old stone winery and its vineyard were abandoned or ignored for decades until the present owners acquired the property in early 69. Directed by attorney and general partner Jim Barrett, the owners restored and expanded the winery, and brought the old estate back to life. Rather than create a tourist center, Barrett kept the winery functional and invested in vineyard development. He also made special efforts to locate and buy the best grapes available while his own vineyards were nonbearing. In early 72, Mike Grgich, then an unknown, was hired as winemaker. Under Grgich's direction, the winery made Chardonnay by blending grapes from Napa and the Alexander Valley, and it was the 73 Montelena Chardonnay that won first place in a well-publicized tasting held in Paris in 76. That victory advanced Montelena's reputation, but it also sidetracked its plan to become known as an estate Cabernet producer.

After Grgich departed in 77 to start Grgich Hills, his successor was Jerry Luper, who had gained a solid reputation with Freemark Abbey. The understudy to both Grgich and Luper was Bo Barrett, the owner's son, who was destined to advance to the winemaking position. Luper's final vintage with Montelena was 81, then Bo Barrett took over. In 1978 the winery's 95-acre estate vineyard, containing 72 acres of Cabernet Sauvignon, came into production. From that year onward, Montelena has emphasized its 100% Estate Grown Cabernet. However, until 1991, it continued making two Chardonnays—Napa Valley and Alexander Valley—both of which were often highly regarded. The Alexander Valley version was discontinued, and today the Napa Valley Chardonnay is made from the Oak Knoll area in southern Napa Valley. Over the years Montelena also enjoyed success with Zinfandel, but in the 90s the winery gradually phased Zinfandel out. A Rhone-inspired red blend named St. Vincent has been added. An early bottled, relatively light style of Cabernet is marketed as "Calistoga Cuvee." Montelena's total annual production remains at the 30,000-case peak, with Cabernet Sauvignon steady at 10,000 cases of the Estate and 5,000 cases of the Calistoga Cuvée.

**Cabernet Sauvignon**

| 77°° | 78° | 79°° | 80 | 81 | 82°° | 83 | **84°°** | **85°°°** | **86** |
|------|-----|------|----|----|------|----|----------|-----------|--------|
| **87°°°** | **88** | **89°** | **90** | **91°** | 92 | **93°** | **94°°** | | |

*Ripe, curranty, and black-cherry fruit with occasional leanings toward overripeness, lots of sweet oak, and fairly massive tannins add up to a series of wines that make up in boldness for what they lack in finesse*

**Chardonnay**

| (Napa Valley) | 86° | 87° | 88°° | 89° | 90 | 91 | **92°°** | 93 | **94°** |
|---------------|-----|-----|------|-----|----|----|----------|----|---------|
| 95 | | | | | | | | | |

*Fairly classic in its focus on ripe, balanced appley fruit, with nuances of butter amidst the toasty oak*

CHATEAU NAPA BEAUCANON   *Napa 1986*   Owned by the de Coninck family of Bordeaux, France, the winery is situated 3 miles south of St. Helena, west of the main wine road. De Coninck operates the second-largest négociant firm in Bordeaux, J. Lebegue, headquartered in St. Emilion. After buying the 65-acre Napa Valley estate in 86, the family subsequently purchased another 190 acres, in two parcels. The larger parcel, 117 acres, is located north of St. Helena, and is now planted half to Chardonnay and half to Cabernet Sauvignon, Merlot, and Cabernet Franc. The second parcel, near the town of Napa, is planted predominantly to Chardonnay. The 86 and 87 vintages were made at other wineries (Domaine de Napa, Vichon) pending completion of its own ultramodern facility. From 88 on, the three primary wines—Chardonnay, Cabernet Sauvignon, and Merlot—have all been estate-bottled. Once the winery was completed, the production increased to the desired 45,000- to 50,000-case level. About half is devoted to Chardonnay, with Cabernet Sauvignon at about 15,000 cases, and Merlot around 10,000 cases a year.

CHATEAU POTELLE   *Napa 1985*   Raised in Bordeaux, where their families were involved in wine, owners Jean-Noël and Marketta Fourmeaux du Sartel were sent by the French government in 80 to study the California wine business. They were impressed enough by its opportunities to decide to join in. In 83, they moved to California and soon began blending and bottling wines under their private label. Most of the first few vintages were aged and bottled at Souverain. Their lineup now consists of Cabernet Sauvignon, Chardonnay, Zinfandel, and Sauvignon Blanc.

As the annual output approached 20,000 cases, they decided to make the full commitment by purchasing land and a facility. First, they acquired a 90-acre vineyard on the Silverado Trail of Napa Valley, and developed that site to Cabernet Sauvignon and related Bordeaux grapes. In the same year they purchased the former Vose Vineyard facility and land, amounting to 270 acres. Situated in the Mount Veeder hills, the winery has 48 acres under vine, mainly Chardonnay, Cabernet Sauvignon, and Zinfandel. These Mt. Veeder estate vineyards are responsible for the deluxe VGS label which is made up of Chardonnay (2,000 cases), Zinfandel (2,000 cases), and Cabernet Sauvignon (600–1,000 cases). A line of lower-priced Napa Valley wines made from valley-grown grapes or from Pope Valley consists of Chardonnay (13,000 cases), Sauvignon Blanc (9,000 cases) and Cabernet Sauvignon (3,000 cases). The winery's current 25,000 cases of annual production will be increasing once its new Mount Veeder planting of 25 acres (Zinfandel, Cabernet, and Chardonnay) reaches maturity. Also, a 40-acre vineyard has been developed in Westside Paso Robles. Its first planting phase included Zinfandel (26 acres) and Syrah (14 acres). The follow-up phase will expand the vineyard by 30 acres as the winery establishes more Zinfandel and Syrah and adds Viognier and Tannat.

### Chardonnay VGS

91   **92°**   94

*Trying for a rich, refined style but sometimes low on overall fruitiness*

### Zinfandel VGS

**90°°**   **92°**   **93**   **95°**

*One of the highest-priced Zinfandels in California, it is ripe, deep, and aggressively oaky, and, while entirely likable, it has yet to measure up to its price tag*

CHATEAU ST. JEAN   *Sonoma 1973*   St. Jean was the first ultra-modern, multimillion-dollar winery to be developed in the Sonoma Valley, perhaps in all of Sonoma County. The wines offered immediately justified the attention to detail as the winery quickly built a strong reputation for vineyard-designated, limited-production white wines. Among its several early successes were Chardonnays from the Robert Young Vineyard and the Belle Terre Vineyard, along with Fumé Blancs from several individual vineyards, particularly La Petite Etoile. Before leaving in 90, winemaker Dick Arrowood also helped expand the late harvest category of dessert wines through a range of *Botrytis*-affected Rieslings and Gewurztraminers.

After several vintages of smooth sailing and critical success, by 82 the winery's production had expanded to over 100,000 cases. The first offering of the long-awaited sparkling wine disappointed for quality and value. The founders, table grape growers from the Central Valley, decided to sell in 84, and after a spirited bidding war, the buyer was Suntory, Ltd., of Japan. The owners reinstated Cabernet Sauvignon, which had been discontinued after 81, and they added Merlot, Pinot Noir, and a Reserve Cabernet. An attractive red Meritage, "Cinq Cepages," has also been added. Several other red wines, produced in limited volume, are available at the winery, such as a Reserve Merlot, Pinot Noir, and three Rhone types, Syrah, Mourvedre, and Grenache. St. Jean's red wine program has grown to 50,000 cases a year. The Reserve Cabernets have been impressive, but the Merlots have enjoyed amazing success in the early vintages. After producing an intensely varietal, often pungent style of Fumé Blanc from the independently owned Petite Etoile Vineyard for many years, St. Jean bought the 62-acre vineyard in 88. The St. Jean Vineyard noted on labels refers to the 55-acre vineyard of Sauvignon Blanc and Chardonnay adjacent to the winery. Overall, St. Jean remains an important Chardonnay producer, even though the quality of its red wines now overshadows the whites. However, its deluxe Chardonnay, the Reserve Robert Young Vineyards, can occasionally compete with the best. After selling the sparkling wine facility and getting out of the bubbly wine segment, St. Jean has expanded production of varietals and blends to the 300,000-cask mark. In 1997 it was acquired by Beringer Estates, which has it running smoother than ever.

## Cabernet Sauvignon

(Laurel Glen)   75   76°   77°°

(Glen Ellen)   76   77°   78°

(Wildwood Vineyard)   78°   79   **80°**

(Cinq Cepages)   **90°**   **91°°°**   **92**   **93°°°**   **94°°**

(Reserve)   **87**   **88°°**   **89°**   **90°°**   **91°**

(regular bottling)   85°   **86°**   **87°**   88°   89   **91°**   **92°**   **93°**

*Older wines were typically bold, tannic, briary, alcoholic, and heavily extracted. Some have aged well; none is especially refined. The newer wines are more restrained, still have plenty of weight, and show more black-cherry fruitiness than before*

## Chardonnay

(Sonoma County)   86   87°   88°   89   90   91   92   93   94   95
96

*Crisp, fruity, moderately oaked style, medium depth*

## Chardonnay

(Robert Young)   79°°   80°°°   81°°   82   83°   84°°   85°   86
87°   88°   **90°**   91   92   93   **94°**   95

*Once among the very best Chardonnays, and still quite good. Many older wines have aged very well. The newer wines show somewhat less depth, but the ripe, luscious, tropical-floral-tinged appley fruit, rich oak, and crisp balance remain in evidence*

## Chardonnay

(Belle Terre)   87°   88   90°   91   92   93°   94   95

*A continuing member of the St. Jean line, this bottling has always shown more oak and stiffness than fruit and roundness*

## Merlot

**90°°**   **91°°**   **92°°**   **93°**   94   **95**

*Ripe, black cherry-like fruit is stiffened by tannins yet remains supple underneath; its price so far has made the wine additionally attractive*

CHATEAU SOUVERAIN *Sonoma 1973* Modeled architecturally upon a hop kiln, this handsome facility has survived several dramatic ownership changes. It was built by Pillsbury in the northwestern corner of the Alexander Valley, and named Souverain of Alexander Valley because Pillsbury was operating another winery in Napa Valley called Souverain of Rutherford. When Pillsbury decided to get out of the wine business, the Sonoma County winery was sold in 76 to a partnership of grape-growers and renamed Souverain Cellars. The close to 300 growers owned acreage in Sonoma, Mendocino, and Napa counties. They agreed to use the appellation North Coast for all their wines, but, as it later turned out, they could agree on little else. Annual production approached 500,000 cases of table wine as the undercapitalized winery struggled into the 80s. A good portion of the large facility was rented to other producers and private brands, who made and/or stored wines there. Winemakers left, and by the mid-80s, it became apparent that the facility and the brand were in serious trouble.

In 86, Souverain Cellars was purchased by Wine World, Inc., the wine division of Nestlé, which immediately renamed it and poured millions of dollars into restoration and modernization. The new owners converted the operation into a line of Sonoma County varietal wines. Vineyard sources had to be lined up through lease or other arrangements, and the owners began developing vineyards adjacent to the Colony facility (see entry) they had bought earlier.

By 90, close to 200 acres were under development in the Alexander Valley and Dry Creek Valley. The wines offered are Cabernet Sauvignon, Zinfandel, Merlot, Chardonnay, and Sauvignon Blanc. Zinfandel is made from the Dry Creek Valley appellation, and the Carneros region supplies Chardonnay. All other bottlings are from the Alexander Valley. Both white wines and the Cabernet have been bottled in a Reserve version. Chardonnay and Cabernet Sauvignon represent close to two-thirds of the annual production, which is growing toward a maximum of 250,000 cases. Quality really turned around in the 90s, as Souverain first made giant quality strides with its Carneros Chardonnay and soon with its three primary reds, Dry Creek Zinfandel, and Alexander Valley Merlot and Cabernet Sauvignon. Each red also often represents good value. Experimental-sized batches of Pinot Noir, Syrah, and Rhone blends all show excellent promise.

### Cabernet Sauvignon

(Regular bottling) 87 88 **89** **90°°** **91°°** 92° **93°** **94°°** **95**

(Reserve) **88** **90°** **92** **93°°** **94°°**

*Since 90, these wines have been ripe, fruity, very high in sweet oak, and moderately long-aging; the Reserve is deeper and carries a tad more oak*

### Chardonnay

86 87 88 **90°** **91°** 92 **93°** **94°** 95 96

*Recent vintages have shown both more oak and more depth of fruit, as well as a more rounded palatal feel*

### Merlot

**86°** 87 88 89 **90°°** **91°°** **92°** 93° 94 **95**

*Like the Cabernet, this wine changed in 90 by showing more fruit, a rounder, more supple palatal feel and richer oak*

### Zinfandel

86 **87°** 88 89 **90°°°** **91°** 92 **93°** **94°** **95°**

*Here is another Chateau Souverain wine which hit its stride in the 90 vintage, although in this case, its continuing track record is more reminiscent of its early history; here, ripeness and oak have not always been accompanied by adequate fruit*

CHATEAU WOLTNER *Napa 1985* Occupying the plateau of Howell Mountain, the historic (ca. 1886) Brun and Chaix building remained inactive from Prohibition until 80. Then the old winery and its 181-acre estate were bought by Francis and

Françoise DeWavrin-Woltner of Bordeaux. Until 83 their family owned the prestigious Château La Mission Haut-Brion. In 82–83, as the old Howell Mountain winery was being restored, the nearby land was cleared and 35 acres were planted to Chardonnay. A total of 55 acres are now under vine, with the eventual goal set at 120 acres.

Given the viticultural history of Howell Mountain and the background of the owners, the decision to focus exclusively on Chardonnay surprised most observers. Having worked with Chardonnay as a winemaker in Meursault, Ted Lemon arrived at Woltner with impressive credentials. Over the first few vintages, the winery produced three vineyard-designated Chardonnays—an estate, the Titus Vineyard, and St. Thomas Vineyard. Each, made in small quantities, was offered to the wine trade on a futures basis. This was an unheard-of practice in California for white wine. Additionally, the first vintages of Chardonnay were priced at levels much higher than the quality merited. It was not until 87 that the wines showed greater depth of flavor and balance. But even now they are among the highest-priced California Chardonnays. The Frederique Vineyard bottling was added in 89, and with the debut of a Howell Mountain bottling in 91, the number of Woltner Chardonnays reached five. To date, their quality has been average, with little more than an infrequent . The overall annual production is now about 12,000 cases.

## Chardonnay

| | | | | | |
|---|---|---|---|---|---|
| (Titus Vineyard) | 89 | 90 | 91 | 92 | 93 |
| (Frederique Vineyard) | 89° | 90° | 91 | 92 | 93 |
| (St. Thomas Vineyard) | **89°** | 90 | 91 | 92 | **93°** |

*This very expensive series of wines has been very high in tasty oak, fairly full-bodied, and firmly structured, but the wines have also been lower in balancing fruit and too frequently have seemed dry and stiff*

CHAUFFE-EAU CELLARS *Sonoma 1971* Until 91 wines from this small winery were bottled under the Vina Vista Winery name. The owners felt that a French-sounding label might improve their fortune. Located in Geyserville, Chauffe-Eau (French for "geyser"—according to the winery) specializes in Cabernet Sauvignon from the Alexander Valley, Chardonnay from the Carneros region and Merlot from Sonoma Valley. Total annual output remains below 1,000 cases. Of the three varietals offered, the full-flavored Cabernet Sauvignon (aged three years in oak) has risen to ° levels in recent vintages.

## Chardonnay

| | | | | | |
|---|---|---|---|---|---|
| 90 | 91° | 93° | **94°°** | **95** | 96 |

*Showing a solid center of appley and slightly citrusy fruit when successful; the wine can be overly oaky when the fruit does not measure up*

CHESTNUT HILL    A San Francisco–based wine importer and wholesaler uses this brand for its negociant wines. Chardonnay and Zinfandel are the two volume leaders, and its Zinfandel is usually from San Luis Obispo. In smaller quantities, Sauvignon Blanc, Merlot, and Cabernet Sauvignon from varying appellations are offered annually. Overall, the output holds steady at 25,000 cases.

CHEVAL SAUVAGE    *(Wild Horse Winery)*    In lieu of a Reserve designation, Ken Volk of Wild Horse is using Cheval Sauvage for his bottlings of specially selected, limited-volume, top-of-the-line wine, including Pinot Noirs from Paso Robles and Santa Barbara as well as one Merlot from Paso Robles. Quantities for each bottling of Cheval Sauvage have ranged from 175 to 250 cases.

CHIMNEY ROCK WINERY    *Napa 1986*    Native New Yorker Sheldon "Hack" Wilson was an executive with Pepsi-Cola International, and for several years was associated with the brewing business in South Africa. When he decided to join the wine world, he searched Napa Valley for an available site and, as an avid golfer, was attracted to property in the Stags Leap District known as the Chimney Rock Golf Course. Buying the land in 80, Wilson removed nine holes, or about 75 acres, and is said by those who play the game to have improved the remaining nine. The vineyard was developed in 81–82, with major emphasis on Cabernet Sauvignon, Merlot, and Cabernet Franc. The winemaking facility was completed in late 89, when the winery was in its fourth vintage. By the early 90s phylloxera had taken over most of the vineyards, and the entire 75 acres had to be replanted. The new vineyard focuses on red varieties—Cabernet Sauvignon, Merlot, and blending cousins—but features tight vine spacing and a wide range of clones and rootstocks. Chardonnay now comes from the Carneros District, and Fumé Blanc is also made from purchased fruit. The winery pins its reputation today on its three estate reds, Cabernet Sauvignon, Cabernet Sauvignon Reserve, and "Elevage," a Meritage produced since 1990. Annual production falls just under 30,000 cases.

### Cabernet Sauvignon

84  **85°°**  **86**  **87**  88  89  **90**  **92**  **94°**  **95**

*Rich, firm, moderately tannic wines, they need to capture enough fruit extract to balance their somewhat tight and reserved style*

### Chardonnay

**84°**  85  **86°**  87  88  90  91  **93°**  **94°**  95

*Medium-depth appley fruit and good crisp acidity, with oak in support; can be somewhat lighter in lesser years*

CHOUINARD VINEYARDS  *Alameda 1985*  Former civil engineer George Chouinard decided to settle down in one place after years of traveling. He and his family bought 100 acres of steep, hilly land a few miles west of Pleasanton. After planting a small (3-acre) vineyard and building a winery, George turned the project over to his son, Damian, who is now the winemaker. Chardonnay and Cabernet Sauvignon grow in the estate vineyard. Additional grapes are purchased from both North Coast and Central Coast appellations. Making most varietals in 200–400-case lots, the winery has reached the 1,000-case-a-year level. About 300 cases of apple wine are also produced by the winery.

THE CHRISTIAN BROTHERS  *Napa 1882*  In mid-89 the wine world, including many Napa Valley residents, was shocked to learn that Grand Metropolitan, the British conglomerate and parent company of Heublein, had purchased the venerable Christian Brothers winery. Run by the teaching order since 1882, the Christian Brothers had moved to the Napa Valley from Martinez in the 20s, devoting winery proceeds to the order's many schools and colleges. The operation at one time included three facilities in Napa and a large winery and brandy-making facility in the Central Valley.

As winemakers, the Christian Brothers produced a large line of varietal and generic wines, along with a line of sparkling wine by the Charmat process. At the height of their winemaking operation, the Brothers produced about 1 million cases of wine a year and a like amount of brandy.

In the 90s the owners shifted all winemaking operations for the Christian Brothers to their facility in Madera, where Almaden, Blossom Hill, and their other low-priced brands are housed. Far removed from Napa Valley, the Christian Brothers now offer a line of inexpensive varietals bearing the California appellation.

CHRISTOPHER CREEK WINERY  *1974*  Known for many years as Sotoyome Winery, this winery has a 10-acre vineyard that contains 3 acres of pre-Prohibition Petite Sirah, 5 acres of Syrah, and the remainder is planted to Chardonnay. Oak-aged Syrah and Petite Sirah represent the majority of the winery's 2,000-case annual production.

CILURZO VINEYARD & WINERY   *Riverside 1978*   Originally this winery was the Cilurzo Piconi Winery, but when the partnership dissolved in 80, Vincent Cilurzo remained on the site and Piconi founded his own wine venture. On his 52-acre estate, Cilurzo had developed 10 acres of vineyard in 68, making it the oldest in the Temecula area. As in many of the early vineyard developments in Temecula, the favorite variety planted was Petite Sirah. A wide range of varietals is now produced from grapes grown within Temecula. Of the 10,000-case annual production, the leaders by volume are White Zinfandel (3,000), Petite Sirah (1,000), Chenin Blanc (1,000), Chardonnay (1,000), Cabernet Sauvignon (1,000), and Sauvignon Blanc (1,000). In recent vintages Petite Sirah has been made in a Nouveau style (once labeled "Full Moon Nouveau") and a regular oak-aged version. A Muscat Canelli labeled "Reindeer Reserve" is bottled in time for the Christmas season. One of the most popular tourist stops, the winery sells much of its production to visitors. Long term, Cilurzo wants to expand his winery's production to 20,000 cases a year.

CINNABAR VINEYARDS AND WINERY   *Santa Clara 1986*   On a hilltop overlooking Saratoga, Tom Mudd and Melissa Frank built a small winery and started a vineyard nearby. Mudd, who was in the mining profession, named his wine venture after the heavy, deep, almost blood-red mercury ore, cinnabar. The steep mountain vineyard covers 24 acres, equally devoted to Cabernet Sauvignon and Chardonnay. The first estate-grown Cabernet was made in 86, the first Chardonnay in 88. The owners, favoring 100% barrel-fermented Chardonnay and 100% Cabernet Sauvignon, are emphasizing estate-grown wines with the Santa Cruz Mountains appellation. Annual production of each estate wine has been averaging 2,000 cases. Recently Cinnabar has also offered Chardonnay and Merlot from the Central Coast and a blended red named "Xcellence." With these wines the total annual output matches the winery's 10,000 cases capacity.

### Cabernet Sauvignon
**86   87   89   90   92   93°**

*Moderately ripe, noticeably tannic wines with black cherry fruit, but lacking in intensity*

### Chardonnay
88   89°   90   91°   92   **93°°   94°°**   95

*Medium-full-bodied, well-balanced wines sometimes lacking in fruit, but special in good years*

CLAIBORNE & CHURCHILL VINTNERS   *San Luis Obispo 1983*   Claiborne (Clay) Thompson and his wife, Fredericka Churchill, are behind this brand, which specializes in white wines. From 83 to 86, Thompson made wines in space leased from Edna Valley Vineyards, where he worked on a part-time basis. Now in its own production facility, this winery offers Riesling, Gewurztraminer, and a Muscat Canelli in a dry style. A blend of the three makes up the fourth wine bottled, "Edelzwicker." Chardonnay and Pinot Noir complete the line. Both the Riesling and the Gewurztraminer succeed more often than not, and the Gewurztraminer is often among the better dry versions. Annual production is at the 4,000-case level.

CLARK–CLAUDON   *Napa 1993*   Owning 20 acres in Howell Mountain, Tom & Laurie Clark cautiously ventured into the winemaking world by making fewer than 200 cases of Cabernet Sauvignon in each of their first three vintages. Their goal is to expand production to 1,000 cases a year. 95 earned °°.

CLAYTON VINEYARDS   *Lodi 1996*   The Clayton family vineyard goes back to 1919, when it contained 20 acres of Zinfandel and a like number of Flame Tokay. In the 1990s the family removed the Tokay and planted 25 acres of Zinfandel, while retaining 15 acres of the best old vine Zinfandel. Making wines in leased space, Clayton produces only Zinfandel. Annual output will remain steady at 1,000 cases over the near term.

CLASSIC WINE CO.   In the 1980s the Franzia family (Fred, Joseph, and John), which operates several large facilities, began acquiring trademarks and inventory of many wineries. Laurier Winery (see entry) and Estrella were among the first acquisitions. More recently, Classic Wine has acquired the trademarks of Hacienda Wine Cellars and Grand Cru Vineyards, in Sonoma Valley, and three brands in Napa Valley, Rutherford Grove, Salmon Creek, and Napa Creek. Classic also developed brands of its own, including Forest Glen Winery, Forest Ville, Foxhollow, Silver Ridge, Douglas Hill, and Montpellier.

CLAUDIA SPRINGS WINERY   *Mendocino 1989*   Home winemaker Warren Hein and longtime friend and San Jose neighbor Bob Klindt formed a partnership and purchased 40 acres in the hills overlooking the Anderson Valley. They have 25 plantable acres near their small winery, but over the first several vintages all Claudia Springs wines have been made from purchased grapes. Chardonnay and Pinot Noir from the Anderson Valley along with a Zinfandel from the Redwood Valley are the primary wines offered. Total production remains under 1,000 cases.

CLINE CELLARS   *Sonoma 1982*   Originally located in the town of Oakley, northeast of Berkeley, Cline Cellars is operated by Fred Cline, who entered the wine business as manager on a farm growing almonds, walnuts, and wine grapes. In 82 he purchased the defunct Firpo Winery, the oldest in the region, and began crushing three red varieties—Carignane, Zinfandel, and Mataro. Until 89, the winery had no refrigeration system, the tanks were redwood, and the fermenters were open-topped redwood vats. White wine production was limited to a few hundred cases. In 87 several wineries working with Rhone varieties discovered that the old California red called Mataro was none other than the prestigious French Rhone variety, Mourvedre.

Holding long-term contracts for 180 acres of the suddenly in-demand variety, Cline began selling Mourvedre to the likes of Bonny Doon and Edmunds St. John. Cline Cellars also began blending and marketing Rhone Valley types, and two bottlings in particular were attractive blends of Mourvedre, Zinfandel, and Carignane. One labeled "Oakley Cuvée" contains over 50% Mourvedre, and the second, "Côtes d'Oakley," is made with about 60% Carignane, 20% Zinfandel. Côtes D'Oakley Blanc, a simple, everyday white, has been added.

In the early 90s, the Clines had moved winemaking operations to the Carneros region of Sonoma, and they established vineyards there that included Syrah, Viognier, and Marsanne. The Oakley vineyards remain the major source of Cline's Rhone-type wines. Within this generally reliable line, the quality leaders have been its Reserve Mourvedre, earning **, and the winery's rich, ripe Zinfandels, both regular and Reserve bottlings. Along with several other wineries, Cline greatly revised and expanded its Zinfandel offerings in the late 1990s. In addition to its Ancient Vines Zinfandel, the winery offers Zinfandel from each of the following single vineyards: Live Oak, Bridgehead, Big Break, and Jacuzzi Family. (Fred Cline's grandfather invented the Jacuzzi whirlpool.) In some vintages, Jacuzzi Vineyard Reserve Zinfandel has been a stand-alone label.

### Zinfandel

| | | | | | | |
|---|---|---|---|---|---|---|
| (Contra Costa County) | 89° | **90°** | **91°°** | 92 | 93 | **94°** |
| (Contra Costa County Reserve) | **89°** | **90°°** | **91°** | 9̶2̶ | 93 | 94 |
| (Bridgehead) | 93 | **94°** | **95°** | 96 | | |
| (Big Break) | **93°** | **95°°** | **96°** | | | |

*Typical of Contra Costa County Zins, the Clines are all ripe, dense, direct and a bit rustic in style with mid-term (3–6 years) aging potential*

CLONINGER CELLARS   *Monterey 1989*   A partnership of four families from the Salinas Valley who have all been involved in local agriculture, Cloninger is specializing in Chardonnay and Cabernet Sauvignon. Barrel-fermented and aged *sur lie*, the Monterey County Chardonnays represent the bulk of the winery's 4,500-case production. Early vintages showed promise.

CLOS DU BOIS   *Sonoma 1976*   As a modest investment, Frank Woods purchased 100 acres of vineyard land in the Dry Creek Valley in 70. The following year he formed a partnership with a college buddy, Thomas Reed, and additional acreage was purchased in the Alexander Valley. When the grape market dipped in 74, the partners decided to try their hand at winemaking. At the Sonoma Vineyards/Rodney Strong facility, they made 2,000 cases of a 74 Chardonnay from Dry Creek Valley. Still in leased space in 77, their first wine from the Alexander Valley pushed production to 6,000 cases. With an improving market for varietal wine in 80, they abandoned their original plan to sell grapes and moved into their own facility, a renovated warehouse in Healdsburg. By then Clos du Bois had 590 acres under vine in the Alexander Valley.

The winery now offers six varietals: Chardonnay, Sauvignon Blanc, Gewurztraminer, Cabernet Sauvignon, Pinot Noir, and Merlot. A series of vineyard-designated wines include two Chardonnays ("Calcaire" in the Alexander Valley, "Flintwood" in Dry Creek Valley) and two Cabernet Sauvignons ("Marlstone," a Bordeaux blend, and "Briarcrest," 100% varietal). Chardonnay is the volume leader, with over 100,000 cases produced, most of that represented by the barrel-fermented version from the Alexander Valley. Both Calcaire and Flintwood Chardonnays are 100% barrel-fermented.

Though no longer the volume leader it was in the 1980s, Merlot remains an important wine at Clos du Bois which presently bottles three versions: Sonoma County, Alexander Valley and Winemaker's Reserve. Now owned by the Wine Alliance (owners of Callaway, Atlas Peak, and William Hill Winery), Clos du Bois has added a Winemaker's Reserve Chardonnay and a Sonoma County Zinfandel to its roster. In 1991 a new winemaking team was in place, and the entire winemaking operation moved into a new, large facility in Geyserville. Production of Cabernet Sauvignon and Fumé Blanc has expanded under present ownership. Volume is steady at 350,000 cases.

### Cabernet Sauvignon

81°  82  83  **84°°**  85  **86°**  87  88  89  **91°**  92°  94

*Ripish, open, juicy, cherry and black-cherry fruit, medium depth, lightly tannic*

### Cabernet Sauvignon

(Briarcrest)  80  81°  83  **84°°**  **85°**  **86°**  87  88°  89  **90°**  92°

*Deeper, slightly tougher, with medium aging potential*

### Chardonnay

86°  87  88°  89  90  91  92  93°  94°  95°

*Clean, straightforward, blossomy fruit, light oak*

### Chardonnay

(Calcaire)  86°  87°  88  89  90  91  93°  **94**  **95°**

*Peachy fruit, slight spice hints, creamy oak, firm balance*

### Marlstone

78  79  80°  81°  82°  83  **84°°**  **85°°**  **86°**  **87°°**  **88°°**  89  **90°**  **91**  92  **93°°**  94

*Mild-mannered in early vintages, the latest efforts are deep, tasty, round, with lots of cherryish and herbal-tinged fruit, filled out by sweet, rich oak*

**Merlot**

82  83  84°  85°  **86°°°**  87°  **88°**  89  90  91  92  93
94  95

*Lots of bright fruit and wonderful balance; elegance in best vintages, but in others wine can be thin, evanescent*

CLOS DU VAL  *Napa 1972*  Owned by John Goelet and managed by Bernard Portet, Clos du Val was an accidental discovery. Goelet, a New York businessman whose family was once involved in the Bordeaux wine trade, asked Portet to search out and study potential winemaking sites. On a brief visit to the Napa Valley one hot summer day in 70, Portet felt a cool breeze as he drove through a particular spot on the Silverado Trail, and realized he had discovered a significant microclimate. A site within that area was for sale, and before long it became Clos du Val.

The winery was up and functioning by 72, producing Zinfandel and Cabernet Sauvignon. The owners developed 140 acres and helped pioneer what is now known as the Stags Leap area. That vineyard contains 100 acres of Cabernet Sauvignon, 20 acres of Merlot, 10 acres of Zinfandel, and 10 acres of Semillon. Merlot, blended with Cabernet, was first offered as a varietal in 77, and Chardonnay joined the winery roster in 78. In 79–80, Clos du Val developed a 105-acre vineyard in the Carneros, containing Chardonnay and Pinot Noir. A third winery-owned vineyard consists of 20 acres of Chardonnay. Cabernet Sauvignon and Chardonnay represent close to two-thirds of the winery's 65,000-case annual output. Zinfandel, Pinot Noir, and Semillon remain on the roster. Since 86, when the winery made its first estate-bottled Carneros Chardonnay, all wines have been estate bottled.

**Cabernet Sauvignon**

73  74°°  75°  76°  77°  78  79°  **80°**  81  82  83  **84°**
**85°**  **86°**  **87**  **88**  **89°**  90  **91**  **92**  93  **94°**

*Tight wines, even when not overly tannic, these refined and somewhat low-keyed efforts carry nicely focused curranty fruit and a generous dollop of creamy, almost milk-chocolatey oak*

**Chardonnay**

(Carneros)  86°  87  88  89  90  91  92  93  **94**  95

*Very well balanced, clean and crisp wines, they show only moderate intensity and can be low in fruit*

**Merlot**

80°  81°  82  83°  **85°°**  86  **87°**  **88°**  89  **90**  **91**  **93°**
**95°**

*Inconsistent to a fault, these wines have ranged from rich, curranty, and well oaked to earthy and vegetal; sweet, creamy oak is always evident*

**Pinot Noir**

80°°°  81°  82°  83  **84°**  **85°**  **86°**  87  **88°**

*Medium-weight, firm, well-constructed, sweetly oaked wines, with moderate-intensity cherry fruit; capable of half a dozen years or more of aging*

**Zinfandel**

78°  79°  80°  81°  82°  83°  84°  **85°°°**  **86°**  **87°°**  **88°**
89  90  91  92  93  94  **95°**

*In the 80s, ripe and fleshy wines, firmed up by imposing tannins, they show the rich oak and keen varietal focus of other Clos du Val reds while carrying greater intensity; from 89 the wines have lost their way*

CLOS FONTAINE DU MONT  *Napa 1991*  After selling the William Hill Winery to the Wine Alliance, William Hill, an incurable developer, formed a new company (Hill & Mayes) and that partnership currently owns Van Duzer wines in Oregon and this brand in Napa Valley. Made in part from Hill's Napa vineyard on the slopes of Atlas Peak, Chardonnay and Cabernet Sauvignon, both labeled "Reserve," are the featured wines to date.

CLOS PEGASE *Napa 1984* The tone for this brand was fixed at the outset in 84, when owner and art collector Jan Shrem selected the controversial post-modernist architect Michael Graves to design the winery. Construction of the multi-million-dollar facility in Calistoga was delayed for a time owing to strong objections from town residents over the building's size and appearance. Since its completion, Clos Pegase has been offering Chardonnay, Sauvignon Blanc, Cabernet Sauvignon, and Merlot. Cabernet Sauvignon comes from the winery's 42-acre Palisades Vineyard north of Calistoga. Planted primarily to Merlot, another 50 acres are located at the winery site.

In 1990 Clos Pegase acquired a 365-acre ranch in the Carneros District and eventually developed more than 200 acres there to Chardonnay and Merlot. The wine roster today consists of three varietals—Chardonnay, Cabernet Sauvignon, and Merlot—and a Meritage-style blend of Cabernet and Merlot labeled "Hommage." As part of a series featuring special artwork, Hommage is the winery's deluxe wine. Over its first decade the winery seemed more intent on making wines with straightforward fruit character. By the mid-1990s the winery's vineyards were in full production, and its primary wines were all estate-grown and -bottled. As the winery moves closer to its annual goal of 50,000 cases, Hommage has emerged as its quality leader.

### Cabernet Sauvignon
85　86°　87°　89　90°　91°　92　93°°　94°　95°

*Made in a light, moderately fruity, refined style, with short to medium aging potential*

### Chardonnay
(Napa Valley)　86　87°　88　89°　90　91　92　93　94°　95

*Like the Cabernet, this wine is geared more toward direct fruitiness and moderate depth*

### Merlot
86°　88°　89°　90　91°　92°　93°　94　95

*The most consistent wine early on for Clos Pegase; the recent results are disappointing*

CLOVERDALE RANCH *(Olivet Lane)* Used for Cabernet Sauvignon and Merlot, this is a label started by the Pellegrini family. The family's 50-acre vineyard in the Cloverdale area of Alexander Valley is planted to Cabernet and other red Bordeaux varieties. To date, the annual production is steady at 1,500 cases.

COBBLESTONE VINEYARDS *Monterey 1993* From a 50-acre vineyard in Greenfield containing 25 acres of Chardonnay, the owners have been producing 200–500 cases of Chardonnay a year as a way to showcase the vineyard. Made in a big, ripe-fruit barrel-fermented style, Cobblestone Chardonnay has developed a following among fans of the style.

CODORNIU NAPA *Napa 1990* The Spanish firm Codorniu, Spain's largest producer of *méthode champenoise* sparkling wine, purchased a 350-acre vineyard and winery site in the Carneros region in 85. By 91, when its first Brut reached the market, Codorniu Napa had developed 50 acres, with a long-term planting goal of 225 acres. Chardonnay and Pinot Noir are the primary varieties planted, but several Spanish white grapes are being grown on a trial basis. With the production of *méthode champenoise* cuvées expected to grow quickly, the winery began making Napa Valley Brut and Napa Valley Rose. However, despite the good quality of both bubblies, sales did not increase at the anticipated rate. In 1997, the owners announced plans to develop a line of varietals. Don Van Staaveren, formerly of Chateau St. Jean, was hired to oversee the production of Chardonnay, Cabernet Sauvignon, Sauvignon Blanc, Pinot Noir, and Merlot. Sparkling wine sales have been steady at 30,000 cases a year.

---

DAVID COFFARO CELLARS    *Dry Creek Valley 1994*    Coffaro had been selling grapes and making wines as an amateur from his 19-acre vineyard since 1979. As a medal-winning home winemaker, he preferred blending wines, and that approach has stayed with him as a pro. His primary wines are an Estate Cuvee (Zinfandel with a splash of Petite Sirah, and Carignane) and a Neighbor's Cuvee (Zinfandel and Cabernet). Carignane and Petite Sirah are also bottled as varietals, and a red Meritage blend of Cabernet and Cabernet Franc is the most recent addition. Most of Coffaro's 2,500-case production is sold as futures, long before the wines are bottled.

---

B. R. COHN    *Sonoma 1984*    Owner Bruce Cohn managed several successful rock groups, and by 74 was wealthy enough to purchase a mature 65-acre vineyard in the Sonoma Valley. From this estate vineyard, known as Olive Hill, the winery grew relatively quickly to 8,000 cases a year. Cohn's 85 Cabernet Sauvignon was one of the first from that great vintage to earn critical praise, and certainly helped the winery's growth. Just over half the output is devoted to Chardonnay. In the 90s the Olive Hill Chardonnays, which were not overly impressive, have been replaced by one from the Sonoma Valley appellation. The Olive Hill Vineyards Cabernet remains the flagship wine, with an annual output of 7,500 cases. The Chardonnay and a few hundred cases of Pinot Noir bring Cohn's total production to 15,000 cases.

### Cabernet Sauvignon

(Olive Hill)    84°°    **85°**    **87°**    **88°°**    **89°°**    90    91    **93**    **94°**    **95°**

*Like the Chardonnay, the Cabernet seems to follow in the no-holds-barred direction, but here the ripe, dense fruit maintains its flavor in the face of the plentiful oak and coarse tannins; the results are long-aging wines of considerable depth*

### Chardonnay

(Olive Hill)    85    86    88    90    91    95    96

*Lots of oak tends to dominate the ripe fruit, but future vintages from this well-situated vineyard could show better balance and earn higher ratings*

---

COLBY VINEYARDS    *Napa Valley 1985*    From its 6.5-acre vineyard on the west side of Napa Valley, Colby makes Chardonnay and Merlot. Both are custom-made at the Rombauer Winery. Made since the 85 vintage, Chardonnay remains the primary wine and accounts for most of Colby's 2,000-case annual output. First bottled in 1996, Merlot should level off at 500 cases.

---

COLGIN CELLARS    *Napa 1992*    Owner Ann Colgin, international art and antique dealer residing in Florida, visited Napa Valley numerous times before deciding to produce wine. On the advice of consulting winemaker Helen Turley, she purchased fruit from the 10-acre Lamb Vineyard located at the base of Howell Mountain and make a 100% Cabernet Sauvignon. Sales to date have been through a mailing list. Initial production of 200 cases will eventually double.

---

CONCANNON VINEYARDS    *Alameda 1887*    Nestled just outside the city limits of Livermore, Concannon was once a cornerstone of the California wine industry. Owned and operated by the Concannon family until 1982, the winery built a sound reputation for both red and white wines. In 62 it bottled the first varietal Petite Sirah, and for many vintages thereafter the Concannons emphasized estate-bottled Petite Sirah and Cabernet Sauvignon. However, by the late 70s, the winery's antiquated facility began to hinder its winemaking, and the winery's staid image did not help. After financing a badly needed renovation program, Jim Concannon sold the winery and vineyard to Distillers Company, a large international corporation. That parent company sold Concannon in early 88 to a partnership headed by winemaker Sergio Traverso and Deinhard of Germany. Traverso, formerly with Domaine Chandon and Sterling Vineyards, reworked the estate vineyard to make Sauvignon Blanc and Cabernet Sauvignon the winery's two leading varietals.

Yet another era began in 92 with the acquisition of Concannon by a limited partnership headed by members of the nearby Wente family. Today, the 150-acre Livermore Estate vineyard yields 40,000 cases a year. Sauvignon Blanc remains the volume leader, followed by Cabernet Sauvignon and Petite Sirah. "Assemblage," an upscale white Meritage that is partially barrel-fermented and oak-aged, completes the Estate-Bottled offerings. Concannon soon added a red Assemblage made from Cabernet Sauvignon, Merlot, and Cabernet Franc. By the late 90s Concannon's vineyard acreage increased to 220, and the winery had introduced a Reserve wine program for Cabernet Sauvignon, Petite Sirah, and Chardonnay that was limited to 2,500 cases a year. A Rhone wine program has been established and to date includes Syrah and a blended red and white. Its midpriced "Selected Vineyards" Chardonnay, Cabernet Sauvignon, and Petite Sirah from the Central Coast continue to be the volume leaders and bring the winery's annual production close to 75,000 cases. Gradual growth will see the winery peak at 90,000 cases a year.

### Cabernet Sauvignon

92　93　94

*Soft, ripe cherry and herb-tinged fruit, light tannins, mild oak, no aging potential*

### Chardonnay

91　93　95°

*Lightly fruity, with citrus and floral elements giving the wine an alluring prettiness in better vintages*

---

CONN CREEK WINERY　*Napa 1974*　Founder Bill Collins was in the electronics industry in Silicon Valley in the late 60s when he bought 55 acres just north of St. Helena. The vineyard contained Zinfandel planted in the 30 s. Collins sold grapes and also increased his vineyard holdings until venturing into winemaking. He had the good fortune to buy 73 and 74 Cabernet Sauvignon from the ill-fated Lyncrest Vineyards. The two Cabernets issued under Conn Creek's label were among the best from each vintage and, along with Zinfandel made from the old vineyards, Conn Creek was off to an excellent start.

In 79 the owner decided to construct a new winery adjacent to Conn Creek. Bringing financial assistance to this project were the former owners of Château La Mission–Haut-Brion, who once owned 25% of Conn Creek and who later founded Chateau Woltner.

Despite continued good fortune with Cabernet Sauvignon, the winery expanded beyond its marketing ability. With inventory threatening to swamp the facility, the winery was sold to Stimson Lane (owners of Chateau Ste. Michelle and Villa Mount Eden). Since then, the roster has been gradually trimmed to two Napa Valley varietals—Cabernet Sauvignon and Merlot. The third major wine is an upscale red Meritage called "Anthology." The combined annual output is now 5,000 cases, and the winery facility has been substantially converted to the storage and bottling of Villa Mt. Eden wines.

### Cabernet Sauvignon

| | | | | | | | | |
|---|---|---|---|---|---|---|---|---|
| (Limited Release) | 79°° | 80° | 81° | 82° | 83° | 84° | 85 | 86 |
| | 87° | 90° | 92° | 93°° | 94° | | | |
| (Reserve/Anthology) | 84°°° | 85° | 86°° | 87 | 91° | 92° | 94 | |

*Always rich and ripe, with fairly prominent oak and a slight tendency toward briariness in some vintages, the Conn Creek Cabernets have been generally consistent*

*performers and have shown an ability to age well; the Reserve picks up the extra oak
and richness that marked the mid-70s efforts from Conn Creek; Anthology appeared
as a Reserve blend of Cabernet and Merlot as of 91*

COOK'S CHAMPAGNE CELLARS    Acquired in 91 by the giant Canandaigua Wine Co.,
Cook's was an old, neglected brand, kicked around for years. Guild bought it in
71, and in 78 decided to use "Cook's Imperial" as a label for a line of low-priced
Charmat process sparkling wines to compete with the enormously successful and
seemingly unbeatable André line. From a modest 10,000-case production in 78,
Cook's enjoyed smooth sailing and was selling over 500,000 cases by 85. In addition to the popular Imperial Brut, Cook's kept expanding its product line, which
now includes Extra Dry, Blush, Spumante, White Zinfandel, and its upscale product (closed with a cork), the Grand Reserve. All sparklers have been identified as
"American Champagne." Cook's is now selling more than 1.6 million cases annually. To capitalize on the name, the winery is now offering varietal wines under the
name of "Cook's Captain Reserve." This low-priced line of table wines includes
Chardonnay, Cabernet Sauvignon, Merlot, and White Zinfandel.

COOPER–GARROD ESTATE    *Santa Cruz Mountains 1995*    A section of the large Garrod
horse ranch was given over to a small vineyard and winery. Its modest output
consists of Chardonnay, Cabernet Sauvignon, and Cabernet Franc. A Reserve
Cabernet is its most successful wine to date.

COPPOLA FAMILY WINES    *(Niebaum-Coppola Winery)*    After Coppola purchased the
Inglenook estate, this label was initially conceived of as a line of wines to make
available at the winery, which has always been a popular tourist destination. As
the tourists line up each day, the Coppola Family line developed a life of its own.
Chardonnay, Merlot, and Cabernet Franc are the headline attractions, but the
winery recently put together a red and white blend—Rosso and Bianco—which
are billed as ideal wines for large family gatherings. Annual output of all wines is
7,500 cases. The Merlot has star potential.

CORBETT CANYON VINEYARDS    *San Luis Obispo 1979*    The biggest winery in the
county, Corbett Canyon did not find smooth sailing in its first decade. Owned
since 88 by the Wine Group (Franzia, Summit), the winery, now a success, was
originally named the Lawrence Winery after its founder, Jim Lawrence, who sold
it to Glenmore Distillers in 82. Winemakers changed with even greater regularity
than owners. The facility remains tucked away in the middle of the Edna Valley,
and buys a considerable percentage of locally grown grapes. To assure itself of a
supply, the Wine Group purchased the 350-acre Los Alamos Vineyard in Santa
Barbara, which today is the primary source of Corbett Canyon's estate-bottled
Chardonnay and Pinot Noir. Most of the winery's 600,000-case output now consists of a line identified as "Coastal Classics." The volume leaders in this line are
Cabernet, Merlot, White Zinfandel, and Chardonnay. A line of Reserve bottlings
consists of varietals from the Central Coast appellation, led by Chardonnay, partially barrel-fermented, Merlot, and Cabernet Sauvignon blended with Merlot.

CORISON WINES    *Napa 1987*    Longtime winemaker Cathy Corison launched her own
brand in 87 after serving as winemaker for Chappellet Vineyards for 10 years. She
specializes in Cabernet Sauvignon from vineyards situated in the mid-Napa Valley, from Yountville to St. Helena. In 1996 she purchased 10 acres of Cabernet
Sauvignon within mid-Napa. This low-yielding vineyard will ultimately be used
exclusively for a single-vineyard Cabernet Sauvignon. Meanwhile, her Napa Valley Cabernet, which has enjoyed great success in the 1990s, remains her primary
wine. Corison's total production is about 2,500 cases.

**Cabernet Sauvignon**
  87°   88°°   89°   90°   91°   92°   93°°   94°   95

*Nicely fruity, richly oaked wines, these Corison efforts have been well-balanced and full of promise for up to a decade of improvement*

CORLEY MONTICELLO VINEYARDS  *(Monticello Cellars)*  The Corley family, owners of Monticello Cellars, introduced this label for their occasional bottlings of limited-volume Reserve-style Cabernet Sauvignon, Pinot Noir, and Chardonnay. The total annual output remains below 2,000 cases.

CORNERSTONE CELLARS  *Napa 1991*  Emphasizing Howell Mountain Cabernet Sauvignon, Cornerstone was founded by former chef and onetime wine merchant Bruce Scotland. Zinfandel debuted in 94 at °°.

### Cabernet Sauvignon
**91**°°  **92**°°  **93**°°  **94**°°°

*Deep, ripe, curranty and highly oaked wines full of aging potential*

COSENTINO WINERY  *Napa 1980*  A one-time wine wholesaler in the Central Valley region, owner-winemaker Mitch Cosentino began making small batches of wine in a rented corner of a warehouse in Modesto. During the first few years, he produced a wide assortment of table wines under the Crystal Valley Cellars brand (revived in 93) and sparkling wines labeled "Robin's Glow." Beginning with the 85 vintage, Cosentino began focusing on Bordeaux varietals—Cabernet Sauvignon, Merlot, and Cabernet Franc—and a Bordeaux blend called "The Poet." He earned critical praise for all four, and his pioneering efforts on behalf of Cabernet Franc paid off with an outstanding 86. That year the primary name switched to Cosentino Winery and by mid-90, Cosentino had finally settled into his new winery in Yountville.

To date most wines have been produced from purchased grapes. Cosentino has 4 acres of Merlot next to the winery. The majority of the reds are grown in Napa, Sonoma, and Lake counties, explaining the frequently used North Coast appellation. Two Chardonnays have been regularly produced, North Coast and a Reserve type from the Napa Valley labeled "The Sculptor." The quantities of each wine offered fall into the 600- to 1,200-case range, with the North Coast bottlings on the high end. "M. Coz" is the name of Cosentino's deluxe red meritage. He also makes wines labeled "The Zin," "The Sem" for Semillon, and "The Neb" for Nebbiolo. Total annual production is at 12,000 cases.

### Cabernet Sauvignon
**85**°  86  **87**  **88**  89  91  94
(Reserve/Meritage)  **84**°°  **85**°°  **86**  **87**°  **88**  **90**°

*Both wines rely heavily on sweet, creamy oak to lift light- to medium-density, currant, and herbal fruit past noticeable tannins; the Reserve is usually a little riper and richer, but not necessarily more ageworthy*

### Chardonnay
86°  87  88  89  90  94

*Toasty, over-oaked wines have often lacked the fruit to bring them into a balanced package*

### Merlot
**85**°  **86**°°  **87**°  88  89  **91**  **92**

*Medium-depth cherry and subtle orange-rind fruit notes are enriched by sweet oak and firmed by light-to-medium tannins*

### Zinfandel
91  92  93  94  **95**°

*Ripe, soft, and often lacking in depth*

COTES DE SONOMA   *(Olivet Lane)*   Owned by the Pellegrini family, this label is found on a series of modestly priced wines. The roster is headed by Chardonnay and Sauvignon Blanc, both fermented in stainless-steel tanks. The red offered is Cabernet Sauvignon. Steady growth has brought annual production to 20,000 cases.

COTTONWOOD CANYON   *San Luis Obispo 1988*   In 88, wine wholesaler and distributor Norman Beko purchased 78 acres of an established larger vineyard in Santa Maria Valley called Santa Maria Hills Vineyard. Using rented space, consulting enologist Gary Mosby (formerly of Edna Valley Vineyards) has been producing barrel-fermented Chardonnay and Pinot Noir for Cottonwood Canyon. The annual production in the early vintages averaged 4,000 cases, 80% of which was Chardonnay.

H. COTURRI & SONS   *Sonoma 1979*   One of the first producers to emphasize the natural, no-chemicals approach to winemaking, Coturri seems to have filled a modest need. This is a family-owned venture, using a slightly expanded shed behind the family home to produce about 2,500 cases a year. Zinfandel and Cabernet Sauvignon are regular items, joined on occasion by Chardonnay and Sauvignon Blanc. The family farms 10 acres, and most of its wines are identified as Sonoma Valley in origin. The reds have generally attracted the most notice, though all too often for the wrong reasons. The Zinfandels in particular tend to be heavy-handed and close to late-harvest in style.

COUNTERPOINT   *(Laurel Glen Vineyards)*   A second label for Cabernet Sauvignon, Counterpoint is a product of owner Patrick Campbell's estate vineyards, but it consists of wines made from young vines and/or wines that do not make it into Laurel Glen's top-of-the-line brand. In recent years, annual output has been at the 3,000-case level.

**Cabernet Sauvignon**

| 87 | 88 | **90°°** | **91°** | **92** | **95** |
|----|----|----------|---------|--------|--------|

THOMAS COYNE WINES   *Alameda 1989*   Using the old stone winery once known as Chateau Bellevue, the oldest winery building in the Livermore Valley, Coyne is emphasizing Cabernet Sauvignon and Chardonnay from the Livermore Valley appellation. On a small-volume basis, Coyne bottles Merlot, Mourvedre, Petite Sirah, Sauvignon Blanc, Zinfandel, and Port. Coyne, also the winemaker for Rosenblum Cellars, intends to expand gradually to a peak of 5,000 cases a year.

ROBERT CRAIG WINE CELLARS   *Napa 1993*   Craig worked with mountain-grown Cabernet Sauvignon when he was assistant winemaker for Hess Collection and Mount Veeder Winery. On his own he produces Cabernet Sauvignon from two mountain appellations (Howell Mountain and Mt. Veeder) and also a Meritage blend named "Affinity" from valley floor vineyards. All three are made in 800–1,000-case quantities. Craig impressed us with his winemaking skills, and his wines have earned rave reviews (°° for the Mount Veeder and Affinity and ° for the Howell Mountain). Chardonnay from Carneros and Syrah have also been made in tiny quantities. Craig is developing a seven-acre vineyard near the town of Napa for Cabernet and related varieties.

CRESTON VINEYARDS & WINERY   *San Luis Obispo 1982*   In the hills of the La Planza Mountain Range, Creston has the distinction of being located at the highest elevation in the county. After a rather flashy beginning when the winery was partly owned by Christina Crawford, daughter of the famous actress, ownership changed in 87 to the Rosenbloom family of Los Angeles. TV game show host Alex Trebek is now majority partner. The 450-acre estate was planted to 155 acres of vineyards in the early 80s. The major varieties contained are Chardonnay, Cabernet Sauvignon, and Sauvignon Blanc. Pinot Noir, Semillon, Chenin Blanc, and

Zinfandel are planted in small amounts. As it expanded to 45,000 cases a year, the winery has enjoyed good sales success with Pinot Noir partially made by carbonic maceration. Cabernet Sauvignon (regular and Winemaker Selection bottlings) and Chardonnay together account for over 50% of total output. Merlot, White Zinfandel, and Chevrier Blanc (Semillon) fill out the roster. We have found the Sauvignon Blanc (blended with Semillon) to range from average to ° occasionally, depending on the level of fruit intensity. Merlot shows steady improvement. Winemaker Victor Hugo Roberts estimates that 50,000 cases is the maximum production goal.

### Chardonnay

84°   85°   87   88°   91   94

*Pleasantly fruity, with appley and occasionally tropical highlights, toasty oak in the background, and good balance*

CRICHTON HALL VINEYARD   *Napa 1985*   Richard and Judith Crichton left their respective careers in merchant banking and teaching behind them in 79 to settle in the Napa Valley and develop their vineyard. The 17-acre spread, planted entirely to Chardonnay, is located on the western foothills of Napa Valley about 3 miles north of Napa. To date, the wines are made in rented space, but aging takes place in barrels owned by the Crichtons. Producing their estate-grown Chardonnay, the Crichtons favor 100% barrel fermentation, partial malolactic fermentation, and aging *sur lie* for approximately eight months. From a first-year production of 1,500 cases, they have now reached their annual production goal of 4,000 cases. After a rough start, the winemaking has settled into a good groove. Merlot and Pinot Noir are now regularly offered, and both have been quite successful and enjoyable. The stylish Pinot Noir is well worth a special search.

### Chardonnay

86   87   88°   89°   90°°   91°°   92   93   94

*In their short history, these wines have ranged from citrusy and pinched to peachy and appley; toasty oak fills in the background*

### Pinot Noir

93°°   94°°   95°

*Fruity and rich with velvety Pinot texture*

CRONIN VINEYARDS   *San Mateo 1980*   Dwayne Cronin is one of several Silicon Valley computer executives who make wine in their spare time. What sets him apart from the others is that Cronin wines, most particularly the Chardonnay, are among the very best made in California, year in and year out. If we had only one Chardonnay to choose, chances are we would select one of Cronin's. The bad news is that Cronin has yet to top the 2,500-case-a-year level, and most of his wines are made in lots of only 150 to 350 cases. As a rule, four Chardonnays are offered—one from Ventana Vineyards in Monterey, another from Napa Valley, a third from Sonoma's Alexander Valley. The fourth bears the Santa Cruz Mountain appellation, and it joined the roster in the late 80s when Cronin's own 1-acre vineyard began bearing. All Chardonnays are barrel-fermented, and given extended *sur lie* aging. Though a little less dramatic, Pinot Noir has also responded well to the Cronin treatment, earning ° on virtually every outing. Cronin has produced a series of red Meritage wine named "Concerto" from Napa's Stags Leap District, and in recent years he has added Cabernet from Santa Cruz Mountains. Neither of these wines, though quite decent, has yet to be of the same high caliber as the Chardonnays. Located in the quaint town of Woodside, the winery is actually in the basement of the Cronins' home. It is not open to the public.

### Chardonnay

(Sonoma County/Alexander Valley)   86°°°   87°°°   88°°   89°   90°
92°°   93°°   94°   95

(Napa Valley) **86°°°** **87°°°** 88°° 89 **90°** **91°** 92 93 **94°**

(Santa Cruz Mountains) 86°° 87°° 88°° 89°° 90 91°° **92°** **93°°** **94°°** 95°

*Each is complex, toasty, buttery, rich, mouth-filling, and filled with fruit, and each carries the stamp of the winemaker in its combination of depth, range, and balance. In rough generalizations, the Sonoma is often the most fruity, the Napa the deepest, and the Santa Cruz Mountains the most complex*

RICHARD CUNEO   *(Sebastiani Vineyards)*   Dick Cuneo was hired by his father-in-law, Gus Sebastiani, and is now the general manager of the large family winery run by his brother-in-law, Don Sebastiani. In 86, when Don took control of the wine company, he rearranged many lines and added this one-wine line as an upscale sparkler. The first offering bearing the Richard Cuneo name was purchased from Sonoma-Cutrer; all subsequent vintages have been custom-made. The wine is made 100% from barrel-fermented Chardonnay, produced by the *méthode champenoise*. It averages three years *en tirage* before being released. The early vintages were uneven in quality.

CUTLER CELLAR   This is a Cabernet Sauvignon–only label, owned by Lance Cutler, the longtime winemaker for Gundlach Bundschu Winery. In the mid-80s, when the owners of Gundlach Bundschu wanted to emphasize estate-grown wines, they decided to cease production of a Cabernet Sauvignon from the neighboring Batto Ranch. Beginning in 85, Cutler took over the contract and has since produced Cabernet Sauvignon that in some years has earned up to °° for its rich cassis and herbal character, balanced by sweet oak. A proprietary blend called "Bearitage" has been somewhat successful. Production is less than 1,000 cases total.

CUVAISON WINERY   *Napa 1970*   During its first decade, this attractive winery on the outskirts of Calistoga seemed to attract confused and confusing owners. Started by two partners from the engineering world of Silicon Valley in 69, it was left in the hands of one partner within its first year. Owner/winemaker Tom Cottrell made nine wines his first year, including a Beaujolais-style Gamay named "Vivace" and other oddities. Within a few years Cuvaison was purchased by a publishing company, Commerce Clearing House, which actually built the present-day winery before selling out in 79 to a Swiss company, Isenhold. Among the primary stockholders of Isenhold was the Alexander Schmidheiny family, which since 86 has owned Cuvaison.

The wine roster of today bears no resemblance to that of the past. In the 70s, Cuvaison became notorious for big, bold, often tannic Cabernet Sauvignons and Zinfandels, both made from old hillside vineyards. Later in the 70s it enjoyed some success with Chardonnay from Winery Lake Vineyard in Carneros. In 79, under the new ownership, Cuvaison acquired 400 acres of prime land in the Carneros and planted more than 300 acres over the next few years. The major varieties established are Chardonnay, Pinot Noir, and Merlot. At one time the owners had considered making sparkling wine and had also thought of building a facility within the Carneros. These ideas were dropped when Cuvaison's Chardonnays from the 85 vintage onward enjoyed unexpected critical and sales success. A Merlot produced in 84 was also among the top ranked of its type, and the winery's planting of Merlot expanded to 20 acres.

By 95 Cuvaison was making 35,000 cases of Chardonnay a year (with further expansion anticipated), 8,000 cases of Cabernet Sauvignon, and about 5,000 cases of Merlot. It occasionally bottles 2,000 cases of Carneros Reserve Chardonnay. Carneros Pinot Noir (1,500 cases.) has become a regular item.

### Cabernet Sauvignon
84°° 85 **86°°** **87°** 88 **89°** **91°°** 92 94

*Owing all of its reputation for Cabernet quality to wines dating from 84 onward, Cuvaison has now established a house style of firm, tight, curranty wines that are high in oak and exhibit a tannic edge in need of many years of aging*

**Chardonnay**

86° 87° 88°° 89 90 91 92 93 94 95°°

*Crisp, appley, and slightly citrusy fruit is supported by rich and toasty oak in this series of moderately deep, exceptionally well-balanced wines*

**Merlot**

84°° 85°° 86° **87° 88°°** 89 **90°° 91° 92°°** 93 94 **95°**

*Well-made, rich wines, high in sweet, ripe-cherryish fruit, and loaded with sweet oak; they seem likely to need fairly long aging on the basis of balance and youthfully coarse tannins*

CYPRESS  *(J. Lohr)*  This line of low-priced varietals was made from purchased wine in the early vintages. Recent bottlings of Chardonnay, Cabernet Sauvignon, Fumé Blanc, and Merlot have been made predominantly from Lohr's vast vineyard acreage in Monterey and in the Paso Robles area. Annual output has been averaging 50,000 cases. Except for the oaky Chardonnay, the wines are lightweights.

D-CUBED CELLARS  *1994*  With three names beginning with the letter"D,"Dwayne D. Dappen had no choice but to use D-Cubed for his brand. Dappen began by making Zinfandel from Howell Mountain and later added a bottling from Napa Valley. His wines are made at Kornell Cellars, where Dappen checks in for his day job as winemaker. Recent vintages show D-Cubed making 1,000 cases of Zinfandel a year, equally divided between Howell Mountain and Napa Valley.

DALLA VALLE VINEYARDS  *Napa 1986*  On a knoll overlooking the intersection of the Oakville Crossroad and the Silverado Trail, the Dalla Valle winemaking facility was completed in the fall of 86. Four years earlier, Gustav Dalla Valle and his wife Naoko developed a 25-acre vineyard in the Oakville area. Dalla Valle had previously been a manufacturer of diving equipment, and was a deep-sea diver himself before entering the wine business at the age of 70. His 25-acre hillside vineyard, situated on the slopes east of the Silverado Trail, is planted predominantly to Cabernet Sauvignon with a few acres of Cabernet Franc and Merlot for blending. Before his death in 1997, Dalla Valle had planted Sangiovese in his vineyard and had introduced a deluxe proprietary blend of Cabernet Sauvignon and Merlot named "Maya." With Tony Soter of Etude overseeing winemaking, the winery came on strong in the late 1990s with its Cabernets and also with a Sangiovese, named Pietre Rosse. Completed in 1986, the winery is designed to produce a maximum of 4,000 cases a year.

**Cabernet Sauvignon**

**86 87° 88 89° 90° 91 92° 93** 94°°° **95°°**

*Always promising, always highly tannic, never quite as deep in fruit as it might, yet collectable for its long-aging possibilities; 94 was a blockbuster*

**Maya**

8̶8̶ **89°° 90°° 91°° 93°° 94°° 95°°**

*As tannic as the Cabernet Sauvignon, but generally much deeper in balancing fruit*

DARK STAR  *Paso Robles 1995*  Owner-winemaker Norm Benson produces a line of red wines from grapes purchased within Paso Robles. To date he has offered Cabernet Sauvignon, Merlot, Zinfandel, and a Meritage blend named Ricordati, which translates as"always remembered."

DE LOACH VINEYARDS  *Sonoma 1975*  One-time San Francisco fireman Cecil De Loach took early retirement in 75 to concentrate on his small vineyard operation in the Russian River Valley. The old 24-acre Zinfandel vineyard he had acquired in 70 was in full production, but a weak demand for grapes in 75 forced him to venture into winemaking. After making only Zinfandel during his first three vintages, De

Loach has become one of the leading Chardonnay producers as well as one of the most reliable brands around. Located west of Santa Rosa, the De Loach winery is surrounded by the 120-acre estate vineyard. Another 75-acre vineyard in the same cool subregion of the Russian River Valley is under long-term lease, and in 90, De Loach purchased an additional 80 acres in a warmer region near Healdsburg suited to Cabernet Sauvignon and related Bordeaux varieties.

Over the first several vintages De Loach developed a good reputation for ripe Zinfandels and spicy Gewurztraminers. In 79, the winery started making White Zinfandel that proved to be a style-setter and a wild commercial success, and it also began earning high marks for Chardonnay in a style combining juicy fruit flavors and early drinkability. By the end of the 80s De Loach was making 25,000 cases of Chardonnay and at least as much White Zinfandel each year. Partially barrel-fermented and aged in French oak for nine months, De Loach Chardonnays have always managed to offer ripe apple appeal and modest depth and complexity when first released. Gewurztraminer is another highly successful varietal produced by De Loach. An early harvest version typically captures varietal intensity in a clean, crisp finish. In some vintages the early harvest ranks among the very best Gewurztraminer of all. Small quantities of late harvest Gewurztraminer are made in certain vintages, and they too are often of ° or °° caliber. Yet another recently successful wine, De Loach Estate Zinfandel is a blend of wines from four old, low-yielding vineyards located near the winery. De Loach has also brought out a lower-priced Chardonnay named "Sonoma Cuvée," and in 91 the winery made its first Merlot. A few years later Petite Sirah from Russian River Valley was added.

De Loach has been making Pinot Noir from his own 9-acre parcel, but the quality and style have varied widely. Sauvignon Blanc of generally average quality and Cabernet Sauvignon fill out the roster. Special lots of limited-production, high-priced, estate-bottled Chardonnay, Cabernet Sauvignon, and Pinot Noir are identified as "O.F.S.," standing for "Our Finest Selection." The total annual production at De Loach is close to 100,000 cases.

### Chardonnay

(Russian River Valley)   86°   87°°   88°°   89°   **90°**   **91°**   **92**   93   94   **95°**

(OFS)   86°   87°   88°°   89°   **90°°**   91   92   **93°°°**   94   **95°**   96

*Immensely fruity, almost juicy in its concentrated, bright style, with pert acidity and toasty oak in support; medium-long aging potential*

### Pinot Noir

(Russian River Valley)   82°°   83°   84   85   86   87   88   89   90   91   **92**   93

(OFS)   88°°   90   92°   **94**   **95°**   **96°**

*Early success has not been often repeated in this variety*

### Zinfandel

(regular bottling)   81   82   83   **84°**   85   **86°**   87   **88°°**   89°   **90°°**   9͎1   **92**   93   **94°°**   **95°**   **96°**

*Filled with ripe, bright, blackberryish fruit and enriched with vanillin oak; medium aging potential; 91 was a surprise, yet quality is down and may stay that way now that the best wine is held back for the single vineyard bottlings*

(Pelletti Ranch)   **90°°°**   **91°°**   **92**   93   **94°**   95°   **96**

(Papera Ranch)   **90°°°**   **91**   **92°°**   93°   94   95°°   **96**

(Barbieri Ranch)   **90°**   **91°**   **92°°**   93   **94°°**   95   **96°°**

(Gambogi Ranch)   **92°**   93   **94°**   95   96

*Deep, fruity, berryish, oaky wines that sometimes give in to overripeness, especially in 95 when the wines ranged in alcohol from 15% to 17%*

DE LORIMIER WINERY    *Sonoma 1985*    In the early 60s Dr. Alfred De Lorimier, a San Francisco surgeon, purchased a home in the Alexander Valley and began developing a vineyard adjacent to it. Located in the northern end of the valley near Geyserville, De Lorimier's home vineyard has been expanded to 64 acres, growing mainly Cabernet, Merlot, Chardonnay, Sauvignon Blanc, Semillon, and Cabernet Franc. In 1995, the owner purchased a 36-acre hillside vineyard in the midsection of the Alexander Valley. This vineyard consists of 15 acres of Chardonnay and 6 1/2 of Cabernet Sauvignon. De Lorimier produces a partially barrel-fermented Chardonnay and four proprietary blends. "Mosaic" is the name given to its red Bordeaux blend; "Spectrum" is the white Bordeaux blend (typically 65% Sauvignon Blanc, 35% Semillon). A late harvest blend of the same two wines fashioned along Sauternes lines is named "Lace." Even the winery's Chardonnay sports a proprietary name, "Prism." Initial production was close to 5,000 cases a year. The winery has the capacity to expand output to 25,000 cases a year.

DE NATALE VINEYARDS    *Sonoma 1985*    The De Natale family owns 7 acres of vineyards on Eastside Road in Healdsburg. With annual production below 1,000 cases a year, the winery is entirely family-run. In small batches averaging between 200 and 300 cases, they have in one vintage or another produced Chardonnay, Pinot Noir, Cabernet Sauvignon, Zinfandel, and Sangiovese. The first vintages of Chardonnay were impressive, and recent Sangiovese vintages have also been good.

DEERFIELD RANCH WINERY    *Sonoma 1982*    Small-scale family winery producing 2,000 cases a year. Wines offered to date are Sauvignon Blanc, Cabernet Franc, Cabernet Sauvignon, Merlot, and Chardonnay.

DEER PARK ESCONDIDO WINERY    *San Diego 1990*    Owned by the Knapps, coprop020proprietors of Deer Park Winery in Napa Valley, this facility produces only Chardonnay. Made from the Knapps' 3-acre vineyard, the Chardonnay is sold to local shops and restaurants in Northern San Diego County. The quality is average.

DEER PARK WINERY    *Napa 1979*    This beautiful old stone winery, built in 1891, went through several ownership changes before it was acquired by two families, the Knapps and the Clarks, refurbished, and put back in operation by the fall of 79. Most of the 48-acre property is steep, rocky hillside, 6 acres of which have been planted to Chardonnay and Sauvignon Blanc. The winery buys Zinfandel and on occasion Chardonnay and Petite Sirah from various growers in Napa Valley. As winemaker, David Clark prefers Zinfandels in a big, ripe style, and usually gives them two years of oak aging. His Napa Valley Zinfandels are generally supple and woodsy, with a hint of fruit. Every now and then he produces a bigger, bolder style of Zinfandel from the Beatty Ranch on Howell Mountain. The winery's total production is about 3,000 cases, with 6,000 set as the maximum level.

DEER VALLEY    *(Paul Masson Winery)*    This was a second label used by Smith & Hook until it was acquired by Paul Masson in 88. In an effort to enter the competitive low-price end of the varietal wine market, Vintners International, Masson's owner, decided to make Deer Valley its major weapon. Canandaigua purchased Deer Valley along with the Paul Masson brand in 1994. All wines are vintaged, and the line presently consists of Chardonnay, Cabernet Sauvignon, Sauvignon Blanc, and White Zinfandel. Sales have reached 70,000 cases a year.

DEHLINGER WINERY    *Sonoma 1976*    Located in the Forestville corner of the lower Russian River Valley, Dehlinger has quietly risen to first-class status. With assistance from his father and brother, Tom Dehlinger planted 14 acres adjacent to the winery. By 80, the winery was producing over 5,000 cases a year. Tom Dehlinger took a degree in biochemistry and went on to study enology at U.C. Davis. Early on, his winery developed a strong reputation for Zinfandel, but was soon performing well with all varietals. In 85 Tom Dehlinger became the sole owner, and the 85 vintage, a highly successful one for the winery, signaled the end of a rough and rustic note and the beginning of a polished, refined winemaking style. At that time the decision was made to produce only estate-grown wines. Unable to buy a suitable vineyard or to grow Zinfandel in his cool-climate locale, Dehlinger ceased making Zinfandel after 83.

Steadily expanding the home vineyard in the 80s, he now has 50 acres planted, mainly to Pinot Noir (20 acres) Chardonnay (15 acres), Cabernet Sauvignon (7 acres), and Merlot (3 acres). Each is made as a varietal. Dehlinger set his sights on Syrah and in 1992 began making blockbuster Syrah from his newly planted 3 acres. He now makes two, an Estate Syrah and a second from the 1-acre Goldridge Vineyard. Recently three Pinot Noirs have been bottled, an Estate, Goldridge Vineyard, and Octagon. All three are often among the very finest made. The rare Octagon bottling is usually made fewer than 200 cases. Also made in small quantities is a blend of Cabernet and Merlot now labeled "Bordeaux blend." A typical vintage gives Dehlinger about 9,000 cases, two-thirds of which are Chardonnay and Pinot Noir.

## Cabernet Sauvignon

78°  79°  80°  82°  83°  **84°**  **85°**  **86°**  87  **88°**  89  90
**91**  **92°**

*Ripish, curranty, somewhat plummy fruit, with occasional cedary or herbal under-tones, medium-rich oak, generally 10-year aging potential*

## Chardonnay

84  85°°  86°  87°  88°  89°  **90°°**  **91°°**  92  93°  **94°**
95°

*Nicely focused appley fruit, frequently with pretty, pearlike overtones, is buoyed by toasty oak and balanced by brisk acids*

## Pinot Noir

82°  83°  84°°  85°°  86°°  **87°°°**  **88°°**  89°°  **90°°°**
**91°°**  **92°°**  **93°°**  **94°°**  **95°°**

*Medium- to full-intensity cherryish fruit, sometimes with black cherry and orange rind, is enriched by oak, firmed by medium tannins, tends to age well*

DEL DOTTO CELLARS   *Napa Valley 1993*   From 10 acres of Cabernet Sauvignon planted in 1983, Dave Del Dotto, former real-estate agent, eased into winemaking by making 500 cases in his first vintage. With Nels Venge of Saddleback Cellars now overseeing winemaking, this team intends to expand annual production to 4,000 cases of Cabernet Sauvignon. 95 was big, rich, tannic and rated at °°.

DELICATO VINEYARDS   *San Joaquin 1935*   Located in Manteca and ranked the seventh largest wine producer in the country, Delicato supplied wines to other brands for many years until it also began bottling its own wines in the early 70s. Until recently, all wines have been made from Central Valley grapes. In the 80s, Sutter Home and other wineries began buying White Zinfandel from Delicato. In the early 80s Delicato, intending to upgrade its quality, had developed close to 300 acres in Clements, not far from Lodi. Then, in 88, it acquired the 13,000-acre San Bernabe Ranch in Monterey County, which contained 8,000 acres of established vineyards.

After that bold move of buying what is probably the world's largest contiguous vineyard, Delicato has expanded production for both its own line and the bulk business. Its Manteca facility now has a storage capacity of 30 million gallons. In 88, a crushing facility was built in Monterey where the grapes are processed. Today, most Delicato generic wines are from the California appellation. At over 100,000 cases, White Zinfandel is the volume leader among cork-finished wines. For the on-premise market, Delicato sells a range of generics and White Zinfandel in 18-liter containers, and that side of the business brings its total production to 2 million cases a year. To date, Monterey County is used for Chenin Blanc, White Grenache, Zinfandel, Sauvignon Blanc, and Chardonnay. In the mid-1990s the owners created the Monterra label, an upgraded line of Monterey varietals.

DEMOOR WINERY   *Napa 1973*   Known from 73 to 83 as Napa Wine Cellars, this winery was operated (often somewhat invisibly) as DeMoor until 1997, when the Rombauer family acquired it and immediately decided to revert back to using the Napa Wine Cellars (see entry) name.

### Cabernet Sauvignon

81°   **82°°**   **83°**   **84°°**   **86**   **87**   **89**

*Ripe, fairly concentrated character, often with a suggestion of dried fruit, enriched by omnipresent oakiness and tending toward an herbal streak in some vintages*

### Chardonnay

84   85°   86   87   88°   89   91   92

*Ripe, not especially fruity wines, high in oak but low in inviting varietal character*

### Zinfandel

84°   85   **86**   **88**   **90**   **91**

*Following the "house" style of emphasized ripeness, these wines have been fairly tannic and well oaked, but not always carrying sufficient fruit*

DEUX AMIS WINERY   Owners Phyllis Zouzounis and Jim Penpraze are indeed two friends who combine their talents to produce a limited line of wines. To date all wines have been made in leased space and are from the Dry Creek Valley appellation. The offerings include Sauvignon Blanc, Zinfandel, and Cabernet Sauvignon. Each at times has displayed good medium-intense character, and the Zinfandel has been a real standout recently. Total annual production is around 500 cases. Since mid-93, Zouzounis has been the winemaker at Mazzocco.

### Zinfandel

88°   **90°°°**   **91°°**   **92°**   **93**   **94**   **95**

*Ripe, generous, berryish fruit is stiffened with about 10% Petite Sirah*

DEVLIN WINE CELLARS   *Santa Cruz 1979*   Located in Soquel, just south of Santa Cruz, Devlin Wine Cellars sells most of its wine from its tasting and sales room. Owner/winemaker Chuck Devlin produces a range of varietals from purchased grapes. In a roster subject to change from year to year, Devlin emphasizes Santa Cruz Mountains Chardonnay, Cabernet Sauvignon, and Zinfandel. The Central Coast appellation is frequently seen on Devlin's Sauvignon Blanc and Merlot, and the Merlots have enjoyed ° success in recent years. A barrel-fermented Santa Cruz Mountain Chardonnay, "Beauregard Vineyard," is Devlin's prestige bottling. However, White Zinfandel is the volume leader in the annual output of 8,000 cases.

DIAMOND CREEK VINEYARDS   *Napa 1972*   This Cabernet Sauvignon–only winery is a great study in making the most from the smallest financial stake. In 67, Al Brounstein left his prospering pharmaceutical business in Los Angeles and moved to Napa Valley. He bought 79 acres of steep, forested land along the mountain ridge west of Calistoga known as Diamond Mountain. He then planted the land to 20 acres of Cabernet Sauvignon with Merlot for blending. Because of the configuration of the site, Brounstein set the vines on three separate blocks which, when each block was made into wine, revealed three distinct personalities. He kept each separate for bottling. Volcanic Hill was the largest parcel, named after the volcanic soils. The parcel opposite it was on red soils and was named Red Rock Terrace. The third, on extremely rocky soil, Brounstein called Gravelly Meadow.

For many years, Brounstein used the services of a part-time winemaker and had his wines crushed and fermented in rented facilities. Once it was in barrels, the wine would be transported to his mountain location.

From 72 to 78, the yields were small, and Diamond Creek did not make more than 1,000 cases total. Over the years Brounstein wisely developed a clientele, and by 80 was able to sell every drop bottled through a mailing list. A fourth vineyard, less than 1 acre, is the Lake Vineyard named after the manmade pond on the property. Usually blended into the Gravelly Meadow, the Lake has been bottled separately on occasion. Diamond Creek averages 2,500 cases a year. It is among the more expensive Cabernets. In the late 80s Brounstein built a compact, efficient winery and barrel-aging room on the property, and everything is state-of-the-art these days.

### Cabernet Sauvignon

(Red Rock Terrace)  73  74  75  77  78°  79°  80°  81°  82°
83°  84°°  85°°°  86°°°  87°  88  89°  90°  91  92°
93°  94  95°°

(Gravelly Meadows)  74  75  76  77  78°  79°  80°  81  82°
83  84°°°  85°°  86°°  87°°  88°  89  90  91°  92°  93°
94°°  95°

(Volcanic Hill)  73  74  75  76  77  78°°  79  80°°  81°
82°  83°  84°  85°°  86  87°  88  89°  90°  91  92  93°
94°  95°

*In the early to mid-70s, these were brutally tannic, overmade wines, whose complexity and depth was often joined by a host of earthy, loamy characteristics. But toward the 80s, the style became moderated just enough to produce cleaner wines, whose somewhat lowered but still mouth-puckering tannins now seemed more reasonably fitted to the rest of the wines' character. Red Rock Terrace is often the most fruity of the wines; Gravelly Meadows tends to be as intense but sometimes slightly less complete; the Volcanic Hill bottling can be a bit drier and thus not quite as able to fight through its bold tannins in lesser vintages. Nonetheless, this trio of wines is fully deserving of the high esteem it has won*

DOLCE  *(Far Niente Winery)*  For several years Far Niente experimented with late-harvest sweet wines along the lines of a French Sauternes. At best a few barrels were made of *Botrytis*-affected Semillon and Sauvignon Blanc. By the 89 vintage, the owners of Far Niente decided to go for the gold and came up with the Dolce name for their late-harvest wine. Made from *Botrytis* Semillon and Sauvignon Blanc, Dolce is barrel-fermented and aged entirely in new French oak for three years. Production varies according to the volume of each vintage but has been averaging 750 cases a year.

DOMAINE CARNEROS  *Napa 1987*  The prestigious name Taittinger appears prominently on the Domaine Carneros label, which is in fact a partnership between Champagne Taittinger, the Kobrand Corporation, a wine importer, and Peter Ordway, who owns the vineyards. Its large chateau-style facility is modeled upon the 18th-century Taittinger residence in Champagne. Located in the Carneros and relying exclusively on fruit grown in that area, Domaine Carneros makes sparkling wine by the *méthode champenoise*. To date its primary wine is a nonvintage Brut. The winery's capacity is 60,000 cases a year, a goal it expects to reach by the end of the decade.

About 110 acres adjacent to the imposing winery are planted to vines; the owners favor Pinot Noir and Chardonnay, but have also planted Pinot Blanc and Pinot Meunier. The initial cuvées of Brut were made from 60% Pinot Noir, 35% Chardonnay, and 5% Pinot Blanc. Like Taittinger Champagne, its French relative, Domaine Carneros, under the direction of Eileen Crane, also hopes to become known for a light-bodied, delicate style of sparkling wine. In furtherance of that goal, it has recently introduced a very delicate vintage Blanc de Blancs, a blend of Chardonnay and Pinot Blanc. Pinot Noir, nonsparkling classic style, was first made in 92, and is sold under the Famous Gate label. In that same vintage the winery created a deluxe Blanc de Blanc (Chardonnay and Pinot Blanc) bubbly named Le Reve.

**DOMAINE DE LA TERRE ROUGE** *Amador 1987* Longtime San Francisco Bay wine merchant Bill Easton began developing vineyards in 85. Located in Fiddletown where he resides, the primary vineyard of 8 acres is planted to Rhone varieties—Syrah, Mourvedre, Marsanne, and Viognier. From his own and neighboring vineyards, Easton has shaped Terre Rouge into a line of Rhone-inspired wines including varietals of Syrah, Mourvedre, Viognier, and two blends. Enigma is the white blend, consisting of Viognier, Marsanne, and Roussanne, and the red counterpart (a blend of Syrah, Grenache, and Mourvedre) is labeled Terre Rouge Noir. Completing the line is a rosé labeled Vin Gris, a quaffable red named Tête-à-Tête, and a sweet dessert wine, Muscat-a-Petits-Grains. Barbera, Zinfandel, and other wines without a Rhone connection are labeled Easton Winery. The combined annual production of both lines is close to the winery's 3,000-case capacity. Long-term annual production of Domaine de la Terre Rouge is expected to be 3,000 cases.

**DOMAINE DU GRAND ARCHER** *(Arrowood Winery)* This is a second label used by Arrowood for Sonoma County varietals made from various batches which either didn't make it into the primary wines or were involved in experimental programs. Chardonnay, Cabernet Sauvignon, and Cabernet Franc Rose are regularly offered. Merlot and Viognier have also been bottled under this name. Except for the Rose, which is not offered under the primary label, Grand Archer wines are aged briefly and sent to market earlier than the Arrowood wines. Annual output ranges between 3,500 and 4,000 cases.

**DOMAINE MONTREAUX** *Napa 1987* Represented by its owners as a separate brand and company, Montreaux is run by Jay Corley, owner of Monticello Cellars, his marketing director, and other partners involved with Monticello in some capacity. The only product is sparkling wine made by the *méthode champenoise;* Montreaux produced its first commercial batch in 83. A separate facility was in place by 87. About 32 acres of Chardonnay and Pinot Noir in the Oak Knoll area are set aside to supply grapes for this brand. The wines used in the cuvée are barrel-fermented and oak-aged. Once selected, the cuvée is given about three years' aging *en tirage.* Typically, the cuvées for the Brut style consist of 60% Pinot Noir, 40% Chardonnay. The early vintages did not live up to all the winemaking attention bestowed upon them, but recent vintages have shown improvement. Production is moving toward a goal of 3,500 cases per year.

**DOMAINE ST. GEORGE** *Sonoma 1986* The old Cambiaso Winery which had muddled along for decades was rechristened Domaine St. George in 86 and began moving on a fast track. A batch of 85 oak-aged Chardonnay was the first wine issued under the Domaine St. George label. The immediate sales success inspired the winery name change and led to its expansion into the low-priced varietal wine market. The facility, located in the northern Russian River Valley, has been upgraded and expanded to handle over 300,000 cases of varietals and proprietary blends. Some of the wines are crushed and fermented at the Sonoma winery, and a bigger portion is bought. Domaine St. George regularly offers Chardonnay, Cabernet Sauvignon, Fumé Blanc, Zinfandel, Chevrier, and blended white and red wines. Confirming its emphasis on the popular and trendy, the winery was the first to bottle a blush Chardonnay. Overall, its quality varies, depending on what is available on the bulk market.

**DOMINUS ESTATE** *Napa 1982* This one-wine producer began with an exciting cast of characters. Dominus Estate is the name of a Bordeaux-style blend created by a partnership, the John Daniel Society. The partners were the daughters of John Daniel, Robin Lail and Marcia Smith, and Christian Moueix, the winemaker-director for the legendary Château Pétrus of Pomerol. John Daniel owned Inglenook Vineyard during its prime years—the 30s to the late 60s. Many of California's most fabled Cabernets, such as the Inglenook Cask Cabernets of 41, 49, 52, 54, 55, 57, 58, and 59, were made entirely or in part from a vineyard that came to be known as Napanook Vineyard.

In 1995 Moueix became sole proprietor of both the vineyard and the brand. After a couple of winemaker changes Moueix installed Jean-Claude Berrouet from Château Petrus as head of winemaking at Dominus. A new facility was built in time for the 1997 harvest. Annual production will remain in the 6,000–8,000-case range. The 125-acre property dates to the 1880s and is located on the western hills near Yountville. In an area proven to be excellent Cabernet turf, Napanook has 50 acres planted to Cabernet and its blending cousins, 20 acres to Chardonnay, and 20 additional acres suitable for planting. Dominus is made exclusively from Napanook Cabernet Sauvignon (75–80%) with Merlot and Cabernet Franc filling it out. The first vintage was 83, a wine that was released a year after the 84, and met with some controversy. While some critics proclaimed Dominus to be an instant legend, we found that the first vintages approached the ° to °° quality, but were neither classic nor the best of their class in the high-priced division.

### Cabernet Sauvignon

| 83° | 84°° | 85° | 86° | 87° | 89 | 90° | 91 | 92 |
|-----|------|-----|-----|-----|----|-----|----|----|

*Immense wines that are bold in curranty fruit, high in rich and creamy oak, and very tannic, they are among the leaders for intensity and drama. But in the early vintages, they also have been bothered by background earthy notes that raise troubling questions about how well they will hold up in the long run*

DOUGLAS HILL WINERY    *Napa 1992*    Owned by the Classic Wine Co., this label appears on Napa Valley Chardonnay and Cabernet Sauvignon.

DOVER CANYON WINERY    *Paso Robles 1994*    Former winemaker at Eberle Winery, Dan Panico ventured out on his own and produces close to a dozen wines. Tops on his list is Zinfandel, which regularly is made from the Jankris Vineyard, and Cabernet Sauvignon from Paso Robles. Panico began on a high note with early vintages of Zinfandel.

DRY CREEK VINEYARDS    *Sonoma 1972*    Owner Dave Stare deserves considerable credit for his pioneering efforts in founding the first small, premium-quality winery in Sonoma County since the end of Prohibition. He was also among the first proponents of the Dry Creek Valley Viticultural Area, and his winery played a key part in the evolution of Fumé Blanc as a varietal, thanks to its pungent, aromatic version. Now, after two expansion stages, Dry Creek is functioning at its maximum capacity of 125,000 cases annually. Fumé Blanc is the major wine, with 28,000 to 30,000 cases made a year, followed by Chardonnay (25–27,000 cases), and Cabernet Sauvignon (10,000 cases). Chenin Blanc, Zinfandel, Merlot, and Petite Sirah fill out the line. Both Gewurztraminer and Johannisberg Riesling have been provided, but were discontinued in the late 80s. Dry Creek Vineyards' Fumé Blanc, tending toward a grassy, pungent style, has succeeded in some years and gone too far in that direction in others. Of late, the winery's Chardonnay has been the best performer. Recently, the much improved Reserve program has consisted of about 3,000 cases of Chardonnay, 100% barrel-fermented, Merlot, and 2,000 cases of a red Meritage. The winery draws from its Estate Vineyards, which consist of 70 acres it owns in the Dry Creek Valley and 32 in the Alexander Valley. It purchases grapes from other vineyards within Sonoma and also within the Delta region, which supplies the winery with Chenin Blanc.

### Cabernet Sauvignon

| 80 | 81 | 82 | 83 | 84 | 85° | 86 | 87° | 88° | 89° | 90 | 91° |
|----|----|----|----|----|-----|----|-----|-----|-----|----|-----|
| 92 | 93 | 94 | 95 | | | | | | | | |

*Always containing Merlot and lately a dollop of Cabernet Franc, the wine can be fruit-focused and clean, with good depth in its best showings, but less complete and a bit too rough at other times*

## Chardonnay

(Sonoma County)   86°°   87   89   90   91   92   93   94°   95
(Reserve)   90   91°   92   94°   95

*Tightly focused fruit, of good intensity and firm balance, is enriched by toasty oak*

## Merlot

88   89°   **90**   **91**   **92**   93   **94**   95

*Typically blended with up to 25% Cabernet Sauvignon and Cabernet Franc combined, but low in fruit nonetheless*

## Zinfandel

(Old Vines)   87   88   89   **90°**   **91**   **92°°**   93   **94°**   95°

*Ripe, berryish, and slightly spicy, but often dry at its heart; recent vintages have been deeper*

DUCKHORN VINEYARDS   *Napa 1976*   A limited partnership of ten families, including Dan and Margaret Duckhorn, this winery is run by the Duckhorns. A banker by profession, Dan Duckhorn became involved in Napa Valley when he was an expert witness in a case involving grape growers. Never much to look at by Napa Valley standards, the winery is located northeast of St. Helena on the Silverado Trail. Ever since its inaugural release of 78 Merlot, Duckhorn has been the most in-demand producer of Merlot, and as a result its usually fine accomplishments with Cabernet Sauvignon and Sauvignon Blanc have taken a back seat. Duckhorn's 6 1/2 acres of Sauvignon Blanc and Semillon now contribute to its annual production of about 7,500 cases of Sauvignon Blanc, about 50% barrel-fermented and often blended with 20% Semillon. They have been rich and attractive enough to earn °° often.

Merlot is bought from several vineyards, including the Three Palms Vineyard in Calistoga and Vine Hill Vineyards in Rutherford, both of which have been individually bottled. The Three Palms Merlots are often the best of the class. The more plentiful Napa Valley Merlot combines fruit from five or six vineyards as a rule, and is usually blended with Cabernet Sauvignon and Cabernet Franc. Duckhorn's Cabernet is often blended with Cabernet Franc and occasionally contains a pinch of Merlot. Production of Three Palms Merlot was reduced by phylloxera during the mid-90s, but Duckhorn is once again making 3,000 cases annually. Paraduxx, a blend of Zinfandel, Cabernet Sauvignon, and Merlot, is new to the roster. Howell Mountain Merlot has replaced Claret, a blend that Duckhorn made in the 1980s.

For over a decade, Duckhorn's Cabernets, limited to about 2,000 cases per year, were among the highest rated of the vintage, and the quality was a little more consistent than was that of its Merlots. In the last few vintages of the 80s, Duckhorn's production increased to about 20,000 cases of red wine—55% Merlot, 45% Cabernet Sauvignon. "Decoy," a second label used for a Pinot Noir today, has also appeared on Cabernet Sauvignon and other wines not making it into the final blends. Since the mid-80s, Duckhorn has acquired 95 acres within Napa Valley, and by the year 2000 the winery intends to own 75% of the grapes it crushes. Its first estate-grown Merlot was made in 95.

## Cabernet Sauvignon

78°°   80°°   **81°°°**   82°°   83°°   **84°°**   **85°°**   **86°°**   87°°
**88°**   **89°**   **91°**   **92°**   **93°**   **94°**   95

*Medium-full-bodied wines, high in curranty Cabernet fruit and rich oak, are seasoned with brushy, briary notes and come with fairly tough tannins; they are tasty, deep, and long aging*

### Merlot

| (Napa Valley) | 79** | 80** | 81** | 82** | 83** | **84*** | **86*** |
|---|---|---|---|---|---|---|---|
| **87*** | **88*** | **89*** | **90*** | **91*** | **92*** | **93*** | 94* | **95*** |

(Napa Valley)  79**  80**  81**  82**  83**  **84***  **86***
**87****  **88***  **89***  **90***  **91****  **92***  **93***  94*  **95***

(Three Palms Vineyard)  78****  81****  83*  **84****  **85***  **86****
**87***  88**  **89***  **90***  **91****  92

(Vine Hill Vineyard)  **85***  86  **87***  **91***

(Howell Mountain)  **90****  **91***  **92***  **93***

*With a decade of outstanding performance behind it, Duckhorn clearly stands as the leading producer of Merlot in California; its Three Palms Vineyard bottling is typically robust and complex, with deep curranty and cherryish fruit emerging as the wine ages through a decade or more of development; the Napa Valley bottling is more directly fruity, less complex but occasionally outperforms its more expensive stablemate when its focused ripe cherry fruit is at its most intense; Howell Mountain is quite brawny.*

DUNCAN PEAK VINEYARDS  *Mendocino 1987*  San Francisco Bay Area attorney Hubert Lenczowski decided to develop a small vineyard on his family's ranch. In the early 80s he laid out 4 acres total to Cabernet Sauvignon, Merlot, and Cabernet Franc on a hillside in an area of Hopland known as the Sanel Valley. By the time of his first crush in 86, Lenczowski had refurbished a two-story barn on a hilltop on the edge of Duncan Peak and converted it into a small winery. The facility has a capacity to ferment and age 500 cases a year. 95 Cabernet earned **

DUNN VINEYARDS  *Napa 1982*  As the winemaker for Caymus Vineyards in the 70s, Randy Dunn established a reputation for outstanding Cabernet Sauvignon. In the late 70s he and his wife, Lori, began reviving an old Cabernet vineyard on their home property west of Angwin in the Howell Mountain appellation. The old 5-acre vineyard was returned to productivity and from it about 500 cases were made in 79. Encouraged by the owners of Caymus, Dunn bonded his winery in 82 and began a distinguished series of Cabernet Sauvignons. His Howell Mountain bottling, produced from his own and a neighboring 5-acre vineyard he manages, started to develop a cult following when the 81 was offered. In the next vintage, Dunn added a Napa Valley Cabernet Sauvignon made from purchased grapes. Dunn's Cabernets have usually been 100% Cabernet and are aged for about two and a half years in small French oak. By the end of the 80s, the annual production of each bottling was 2,000 cases. Dunn has also been an active consultant, and in the 80s his talents were brought to bear on the early vintages of Cabernet Sauvignons bottled by La Jota, Grace Family, Livingston, Pahlmeyer, and others.

### Cabernet Sauvignon

(Howell Mountain)  79  **80***  81*  **82****  **83****  **84****  **85***
**86****  **87****  **88***  **89***  90**  91**  94**

(Napa Valley)  **82****  **83***  **84****  **85****  **86****  **87****  **88***
**89***  90****  91*  92**  93  **94***

*Deep, ripe, concentrated, immensely fruity wines, broadened by gobs of rich, sweet, creamy oak and carrying the structure and depth for long aging, Dunn Cabernets are arguably the best of breed in recent years. The Howell Mountain is the tougher, more briary wine, while the Napa Valley is somewhat smoother and richer*

DUNNEWOOD VINEYARDS  *Mendocino*  1988 Introduced in 88 by Guild, then its parent company, Dunnewood began on an upbeat note. The quality of its first wines, particularly its 84 Reserve Cabernet Sauvignon from Napa Valley and 88 Napa Chardonnay, caught everyone's attention. But then the quality declined. When Guild was acquired by the giant Canandaigua Wine Co. in 91, the new owner upgraded the Dunnewood name by focusing on a line of North Coast varietals—Chardonnay, Cabernet Sauvignon, and Merlot. The line extends to Sauvignon Blanc, Pinot Noir, Zinfandel, and White Zinfandel. Recently, Dunnewood has in-

troduced an upscale line of limited volume wines under the "Dry Silk" designation. To date, this line consists of Carneros Chardonnay, Alexander Valley Cabernet Sauvignon, and Napa Valley Cabernet Sauvignon. Both the North Coast and
Dry Silk wines are priced modestly. Annual output is close to 300,000 cases.

DURNEY VINEYARD   *Monterey 1977*   William Durney and his wife, author Dorothy
Kingsley, were the first to establish vineyards in the Carmel Valley. Situated on a
series of ridges in a woodsy, remote sector of the valley, the vineyard was started
in 67 and now covers 85 acres. The principal varieties planted were Cabernet
Sauvignon, Riesling, Chardonnay, and Chenin Blanc. In 86 and 87 the winery
made no wine under its label, and production was not resumed full scale until the
90 vintage. After the death of Mr. Durney in 89, the winery muddled along until
it was purchased in 94 by a British group headed by investor Gilbert Heller. Since
then the estate vineyard has been enlarged to 120 acres total, with 40 acres
planted to Merlot. With vineyard maturity, Durney's annual production of 30,000
cases will emphasize Cabernet Sauvignon, Merlot, and Chardonnay. When bottled, Reserve Cabernet Sauvignon has often proved to be exceptional. Pinot Noir
and Chenin Blanc fill out the roster. Occasionally the winery uses "Cachagua" as
a second label for Cabernet and Chardonnay.

### Cabernet Sauvignon

**78°°   79°   80°   81°   82°   83°   84̶   90°**

*Consistently good, usually rich in sweet oak, sometimes too much ripe fruit; light-
medium tannins and good depth combine to give aging potential*

DUTCH HENRY WINERY   *Napa 1989*   Located along the Silverado Trail, this family-
owned, unpretentious winery sells most wines at its cellar doors. From its 4-acre
vineyard and leased vineyards, Dutch Henry offers Cabernet Sauvignon, Merlot,
Chardonnay, and Claret, a generic red. Annual production is 2,000 cases.

DUXOUP WINE WORKS   *Sonoma 1981*   Named after the Marx Brothers movie *Duck
Soup,* this winery makes only red varietals. It owns no vineyards, so all grapes are
purchased, with most of the wines originating in the Dry Creek Valley. Over recent vintages it has made Syrah, Zinfandel, Napa Gamay, and Charbono. The Zinfandel has been quite erratic and sometimes unpleasant. The others, notably the
Charbono from Napa Valley and the Dry Creek Valley Syrah, offer solid character
in a ripe, fruity style. The Gamay is the one wine rising above average in some vintages. Total annual production is at the maximum 2,000-case level.

EBERLE WINERY   *San Luis Obispo 1982*   Gary Eberle came to Paso Robles in 77 to serve
as winemaker for Estrella River Winery, the ambitious winery and vineyard project founded by his stepbrother. After the 81 vintage, Eberle left to start his own
much smaller winery about 3 miles away. For several vintages, Eberle's wines
were made from his former winery's vineyards. Now, he has 38 acres of his own,
planted primarily to Cabernet Sauvignon, Viognier, and Chardonnay. From purchased grapes, Eberle makes "Paso Robles" Zinfandel, Cabernet Sauvignon,
Syrah, and Chardonnay, along with a sweet-finished Muscat Canelli. He favors
unblended Cabernet Sauvignon, while his Chardonnays are fermented in
stainless-steel tanks with about 50% going through malolactic fermentation. In
certain vintages, Eberle selects the best barrels in the cellars to produce a Reserve
Cabernet. In the 1990s Eberle expanded his interest in Rhone wines and now offers Viognier, Grenache, Côtes-du-Robles (blend of Syrah and Cabernet), and
single-vineyard Syrah from both Steinbeck Vineyard and Fralich Vineyard. Occasionally he offers Zinfandel from Steinbeck Vineyard and Sauret Vineyard. Representing close to one-third of the winery's 18,000-case annual output, Cabernet
Sauvignon remains the flagship wine.

ECHELON   *(Chalone Estates)*   In 1998 Chalone Estates, in the midst of many changes,
introduced this brand for Central Coast Chardonnay and Pinot Noir. Marketed at

competitive price levels, both wines are made under the supervision of Larry Brooks, the longtime winemaker for Acacia, part of Chalone Estates. Initial quantities of 60,000 cases for Chardonnay and 20,000 cases of Pinot Noir indicate Echelon will likely become the company's big-volume brand.

TOM EDDY WINES   *Napa Valley 1991*   Well-traveled veteran winemaker Eddy (formerly with Inglenook, Souverain, and Christian Brothers) set up a consulting business along with a small-volume wine brand. Since 1991 he has been buying grapes from several vineyards within Napa Valley to produce a 100% Cabernet Sauvignon. Aged more than two years in barrel and one in the bottle, Eddy's Cabernets have been rightfully praised for their intense flavors and balance. Production remains in the 400–500-case-a-year range. Price is more than $50 a bottle. 94 Cabernet earned °°.

EDIZIONE PENNINO   *(Niebaum-Coppola Estate)*   Francis Ford Coppola's grandfather was Francesco Pennino, the well-known musician and composer whose music company was named Edizione Pennino. With a little urging from his grandmother, Coppola revived the name and logo for this label, which to date has appeared only on Zinfandel. The first vintages were big, richly flavored, and well orchestrated. Production remains modest at 300 cases per year.

**Zinfandel**

**91°°   92°°°   93°°   94°°   95**

*Ripe blackberry fruit with shadings of ripe raspberry is filled out by rich, creamy oak in balanced, carefully crafted wines*

EDMEADES VINEYARDS   *Mendocino 1972*   One of the pioneers of the Anderson Valley, this winery and it 62-acre vineyard enjoyed some success in the 1980s only to slowly deteriorate from neglect in the late 1980s. Closed by the Edmeades family, the property gathered dust and tumbleweed until it was acquired by Kendall-Jackson Winery in 1992. Since then, the winery has been spruced up a little and the vineyard has been replanted to Chardonnay and Pinot Noir. In addition to making varietal wines from those two grapes, Edmeades is emphasizing small-lot production of Gewurztraminer and vineyard-designated Zinfandel from some of the oldest vineyards (Zeni, Ciapusci) in the Anderson Valley. Reaching out into the Redwood Valley, Edmeades has offered Zinfandel and Petite Sirah from Eaglepoint Vineyard. As production grows toward the 6,000-case goal, the Mendocino appellation Zinfandel is the major wine in the lineup.

EDMUNDS ST. JOHN   *Alameda 1985*   Located in Emeryville, this winery operated for two years as the East Bay Wine Works before assuming its present name. Former wine retailer Steve Edmunds began his professional winemaking career by blending a white wine, "Melange," and a red, "Petit Rouge." In 86 he began applying his blending skills to Rhone Valley grapes and wine types, and became one of the key members of the so-called Rhone Rangers. Edmunds ferreted out Syrah from Sonoma, Mourvedre from Oakley in Contra Costa County and Mount Veeder in Napa, and Grenache from Mendocino and Washington State. He has experimented with numerous combinations, only a few of which have been marketed. His small regular production consists of Zinfandel, "Côtes Sauvage" (a proprietary blend of Syrah, Grenache, and Mourvedre), and Syrah and Grenache. Edmunds has tried his hand with many different varieties including Viognier, Pinot Grigio (Pinot Gris), Cabernet Franc, and likely any other type of wine that might prove to yield interesting wine. To date, he has put his signature on some truly outstanding Syrah and Zinfandel, and is a leader in the world of Rhone blends with his Côtes Sauvage. In the late 80s he began developing 20 acres in the southern part of El Dorado County, a region supplying Grenache and Syrah for his label. The annual production will remain under 5,000 cases until the El Dorado plantings come into full production.

**Syrah**

89° 90°°° 91°°° 92° 93°° 94°°

*Deep, ripe, fruity, and tannic, this is a full-blown "big" wine*

**Zinfandel**

86°° 87°° 88 90°° 91°° 92 93° 94 95

*Ripe, brawny, deeply flavored wines capable of aging for half a decade or more; 88 was an overripe anomaly; recent wines from Amador County have lacked the usual swagger*

---

EDNA VALLEY VINEYARDS *San Luis Obispo 1980* A joint venture between Chalone Wine Group and Paragon Vineyards, Edna Valley Vineyards enjoyed a really good run of Chardonnay vintages in the 1980s. In the early 1990s its wines fell back into the pack, but a new winemaking team and new production facility have combined to put the winery back on track. From Paragon's impressive 756-acre vineyard, the winery produces about 70,000 cases of Chardonnay and 2,000 cases of Pinot Noir. Edna Valley also has added a series of limited production wines such as Pinot Blanc, Vin Gris, and a Brut Sparkling wine from the Edna Valley appellation along with Cabernet from Paso Robles, Syrah from Santa Barbara, and Viognier from Templeton. However, the winery's reputation rides with Chardonnay, which is once again among the best values.

**Chardonnay**

84°° 85° 86° 87°° 88°°° 89° 90° 91 92 93 94 95° 96°°

*Ripe fruit comes balanced by ample acidity, and the wine can be both rich and complex in its combination of oak and roasted-grain elements*

---

EHLERS GROVE *Napa 1993* Tony Cartlidge, Paul Moser, and Don Spirlock, the Napa Valley team that created Stratford and Canterbury in the 1980s, formed Ehlers Grove after relinquishing their domestic interests in Strartford and Canterbury. After renovating and renaming the historic Ehlers Lane Winery north of St. Helena, the partners set out to produce Chardonnay, Sauvignon Blanc, and Cabernet Sauvignon labeled Ehlers Grove. Cartlidge & Browne remains an affiliated label for Chardonnay.

---

ELAN *Napa 1995* Owning 13 acres and leasing a neighbor's 10-acre vineyard, Atlas Peak resident Pat Smith made 150 cases of Cabernet Sauvignon in his debut vintage. He intends to build a winery and eventually bottle 2,000 cases of Cabernet Sauvignon (blended with Merlot and Cabernet Franc) by the year 2001.

---

ELKHORN PEAK CELLARS *Napa 1992* From the family's 8-acre vineyard planted in 1983, Ken Nerlove focuses on Chardonnay and Pinot Noir. The winery's first vintage of 1992 yielded 500 cases, and Elkhorn Peak has set 2,000 cases as its maximum production goal. Located east of the Carneros district and overlooking the San Pablo Bay, the winery's vineyard falls within Southern Napa Valley's Jamieson Creek, a cool climate region with considerable room for vineyard expansion. The Pinot Noir offers plenty of deep fruit.

**Chardonnay**

93 94° 95

**Pinot Noir**

93° 94°° 95°

---

EL MOLINO WINERY *Napa 1981* Having restored a winery and aging caves that were built in 1871 and operated until 1920, Reg Oliver produces only high-priced Pinot Noir and Chardonnay. His Pinot Noir is whole cluster–fermented in small vats. Aged entirely in new French oak barrels, the Pinot Noirs display richness, but the early vintages were erratic in quality. The Chardonnays, produced from a vineyard owned by Oliver, have been more worthwhile in recent vintages. Annual production is 2,000 cases.

### Chardonnay

89   90°   91°   92°   93°   **94°°**   95   **96°°°**

*Rich, oaky notes season the ripe fruit in this full-bodied wine*

### Pinot Noir

87°°   88   89°   **90°**   **91°°**   92°   **93°**   94°

*Ripe, fleshy, deep flavors are highlighted in this ageworthy Pinot*

---

ELIZABETH VINEYARDS   *Mendocino 1987*   In the middle of the Redwood Valley, Betty Foster and family planted 40 acres of vines in the 70s. The name Elizabeth is that of her first granddaughter. While selling the crop to numerous Mendocino producers as well as to the Robert Mondavi Winery, Simi, and Souverain, the owner began testing the winemaking world in 87. Only Sauvignon Blanc and Zinfandel are made, and the production will be confined to 200 cases of each varietal.

---

ELLISTON VINEYARDS   *Alameda 1983*   The name Elliston is taken from the historic 17-room mansion located in the Sunol Valley, south of Pleasanton, purchased by the current owners in 69. After refurbishing the house and grounds, the Awtrey family converted the carriage house into a small winery, planted 3 acres to Chardonnay, hired a winemaker, and ventured into the wine business. Selling wines directly to visitors, the winery produces 2,000 cases per year. Over the first several vintages, it made Chardonnay, Pinot Blanc, and Pinot Gris, along with Cabernet and Merlot. All are from the Sunol Valley appellation. Elliston was the first California producer of Pinot Gris, a variety sparking great interest in Oregon. The winery currently plans to emphasize that variety along with Chardonnay and Pinot Blanc.

---

ELYSE WINE CELLARS   *Napa 1987*   This small winery is owned by Nancy and Ray Coursen of Napa, who have been focusing early on Zinfandel from a single vineyard in West Rutherford. The Morisoli Vineyard was established in 15, and today it remains a field blend of Zinfandel, Petite Sirah, and miscellaneous reds. Elyse Zinfandels are aged for one year in a combination of French and American oak. The Coursens expanded their line in the 1990s and are now making a Howell Mountain Zinfandel, a special batch of Napa Valley Zinfandel named "Couer du Val," and a blended red, "Nero Misto," which translates into "mixed black varieties." Cabernet Sauvignon joined the team in the early 90s. The production is increasing toward 5,000 cases a year. This label's quality level has been impressive from the outset.

### Zinfandel

| (Morisoli) | **87°** | **88°** | **89°°** | **90°°** | **91°°** | **92°** | **93** | **95** |
| (Howell Mountain) | **91°°°** | **92°°°** | **93°** | **94°°** | | | | |

*Very solidly constructed, ripe, richly oaked wines, capable of improving with cellar aging*

---

EOS WINERY   *Paso Robles 1996*   Eos is a partnership between members of the Archiero family and Young's Market, a major wine distributor. With Tom Eddy supervising winemaking, the Eos line of Paso Robles varietals consists of Chardonnay, Cabernet Sauvignon, Zinfandel, and Petite Sirah.

---

ESTANCIA VINEYARDS   *(Franciscan Vineyards)*   Around 86, following its umpteenth reorganization, Franciscan Vineyards introduced Estancia as the label for wines made from its holdings in the Alexander Valley. Ever since then Franciscan Vineyards has been used only for Napa Valley wines from its Oakville Estates. To start with, the Estancia lineup consisted of Alexander Valley Cabernet Sauvignon, Chardonnay, and Fumé Blanc, grown in the winery's 325-acre vineyard. Presented in a handsome package, the three varietals were marketed as "values for the money." Estancia achieved its goal most often with Cabernet Sauvignon made in a moderately fruity, soft, slightly herbaceous style. However, the owners soon purchased 500 acres of vineyards in Monterey County, and over the next few years entirely reorganized the Estancia line. From its Monterey holdings, Estancia concentrates on white wines, primarily Chardonnay, Sauvignon Blanc, and a white Meritage blend. The latter is 100% barrel-fermented and *sur lie* aged in small oak barrels. Chardonnay (50% barrel-fermented) represents 85% of the Monterey County production, which is close to 150,000 cases. From its Alexander Valley acreage, Estancia now bottles only red wines, led by Cabernet Sauvignon, Merlot, Meritage, and Sangiovese. Altogether, the reds add up to 40,000 cases, 75% of which is Cabernet Sauvignon. Most Estancia wines are attractively priced and occasionally earn good-value ratings. The standout to date has been the red Meritage, a wine of ** potential. Sangiovese also shows great potential, as also does Duetto, a blend of Cabernet Sauvignon and Sangiovese.

## Cabernet Sauvignon

(regular bottling)   87°   88   89   90°   91   **92°**   93   94

(Meritage)   87°   88°°   89   **90°**   **92°**   **93°**   **94°**   **95°**

*The popularly priced regular bottling is often a good value for its youthful, cherryish fruit while the Meritage, albeit in the $20 price range, also earns it spurs for values and for mid-term ageworthiness*

ESTATE WILLIAM BACCALA   *Mendocino 1993*   When he acquired the former Tijsseling winery in 93, Baccala was returning to Mendocino, where he founded this brand in the early 80s. After selling his winery and moving his winemaking operations to Sonoma County in 86, he concentrated upon developing a line of négociant wines under the Zellerbach Vineyard brand. Production of the Baccala line of wines was virtually halted. Now back close to where he started, Baccala is making Merlot and Old Vine Zinfandel. Initial production of Estate William Baccala wines was 5,000 cases total. Baccala still owns the Zellerbach brand (see entry).

ESTRELLA RIVER WINERY   *San Luis Obispo 1977*   Estrella River was the first major winery and vineyard development in San Luis Obispo County. The original partners included Gary Eberle, who started his own winery later on, and onetime football hero Rocky Bleir. By the early 70s the partnership had developed over 700 acres of vineyards. Increasing the production of wine, by 80 Estrella River was making close to 100,000 cases. After many further ups and downs, the facility and 560 acres of mature vineyards were acquired in 88 by the Nestlé Corp., the owner of Beringer, Chateau Souverain, Deutz, and other brands. The Estrella Winery brand was kicked around by a few people before being picked up by Classic Wine Co., a large wine distributor in California. The Estrella name is now attached to Cabernet Sauvignon, Chardonnay, White Zinfandel, and generic wines, all most often seen in supermarkets.

ETUDE   *Napa 1985*   Tony Soter, a highly regarded consultant and former winemaker for Chappellet and others, owns Etude. To date he has produced only Pinot Noir and Cabernet Sauvignon. All fruit for Etude is purchased from Napa Valley growers, with Pinot Noir made from three vineyards in the Carneros, and Cabernet from several vineyards in mid–Napa Valley. Soter, who serves as winemaker for Spottswoode, blends about 12% Merlot and 10% Cabernet Franc into Etude's Cabernets. Renting space in another facility, Soter has been making about 3,000 cases of each wine a year. Etude's sturdy, ageworthy Pinot Noirs have attracted more interest and have earned ** in several vintages.

## Cabernet Sauvignon

85   **86°°**   **87°**   **89°**   **90°°**   **91°°**   **92°**   93°°°

*Fleshy wines, high in extract and tannin, and fairly direct in their dense, ripe cherry and sweet oak character; they should age well but will always be more bold than refined; 88 not offered*

**Pinot Noir**

84•• 85••• 86• **87**•• **88**•• 89• **90**•• 91•• **92**•• 93•
**94** 95•

*Like the Cabernets, these wines are deep in character and appear to have the balance and backbone for long aging; their Pinot Noir heritage shows in the rich, broad fruit and supple, almost velvety texture, set within fairly bold tannins*

EVENSEN VINEYARDS & WINERY  *Napa 1979*  Located on winery row in Oakville, this winery is operated by the Evensen family as a part-time project. For many years they sold the fruit from their 5 acres of Gewurztraminer. In 79, working in the basement of their home, Dick and Sharon Evensen produced a few hundred cases of dry-styled Gewurztraminer. Over the years, the production of Gewurztraminer has averaged about 700 cases. The Evensen home vineyard now has 1 acre of Chardonnay, which will yield about 200 cases a year.

EXPRESSIONS  *(Glen Ellen Winery)*  Presented in a bright, upscale package, the Expressions line of varietals represented a departure for Glen Ellen Winery. Though still modestly priced and often representing good value, the wines were made in small volume from prestigious appellations. The value leaders to date are Sonoma County Chardonnay and Merlot, Napa Sangiovese, and North Coast Cabernet Sauvignon. Viognier and Zinfandel complete the line.

FALLENLEAF VINEYARDS  *Sonoma 1986*  Planted in the early 80s, Fallenleaf's 15-acre vineyard falls partly within the Carneros appellation and partly within Sonoma Valley. The winery's first several vintages were custom-crushed at Bouchaine, and only Chardonnay and Sauvignon Blanc have been produced. Because the appellation boundary runs through its vineyard, the winery bottles two Chardonnays—Sonoma Valley and Carneros. By 90 production was at the 3,000-case level, with equal emphasis on Chardonnay and Sauvignon Blanc.

FANUCCHI WINERY  *Russian River Valley 1995*  Definite old-time growers, the Fanucchi family bought an old Zinfandel vineyard in 1906. In 1984 10 acres were developed to an esoteric white grape, Trousseau Gris. Grapes were sold to several wineries until the mid-1990s, when Peter Fanucchi decided to make wines. His Zinfandel from old vines was joined by a rare Trousseau, and the Zinfandel was immediately among the most expensive, and occasionally among the best.

FAR NIENTE WINERY  *Napa 1979*  Founded in 1885, the Far Niente Winery was abandoned at Prohibition, and remained a hollow shell until Gil Nickel came along in 78 to revive it. With neighboring vineyard owner Dick Stelling, and John Nickel, his brother, Nickel completely restored the original winery, which is set back from the wine road just south of the Robert Mondavi Winery. During its first three vintages Far Niente produced its wines in a rented facility and released only Chardonnay in a ripe, well-oaked, sometimes heavy-handed style. In 82 its first Cabernet Sauvignon was rich, ripe, and also tannic. However, as production of Chardonnay grew to 25,000 cases, and Cabernet (blended with Cabernet Franc and Merlot) grew to 10,000 cases, the quality has improved. On occasion, the winery produces a sweet dessert wine named "Dolce," made from *Botrytis*-affected Sauvignon Blanc and Semillon. In 90, Far Niente added 15,000 square feet of man-made aging caves, which completed the restoration and expansion of this showcase facility.

**Cabernet Sauvignon**

82 83 84 **85**• **86**••• 87 **88**• 89• 90• **91**•• **92**•
**93** **94**• **95**••

*Marked by inconsistency, these wines are always ripe and oaky, with medium tan-nins, but have only delivered a full measure of ripe cherry and curranty fruit in some recent vintages*

## Chardonnay

84   85°   86   87°   88   89   90   91   92   93   94   95°

*Always high in toasty oak character and medium-full-bodied, the wines have often been low in vitality and, as a result, have sometimes carried an exaggeratedly dry, smokey quality*

---

FARELLA–PARK VINEYARDS   *Napa 1985*   The Farellas, Frank and Annie, own a 28-acre vineyard in the eastern hills of the Napa Valley. It consists of 12 acres of Chardon-nay, 7 of Sauvignon Blanc, and 9 of Cabernet Sauvignon and Merlot. After plant-ing the vineyard in 79, they sold most of the crop to the Robert Mondavi Winery, keeping a few tons to produce wine. Their son, Tom, is an enologist (formerly of Preston Vineyards) who assists with the family operation. At full capacity their small winery can handle 500 cases a year. The mainstays bottled are Chardonnay, Sauvignon Blanc, Cabernet Sauvignon, and Merlot.

---

GARY FARRELL WINES   *Sonoma 1981*   Starting in the cellars of Davis Bynum in 78, Gary Farrell worked his way up the ladder and has toiled as winemaker for both Bynum and J. Rochioli. Now, while still winemaker for Davis Bynum, he continues mak-ing wines under his own brand as he has since 82. Using his own barrels and a corner of the Bynum winery, Farrell produces small batches of varietals from spec-ified vineyards in the cool sectors of the Russian River Valley appellation. He has shown flashes of brilliance with Chardonnay and with Pinot Noir. In 87, he stopped making Sauvignon Blanc and added Cabernet Sauvignon and Merlot. Both varieties, grown in the Danielik Vineyard (referred to as "Ladi's Vineyard" on labels) east of Santa Rosa, have been very successful in their initial efforts. Farrell's Merlot from "Ladi's Vineyard" can be exceptional. Pinot Noir from the Howard Allen Vineyard, bordering Rochioli's property, usually shows more earthiness than the Russian River Valley bottling. Pinot Noirs from Bien Nacido in Santa Bar-bara, from Floodgate Vineyard, and from other tiny vineyards in Anderson Valley also have been made. Farrell's production is holding steady at 3,500 cases a year. He has set 4,500 cases as the maximum.

## Cabernet Sauvignon

(Ladi's Vineyard)   **88°**   **89°**   **90°°**   **91°**   92

*Moderately ripe in black-cherryish fruit and high in creamy oak, this wine tends at times to a slight narrowness*

## Merlot

**90°°°**   **91°°**   92   **93°°**   **94°**   95

*Much like the Cabernet, but more supple in texture*

## Pinot Noir

(Howard Allen Vineyard)   85   **86°**   **87°**   **88°°°**   **90°°**   **91°°°**   **92°°**   **94°°**   **95°**

(Russian River Valley)   **82°°**   **84°°°**   **85°**   86   **87°**   **88°**   89   **90°**   **91°**   92°   93   **94°°**   95   **96°**

*Ripe grape aromas redolent of cherries and enriched by oak, together with mouth-filling flavors, good balance; the lesser efforts have shown foresty, mushroomy notes*

## Zinfandel

**90°°**   **91°**   **92°**   **93°°**   **94°**   95

*Filled with focused berryish fruit enriched with sweet oak*

---

FENESTRA WINERY   *Alameda 1976*   A family-owned brand without vineyards, Fenestra remains small and competitive. Owners Lanny and Fran Replogle made wines in several locations prior to setting up their present facility in the Livermore Valley. Replogle, a chemistry professor at San Jose State, finds the time to make 4,000 cases a year. His production includes numerous small batches of as many as eight varietals. Buying grapes from three primary appellations—Livermore Valley, Monterey County, and Santa Clara County—he regularly offers Cabernet Sauvignon, Merlot, Chardonnay, Semillon, and Sauvignon Blanc among the varietals. A generic red is named "True Red" in honor of George True, founder of the now historic winery. Mourvedre and Pinot Gris are recent roster additions. The long-term production goal is 10,000 cases a year.

FERRARI–CARANO VINEYARDS  *Sonoma 1981*  In 79, Don Carano, owner of the El Dorado Hotel in Reno, bought vineyard land in the Alexander Valley near the town of Geyserville. He later purchased additional vineyard sites in the middle of Alexander Valley and in Dry Creek Valley, where he eventually built the winery. After his first two vintages, Carano acquired more vineyards in Knight's Valley and in the Carneros, where he now has 39 acres of Chardonnay. All told, the winery has 450 acres under vine in twelve separate sites. The primary varieties planted are Chardonnay, Sauvignon Blanc, Cabernet Sauvignon, and Merlot. With the release of its first vintages of Fumé Blanc and Chardonnay, the winery got off to an excellent start. The barrel-fermented Chardonnay was an immediate success, and it has been joined by a Reserve version (strongly oaked) limited to about 300 cases total. Made in a brisk, floral-weedy, youthful style, the Fumé Blanc is of ° caliber. Both Cabernet Sauvignon and Merlot are blended with other Bordeaux varieties. In the 90s, the winery issued a Reserve Meritage red, aged four years in its cellars, and added "Siena," its proprietary red blend of Cabernet Sauvignon and Sangiovese. A limited-edition Chardonnay Tre Terre Vineyard was added in the mid-90s and has usually been as fine and rich as the Reserve. As the winery continued vineyard development and replanting throughout the 90s, it relocated most red varieties to hillside and mountain sites. As of 94 the Red Meritage has been named Tresor. The owners have completed an impressive 15,000-square-foot hospitality center, named "Villa Fiore." Total annual production will peak around 175,000 cases.

### Cabernet Sauvignon

86°   87°   88°   89   90   91°°   92   93°   94°

*After years of good results with ripe but somewhat limited fruit, 91 came up with deep, supple fruit and white, and lots of complementary oak*

### Chardonnay

(regular bottling)   85°°   86°°   87   88   89°   90°   91°   92   93°   94°   95°°

(Reserve)   86°°°   87°   88°   89°°   90°°   91°   92   93°   94°°

*Bright, fresh appley fruit and lots of toasty oak are combined in wines that are balanced, lively, and deeply flavored; the Reserve is the richer of the two*

### Merlot

86   87   88°   89   90   91°°   92°   93   94°   95°

*Like the Cabernet, this wine was rounder and richer in 91*

### Zinfandel

91°   92°°   93°°°   94°°   95

*Typical Dry Creek berries and spice; these wines have noticeable tannins and will age well*

GLORIA FERRER  *Sonoma 1982*  The owners of Freixenet, the popular Spanish sparkling wine, launched this brand of *méthode champenoise* sparkling wine in 86. The new winery and large aging cellars located in the Sonoma-Carneros region were ready in mid-88. On 160 acres of former pastureland, the winery, headed by the eldest son of Freixenet's owners, Jose Ferrer, and his wife, Gloria, now has 50 acres planted to Pinot Noir and Chardonnay. The winery's list of offerings, each of which finds Pinot Noir the dominant grape, is keyed on the nonvintage Brut and a vintaged Brut dubbed "Royal Cuvée," aged longer on the yeasts and made from 60% Pinot Noir. A third but limited-volume sparkler is the vintaged "Carneros Cuvée," made exclusively from grapes grown in the Carneros district. With a production capability of 80,000 cases, the winery experienced slow growth over its first decade. As a result, it added nonsparkling Pinot Noir and Chardonnay, both of which performed well enough to encourage expansion. A Late Disgorged Brut has emerged as the winery's best bubbly in a classic style. The Chardonnay has rated ° in recent vintages.

FETZER VINEYARDS   *Mendocino 1968*   Former lumberman Barney Fetzer planted a few acres of vines on a ranch he bought in 58. After selling the crop for several years, he decided to produce Zinfandel and Cabernet Sauvignon in 68. With his sons John and Jim, he restored an old stone winery northwest of Hopland, and the Fetzers were in the wine business. They soon outgrew that tiny facility and kept on expanding production throughout the 70s. After their father died, the entire family became involved in the winery operation. Fetzer earned an early reputation for sturdy red wines, especially Zinfandels from the Scharffenberger Vineyard, Ricetti Vineyard, and their own vineyard. The winery also made heavyweight Petite Sirahs in the 70s. As the overall production grew, the Fetzers shunned advertising and concentrated upon marketing through a strong national network of wholesalers. They also kept prices below their competition during the expansion years.

In the early 80s, with winemaker Paul Dolan at the helm of a separate facility for white wines, the winery made remarkable improvements in the quality of its Chenin Blanc, Riesling, and Gewurztraminer. Each was made in a slightly sweet to sweet style, but with such forthright fruitiness and balancing acidity that the wines succeeded. When the blush wine era began in California, Fetzer was flexible enough to seize the opportunity, and before long was making four blush wines, including an ever popular White Zinfandel. The blush wine sales grew to such a volume that they were given the winery's second label, "Bel Arbres Vineyard," changed in 89 to Bel Arbors (see entry).

By the late 80s Fetzer was operating three winemaking facilities and Valley Oaks, a vineyard as well as a garden/entertainment center. With over 2,000 acres owned, and another 2,000 acres under long-term contract, the winery was making wines from many California growing regions. Fetzer was also among the first to use wines from Washington and Oregon in its Bel Arbors line. Two varietals took on proprietary names—Valley Oaks Cabernet Sauvignon and "Sundial" Chardonnay—and the sales success of the latter soon exceeded the supply from the Fetzer Sundial Ranch. Though many other producers had given up on Gewurztraminer, Fetzer began pushing it in the late 80s and now makes over 300,000 cases of a frequent ° version.

In mid-92, for a reported $100 million, the Fetzer family sold the winemaking facilities and the Fetzer brands, including Bel Arbors, to Brown-Forman, national marketing agents for Jack Daniel's, Bolla, Korbel, Noilly Prat, and many others. But the Fetzers retained ownership of most of the vineyards, and agreed to sell their grapes to the former winery, which was being managed by Paul Dolan. For several vintages Fetzer focused on what is now the "Barrel Select" line of Chardonnay and Cabernet Sauvignon. Entirely barrel-fermented, the "Barrel Select" Chardonnay is a blend of grapes from four regions. The "Barrel Select" Cabernet Sauvignon, aged entirely in small French oak, wins plaudits for quality and value. The winery has expanded the production of its Eagle Peak Merlot, and Echo Ridge Sauvignon Blanc. An early advocate of organic grape growing, Fetzer now has 400 acres of certified organic vineyards. Its line of organic wines is Bonterra (see entry), which has grown rapidly. More recently the winery has focused on its small-batch Reserve wines. Originally setting out to repair oak barrels, Paul Dolan set up a cooperage house next to the winery. Within a few years the business expanded into barrel building and evolved into a separate company, Mendocino Cooperage. This company now produces close to 100,000 oak barrels a year from both American and French oak. Its barrels are used by 200 wineries, including Fetzer. The flagship wines are labeled Reserve and include Cabernet Sauvignon, Chardonnay, Pinot Noir, and Petite Sirah. Fetzer's annual production is pushing 2.5 million cases.

### Cabernet Sauvignon

(Barrel Select)   82   83   84°   85°   86°   88   89   **90°**   **91°**   **92** 93°   **94**

*Ripish, cherryish fruit with sweet oak, supple texture with moderate tannins for moderate ageability*

### Chardonnay

(Barrel Select)   86°   87   88°   89   90   91°   92   93   95

(Special Reserve)   86°°   88   89°   90°   91°   **95**

*The upscale models, ranging from the moderately oaked, usually dependable Barrel Select to the fairly oaky and rich Reserve, have both offered good value when in peak form*

### Zinfandel

(Ricetti Vineyard / Special Reserve / Barrel Select—as of 88)   81°   82° 83°°   85°   86°   88°   **89°**   **90°**   **91°**   **92°**   **93**   94

*Usually tough, tight, hard, concentrated, deep blackberryish fruit, substantially oaked, long-aging*

---

FICKLIN VINEYARDS   *Madera 1946*   California's first port specialist, Ficklin is still turning out some of the very finest. Over the years the Ficklins have developed 35 acres planted to traditional port varieties such as Tinta Cao, Tinta Madeira, Souzao, and Touriga. Most of the family's winemaking efforts go into the Tinta Port, a smooth, delicious blend that often improves with age. However, seven times over its first fifty years, Ficklin has bottled a Vintage Port. More recently it came out with a heavenly Tawny Port. Only 1,000 cases of the Tawny are produced, and approximately 10,000 cases of Tinta Port are bottled each year.

---

FIDDLEHEAD CELLARS   *Napa 1989*   Owner Kathy Joseph made wines for the Robert Pecota Winery for several years. Preferring to be on her own, she founded Fiddlehead and now enjoys controlling every function from production to marketing. Renting space in the Edna Valley, she has made small batches of Pinot Noir from the Santa Maria Valley and Oregon's Willamette Valley. She also makes a barrel-fermented Sauvignon Blanc from the Santa Ynez Valley. A few cases each of a Red and White Table Wine round out the roster. To date, her efforts have produced spectacular Pinot Noirs and excellent Sauvignon Blancs. Total production approaches 1,000 cases per year.

### Pinot Noir

(Santa Maria Valley)   90   **91°°**   **92°**   **93°**

(Willamette Valley)   **92°°**   **93°°°**   **94°**   **95°**

*Rich, supple, deep Pinots, they are balanced and ageworthy*

---

FIELD STONE WINERY   *Sonoma 1977*   With its tasting room built into the underground cellars and the winery itself surrounded by oak trees, Field Stone is one of the more picturesque wineries in the Alexander Valley. The winery began by focusing on white and rosé wines, but by 82, when under new management, it began stressing red wines, mainly Cabernet Sauvignon and Petite Sirah. Cabernet Sauvignon represents 70% of the 130 acres planted, Petite Sirah accounts for 10%, and the remaining 20% consists of several white varieties, including Viognier. Once bottled under several vineyard designations, Cabernet Sauvignon production has been trimmed to a regular and a Reserve. In recent vintages Field Stone has shown improvement with both Gewurztraminer and Cabernet Sauvignon. Sauvignon Blanc, Sangiovese and Chardonnay complete the line. Since the late 80s, Chardonnay has been obtained from Carneros and the Russian River Valley areas. Visitors and regular mailing-list customers purchase about one-third of the 12,000 cases produced per year. The winery is gradually expanding to the 20,000-case level.

### Cabernet Sauvignon

86° 87 88 **89°** 90 **91** 92 93 **94°**

*Moderately fruity, moderately deep, and moderately successful in a medium to medium-full-bodied style*

### Chardonnay

88° 89° 90 91 92 93 94 95

*Clean but somewhat understuffed, mildly oaked wines*

FIFE VINEYARDS *Napa 1991* After serving as president of Inglenook and vice president of Beaulieu, Dennis Fife decided to leave the corporate world and develop his own label. The roster has expanded each year and is now quite lengthy. Most wines are made from his three vineyards. One is adjacent to his home in the Spring Mountain District, where he grows Cabernet Sauvignon. He also owns the Larkmead Vineyards north of St. Helena, which contains Cabernet Sauvignon and Cabernet Franc. The third site is in Mendocino's Redwood Valley, which Fife acquired when he bought the Konrad Winery. From Mendocino, Fife is now making Zinfandel and Petite Sirah from the Redhead Vineyard, Sangiovese, and a red Rhone blend. From the Napa Valley appellation, Fife's lineup includes Old Vine Zinfandel, Cabernet Sauvignon (regular and Reserve), Merlot, Cabernet Franc, and a blend named Max Cuvee, based on Syrah, Petite Sirah, Zinfandel, and other reds. Recently Barbera from Lodi has joined the Fife team. Annually, Fife makes 4,000 cases. The house style favors extract and tannin.

### Zinfandel

(Les Vieilles Vignes) **91 92°° 94° 95° 96°**

(Redhead Vineyard) **94° 95 96**

*Ripe, firm, berryish, a bit tight in structure when young, usually with good depth*

FIRESTONE VINEYARD *Santa Barbara 1974* Early vinous settlers in the Santa Ynez Valley, the Firestones began developing their estate vineyard in 73. A stunning facility and visitors center were ready, though incomplete, in time for the 75 harvest. Both the name Firestone and the scope of the investment (265 acres of vineyards) in an unknown region meant that the winery would be closely watched from the start. In 76 and 77, its Pinot Noirs were highly successful, but then and long after, its Cabernet Sauvignon and Merlot contained damaging degrees of vegetal character. As the winery grew to 80,000-case-a-year level, Firestone worked hard to develop a reputation for Johannisberg Riesling in a medium-sweet style. Floral and fruity, with medium-deep flavors and excellent balance, its Rieslings are frequently in the ° category, occasionally rising to °° . The slightly sweet Gewurztraminer is capable of reaching °° quality.

Beginning in 85, Firestone's Merlots started to earn recognition for early enjoyment and an infrequent as the vegetal component was brought under control. A similar over-grassy-weedy streak to the Sauvignon Blanc has been toned down by barrel fermentations and by the addition of about 8–10% Chardonnay. Generally, the winery's Sauvignon Blancs offer exotic aromas, but are somewhat lacking in vitality. A similarly disconcerting muddled impression marred the Chardonnays up to the late 80s. From the mid-80s, the Cabernets, unlike their heavy-bodied, often overly herbal predecessors, have turned out to be enjoyable in a soft, undemanding style. A slightly sweet Rosé of Cabernet, first produced in 75, still enjoys some popularity. By the mid-90s, the next generation, Adam Firestone, was running the winery, which had undergone a complete renovation and had expanded its vineyard holdings. Led by Chardonnay (128 acres), Merlot (118 acres), and Cabernet Sauvignon (114 acres), Firestone now owns over 500 acres. Part of its old Riesling acreage was converted to Viognier, and its Syrah acreage has grown to 20. Though still making delightful Riesling and crisp, dry Gewurztraminer, Firestone now emphasizes Chardonnay, Cabernet, Merlot, and Reserve reds that are blends of Cabernet, Merlot, and Cabernet Franc. In the 90s the winery has enjoyed great success in the export market, selling over 10,000 cases a year to the UK. It annual production today is closing in on 100,000 cases. It has the estate acreage to grow comfortably to 125,000 cases.

### Cabernet Sauvignon

78°   79   81   82   83°   84°   85   86   87   88   90   92

*Now made in a lighter style that preserves fruit and acid and avoids vegetal and soft-structured tendencies*

### Chardonnay

86   87   88   89   90   91°°   92°   93   94   95

*Fruity, firm, noticeable oak, somewhat low in intensity; disappointingly inconsistent*

### Merlot

82   84   85   86°   87   88   89   **91**   92   93

*Like the Cabernet, this one is now lighter, fruitier, better but not very special*

FISHER VINEYARDS   *Sonoma 1979*   Fred Fisher, a descendant of the automotive "Body by Fisher" family, established his winery on the Sonoma County side of the Mayacamas Mountains. In 73 the hillside vineyard was developed and now covers 25 acres. The winery owns another 50 acres situated at the northern, warmer end of the Silverado Trail in Napa Valley. In both locations, Cabernet Sauvignon, Merlot, and Chardonnay are the only varietals planted. The winery's primary Chardonnays carry the Napa/Sonoma appellation and are a blend of hillside and valley floor grapes. The reserve versions of Chardonnay, labeled "Coach Insignia," have ranged in quality from excellent to good. The "Coach Insignia" Cabernet Sauvignon, made exclusively from the Sonoma hillside acreage, was also introduced with the 84 vintage. By the end of the decade Fisher had added an estate-grown Merlot to the roster and two vineyard-designated wines—""Whitney's Vineyard" Chardonnay, made from its oldest 4 1/2-acre mountain vineyard, and a "Wedding Vineyard" Cabernet from its 8-acre mountain parcel. Today, the winery favors natural yeast fermentation for all its wines. In recent years the Coach Insignia bottlings have been averaging about 2,000 cases each. The entire line is holding steady at 8,000 cases a year.

### Cabernet Sauvignon

(Coach Insignia)   84°   **85°°**   **86°**   **87°°**   89°   **90°**   **91°**   **92** 93°°   **94°**   **95**

*Deep in handsomely rendered varietal fruit, and showing lots of rich oak, the wine can be high in tannin and very tight when young*

### Chardonnay

(Napa/Sonoma/Whitney's Vineyard)   85   86°   87   88   89°   90 91°   92   93

*Medium-depth fruit, with toasty oak in better vintages, but showing less focus and depth in other years*

### Chardonnay

(Coach Insignia)   84°   85°   86°°   87   88°   90°°   91   92 **93°°**   **96°**

*Usually rich in ripe appley fruit, and rich in toasty oak, the wine lives up to its special billing in many years*

**Merlot**
**91   92   93   94°°**

*Ripe cherry and dried brush notes, moderate tannin, generally ageworthy*

FITCH MOUNTAIN   *Sonoma 1985*   A negociant brand operating in Sonoma County, Fitch Mountain is owned by Greg Smith, who is also co-owner of Optima. Using his own cooperage and a rented facility, Smith blends, ages, and bottles wines he purchases. His output depends on the availability of grapes, and therefore has varied from year to year from as many as 20,000 cases to as few as 2,000. Given a choice he prefers offering Zinfandel, Cabernet Sauvignon and, from time to time, Chardonnay and Merlot. Most wines have come from Sonoma County, a few from Napa Valley. In better years, Fitch Mountain wines offer good value. The brand is named after a real Fitch Mountain, visible from the barrel-aging cellar/warehouse in Healdsburg.

FITZPATRICK WINERY   *El Dorado 1980*   Situated in the southern end of the county, Fitzpatrick was known originally as Somerset Vineyards. It was renamed Fitzpatrick in 85. Over the first several vintages, the winery produced a range of table wines. In the late 80s the owners of this small winery decided to diversify and developed a popular bed-and-breakfast complex. Directed by Brian Fitzpatrick, the winery has a 15-acre vineyard, which yields Cabernet Sauvignon, Chardonnay, and Syrah. Its Zinfandels originate in Amador's Shenandoah Valley. Over its early history, the winery has bought Zinfandel from many individual growers. Additionally, it makes White Zinfandel and a blend of Zinfandel and Petite Sirah named "King's Red." The winery's annual output has reached 4,500 cases. In the long term, the winery has set 7,000 cases as its target maximum.

FLEUR DE CARNEROS   *(Carneros Creek Winery)*   This label is used for the winery's light-bodied, fruit-filled style of Pinot Noir, similar to Saintsbury's "Garnet."

FLORA SPRINGS WINERY   *Napa 1978*   In 77 Jerry and Flora Komes purchased an old winery (ca. 1888) and vineyard once used by Louis Martini for barrel-aging sherry and other wines. Komes had retired from Bechtel Industries and looked on the Napa Valley acquisition as a means of producing retirement challenges. When Julie Komes Garvey, her husband, Pat, and her brother John became interested in moving to Napa, the family's plan changed. Julie and Pat Garvey purchased additional vineyard land, and the family winemaking venture began. They restored the old stone winery nestled against the western Rutherford hills, and replanted the adjacent 50-acre vineyard to Cabernet Sauvignon, Merlot, and Cabernet Franc. Now known as the Komes Ranch, this vineyard is responsible for the winery's upscale red Meritage, "Trilogy." The winery has other vineyards in Napa Valley, bringing the total to 400 acres.

Close to 75% of the crop is sold, making the grape business an important part of this operation. Both the Komes Ranch and the Garvey Ranch are in the Rutherford Bench region and grow mostly Cabernet Sauvignon and Merlot. In the cooler growing area of Yountville, the Crossroads Ranch grows most of the winery's Sauvignon Blanc. As an important grape grower, Flora Springs owns 119 acres of Cabernet Sauvignon, 72 acres of Chardonnay, 69 acres of Sauvignon Blanc, and 36 acres of Merlot. Most of its vineyards were replanted in the 1990s, and the owners shifted their Chardonnay acreage to the Carneros District and other cooler sites and planted Merlot and Cabernet in Rutherford, where Chardonnay once grew. With the addition of Pinot Noir, Sangiovese, and Zinfandel, today's wine roster favors red wines. Cabernet Sauvignon and Merlot are the leaders. Three Cabernets are offered: Reserve, Napa Valley Estate, and Cypress Ranch. A like number of Merlots consist of Napa Valley Estate, Reserve, and Windfall Vineyard. Pinot Grigio is a newcomer to the white lineup, which is headed by two Chardonnays (Barrel-Fermented Napa and Carneros) and Sauvignon Blanc. Its two upscale, proprietary blends—Trilogy and Soliloquy—are the flagships of the Flora Springs label. The winery's annual output remains constant at 25,000 cases.

### Cabernet Sauvignon

(Napa Valley)  80°  81°  82  83  84°  **85°°**  86  87  88  89
90  95

(Reserve)  **89  90  93°**

*Capable of possessing deep fruit, well supported by rich oak, and made ageworthy by fairly bold tannins; the Cabernet is light and early-maturing, and the Reserve is deeper and more oaky*

### Chardonnay

(regular bottling)  86°  87°  88  89  90  91  93

(Barrel Fermented)  86°°  87°°  88°°  89°°  90  91  92  93
94  **95°**

*Both wines have good fruit and good balance; the Barrel Fermented is richer, deeper, and oakier, but has not shown well recently*

### Merlot

(Napa Valley)  **85°°**  86  **87°**  88  89  90  91  92  93  94
**95  96°**

*Typically possessed of ripe cherry fruit, buttressed by oak, the wine can be rich and supple in top vintages*

### Trilogy

**85°  86°  87°  88°  89°  91°°  92°°°  93°**

*A blend of equal parts Cabernet Sauvignon, Merlot, and Cabernet Franc, it is medium in depth and tough in structure; in spite of the above-average quality, this wine has not yet fully lived up to its pedigree in most years*

---

THOMAS FOGARTY WINERY  *San Mateo 1981*  The winery, perched on the northern end of the Santa Cruz Mountains appellation, is owned by Thomas Fogarty, a cardiovascular surgeon practicing in Palo Alto. He purchased 300 acres of land in 68 in what is locally known as the Portola Valley, began planting vineyards in 78, and added to them in 80. His 24-acre estate vineyards consist of Chardonnay (18) and Pinot Noir (6). The winery was built in 81, and winemaker Mike Martella has been involved since then. Fogarty emphasizes Chardonnay and Pinot Noir, and has produced numerous versions from many regions and vineyards. Among today's offerings are an Estate Reserve Chardonnay, Santa Cruz Mountains Chardonnay, and after a long hiatus, Monterey Chardonnay. Estate Reserve Pinot Noir and Santa Cruz Mountains Pinot Noir are regularly offered and are the most exciting wines. On occasion one encounters Cabernet Sauvignon from Napa Valley and Merlot from Fogarty's young vineyard. Gewurztraminer is another winery specialty. Usually made in a dry style, Fogarty Gewurztraminer°°-°°° often ranks among the very best, with rich varietal spice and great balancing acidity. Fogarty usually produces them from Monterey or the Santa Cruz Mountains, but the winery has recently (and quite successfully) experimented with Dry Gewurztraminer from the Willamette Valley. Sparkling wines (Brut, Blanc de Noirs) and an Estate Sangiovese are the latest additions sold mostly at the winery. Total production is close to the 7,500-case maximum, about half devoted to Chardonnay.

### Chardonnay

(Edna Valley–Paragon Vineyard)  86  87  88°  89  90

(Santa Cruz)  86  87  88  90  91  92°  **94°  95°°**

(Ventana Vineyards)  87°°  88  89  90°°  95

*Always oaky and typically trying for richness and complexity, these wines have all too often been overdone and lacking in the fruit depth needed to keep them in balance*

---

FOLEY ESTATE WINERY  *Santa Barbara 1997*  The former Curtis Winery was acquired in 1997 by William Foley II, who also purchased 46 acres of vineyards. Foley intends to continue making Cabernet Sauvignon and Merlot from the La Cuesta Vineyard. Chardonnay and a Reserve Chardonnay also are offered. The winery's capacity is 8,000 cases.

FOLIE À DEUX WINERY    *Napa 1981*    Both the name and the whimsical label helped to focus immediate attention on co-founders Larry and Eva Dizmang's shared fantasy. Folie à Deux specializes in Chardonnay and Cabernet Sauvignon. Always a favorite, Chenin Blanc was made into a dry, oak-aged serious wine for several years. But in the 90s the founders were headed for divorce court and the winery, suffering from a lack of attention, eventually was heading toward foreclosure by the bank. In 1995, the winery and its 22-acre vineyard were acquired by a limited partnership headed by Dick Peterson, one-time winemaker for Beaulieu who for many years ran the Monterey Vineyard. Peterson is maintaining the Napa Valley roster by emphasizing Chardonnay, Merlot, Cabernet Sauvignon, and Chenin Blanc. He is also making the popular sparkling wine named "Fantasie," a blend of Chardonnay and Muscat. In 1997 Scott Harvey (ex-Redwood winemaker) joined the team. Harvey immediately added his favorite red wines from Amador County, which also had developed quite a following, such as Old Vine Zinfandel, Barbera, Syrah, and Sangiovese. Today the winery consists of two separate lines from Napa Valley and Amador County. They combine for 35,000 cases a year.

**Chardonnay**

83°°°   84   85°   86°   87°   88°   90   95

*After starting out with near-perfection, this wine has settled into a pattern of offering satisfying, somewhat appley, medium-depth fruit, and slightly toasty oak*

FOPPIANO VINEYARDS    *Sonoma 1896*    This historic family-run winery produces close to 200,000 cases a year under three labels. Located southwest of Healdsburg, the old facility has been significantly modernized, though from the outside it still looks like a remnant of a bygone era. Beginning in the late 60s, the Foppiano brand moved away from its jug-wine emphasis and entered the varietal wine market under the Louis J. Foppiano label (now Foppiano Vineyards). The first varietals to earn modest critical praise were Petite Sirah and to a lesser degree, Cabernet Sauvignon. A limited-volume Reserve Petite Sirah, aged entirely in French oak barrels, was joined by a limited-production Reserve Zinfandel in 87. Merlot was added in the 90s.

The Foppiano family owns 160 acres under vine, the leading varieties being Chardonnay (30 acres), Cabernet Sauvignon (24 acres), and Petite Sirah (20 acres). With all its vineyards situated in the Russian River Valley region, Foppiano's estate-grown wines carry that appellation. A separate line of white wines named "Fox Mountain" (see entry). To also help sever the association of the Foppiano name with jug wines, the winery markets close to 150,000 cases a year of low-priced varietals and generics under the "Riverside Vineyard" label (see entry). The total amount of wine labeled Foppiano Vineyards is close to 30,000 cases a year.

FOREST GLEN WINERY    *(Classic Wines)*    Viewed by its parent company as a mid-level brand, Forest Glen is led by its Barrel Select Merlot and a partially barrel-fermented Chardonnay, both of which are heavily promoted. The line includes Shiraz and Cabernet Sauvignon. All wines are "California" in appellation.

FOREST HILL VINEYARDS    *Napa 1987*    David Manace, a plastic surgeon in San Francisco, purchased a vacation home in St. Helena in 1982. After making wines as an amateur for a few years, he decided to specialize in barrel-fermented Chardonnay. Buying grapes from two local vineyards, he made 200 cases his first year, and has gradually increased production each year, setting 1,000 cases a year as the maximum. The bottle chosen for Forest Hill Chardonnay is an unusual crystal-clear Burgundy bottle and, for an added touch, each is offered in a custom-made wooden box.

### Chardonnay

| 87 | 88° | 89 | 90° | 92 | 93 |
|---|---|---|---|---|---|

FOREST VILLE  (*Classic Wines*)  This brand covers a line of inexpensive varietals from the obligatory trio of Cabernet, Chardonnay, and White Zinfandel to less-likely wines such as Merlot, Gewurztraminer, and Riesling.

FORMAN WINERY  *Napa 1983*  In 68 the newly formed Sterling Vineyards picked 24-year-old Ric Forman as its first winemaker. Heading Sterling's wine program until 77, Forman became known for a series of barrel-fermented Chardonnay, Cabernet Sauvignon, and for his contributions to the styling of Sauvignon Blanc and Merlot. When Sterling was sold to Coca-Cola of Atlanta in 77, Forman became partners with Sterling's founder, Peter Newton, helping to develop vineyards and making the first few vintages of a winery that reportedly was to be named Forman Winery, but ended up as Newton Vineyard.

Forman left Newton in early 82 to start his own winery on Howell Mountain. He planted 6 acres to Cabernet on the hillsides near the winery, and has expanded that initial block to 47 acres. His Chardonnay is obtained from a vineyard in the valley floor area of Rutherford. All Forman Chardonnays are barrel-fermented. With Cabernet Sauvignon, Forman almost always adds Merlot and sometimes Cabernet Franc. Aging in French oak for close to two years, Forman's Cabernets have been among the richest made. He produces a maximum of 2,000 cases each of Chardonnay and Cabernet. A second label, "Chateau La Grande Roche," has been set aside for a Grenache and any lower-priced wines he might wish to produce.

### Cabernet Sauvignon

| 83°° | 84°° | 85°°° | 86° | 87 | 88°° | 89 | 90° | 91 | 92° | 93 |
|---|---|---|---|---|---|---|---|---|---|---|
| 94 | 95° | | | | | | | | | |

*Deep, handsomely crafted fruit is set with a solid framework of tannins in a wine that seems capable of aging well for a decade or more*

### Chardonnay

| 84° | 85°° | 87° | 88° | 89 | 90° | 91° | 92° | 93 | **95** | 96 |
|---|---|---|---|---|---|---|---|---|---|---|

*Always complex in its far-ranging, toasty, roasted-grain qualities, this appley, citrus-tart wine sometimes founders, due to a shortage of essential fruit to balance its diverse and demanding character*

FOUNTAIN GROVE  (*Godwin Winery*)  One of the oldest names in California wine history, Fountain Grove, located north of Santa Rosa, was a 400-acre vineyard and bustling winery in the early 1900s. The name was barely kept alive until the 1960s. In 1998 Richard Godwin, owner of Mark West Vineyard and Martini and Prati, revived the brand and brought out Cabernet Sauvignon, Merlot, and Chardonnay. Bearing a California appellation, these three were priced appropriately at the low end. Viognier and "Aestivossa," a red Meritage, complete the roster.

FOX HOLLOW  (*Classic Wines*)  This brand to date has included Chardonnay from Monterey, Cabernet Sauvignon from Paso Robles, and Merlot from varied appellations.

FOX MOUNTAIN  (*Foppiano Vineyards*)  Fox Mountain represents Foppiano's white wine line. Only a Sauvignon Blanc and Chardonnay are offered, and each consists of about 2,000 cases.

FOXEN VINEYARD  *Santa Barbara 1987*  This winery is a joint effort between partners Bill Wathen and Richard Dore. One-time vineyard manager for Rancho Sisquoc and Chalone, Wathen is the grape buyer for the joint venture. Dore (a member of the Foxen family) managed the large Foxen cattle ranch in the northern corner of Santa Barbara County. Over the first vintages, an assortment of wines were made from purchased grapes grown in several Santa Barbara County appellations. The winery's emphasis is Cabernet Sauvignon, Chardonnay, Pinot Noir and Chenin Blanc. The owners have established a 10-acre vineyard in the Santa Maria Valley adjacent to their winery, with 5 acres of Chardonnay and the rest planted to Cabernet Sauvignon, Merlot, and Cabernet Franc. With a long-term contract with Bien Nacido Vineyard, Foxen now regularly offers Pinot Noir from that vineyard. Syrah is the latest addition. With vineyard maturity, the owners plan to level off at 3,000 cases per year.

### Chardonnay

88　89　90　92　93　94

### Pinot Noir

89　91　92°　**93°**　**94**　**96°°**

*Fairly full-bodied, ripe-tasting wines with distinct herbal/brushy overtones*

FRANCISCAN VINEYARDS　Napa 1973　Now on solid footing after what still ranks as one of the roughest starts by any winery in memory, Franciscan sits in the middle of Rutherford on the main wine road. The founders, now long forgotten, went out of business before their first wines were bottled, and Franciscan continued on a roller coaster until 79, when its fifth ownership began. Now in the hands of its sixth owner, a 50–50 partnership between the Peter Eckes firm of Germany (the fifth owner) and Augustus Huneus, who also owns Mount Veeder Vineyards, and Quintessa. Franciscan's five wines—Chardonnay, Cabernet Sauvignon, Merlot, Zinfandel, and a red Meritage—also bear an "Oakville Estate" designation. The owners have 240 acres under vine in Oakville. In 90, they bought 270 acres on the western side of the Silverado Trail, of which about 200 acres will be planted to the five red Bordeaux varieties. This vineyard will eventually supply most of the fruit for Magnificat, Franciscan's Meritage Red. Chardonnay (50% barrel-fermented) and Cabernet Sauvignon (blended with 10%–15% Merlot) are the mainstays in the line. The winery also bottles two limited-edition Chardonnays: the 100% barrel-fermented Reserve (less than 1,000 cases) and the wild-yeast-fermented, unfiltered Chardonnay, called "Cuvée Sauvage" (3,000 cases). "Estancia" (see entry) is under the same ownership. The annual production of Franciscan Vineyards is steady at 60,000 cases.

### Cabernet Sauvignon

(Napa Valley)　83　84　85°　86　**87**　**88**　89　**90**　**91**　92　93　94　**95°**

(Meritage/Magnificat)　**85°**　**86°**　**87°**　88　89　**90°**　**92**　**93°°**　**94°**

*Soft, ripe, cherry and herb-tinged fruit; moderate tannin; occasionally attractive in the short term; Magnificat is blended with Merlot and Cabernet Franc and is more ageworthy*

### Chardonnay

(regular bottling)　86　87°　88°　89°　90°　92　**93°**　94　95　96°

(Cuvée Sauvage)　88°　89　90°　91°　92°　93°　94°°　**95°°**

*Direct, presentable wines with medium-depth fruit and just enough oak for a suggestion of richness; Cuvée Sauvage, fermented with wild yeasts, is a bigger, richer wine*

### Merlot

83°　84　85°°　86°　87°　88　89　90　**91°**　**92**　**93°**　**94**　95°

*Generally attractive, ripe and round fruit, with sweet oak creaminess and moderate tannins combined in wines of short- to medium-term appeal*

### Zinfandel

**88°°** 89 **90°** **91** 92 **93°** 94 95

*Berryish fruit, sometimes on the dry side, combines with sweet oak in this medium-full-bodied wine*

---

FRANUS *Napa 1993* Formed by Peter Franus after he departed as winemaker at Mount Veeder Winery, this winery specializes in Zinfandel. Franus prefers making Zinfandel from old vines within the Mount Veeder appellation and has bottled as many as three separate vineyard-designate Zinfandels in a given year. Quality is generally above average.

---

FRANZIA *San Joaquin 1906* The Franzia family, which founded the winery and operated it until 73 as Franzia Brothers, sold both winery and name to Coca-Cola of New York. Today's parent company is the corporation named the Wine Group, which owns Corbett Canyon among other wine properties. Franzia covers a broad line of table wines, varietals and generics, along with low-priced sparkling wines and wine coolers. Ripon is the hometown of the primary production facility, which bottles over 8 million cases a year. Much of that total goes into the world with the Summit label attached, and most of Summit's business is the bag-in-the-box trade. Franzia's line of varietals is led in volume by White Zinfandel, White Grenache, French Colombard, and Chenin Blanc.

---

FREEMARK ABBEY WINERY *Napa 1967* This site was first home to a winery in 1886, and the original Freemark Abbey sign went up in 39. That operation continued until the late 50 s, with the official door-closing taking place in 62. By 67, however, it had been revived and the winery restored by a partnership of seven, most with deep Napa Valley roots. Longtime resident Chuck Carpy headed the group, which included the well-known vineyardist Laurie Wood, and the now legendary winemaker Brad Webb. A fourth partner, Bill Jaeger, later became better known for running Rutherford Hill Winery. Webb, who had been with Hanzell, guided the early winemaking at Freemark Abbey as a consultant. Among many of his contributions, Webb was a proponent of French oak aging for Chardonnay, was among the first to use Nevers oak, and began blending Merlot in Cabernet Sauvignon as early as 68.

By the late 60s and early 70s, Freemark Abbey had become a quality name to every wine lover. Petite Sirah rose to prominence in that era due largely to such highly praised versions as the 69 and 71 made from the York Creek Vineyard. From the Bosché Vineyard in the Rutherford Bench, the winery has since 70 produced a noteworthy series of Cabernets. Among its other credits, Freemark Abbey made an enormously appealing dessert-style Riesling in 73 called "Edelwein" that ranks even today among the finest of its late-harvest type.

Since the early 80s, the winery slipped back a little with its Cabernets, but has been turning out generally acceptable Chardonnays. As production edged toward the full-capacity level of 30,000 cases, the winery trimmed its line to Chardonnay (Napa Valley) and a 100% barrel-fermented "Carpy Ranch") and three Cabernet bottlings (Napa Valley, "Bosché," and "Sycamore Vineyard"), with limited amounts of Riesling. Merlot joined the roster in the 90s. Normally, the winery makes a slightly sweet Riesling with about 1.5% residual sugar. In years when *Botrytis* concentrates the grapes, Freemark Abbey makes the late-harvest wines called "Edelwein" for residual sugar near 10%, or "Edelwein Gold" when the sweetness level is close to 20%.

### Cabernet Sauvignon

(Napa Valley) 78° 79 80 81 82° 83 84 85 86 **87**
88 89 **90°** **91** **92°** **93°** **94°**

(Bosché) 70°° 78° 79 80 81 82° 83 84° 85 **86**
**87°**

(Sycamore) **85°°** **86**

*Over two decades of making Cabernet Sauvignon, Freemark Abbey has garnered precious few high ratings for its stable of light-to-medium-depth, cherry and herb-flavored wines*

## Chardonnay

| | | | | | | | |
|---|---|---|---|---|---|---|---|
| (Napa Valley) | 86°° | 87 | 88° | 89 | 90 | 91 | 93° | 94 |
| (Carpy Ranch) | 88 | 89°° | 90 | 92° |

*In the early to mid-70s, Freemark Abbey Chardonnays were considered among the best in California; but following a spectacular wine in 75, things went somewhat downhill, and the wines rarely were able to recapture the bright, luscious fruit that had been their early hallmark. Now, even in their better performances, they tend to be stiff and green-appley, with toasty oak in the background*

## Merlot

90   91   92   **93°**   **95°**

*Cherryish fruit, touches of herb, sweet oak in a supple package*

FREY VINEYARD    *Mendocino 1980*    Owned by the large (12 children at last count) Frey family, this winery is located in the northern end of the Redwood Valley. Patriarch Dr. Paul Frey was a physician at the Mendocino State Hospital when he purchased the old ranch in 61. A few years later he planted a 40-acre vineyard, and little by little the family edged into the grape business, using organic farming methods. After a few wineries earned plaudits for wines made from Frey's grapes, in 80 they decided to produce wines themselves. Frey wines are made without sulfur dioxide, and all grapes fermented by the winery are grown organically. The winery is a collection of used equipment; many of the fermenting tanks were once used and abandoned by dairies. Though the quality has been quite uneven, the Freys have enjoyed the advantages of good timing. An interest in organic wines pushed their production from 5,000 cases in 86 to close to 15,000 in 95. The current lineup includes Zinfandel, Syrah, and several vineyard-identified and one Reserve-type Cabernet Sauvignon. The white wines, fluctuating more widely in quality, include Gray Riesling, Colombard, and Gewurztraminer.

## Zinfandel

88°   8̶9̶   90   91   9̶2̶

*Whether because of the vagaries of organic winemaking or inconsistent levels of skill, these wines have often been deeply troubled*

FRICK WINERY    *Santa Cruz 1977*    After making their first two vintages in an abandoned gas station in Bonny Doon, Bill and Judith Frick moved into their first "real" facility in the city of Santa Cruz. They produced wines at this location through 88, made entirely from purchased grapes. Their major emphasis fell on barrel-fermented Chardonnay and Pinot Noir, both from the Central Coast, and on Zinfandel and Petite Sirah. A small batch of Grenache plus blended generic wines often filled out the 3,500-case-a-year line. After a long search for a new location, the Fricks moved in late 88 to a vineyard and winery site purchased in the Dry Creek Valley of Sonoma County. The hillside vineyard contained 5 acres of mixed reds such as Zinfandel and Gamay, and the Fricks have added 4 acres of Syrah. Today's wine roster is led by Syrah, Petite Sirah, and a bright, zesty Cinsault rose.

J. FRITZ CELLARS    *Sonoma 1979*    Set back into the hillside, J. Fritz Cellars is a charming winery with an underground aging cellar. It is located at the northern end of Dry Creek Valley. The Fritz family owns three separate vineyards in the Dry Creek Valley that combined total 90 acres and has another 35 acres in the Russian River Valley under long-term lease. Over the first several vintages, the production of Fritz wines has fluctuated widely. To varying degrees, the facility had been involved in custom-making wines for others, and has sold some of its grapes, depending on the demand. Over the years the Chardonnays have come from numerous appellations, but Fritz has settled on Sonoma County as its primary Chardonnay, which is occasionally accompanied by a Reserve from Russian River Valley. Sauvignon

Blanc is the second most prominent varietal. More often than not Fritz's Sauvignon Blancs offer an abundance of lively fruit flavors and earn **°** and frequently even **°°**. Zinfandel from old vines in Dry Creek Valley has reached above average quality levels recently. Merlot and Cabernet Sauvignon, both from Dry Creek Valley, are made in limited quantities. Winemaker Helen Turley of Marcassin (see entry) came on board as a consultant in the late 90s to create a series of single-vineyard Chardonnays, single-vineyard Zinfandels, and to upgrade Cabernet Sauvignon.

### Chardonnay

85  86  87  88  90  91**°**  92  93  94

*The winery's regular bottling Chardonnay has won few fans to date*

### Zinfandel

83**°**  84**°**  86  87**°**  88**°°**  89**°**  **90°°**  **91°**  92  **93°**  **94°**
**95°**

*Medium ripe, with black-cherryish fruit and reasonable depth, moderate tannins for ageworthiness; 88 was near-classic; overall consistency has been admirable*

---

FROG'S LEAP WINERY  *Napa 1981*  Larry Turley, a physician in the trauma ward at a nearby hospital, bought property in Napa Valley once used to raise frogs whose legs were destined for the restaurant trade. In 78 he planted 1 acre to Sauvignon Blanc, and converted the old livery stable into a winery, choosing a name and a label design aimed at poking fun at the highly successful Stag's Leap Wine Cellars. The joke happily backfired when the overall quality of Frog's Leap Sauvignon Blanc, along with the artistic merits of the label, brought considerable recognition to the winery. Within a few years winemaker John Williams (ex–Spring Mountain) became a partner, and through his full-time efforts the winery was able to grow in size and expand its varietal roster.

Williams and Turley seemed to be having fun as they brought production to the 50,000-case level. However, the partners differed on key points and in 1994 decided to go their separate ways. Turley founded Turley Cellars (see entry). Williams and his wife, Julie, keep the Frog's Leap trademark and the grape contracts, and purchased an old winery and vineyard in the Rutherford area. They quickly transformed the old winery into an operational facility, and by the 94 harvest they were making Frog's Leap wines as they had before. They acquired 37 acres planted to Sauvignon Blanc and Merlot, and the Williamses retained their 10-acre vineyard planted to Zinfandel. Today, 50% of their 50,000-case production is Sauvignon Blanc; the remainder is equally divided between Carneros Chardonnay, Napa Merlot, and Napa Zinfandel. On occasion, especially in a Leap Year, they try to produce a late-harvest-style Sauvignon Blanc dubbed "Late Leap."

### Cabernet Sauvignon

82  83**°°**  84**°**  **85°**  **86°**  **87°°**  88  89  **90°°**  **91**  92  **93**
**95°°**

*Not the most elegant wine around, this one impresses for its intensity, breadth, and aging potential, as well as for the value it offers when it occasionally earns very high ratings. Its character favors black cherry and faint notes of herbs, with tinges of orange rind and mint showing up from time to time, while noticeable astringency suggests several years of cellaring*

### Chardonnay

(Napa Valley)  86  87**°**  88

(Carneros)  86  89  90  91**°**  92  94  95

*Straightforward, mild, appley fruit, often with citrusy and blossomy aspects, carrying background notes of toasty oak in wines that are usually low to medium intensity*

### Merlot

**90°**  **91°**  **92°**  **93°**  **94**

*This new addition to the Frog's Leap lineup has shown good depth to cherryish and curranty fruit buttressed by creamy oak and firmed by light-medium tannins*

**Zinfandel**

85° 86 87°° 88° 89° **90° 91° 92 93** 94 95

*In its best showings, the wine has managed to find admirable balance between ripeness and black-cherry fruitiness; sweet oak and medium tannins are constants*

GABRIELLI WINERY *Mendocino 1989* Located in the northern Redwood Valley, Gabrielli is a partnership of several local families. Gabrielli has been producing barrel-fermented Chardonnay, two strapping Zinfandels (the regular and Reserve bottlings both contain a dollop of Petite Sirah), Riesling (atypically barrel-fermented), and "Ascenza," an unusual white proprietary blend of Riesling, Chenin Blanc, and Chardonnay, combined prior to fermentation in small oak barrels. The Zinfandels have enjoyed early success. While most grapes for the line are purchased from several Mendocino County growers, the partners own a 13-acre vineyard planted to Sangiovese and Syrah. While the estate Sangiovese and especially the Syrah show considerable promise, they reinforce the winery's take-no-prisoners style. Annual production of 5,000 cases is expected to grow to a maximum of 20,000.

**Chardonnay**

(Mendocino)  90°  91°  92°°  94°

(Reserve)  90°  91°  92°  94  **95**

*Both wines have shown attractive fruit in a direct, slightly citrusy style; Reserve is somewhat oakier*

**Zinfandel**

(Mendocino)  **90°  91°  92°**  93  **94  95**

(Reserve)  **90°  91°  92°  93  94°**

*Moderately bold, berryish wines*

GAINEY VINEYARDS *Santa Barbara 1984* The Gainey family, like many of their neighbors, live on a large ranch in the Santa Ynez Valley. Their 1,800-acre spread is home to a variety of crops and farm animals. Gainey Vineyards began to receive attention in the early 80s, and today the winery has 60 acres planted to several varieties. About one-third of Gainey's output is Chardonnay, its most consistently good wine, with Johannisberg Riesling accounting for 22%. As the winery grows to its targeted annual maximum of 15,000 cases, Cabernet Sauvignon and Merlot together represent 30% of the annual emphasis. Both Pinot Noir and Sauvignon Blanc are regularly made, but in small quantities. In recent years, the Limited Selection Savignon Blanc has been outstanding (up to °°°). In some vintages, Gainey's Pinot Noir is a distinctive wine earning °°. The winery sells a significant portion of its wines from the tasting room or through its mailing list.

**Chardonnay**

(Santa Barbara County)  86°  87  88°  89  90°  94  **95°**

(Limited Selection)  88°°  89°  90  **94°°  95°°**

*Usually showing lots of fruit, the Reserve has an extra measure of aging potential*

GALANTE FAMILY WINERY *Monterey 1994* In 1968 the Galante family bought a 700-acre cattle ranch in the Carmel Valley. After becoming disillusioned with the cattle business, the family planted 50 acres to vines in 1983. Cabernet Sauvignon was the featured variety, and for several years Morgan Winery purchased the majority of the fruit. In the 90s the Galantes began constructing their winery, which was in full operation by the 94 crush. Cabernet Sauvignon is the major wine, and in most vintages, Galante bottles Cabernets from two distinct vineyards, Red Rose Hill and Blackjack Pastures. A few hundred cases each of Merlot and Sauvignon

Blanc push annual production to 2,500 cases, about a third of Galante's expected optimum level.

E. & J. GALLO WINERY  *Modesto 1933*  Brothers Ernest and Julio Gallo started out in 33 with a $500 bank loan to purchase winemaking equipment. Today, Gallo is the largest wine company in the world, operating five facilities in California and selling about 70 million cases a year. Headquartered in Modesto, the Gallos rose to prominence on the strength of generic wines in jug bottles with screw caps, promoted—as with their extensive lines of table, sparkling, and dessert wines—by savvy marketing techniques. In the 60s and early 70s, Gallo's Hearty Burgundy was a perennial best-seller, while in the mid-70s its Chablis Blanc took over the top spot. Though the Gallos own over 4,000 acres of vineyards, they are the biggest customers for grapes grown in Sonoma County, Mendocino County, Napa Valley, and Monterey County. Milestones for the Gallos include the debut of varietal wines with cork closures in 75, and the completion in 78 of a massive aging cellar housing thousands of 3,000-gallon-capacity oak uprights. This cellar enables Gallo to offer Chardonnay, Cabernet Sauvignon, and Zinfandel under the "Reserve Cellars" designation. At their Modesto winery, the Gallos manufacture their own bottles, averaging about 2 million per day.

In addition to the Modesto facility, Gallo Winery operates others in Fresno, in Livingston, and in the Dry Creek Valley of Sonoma County. In the 80s the Gallos began paving the way for an eventual shift of emphasis, not of volume, to Sonoma County. After buying the former Frei Brothers Winery in 77, they have expanded that facility in Sonoma County to its present capacity of 9 million gallons. New vineyards have been developed in several Sonoma locations. To date, Gallo has established 800 acres in the Dry Creek Valley with emphasis on Cabernet and Zinfandel, and 400 acres in the Russian River Valley planted primarily to Chardonnay and Pinot Noir. It has also developed a 200-acre site north of Geyserville that contains Cabernet and Zinfandel. Wines from the Sonoma County project are labeled Gallo Sonoma (see entry).

However, Gallo's strength is in generic wines with California as their appellation. With a combined storage capacity of 330 million gallons, Gallo has a 34% share of the entire U.S. wine market and, in the generic wine category, its sales represent 45% of the jug-wine business. These figures take into consideration the myriad of labels used in addition to Gallo Winery. The most significant of these are Carlo Rossi (Chablis, Rhine, and Rosé), André and Tott's for sparkling wine, Livingston Cellars for a good Cream Sherry and other fortified wines, and Ballatore Spumante. Bartles & James reigns as the best-selling cooler, and E & J is the best-selling brandy. William Wycliff is a label for the restaurant and bar trade. All are owned by Gallo.

From time to time, we have found Gallo's Reserve Sauvignon Blanc, made in an accessible, light style, to be pleasant and a good value. And in the low-priced sparkling wine category, "Tott's Reserve" is sometimes a cut above the competition.

GALLO SONOMA  *(E. & J. Gallo)*  The long-awaited vinous results of Gallo's vineyard developments in Sonoma County appeared with a great deal of media fanfare. Gallo made headlines with its very expensive Estate Bottled Reserve Chardonnay (100% barrel-fermented in French oak) and Estate Bottled Cabernet Sauvignon. Only 4,000 cases of each were made in the inaugural vintage of 1990, but the story took on added significance since the wines appeared shortly after the accidental death of Julio Gallo, the mastermind of the Sonoma project. Though obviously priced high for shock value, the Estate Cabernet Sauvignon and Chardonnay have been impressive in each vintage and usually approach the °° range. As its more reasonably priced Sonoma line unfolds, Gallo's long-term plan is to highlight Sonoma's subregions and its own vineyards. To date its leading Dry Creek Valley wines are Cabernet Sauvignon, Merlot, and Zinfandel, and one white, Chardonnay from the Stefani Vineyard. The Alexander Valley wines, labeled

Barrelli Creek, are Cabernet Sauvignon, Zinfandel, Valdiguie, Barbera, and San-giovese. The latter two are first-class but still in the experimental stage. Chardon-nay from the Laguna Vineyard is its primary Russian River Valley entry, but vineyards in the area are being developed to Pinot Noir, with Syrah and Viognier in the testing stages. With more than 2,000 acres planted and more anticipated in the key Sonoma County region, Gallo Sonoma is just getting under way. To date, though rich in varietal character and fairly priced, the Zinfandels have a tendency to be a little heavy-handed. However, Chardonnay in all of its guises has been a pleasant surprise.

### Cabernet Sauvignon

(Northern Sonoma Estate)    **90°°**    **91°°**    **92°°**    **93°°**

(Frei Ranch)    **92°**    **93°**    **94°°**

(Stephani Vineyard)    **93**    **94**

### Chardonnay

(Estate)    91°    92°    93°    **94°°**    95°

(Stefani Vineyard)    **94°**    95

(Laguna Ranch)    94°    95    96°

### Zinfandel

(Frei Ranch)    90°    91°    92°    93    94°

---

GAN EDEN WINERY    *Sonoma 1985*    Located within the Green Valley appellation of Sonoma County, Gan Eden Winery was designed to produce certified kosher wines. Its line of varietals is made from Sonoma County grapes, primarily from the Alexander Valley. The line consists of Cabernet Sauvignon, Chardonnay, Black Muscat, Gewurztraminer, and Fumé Blanc. Over its early history, the quality lead-ers to emerge are Cabernet Sauvignon and Chardonnay. With dense black-cherry fruit and deep, yet soft flavors, the Cabernet Sauvignons, which can be unde-pendable, have at times earned up to °°. In a style accentuating lemony fruit, vanillin oak, and bright acidity, its Chardonnays have been of ° caliber. Annual production has grown to 15,000 cases; the winery's full capacity is 40,000. The winery was unable to continue its initial quality performance, and has become slightly erratic. However, it remains a name to follow for quality kosher wines.

---

GARLAND RANCH    *(Chateau Julien)*    Presented by the owners of Chateau Julien as a line to compete in the mid-priced category, Garland Ranch wines are usually from the Central Coast appellation. As a rule Garland Ranch offers Sauvignon Blanc, Cabernet Sauvignon, Chardonnay, and Merlot. The annual output has been about 10,000 cases over recent years.

---

GAVILAN VINEYARDS    *(Chalone)*    Over its history this second label has been attached to a wide variety of wines from numerous appellations. For several years, the wines were bottled at Carmenet (part of the Chalone group of wineries) in Sonoma Valley. Currently they are bottled at the Chalone winery in Monterey County, and the label appears on wines made by Chalone that for one reason or another are not used for the primary label. The most recent reason for the increase of Gavilan wines is that the label is being used for wines made from young vines on the Chalone Pinnacles estate. Annual production of Gavilan has, as a result of vineyard expansion at Chalone, surpassed 10,000 cases a year. Most of that is Chardonnay. The line includes Chardonnay, Chenin Blanc, Pinot Noir, and Pinot Blanc. 95 was the final vintage for this label. See "Echepon" for the Chalone group's new entrant in the lower-priced arena.

### Chardonnay

88°    89°    90°    91    92    93

*Toasty oak overlies green appley, slightly citrusy fruit in this consistent second label*

**DANIEL GEHRS VINEYARDS** *Santa Barbara 1993* Veteran winemaker, Dan Gehrs, developed his own line of wines as a sideline. Most of his 3,500-case annual output consists of white wines, with a fruity Cabernet Franc from Santa Barbara being the sole red. The whites, which are all grown in Monterey's Carmel Valley, are headed by Fume Blanc, Chenin Blanc (barrel fermented), Muscadet (no oak), Pinot Blanc (barrel fermented), and a white table wine blend of Chenin Blanc and Chardonnay.

**GEORIS WINERY** *Monterey 1989* Walter Georis owns the highly praised Casanova restaurant in Carmel, and in the early 80s decided to develop a vineyard near his home in the Carmel Valley. On a site northeast of Durney Vineyards, Georis planted 15 acres to Merlot, Cabernet Sauvignon, and the three other Bordeaux red varieties. In 86 he made about 400 cases of Merlot at Morgan Winery. A small winery was built by 89, and Georis intends to specialize in Merlot and a proprietary red Bordeaux blend. Production has remained minuscule.

**GERWER WINERY** *El Dorado 1983* The Gerwers presently occupy land that was the site for a test plot and experimental vineyard for El Dorado County set up by the University of California in 67. Encouraged by the results, Vernon Gerwer and his family began developing their own 12-acre vineyard in 79. On a 40-acre parcel south of Somerset at the 2,600-foot level, they planted Ruby Cabernet, Sauvignon Blanc, Semillon, and Petite Sirah. Chenin Blanc and Zinfandel (to produce White Zinfandel) are made from grapes grown by their neighbors. The winery, known for a few years as Stony Creek, changed to the family name in early 83. Since then, its production has reached 5,000 cases; with the expansion of their vineyard to 20 acres, the Gewers intend to level off at 8,000 cases a year.

**GEYSER PEAK WINERY** *Sonoma 1972* This ancient bulk wine producer, founded in 1880, was brought back to life when Schlitz of Milwaukee acquired it from the Bagnani family in 72. The beer company modernized and expanded the facility, located a mile north of Geyserville. Within three years, the winery was cranking out 200,000 cases of varietals and generics. Under Schlitz ownership, this winery was the first to make and sell wines in a can, wines in the bag-in-the-box, and wines in a plastic container. Its line of cheap generics expanded to the point where it was finally given its own name and label, "Summit." With Summit leading the way, the winery was making over 1 million cases by the end of the 70s. Geyser Peak acquired 600 acres of vineyards and a reputation for making wine almost as bland in character as most beer. In 83, after Schlitz was taken over by another major brewery, the winery became the property of the local Trione family, which gradually discontinued the novelty packaging and eventually disposed of the Summit brand. Vineyard acreage grew to 1,150 acres.

Under the Triones' leadership, the winery began to focus on a line of varietals, most of which were in the mid-price range or lower. In 89, the next chapter opened as the winery entered into a 50-50 partnership with Penfolds, the largest and most widely distributed brand of Australian wines. A new winemaker from Australia, Daryl Groom, was brought in to run the winery. After Penfolds became entangled in a complicated corporate takeover in early 92, Trione bought out Penfolds to become sole proprietor again. Since then the line has been trimmed from 800,000 cases to half that by dropping the large-volume, low-profit generic wines and White Zinfandel. Definite quality breakthroughs first became evident when all of the 89 s were marketed. Today the leading varietals by volume are Chardonnay (regular and Reserve), Soft Johannisberg Riesling, Sauvignon Blanc, and Semchard, a blend of Semillon and Chardonnay that has long been popular in Australia. The Soft Riesling, made in a low-alcohol, medium-sweet style, is a frequent crowd-pleaser with the balance needed to keep it at the ° level. Substantial improvements have recently been achieved in the winery's Merlot, Sauvignon Blanc, and Cabernet Sauvignon. "Reserve Alexandre" and "Chateau Alexandre" identify its Meritage red and white versions. Daryl Groom added a Syrah which he insists on labeling "Shiraz." Its production of Shiraz will expand in the 90s. He also has made complex Reserve Cabernet Sauvignon, and is making small lots of Reserve Shiraz. Trione plans to keep production at between 450,000 and 500,000 cases. "Canyon Road" (see entry) is a revamped second label. In 95 the winery introduced the "Venezia" label (see entry) for Sangiovese and other wines made in small quantities. Geyser Peak, related brands, and adjacent vineyards were acquired in 1998 by Fortune Brands, Inc.

## Cabernet Sauvignon

(Alexander Valley)   82   83   84   85   **89**   90   91   **93**   95

(Reserve)   85   **87°**   **90**   **91°°°**   **92°°°**   **94°**

*Ranging from light and fruity to light and uninteresting, this one can be a good value in its better years; the Reserve is bigger and better*

## Chardonnay

(Sonoma County)   86   87   88   89   90   92   93   94   95

(Reserve)   92   93   **94°°**   **95°**

*The Sonoma County bottling has been light and vaguely floral, but usually lacking substance; the Reserve is riper, richer, oakier and better*

## Merlot

85   86   87   88   89°   **90°**   **91°**   **92°**   93   **94°**   95

*Upgraded into a fruity, moderately rich wine under winemaker Groom*

## Reserve Alexandre

84°   85   87   **90°**   **91°°**   **92**   **93°**   **95°°**

*Lately containing about 40% Cabernet Sauvignon with 15-30% each of Cabernet Franc and Malbec, this wine tries, by content at least, to make a quality statement; it succeeds on occasion*

---

GIRARD WINERY   *Napa 1980*   The family-owned and -operated winery was founded by Stephen Girard, Sr., and run by Stephen Jr. until it was sold in 1997 to Leslie Rudd. In 74 the Girards bought 60 acres with 44 planted to vines surrounded by an oak grove. Located on the midsection of the Silverado Trail in Oakville, the site contained Cabernet Sauvignon established in 68. Retaining the Cabernet and a small Chardonnay planting, the Girards improved the old vineyard and added Chenin Blanc in 77. By 80, the Girards were building a winery, and two years later they bought over 400 acres of hillside property on Mount Veeder, eventually planting 40 acres to Cabernet Sauvignon, Cabernet Franc, Chardonnay, and Semillon.

With emphasis on Chardonnay, Cabernet Sauvignon, and Chenin Blanc, Girard was making about 17,000 cases by 90. A Reserve Cabernet Sauvignon, a Reserve Chardonnay, and a regular Semillon were each made in 500-case quantities. In the mid-80s, Girard planted 25 acres of wine grapes on land it owns in southern Oregon. With Carl Doumani, owner of Stags' Leap Winery, as his partner, Girard now runs the Benton Lane Winery in Oregon. In 1998 Leslie Rudd changed the winery's name to Rudd Estate and hired David Ramey (ex-Chalk Hill and ex-Dominus) to take over winemaking.

## Cabernet Sauvignon

(regular bottling)   80°°   81°°   82°   83   **84°**   85°   **86**   87°
88   **90°°**   **91°**   **93°**   **94°**

(Reserve)   83   **84°°**   **85°**   **86°**   88   89   **90°°**   **91°**   9̶2̶   **93°**
**94°°**

*High in ripeness and oak, these well-stuffed wines rarely lack personality but can become overblown, over-oaked, and too tough in tannin; the hillside-grown Reserve goes in the same direction but is generally the bolder of the two*

### Chardonnay

(regular bottling)   84   85   86°   87   88°°   89   90°   91°   92   93°°   94

(Reserve)   86°°   87°   89°°   90   92°   93° · 94°

*The Reserve bottling often carries the richness and depth of grand Chardonnay, although at times it can be almost too oaky*

GLASS MOUNTAIN   *(Markham Winery)*   Added in 90, this second label is used for moderately priced Petite Sirah, Cabernet, Merlot, and Chardonnay.

GLEN ELLEN WINERY   *Sonoma 1980*   Within the borders of the quaint town of Glen Ellen, the Benziger family updated an old facility in the western hills of the Sonoma Valley. On beautifully terraced hillsides, they established an 85-acre vineyard. The first wines offered under the Glen Ellen Winery name were inexpensive Cabernet Sauvignon and a red generic blend bought readymade, only to be blended and bottled. Both wines were adorned with a folksy-looking label and given the designation "Proprietor's Reserve." Patriarch Bruno Benziger, a successful importer and marketing executive with the Park-Benziger spirits importing company in New York, soon proved equally adept at building a wine brand through clever merchandising. As the demand for the first two wines increased, Glen Ellen Winery added a low-priced Chardonnay which enjoyed extremely rapid sales growth. Unintentionally, the winery had created a new industry category called "fighting varietals," which are inexpensive and designed for popular appeal.

By the end of the decade, Glen Ellen Winery had developed an elaborate network for buying, blending, and bottling bulk wines, which allowed its annual sales to grow to over 3 million cases. All of the Proprietor's Reserve wines are blends of wines and grapes purchased from numerous sources and regions throughout California. In 85–86, the family slowly introduced wines under yet another brand, M. J. Vallejo (see entry), covering a line similar to those under the Glen Ellen Winery. In 1994 the Benzigers sold Glen Ellen and M. G. Vallejo to Heublein, which has continued to offer the same products. Sales are steady at 3 million cases annually.

Under the Glen Ellen Winery "Proprietor's Reserve" label, the wines offered are Cabernet Sauvignon, White Zinfandel, Chardonnay, Chenin Blanc, Sauvignon Blanc, Gamay Beaujolais, and Red Table and White Table wine.

GLORIA FERRER CHAMPAGNE CAVES   *Sonoma 1988*   The well-known Freixenet company of Spain developed vineyards and built a large facility in the Sonoma sector of the Carneros district. Over 100 acres have been planted to Pinot Noir and Chardonnay. Sparkling wine is the main thrust, but in the mid-90s Gloria Ferrer began making Pinot Noir and Chardonnay table wine as well as a line of sparklers. Brut aged for two years en tirage is the main bubbly offered, followed by a Blanc de Noirs (over 90% Pinot Noir), and a Brut Rose. The winery's vintage sparkler is labeled "Brut Royal Cuvee," and this cuvee is a 50-50 blend of Pinot Noir and Chardonnay aged on the yeast for over four years. The style of the Brut shows typical California bright fruit and moderate yeastiness. Overall, the quality is good and these sparkling wines are pleasant and affable. We feel the Blanc de Noirs is its most attractive offering. Annual, production of the sparkling wines is steady at 45,000 cases.

GODSPEED VINEYARDS   *Napa 1986*   Owner Larry Stricker developed 22 acres to Cabernet Sauvignon and Chardonnay in the Mt. Veeder district. An architect who worked on many resorts (the Desert Springs Resort and Spa and the Mauna Lani Bay Hotel are the best known), Stricker is moving toward an annual production of 3,000 cases. With the intention of marketing the lion's share to those resorts he helped design, Stricker has split the winery's output evenly between Cabernet and Chardonnay.

GODWIN FAMILY WINES   *Sonoma 1994*   Richard Godwin, an engineer by profession, developed 44 acres of Chardonnay on his 150-acre ranch in the Alexander Valley. In the mid-1990s he acquired Associated Vintage Group, a producer of wines for dozens of other labels. He later acquired Mark West Vineyards and Martini & Prati. The Godwin label is seen on 100% barrel-fermented Alexander Valley Chardonnay, which accounts for most of the 2,000-case production. Merlot has recently been added to the line.

GOLD HILL VINEYARDS   *El Dorado 1986*   Gold Hill is located in the town of Coloma, a mile south of Sutter's Mill, where gold was discovered. Owner Hank Battjes acquired part of an experimental vineyard planted in the mid-60s and has since expanded it to 35 acres. Chardonnay at 15 acres is the prime variety, followed by Cabernet Sauvignon at 13 acres. A few acres each are planted to Merlot, Cabernet Franc, Chenin Blanc, and Riesling. Chardonnay represents 70% of the total annual output. Limited amounts of Cabernet, Merlot, and Cabernet Franc are offered. With vineyard maturity, Gold Hill will build to the 8,000-case level. Some wines are sold under the "Coloma Gold" label.

GOLDEN CREEK VINEYARD   *Sonoma 1983*   Owner-winemaker Ladi Danielik was born in Czechoslovakia and emigrated to the U.S. in 68, coming to California in 77, where he bought 70 acres of land a few miles northeast of Santa Rosa. On steep hillsides he planted 12 acres to Merlot and Cabernet Sauvignon, and two white varieties, Sauvignon Blanc and Gewurztraminer, which were eventually budded to more Cabernet and Merlot. The Cabernet and Merlot have been more successful, as has been a blend of the two termed "Caberlot." Production has varied from 500 cases a year to just over 1,000, depending upon sales. When the production is low, the owner has a ready market for his grapes.

GOLDEN EYE VINEYARD   *Mendocino 1996*   Wine-knowledgeable bird lovers recognizing Golden Eye as a duck might logically deduce that this label belongs to the owners of Duckhorn Vineyards. Sure enough, in late 1996 Duckhorn acquired the former Obester winery and 85-acre property in Mendocino's Anderson Valley for the purpose of becoming a Pinot Noir producer. The vineyards now cover more than 100 acres and have been planted to numerous combinations of Pinot Noir clones and rootstocks. Golden Eye's first Anderson Valley Pinot was made in 1997. Trials are under way with white varieties, and this winery is considering Pinot Blanc as a real possibility.

GOODE-READY   *(Murphy Goode Winery)*   A label introduced in 91 for an early-maturing style of Cabernet Sauvignon. The name is taken directly from two winery principals, Dale Goode and Dave Ready. The owners are ready to use Goode-Ready whenever they encounter a vintage in which some batches from their estate vineyards yield light-style wines.

GOOSECROSS CELLARS   *Napa 1985*   Goosecross was founded by the Gorsuch family, whose name in Old English literally translates into "when the goose crosses." In the early 80s Ray Gorsuch bought a vineyard on State Lane in Yountville and developed the family's 10 1/2-acre Chardonnay estate. Until 85 all grapes were sold, and Far Niente and Burgess Cellars were among the several buyers. His son, Geoff Gorsuch, runs the winery operation and manages the vineyard today. Chardonnay is produced, the flagship wine being the estate-bottled version. The winery added Cabernet Sauvignon from Howell Mountain in the early 1990s. In 1996, with the acquisition of the Pradel Winery and vineyard, it added Yountville Cabernet Sauvignon to the roster. Limited (200-case) Edition, Artist Series Cabernet is named Aeros. Production has edged up close to the winery's 8,000-case capacity. The winery's production goal is 8,000 cases.

### Chardonnay

(Napa Valley)   85   86   87°   88   89   90°   92

*Plenty of oak, often in search of fruit, has left these wines somewhat monodimensional*

GRACE FAMILY VINEYARD   *Napa 1978*   Planning to move his brokerage business to the country, Smith Barney stockbroker Dick Grace and his wife, Ann, bought a home in St. Helena in 74. Two years later they planted 1 acre of Cabernet Sauvignon adjacent to their home, making their first small crop into wine at Caymus Vineyard in 78. From then until 83 the Grace Family Cabernet was bottled as a vineyard-designated wine under the Caymus label. Because the wine made was of fine quality and extremely scarce, Grace Family Cabernet attracted strong interest from collectors. Dick Grace further added to the winery's cult following by regularly contributing special bottles of his Cabernet Sauvignon to a dozen or more charities. In large format bottles, Grace Family wines often sold for record-setting prices. In many other ways, Grace raises funds for worthwhile charities and causes. The Cabernets, which are always 100% Cabernet, are aged close to three years in new French oak barrels. Generally, his two-acre vineyard yielded 200 cases a year. In 1995, he removed one diseased acre, so production in the following few years has been reduced until the new vineyard reaches productivity. Two other tiny-production wineries make their wines in the Grace Family winery. Hartwell Vineyard (see entry) and Vineyard 29 both specialize in Cabernet Sauvignon. All wineries share winemaking services which today are provided by Heidi Barrett and in past vintages have been handled by Gary Galleron and Randy Dunn. Sales of Grace Family wines are mainly by mailing list.

GRAESER WINERY   *Napa 1985*   Richard Graeser inherited an old estate and 45 acres of mountainous property in 84. His parents had purchased the property in 58 and used it for many years as a summer home. With years of experience as a farmer in the Bakersfield area, Graeser decided to try his hand at grape-growing and winemaking. Intending to specialize in a Cabernet Sauvignon blend from the mountain vineyard, he planted 9 1/2 acres in 84–85 to Cabernet Sauvignon, Cabernet Franc, and Merlot. Located on the Petrified Forest Road about a mile north of Calistoga, Graeser Winery began by making Cabernet Sauvignon, Semillon, and Chardonnay from purchased grapes. Nowadays Graeser is specializing in estate-grown Cabernet Sauvignon, Merlot, and Cabernet Franc, along with Chardonnay and Semillon made from purchased Napa Valley fruit. Production of the three estate-grown red varietals has approached 5,000 cases a year, with Cabernet accounting for well over 50% of the total. The facility allows for gradual production increases to a maximum of 8,000 cases a year.

GREGORY GRAHAM   *Sonoma 1994*   Graham is full-time winemaker for Rombauer Cellars, where he also oversees production of a dozen other brands custom-made at Rombauer. His own label so far has consisted of a few hundred cases of some of the finest, most enjoyable Viogniers yet made this side of the Rhone Valley. In most vintages he has been offering Viognier from both the Knights Valley and the Napa Valley. In most vintages, both versions are superb.

GRAND CRU VINEYARDS   *Sonoma 1970*   Walt and Tina Dreyer, one-time owners of Oroweat Bread, bought the winery in 1981. Under their ownership, production increased to over 50,000 cases, with the addition of a White Zinfandel, and a low-priced Sauvignon Blanc and Cabernet Sauvignon under the California appellation. Over the next few years the Dreyers made many changes in the product line, looking for the right mix, but nothing seemed to click. They added a Chardonnay; they introduced wines under the Dreyer label. By 92 they were unable to arrest the financial slide, and eventually the banks foreclosed. The trademark and the inventory were purchased by the Classic Wine Co. in 1994. Today the owners bottle Merlot and other varietal that are similarly low-priced.

GRANITE SPRINGS WINERY   *El Dorado 1981*   With a name reflecting the granitic soils prevalent throughout its vineyards, Granite Springs is a family-owned winery. In

79, owner-winemaker Les Russell developed a 24-acre vineyard planted to Cabernet Sauvignon, Sauvignon Blanc, and Zinfandel, with small amounts of Chenin Blanc, Petite Sirah, and Muscat Blanc. Beginning with an annual production of 2,700 cases, the winery has grown to its maximum of 10,000 per year. Within its first decade, Granite Springs established solid winemaking credentials by turning out well-made White Zinfandels and Chenin Blancs, both in a slightly sweet style. Its estate-bottled Petite Sirah also ranked as one of the better versions of the varietal. Made to last, the Petite Sirahs have earned * in most vintages; the winery's Reserve Zinfandel has occasionally been a ** performer. The Chardonnay to date has been inconsistent. Port production has been given attention by winemaker Russell, who has experimented with both Zinfandel and Petite Sirah, individually and combined.

GREEN & RED VINEYARD   *Napa 1977*   Jay Heminway abandoned the teaching profession and moved to the Chiles Valley in 70, purchasing a 160-acre farm that had fallen into neglect. By 72 he had developed a 16-acre vineyard on a site that ranges in elevation from 900 to 1,500 feet, and where, Heminway believes, two distinct microclimates exist. On the lower levels he planted 9 1/2 acres of Chardonnay, and along the higher contours 7 1/2 acres of Zinfandel. The soils also vary, red iron mixed with green serpentine being the most common; these soil types explain the vineyard's name. However, the winery's main focus is its regular Zinfandel, usually made in a tannic style, and estate-grown Chardonnay. They represent 80% of the winery's annual output, which will level off at 5,000 cases a year. The Zinfandel occasionally rises to * rating.

GREENSTONE WINERY   *Amador 1980*   The Greenstone Winery rests on a gentle knoll in the middle of a 40-acre ranch in a part of Amador County known as Jackson Valley. A partnership of two families, Greenstone offers a range of table wines and fortified wines. Beginning in 80, a 30-acre vineyard was planted to French Colombard, Chenin Blanc, Zinfandel, Sauvignon Blanc, Cabernet Sauvignon, Muscat Blanc, and Palomino (used for sherry). Slightly sweet, picnic-style White Zinfandel and Colombard account for over 50% of the annual 10,000-case production. Most wines are made from Greenstone's own vineyards, with the exception of a Zinfandel Port from Calaveras County. Long-term, the winery will level off at 20,000 cases a year.

GREENWOOD RIDGE VINEYARD   *Mendocino 1980*   On an isolated southern ridgeline at the 1,200-foot level, the Greenwood Ridge winemaking facility can be found in a pretty, pastoral setting. A tasting room was later built on the floor of the Anderson Valley to connect the winery to the world. Owner Allan Green left the graphic arts profession and bought an old vineyard, once owned by Husch, not far from the Dupratt Zinfandel vineyard which sells to Steele Wines. Green redeveloped his vineyard and now has roughly 4 acres each of Riesling, Cabernet Sauvignon, and Merlot. He purchases Chardonnay from the Redwood Valley, Zinfandel from Sonoma County, Sauvignon Blanc and Pinot Noir from Mendocino County. The winery has produced a string of excellent White Rieslings in a slightly sweet style, which have often been ** beauties. The Zinfandel, Pinot Noir, and Sauvignon Blanc have risen above average. Green continues to work with Cabernet (regular and reserve) and with Merlot, both tending to be likable wines with a touch of herbaceousness in their youth. On occasion both Merlot and Pinot Noir have ranked among the very best from a particular vintage. The winery has reached its maximum capacity of 8,000 cases.

## Cabernet Sauvignon

89   **90**   91   **92°°**   94   95

*Firm and oaky but lacking depth; 92 surprised*

## Chardonnay

(Dupratt)   90°   92   94°   95   **96°**

*Sometimes underfilled, the wine can show attractive ripe apple and citrus fruitiness enhanced by oaky and leesy notes*

### Merlot

88  **89°**  **91°**  **92°°°**  **93°°**  94°  **95°**

*Blended with about 20% Cabernet, this wine is rich, supple, and in 92 showed depth matched by few Merlots*

### Zinfandel

(Scherrer Vineyard)  89°  **90°**  91  92°  **93°°**  **94°°°**  95  **96°**

*Often superb, deep and ripe fruit with mid-term aging possibilities*

GRGICH HILLS CELLAR  *Napa 1977*  The partners behind this successful winery are Mike Grgich, the winemaker, and Austin Hills, the vineyard owner and developer. Though not as well known in wine circles as Grgich, Austin Hills comes from a San Francisco family that once owned Hills Bros. Coffee, and was involved in the family business until it was sold in 76. At that time he decided to expand his small vineyard located in Rutherford and to venture into wine production. In early 77 he and Grgich, who had been with Chateau Montelena, became equal partners. Born in Desne, Croatia, in Yugoslavia, Grgich emigrated to the U.S. in 58. He began his California winemaking experience with the original Souverain as Lee Stewart's apprentice. He later worked for the Christian Brothers, Beaulieu Vineyard, and the Robert Mondavi Winery, where he remained until going to Montelena as head winemaker in 72. It was during his tenure that Montelena produced the 73 Chardonnay that bested its French counterparts in the now famous 76 tasting held in Paris.

The new Grgich Hills winery was barely finished in time for the 77 harvest. The wines produced were Chardonnay, Zinfandel, and Johannisberg Riesling in a slightly sweet style. A Fumé Blanc was added to the line in 81, and the first Cabernet Sauvignon vintage was 80. Using Chardonnay from the Hills vineyard in Rutherford, Grgich was performing at the ° level from the beginning. Changes in winemaking have been implemented gradually. In 85, Grgich introduced partial barrel fermentation; by 87 he was fermenting 100% of the Chardonnay in Limousin barrels. Malolactic fermentation has just about always been prevented in Grgich Chardonnays, as it also is in Zinfandels. The grape sources for Chardonnay are four vineyards in Napa Valley: Rutherford, Yountville, north of Napa, and Carneros. The Fumé Blanc is made primarily from the winery's Olive Hills Vineyard in Napa. Grgich plays down the grassy-herbal side of Fumé Blanc to emphasize ripe fruit, balanced and substantial flavors in an oak-enriched style that varies between ° and °° performances. Aging his red wines in a combination of American and Nevers oak barrels, Grgich also prefers Zinfandel from old, nonirrigated hillside vineyards, and he has found an appropriate source in the Alexander Valley. The quantity of Cabernet Sauvignon was small in 80 and 81, but with the 84 vintage grew to 10,000 cases a year. Grgich Cabernets are grown in the winery's Yountville vineyard and blended with Merlot before being aged for two years in both French and American oak. By 90 the winery was at its capacity level of 30,000 cases. Chardonnay accounts for over 30% and Fumé Blanc for 20%, with Zinfandel and Riesling combining for 15%.

### Cabernet Sauvignon

81°°  82°  83  **84°**  **85°°**  **86°**  **87°**  88  89  **90**  **91**  **92°**
**93**  **94°°**

*Fairly full-sized Cabernet sometimes showing more ripeness, tannin, and oak than restraint; the wine succeeds when its fruit is able to match up with its ambitions*

### Chardonnay

86°°  87°°  88°  89°  90  91°  92  93  **94°**  **95°**  **96°**

*High in oak and high in appley fruit, with somewhat stiff acidity in the background, this wine is among the standard-setters for California Chardonnay*

## Zinfandel

78••• 79 80••• 81•• 82••• 83• 84• 86 **87**•• 88
**89**• **90**• 91 **92** **93**• **94**•• **95**•

*Always a wine heading toward overripeness, it has seemed to lose its massive berry-
ish center in recent years and no longer is able to command top ratings or be worthy
of lengthy cellar aging*

GROTH VINEYARDS & WINERY   *Napa 1982*   One-time president of Atari and former
accountant Dennis Groth decided to invest in the grape and wine world in 81. He
bought two vineyards in Napa Valley, the Oakcross Vineyard in Oakville containing 68 acres of Cabernet Sauvignon (all planted in 74) and 32 acres of Chardonnay, and the Hillview Vineyard just south of Yountville, with 28 acres of Sauvignon
Blanc, 12 acres of Merlot, and 3 acres of Chardonnay. Construction of a winery in
Oakville was finally completed in 89. Until then, the wines were fermented in one
location, aged in another, and bottled in a third. In 90, all winemaking was
brought together under one roof and the winery was close to its production capacity of 40,000 cases. Making only estate-grown wines, Groth produces 20,000
cases of Cabernet Sauvignon (with about 10% Merlot), and 10,000 cases each of
Sauvignon Blanc and Chardonnay. Cabernet Sauvignons, regular and limited-
volume Reserve, have been the winery's strong calling card; but, except for the
spectacular mid-80s vintages, its record has been surprisingly inconsistent.

## Cabernet Sauvignon

82• 83• **84**• **85**•• **86** **87** 88 89 **90**• 91 92̶ **93** **95**
(Reserve) **85**••• **86**•• **87**•• 88 89̶ 90̶ 91 **94**•

*Loaded with sweet oak, sometimes at the expense of the fruit, this wine is usually
well proportioned, otherwise with medium tannins adding to the notion that it will
age well; 89 and 90 Reserves were dirty aberrations*

## Chardonnay

86• 87 88• 89 90••• 91 92 **93**• **94**•• 95

*Omnipresent, heavy-handed oak often outdistances the appley fruit; but when the
wine is in balance, it is attractive to fans of the toasty, fleshy style*

GROVE STREET WINERY   *Sonoma 1990*   Soon after investor Bill Hambrecht became sole
proprietor of Belvedere Winery (see entry), he began reshaping his second label
(Discovery Series) into what is now Grove Street Winery. This line of inexpensive
wines includes Chardonnay, Cabernet Sauvignon, California White Zinfandel,
and Malbec from Argentina. The annual output has reached 75,000 cases.

GUENOC WINERY   *Lake 1981*   This winery and estate are owned by the Magoon family, which acquired 23,000 acres in the early 60s in exchange for land in Hawaii it
gave to the University of Hawaii. The winery is in Middletown, about 20 miles
north of St. Helena. Part of the Magoon property, approximately 4,000 acres, was
once owned by the famous Victorian actress Lillie Langtry, who lived there from
1888 to 1906. The Magoons restored the Langtry House, and have used the historical connection in their publicity. Beginning in the late 60s they developed
vineyards in and around the former Langtry estate, and also in a part of their
ranch that falls within Napa County.

The Guenoc Winery today has 385 acres of vineyards; the leading varieties are
Chardonnay, Cabernet Sauvignon, and Sauvignon Blanc. Walt and Roy Raymond
of the Raymond Vineyards in Napa Valley helped develop the vineyards, and the
first vintage produced, the 76, was made by Walt Raymond. By 80 the Magoons
had built their own winery and begun making a line of varietals, mostly from their
own grapes. Magoon defined the Guenoc Valley well enough to have it become
approved as a Viticultural Area in 81. Most of his vineyards are in the Lake County
part of Guenoc Valley, but Magoon decided to plant Cabernet Sauvignon and all
related varieties in a lower-elevation site in the northern corner of Napa County.

Over the years, Guenoc Winery has frequently altered its wine roster. For a few vintages it made a name for itself with its Petite Sirahs and heavy-bodied Zinfandels. Its Chardonnay has earned ° but has been highly variable. When the tannins are under control, the winery's Zinfandel can rise above average. Its most recent releases of Sauvignon Blanc and Cabernet have been well made, and represent good values. Several different Reserve designations have been tried and discarded, and the Reserves are currently labeled under vineyard designated names. The most impressive, as well as most expensive, wines are the Meritage red and white marketed under the "Langtry" label. Altogether, total annual output is 85,000 cases. The winery's capacity is 110,000 cases.

### Chardonnay

| | | | | | | |
|---|---|---|---|---|---|---|
| (Guenoc Valley) | 89 | 90° | 91 | 92 | 93 | 95 |
| (Guenoc Valley-Reserve) | 88° | 89 | 90 | 91 | 92°° 93 | **94°** **95°°** |

GUGLIELMO WINERY   *Santa Clara County 1925*   Located in the Morgan Hill area, this family-owned winery is now in the hands of the third generation. In the 60s and into the early 70s, under the "Emile's Private Stock" brand, it produced large quantities of jug wines for many restaurants in Northern California. The family name, Guglielmo, is often highlighted on a limited line of Reserve varietals from Santa Clara Valley. The most consistently successful wine is a Reserve bottling of "Claret," blended from family-grown Zinfandel and Petite Sirah. Though the winemaking style retains a rustic touch, the red varietals—Zinfandel, Cabernet Sauvignon, and Merlot—are often more than decent wines in a relatively inexpensive price range. Chardonnay and Johannisberg Riesling are from the Monterey County appellation. Total annual output is around 75,000 cases.

GUILLIAMS VINEYARD   *Spring Mountain District 1972*   Early arrivals in the Spring Mountain, John & Shawn Guilliams developed 7 acres on hillsides near their home. They produce only Cabernet Sauvignon (blended with Cabernet Franc and Merlot), and typically age each vintage three years in oak and one in bottle before selling it. Production ranges from 1,000 to 1,400 cases per annum.

GUNDLACH–BUNDSCHU WINERY   *Sonoma 1973*   This family-owned winery can trace its history back to 1858. Prior to Prohibition, the name was well regarded for a range of table and fortified wines, and from the time of Repeal until it reopened as a producer, Gundlach-Bundschu's vineyard was a favorite of many producers within the area. Under the direction of Jim Bundschu, the winery started on a small scale in 73. Growing steadily each year, it has leveled off at 40,000 cases a year. The Bundschus own 375 acres of vineyards and still sell a portion of their crop to others. The original 125-acre family vineyard, referenced on labels as "Rhinefarm," is located in the Sonoma-Carneros appellation. Another family-owned vineyard with 150 acres is located east of the town of Sonoma. The winery has preferred to use Sonoma Valley as the appellation. In its initial vintages, it promoted an obscure white varietal, Kleinberger, and gained some critical attention for its ripe, brawny Zinfandels.

Quality rose higher in 80, a year in which the winery began producing Merlot in a big, rich style and Gewurztraminer that in some vintages was intense in character and balanced. Throughout the 80s Gundlach-Bundschu performed well, with the exception of a Zinfandel wandering to the overripe end of the spectrum. Cabernet Sauvignon from the neighboring Batto Vineyard was bottled from 77 to 84. Today, the winery concentrates on estate-grown wines, making a Rhinefarm and a Rhinefarm Reserve Cabernet Sauvignon. Chardonnay in a fruity, moderately oak-influenced style has been consistently solid and often represents good value. Occasionally, Gundlach-Bundschu's vintages of Pinot Noir display some finesse and rise to ° levels. Finished in a relatively dry style, Gewurztraminer ranks in the ° range in most vintages. Cabernet Franc and two low-priced blends, "Sonoma Valley White" and "Sonoma Red," complete the line. Overall, Gundlach-Bundschu is a reliable brand offering good value in many of its wines.

### Cabernet Sauvignon

80° 81° 82° 83 84° **85°** 86 **87°** **88°** 89 **90** 91
**92** 93

*Typically showing ripe, cassislike fruit, medium-full body, and herbal leanings in a medium-aging style*

### Chardonnay

(regular bottling) **86°°** 87 88 89 90 91 93 94

(Special Selection) 86 87 88 **90°** **91°** 93

*Straightforward, somewhat appley fruit, moderate oakiness, medium depth, good balance; good value in best vintages*

### Merlot

80° 81°° 82°° 83° 84° 85°° **86°°** **87°** **88°** **89°** 90
**92** **93** **94** **95**

*Very ripe style that skirts the boundaries of acceptability, but is kept in check by enormous fruit, rich oak, and tannic structure*

### Zinfandel

(Rhinefarm Vineyard) 85° 86 87 88 89 90° 91° **93°**
**94** **95°**

---

**HACIENDA WINERY**   *Sonoma 1973*   In the 80s Hacienda reached its optimum level of 30,000 cases a year, with Chardonnay and Chenin Blanc (from the Delta region) representing more than half of the total. Purchased in 93 by Classic Wines Co., the Hacienda brand is now similar to a negociant label and has given up its high-caliber intentions.

---

**HAFNER VINEYARD**   *Sonoma 1982*   The Hafner family began developing vineyard in 67, and 90% of the acreage consists of Chardonnay and Cabernet Sauvignon. In 82 the Hafners built a small winery with the intention of making modest quantities of wine. By 85, they expanded the facility and developed a direct-marketing mailing-list program. Hafner's annual production has reached the maximum of 7,500 cases of Chardonnay and 2,500 cases of Cabernet Sauvignon. Occasionally, a late harvest Riesling is made with varying levels of *Botrytis.*

---

**HAGAFEN WINERY**   *Napa 1979*   In Hebrew, *hagafen* means "the vine," and Hagafen was the first kosher-wine specialist on the North Coast. Founded by Zach Berkowitz and Ernie Weir, who has always served as winemaker and is now sole owner. For three or four years, Hagafen attracted some media attention, but the quality was a little uneven. From a high mark of 5,000 cases, the winery's production at one point dipped to below half that, and now seems settled on 3,000 cases a year. Pinot Noir, Chardonnay, Riesling, and about 1,000 cases of Cabernet Sauvignon account for virtually all of the output.

### Chardonnay

87 88 89 90 91 94 95

---

**HAHN ESTATE**   *Monterey*   With vineyards in the Santa Lucia Highlands and the Aroyo Seco appellations, the Hahn family now have a total of 1,400 acres. Restricting its Smith & Hook label to upscale Cabernet Sauvignon and Merlot, the family produces a full line of modestly priced wines labeled Hahn Estate. Chardonnay is the volume leader and in most vintages represents good value in a fruity, round style. Annual output is 75,000 cases, with steady growth likely to continue.

---

**HAMEL WINERY**   *Sonoma 1995*   As winemaker for Preston Vineyards in Dry Creek Valley, Kevin Hamel was among the first to explore Syrah and other Rhone varieties. As a part-time project he has developed his own brand, which only offers Syrah.

Buying grapes from small vineyards in the warmer parts of Russian River Valley and Dry Creek Valley, Hamel has bottled 500 cases in each vintage to date. In a rich, long-lived style, Hamel Syrahs have ranked among the best made, earning °° in each of its first two outings (94 and 95).

HANDLEY CELLARS   *Mendocino 1978*   After gaining winemaking experience first at Chateau St. Jean and next at Edmeades Vineyard, winemaker Milla Handley went on to start her own winery in Philo, at the western edge of the Anderson Valley. The first few vintages of barrel-fermented Chardonnay from her parents' vineyard in Dry Creek Valley received considerable critical praise. Her father owns 20 acres in southern Dry Creek Valley, planted mostly to Chardonnay and Sauvignon Blanc. A 20-acre vineyard surrounding the winery was planted to Chardonnay and Pinot Noir. By the mid-80s the winery was producing two Chardonnays (Dry Creek Valley and Anderson Valley), Gewurztraminer, Pinot Noir, and Sauvignon Blanc, also from Dry Creek Valley. The overall quality level is solid. A small-scale sparkling wine program is under way as Handley makes both a Brut and a Rosé sparkling wine by the *méthode champenoise*. Total production for the sparklers remains under 1,000 cases a year. The winery's maximum production capacity is 12,000 cases. Its most exciting wines today are the sparklers—the Brut Rosé and the Blanc de Blancs.

**Chardonnay**

(Dry Creek Valley)   83°   84°   85°°   86°   87°°   88   89   90
91   92   93   94   95°

*Medium-intense fruit, floral notes, and toasty oak are presented in a firmly structured, medium-long-aging wine*

HANNA WINERY   *Sonoma 1985*   Owner Dr. Elias Hanna, a heart surgeon, established his winery on his 35-acre estate a few miles west of Santa Rosa. After developing 10 acres of Chardonnay adjacent to the winery, he purchased 100 acres in the Alexander Valley and over time 60 acres were planted to Chardonnay, Sauvignon Blanc, Cabernet Sauvignon, and Merlot. The first crush in 85 amounted to 8,000 cases, and within its third harvest the winery has grown to the 25,000-case level. All wines, including the barrel-fermented Chardonnay, Sauvignon Blanc, Merlot, Zinfandel, and Cabernet Sauvignon (blended with Merlot), are of above-average quality. While each is relatively successful, Cabernet Sauvignon and Chardonnay have led the way. Hanna's annual production will level off at 50,000 cases.

**Cabernet Sauvignon**

**86°°**   87   **88°**   **90**   91   **92°**   **93°°**   **94**   **95°**

*Capable of being ripe and fruity, with good depth and aging potential, this is one to watch in future years*

**Chardonnay**

86°°   87   88°°   89   90   91°   92   93°   **94°**   **95°**
**96°**

*Fruity, with some hints of juiciness; rich oak*

**Merlot**

90   **91**   **92**   **93°**   **94°**   95

*Ripe, round, oaky when good, but thinner in lesser vintages*

HANZELL VINEYARDS   *Sonoma 1956*   This was the original showcase winery, and one of the few successful small wineries after Repeal whose wines inspired many others to follow in its path. Hanzell was designed by the late Ambassador James Zellerbach, who modeled it on Clos de Vougeot in Burgundy. Located in what is still a remote hillside region along the eastern edge of the Sonoma Valley, Hanzell has 33 acres planted to well-established Chardonnay and Pinot Noir. Among its many accomplishments, the Hanzell winery emphatically introduced French oak barrels for aging and also for barrel fermentations of Chardonnay. It was also a technical leader for Pinot Noir in its small-batch approach, with frequent punching down of the cap for extraction.

For many years Hanzell's wines set high standards. The Chardonnays have always been made in a ripe style, with considerable oak influence. Though less consistent by far, Hanzell Pinot Noirs are big, ripe, and intense, with varying degrees of complexity and balance. The full-blown, large-scale style of both wines reflects the microclimate, which has always seemed best suited to Cabernet Sauvignon or possibly Zinfandel. Total annual output is fixed at 3,000 cases. The winery and beautiful grounds are closed to the public. They are owned by the Barbara de Brye estate of Canada.

### Cabernet Sauvignon

82   83°°   84   85°   86°   87°   88°   89°   92

*Potentially the best wine to come from Hanzell, it follows the winery's expansive style in its ability to offer ripe, deep character; but somehow its promise has not yet been realized*

### Chardonnay

83°°   84°   85   86°°   87°   88°°   89   90°   91   92   93   94

*Near to overdone in every vintage, at its best it manages sufficient fruit to balance its ripeness and heavy oak and is exciting for fans of the style*

### Pinot Noir

78°°   79°   80°   81°   82   83   84°   85°   86°   87   88   89
90   92

*Almost always too ripe to be called classical Pinot Noir, the wine can be deep in character, if often somewhat wanting in fruit*

HARLAN ESTATE WINERY   *Napa 1990*   A partner in Merryvale Vineyards and in the Meadowood Country Club, real estate developer H. William Harlan began acquiring prime vineyard land in the 1980s. Today he owns 230 acres, and has planted 33 acres to Cabernet Sauvignon and related blending varieties. Tucked up against the western hills, Harlan's hillside vineyard overlooks Far Niente Winery in the Oakville area. After a few practice rounds, Harlan made his first estate red (predominately Cabernet Sauvignon) in 1990. Made by Bob Levy in collaboration with Michel Rolland of Bordeaux, Harlan Estate Cabernets have been amazingly concentrated and polished. Quickly awarded cult status by the wine media, the wines are now among California's most expensive and most difficult to locate when new. Recently even older vintages have been among the most in demand at wine auctions. Production, currently at 1,200 cases, will gradually increase to an optimum of 2,500 cases.

HARRISON VINEYARD   *Napa 1988*   In 87 Lyndsay Harrison purchased a mature 17-acre vineyard located on the eastern hills of the Napa Valley. Encouraged by neighbor Bob Long of Long Vineyards, Harrison arranged to have the first vintages custom-made by Pecota Winery. Harrison's Chardonnay is barrel-fermented, undergoes complete malolactic fermentation, and ages six months *sur lie*. Grown on the steeper hillsides near Pritchard Hill, Harrison's Cabernet is 100% varietal and is given two years' aging in small French oak. The Harrisons built a small winery and aging caves in 1994. Vintages have been averaging 1,200 cases of Chardonnay and 900 of Cabernet a year. Merlot and Zinfandel named Zebra are produced from neighboring vineyards.

### Cabernet Sauvignon

89   90°°   91   92°°   93   94   95°

*Capable of being deep, tight, and ageworthy*

**Chardonnay**

89   90   91   93°°   94°   95

*Like the Cabernet, this wine tends to ripeness and weight*

HARTFORD COURT   *Sonoma 1994*   After acquiring the practically new facility built for Laurier, Jess Jackson (Kendall-Jackson) renamed it Hartford Court. The winery's specialty is limited-volume, often vineyard-designated Zinfandels from the Russian River Valley. There are also Pinot Noir and Chardonnay from Jackson's 20-acre Arrendell Vineyard and from the Sonoma Coast appellation. To date production hovers around 2,000 cases. Both Pinots and Zins have earned up to °° in first vintages.

HARTWELL VINEYARD   *Napa 1990*   From his 2-acre Cabernet Sauvignon vineyard in the heart of the Stags Leap area, Bob Hartwell produces 200 cases a year. Hartwell planted this vineyard to the Bosche clone from cuttings obtained from the Grace Family Winery. From the Sunshine Vineyard, a nearby second vineyard covering 10 acres, Hartwell produces 700–800 cases of Cabernet Sauvignon. The Grace clone Cabernet is made at Grace Family Vineyard; the Sunshine Cabernet at Hartwell's small underground winery in Stags Leap. Both Cabernets enjoy a strong following.

HAVENS WINE CELLARS   *Napa 1984*   Between 84 and 89, owner-winemaker Mike Havens rented space in other facilities to produce his wines. Havens, a former English professor at UCLA, transferred to U.C. Davis in order to learn more about enology and viticulture. In 83 he purchased property next door to the Truchard Vineyard in the Carneros, and has been purchasing grapes from Truchard to supplement his own crop since the first crush in 84. The Havens wine roster consists of Sauvignon Blanc, Chardonnay, and Merlot, the latter representing two-thirds of the winery's total annual production of 4,500 cases. Havens blends as much as 20% Cabernet Franc into his Merlot. Among the first to produce Syrah from Carneros, the winery now offers a Reserve Syrah as well as a Reserve Merlot.

**Merlot**

| | | | | | | | | | |
|---|---|---|---|---|---|---|---|---|---|
| (Napa Valley) | 86 | 8̷7̷ | 88° | 89° | 90° | 91 | 92 | 93° | 94 | 95° |
| (Carneros Reserve) | 87° | 89° | 90°° | 91°° | 92°° | 93°° | 94°° | 95° |

*Nicely focused Merlots, the Napa Valley has been less complete than the Reserve, which has performed admirably in every outing to date*

**Syrah**

92°°   93°   94   95°

*Ripe, spicy, sturdy wines*

HAWK CREST   *(Stag's Leap Wine Cellars)*   This second label first appeared in 74 on a bottle of Riesling, and by 76 was being used for Cabernet Sauvignon that did not make the cut for the primary brand. It lurched along in no particular direction until the early 80s, when it became a full-fledged line of competitively priced, ready-to-drink varietals. Made from purchased grapes or purchased wines, and often a combination of the two, Hawk Crest wines have carried many appellations. The majority are California and North Coast. The present lineup consists of Chardonnay, Sauvignon Blanc, Cabernet Sauvignon, and Gamay Beaujolais. Annual output of about 90,000 cases is led by Chardonnay, Merlot, and Sauvignon Blanc in terms of volume and consistent quality.

HAWLEY WINES   *Sonoma 1996*   After guiding Clos du Bois through its expansion era in the 1990s, winemaker John Hawley joined the fast-growing Kendall-Jackson company in the 1990s. Now working part-time as a consultant, Hawley is making Merlot and Viognier from his seven-acre hillside vineyard in the Russian River Valley.

HAYWOOD WINERY    *Sonoma 1980*   Between 76 and 78, Peter Haywood developed a 90-acre vineyard on steep terraces and hilly terrain in a secluded valley northeast of the town of Sonoma. A decade later he planted 18 additional acres of Cabernet Sauvignon and Merlot. The primary varieties cultivated are Zinfandel, Cabernet Sauvignon, Zinfandel, and Merlot. At times, the winery has made a Zinfandel in a ripe style that has earned our strong praise. Los Chamizal Vineyard, the original estate vineyard, is the origin of Haywood's Zinfandel. In 91 Racke, owners of Buena Vista, acquired a controlling interest in Haywood and moved the winemaking operation to Buena Vista in the Carneros district. The lineup has been changed to include low-priced "Vintner's Select" Chardonnay and Cabernet Sauvignon bearing the California appellation. These two wines combine for a total of 200,000 cases a year. The Estate Zinfandel averages 4,000 cases a year. Rocky Terrace Zinfandel is an up-scale, deep and successful bottling in its first appearances (°° for 93; ° for 94)

### Cabernet Sauvignon

81    82    83°    84°    **85°**    **86**    **87**    **88**

*Typically blended with a portion of Merlot (12–18% in most recent vintages), the wine tends toward tannic toughness that can all but cover the underlying black-cherryish fruit*

### Chardonnay

84°    85    86    87    88    89°

*Mixed results from a wine that can be coarse and closed-in if the fruit is not up to snuff*

### Zinfandel

81°°    82°    83°°    84°°°    85    86    **88°°**    **89°**    **90**    91    **92°**
94    **95**

*After a string of hits, the wine has fallen off in some recent years but, at its best, is full of ripe and rich, well-focused Zinfandel fruit*

HEITZ WINE CELLARS    *Napa 1961*   This winery is located to the east of the Silverado Trail in an isolated area in mid–Napa Valley. Originally housed in the small building in St. Helena that now serves as its sales room, Heitz Wine Cellars began as a bottler of an assortment of wines, some purchased and blended and finished by winemaker Joe Heitz. Heitz made his first Cabernet in 65, and the next year had the good fortune of being offered the opportunity to make Cabernet from a single vineyard located in Oakville named Martha's Vineyard. It is the series of Martha's Vineyard Cabernets that placed Heitz Cellars at center stage. The 68 vintage was the first highly acclaimed bottling, and the 70 received even better reviews. Martha's Vineyard, a 34-acre parcel in the foothills west of Oakville, is sold only to Heitz, who makes about 4,000 cases of Cabernet from it each year. Over the years he has also made Cabernet from the Fay Vineyard (now owned by Stag's Leap Wine Cellars), and from Bella Oaks (owned by Belle and Barny Rhodes, who developed the first 12 acres of Martha's Vineyard in 60).

A Napa Valley bottling of Cabernet is a regular part of the roster, first made from purchased grapes but since 86 from a newly acquired 75-acre vineyard on the Silverado Trail. The winery now owns a total of 115 acres. Heitz believes in making 100% Cabernet Sauvignon, and all of his bottlings age in French and American oak. In the late 60s and early 70s, he was highly regarded for Chardonnay, but many vintages have come and gone since a Heitz Chardonnay has earned a kind word.

The only Heitz wine worthy of any notice after Cabernet is Grignolino, made into a pleasing regular bottling and a rosé. By the end of the 80s the winery's annual production was 35,000 cases. From its sales room in St. Helena, Heitz offers a lengthy list of older vintages, and every February makes its first offering of a new vintage of Martha's Vineyard. Many people, ourselves included, maintain that the

68 and 74 Martha's Vineyard Cabernets are among the best wines ever produced in California. Characteristically, the independent-minded Mr. Heitz thinks the 69 is his top effort. Many people, ourselves included, believe that beginning in 1985 the overall quality has slipped and that there has been a degree of unaccountable mustiness in Heitz's Cabernets, and, more recently, also in the Chardonnays and Pinot Noir. Mr. Heitz never shared that opinion, and the problem has disappeared by now. After the 1992 vintage, Martha's Vineyard was pulled and replanted in its entirety, leaving a gap in vintages until 1996.

### Cabernet Sauvignon

(Martha's Vineyard)  68°°°  69°°  70°°°  72°°  73°°  **74°°°**
**75°°°**  76°°  77°°  **78°°**  **79°°**  **80°°**  **81°°**  82°  **83°°**
**84°°**  85°  **86°**  87  88  **89°°**  **90°**  91  92

*Clearly among the stars in California's Cabernet galaxy, this deeply curranty, always minty/eucalyptus-toned, long-aging wine has earned a strong following for its two-decade record of outstanding performance; a slight fall-off has been noticeable as the vineyard has aged, and the 88 was less than stellar*

### Cabernet Sauvignon

(Bella Oaks)  76°°  77°°°  78°°°  **80°°**  81°  82  83  **84°**
85  **86**  **87°**  8̶8̶  89  **90°**  93

*Softer and focused on ripe cherry fruit, with hints of herbs and occasionally of brush and dried bark, this wine can be round and rich in some years, but has recently lacked the depth and prettiness that characterized its early vintages*

HENDRY VINEYARDS  *Napa 1995*  George Hendry, a nuclear physicist who designs and manufactures particle accelerators, also owns and manages one of the most prominent vineyards. From 80 acres planted in the early 1970s the Hendry family has expanded its holdings to 115 acres today. Over the years Hendry sold to many producers, and rose to prominence when Rosenblum Cellars and Franus began making Zinfandel labeled Hendry Vineyard. Located in southwestern Napa Valley, the vineyard contains Zinfandel, Pinot Noir, Chardonnay, and Cabernet Sauvignon. As a wine producer, Hendry makes wines from each varietal, but his emphasis falls on a specific block each wine is made from to demonstrate microclimates. He has made bold versions of Zinfandel° and Cabernet Sauvignon° to date. With annual production scheduled to grow to the 6,000-case level, half of the total will continue to be Zinfandel.

BARON HERZOG WINE CELLARS  *Santa Clara 1994*  One of the largest and most successful producers of California kosher wine, Herzog offers a full line of varietals. Its White Zinfandel represents about one-third of the winery's 115,000-case annual sales. Chenin Blanc and Johannisberg Riesling are often award-winners at various competitions, and the Chardonnay and Cabernet Sauvignon are true to type and good wines for the money. Herzog's top-of-the-line wines are its Limited Edition Cabernet Sauvignon and another Cabernet labeled "Special Reserve."

THE HESS COLLECTION  *Napa 1982*  Swiss-born Donald Hess came to California seeking new sources of mineral water to expand Valser, his mineral water business. Wine caught his attention, and in 78 he purchased 550 acres of land on Mount Veeder from William Hill. Over the next several years he developed vineyards in Napa Valley that now cover 400 acres, equally divided between Chardonnay and the Cabernet complex—Cabernet Sauvignon, Merlot, Cabernet Franc, Malbec, and Petit Verdot. Part of his expanded holdings came in 86 when he purchased the historic Mount La Salle Winery, owned and operated by the Christian Brothers, who had decided to consolidate their winemaking operations. After renovating the large facility, Hess chose to build up his brand slowly, and until 88 sold most of the production to other wineries. The winemaking style favors barrel fermentation for the Chardonnay, and extended maceration and long barrel aging (two years) for the Cabernet. The winery also produces a Reserve Cabernet in limited quantities, which has risen to °°° in some vintages, although both Cabernets have been inconsistent of late. The Chardonnays have on occasion reached °. In the 90s Hess has also developed 240 acres in the American Canyon region in southern Napa, and this vineyard has become the backbone of Hess Chardonnay. The winery will continue to produce Mt. Veeder Chardonnay, but only in small quantities. A Pinot Noir from Santa Maria Valley has been added, and production of that wine has reached 5,000 cases. Hess's intention, as production moves closer to its 40,000-cases-per-year goal, is to emphasize Cabernet Sauúvignon and to maintain Chardonnay production at the 15,000-case level.

The "Collection" in the brand name refers to the 13,000-square-foot art gallery that Hess built in the winery to display his hundreds of paintings to the public.

HESS SELECT   *(The Hess Collection)*   Created in 1989, Hess Select is a second label first used for Chardonnay made by the Hess Collection winery in Napa Valley. Cabernet Sauvignon has been added to the line recently. These wines are identified by a California appellation, but most of the grapes used originate in Hess's 350-acre vineyard near Soledad in Monterey County. Simple, fruity, and given short-term aging, the Hess Select wines are produced in the large Napa Valley facility. Each has been cited for its good value. Hess Select's output is 65,000 cases a year.

HIDDEN CELLARS   *Mendocino 1981*   Located in Talmage east of Ukiah, Hidden Cellars is now making close to 15,000 cases of table wines. In the beginning, managing partner Dennis Patton emphasized white wine production. Over the first few vintages the results were somewhat uneven. Starting in 86, Hidden Cellars began to improve as its Sauvignon Blanc and Chardonnay displayed better character and balance, and the 86 Zinfandel confirmed the upward course.

Nowadays, Patton buys all grapes from within Mendocino County and is offering a medium-intense Sauvignon Blanc of ° caliber. He ferments 75% of his Sauvignon Blanc in oak, and ages the wine *sur lie* for about nine months. "Alchemy" is a proprietary blend of Semillon and Sauvignon Blanc that is barrel-fermented, aged *sur lie,* and surprisingly big and rich, though not to everyone's liking. By the mid-90s the winery's owners decided to emphasize red wines from several old vineyards scattered throughout Mendocino and grouped these wines along with its top-level Chardonnay under the Mendocino Heritage moniker. This line of limited-edition reds includes Old Vine Zinfandel, Sorcery (a field blend of Zin and other reds), and single-vineyard Zinfandels from Hildreath Ranch and Eaglepoint. Old Vine Petite Sirah and Eaglepoint Petite Sirah are also part of the Heritage line. Though the quality has varied, these Heritage wines are never shy and tend to be in a shoot-from-the-hip style.

### Chardonnay

86   87°   88°   89   90°   91   92   93   94

*Now showing solid middle-of-the-road varietal character, backed up by oak and ample acidity*

### Zinfandel

(Pacini Vineyard to 89/Mendocino 90 to present)   82   83   84   85
86°°   87°   **88°   89   90   91°   92   93   94°   95**

*After a wobbly start with good grapes, quality has come up, and the latest efforts have shown greater fruit and depth*

WILLIAM HILL WINERY   *Napa 1976*   After graduating from the University of Oklahoma, William Hill earned an MBA at Stanford and by 74 was deeply involved in vineyard development. Hill started producing wines in rented facilities in 76, and by the end of the 80s he was making over 45,000 cases a year of Chardonnay and 20,000 cases of Cabernet Sauvignon.

In 1992 Allied-Lyons, owners of Clos du Bois, Callaway, and Atlas Peak, purchased the William Hill trademark, winery, and most of the assets, including the

115-acre vineyard adjacent to the winery. Long-term contracts enable the new owners to continue making Cabernet from the Mount Veeder area and Chardonnay in part from the Carneros district. Allied-Lyons added Merlot to the William Hill line, which is holding steady at 100,000 cases per year. With Jill Davis (ex–Buena Vista) coming on board as winemaker in 1994, the winery has steadily improved its Reserve wine program. Overall, Chardonnay and Cabernet Sauvignon account for most of the annual output.

### Cabernet Sauvignon

(Gold Label/Reserve)   82°°   83°°   84°°   **85°**   **87°**   8̶8̶   89   9̶0̶   92

*Ripe and briary with solid tannin, the wine usually has sufficient fruit for balance; late results have been problematic*

### Chardonnay

(Gold Label/Reserve)   86°°   87°°   88°   89   90   92   94

*Oaky and ripe with appley fruit at the center*

---

PAUL HOBBS CELLARS   *Napa 1991*   Hobbs, a well-traveled winemaker, honed his skills at Simi and at other California wineries before making a name for himself in South America, where he has worked for several wineries in Chile and Argentina. As the head of a limited partnership, Hobbs rents space and makes his wines at the Kunde Estate Winery. He produces Chardonnay, Pinot Noir, and Cabernet Sauvignon from the Carneros appellation on a regular basis. Howell Mountain Merlot is made from time to time. Production is moving toward a 5,000-case annual limit.

---

HONIG CELLARS   *Napa 1980*   In 66 Louis Honig bought a 67-acre ranch and old vineyard from Charlie Wagner of Caymus. The vineyard was renamed HNW and the Honigs ventured into the grape-growing business. By 80 Bill Honig, Louis's son, and Daniel Weinstein, his son-in-law, began guiding the enterprise into winemaking. The Honig vineyard is highly esteemed for Sauvignon Blanc, and has sold grapes to many wineries. Honig Cellars made only Sauvignon Blanc, until adding Chardonnay and Cabernet Sauvignon in 87. The 67-acre vineyard, after several changes, now consists of 29 acres of Sauvignon Blanc, 18 acres of Cabernet Sauvignon, 4 acres of Merlot, and 6 acres of Chardonnay. With close to 10,000 cases a year of Sauvignon Blanc, Honig has steadily improved its performance and in recent vintages has been a consistent ° version with excellent depth. With vineyard maturity, Cabernet Sauvignon production should level off at 3,000 cases and Chardonnay at a little over 1,000 cases a year. Since it opened, the 30,000-case-capacity facility has custom-made wines for many clients. For their own brand, the Honigs see 13,000 cases as maximum.

---

HOP KILN WINERY   *Sonoma 1975*   Located in the Russian River Valley, this winery, a converted hop kiln, is a state historical landmark. Surrounded by its 65-acre vineyard, Hop Kiln produces eight varietals, two blends ("Marty's Big Red" and "A Thousand Flowers White"), and an unusual sparkling wine named "Verveux." Even since it began, the winery has been best known for sturdy reds, particularly its intense, heavy-bodied Petite Sirah and its compact, ripe Zinfandel. Both red varietals are produced from nonirrigated vineyards. "Primitivo" is the name reserved for wine made from the oldest Zinfandel vines on the estate, and Hop Kiln has the distinction of bottling the first U.S. wine labeled "Valdiguie," the authentic name for what's commonly called Napa Gamay. Hop Kiln's Valdiguie is made in a medium-bodied style. Occasionally, a dry-finished, assertive, and unusually full-bodied Gewurztraminer rises to the ° level. However, sustained success with red wines prompted Dr. Marty Griffin, Hop Kiln's owner, to expand its production of Cabernet Sauvignon. In the late 80s, the winery planted 10 acres to Cabernet, and purchased enough grapes from growers to produce over 1,000 cases of

Cabernet. Currently, the winery's total production is 9,000 cases a year. It remains one of the more rewarding wineries to visit.

### Zinfandel

83  84°  85°  86°  **87°°**  **88°**  89°  **91°**  **92°**  94  95  **96**

*More power than finesse is packed by this very ripe, gutsy wine, which is not designed for the faint of heart*

---

ROBERT HUNTER WINERY  *Sonoma 1980*  This off-again, on-again winery specializes in *méthode champenoise* from the Hunter Vineyard in the Sonoma Valley. It was in operation from 1980 through 85, and then production was interrupted until 1991 when Hunter produced 1,000 cases of its Brut de Noirs. A blend of Pinot Noir and Chardonnay, the Brut de Noirs receives 2 1/2 years en tirage.

---

HUSCH VINEYARDS  *Mendocino 1968*  As the first winery after Prohibition to open in the Anderson Valley, Husch struggled through its early few pioneering vintages. Founder Tony Husch worked hard and achieved moderate success, but decided to sell the winery in 79 to the Oswald family, longtime grape growers who owned the 110-acre La Ribera Vineyard near Ukiah and another 50 acres in Anderson Valley. The Oswalds invested in winery equipment and improved the facility. Under their ownership, Husch steadily improved, and today puts out a line of reliable varietals ranging from average to ° without wide variations.

From the Anderson Valley appellation, Husch offers Gewurztraminers which are often superb, along with an increasingly enjoyable Pinot Noir. Sauvignon Blanc, Cabernet Sauvignon, Chenin Blanc, and Chardonnay are from the Mendocino appellation, usually made entirely from the winery's La Ribera Vineyards near Ukiah. One of the most consistent wines on a ° track is Husch's always likable Chardonnay. Partially barrel-fermented, Husch Sauvignon Blanc has earned °. Husch has added a Reserve Pinot Noir, and its version of a Reserve Cabernet Sauvignon is its often high-quality wine labeled"North Field Select"Cabernet. La Ribera Vineyards is a name used for a second level of Cabernet Sauvignon and blended white. All told, Husch makes 25,000 cases a year.

### Chardonnay

86°  87°  88°  89  90  91  92  93  95

*Consistently fruity and firmed by perky acidity, medium-bodied, quietly okay; a good value in every vintage to date*

### Cabernet Sauvignon

(La Ribera Vineyards)  87  **88°**  89  **90**  91°  92  **93**  95

*Mid-sized, moderately fruity wines*

### Pinot Noir

86°°  87°  **88°**  89  90  **91°°**  92  93  **94°**  95

*Mid-priced and a good value when it succeeds; the wine offers cherryish fruit and can enjoy a certain supple palate feel*

---

IMAGERY SERIES  *(Benziger Winery & Vineyards)*  Started in 87, this line evolved from experiments with unusual varieties grown in unusual locations, or with wine grapes on the endangered-species list. Among the many lesser-known varietals bottled are Aleatico, Trousseau, and Zinfandel Port. Specially promoted through Benziger's tasting room, the Imagery Series wines often have specially commissioned designer labels. Having evolved into a separate and successful brand on its own, Imagery Series regularly offers Petite Sirah, Pinot Blanc, Malbec, Cabernet Franc, and Viognier.

---

INDIGO HILLS  *(Gallo)*  One of several snazzy new labels created by Gallo with no mention of the Gallo name, Indigo Hills is seen on wines bearing either North

Coast or Mendocino place-name. Chardonnay carried the Mendocino appellation with Pinot Noir, Zinfandel, and Sauvignon Blanc all labeled North Coast. Generally these wines were correct and offered decent flavor for the price. A sparkling Brut Chardonnay made by the *méthode champenoise* also was on the roster.

INGLENOOK—NAPA VALLEY    *Napa 1879*    From the time Gustave Niebaum founded Inglenook until his grandnephew John Daniel, Jr., sold it in 64, Inglenook was known as a pioneer and as a producer of high-quality wines, particularly Cabernet Sauvignon. Under the direction of the Daniel family, Inglenook offered a regular and a Special Cask Cabernet Sauvignon (introduced in 49) from its holdings adjacent to the winery located on the west side of the wine road in Rutherford. Up until the early 60s, Inglenook's Cabernets competed head-on with those from Beaulieu and Charles Krug.

In 64 the winery and most of its acreage (except for the 100 acres known as Napanook) were purchased by Allied Grape Growers. In 69, they were in turn bought by giant Heublein, which expanded production throughout the 70s. The name Inglenook was extended to cover "Inglenook Navalle," which relied on grapes grown in the Central Valley where the bottling occurred. This volume-oriented Navalle jug line all but ruined Inglenook's once-high reputation.

In 79, faced with a faltering image, Heublein's wine division tried to reverse direction and initiated a major revitalization program. This included restoring the old winery, replanting the original vineyard, and improving the quality of the wines bottled. In 83, "Reunion," a new proprietary wine made primarily from Cabernet Sauvignon, appeared. Made from the original vineyards used by John Daniel, Jr., to produce Inglenook's fabled vintages, Reunion has earned ° and °° in its early issues. However, as hard as they tried, the owners were unable to reverse the situation, and sales of Inglenook's Cabernets and all their other wines steadily declined in the 80s. The tasting and sales rooms, the barrel room, and the 72-acre vineyard in Rutherford containing the once-prized Cabernet Sauvignon vines were acquired in 1995 by Francis Ford Coppola, whose winery is Niebaum-Coppola (see entry). The once proud Inglenook name is now reduced to the jug wines of Inglenook Navalle (see next entry), and all Napa Valley references are for historical purposes only.

### Cabernet Sauvignon

80°    81    82°    83°    85°    86    87°    89

*A direct, ripe cherry and curranty offering, with moderate oak, and evident but unimposing tannins*

### Chardonnay

(regular bottling)    84    85    86°    88    89    90    91

(Reserve)    84°    85°    86°

*Straightforward, presentable wines, with citrus, apple, and oak qualities; medium depth at best for the regular bottling and more obvious oak in the Reserve*

### Merlot

(Reserve)    83°°    **85°°**    86    **88°**

*Save for the 86, which was out of form, this has been a fruity, rich, firm wine, which has handsomely combined moderately deep cherry and currant character and creamy oak*

INGLENOOK NAVALLE, NAVALLE SELECTIONS    *(Inglenook)*    Today, the primary label for a line of inexpensive varietals is "Navalle Selections." It covers Chardonnay, Sauvignon Blanc, Cabernet Sauvignon, and White Zinfandel, all from the California appellation and all bottled in 750-ml and 1.5-liter containers. Navalle Selections is headquartered in Madera, where Heublein operates a large facility also used for Almadén Vineyards, Blossom Hill, Sylvan Springs, and others. However, Heublein continues using the Inglenook Navalle name, primarily for generics in magnums and for a line of varietals and generics sold in 18-liter bag-in-the-box containers. Brands with Navalle in their name represent annual sales of 2.5 million cases.

IRON HORSE VINEYARDS   *Sonoma 1978*   This winery is known more for its sparkling wines than for its agreeable but not quite as successful table wines. In 76 owners Audrey and Barry Sterling purchased an old estate and 300-acre ranch that was once a railroad stop named Iron Horse. A corporate attorney, Barry Sterling took on one-time vineyard manager Forrest Tancer as a partner in the establishment. Situated in a cool growing region near Sebastopol in Sonoma's Green Valley, the surrounding vineyards, first developed independently by Tancer, now cover 110 acres, evenly divided between Chardonnay and Pinot Noir. Another vineyard in the warmer Alexander Valley contains 44 acres and is planted to Cabernet Sauvignon (20 acres), Sauvignon Blanc (12 acres), Cabernet Franc (3 acres), Viognier (14 acres), and Sangiovese (3 acres).

In its first decade, Iron Horse developed a strong following for its barrel-fermented, rich, balanced Fumé Blanc, a frequent ° performer that rises to °° on occasion. Recent vintages of the enticing Fumé Blanc have contained as much as 25% Viognier. Introduced with the 80 vintage, the winery's sparkling wines started on a small scale but have grown in quantity and in quality. Both the Brut and Blanc de Blancs have been in the °°° category on several occasions. It offers two other sparklers in significant quantities—a Blanc de Noirs labeled "Wedding Cuvée" and a strawberry-pink Brut Rosé. Iron Horse has also experimented with two late disgorged sparkling wines, a "Vrais Amis Brut" and a "Late Disgorged Brut." Both are aged for over five years *en tirage*, varying ever so slightly only in the dosage. After the 84 vintage, Cabernet Sauvignon was replaced in the roster by "Cabernets," a blend of Cabernet Sauvignon and Cabernet Franc. For volume, Chardonnay is the winery's major varietal. Barrel-fermented, it displays apple character in a crisp, lemony style. Pinot Noir completes the line.

Total production at Iron Horse is 32,000 to 34,000 cases a year, equally divided between table wine and sparkling wine. Lesser-quality, early-maturing Pinot Noir has been bottled under the "Tin Pony" second label. In the 90s, Iron Horse and Laurent Perrier of Champagne hooked up in a joint venture to produce sparkling wine from vineyards in the Sonoma Green Valley.

### Cabernet Sauvignon/Cabernets

| 80 | 81 | 82° | 83° | 84° | **85** | **86°** | **87°°** | 88 | 89 | **90°** | **91** |
|----|----|-----|-----|-----|--------|---------|----------|----|----|---------|--------|
| **92°** | **93** | **94°** | **95°** | | | | | | | | |

*Now containing about 35% Cabernet Franc, this tight, black-cherryish wine has needed more depth of character to measure up, regardless of title and blend changes*

### Chardonnay

| 84° | 85 | 86° | 87° | 88° | 89° | 90° | 91° | 93 | 94 | 95 | 96 |
|-----|----|-----|-----|-----|-----|-----|-----|----|----|----|----|

*Blossomy fruit with citrusy overtones and background oak are carried in a typically medium- to medium-full-bodied wine, whose crisp acidity usually takes an extra year or two to soften*

IRONSTONE VINEYARDS   *Calaveras 1989*   Longtime diversified farmers and grape growers in the Lodi district, the Kautz family expanded their farming operations into Murphys, a small town in Calaveras County. By 1989 they were expanding their vineyards and building a large winery that ended up being seven stories high. It is the major tourist facility today. There is also a large underground aging cave, and the owners also made a major investment in the latest winemaking equipment. Now, with approximately 4,200 acres of vineyards established, the family intends to keep on planting over the next decade. The leading wines produced are Chardonnay, Cabernet Sauvignon, Cabernet Franc, Merlot, Shiraz, and Symphony. In the Gold Rush area Kautz has created a tourist destination with a theater and entertainment facilities to go along with cooking demonstrations and wine events. All wines are modestly priced, and we find much to like about the reds in general and the Shiraz in particular. Annual production quickly hit 250,000 cases and is expected to double by 2001.

---

**"J"** *Sonoma 1987* Jordan Vineyards created a separate facility for its brand of *méthode champenoise* sparkling wine which to date consists only of a Brut. Made from roughly equal parts of Chardonnay and Pinot Noir, the Brut ages for 3 1/2 years of the yeast before being disgorged. After a surprisingly ordinary first effort, "J" has quickly moved up the quality ladder to challenge the state's leaders. In the 1990s the quality seems to improve with each vintage, and the magnums, which are aged longer, have been simply unbeatable. In 1997 Judy Jordan, who runs the sparkling wine business, purchased the Piper-Sonoma facility and 118 acres of prime vineyards in the Russian River Valley. J now owns 170 acres, and the annual production of sparkling wine is 30,000 cases. On a limited basis it produces non-bubbly Pinot Noir and Pinot Gris.

---

JADE MOUNTAIN WINERY *Napa 1984* Sharing space at the White Rock Winery in Napa Valley. Jade Mountain began making Rhone-style wines in the late 80s. Most of the wines are made from purchased grapes, but owner Jim Paras developed 22 acres in the Mt. Veeder area to Syrah and Viognier. Currently producing two Syrahs, one from Paras Vineyard and the other from Hudson Vineyard in the Carneros District, Jade Mountain has recently added Viognier from Mt. Veeder, Mourvedre from Contra Costa, and Merlot from Napa Valley to its varietal roster. Using Cabernet and sometimes Merlot to blend with Mourvedre and Syrah, Paras continues making three red blends with a southern France accent. La Provencale (Syrah, Mourvedre, and Grenache) is the smoothest and often rates °°. Les Jameux (Mourvedre and Cabernet) and "Côtes du Soleil" (Mourvedre, Syrah, and Cabernet) are both long-agers and have also been well received. Annual production is holding steady, at 7,500 cases.

---

JAFFURS WINE CELLARS *Santa Barbara 1994* Owner/winemaker Craig Jaffurs is one of several dynamic Rhone wine specialists popping up in Santa Barbara. Owning no vineyards, Jaffurs buys from three highly regarded vineyards: Thompson Vineyard (Syrah), Bien Nacido (Viognier, Syrah), and Stolpman Vineyard (Syrah, Grenache, Mourvedre, Viognier, Roussanne). As production has grown to close to 3,000 cases, Jaffurs offers Syrah, Viognier, Grenache, and Matilija Cuvee (Mourvedre, Syrah blend). In the early rounds Jaffurs showed a skilled hand with Syrah from both Thompson Vineyard and Santa Barbara County, and he has also made one of the most impressive Grenache wines yet made in California. Clearly Jaffurs is an up-and-coming producer.

---

TOBIN JAMES WINERY *San Luis Obispo 1985* After winemaking stints at Eberle and Estrella River Winery, James launched this brand by renting space here and there. Today he is the consulting winemaker for Peachy Canyon Winery, where he also produces his own wines. To date, all wines have been made from the Paso Robles appellation, with the primary emphasis falling on Zinfandel. James also offers Cabernet Sauvignon, Chardonnay, Pinot Noir, and Merlot, and these wines bring the total production up to an average of 7,500 cases a year. In the early 90s, he began developing a 40-acre site within Paso Robles, and the leading varieties planted are Zinfandel, Cabernet Sauvignon, and Syrah. The winery enjoys a cult following for its Zinfandels (as many as five bottling appear per vintage) and for Syrah.

---

JARVIS WINERY *Napa Valley 1992* On a beautiful site in the southeastern hills of Napa Valley, William Jarvis constructed an impressive underground winery and developed 40 acres of vineyards. Cabernet Sauvignon was emphasized right out of the gate, but Chardonnay has edged up in quantity lately. Cabernet Franc has become a regular item, and occasionally a small batch Cabernet Sauvignon named Lake

William is bottled. As annual production moves close to 5,000 cases, we have found the prices and the quality to be high.

JEKEL VINEYARDS   *Monterey 1978*   One of the first wineries to commit itself to Monterey County, Jekel began by developing vineyards in the Greenfield area in 72. Founded by twins Bill and Gus Jekel, the winery and vineyards have been under the control of Bill and his wife, Pat, since 86. The winery continues to enjoy a reputation for consistency with Johannisberg Riesling. Chardonnay, made in regular and Private Reserve bottlings, is the major variety, planted at 116 acres, while at 80 acres Cabernet Sauvignon and its consorts (Merlot and Cabernet Franc) follow in importance. Recently the winery has been making Chardonnay from its Gravelstone Vineyard. Cabernet and related varieties are grown in the Sanctuary Vineyard, and the red Meritage is named Sanctuary. Current production of 85,000 cases is expected to double over the next decade. Limited amounts of Muscat Canelli and Cabernet Franc are regularly offered. All wines carry the Arroyo Seco appellation. Early in 92 the winery was sold to Brown-Forman, the successful marketing company that handles Italy's Bolla and California's Korbel and also owns Fetzer Vineyards.

### Chardonnay

86   87°   88°   89   90°   93   94   9̶5̶   96

*Fighting a tendency to be over-oaked and lacking in fruit, the wine succeeds best when it is able to capture elements of brightness and balance that keep its ripe, appley fruit at the center of attention*

JEPSON VINEYARDS   *Mendocino 1986*   Banker and entrepreneur Robert Jepson bought the winery, inventory, and vineyards of the former William Baccala Estate (founded 82) in 86 and was able to have Jepson wines on the market within a few months of the purchase. The winery is situated between Hopland and Ukiah, with its 108-acre vineyard located across the road to the east. Chardonnay and Sauvignon Blanc represent about 90% of the total acreage and are the primary wines produced. A Reserve Chardonnay, 100% barrel-fermented, is made in small volume. About 10 acres of French Colombard, used for a generic white table wine, are adjacent to the winery. In 88 the winery introduced its line of *méthode champenoise* sparkling wine. Made 100% from Chardonnay, the winery's Brut Blanc de Blancs has been of ° quality. Jepson also produces a brandy made by the pot-still method. This Cognac-style brandy is well worth seeking out, but the annual output is small (less than 500 cases). Its Blanc de Blancs production averages 3,500 cases. Though Pinot Noir and Viognier have been added recently, Jepson's Chardonnay and Sauvignon Blanc remain the mainstays and currently account for most of the 17,000 cases produced each year. With expansion of the facility, annual total production could grow to 30,000 cases.

### Chardonnay

85°   86   87°   88   90°   91   92   93°   94   95   96°

*Straightforwardly fruity, tending toward apples, with hints of blossoms, quietly oaked, well balanced*

JOHNSON'S OF ALEXANDER VALLEY WINES   *Sonoma 1975*   Back in the late 60s the Johnson brothers converted 50 acres of pears and prunes to vineyards. After selling grapes for a few years, they branched out into winemaking, building a small winery next to the vineyards in the heart of the Alexander Valley. Within a decade, they were producing a fairly wide range of varietals. Blush wines—White Zinfandel and Pinot Noir Blanc—were added to bring their annual output close to 10,000 cases by 85. They focus production today on White Zinfandel, Cabernet Sauvignon, Chardonnay, and Johannisberg Riesling. Most of the current production is sold direct from their tasting room. To date, the winery's quality record has generated very little acclaim.

JORDAN VINEYARDS   *Sonoma 1976*   The imposing Jordan Winery is situated on a hill-top east of Healdsburg. The winery, which is not open to the public, draws from its 200 acres of Cabernet Sauvignon and Merlot, and 50 acres of Chardonnay. All varieties are planted in the Alexander Valley and contribute to an annual production of 85,000 cases. The winery's mainstay, Cabernet Sauvignon, accounts for 60,000 cases. Owned by Tom Jordan, a geologist specializing in oil exploration, the winery had developed a special cachet even before it marketed its second vintage. At first, only Cabernet Sauvignon was to be produced. Debuting with a well-reviewed 76 Cabernet, the winery was able to make its first estate-bottled offering in 1978. From that time on, Jordan has followed a relatively long aging program, in which a new vintage is released about four years after the harvest. Situated in a low-lying area close to the river's edge, the estate vineyards have to be carefully cultivated to try to control excessive vigor, which can contribute to a herbal-vegetal character.

Over the first 10 vintages, Jordan's Cabernet did not quite live up to the high expectations. Even though most Cabernet vintages have, with the exception of the dismal 82, been enjoyable, only a few standout vintages have been awarded °°. The caveat among those who fault Jordan Cabernet is its early appeal and lack of ageability. Over the first decade, Jordan's Chardonnays were full-bodied and well-oaked, but only rarely rose above average quality. In 1989, to remedy the situation, Jordan planted 100 acres of Chardonnay in the Russian River Valley. Fruit from this vineyard, which is expected to add lively fruit flavors and crisp acidity, first made its way into Chardonnay in the 92 vintage. Neither the Cabernet Sauvignon nor the Chardonnay, even in better years, has been good enough to stand at the top of its class.

### Cabernet Sauvignon

80°°   81   82   83°   84°   85°   **86°**   **87°**   88   89   90   **91**
92   94

*Soft, ripish, black-cherryish, and cedary character, sometimes high in herbal notes, lightly tannic, and supple on the palate; recent years have lacked fruit*

### Chardonnay

86°   88   89   90°   91°   92   93   94   95

*Oaky, somewhat firm wines with apple, citrus, and hints of tropical fruits*

JORY WINES   *Santa Clara 1986*   Occupying space in a large, historic winery in Los Gatos, Jory makes the majority of its wines from the local Santa Clara area. The specialties are Chardonnay (regular and Reserve) and Pinot Noir, which account for over 60% of its 5,000-case output. In small lots of 300 to 500 cases it also offers Pinot Blanc, Merlot, Mourvedre, and a *méthode champenoise* Champagne called "Mistral." Jory's most distinctive wines have been its idiosyncratic blends, with their unusual proprietary names and accompanying labels. The most flavorful is "Red Zeppelin Reserve," made in part from Mourvedre. Others in this humorous vein are a "Bon Jory Red," a "White Zeppelin" "Blimp de Blanc," and "Claret" "Old Barrister." Despite a record of inconsistent quality thus far, the owners are having fun.

JOULLIAN VINEYARDS   *Monterey 1987*   Located in the Carmel Valley, Joullian is neighbor to Durney Vineyards. Co-owner and winemaker Ray Watson is a former wine merchant whose brother is the pro golfer Tom Watson. Inspired by early vintages of Durney Cabernet, Watson purchased the large ranch in 82, and since then has developed 40 acres of vineyards. The leading varieties are Cabernet Sauvignon, Merlot, Chardonnay, Sauvignon Blanc, and Semillon. After producing experimental-size quantities in its first two vintages, Joullian managed its first substantial crush in 88, when it produced 1,000 cases of barrel-fermented Chardonnay, 1,000 cases of Sauvignon Blanc (blended with 15% Semillon), and 600 cases of Cabernet Sauvignon (blended with Merlot and Cabernet Franc). With vineyard maturity, Joullian is expected to produce 10,000 cases a year, 50%

consisting of Cabernet Sauvignon, 25% of Chardonnay, and 25% Sauvignon Blanc. Over the early vintages the winery used the "Cepage" label for small-batch bottlings.

JUDD'S HILL    *Napa 1989*    Founder and owner of Whitehall Lane Winery until 1988, Art Finkelstein purchased a terraced hillside vineyard in the hills east of St. Helena in 1985. By the 89 harvest he had built a small winery on Judd's Hill overlooking the 7-acre vineyard. Only Merlot and Cabernet Sauvignon, the latter field-blended with Merlot and Cabernet Franc, are produced here. Both are aged for two years in a combination of French and American small oak barrels. A maximum of 2,000 cases are produced per year.

### Cabernet Sauvignon
89    90°°    91    92    93°    95°°

*Concentrated slightly briary, compact and moderately tannic wines*

### Merlot
93°°    94°    95

*Only slightly less dense and tough than the Cabernet but equally deep in character*

JUSTIN VINEYARDS & WINERY    *San Luis Obispo 1987*    An investment banker for two decades, Justin Baldwin branched out into the grape and wine business in 82, acquiring 165 acres of land in the Paso Robles appellation. His 65-acre vineyard, located 15 miles west of the town of Paso Robles, is the most westerly of any in the area. Specializing in three wines—Chardonnay, Cabernet Sauvignon, and a red Bordeaux blend—he planted 30 acres of Chardonnay, 25 acres of Cabernet Sauvignon, and 5 acres each of Merlot and Cabernet Franc. Baldwin prefers wines that are ripe and full-bodied, and his Chardonnays are 100% barrel-fermented in new oak. Over the first several vintages, the production held at 8,000 cases. Red wines—the Cabernet Sauvignon (100% varietal) and "Isosceles," a Meritage blend of Cabernet, Merlot, and Cabernet Franc—are aged about 3 years in small oak barrels. "Justification" (a blend of Cabernet Franc and Merlot) is made in a relatively lighter, elegant style. "Obtuse" is Justin's version of an American Port made from Cabernet Sauvignon. From time to time the winery bottles small amounts of Merlot and Cabernet Franc. When the estate vineyards are mature, production will grow to 30,000 cases a year.

### Isosceles
91    92°    93    94°    95

*About 2/3 Cabernet Sauvignon with varying proportions of Cabernet Franc (up to 25%) and Merlot, the wine favors ripeness and mass over finesse*

KALIN CELLARS    *Marin 1976*    Owner Terry Leighton is a microbiologist at U.C. Berkeley, and a winemaker in his spare time. Using a warehouse in the town of Novato, he produces Chardonnay, Pinot Noir, Semillon, Cabernet Sauvignon, and sparkling wines. In a typical year Kalin bottles several Chardonnays, and in recent vintages the recurring appellations have been Livermore Valley, Potter Valley, Russian River Valley, and Sonoma Valley. In addition, he identifies the grower by a system of lettered cuvées. Kalin Chardonnays, often highly rated and earning °° for both Cuvée "LV" and Cuvée "W," are barrel-fermented, and pushed to the max. Usually they display a strong oak component and depth, and often are successful, albeit in a weighty, viscous style. Pinot Noirs are highly variable. Barrel-fermented Semillons from the Livermore Valley are often among the most noteworthy efforts with the varietal. Production, including a few hundred cases of sparkling wine made by the *méthode champenoise*, is at the facility's capacity level of 6,000 cases.

KARLY WINES    *Amador 1979*    A family-owned and -operated winery, Karly developed a 17-acre vineyard in the 70s. Larry "Buck" Cobb and his wife, Karly, planted Zinfandel and Sauvignon Blanc, with a small amount of Petite Sirah. The latter, sometimes blended into the winery's Zinfandel, is most often bottled as a limited-volume varietal. Over its first decade, Karly produced Chardonnay from different sources within the Central Coast region and then shifted to Napa Valley for Chardonnay. Karly's Amador Sauvignon Blancs, big-bodied wines with a creamy oak texture and a figgy character, have risen on occasion to ° level. Though somewhat erratic, Karly's Zinfandels (about 2,500 cases per year) belong to the big, brawny, no-holds-barred school. This also holds true for the vineyard-designated "Sadie Upton" Zinfandel. "Warrior Fires" is an apt name for one of the more impressive versions of superripe, powerhouse Zinfandels, a style back in vogue in the 90s. Syrah is now a regular part of the lineup, and Grenache is a recent addition. The winery's annual output is close to the 9,000-case maximum.

## Zinfandel

(Amador County)   80°°   81°   82°   83°   84   85   86°   87   88   89°   **90**   **91**   **92**°   93   **94**°   **96**

*Ripe, brawny, full-bodied, sometimes tarry and bordering on the overripe, usually rich in creamy oak*

(Warrior Fires)   **94**°   **95**°°

---

KEEGAN CELLARS   *Sonoma 1995*   Pinot Noir from the Russian River Valley is the headline attraction produced at this small cellar. Owner and onetime vineyard supervisor and marketing director, now turned winemaker, Eugenia Keegan buys Pinot Noir from several growers and then follows traditional methods to make her elegant style of wine. Also part of this one-person show are an unfiltered Chardonnay and Zinfandel, both from Sonoma County. Annual production of 1,000 cases is steady, with Pinot Noir accounting for more than 60%.

---

ROBERT KEENAN WINERY   *Napa 1977*   In the early 70s, Robert Keenan purchased the defunct Conradi Winery, a 176-acre estate located at the 1,700-foot level on Spring Mountain. Conradi began operating in 1904, but did not recover after Prohibition. Some 62 acres were planted by Keenan to Cabernet Sauvignon, Chardonnay, Cabernet Franc, and Merlot. A stone winery was set into the hillside for natural cooling. In 78, because his own vineyard was not then in full production, Keenan was purchasing grapes from Winery Lake Vineyard, a famous vineyard in the Carneros region. To obtain that grower's Chardonnay in sufficient quantity, Keenan took more Merlot than was needed for blending with Cabernet Sauvignon. As a result of the surplus, he reluctantly bottled Merlot as a varietal, but the quality of that first bottling earned such high praise that Merlot became a regular and successful part of the line. Keenan's Merlot is blended with Cabernet Franc, and its production has been holding steady at 3,000 cases. Also at the same production level, the Cabernet Sauvignon is softened by the addition of Merlot and Cabernet Franc. In an average year, enough Cabernet Franc remains to allow Keenan to bottle about 1,000 cases of that varietal. Having produced two Chardonnays for close to a decade, Keenan dropped "Ann's Vineyard" Chardonnay after 1989, and today makes about 3,500 cases of a Napa Valley Chardonnay only. Merlot is our favorite Keenan offering of late.

## Cabernet Sauvignon

78°   79°°   **80**°°   81   82°   **83**°°   **84**°   **85**°   **86**°°   87   88°   **92**   **93**

*Medium-density cherry, currant, and quietly herbal fruit is firmed by noticeable tannin in this series of ageworthy wines*

## Chardonnay

(Napa Valley)   86°   87   88°   89°   91   92   93
(Ann's Vineyard)   86°   87

*The Napa Valley bottling is the bigger, richer, of the two, while the Ann's Vineyard wine offers tighter, more wiry fruit*

**Merlot**

82°° 83°°° 84°° 85° **86°** 87 **88°°** 89 92° **93°°**
94° 95°

*Rated among the top Merlots in many vintages, the wine is rich, round on the palate,
and fairly deep in ripe cherry fruit; its medium tannins have helped it to age well*

KENDALL-JACKSON VINEYARDS *Lake 1982* Starting out with modest goals, San Francisco attorney Jess Jackson bought a vineyard near Clear Lake in the early 70s. His grapes were sold for a few years, until he decided to make wine under the Chateau du Lac brand. Shortly after changing the name to Kendall-Jackson, Jackson entered the battlefield with an 82 Chardonnay, a blend of grapes from several regions that carried the California appellation. Produced even before the winery was completed, this first Chardonnay was widely appealing and a critical success. With the 83 vintage, Jackson hired Jed Steele as winemaker, and the combination clicked. From that year on, the brand grew, the success stories multiplied, and Jackson began expanding his vineyard and wine empire. Steele, formerly of Edmeades Vineyards in Mendocino's Anderson Valley, proved to be a master blender, maker of larger and larger blends of Chardonnay from North Coast and Central Coast grapes. At the same time, he produced an array of small-batch Zinfandels (Dupratt-DePratie Vineyard, Mariah Vineyard, Zeni, and Ciapusci Vineyard). In 85 he elevated Kendall-Jackson Cabernet to the big time with a Cabernet-Bordeaux blend named "Cardinale." In 86 a limited-volume Syrah from the cool-climate Durell Vineyard was added to his credits.

While Steele was crafting a wide array of good to often excellent wines that varied in volume from a few hundred cases to more than 500,000 cases, Jackson was on a veritable shopping spree. He formed a partnership that purchased 1,200 acres in Santa Barbara County's Santa Maria Valley in 1988 to supply grapes for a winery named Cambria Winery & Vineyard that he built there. In 88 Jackson also purchased Edmeades in the Anderson Valley, Steele's old hangout; and in 89 he bought the winery and vineyard in Sonoma County known as Zellerbach (renamed Stonestreet). At his original winery in Lake County, Jackson still has an 80-acre vineyard, which brings his total planted acreage to about 5,000. The Lake County property is now making wines as Lakewood (see entry). In the early 90s Jackson and Steele had a few differences and parted company, which led to a protracted and rather nasty legal feud in 1992. Undaunted, Jackson soon purchased the large-volume custom winemaking facility in Geyseville known as Vinwood. This winery has been expanded and now houses most of his white wine production. Jackson went on to acquire Robert Pepi Winery in Napa, the former Laurier Winery in Russian River Valley which is now Hartford Court, as well as La Crema Winery in the same appellation. He has also created wine brands from scratch, such as Kristone, Camelot, and Lokoya. Overseas, he owns Villa Arceno in Chianti, Vina Calina in Chile, and Mariposa in Argentina.

After many roster and nomenclature changes, the Kendall-Jackson offerings have been pared down to two broad lines of varietal wines, both using the California appellation. The biggest and moderately priced line is the Vintner's Reserve, which includes Chardonnay, Cabernet, and other typical varietals as well as Cabernet Franc, Viognier and Syrah. The second is dubbed "Grand Reserve" and it includes Chardonnay, Merlot, Pinot Noir. Cabernet Sauvignon, and Cabernet Franc. The two Meritage blends—Cardinale, the high-priced red, and "Royale," the white blend of Semillon and Sauvignon—are not part of either line. The quality achievements for several wines, notably Chardonnay, Pinot Noir, and Merlot are amazing considering the sheer growth of this brand. By the late 1990s Jackson had developed more than 2,000 acres in Sonoma County, including hundreds of acres in the coolest coastal sites which are heavily planted to Pinot Noir. A program of single-vineyard varietals is well under way and began with Cabernet Sauvignon Buckeye Vineyard (Alexander Valley region) and Chardonnay from Paradise Vineyards (Monterey County). In 1985 Kendall-Jackson made 64,000 cases, and its current annual production is about 3 million, with close to 2 million consisting of its Vintners Reserve Chardonnay. To meet the demand, Kendall-

Jackson built a winery with a case capacity of 1.3 million a year in Monterey County, where Jackson owns or controls more than 2,500 acres.

### Cabernet Sauvignon

(Lake County and Vintners Reserve)    83    84    86    **87°**    88    89
**90°°**    91    92    93    94    95

(Grand Reserve)    **85°°**    **86°**    **87°°**    **88°**    **90°**    **91°**    **92°**    **93°°**
**94°°**

*With Vintner's Reserve having become all too ordinary, the Grand Reserve has moved upscale and is ripe, rich, oaky and somewhat open*

### Chardonnay

(Vintner's Reserve)    86°    88°    89    90    91°    92    93°    94°    95
96

*The quintessential "popular-styled" Chardonnay, it is always fruity, a little on the blossomy side, usually slightly sweet-tasting without being cloying, and meant to be drunk young*

### Chardonnay

(Grand Reserve)    86°    87°°°    88    89°°    90°°    91°    **92°°**    **93°**
**94°**    **95°°**    **96**

*Barrel-fermented and often showing more depth and range than the Vintner's Reserve, as well as more aging potential, the wine is nonetheless oriented to appley and lightly floral fruit, with oak showing up in a supporting role*

### Merlot

(Vintner's Reserve)    88°°    89    90    **91°**    **92**    93    94

(Grand Reserve)    **92°**    **93**    **94°**

*Cherryish fruit, often with hints of berries and herbs, is sweetened by creamy oak; the Grand Reserve has more ripeness and depth*

### Pinot Noir

(Vintner's Reserve)    89°    90    91    **92°**    93    **94**    95°

(Grand Reserve)    **92°**    **93**    94

*Supple, moderately rich wines with the Grand Reserve carrying lots of oak*

---

KATHRYN KENNEDY WINERY    *Santa Clara 1979*    Originally the vineyard was established by Kathryn Kennedy to discourage developers in the area who wanted to build a road through an open field adjacent to her home. In 1973, 8 acres were planted (now it is 9 1/2) to Cabernet Sauvignon, and the first wine was made in 79. The small winery is located close to the original Paul Masson Winery in Saratoga. The annual production of Cabernet Sauvignon from the nonirrigated vineyards varies widely, but averaged 500 cases a year in the 80s. Approximately 1,000 cases a year is the maximum production goal for the Santa Cruz Mountains appellation Cabernet Sauvignon. Syrah and "Lateral," a Bordeaux blend of Merlot and Cabernet Franc from purchased grapes, are the only other wines produced. The quality for the estate Cabernet has been generally above average, and most vintages seem capable of medium- to long-term aging.

### Cabernet Sauvignon

84    **85°**    **86°**    **87**    89    90    **91°°**    **92°**    **93°**

*Big, ripe, tannic wines, they are long-aging and expensive*

---

KENWOOD VINEYARDS    *Sonoma 1970*    Within its first decade, the founding partners transformed an old jug-wine facility in the Sonoma Valley town of Kenwood into a modern winery offering a range of varietals. In the early years, winemaker Bob Kozlowski was responsible for many top-notch reds. Partners Mike and Marty Lee, along with John Sheela, their brother-in-law, kept plugging away and over the next few years transformed Kenwood into a first-class, full-range winery, offering good- to excellent-quality red and white varietals. With the release of its 83 Sauvignon Blanc, a °°° classic, Kenwood entered a new era. Its best-selling varietal is Sauvignon Blanc, which continues to be among the best of each vintage even as annual production approaches 50,000 cases. The second leading wine is now Chardonnay, with over 25,000 cases made, spread out over three bottlings (Sonoma Valley, Beltane Ranch, and Yulupa Vineyard).

A sentimental favorite among the founders, Zinfandel (the 70 vintage was the first Kenwood wine to gain wide critical praise) has been produced every year. In 75, Kenwood made a special batch of ageworthy Cabernet Sauvignon and commissioned an artist to design a label for it. This "Artist Series" of Cabernet Sauvignon became one of the most sought-after of its type; however, production is limited to 2,500–3,000 cases. As of 89, Merlot has joined the roster. Buying most grapes from Sonoma County, Kenwood prefers Sonoma Valley as its source. The winery has expanded its own holdings to include 135 acres of estate vineyards. However, Kenwood enjoys an exclusive relationship with the 110-acre Jack London Ranch, from which it makes vineyard-designated Pinot Noir, Cabernet Sauvignon, and Zinfandel. In recent vintages Kenwood has offered Zinfandels from Sonoma Valley and Lodi as well as from single vineyards such as Jack London Ranch, Nuns Canyon, Nora's Vineyard, Barrica Vineyard, and Mazzoni Vineyard. A Reserve Sauvignon Blanc is new and often incredibly rich. In 98 the winery was sold to Gary Heck of Korbel, who also owns Lake Sonoma Winery and Valley of the Moon Winery. All told, the winery has 450 acres under long-term contract. Its annual production is over 200,000 cases.

### Cabernet Sauvignon

(Sonoma Valley)   78°   80   81   82   83°   84°°   **85°°**   **86°**
**87°°**   88   **89°**   **90**   **91**   **92**   93   **94**   **95°**

*The most variable of Kenwood's Cabernets tends to be big, ripe, black-cherryish, moderately dense in warm years and a little on the understuffed side in others*

### Cabernet Sauvignon

(Jack London Vineyard)   78°°   79°°   80   81   82   83°°   **84°°**
**85°**   **86°**   **87°**   **88°**   **89°°**   **90°°**   **91°**   **92**   93

*Usually bold, brawny wines, full of briary, brambly spice and tight, black-cherryish fruit, wrapped in long-aging tannins, this one is the toughest of the three Kenwood Cabernets*

### Cabernet Sauvignon

(Artist Series)   78°   79°°   80   81   82°   83°°   **84°°**   **85°°°**
**86°°°**   **87°°**   **88°**   89   **90**   **91°°**   **92°**   **93°**

*The rich and deep centerpiece of the Kenwood line, this wine matches the Jack London in aging potential but usually surpasses it in pure Cabernet-focused, balanced, youthful fruit*

### Chardonnay

(Sonoma Valley)   84°   85°   86°   87°   88°   91°   92°   93   94
95

*Recently less successful, these wines offer medium fruit with toasty oak accents in better years*

### Merlot

(Sonoma Valley)   89   **90°**   91   **92°**   **94°**   **96°**
(Jack London Vineyard)   **91°°**   **92°**   **94°**

*In the Kenwood fashion, the regular bottling is ripe, of moderate depth and has light-medium tannins, while the Jack London bottling is deep, very concentrated in good vintages and can be long-aging*

### Zinfandel

79°°   80   81°   82°   83°   84°°   85°°   **86°°**   **87°**   88   **89**
**91°°**   **92°°**   **94**   **95**

*Ripe, deeply fruited, well focused, solidly structured, and proven to be ageworthy, these wines have become less deep in fruit of late*

**KENWORTHY VINEYARDS** *Amador 1979* The Kenworthy family specializes in Zinfandel grown in its 8-acre estate vineyard. Made by John Kenworthy, the heavy-duty Zinfandel accounts for over half of the winery's 2,000-case-a-year maximum output. Chardonnay and Cabernet Sauvignon, made from El Dorado grapes, represent the remainder of the production.

**J. KERR WINES** *Santa Barbara 1986* After stints with Chalone, Jekel, and Ventana Vineyards, John Kerr returned to his hometown area of Santa Barbara to work as a consulting enologist. He is a consultant for other wineries, and is developing his own brand. Barrel-fermented Chardonnay is Kerr's first love, and some of his early vintages have reached the °° level. Over the long term, with the completion of his own facility, Kerr would like to expand to 5,000 cases.

**KEYHOLE RANCH** *Sonoma 1996* Operated by the Seghesio family as a stand-alone brand, Keyhole Ranch consists of Pinot Noir from the family's 30-acre Russian River Valley vineyard. Annual output is expected to grow to 5,000 cases.

**KISTLER VINEYARDS** *Sonoma 1978* Perched on an isolated ridge of the Mayacamas Mountains some 2,000 feet above the Sonoma Valley, Kistler's original 35-acre vineyard was planted to Chardonnay and Cabernet Sauvignon. But Kistler's amazing success with Chardonnay led to the removal of Cabernet in favor of more Chardonnay. This original vineyard is now the source of Kistler's Sonoma Valley, "Kistler Vineyard" Chardonnay. This first-class producer has emphasized small-batch, vineyard-designated Chardonnays and Pinot Noirs from its own vineyard and other sources. After an excellent beginning, Kistler fell back for a few years as if to repent for an ill-fated 80 Chardonnay. By 85 it was again in top form and has become one of the outstanding Chardonnay producers. Owned by Steve and John Kistler and winemaker Mark Bixler, the winery adheres to the traditional, minimal-handling school of winemaking. Its Chardonnays are barrel-fermented and undergo complete malolactic fermentation.

The current roster of vineyard-designated Chardonnays consists of Dutton Ranch, Durell Vineyard, McCrea Vineyard, Vine Hill Road, and Kistler Vineyard. Recently Kistler has added a Sonoma Coast Chardonnay (6,000 cases) and a special Cuvee Chardonnay (500 cases). In 86 Kistler purchased a mature 20-acre vineyard in southwestern Sonoma County. In 1992 this Russian River Valley site, known as Vine Hill Vineyard, encouraged the owners to build a winery there, which was designed by them to produce their style of Chardonnay and Pinot Noir. With annual production of 12,000 cases consisting mostly of Chardonnay, Kistler is moving ahead to achieve similar success with Pinot Noir from Vine Hill Vineyard and other sites falling within the Russian River Valley appellation.

**Cabernet Sauvignon**

(Kistler Vineyard)   **85°°   86°°   87°   88°   90   91°°   92°**

*Seemingly destined to make its place among the top Cabernets grown in California, this one is deep in curranty and black-cherryish fruit, tight in structure, and loaded with aging potential*

**Chardonnay**

(Dutton Ranch)   84   85°°   86°°   87°°   88°°   89   **90°°°   91°
92°   94°°°**

(Durell Vineyard)   86°°°   87°°°   88°   89°°   **90°°   91°°**   92
**93°°   94°°**   95

(Kistler Vineyard)   86°°°   88°°°   89°   **90°°°   91°°°**   92°°
**94°   95°°**

(McCrea Vineyard)   88°°°   89°°   **90°   91°°   92   94°°°   95°°**

*With its recent vintages, Kistler has reestablished its place among the top handful of Chardonnay producers in California. All of its wines have possessed depth of fruit, complexity, and aging potential. The Dutton often follows a more floral line than the others, while the Kistler seems to be the most durable*

KONGSGAARD VINEYARD   *Napa 1996*   Longtime winemaker for Newton and currently with Luna, John Kongsgaard also oversees his family's 10-acre Chardonnay vineyard in southern Napa. In 96 he produced a few hundred cases of awesome Chardonnay from this hillside vineyard. It was barrel-fermented and bottled unfiltered. Optimum annual output is in the 500-case neighborhood.

KORBEL CHAMPAGNE CELLARS   *1862*   California's leading volume producer of *méthode champenoise* sparkling wine, Korbel is approaching its production goal of 1.5 million cases. The beautiful old winery is located along the western edge of the Russian River Valley a few miles west of Guerneville. In the distant background one can see part of Korbel's 600-acre vineyard, which supplies a small portion of the winery's crush needs. Grapes are contracted from throughout the state as the winery concentrates on making its line of sparkling wines—Brut Natural, Brut, Blanc de Blancs, Blanc de Noirs, and Rosé. The Brut is the top seller, and accounts for over 700,000 cases a year. By contrast, the winery's Blanc de Noirs (100% Pinot Noir) and Blanc de Blancs (100% Chardonnay) are each made in quantities of about 10,000 cases.

Le Premier, an upscale vintage dated sparkler has been added to improve the winery's faltering image. Even the once highly touted Natural and Blanc de Blancs have suffered from a diffuse, muddled impression in some recent releases. The Brut Rosé (not to be confused with the sweeter Rosé) has been consistently enjoyable, however. The winery's Blanc de Noirs along with the Brut Rosé were the quality leaders at the end of the 80s, each achieving ° ratings. In the 90s the market for sparkling wine declined, and Korbel returned to bottling Cabernet and Chardonnay. Korbel is also a leader in the field of California Brandy, with annual sales in excess of 400,000 cases.

HANNS KORNELL CHAMPAGNE CELLARS   *Napa 1952*   Hanns Kornell made his first bubbly in a makeshift cellar in Sonoma County. In 58 he purchased the defunct Larkmead Winery north of St. Helena, and settled in to make a range of sparkling wine. Following German practice, Kornell purchased readymade batches of wine, usually from the Riesling grape, and made them sparkle by the *méthode champenoise.* Some historians maintain that Kornell was the first in California to adopt this traditional French method. From the 50 s to the late 70s, Kornell produced a range of generally popular sparklers, all displaying their Riesling parentage. But sales had been slipping steadily in the 80s, falling below 70,000 cases a year. In 93 the facility was purchased by Rombauer, who is keeping the Kornell name alive through token amounts of sparkling and table wines.

KRISTONE   *Santa Barbara 1991*   Part of the Kendall-Jackson wine empire, Kristone is the company's entry in the upscale sparkling wine world. Winemaker Harold Osborne (ex-Schramsberg) works within the Cambria facility to produce a line of sparkling wines, using grapes predominantly from Santa Maria Valley. With his sights on a big, bold style of wine, Osborne uses riper than normal fruit, ages his cuvees in oak barrels, and then gives the cuvees an average of three years' aging *en tirage* prior to final bottling. Critical reception to the Blanc de Blancs, Blancs de Noirs and Rose have been mixed. Based on the early vintages we recommend the Rosé but also suggest that adventurous types try the others.

CHARLES KRUG WINERY   *Napa 1861*   Charles Krug, a Prussian emigrant, arrived in San Francisco in the 1850 s. He started a vineyard and built the winery bearing his name in 1861. Krug died in 1892, and although his winery was relatively large, the quality achievement during his reign is unknown. In 43, Cesare Mondavi, who was running a successful winery in Lodi as well as in St. Helena at the Sunny St. Helena Winery, purchased the Krug property in order to expand his family enterprise. The next year the Mondavi era began as their first wines were made in the original cellar and aged in the carriage house. Cesare Mondavi ran the Krug Winery with his two sons, Peter, who focused on winemaking and production, and an older brother, Robert, who handled marketing and promotions. Krug is usually credited with introducing temperature-controlled fermentation and sterile filtration during this period, and for performing breakthrough research into oak aging and the use of French oak barrels. The California style of slightly sweet, fruity Chenin Blanc is said to be a Krug innovation.

In 59 Cesare Mondavi died, leaving the winery in the hands of his wife, Rosa, their two sons, and one daughter. This working relationship began to unravel as the brothers, both strong-minded, collided on many issues. The well-documented account has Peter Mondavi gaining control, while Robert, eased out, left in 66 to start his own winery. A long legal battle followed, and when it was finally resolved in the late 70s, Robert won on almost every count and was awarded money, wine, and vineyards from the Krug Winery. For the next several years Krug was forced to work on a frugal budget and the winery failed to keep up with the fast-moving competition.

Its Cabernets, including a 3,000-case-per-year Reserve line labeled "Vintage Selection," were standouts in the 50 s and 60s. We find that Krug's Cabernets diminished in intensity and appeal after 1971. Despite long efforts since then to reinstate the Cabernets to their former glory, the first positive signs did not appear until the 85 and 86 vintages of the "Vintage Selection" bottlings.

Currently, the winery owns or controls 1,000 acres of vineyards scattered throughout Napa Valley. Two vineyards in the Carneros grow Chardonnay and Merlot, and the winery is surrounded by over 100 acres on the original ranch. Krug is currently developing vineyards on 600 acres it owns in Yolo County. Krug's wine roster in addition to two Cabernet bottlings now includes Chardonnay, Sauvignon Blanc, Merlot, and Pinot Noir. In the 80s the winery's output varied from one year to the next, but more recently it has made approximately 150,000 cases of varietals a year, of which 30% is Cabernet Sauvignon.

After years of neglect, the winemaking facility has been renovated and brought up to contemporary standards. However, the first signs of quality improvement were signaled by the 86 Special Selection Cabernet Sauvignon and recent vintages of Carneros Reserve Chardonnay. In the late 1990s Krug continued to make quality improvements as it added an impressive Reserve Merlot, and both its Sangiovese and Red Meritage named Generations showed that the winery was back on track. C. K. Mondavi Vineyards (see entry) is Krug's line of cheaper wines.

### Cabernet Sauvignon

(Napa Valley)  84   85   86   87   88   89   90   91   92
93   **94°**   95

*An unenviable record of underfilled, uninteresting wines; in 94, at least, Krug came through*

(Vintners Selection)   84   85°   86°   88   **91°**

*Sometimes ripe enough and deep enough to merit commendation, but the current record, like the long-term record, is spotty at best*

---

KUNDE ESTATE WINERY   *Sonoma 1990*   Having planted vines in the hills of Kenwood in 1904, the Kunde family was a highly regarded grape grower and wine producer until they closed down the winery operation in 44. From then until 90, when they opened their new facility, the Kundes sold their entire crop to Sebastiani Vineyards and other nearby producers. The family now owns 750 acres of vineyards divided among three ranches: Wildwood, Kinneybrook, and Bell. Cabernet Sauvignon (75 acres), Chardonnay (170 acres), Merlot (110 acres), and Sauvignon Blanc (60 acres) head a lengthy list of varieties planted. As annual production expands from 50,000 to 100,000 cases, Cabernet Sauvignon and Chardonnay are the volume leaders. A Reserve program consists of Chardonnay (100% barrel-fermented) and Cabernet (blended with Merlot and Cabernet Franc). Sauvignon Blanc (blended with Semillon), Merlot, and Zinfandel from the winery's oldest vines round out the roster. Chardonnay is the overall quality leader, with three noteworthy versions offered each vintage: Reserve, Wildwood Vineyard, and Kinneybrook Vineyard.

### Chardonnay

90° 91°° 92° 93 94 95 96

*Oaky, moderately ripe, appley, medium-full-bodied*

(Reserve) 90°°° 92° 93° 94° 95°°

(Kinneybrook Vineyard) 92° 93° **94°** **95°°**

(Wildwood Vineyard) 92 93 **94°** 95

### Merlot

**91** **92** **93** 94° **95°**

*Medium full-bodied wines with ripe cherry fruit; mid-term aging potential*

### Viognier

92°° 93° 94° 95° 96 **97°°**

*Medium-depth wines showing fruity, sometimes slightly floral Viognier character*

---

LA CREMA *Sonoma 1979* This winery started out located in a dreary warehouse in Petaluma, where it made only Pinot Noir and Chardonnay. The winery's name then was La Crema Vinera, and its emphasis was on small-batch, vineyard-designated wines made with minimal clarification. The wines made varied widely in quality. In 84 the winery was acquired by Jason Korman with a new name, La Crema, the winery continued purchasing Pinot Noir and Chardonnay from several vineyards. However, it simplified its line by offering only a regular and Reserve version of each varietal. The brand grew quickly to the 60,000-case-a-year level.

In 1986 the owners, however, were on the ropes financially, and were unable to last many more rounds. They filed for bankruptcy, and the banks eventually assumed control of La Crema. In 93, Kendall-Jackson purchased the trademark and is now producing La Crema wines at a new winery in the Russian River Valley. A nearby vineyard grows 33 acres of Chardonnay and 11 acres of Pinot Noir. La Crema is currently producing 100,000 cases a year.

### Chardonnay

(regular bottling) 86 87° 88 90 92 93 94° 95

(Reserve) 86°°° 87°° 89 92° 93° **94°°** 95

*Both wines are balanced, somewhat appley, and well oaked in composition, but the Reserve seems to find extra measures of depth and richness that have been wanting in the regular edition*

### Pinot Noir

83° 84° 85° 86° 87 88 91 **92°** 93 **94°°** 95

*Relatively direct cherry and herb style, with moderate depth and short-term aging potential*

---

LAETITIA VINEYARDS *Arroyo Grande Valley 1994* Laetitia, the varietal wine reincarnation of Maison Deutz, was formed once the Deutz partnership dissolved. Anticipating the change, the winemaking staff had played a few practice rounds by making Pinot Noir under the Carpe Diem label. Using the same facility, vineyards, and winemaker, Laetitia produces Chardonnay, Pinot Noir, and Pinot Blanc. In most vintages 500–600 cases of each varietal are offered as a Reserve. Divided into three parcels—La Colline, Clos Laetitia, and Les Galets—the 187-acre vineyard will enable the winery to expand total production quickly, to 15,000 cases a year.

LA JOTA VINEYARD CO.   *Napa 1985*   Encouraged by his home winemaking experiences, Bill Smith began looking for a vineyard where he could grow grapes and continue his amateur winemaking. Smith, an executive with an oil exploration company, and his wife, Joan, wanted to be weekend vineyardists. In 74 they discovered the remains of the pre-Prohibition La Jota Winery, on Howell Mountain, and bought it along with the surrounding property. Abandoned during Prohibition, the original stone winery was built in 1895 by Frederick Hess. Starting gradually with a few acres of Cabernet Sauvignon, the Smiths developed 30 acres to Cabernet Sauvignon and Zinfandel. Dissatisfied with the grape market, they began making wine with the help of a neighbor, Randy Dunn.

In 82 they produced their first estate-grown Cabernet, and a year later they made their first estate-grown Zinfandel. Aged for close to 2 years in Nevers oak, the Cabernets are blended with 5% to 10% Merlot and Cabernet Franc. Over the years their Zinfandel vineyard was converted to Cabernet Franc and to Viognier. Among the first to make Viognier, the Smiths produced a few hundred cases in 86, and are now up to about 700 cases from their 3 acres. After experimentation, Bill Smith is making Cabernet Franc in two styles—one light and fruity, the other full-bodied and ageworthy. The winery's mainstay, Cabernet Sauvignon, is made from the estate's 20 acres of that grape, and production is level at 3,000 cases. As of 1991 La Jota has been selecting the top 50% of its Cabernet, which is bottled under "Anniversary Release" designation. Smith's Pinot Noir from the Sonoma Coast appellations are labeled W. H. Smith Wines (see entry).

### Cabernet Sauvignon

(Howell Mountain Selection)   **91°**   92   **93**   **94°°**   **95°**

(Howell Mountain to 90; Anniversary bottlings 91 and thereafter)   82°
83°°   **84°**   **85°**   **86°**   87°   **88°**   89°   **90**   **91°°**   92°°°
**93°°**   94°°°   95°°°

*Firm, ageworthy, tightly bound wines, these ripe and rustic offerings have been more notable for their perceived aging potential and Howell Mountain appellation than for their depth of fruit; with 91, the best fruit was directed to the Anniversary bottling and the results justify the decision*

LANG & REED WINE CO.   *Napa 1995*   Twenty-year wine marketing veteran John Skupny launched his own brand by focusing on Cabernet Franc from Napa Valley. To date he has offered two styles, an early-maturing fruit forward style and an ageworthy version labeled "vin de garde." Both were among the better-balanced Cabernet Francs on the market. Production falls a little short of 1,000 cases a year.

LAKE SONOMA WINERY   Sonoma 1977   Originally known as Diablo Vista Vineyards, this winery was founded in Benicia in Contra Costa County. The winery was purchased in 82 by the Polson family, which owned vineyards in the northern part of Dry Creek Valley. A winemaking facility was built in stages and was finally completed in 90. The 10-acre vineyard is located near Lake Sonoma Dam, and the primary varieties grown are Zinfandel, Sauvignon Blanc, Cabernet Sauvignon, Merlot, and Chenin Blanc. Zinfandel and Sauvignon Blanc are the mainstays in the present output of 3,000 cases. The winery was among the first to offer Cinsault, a minor Rhone Valley red. From its own vineyards and purchased grapes, Lake Sonoma was purchased in 1997 by Gary Heck of Korbel and Kenwood Vineyards. Adjacent to the winery, he established a microbrewery. The winery produces about 5,000 cases a year.

LAKESPRING WINERY   *Napa 1980*   This winery was founded by the Battat family, and run by the three Battat brothers—Frank, Harry, and Ralph—and their families. They planted 10 acres to Chardonnay. In addition to its Chardonnay, Lakespring produces Cabernet Sauvignon, Merlot, and Sauvignon Blanc. Tired of the business, the Battat brothers sold the label and the name Lakespring to their national distributor, the New York–based importer Frederick Wildman and Son. Wildman now has the line of Lakespring wine made under contract at a large facility. The roster remains unchanged, consisting of Napa Valley Cabernet Sauvignon, Chardonnay, Merlot, and Sauvignon Blanc. Wildman sees 36,000 cases as a desired annual output.

LAKEWOOD VINEYARD   *Lake 1990*   Housed in the original winery in Lakeport where the Kendall Jackson brand was established in the 1980s and relying on the nearby 72-acre vineyard, this brand was created by owner Jess Jackson for varietals made from Sauvignon Blanc and Semillon. "Chevriot," a Meritage blend of barrel-fermented Semillon, and Sauvignon Blanc is also made. The Sauvignon Blanc is crisp and pleasing. While the Chevriot displays the most oak influence and depth, it has been an inconsistent performer. Annual production remains steady at 2,000 cases.

LAMBERT BRIDGE   *Sonoma 1975*   Located in the Dry Creek Valley, Lambert Bridge began in 69 when proprietor Jerry Lambert purchased the present 119-acre site. By 73, with his vineyard established to Chardonnay and Cabernet Sauvignon, and a fraction to Merlot. The vineyard was then expanded to 76 acres divided into three parcels. Over its first decade, the winery specialized in three varietals— Chardonnay, Cabernet Sauvignon, and Merlot—and prided itself for producing only estate-grown wines. But both its Chardonnay and Cabernet Sauvignon met with extremely mixed reviews. The winery added Fumé Blanc to its line. And it began producing Reserve-type wines—Chardonnay"Tête de Cuvée"and"Library Reserve" Cabernet Sauvignon, both from the Dry Creek Valley appellation. But after losing a protracted legal battle against its national distributor, the winery closed down in late 92. It was reopened in 1993 after being acquired by the Chambers family. With Julia Iantosca as winemaker, Lambert Bridge has gradually shifted emphasis to Merlot, Chardonnay, and Fumé Blanc. A limited edition and impressive new red Meritage is Crane Creek Cuvée from Dry Creek Valley. Zinfandel also is a regular in the lineup. As annual production works its way back to 18,000 cases, the winery sells more than half to visitors.

### Cabernet Sauvignon

84   **85°**   **86°°**   **89°°**   **91°°**   **92°**   **95°**

*Black-cherry fruit is combined with ample oak in a medium-full-bodied wine of supple, moderately tannic structure*

### Chardonnay

**85°**   **86°**   88   **89°**   **90°**   **92°°**   93   **94°**   95

*Floral and direct apple tones are presented in a crisp, firm style, amenable to a few years of development in the bottle*

LAMBORN FAMILY VINEYARDS   *Napa 1982*   Bob Lamborn, a private investigator in the Oakland area, bought 30 acres of secluded land on Howell Mountain in 73, intending to use the property as a rural retreat. Upon hearing from his neighbors that a famous vineyard once occupied the site, he cleared the land and planted 9 acres to Zinfandel. In 79, with his neighbor Randy Dunn acting as winemaker, Lamborn produced 100 cases. A decade later he was making 1,100 cases a year in his own tiny winery. As production expands to the 2,200-case level, he purchases Zinfandel from the neighboring Beatty Ranch. Aged in a combination of French and American oak for an average of 18 months, Lamborn Zinfandels are ripe and jammy, in a style typical of the area. With another 10 acres plantable, Lamborn has been adding Sangiovese.

### Zinfandel

84°°   **85°**   **86°**   87   **88°°°**   89   **90**   91   **93**   **94°**   **95°**

*Ripe-berry fruitiness, with briary and spicy notes, comes in a firm, full, and tannic package that is not always up to its brusque exterior; the 87 was a bit of a clinker; the 88 was one of the finest*

LANDMARK VINEYARDS    *Sonoma 1974*    Landmark tried out a number of wines over its first decade. Founded by the Mabry family, owners of several vineyards in Sonoma, the winery was located in Windsor until 88, when it finally fell victim to urban encroachment and real estate developers. Bill Mabry, who was then the managing partner and winemaker, decided he could not stop progress, and relocated to a site north of Kenwood in the Sonoma Valley where a new 40,000-case winery was readied for the 90 harvest. Now owned by Demaris Ethridge, Landmark has scaled back production to Chardonnay and Pinot Noir. As of the late-90s, the Chardonnays are labeled "Overlook" and "Demaris Reserve." The "Overlook," made from the winery's 13-acre vineyard, is holding steady at 7,500 cases. The quality of both took a turn for the better in 1993 with the entrance of Helen Turley as a consultant. Turley also has encouraged the production of a few barrels of Pinot Noir. Though available only at the winery, the Pinot Noir is worth a special trip.

### Chardonnay

| | | | | | | | | | |
|---|---|---|---|---|---|---|---|---|---|
| (Sonoma County/Overlook) | 86 | 88 | 89 | 90 | 92 | 93 | 94 | 95 | 96 |
| (Demaris Reserve) | 88 | 89° | 90 | 92 | 93°° | 94° | **95°** | **96°°** | |

*Showing appley and somewhat floral fruit in good years, the Sonoma County/Overlook wine continues to have a spotty track record; the latter wine, higher-priced, has deeper fruit and more oak*

LANG WINES    Commercial pilot Bob Lang helped develop a 160-acre vineyard in the Sierra Foothills. The leading varieties in this vineyard, named "Twin Rivers Vineyard," are Zinfandel and Sauvignon Blanc. To help promote the sales of grapes, Lang decided to produce a few hundred cases of Zinfandel per year. Made at the Granite Springs Winery, Lang Zinfandels are full-bodied and often exemplary of the region.

LA SIRENA    *Napa Valley 1994*    This label is owned by Heidi Barrett, well-known consulting winemaker for Screaming Eagle, Grace Family, Hartwell, Vineyard 29, and previously with Dalla Valle and Buehler. She is making Sangiovese from a vineyard in Pope Valley as well as a tiny quantity of Cabernet Sauvignon, her specialty. Combined annual output is 500 cases.

LAS MONTANAS WINERY    *Sonoma 1982*    Literally a one-woman show, Las Montanas is a small (1,500 cases a year) winery located on the steep hillsides overlooking the Sonoma Valley. Owner-winemaker Aleta Apgar is adamant about making only natural (chemical-free) wines from grapes farmed organically. She has 3 acres adjacent to the winery, and they provide most of the fruit needed to produce 400 cases each of Cabernet Sauvignon and Zinfandel. Though the quality is slightly erratic, the Zinfandel has on occasion been extremely attractive in a ripe-berry style.

LAS VINAS    *San Joaquin 1986*    The Cotta family (John, Jim, and Joe) owns 800 acres of vineyards within the Lodi region. With John as the winemaker, they are producing a line of varietal wines from their vineyard. Most of their crop is sold to wineries within the general vicinity. The major varietals produced, in order of importance, are: Cabernet Sauvignon, Sauvignon Blanc, Symphony, Chardonnay, and Zinfandel. A medium-sweet blended blush wine goes by the proprietary name of "Amorosa." On occasion, Symphony is produced in a late harvest style. The winery's annual production goal is 15,000 cases a year.

LAURA'S VINEYARD    *Paso Robles 1996*    Patrick O'Dell, who owns Napa's Turnbull Cellars, acquired an established but neglected vineyard in Paso Robles and also purchased 250 acres of potential vineyard land surrounding it. O'Dell has increased the planting of Cabernet and Chardonnay and added new blocks of Syrah, Viognier, Barbera, and Sangiovese. As he did with Turnbull, O'Dell will build this brand slowly. The most promising wines are Zinfandel and Syrah.

LAUREL GLEN VINEYARDS  *Sonoma 1980*  Owner and winemaker Patrick Campbell makes Cabernet Sauvignon from 35 acres located on the rocky slopes high above the Sonoma Valley. His vineyard falls within the Viticultural Area he identified and promoted as Sonoma Mountain. Campbell made wines as an amateur in the 70s, and also sold some of his grapes to Chateau St. Jean and others before going professional in 81. He began developing his vineyard in 68, and with gradual expansion the vineyard now consists of eight distinct blocks, all east-facing at the 1,000-foot-elevation level. So situated, the vineyards are above the frost line, and the eastern exposure protects the vines from intense late-afternoon heat during the growing season. Both Cabernet Franc and Merlot are grown, but mainly as blending candidates, should they be needed.

For his Cabernet Sauvignon, Campbell begins by harvesting the crop from each block separately, and then uses open-top fermenters and allows the temperature to approach 90°F. Clarification is accomplished in most vintages by frequent rackings. For aging, he uses mostly new Nevers oak, and allows the wine to spend close to two years in small oak barrels. As a rule, Laurel Glen Cabernets are impeccably made, and offer deep, intense fruit. Batches of wine not used in the final master blend are sometimes bottled and sold as "Counterpoint." The maximum annual production is 5,000 cases. Campbell has also added "Terra Rosa," a Cabernet he purchases and ages before bottling, and "Reds," a low-priced red wine that in recent years has come from Chile.

### Cabernet Sauvignon

81°  82  83°  **84°**  **85°°°**  **86°°**  **87°**  **88°**  89  **90°°**  91
**92°°°**  **93**  **95**

*Deep black-cherry fruit, hints of cocoa and herbs, rich oak, and a tannin-firmed, supple texture combine in wine of good aging potential*

LAURIER VINEYARDS  *(formerly Domaine Laurier)*  *Sonoma 1978*  Under the direction of the Shilo family, its founders, the winery gradually expanded over its first decade to produce 12,000 cases by 88. However, in early 89 the winery was sold. Later that year the well-known winemaker Merry Edwards (justifiably famous for her Chardonnays at Mt. Eden, Matanzas Creek, and Merry Vintners) joined the winery. Edwards's style of winemaking is based on 100% barrel-fermented Chardonnay, and the small-batch method with frequent punching down for Pinot Noir. She produced two vintages before bankruptcy forced closure of the facility. The brand was acquired in 91 by Classic Wines. Edwards was retained as winemaker. In rented space, she continues to make barrel-fermented Sonoma County Chardonnay, and Pinot Noir, and will oversee expansion to 11,000 cases per year.

LAVA CAP VINEYARD  *El Dorado 1986*  Situated northeast of Placerville on a rocky ridge that is unusually rich in volcanic soils, Lava Cap is family-owned and -operated. Its 30-acre vineyard located at the 2,600-foot elevation was developed in 81. The vineyard contains Chardonnay, Merlot, Sauvignon Blanc, Cabernet Sauvignon, and Zinfandel. A generic wine, Lava Cap Red (a blend of Cabernet Sauvignon and Zinfandel), and Petite Sirah complete the line of this 7,000-case producer. In the 90s, Lava Cap emerged as one of the stars of the region. It has been successful with Merlot, Cabernet Sauvignon, and Chardonnay, especially with the Reserve Chardonnay.

### Chardonnay

(El Dorado)  90°  91°  **92°**
(El Dorado Reserve)  89°°  90°  91°  92°°  **94°**  **95°**

*Both wines are overachievers at their very enticing price levels; both have good fruit, moderate oak, and an open, easy-to-like structure*

DANIEL LAWRENCE CELLARS  *Sonoma 1995*  This line of varietals was launched by wine business veteran Dan Horsch. His lineup includes the usual suspects—

Cabernet, Chardonnay, and Zinfandel—along with Syrah, Sangiovese, and Merlot. Reserve bottlings of Chardonnay and Syrah also have been offered. In the early rounds all wines, with the exception of the Contra Costa–grown Zinfandel, were made from North Coast appellations. The owners have projected 15,000 cases a year as their maximum.

KARL LAWRENCE CELLARS  *Napa 1991*  Though firmly ensconced as winemaker at Sequoia Grove Vineyard, Michael Trujillo developed this Cabernet-only label in partnership with longtime friend Brian Henry. Karl and Lawrence are the middle names of the partners. Since 1991 their Cabernet Sauvignon has combined fruit from two highly acclaimed sources, the Morisoli Vineyard in Rutherford and the Lamb Vineyard near Howell Mountain. Over the first several vintages annual production has averaged 650 cases. Both partners agree that growth to 1,000 cases a year is possible.

LAZY CREEK VINEYARDS  *Mendocino 1973*  Founded by former restaurateur Hans Kobler and his wife, Theresa, Lazy Creek is located in the Anderson Valley just west of Philo. The small, cozy winery is surrounded by 20 acres planted to Gewurztraminer, Pinot Noir, and Chardonnay. The winery is best known for its first-class Gewurztraminers, which usually rank among the very best in the state. The style of recent vintages has been opulently spicy and flowery and finished with a slight sweetness. Its Pinot Noir in the mid-80s began to earn * in a style that displays cherry-berry characteristics with moderate intensity. In a fruity, well-made style, Lazy Creek Chardonnays are usually pleasant. A Red Table Wine made from left-over Pinot Noir is made in most years to accompany the three varietals. Total production approaches 4,000 cases.

LE DOMAINE  *(Almadén Vineyards)*  This once highly visible line of moderately priced sparkling wine was acquired in 87 by Heublein Wines, which also owns Inglenook, Beaulieu, and the Christian Brothers. At one time Le Domaine's offerings were produced by the transfer process and the quality was decent and remained so for several years. The two current bottlings, Brut and Extra Dry, are made by the Charmat process and tend toward the dull, sweet side of their respective categories.

LEEWARD WINERY  *Ventura 1979*  After some success as home winemakers, partners Chuck Brigham and Chuck Gardner decided to go commercial in 79. However, until they moved into a full-scale winery in 82, they continued to make wine in their basement. From the very first vintage, Chardonnay has been the major wine by volume. Stressing barrel fermentations, French oak aging, and malolactic fermentations, Leeward built a reputation for full-blown Chardonnays. Today, 90% of its annual 15,000-case production is Chardonnay. Cabernet Sauvignon from the Alexander Valley, Coral, and a few hundred cases of Merlot round out the line.

**Chardonnay**

| (Edna Valley) | 86 | 87 | 88 | 89 | 90 | 91° | 92 | 93 | 95 |
|---|---|---|---|---|---|---|---|---|---|
| (Central Coast) | 86° | 87 | 88 | 89° | 90 | 91° | 92 | | |
| 93 | 95 | | | | | | | | |

*Always oaky, and typically full of winemaking nuances, these wines have all too often lacked the necessary core of fruit to balance their other parts*

LEWIS CELLARS  *Napa Valley 1994*  Randy Lewis, a former race driver with many appearances at the Indy 500, began his wine career as a partner in Oakville Ranch Vineyards. When that partnership dissolved, Randy founded Lewis Cellars, which has been making Cabernet Sauvignon and Chardonnay from the Oakville region. Both Reserve Chardonnay and Reserve Cabernet have been standouts in most vintages. Total production has reached 2,500 cases. Merlot, recently added, is also impressive.

## Cabernet Sauvignon
**92  93°°**  94°°  95°°

*Deep and keenly focused black cherry and dried currant fruit is topped by rich oak and firmed up by youthful tannins; expect 10 or more years of cellaring improvement*

## Chardonnay
93  **94°°  95°°**

*Ripe, deep, solid Chardonnay, high in oak*

## Merlot
**94°°°  95°°°**

*A beautiful, deep, fruity, rich first effort filled in further by Cabernet Sauvignon (18%) and Cabernet Franc (6%); 95 followed suit*

LIBERTY SCHOOL  *(Caymus Vineyards)*  Introduced by Caymus in 75 as a way to sell left-over Cabernet Sauvignon, Liberty School evolved into a full-scale brand. The name derives from the nearby schoolhouse attended by owner Charles Wagner as a schoolboy. Liberty School's line now consists of Chardonnay and Cabernet Sauvignon. Liberty School wines are now made in Paso Robles in partnership with the Hope family, whose vineyard supplies much of the wine. Liberty School is bottling and selling 45,000 cases a year. Overall, its quality performance has been among the best of the many second labels.

LIMERICK LANE CELLARS  *Sonoma 1988*  Located in the Russian River Valley, Limerick Lane produces only Zinfandel. Sauvignon Blanc production ended after 1993. All Zinfandel crushed is grown in the adjacent 30-acre Collins Vineyard, owned by partner Michael Collins. Each vintage is barrel aged in a combination of French and American oak for about 14 months. A few vintages have earned °° to date; the winery's style, when it is on target, is a beautiful combination of deep fruit and lively, zesty ripe berry flavors. Annual output of 2,500 cases will eventually grow to 6,000 cases.

## Zinfandel
(Collins Vineyard)  **93°  94°°  95°  96°**

*Ripe, berryish, deep and somewhat spicy, high in oak and moderately tannic*

LIPARITA WINERY  *Napa 1988*  On a site said to have been the home of a winery prior to Prohibition, San Franciscan Robert Burrows has revived the Liparita brand and developed a vineyard. Located on Howell Mountain, the vineyard, now covering 80 acres, is planted to Chardonnay, Cabernet Sauvignon, Merlot, and Sauvignon Blanc. In 87 the owner asked winemaker Merry Edwards to make an experimental batch of Chardonnay to officially reinstate the Liparita name. In the early vintages, both the Merlot and the Cabernet have offered tremendous depth, and the Cabernets have reached the °° level more than once. Seven vintages of Chardonnay have yielded no hits. Burrows sold the Howell Mountain vineyard to Kendall-Jackson in 1997. Since then he has been buying Merlot and Chardonnay from the Carneros District, and Cabernet Sauvignon and additional Chardonnay from growers in the mid–Napa Valley and several mountain vineyards. Liparita's production is steady at 3,000 cases, evenly divided among Chardonnay, Cabernet, and Merlot.

## Cabernet Sauvignon
**90°°  91°°  92  93**  94°°

*Deep, concentrated, well-oaked, curranty, briary, tannic wines that will age a decade and more*

LITTORI  *Napa Valley 1993*  Ted Lemon, longtime winemaker for Château Woltner, focuses his esoteric Littori brand on Chardonnay and Pinot Noir from cool sites in

Sonoma and Mendocino Counties. To date his wines include Chardonnay from Hirsch Vineyard in cool western Sonoma, and Pinot Noir from One Acre Vineyard in Mendocino's Anderson Valley.

LIVERMORE VALLEY CELLARS  *Alameda 1978*  About midway between Livermore and Pleasanton, this family-owned operation sold grapes to Wente and others for several years. By 78, owner Chris Largis began making wines from a portion of his mature, 34-acre, dry-farmed vineyard. All grapes are white, but the varieties represented a mix of old and contemporary, obscure and common. Golden Chasselas and other museum pieces grow alongside Gray Riesling, French Colombard, and Chardonnay. One vineyard parcel is a mixed planting of Chenin Blanc, Pinot Blanc, and other varieties, picked and crushed together to produce a generic white. Chardonnay and dry-style Colombard are mainstays in this 3,000-case winery.

LIVINGSTON VINEYARDS  *Napa 1987*  John and Diane Livingston own a 10-acre vineyard on the western edge of the Rutherford Bench. The pre-Prohibition vineyard was replanted to Cabernet Sauvignon in 69. Named Moffett after Diane's family, the vineyard supplied grapes to many Napa Valley wineries until the Livingstons decided to custom-crush in 84. A small winery has been built on the property. First vintage in 84 yielded 900 cases. The optimum annual output for Moffett Vineyard is pegged at 2,000 cases. Both Cabernet Franc and Merlot have been used in the blend. Livingston prefers to age the Moffett bottling at least two years in small oak barrels. In 89 a Napa Valley Cabernet from purchased grapes was added, and about 2,500 cases of this "Stanley's Selection" Cabernet are produced each year. Early vintages were made by Randy Dunn, but since 1996 John Kongsgaard (formerly of Newton) has supervised production. The winery has added a few hundred cases of Chardonnay and Syrah to its roster.

### Cabernet Sauvignon

(Moffett Vineyard)  84°°  **85°°**  **86°°°**  87  88°  **89°**  **90°**
**91°**  92  93  94

(Stanley's Selection)  89°  90°  **91°**  92  **93°**  94

*Deep, curranty, often somewhat loamy, and rich in creamy oak, the wine is supple and inviting at the center but also has plenty of tannin for backbone and ageworthiness*

LOCKWOOD VINEYARDS  *Monterey 1989*  A limited partnership of growers owning 1,600 acres of vineyards in the Salinas Valley, Lockwood markets Chardonnay, Pinot Blanc, Riesling, Cabernet Sauvignon, Merlot, and Muscat Canelli. Except for its limited line of Partners Reserve wines, Lockwood's prices are well within reason, making its Pinot Blanc, Sauvignon Blanc, and, on occasion, its Chardonnay candidates for good value citations. The pricier Reserves have a tendency to go over the top, and the Chardonnay and Pinot Blanc are both oak-laced. Chardonnay accounts for one-third of Lockwood's annual output and will remain the leading varietal as the winery grows toward the 50,000-case level.

LOGAN WINERY  *(Talbott)*  Not long after the Talbotts saw a sufficient demand for their high-priced Chardonnay, they introduced a less expensive Chardonnay under the Logan name. Grown in the same vineyards of Monterey's Salinas Valley, Logan Chardonnay is also barrel-fermented. Owner Robb Talbott named this label after his son, Logan. Annual output has ranged from 4,000 to 5,000 cases. The quality has been surprisingly erratic, especially in view of the success enjoyed by the main brand.

J. LOHR WINERY  *Santa Clara 1974*  Taking over an old brewery site in downtown San Jose, owner Jerry Lohr and a since departed partner, Bernie Turgeon, built a winery and tasting room. In the early 70s, they were both successful in the custom home construction business and invested in a vineyard site in the Greenfield area of Monterey County. When the 280-acre vineyard was reaching maturity, they began producing a hit-or-miss line of wines, led by a slightly sweet Johannisberg Riesling. After 84, when Lohr took charge of the operations, the winery changed direction with the help of a marketing partnership with the Wine Trust. By 90 many changes were being felt.

With vineyards in four regions, J. Lohr now owns or controls 1,100 acres. A line of upscale varietals has evolved, a few featuring vineyard designations and others being marketed under the "J. Lohr Estates" banner. In Monterey County, the winery's 55-acre Cypress Vineyard yields its Reserve Chardonnay. The major J. Lohr Estates wine is the "Riverstone" Chardonnay from Monterey. The original 335-acre Greenfield holding grows several varieties and contributes to the regular J. Lohr Winery bottlings of Chardonnay, Gamay, and Johannisberg Riesling.

The fourth vineyard, Seven Oaks, is in Paso Robles, and its 454 acres are used mainly for Cabernet Sauvignon, Merlot, and Syrah. J. Lohr's vineyard-designated wines added an emphatic note of seriousness to a winery enjoying success with its consistently zesty, fruity, and popular Monterey Gamay that earns °, and White Zinfandel. Though both the "Bay Mist" Riesling and "Wildflower" Gamay remain on the roster, it is Lohr's "Riverstone" Chardonnay (80,000 cases) and the "Seven Oaks" Cabernet (50,000 cases) that have emerged as key players. Both frequently earn "good value" citations. The winery also makes 1,000 cases of pricier, super-premium Cabernet Sauvignon under the "VS" for very special designation. Annual production for J. Lohr is over 300,000 cases, with 400,000 set as the maximum. The winery also has a growing second label, "Cypress" (see entry).

## Chardonnay

(Greenfield/Riverstone)   **84**   85   86   87   88°   89   90°°   92   93   94   95   96

*Floral-toned fruit and candied flavors make this an unusual entrant in the Chardonnay field; the 90 was deeper and had more obvious oak*

**LOKOYA WINERY** *Napa 1994* The unifying theme in this Kendall-Jackson brand is the use of mountain-grown vineyards. Having acquired Liparita Vineyard in Howell Mountain and other vineyards in the Mount Veeder region, Jackson created Lokoya for limited-edition Cabernet and Chardonnay. To date the wines, which are made at Cardinale in Napa Valley, include Mount Veeder Cabernet, Howell Mountain Cabernet, and Chardonnay.

**LOLONIS WINERY** *Mendocino 1982* The Lolonis family established a vineyard in the Redwood Valley about 2 miles north of Lake Mendocino in 21. Situated on the slopes at the 1,000-foot elevation, Lolonis Vineyard sold its grapes to home winemakers during Prohibition and for many years afterwards. Grapes were sold to wineries and blended until Fetzer Vineyards began producing a vineyard-designated Lolonis Zinfandel in the early 70s and continued throughout the 80s. These Zinfandels by Fetzer were often big, intensely flavored, and powerful versions that were well received. Over the years the dry-farmed Lolonis vineyard was expanded to its present 300 acres, and the major varieties planted are Chardonnay, Zinfandel, Cabernet Sauvignon, Merlot and Sauvignon Blanc. Many wineries buy Lolonis grapes, among them Fetzer, Parducci, and Steele Wines, which bottles a Lolonis Chardonnay. In the early 80s Lolonis began producing wines from its own vineyard; while emphasizing Chardonnay and Fumé Blanc, it also made Merlot, Cabernet Sauvignon and Zinfandel. The quality overall has been average, and the Chardonnays have been ripe in fruit and full-bodied, typical of the vineyard. Total production is approaching 30,000 cases a year, led by Chardonnay and Zinfandel. Lolonis completed a new winery in time for the 97 harvest. Zinfandel is its best wine, and we have often recommended both the Mendocino and the Reserve bottlings as among the best from Mendocino and good values to boot.

**Merlot**

93°°   94   95°

*Big, ripe, highly oaked, coarsely tannic wines*

**Zinfandel**

(Mendocino County)   90   91°   94°°   95°°   96°

(Private Reserve)   88°   89   90°   93   94°   95°°

*Ripe, berryish, straightforward, the Reserve is often bigger and oakier but not always with more Zinfandel fruit, especially in recent vintages*

LONETREE WINERY   *Mendocino 1994*   After selling the sparkling winery he founded, John Scharffenberger decided to produce nonsparkling wines from his family's 75-acre vineyard in the rolling hills of Redwood Valley. Known as Eaglepoint, the vineyard continues supplying grapes to Edmeades, Fetzer, and others. As a producer, Lonetree offers only red wines, Zinfandel, Syrah, and Sangiovese. As its output gradually expands to 2,000 cases, Lonetree has shown promise with all three. The odds-on favorite appears to be Syrah.

LONG VINEYARDS   *Napa 1977*   When Zelma Long was a winemaker at the Robert Mondavi Winery, she and her husband Bob lived near the town of Angwin in the northeastern corner of Napa. As a weekend project, they planted 12 acres of Chardonnay and 4 of Riesling along the rocky hillside. Early vintages were sold to Mount Veeder Vineyards, which produced superb Long Vineyard Chardonnay in the mid-70s. As they eased into wine production, the Longs made excellent Chardonnays from their own fruit. In 81, Zelma Long became head winemaker for Simi Winery, and shortly thereafter the couple divorced. Still co-owners of this winery, they now have 16 acres of Chardonnay. The production is still headed by Chardonnay (barrel-fermented) and Riesling in a medium-sweet style, both from the home vineyard. Sauvignon Blanc (blended with about 20% Chardonnay) comes from the Carneros District. In addition, Long also offers Pinot Gris and about 200 cases of Cabernet Sauvignon. From 1979 to 93 the Cabernet came from the University of California's Experimental Vineyard in Yountville.

In 1990 Bob Long planted 1 acre of Cabernet Sauvignon in his vineyard, and in 94 he began making Cabernet only from this home vineyard. Long is currently bottling about 2,500 cases a year, with Chardonnay accounting for three quarters of the total. When the vines are fully developed, Long plans to make 3,000 cases annually. Each of the wines produced has been among the best from time to time.

**Cabernet Sauvignon**

83°   84°   85°   86   87°   89   90   92   93   95°

*Well-fruited wines, high in oak and massively tannic, they may last for decades but seem a little overdone*

**Chardonnay**

86°   87°   88°   89°   90°°   91°°   92°   93°   94°   95   96

*The first vintages (going back to the mid-70s) from this vineyard were more fruity than wines of the mid-80s, which are clean, well-oaked, somewhat complex, yet also somewhat stiff and citrusy; recent vintages have returned to form*

RICHARD LONGORIA WINES   *Santa Barbara 1982*   Rick Longoria has been making wines in Santa Barbara County since 76. He and his wife work together on this family wine venture. Production has been limited to Pinot Noir from Bien Nacido, along with Merlot, Cabernet Franc, and Chardonnay from Santa Ynez.

LUCAS WINERY   *San Joaquin 1978*   Among a handful of family-owned wineries in Lodi, Lucas Winery specializes in Zinfandel. In 77, the Lucas family (Dave and Tamara Lucas) acquired property that included a 30-acre vineyard. About 18 acres consisted of old Zinfandel, with the remainder planted to Tokay. In 79 their first

Zinfandel was made, and ever since they have been using the oldest vines to make about 1,000 to 1,200 cases a year. As a rule, the Zinfandel is aged in French oak for about a year and a half. During the White Zinfandel boom period, the winery's output varied. The old Tokay acreage was removed in the late 80s to make room for other wine varieties.

LUNA VINEYARDS   *Napa Valley 1996*   Occupying the former St. Andrews Winery along Napa's Silverado Trail, Luna is operated as a separate corporation by several key principals of Beringer Estates. Winemaker John Kongsgaad (ex-Newton) came aboard in 1996 to guide the production of Merlot, Sangiovese, and Pinot Gris. Departing from the norm, the early vintages of delightful Sangiovese were blended with Merlot and Syrah. Both the Merlot and the Pinot Gris also started off well above average in quality. Merlot at 5,000 cases tops the roster of this 12,000-case winery.

LYETH WINERY   *Sonoma 1981*   The Lyeth Winery, named after founder Chip Lyeth, was among the first to apply the estate wine concept as it is defined in the region of Bordeaux to California winemaking and labeling.

In 88, when it was producing about 28,000 cases a year, the winery and vineyards were acquired by Vintech, an ill-conceived investment company that quickly went belly-up. After selling the vineyards to Gallo in 91, the owners soon filed for bankruptcy. In early 92 the trademark Lyeth and its wine inventory were purchased by Jean-Claude Boisset. (The winemaking facility stood empty for a year until Silver Oak Cellars of Napa bought it in 93.) Since 1989, all Lyeth wines have been made from ready-made wines purchased in bulk. Recent Chardonnays have not excited.

### Lyeth Red

81°°   82   83°   84°   **85°**   **86°°**   **87**   88   **90°**   **91**   **92** 93

*More complex in the telling than in the bottle, this blended wine is typically fruity in a cherryish, slightly herbal vein, and has good structure for several years of aging potential*

LYNMAR WINERY AT QUAIL HILL   *Sonoma 1994*   Planted in the early 1970s, Quail Hill Ranch consists of 40 acres of Pinot Noir and Chardonnay. Until Lynmar was formed, several important Pinot Noir producers made Quail Hill vineyard-designated bottling. As a producer, Lynmar offers about 1,000 cases of Pinot Noir and 400 of Chardonnay. Showing little restraint, the winemaking style in the early rounds was heavy-handed when it came to oak. However, the mature, nonirrigated vineyard is a proven one, and that is good reason to keep an eye on Lynmar in the future.

LYTTON SPRINGS WINERY   *Sonoma 1975*   Located on the northwestern edge of Healdsburg that separates Dry Creek from the Alexander Valley, Lytton Springs was known first as a vineyard. It has 150 acres, including 50 of Zinfandel planted in the early 1900 s. This parcel of old vines, possibly the oldest in Sonoma County, is known as the Valley Vista Vineyard. Ridge brought Lytton Springs to our attention ln 72 when it made a vineyard-designated Zinfandel. The vineyard's owners, inspired by the recognition, established their own winery in 77, and have always made Zinfandel their mainstay. As a producer, Lytton Springs turned out Zinfandels that were often intense, sometimes close to late harvest in style, and brawny but not always cleanly made. In the early 80s the winery had developed a full line.

By the late 80s the winery was wisely concentrating on Zinfandel, bottling about 7,000 cases of a regular version and 1,000 of a Reserve. In a surprise move, Ridge Vineyards reentered the picture in 91 and bought the vineyard and winery. Since then it has selected a portion of the Zinfandel for its "Ridge" label and made a small amount of Zinfandel under the "Lytton Springs" label. The winemaking takes place in Ridge's Santa Cruz Mountain facility. Meanwhile, the former Lytton Springs winery is primarily a sales and tasting room. After 94, the separate Lytton Springs label disappeared.

### Zinfandel

79** 80 81 82** 83*** 84** 85* 86 87*** 88**
89 91* 92 93* 94

*Full-blown, ripe, dense, rich, oaky, tannic, alcoholic; incredible when right, often disastrous when not*

MACROSTIE WINERY    *Sonoma 1988*    After leaving his post as winemaker at Hacienda Winery, where he served from 75 to 87, Steve MacRostie formed his own family wine company. His focus is on Chardonnay grown by Sangiacomo, one of the biggest independent vineyards in the Carneros District. His approach is to whole-cluster press the grapes and then ferment the juice entirely in oak barrels. The wine is aged for several months *sur lie.* In 89 he was a consultant to several winemakers, and moved his own operation into the Roche Vineyards in the southern Carneros. He became the consulting enologist for Roche before its first harvest. MacRostie Chardonnay represents 80% of the winery's 6,000-case-a-year output. Pinot Noir and Merlot both joined the roster in the 90s but results have been less consistently happy than for the winery's Chardonnay.

### Chardonnay

87* 88 89* 90* 91* 92* 93* **94*** **95**** 96*

*Firm fruit and suggestions of complexity in early vintages have continued and give admirable consistency to MacRostie's Chardonnays*

MADRONA VINEYARDS    *El Dorado 1980*    With 35 acres planted along a ridgetop at the 3,000-foot level, Madrona can claim to have vines growing at the highest level in the state. Located 5 miles east of Placerville, the vineyard is owned by Dick Bush, who established it in 73 with the intention of selling all of the crop. When the grape market proved difficult, he built a winery and began making wines in 80. Most of the winery's production is from his own vineyard, which contains Cabernet Sauvignon, Merlot, Cabernet Franc, Zinfandel, Chardonnay, Johannisberg Riesling, and Gewurztraminer. All are made as varietals. On occasion a portion of his Riesling develops *Botrytis* and a late harvest version is produced. Overall the winery has enjoyed modest success. The reds—Cabernet Sauvignon, Zinfandel, and Quintet, a Meritage—are the best bets here. Whatever slight blemishes they may have are nicely compensated for by ripe flavors and modest prices. The winery's annual production target is 10,000 cases.

MAHONEY ESTATES    *Napa 1992*    Francis Mahoney, co-owner of Carneros Creek Winery, created this label for Pinot Noir from one of his favorite parcels, the Las Piedras Vineyard. Located in the Carneros District on the southern edge of Carneros Creek's vineyard, this 4½-acre site, which was planted in 1988, has soils characterized as pure shale, making it extremely well drained. On average Mahoney produces 700 cases, with 1,000 cases a year seen as maximum.

MAISON DEUTZ WINERY    *San Luis Obispo 1981*    A joint venture between Deutz Champagne of France and Beringer Estates, Maison Deutz enjoyed some success with its sparkling wines before the partnership dissolved in 1996. The winery and vineyards are now part of Laetitia Vineyards (see entry). For now, the new owners are keeping Maison Deutz alive as a sparkling wine brand, but production has been drastically reduced as they concentrate on Laetitia.

MANZANITA    *Napa 1980*    This is a label owned by Steve Koster, a longtime resident of Napa Valley who has designed numerous wineries. Using leased space and operating part-time, he has regularly made Napa Valley Chardonnay and Cabernet Sauvignon. Manzanita Chardonnays are 100% barrel-fermented, and about one-third goes through malolactic fermentation. The Cabernet Sauvignon, usually softened with Merlot, is aged for two years in small French oak barrels. On average, Manzanita makes about 1,500 cases of Chardonnay and close to 1,000 cases of Cabernet Sauvignon per year.

MARCASSIN WINERY  *Sonoma 1990*  This small winery located in western Sonoma County is specializing in Chardonnay and Pinot Noir. Its owner-winemaker, Helen Turley, developed a following during stints as winemaker at Stonegate, B. R. Cohn, and Peter Michael Vineyards, where she made some exciting Chardonnays. On her own, she prefers to work with grapes grown in cool climates. She has been buying Chardonnay from the Carneros district and also from the Lorenzo Vineyard near the coastal town of Occidental. The first vintages produced only 250 cases of each; the quality was high. As of the late 90s, Marcassin has been making Pinot Noir and Chardonnay from its own 10-acre vineyard situated in the cool-climate hillsides of the Sonoma Coast.

MARCELINA VINEYARDS  *(Gallo)*  Debuting in 1997, Marcelina represented Gallo's first wines to bear a Napa Valley appellation. Displaying on-target varietal character, both Chardonnay and Cabernet Sauvignon were well received by critics despite being priced slightly on the high side.

MARIETTA CELLARS  *Sonoma 1980*  Heavyweight red wines are the major focus of this owner-operated winery. Winemaker Chris Bilbro, whose family once owned Bandiera, buys grapes from within Sonoma County to produce 10,000 cases a year. The mainstays are Zinfandel and Cabernet Sauvignon, both made in a somewhat rustic style, and a country-style blend, "Old Vine Red." Zinfandel has occasionally earned ° and more. A recent addition to the line, Angeli Cuvee (a blend of Zinfandel with Petite Sirah and Carignane) earned °°° for the 94 vintage.

### Cabernet Sauvignon
81°  82°  83  84  85  **87°**  91  **95°**

*Following the house style, this wine is typically rough, ripe, sometimes hinting at tar, and best suited to burgers and steaks hot off the barbecue*

### Zinfandel
82  83°°°  84  85°  86°  **87°**  **88°**  **90°**  **91**  92  **93°** **94°°**  95

*A berryish version of the Cabernet, it has been enjoyable and attractively priced in better vintages*

MARILYN MERLOT  This play on words, which may seem a tasteless joke to some, is in fact a private label owned by Nova Wine Partners in St. Helena. First made in 85, so far each vintage uses a different photograph of Marilyn Monroe on the label, and the name is written across the label in a lipstick-smear script. Part of the proceeds go to her estate. Except for 87, the wines have carried a Napa Valley appellation, with all grapes originating in the Napa Valley. (When it became difficult to find sufficient Merlot from Napa in 87, wines from the French region of Aude were used.) The annual output has increased to over 5,000 cases.

MARKHAM VINEYARDS  *Napa 1978*  Founder Bruce Markham bought an old, defunct winery north of St. Helena along with some choice acreage in the Yountville area. Within a year the large (1-million-gallon-capacity) winery was cleaned up and ready to crush, both for Markham's own brand and for others on a custom-crush basis. Despite his background in the advertising profession, Markham never really generated much publicity for his own winery. He may have gotten off on the wrong foot by offering high-priced Muscat de Frontignan and Gamay Beaujolais Blanc as his first releases.

One of the primary vineyards Markham purchased was a 100-acre plot in Yountville that came with a rich history. It once belonged to the Van Loben Sels

family, who owned Oakville Vineyards (now defunct) and produced a few exciting Cabernet Sauvignon vintages from 68 to 77. Even though Markham is located
between the frequently visited Charles Krug Winery and Sterling Vineyards, the
plain-looking Markham facility did not attract the attention of tourists until its
major facelift in 89. By then Markham was gone, having sold his winery in early
88 to Mercian of Japan. Markham's annual output had reached 18,000 cases by
80, and stagnated at that level until 88. By the mid-80s, however, the winery was
beginning to earn ° and °° for its Merlots and Cabernet Sauvignons, and by 87
was on a positive course.

Under the new ownership, the vineyards have been expanded. The largest
planting is in Yountville, with all 100 acres now devoted exclusively to Cabernet,
Merlot, and Cabernet Franc. In Napa, the winery has a 70-acre parcel called Hopper Creek Ranch, with Chardonnay and Sauvignon Blanc predominating. In a
sector of Calistoga at moderate warmth and high elevations, the winery has 60
acres under vine, with 49 acres of Cabernet and 11 of Merlot. In order to meet the
demand for Merlot, it has been buying grapes from within Napa Valley. As its annual output hits the 75,000-case mark, halfway to its projected maximum,
Markham is focusing attention on Merlot (blended with Cabernet Sauvignon),
Cabernet Sauvignon, and Chardonnay. Sauvignon Blanc became an important
wine in the 90s. On a limited scale, Markham makes Muscat Blanc, and also two
upscale, Reserve-type wines, Laurent Chardonnay and Limited Red (Meritage).
Glass Mountain (see entry) is Markham's second label. Mercian, Inc., the winery's
owner, is involved in vineyard properties throughout the world and is Japan's
largest wine company.

### Cabernet Sauvignon

78°   79°   80°°   81°°   82°   83°°   **84°°**   **85°°**   **86°°**   87
88   **90°**   **91°**   **92**   **93**

*Once our candidate for the best-kept secret among high-quality Cabernet Sauvi-*
*gnons, inconsistent results in recent years have robbed this often attractive wine of*
*its special cachet*

### Chardonnay

86   87   88   89   90°   91   93°°   94°   95°

*Improved recent results are keyed on clean, oaky, decently fruity wines*

### Merlot

81°°   82   83°   84°   **85°°°**   **86°°**   87   **88°**   89°   90   **91**
**92°**   **93°°**   **94°**

*Attractive ripe, bright, cherrylike fruit, sweetened by a nice touch of oak, comes with*
*just a bit of tannic coarseness to encourage a few years of cellaring without interfer-*
*ing with the wine's early drinkability; 90 was a soft, dull departure from form*

MARTIN BROTHERS WINERY   *San Luis Obispo 1981*   Located east of Paso Robles, the
Martin winery has grown from a tiny renovated dairy barn to a mid-sized, modern facility. Run by the entire Martin family, the winery is surrounded by the
family-owned 70-acre vineyard. Although the volume emphasis has fallen on
White Zinfandel, Chenin Blanc, and Chardonnay over the first several vintages,
the Martins have tried hard to generate interest in Nebbiolo and other Italian
grape varieties. After making their first Nebbiolo in 84 from Amador County, they
have relied on various sources while awaiting full maturity of their own acreage.
The winery currently offers two bottlings of Nebbiolo: a 3,000-case regular bottling with a California appellation, and a 300-case Reserve-style Nebbiolo aged
for two years or more in small oak barrels. The owners have recently been marketing their Zinfandel under the name "Primitivo." Among several unusual offerings, the Martins have been making a high-priced blend of Cabernet Sauvignon
and Sangiovese called "Etrusco," a few hundred cases of Aleatico, and 100 cases
of a Grappa made entirely from Nebbiolo. With the addition of Pinot Grigio and
Sangiovese to the lineup, the Martin Brothers are down to Chardonnay as the

only wine without an obvious Italian connection. Nebbiolo Vechio, the Reserve bottling, is the most fascinating wine, but the Cabernet Etrusco is also unusual and worth exploring. However, the raging sales success at 10,000 cases a year is Moscato Allegro, a low-alcohol, fizzy, very sweet, and apparently widely enjoyed aperitif-style wine. Now making 18,000 cases per year, the winery has set its maximum at 20,000 cases.

MARTINELLI VINEYARDS  *Sonoma 1987*  In the grape-growing profession since 05, the Martinelli family began producing small amounts of wines in 87. Zinfandel, Gewurztraminer, Pinot Noir, and Chardonnay are the primary varieties found in its Russian River Valley vineyard. Planted in 1904, the 4 acres of Zinfandel are located on the steepest hillside (known as Jackass Hill), Martinelli focuses on Chardonnay, Pinot Noir, Gewurztraminer, and Zinfandel, and its annual production is approximately 2,000 cases.

MARTINI & PRATI WINERY  *Sonoma 1881*  One of Sonoma's oldest wineries, Martini & Prati made bulk wines for other producers such as Gallo and Paul Masson until most of its markets dried up in the 1990s. Through a partnership with Associated Vintage Group, which owns Mark West, the winery has been revived as a producer. Though it still houses old redwood tanks and open-top concrete fermenters, the winery is making a variety of wines today, most with an Italian theme. The primary wines are Barbera, Sangiovese, Zinfandel, and a blended red named Sant Elmo. It also encourages guests to fill their own jug bottles at the winery.

LOUIS M. MARTINI WINERY  *Napa 1922*  One of the most revered wine families, the Martinis have always seemed to pride themselves on a low-keyed, no-frills approach to the wine business. From 34, when Louis M. Martini made his first vintage in Napa Valley, to the early 70s, Martini enjoyed a following for its red wines, Cabernet Sauvignons, Zinfandels, and Barberas. In 57 Louis M. turned the reins over to his son, Louis P. Martini, who operated the winery in much the same fashion. Today, his two children, Carolyn and Michael, have taken on full responsibilities as, respectively, president and head winemaker, although the senior Martini remains active in day-to-day operations.

Prior to 80, the winery was producing about 400,000 cases, with strong emphasis on red wines, but to many people it seemed to be resting on its laurels. Martini Cabernet Sauvignons from the 40 s, 50s, and 60s—Special Selection and/or Private Reserve—were held in the same high esteem as Inglenook's and Beaulieu's Cabernets. Martini Cabernets tended to be less intense than the competition, but responded exceptionally well to bottle aging, and in our experiences Martini Cabernets in 51, 57, 58, and 68 Lot 4 rank among the finest tasted. The winery offered three bottlings of Cabernet Sauvignon, the California appellation being the mainstay. For the Special Selection, the winery would set aside the best 10% from a given vintage, while the Private Reserves through the mid-50s often came from the Monte Rosso Vineyard in Sonoma Valley, and thereafter were often Cabernets given extended bottle aging by the winery. After the 70 vintage, the winery's Cabernets failed to keep pace. Martini was also highly regarded for Barbera, an occasional vintage of bone-dry Gewurztraminer, a white varietal known as "Folle Blanche," and for Moscato Amabile, a semi-sparkling wine sold at the winery. The winery produced and bottled the first commercial Merlot (a blend of 68–70) from California.

Despite its record and its honest pricing, the Martini Winery failed to sustain interest after the early 70s. The style of many red wines, derived from aging in large redwood vats, was out of sync with the times. By the end of the 80s, needed changes had been made. All the old redwood cooperage had disappeared, and small oak barrels aging both red and white wines lined the walls. Although Cabernet Sauvignon is still the volume leader, Merlot and Chardonnay follow right behind it. The new Martini offers three categories of table wine. Its modestly priced varietals from Napa Valley, Sonoma County, or North Coast appellations now number a dozen. The Reserve program consists of four Napa Valley varietals—Cabernet Sauvignon, Petite Sirah, Merlot, and Chardonnay. A series of "Vineyard Selection" varietals is at the top end of the price scale and includes Monte Rosso Cabernet Sauvignon, Monte Rosso Gnarly Vines Zinfandel, and Folle Blanche.

Of the winery's 1,000 acres established to vines, over 50% fall within Napa Valley, about 35% in Sonoma County, and the remainder in Lake County. The annual output of varietal wines is 135,000 cases. Martini's recent wines remain low in intensity and in quality, and usually rank as no more than acceptable save for a few special bottlings.

### Cabernet Sauvignon

(Monte Rosso Vineyard) **84°** **85** **87°** 89° **90** 91 **94°** **95°**

*Typically sturdy wines big in structure but not always in fruit*

MASON CELLARS   *Oakville 1993*   With more than 25 years of winemaking experience in the Napa Valley, Randy Mason, who currently oversees activities at Napa Wine Cellars, started his own brand as a serious sideline. It offers Merlot and Sauvignon Blanc from well-established vineyards in the Yountville District. During his 26-year stint with Lakespring Winery, Mason made Sauvignon Blanc from the Yount Mill Vineyard. His experience has paid off, as his own Sauvignon Blanc from this vineyard has reached * levels. Annual output consists of 4,000 cases of Sauvignon Blanc and 1,500 of Merlot.

MASSON VINEYARDS   *Monterey 1852*   Paul Masson founded his winery in Saratoga, part of today's Santa Cruz Mountain appellation. He developed a brand that was among the best known in California, both during his reign and long after his death. Known as Paul Masson Vineyards, the original mountain winery was purchased by Joseph E. Seagram in 43, and under its ownership production was expanded to a full line of table (varietal and generic), fortified, and sparkling wines. Concentrating on nonvintaged table wines in the 60s, Masson offered consistency but rarely great quality. Annual output grew to close to 8 million cases, as Seagram augmented production by operating a large facility in Soledad in Monterey County, even larger facilities in the Central Valley, and maintained both its modern Champagne Cellars and historic mountain winery in Saratoga.

By the mid-80s, Masson owned 4,500 acres of vineyards in Monterey County, and was turning out a line of varietals from Monterey that failed to win any kind of following. In 87 Vintners International acquired Masson, along with Taylor California Cellars and Taylor of New York. Shortly thereafter, all Masson operations were shifted to Soledad and to a large production facility in Madera. By the end of the 80s, the management had gone through some reshuffling and had sold all of the original vineyards. The winery purchases most grapes under contract, and the present Vintners International partnership brings 1,500 acres in Monterey into the fold. The lion's share of the business remains generic bottlings, including 600,000 cases of wines in Masson's carafe container. The present owner is the Canandaigua Wine Co., California's second largest. Overall, annual sales are close to 3.5 million cases.

MATANZAS CREEK WINERY   *Sonoma 1977*   From very modest beginnings (3,000 cases made in a converted barn in 77) Matanzas Creek has grown moderately in size and exponentially in reputation. In 74, 22 acres were planted to Chardonnay and Merlot in what was then a remote part of Sonoma County called the Bennett Valley, midway between Santa Rosa and Kenwood. Initial success with Chardonnay encouraged the owners, Sandra and Bill MacIver, to add 20 acres of Chardonnay and some Cabernet Sauvignon. After a few vintages and a change in winemakers, Matanzas Creek dropped its erratic Pinot Noir and by 84, with production up to 8,000 cases, it constructed a new, ultra-modern winery with a much greater production capacity. Having earned °°° for its Chardonnays and critical acclaim for its Sauvignon Blancs, the winery, to the surprise of many, made a major commitment to Merlot by phasing out its Cabernet production. Today, three varietal wines are made. Chardonnay, in a barrel-fermented style, is the most important, with 18,500 cases produced. Sauvignon Blanc (about 8,500 cases), aged in oak and usually blended with Semillon, is a trendsetter with the complexity and balance to earn ° regularly and °° on occasion. It also has some aging potential. Merlot (5,000 cases) is usually blended with Cabernet Franc and Cabernet Sauvignon, and then aged in new French oak. Future increases in annual output will likely be in Merlot. In 1990 Matanzas Creek selected nine barrels of Chardonnay for extended aging and special treatment. That wine was labeled "Journey" and, retailing for $70 a bottle, was the most expensive Chardonnay ever. "Journey" has evolved to include a comparably rare (144 cases total), expensive ($125 a bottle), and extraordinary Merlot.

### Chardonnay

86°° 87°°° 88°° 89° **90° 91° 92°° 93°° 94°** 95 96°

*Enormous depth of flavor, showing ripe, appley fruit, augmented by rich, toasty oak with balance provided by ample acidity; medium-length aging potential*

### Merlot

82° 83°° 85 **86° 87°° 88°** 89 **90°° 91°° 92°°°**
**93°° 94°° 95°**

*Typically on the very ripe side and often including nuances of brush, herbs, and cocoa to deep fruit; extraordinary track record*

MAYACAMAS VINEYARDS   *Napa 1941*   A good choice as the prototype of the boutique winery, Mayacamas began to assume its present shape in 41, when Jack and Mary Taylor bought a long-abandoned stone winery and distillery, both built in 1889. Jack Taylor was an executive with Shell Oil, and he and his wife wanted a simpler lifestyle. An old vineyard was planted to Pinot Noir and Chardonnay along extra-wide terraces on the steep hillsides. Situated on the slopes of Mount Veeder at the 2,000-foot elevation level, the vineyard proved difficult to farm and experienced low yields owing to deer and bird damage. After some success with their Chardonnays, the Taylors gave up on Pinot Noir and planted Cabernet Sauvignon. For several vintages in the 60s, Philip Togni was the winemaker at Mayacamas.

By 68, weary of the pace, the Taylors sold the winery to Bob and Elinor Travers, owners ever since. The winemaker for them in 68–72 was Bob Sessions, who went on to work at Hanzell. The Traverses have expanded the vineyard to 55 acres and concentrate on Cabernet Sauvignon and Chardonnay, along with limited amounts of Sauvignon Blanc, Pinot Noir, Zinfandel, and Merlot. A late harvest Zinfandel appears every now and then. About 2,000 cases of Cabernet Sauvignon are made each year. Mayacamas Cabernet is 100% varietal and usually tannic. During the 70s its Cabernets enjoyed a well-deserved following, but they have not been among the quality leaders in recent vintages. Mayacamas also makes about 1,000 cases of barrel-fermented Chardonnay. Most of the winery's production is sold through a mailing list and the winery has dropped out of the ranks of the top producers.

### Cabernet Sauvignon

70°° **73°° 74°°** 78 **79° 80 81°** 82 84 85 86 88
90

*Even now, older Mayacamas wines are among the best of their vintages; sadly, the winery's more recent efforts have lacked the fruit to bring the wine into focus and, as a result, it has lost a good deal of standing among top producers*

MAYO FAMILY WINERY   *Sonoma Valley 1993*   This small-scale family winery makes 2,000 cases a year and sells most of it from the sales room. Mayo offers Chardonnay, Pinot Noir, Zinfandel, Merlot, and Cabernet Sauvignon.

MAZZOCCO VINEYARDS  *Sonoma 1984*  Dr. Thomas Mazzocco is a famous eye surgeon practicing on the West Coast who acquired an 18-acre vineyard in the Alexander Valley. This vineyard is named River Lane, and contains 18 acres of Chardonnay. Another vineyard in the Dry Creek Valley has 13 acres planted to Cabernet Sauvignon and its blending varieties. Through 1990 Mazzocco was earning high praise for its "Dry Creek" Zinfandels. The winery was on a fast course to produce 35,000 cases a year when Dr. Mazzocco decided to sell it in 90 to Vintech, an investment firm that went out of business within a year. In 91 Mazzocco bought his winery back and decided to scale the operation down to 15,000 cases a year. About 50% of the total output is "River Lane" Chardonnay, with Zinfandel holding steady at 4,000 cases and Cabernet Sauvignon at 2,000 per year. "Matrix," a red Meritage bottling of 1,000 cases, is from the estate vineyards, as is the winery's 300-case bottling of Merlot. Recently, several single-vineyard Zinfandels from the Dry Creek and Alexander Valley regions are made in 100–200-case lots.

### Cabernet Sauvignon

**86°  87°°  88  89  91°°  92  93**

*Following a ripe, rich style, with both depth and tannins for medium-term aging, the wine leans toward fullness without sacrificing balance*

### Chardonnay

(River Lane Vineyard)  86  87°  88°°  89  91°  **92°**  93  **94°  95°**  96

*Well-balanced, appley fruit, and noticeable oak*

### Zinfandel

86°°°  **87°°°  88°°**  90  91  92  93  94  95

*After early successes, the wines have been less deep*

---

PETER MCCOY VINEYARDS  *Sonoma 1984*  McCoy, a CPA in San Francisco, has reserved a place for himself in history as the first to make Chardonnay from the Knights Valley appellation. Beginning in 80, he planted 15 acres on rocky soils and dubbed that vineyard Clos des Pierres. The Chardonnays are 100% barrel-fermented in French oak. When the vineyard reaches full maturity, McCoy's production will peak at 3,500 cases.

### Chardonnay

84°  86°°  87°  88°  90°  92°  93°

*Lots of toasty oak from barrel fermentation is positioned atop solid, deep varietal fruit, while ample acidity assures both balance and ageworthiness*

---

MCDOWELL VALLEY VINEYARDS  *Mendocino 1979*  In 70 Richard and Karen Keehn purchased a large ranch situated 4 miles east of Hopland. It was their intention to develop a vineyard and sell the fruit. Within a few years they had not only developed the original vineyard site but had also expanded it to over 300 acres. For several years they sold their grapes, but in early 79 they decided to start their own winery. The varieties grown and made into wines changed with the times.

In 81 the Petite Sirah, which consisted of 36 acres, was identified by experts as the French Syrah, giving McDowell one of the oldest and largest plantings of Syrah in the state. In 82 they began labeling their wine "Syrah." A new winemaker hired in 85 experimented with Grenache and Syrah, and with newly planted Rhone varieties—Mourvedre, Marsanne, and Viognier. By 89 McDowell was producing modest amounts of wines made from Rhone varieties.

With annual production topping 125,000 cases, the winery was not very profitable. In 1994 the Keehns sold the facility and the surrounding 36 acres to the Associated Vintage Group, a custom-winemaking company, and since then that firm has been custom-making McDowell's line of Rhone wines. McDowell's acreage has been replanted in the 90s and now consists of 125 acres total, led by Syrah (66 acres) and Viognier (26 acres). Its major wines are Syrah (blended with

Viognier), Viognier, Grenache, and Marsanne. With annual production at 25,000 cases, McDowell makes both a Mendocino Syrah (14,000 cases) and an Estate Syrah (2,500 cases). Both are better than anything seen from McDowell in the more traditional varieties.

### Cabernet Sauvignon

81° 82° 83° 86 87 88 89 91 94

*Early vintages showed good fruit and depth, but later wines have been more ordinary and not worth following*

### Chardonnay

86 87 88 90° 91 92

*The winery has experienced limited success with wines that are thin and mildly fruity with floral overtones; the home-grown version is noticeably oaky*

---

MCHENRY VINEYARD *Santa Cruz 1980* After retiring in 74 from his position as Chancellor of the University of California at Santa Cruz, Dean McHenry tended to his 4-acre vineyard adjacent to his home in the Santa Cruz Mountains. Beginning in 77, with the help of his family, he became a home winemaker and won several awards. With his son Henry McHenry, a professor from U.C. Davis, serving as winemaker, they went pro in 80, making a total of 300 cases. At 3.3 acres of Pinot Noir and 1 acre of Chardonnay, the winery's maximum annual output will remain below 500 cases. Most of the output is sold at the winery located on Bonny Doon Road or at retail in the San Francisco Bay Area. Both wines reach ° status on occasion.

---

THE MEEKER VINEYARD *Sonoma 1984* On a 215-acre ranch in the Dry Creek Valley, Los Angeles attorney and investor Charles Meeker has set up his small winery. With a 60-acre vineyard on the hillsides in northwestern Dry Creek, Meeker is producing Zinfandel, Cabernet Sauvignon, and Chardonnay. Zinfandel has emerged as the leader, with both a regular and a Reserve-type "Gold Leaf" bottling. Cabernet Sauvignon, Chardonnay, and a generic red blend fill out the line. Annual production remains steady at 3,500 cases.

### Cabernet Sauvignon

84° 85° 86 87 90 91°

*Bold, ripe, immensely tannic wines requiring long aging are the rule here, but the fruit seems unlikely to measure up to the demands of a decade or more of cellar aging*

### Zinfandel

(Dry Creek Valley) 84°° 85° 86° 87 88 89 90 91° 92° 93° 94

*Like the other Meeker wines, this one is made in a no-holds-barred style featuring ripeness and oak in abundance; it can be among the better examples of Dry Creek Zinfandel, but occasionally needs more depth to match its abrasive tannins*

---

MENDOCINO HILLS VINEYARDS *Mendocino 1989* Dick Sherwin owned Lytton Springs Winery for many years. Before selling it to Ridge in 91, he also produced Cabernet Sauvignon from a vineyard he owns in the Hopland area of Mendocino County. He retained the vineyard, and created this label for his Cabernet Sauvignon. Over the first vintages it was made in a rugged, tannic style but with enough deep fruit to provide balance. Annual production remains at 2,000 cases.

---

MER SOLEIL *Monterey 1992* Chuck Wagner, whose family owns Caymus Vineyards, dropped Napa Valley Chardonnay from the roster some years ago, but he never gave up the idea of making Chardonnay from another region. His search for a special site eventually brought him to Monterey, where he purchased a 43-acre vineyard and an old farmhouse in the Santa Lucia Mountains. After converting the barn into a winery, Wagner produced 1,200 cases of full-bodied, barrel-fermented Chardonnay in his first vintage. His goal is to expand Chardonnay production to 5,000 cases a year. His wines were first called "Mer et Soleil."

### Chardonnay

93°°°   94°°   95°

*Rich, fairly deep, appley and slightly citrusy wines with a full complement of toasty oak*

---

MEREDITH VINEYARD ESTATE   *Russian River Valley 1997*   After 25 years of making wines for many leading wineries (Mount Eden, Matanzas Creek, and Laurier) Merry Edwards is doing what she has always wanted to do: make limited amounts of Pinot Noir her way. Her way involves planting a special site (southeast-facing slopes) in the Russian River Valley. Teaming up with partner Bill Bourke, she planted the 24-acre vineyard to several Dijon clones, the Swan clone, and the Mount Eden selection she isolated and propagated in the late 1970s. The early vintages are being made from some of the finest local vineyards, but eventually the 2,400-case annual output of Pinot Noir will be entirely estate-grown.

---

MERIDIAN CELLARS   *San Luis Obispo 1984*   Chuck Ortman, one of the first young winemakers to make a name for himself in the 70s, owned this brand before selling it to Nestlé in 88. After buying the former Estrella River Winery facility in Paso Robles, but not the brand, and 560 acres of vineyards, Nestlé hired Ortman to be the winemaker and acquired the name Meridian in the deal. In the 60s, Ortman began his career at Heitz Cellars, and then moved on to become winemaker for Spring Mountain Winery. With them, he was responsible for several fine vintages of Chardonnay, Cabernet Sauvignon, and unusually rich Sauvignon Blancs. Ortman left Spring Mountain and then consulted to several wineries—Far Niente, Shafer, Fisher, Keenan, and Cain—before starting Meridian in 84. With the new Meridian, Ortman began by making two Chardonnays, Edna Valley and Santa Barbara County. The first vintages yielded close to 30,000 cases total. As the name gains recognition, the winery will expand production to 100,000 cases a year. Chardonnay dominates the volume, but Cabernet Sauvignon, Syrah, and Pinot Noir are also being made by Meridian. In general, Meridian wines offer immediate appeal and are attractively priced. The Reserve Chardonnay and Pinot Noir sometimes rise to star levels, and the fruit-filled Syrah is worth checking out.

### Chardonnay

| (Santa Barbara County) | 88° | 90 | 91° | 92 | 93 | 94 | 95 | 96° |
|---|---|---|---|---|---|---|---|---|
| (Edna Valley) | 88° | 89° | 90° | 91° | 92° | 93 | **94°** | **95°** | **96°** |

*The less expensive Santa Barbara County bottling has lacked the medium-depth fruit which has generally shown up in the Edna Valley wine*

### Pinot Noir

90°   91   92°   94   95°   96

*Direct, moderately fruity, easy-drinking and priceworthy when successful*

---

MERRYVALE VINEYARDS   *Napa 1983*   Founded by five partners, three in real estate and two in the wine business, Merryvale burst onto the scene with great promise. Merryvale was the brainchild of partner Bill Harlan, who in addition to developing and owning offices in San Francisco also owns the Meadowood Club in St. Helena, a resort which is home to the annual Napa Valley wine auction. Jack Schlatter, a Swiss entrepreneur, became sole owner in 96 after Harlan left to begin Harlan Estate (see entry). The winery's 30-acre vineyard contains Cabernet, Merlot, and other Bordeaux varieties. The roster is currently headed by Profile, a red Meritage, and Silhouette, its limited-edition Chardonnay. An impressive line of Reserve bottlings includes Chardonnay, Cabernet Sauvignon, and Merlot. Starmont Chardonnay, Hillside Cabernet Sauvignon, and Vignette (white Meritage) are more widely available wines and represent almost 50% of the winery's 45,000-case annual production.

### Cabernet Sauvignon

**88  90°°  91°°  92  93°°  94°°**

*This wine has shown deeper fruit than Merryvale's "Profile," which is also Cabernet-based*

### Chardonnay

(regular bottling/Starmont)   86   87   88°   89   90   91°
92   93   94°   95   96

(Reserve)   90   **91°°**   92   93   94°

*No shrinking violet, this brashly oaked, tight, but solidly fruity wine will appeal to fans of expansive Chardonnays; the Reserve offers even more of the same*

### Merlot

**89°°  90°°  91**  92  93  **94°°  95°°**

*Generally fruity, rich and moderately tannic, it stumbled in 92*

### Red Table Wine Profile

**83°°°**  84  **85°**  **86**  **87°**  **88°**  89  **90**  **91**  **92**  94°°

*Somewhat inconsistent to date but never lacking for size, this one can be wonderfully fruity and full of rich oak at its best; even in lesser years, it has the capability to improve for up to a decade in the bottle*

---

PETER MICHAEL WINERY   *Sonoma 1988*   In the early 80s, London-born businessman Peter Michael acquired vacation property on a knoll overlooking the Knight's Valley. In 84 he was encouraged to develop a vineyard which is located at the 1,700–2,000-foot-elevation level. Cabernet, Merlot, and Cabernet Franc were the main varieties planted in the 23-acre site. In 88, 25 additional acres of the same varieties were developed. Chardonnay from the Gauer Ranch in the Alexander Valley was the first wine to be released. Made in the traditional Burgundian manner—barrel fermentation in new oak—the inaugural Chardonnay release was a °°° success. A new winemaking facility with several unusual touches was fully operational by 89. The winery was divided into two separate sections, one for red winemaking, the other for Chardonnay. A special barrel-fermentation room controls both the temperature and the humidity for Chardonnay production and aging. The winery has produced blockbuster Chardonnays from Howell Mountain in Napa Valley and from the Alexander Valley, a bottling labeled "Mon Plaisir." It has also been making a Sauvignon Blanc from Howell Mountain. Through long-term contracts with the Gauer Vineyard in Alexander Valley, and Morelli Vineyard, a new vineyard it developed in western Sonoma, Peter Michael is offering six single-vineyard Chardonnays. Mon Plaisir, Cuvée Indigene, and Point Rouge are Chardonnays from parts of the Gauer Ranch, and Belle Côte, La Carrière, and Morelli Vineyard are from estate vineyards. The only red, Les Pavots, a Meritage blend favoring Cabernet Sauvignon, is from the estate vineyard. Annual production is approaching 12,000 cases.

### Cabernet Sauvignon

(Les Pavots)   88   89   90   **91°**   **92°**   **93°°**   95

*Very tough wines in want of much bigger fruit in most vintages*

### Chardonnay

87°°°   **88°°**   **90°°**   91   92°   93   **94°°**

*Debuting with one of the best Chardonnays in years, and following with an impressive second wine, this producer will be one to watch; the wines to date have been rich, complex, deep, and fairly pretty; 91 had everything but the fruit*

---

MICHEL–SCHLUMBERGER   *Sonoma 1987*   Founder Jean-Jacques Michel, an investment banker originally from Switzerland, purchased land and began developing 50 acres of vineyards in the western Dry Creek Valley. About half of the total acreage is devoted to Chardonnay; the rest is planted to Cabernet Sauvignon (14 acres),

Merlot (8 acres), and Cabernet Franc (4 acres). The rather elaborate Mediterranean-style wine facility and adjoining estate were fully operative by the 86 harvest, while wines from 84 and 85 were made at another winery. A change in winemakers occurred in 89. By the early 90s it was making close to 15,000 cases of Cabernet Sauvignon and 10,000 cases of Chardonnay. However, even after the recent addition of a Merlot and a Reserve Cabernet Sauvignon to its roster, this winery remained an underachiever over its first decade. In 93, Jacques Schlumberger, whose family produces wines in Alsace, took over as majority owner and immediately changed the winery's name, but to date, results have not improved.

### Cabernet Sauvignon

84°  86°  87  88  89°  90  91  92  93  94

*Typically blended with 15% Merlot and 10% Cabernet Franc, the wine has been moderately fruity and quietly oaked; aging potential has been a plus*

---

MIETZ CELLARS  *Sonoma 1989*  Keith Meitz, a member of the Santa Rosa Fire Department, began growing grapes as a sideline in the early 80s. Today he has his main vineyard in the Russian River Valley and a smaller one in Dry Creek Valley. Merlot and Cabernet predominate, but Meitz has added Cabernet Franc for blending. Most of the crop from his 20-acre vineyard is sold, with Merlot the only wine made by Meitz. Usually blended with Cabernet Sauvignon and Cabernet Franc, his Merlots have enjoyed some critical success. In a few years, the winery's annual output will level off at 2,400 cases.

### Merlot

89  90°  91°  93  94°

*Ripe, somewhat narrow, oaky and fairly tannic wines*

---

MILANO WINERY  *Mendocino 1977*  Located in Hopland, Milano is a compact winery that is a refurbished hop kiln. Over its first few vintages, the winery offered an array of wines from Mendocino and Sonoma County appellations with variable quality results. In 80 the ownership was restructured, and the winery came into the control of the Milone family. Jim Milone is both director of operations and winemaker and is emphasizing Chardonnay, Cabernet Sauvignon, and Zinfandel. Production, due to slow sales, has since been reduced to 2,000 cases, though the owners plan to work their way back to 5,000 cases a year. All wines offered are produced from the family's 60-acre vineyard, located a short distance from the winery.

---

MILAT VINEYARDS  *Napa 1986*  Brothers Bob and Mike Milat, longtime residents of St. Helena, own a 22-acre vineyard established in the late 40 s. They were content to sell their grapes to local wineries until the mid-80s. After seeing so many of their BMW-driving customers become successful wine producers, they decided to join in. A cozy winery and tasting room were built close to the wine road a little south of St. Helena. Their marketing plan was to sell all wines direct from the centrally located winery. As the output grew to 2,500 cases, they focused on White Zinfandel, Chenin Blanc (below 1% sugar), Sauvignon Blanc, Chardonnay, and Cabernet Sauvignon.

---

MILL CREEK VINEYARDS  *Sonoma 1974*  Located at the southern end of the Dry Creek Valley 5 miles due west of Healdsburg, Mill Creek is owned and operated by the Kreck family. The Krecks first planted vines in 65, and the family vineyard, always weighted toward Cabernet Sauvignon, now covers 75 acres. In 77 the first harvest from young Cabernet vines yielded a wine so light in color that it was bottled and dubbed "Cabernet Blush." When the blush wine era arrived in full, Mill Creek had the trademark rights to the Blush name and was paid royalties by those using it. By 82 the winery had been expanded to include a visitors facility and picnic grounds. The winery sells a high percentage of its 15,000-case annual output direct from the tasting room.

A full line of table wine is made, including five reds (Cabernet Sauvignon, Zinfandel, Merlot, Pinot Noir, and Old Mill Red) and three whites (Chardonnay, Sauvignon Blanc, and Gewurztraminer). The inconsistency that characterized Mill Creek in the 80s has given way to a line of wines featuring correct varietal character in the whites and an attractive fruit-driven Merlot. The Merlot along with the Sauvignon Blanc and Chardonnay have often stood out as good-value wines.

MIRABELLE   *(Schramsberg Vineyards)*   In the early 90s the once-staid Schramsberg Vineyards aggressively launched several new types of sparkling wine. Mirabelle represents Schramsberg's foray into the world of mid-priced bubbly. Produced from Pinot Noir and Chardonnay and made by the *méthode champenoise,* both the Brut and Brut Rosé are non-vintage wines bottled under the North Coast appellation. The early bottlings of the Rosé offered more freshness and appeal, and were more of a real bargain.

MIRASSOU VINEYARDS   *Santa Clara 1966*   A family winery that is now run by the fifth generation, Mirassou produced bulk wines for decades. Since entering the bottled-wine world in 66, the winery has grown to the 350,000-case-per-year level. It has not reached that level easily or without experiencing serious setbacks along the way. With the winemaking facility located in the Evergreen area south of San Jose, the winery maintains 200 acres of vineyards within Santa Clara County and has another 600 acres under vine in northern Monterey County. Most of the vineyard land once owned or leased by the winery was giving over to houses in the early 60s. In 66–67, the Mirassous began developing vineyards in Monterey to supply anticipated needs. Throughout the 70s and even into the early 80s, the Mirassous continued making red wines that were not always acceptable and correct.

In recent years the winery has changed its vineyard focus by removing Zinfandel and some of its Cabernet from Monterey. Buying some fruit from Napa Valley, it has begun to offer Cabernet Sauvignon with a California appellation and Merlot from the Central Coast. Its production level breaks down into 70% white wines, 20% reds, and 10% sparkling wine. The volume leader is White Zinfandel, followed by Chardonnay, Monterey Riesling, and White Burgundy. The latter, often a good value, is made predominantly from Pinot Blanc. The *méthode champenoise* sparkling wines are beginning to earn recommendations after years of erratic performance.

Beginning in 89, Mirassou sparkling wines have been made in a separate facility. Over the years the special designation for limited-volume table wines has been "Harvest Reserve," but until recently only an occasional Pinot Noir and Chardonnay bottling lived up to that title; in the 90s, Mirassou's regular and Reserve Chardonnays have earned above-average quality ratings. The winery has set 500,000 cases a year as its maximum production level for all wines.

### Chardonnay

(Monterey County)   84   85   86   87   88°   89   90°   91   93   94   95

(Harvest Reserve)   89   90°   91°°   92°°   93   94   95°°

*The Monterey County wine carries quiet suggestions of flowers and pears in a balanced but rarely inviting presentation; the Harvest Reserve has more intensity and character, and has been Mirassou's best wine for some time now.*

CHARLES B. MITCHELL VINEYARDS   *El Dorado 1993*   Like many wineries in the foothills, Mitchell sells a high percentage of wine direct to visitors. With 20 acres planted, Mitchell purchases additional tonnage to produce over a dozen different wines. The top-sellers are his Reserve Petite Sirah, Euphoria (barrel fermented Sauvignon Blanc), Merlot, and Zinfandel. Annual output is steady at 12,000 cases.

C. K. MONDAVI WINES   *(Charles Krug Winery)*   This label covers a large-volume line of low-priced varietals—Chenin Blanc, Sauvignon Blanc, Chardonnay, Zinfandel, and Cabernet Sauvignon. The roster is headed by Chardonnay and Cabernet. Annual sales are now level at 500,000 cases.

---

ROBERT MONDAVI WINERY    *Napa 1966*    After being forced out of Charles Krug Winery, a winery owned by his family, Robert Mondavi formed his own company in 66 and built a new winery in Oakville. At first he worked with his son Michael, but within a year he was joined by his other son, Tim, and his daughter Marcie. Robert was able to finance the development and start-up operation through a 50–50 partnership with Rainier Brewing Company of Seattle. The winery at the time was the first new one built in Napa Valley since Prohibition, and was also to become known as an ultra-modern, highly experimental, high-tech facility. All tanks for fermentation and storage have always been monitored by computer, and Mondavi conducted untold experiments in what evolved into a winery within a winery experimental lab.

The use of oak was a subject of endless experiments, and the winery was soon overflowing with barrels of all sizes from every known cooper in the world. Early in its history, the Robert Mondavi Winery rescued Sauvignon Blanc from oblivion by popularizing a dry, oak-aged style under the name Fumé Blanc. In 78, Rainier's interest was purchased and the winery became a wholly owned family project. Shortly thereafter the winery's production reached 350,000 cases, and it owned 1,000 acres of vineyards adjacent to the winery and in other Napa Valley sites. In 79 Mondavi revamped an older winery in Woodbridge, near Lodi, and transferred the production of his lower-priced line of Cabernet Sauvignon, Sauvignon Blanc, Chardonnay, and White Zinfandel. These wines evolved from a trio of table wines (red, white, and rosé) introduced in 75. They are currently labeled "Robert Mondavi Woodbridge" (see entry). Opus One (see entry) was yet another Mondavi project that became a reality in 79.

Amidst amazing expansion marked by the uncanny promotional knack of its proprietor, Robert Mondavi Winery earned worldwide recognition for its wines, especially the Cabernet Sauvignon. Now making both a regular and Reserve (the initial vintages were labeled "Unfiltered"), Mondavi has fiddled with the style of each Cabernet bottling over the years. By the mid-80s the regular Cabernet was styled to be varietally correct, early maturing, and attractive to restaurateurs, whereas the Reserve Cabernets had become fatter and more ageworthy. However, Pinot Noir, both regular and Reserve versions, demonstrated great improvement. Robert Mondavi Chardonnays have been generally consistent, but ironically, Fumé Blanc, once the winery's flagship, has been less successful of late, although the Reserve Fumé Blanc remains among the very best of the type.

The Mondavi roster today is greatly reduced in the number of varietals offered, but the winery tends to make each varietal under multiple designations/appellations. Wines currently marketed made from Sauvignon Blanc grapes are Fumé Blanc, Reserve Fumé Blanc from To-Kalon Vineyard and a Sauvignon Blanc from Stag's Leap, which was first offered in 1993. There are three Chardonnays and three Pinot Noirs: Napa Valley, Carneros, and Reserve. Cabernet bottlings are also a trio: Napa Valley, Reserve, and Stags Leap. As of now only one Zinfandel and one Merlot are bottled. Beginning in 1986, Mondavi bottled his Reserve Cabernet unfiltered, and as of now, the winery is bottling almost all of its wines unfiltered. Also, about 50% of Mondavi's Chardonnays are fermented by native yeast. A small sparkling wine program got under way with the debut of a long-aged Brut Reserve and Brut Chardonnay. The winery's leading wine in volume is Chardonnay at 200,000 cases, followed by Cabernet Sauvignon at 100,000 cases. With annual production close to 500,000 cases, Mondavi purchases about half of all the grapes it crushes. A vineyard in the Carneros was established in 88, and brought 480 acres (mostly of Pinot Noir and Chardonnay) into the fold. All told, Mondavi now owns about 1,500 acres in the Napa Valley and controls another 1,000 acres. Included in its Napa holdings are 400 acres of Cabernet Sauvignon. Mondavi also owns close to 500 acres in Santa Barbara County. In 93, the winery went public with a stock offering to raise money for redevelopment; however, the Mondavi family retains 72% ownership and 95% of voting control. Other California wineries owned by Robert Mondavi or his family are Byron Winery, Opus One (50%), and Robert Mondavi–Woodbridge. The winery also produces Mondavi "Coastal" wines, a line of varietals made from Mondavi's 1,800 acres of vineyards in Santa Barbara and Monterey. Sales of Robert Mondavi Coastal Wines exceed 700,000 cases a year. The former Vichon Winery in Oakville now houses La Famiglia di Robert Mondavi, a 25,000-case-a-year line featuring Barbera, Sangiovese, Pinot Grigio, Tocai, and other wines of Italian descent. In the late 1990s, Mondavi Winery went to France to produce a line of French varietals labeled Vichon Mediterranean, and within two years sales were pushing 500,000 cases. A joint venture between Mondavi and Frescobaldi of Italy has given birth to Luce and Lucente, red wines from Montalcino. A similar partnership with Caliterra of Chile resulted in the creation of Sena, a high-priced Chilean Cabernet Sauvignon.

### Cabernet Sauvignon

(regular bottling)  68°°  70°°  73°  74°°  75°  76  77  78  79°  80  81  82  **83°**  **84°**  **85°**  **86°**  **87°**  **88**  89°  **90°°**  91  **92°**  **93°**  **94°**  **95°**

*Among the best Cabernets in the early 70s, this wine has been made in a softer, more drinkable style for over a decade now; it retains generally attractive fruit, has a softly oaky veneer, and carries moderate tannins*

### Cabernet Sauvignon

(Reserve)  71°°  73°°°  74°°°  75°°  76°°  77°°  78°  79°°  **80°°**  **81°°**  **82°°**  **83°°**  **84°°**  **85°°**  **86°°°**  **87°°**  **88°°**  **89°°**  **90°°**  **91°°**  **92°°**  **93°**  **94°°°**  **95°**

*Rich, refined, balanced wines, deep in curranty and ripe cherry fruitiness and sporting lots of creamy oak, these attractively supple wines are buttressed by plentiful but never overwhelming tannins, and are among the most elegant offerings within Cabernet's upper echelons*

### Chardonnay

(Napa Valley)  86°  87°  88  89  90  91  92  93  94  95
(Carneros)  **91°**  **92°**  **93°°**  **94°**  **95°**

*Limited in fruit and limited in range, this small-hearted Chardonnay wins few friends; the Carneros has a bit firmer style and decidedly more depth than the Napa Valley bottling*

### Chardonnay

(Reserve)  84°°  85°°  86  87°°°  88°°°  89  **90°**  **91°**  92  **93°°**  **94°°**  **95°**

*Round, mouth-filling, deeply drawn wines, these complex Chardonnays combine appley fruit with oaky and roasted-grain notes; superb balance will keep the best efforts in good shape for many years of cellaring*

### Merlot

**89°**  **90**  **91°**  92  **93**  **94°**  **95°**

*Nicely polished Merlot varietal fruit with cherryish and slightly herbal character*

### Pinot Noir

(regular bottling)  80°  81°  82°  83°°  84°°  85°  86  **87°**  **88**  **89°**  **90**  **91°**

(Reserve)  80  81°°  82°°  83°°  84°  86  **87°°**  **88°°**  **89°**  **90°°**  **91°°°**  **92°**  **93**  **94°**  **95**

*Somewhat closer in character and style than the other Mondavi pairings, these wines are supple, somewhat velvety, and balanced; both have cherry and black-cherry fruit and rich oak. The Reserve is clearly the deeper and longer-lasting, often with more range*

ROBERT MONDAVI WOODBRIDGE    *(Robert Mondavi Winery)*    In the 80s this label experienced rapid growth and for several years was the cash cow keeping the Robert Mondavi clan happily together. All wines are produced in Woodbridge, far away from Napa Valley, where the winery can draw from Lodi and other high-yielding vineyard districts. With production close to 5 million cases annually, Chardonnay, Cabernet Sauvignon, and Sauvignon Blanc, all subtitled "Barrel-Aged," drive the line. Zinfandel, regular and blush, and Chenin Blanc are also bottled.

MONT ST. JOHN CELLARS    *Napa 1979*    The Bartolucci family, owners of the Mont St. John Cellars and the estate vineyard known as Madonna Vineyards, is one of the old and most important families in Napa Valley. In 22, the family acquired a winery and 24 acres of vineyards offered through an auction. After Prohibition, it operated the Madonna Winery, which at one time was the 12th largest in California. In 71, confronted by "an offer they could not refuse," the Bartoluccis sold the winery and vineyard in Oakville, and the buyers started the ill-fated but often exciting Oakville Vineyards. Afterwards, Buck Bartolucci used his share of the proceeds to buy 160 acres in Los Carneros. Over the next few years, he developed new vineyards, and ended up with 140 acres planted.

By 79 Buck and his father had built a small winery in Los Carneros. During the 80s the Bartoluccis sold most grapes, notably their Pinot Noir and Chardonnay, to the likes of Acacia, Robert Mondavi, and Joseph Phelps. For years both Acacia and Bargetto made a Pinot Noir, Madonna Vineyard, from Bartolucci's grapes. As its own wine producer, Mont St. John Cellars expanded gradually, and by 90 was at the 15,000-case-a-year mark. It has shown promise at times with Pinot Noir and with recent vintages of Cabernet. Chardonnay represents about one-third of the winery's total production, with Cabernet Sauvignon and Pinot Noir combining for one-third. All other varietals—Gewurztraminer, Johannisberg Riesling, and Muscat—are made in lots of 500 cases and are available primarily at the winery. The annual output will level off at 22,000 cases.

MONTHAVEN VINEYARDS    *1993*    Representing the top of the line for Golden State Vintners, a large Central Valley company that operates a large production facility in Napa Valley, Monthaven is a line of modestly priced Napa wines made at the company's St. Helena facility. So far Monthaven's Chardonnay, Cabernet Sauvignon, and Sauvignon Blanc have all offered fairly good value.

MONTE VOLPE VINEYARDS    *Mendocino 1990*    Winemaker Greg Graziano (Domaine Saint Gregory) has teamed with vineyardist Lowell Stone to produce a line of Italian-type wines. Located in Talmage, Stone's vineyard is named Fox Hill, which in Italian is Monte Volpe. It contains an old parcel established to Nebbiolo, and the partners have added Sangiovese and Pinot Grigio as well as a few acres of Barbera, Dolcetto, and Tocai Friulano, an obscure white grape native to Northern Italy. Early vintages of Barbera and a Moscato have met with critical success. Monte Volpe's annual output will grow from its initial 2,000-case total to a maximum of 5,000 cases.

MONTEREY PENINSULA WINERY    *Monterey 1974*    Founded by two dentists in the Monterey Bay area, this winery developed something of a maverick reputation during its first vintages. The original building serving as its winery until 86 was a slightly restored restaurant, and along with the basic equipment within, the overcrowded premises added to the "devil-may-care" feel. However, Monterey Peninsula made several exceptional wines, and for many years it was the only producer of first-rate Cabernet Sauvignon from Monterey County. In the 70s it was also highly involved in the Zinfandel revival, and for many vintages produced as many as eight separate bottlings.

After moving into a bigger, more efficient facility in 86, the winery began emphasizing Monterey-grown wines, led by Cabernet Sauvignon, Merlot, Chardonnay, and Pinot Blanc. It uses "Doctor's Reserve" as a designation for the best Cabernet, Merlot, and occasionally best Zinfandel from a particular vintage. The winery regularly makes Chardonnay (barrel-fermented) from the Sleepy Hollow Vineyard in Monterey, Pinot Blanc (barrel-fermented in neutral oak) from the Cobblestone Vineyard in Monterey, and Pinot Noir. Its often praiseworthy Cabernet Sauvignon (2,500 cases) and an usually exceptional Merlot (1,000) represent close to half of the winery's production. An unusual, long-aged, blended red (Petite Sirah with Zinfandel) is called Black Burgundy. The winery's more conventional, jug-style blended white and red table wines are sold under the Big Sur label. With production at 10,000 cases, the winery was acquired in 1995 by Rutherford Benchmarks, a marketing company that also owns Quail Ridge in Napa.

MONTEREY VINEYARD    *Monterey 1973*    Now an elaborate 2-million-gallon-capacity winery, the Monterey Vineyard began with a well-known winemaker and great aspirations for varietal wines from Monterey, an unproven growing region. Winemaker Dick Peterson arrived from Beaulieu Vineyard to direct production, and the erudite Gerald Asher, author and essayist for *Gourmet,* joined him as marketing director. However, over the first few vintages the wines were not well received. The whites were excessively grassy and intense; the reds bordered on the vegetal. The whole venture never really got off the ground and was beginning to disintegrate fast. Peterson soon found himself the sole owner and winemaker until Coca-Cola of Atlanta came along to buy the winery in 77. The Coke team used Peterson to create many wines for their new low-end brand, Taylor California Cellars. Slowly, they made changes in the product line, bringing respectability to Monterey Vineyard.

In 83 Coca-Cola of Atlanta sold its various wine interests to Joseph E. Seagram. Amidst many changes, all the varietal wines still originate in Monterey County. The winery now controls 1,200 acres of vineyards, with Cabernet Sauvignon, Chenin Blanc, and Chardonnay the most widely planted. Its two best-selling varietal wines are Chardonnay and Merlot. Two lines of varietals are offered. The primary one consists of Cabernet Sauvignon, Merlot, Chardonnay, Sauvignon Blanc, White Zinfandel and Zinfandel. A limited-volume, pricier line of "Limited Reserve" wines is composed of Chardonnay, Cabernet Sauvignon, and Pinot Noir. All the wines, including the Reserves, are low-priced; the quality is average. Annual production is around the 600,000-case mark.

MONTEVINA WINERY    *Amador 1973*    A key player in the revival of Amador County, Montevina was the first new winery established in the Sierra Foothills after Prohibition. Between 72 and 74, it developed its 80-acre vineyard in the Shenandoah Valley, consisting of Sauvignon Blanc (29 acres), Zinfandel (22), Cabernet Sauvignon (15), and Semillon (10). From 73 to 82, the winery was directed by winemaker Cary Gott, who developed a reputation for several types of Zinfandel along with an innovative streak. Montevina was among the first to make a Nouveau-style Zinfandel (labeled "Nuevo") by carbonic maceration, and also a White Zinfandel, made in a bone-dry style.

In the 80s production increased as the winery attempted to emphasize whites such as Chardonnay from purchased grapes and Sauvignon Blanc and Semillon from the estate vineyard. After a family dispute, Gott left, and for a time the winery lost any sense of direction. In late 88 the winery and vineyard were bought by the Trinchero family, owners of Sutter Home Winery in Napa Valley. They have since added 150 acres of red grapes, primarily Zinfandel, with 30 acres of Sangiovese. Its 70 acres of Barbera makes Montevina the largest grower of that variety outside of the Central Valley. Wines on the roster made from estate grapes are Zinfandel, Zinfandel Reserve, Barbera, Brioso (a light style of Zinfandel), Montanaro (blend of Zinfandel and Barbera), Matrimonio (Sangiovese, Barbera, Nebbiolo, and Refosco), Sangiovese, and Aleatico. In recent vintages Zinfandel has returned to top form, and Barbera is not far behind. Long-term, the owners believe Sangiovese will be the superstar. Reserve-level Barbera, Sangiovese, and Zinfandel are sold under the Terra d'Oro label. Combined annual production is close to 50,000 cases.

### Zinfandel

| 87 | 88 | 89* | 90* | 93 | 94 | 95* |
|----|----|-----|-----|----|----|-----|

*Changes in style have made this one hard to follow through its many variations in name, depth, and tannin levels; recent efforts have been ripe and open*

---

MONTICELLO CELLARS  *Napa 1980*  Thomas Jefferson happens to be one of Jay Corley's personal heroes, so when Corley ventured into the grape-growing business, he named his company Monticello. In the early 70s, Corley was operating a successful real estate and insurance business in Los Angeles, and among several investments he bought a former prune orchard in Napa Valley located just north of the town of Napa. He planted the site to vines, and sold all of the first several harvests from the 125 acres. However, by 80 Corley began easing into winemaking, producing his first two vintages at a neighboring facility. His own winery was built in time for the 82 crush. As a grower, Monticello initially specialized in white varieties—Chardonnay, Sauvignon Blanc, and Gewurztraminer. While still selling many tons of grapes, it now buys some Cabernet Sauvignon and Merlot to use in its expanding red wine program. Cabernet Sauvignon now accounts for half of the winery's production. The "Jefferson Cuvée" Cabernet is a fruit-oriented version softened with Merlot. Another Cabernet, made in a riper and longer-lived style, is named "Corley Reserve." Monticello's Corley Reserve Chardonnay is entirely barrel-fermented and "sur lie," aged in French oak for a year. The less expensive Estate Chardonnay spends less time in new oak barrels. Occasionally the winery makes a Sauternes-style wine from Semillon with *Botrytis*, and that wine is labeled "Chateau "M'.""

Recent vintages of Pinot Noir are light in color but promising. Merlot has recently joined the line. Corley is also actively involved in Domaine Montreaux.

### Cabernet Sauvignon

| (Corley Reserve) | 82* | 84* | 85* | 86* | 87** | 89 | 90 |
|------------------|-----|-----|-----|-----|------|----|----|

| (Jefferson Cuvée) | 82** | 83*** | 84 | 85 | 86** | 87 | 88 | 89 |
|-------------------|------|-------|----|----|------|----|----|----|
| 92 | 93 |

*Proving that bigger is not always better, the Jefferson Cuvée has turned out to be the more attractive wine over the years for its better fruit; if not as tough as the Corley, it will age perfectly well for up to a decade or more in its better vintages*

### Chardonnay

| (Corley Reserve) | 84 | 85* | 86** | 87 | 88 | 89 | 90 | 92 | 93 |
|------------------|----|-----|------|----|----|----|----|----|----|

| (Jefferson Cuvée) | 84* | 85* | 86* | 87 | 88 | 90* |
|-------------------|-----|-----|-----|----|----|-----|

*Though not exhibiting the range of its oakier sibling, the Jefferson is capable, in most years, of being an accessible, fruity, crisp, and clean Chardonnay, while the Corley, when it succeeds, relies on wood and ripe grape character*

---

MOONDANCE CELLARS  *Sonoma 1992*  Located near the town of Sonoma, Moondance is a family-owned 5,000-case winery. Almost every bottle made is a red wine, and the favorites among its customers are Cabernet Sauvignon and Merlot.

---

MORGAN WINERY  *Monterey 1982*  As winemaker for Durney Vineyards in Carmel and Jekel Vineyards in the Salinas Valley, Dan Lee had the opportunity to acquire first-hand knowledge of many vineyards within Monterey County. In the early 80s when working for Durney, he began developing his own brand. In the beginning Morgan was to be a Monterey County Chardonnay–only label. Enjoying critical success for his Chardonnays, Lee added Sauvignon Blanc and Zinfandel from the Alexander Valley. By 86 Lee decided to make Morgan his full-time project and opened a small facility in Salinas. Purchasing grapes for all wines, Lee produces a Monterey Chardonnay by blending fruit from six separate vineyards. Barrel-fermented in heavily toasted French oak from Burgundy, Morgan Chardonnays undergo partial malolactic fermentation before being aged for close to a year *sur lie*. An occasional Reserve Chardonnay is given longer barrel and bottle aging.

Partially barrel-fermented in less toasty oak, Morgan's Sauvignon Blanc (blended with 5–10% Semillon) originates in the Alexander Valley. A low-yielding hillside vineyard in Carmel Valley remains the source for Cabernet Sauvignon, which Lee ferments at relatively warm temperatures and confines to 100% varietal composition. The California appellation Pinot Noir is from grapes grown primarily in the Carneros, with a small portion from Monterey. Recent vintages of Reserve Pinot Noir from Carneros and from Monterey have reached °° and ° quality, respectively. Zinfandel from Alexander Valley completes the line.

Overall Dan Lee has turned out such magnificent Morgan Chardonnays (up to °°° ) that his other wines often go unnoticed. However, this talented winemaker has been successful with all wines. The Sauvignon Blanc, rich and creamy, is usually varietally precise and elegant enough to earn °° . As production edges toward the 20,000-case annual goal, 50% consists of Chardonnay and 25% is Sauvignon Blanc.

## Cabernet Sauvignon
86°° 87° 88 89° 90° 91°

*Impressively stuffed, medium-full-bodied, rich and ripe wines which, from all indications, should age well*

## Chardonnay
(regular bottling)  84°°  85°°°  86°°  87°  88°°  89°
90°°  91°  92  93°  94  95°  96°

(Reserve)  87°°  88°°  89°°  90°°  91°°  92°  93°  94°
95°°

*These wines' impressive track records have been achieved with a string of deeply fruited, pineappley, and sometimes citrusy efforts, buttressed by toasty oak and hints of roasted grains. They place Morgan among the top Chardonnay producers in the state*

## Pinot Noir
(California)  86  **87°**  88  **89°**  **90°**  91  **92°**  **93**  **94**  95
(Carneros Reserve)  **90°°**  **91°°**  **92**  **94°**
(Monterey Reserve)  **90°**  **91°**  **92°**  93  **94**  **95**  **96°**

*Medium-ripe fruit and rich oak are combined in these attractive, ageworthy wines; the Reserves are that much deeper in most vintages*

MOSBY WINERY AT VEGA VINEYARDS  *Santa Barbara 1979*  Owned and operated by the Mosby family, this winery used the name of Vega Vineyards until the family name was added recently. The facility occupies a renovated carriage house in the Santa Ynez Valley. With 34 acres developed on two separate parcels in the area of Buellton, the winery produces Gewurztraminer, Johannisberg Riesling, Chardonnay, and Pinot Noir in both a conventional and "Blanc" style. For several years, the Mosbys have called the Pinot Noir-Blanc "Pineau." Every now and then a late-harvest, *Botrytis*-affected Riesling is produced. Throughout the winery's history, the overall quality has varied considerably. In the late 80s Mosby began offering a series of limited-volume wines from Italian varieties, such as Nebbiolo, Brunello, and Primitivo. It also produces Grappa and several *eaux de vies*. Over its first decade, as Vega or as Mosby Winery, the wines have been made by owner Bill Mosby. The annual production goal is 10,000 cases.

MOUNT EDEN VINEYARDS  *Santa Clara 1972*  In the early 40s, Martin Ray left Paul Masson Winery and developed vineyards and a winery which he operated until 72 as Martin Ray Vineyards. Ray was a strong-minded individual, who was often involved in controversy over finances and winery control. After protracted legal battles among investors which culminated in the removal of Ray from the winery, the property was split by a court order. The bigger vineyard parcel and the original winery on the steep mountainside overlooking the Santa Clara Valley were renamed Mount Eden Vineyards. The lower, smaller portion was taken over by the

Ray family and operated as Martin RayVineyards. Since 72 the Mount Eden winery, also no stranger to controversy, has made three wines from its 36-acre vineyard. Both Chardonnay and the Pinot Noir (originally planted in 43) are located at the highest elevations—1,800- to 2,000-foot level. Cabernet Sauvignon is established in the lower parcel at the 1,400-foot level. The crop from these old, unirrigated vines planted on thin mountain soil is extremely small. Since 1992 the Cabernets from this old parcel have been bottled separately as Estate Old Vines.

In the 80s, the acreage of Cabernet Sauvignon was expanded to 20. At times Mount Eden has made spectacular, rich vintages of Chardonnay in a ripe, barrel-fermented vein, and highly extracted Cabernet Sauvignon. Pinot Noirs have performed erratically. However, after a slump in the early 80s, the winery, under the guidance of winemaker Jeffrey Patterson, began returning to form in 84. In a typical year it makes 500 cases of estate-bottled Chardonnay and Pinot Noir. The production of Cabernet should double to 1,000 cases with vineyard maturity. Following a traditional approach, its Cabernets are aged two years in French oak and two years in bottle before being sold. The volume wine (3,000 cases) is a Chardonnay from the MacGregor Vineyard in Edna Valley. It too is a full-blown, barrel-fermented wine, though usually less rich than the winery's estate Chardonnay.

### Cabernet Sauvignon

(Santa Cruz Mountains to 88; Old Vines to present)　73••• 74•• 75•
76•• 77• 78•• 79• 80 81•• 82 83 **84**•• **85**• **86**••
**87 88**• **89 90**•• **91 92 93 94**•

*Gone are the days of waiting 10 to 15 years for this wine to become somewhat accessible (although the still-evolving 73 ranks as one of our all-time favorites) and now one can taste the deep, curranty, briary, somewhat rooty and bell-peppery fruit through the tannins at an earlier age*

### Chardonnay

(Estate)　86••• 87••• 88••• 89• **90**••• **91**•• 92 **93**•••
94• 95

*An enviable track record in the last few vintages has lifted this deep, rich, toasty, appley, fleshy, and well-balanced wine to stardom*

### Chardonnay

(Edna Valley)　87• 88• 89• 91• 92• 93 94• 95 96

*In the rich Mount Eden style, the wine is both oaky and nicely fruity, but has less range and substance than its more expensive running mate*

### Pinot Noir

80 81 82 83 84•• 85 **87**••• **88**•• 89 **90**• 91 **93**•
**94**

*At its inception, in 72, this was one of the few true standouts among California Pinot Noirs, but lately it has had a difficult time and all too often fails to deliver the ripe, deep, black-cherryish fruit and rich, loamy, slightly leafy nuances that have been its hallmark in the best vintages*

MOUNT MADRONA *(St. Supery)* Introduced in 1994, this label is found on kosher wines produced by St. Supery. Napa Valley Cabernet Sauvignon and Chardonnay top the roster of this 5,000-case-per-year label.

MOUNT PALOMAR WINERY *Riverside 1975* One-time merchant seaman, tuna fisherman, and U.S. Army officer John Poole owned and operated the popular radio station on Catalina Island, KBIG, before entering the wine business. He left radio in 69, attracted by the opportunity to buy vineyard land in Temecula. His vineyard, the Long Valley Vineyard, was among the first in the area. Once covering 150 acres, it now contains about 100 acres. Poole acted as winemaker for the first vintage in 75, and for the next hired Joseph Cherpin. In the early vintages the winery's line was slanted toward slightly sweet table wines (including a Cabernet Sauvignon) and sherries, selling many wines directly from the tasting room. In 81 the owner revamped the vineyards, removing several varieties that performed poorly and replacing them with Chardonnay and Sauvignon Blanc. A few acres have been planted to Sangiovese.

With 32 acres planted, Chardonnay is the volume leader. As the winery moves toward its ultimate production goal of 30,000 cases, its white wines represent 80% and blush wines 10% of the total. Its large visitors center is one of the most popular in the area, and several wines—Cream Sherry, Gamay Beaujolais Nouveau, and the occasional late harvest Riesling—are sold only at the winery. Castelletto (see entry) is the winery's label for Italian-style wines. Rey Sol (see entry) is a separate label for Rhone-inspired wines. To date, the highest quality has been achieved with its Chardonnays (both regular and Reserve bottlings), which rank among the finest from the region.

MOUNT VEEDER WINERY  *Napa 1973*  In the mid-1960s, founders Mike and Arlene Bernstein planted 20 acres on the steep slopes of Mount Veeder. Among the first vintages, the winery offered rich, brawny Cabernet Sauvignons, often on the weedy-green olive side, and an often fantastic, rich, barrel-fermented Chenin Blanc. Enamored of immense, ripe Zinfandels (73 was a classic). Bernstein also went out of his way to make them in both standard and late harvest styles. Chardonnay from the Long Vineyard was made for several vintages, and there were several successes. By 80, when its annual production had reached 4,000 cases, the winery was more of an artistic success by virtue of its "interesting" wines than a commercial success. The low-yielding vineyards turned out to be extremely labor-intensive to farm.

In 82 the winery and the 80-acre estate were sold to the Matheson family. The vineyard was expanded to 23 acres, with 6 to Chardonnay, 12 to Cabernet Sauvignon, and the remainder to other Bordeaux red varieties. Buying additional grapes, the winery was making 5,000 cases by 85. It remained at that level until June 89, when the winery was sold again, this time to Agustin Huneeus and the Eckes family, owner of Franciscan Vineyards. From its 40-acre vineyard, the winery has set 8,000 cases as its annual goal, with Cabernet Sauvignon. Estate Reserve (red Meritage), Merlot, and Zinfandel representing the entire line.

### Cabernet Sauvignon

(regular bottling)  74°°  75°°  76  77  78  79°  80°  81°°
82  83  84  **86**  **87**  **88°**  **89°**  **90°°**  **91°°**  **92°**  **93°**
**94°°**  **95**

(Reserve)  **89°**  **90°°**  **91°°°**  **92°°**  **93**  **94°**

*The deep and long-lasting fruit captured in the early vintages seems to have been lost in the more recent offerings; as a result, the wines of the mid-80s turned out stiff, hard, and ripe, without the necessary center of fruit to bring them into balance; success returned in the late 80s and has continued since*

### Chardonnay

84  85°  86  87  88  89  90  91  92

*Firmly structured but sometimes lacking in depth, the wine tends toward apples and citrus, with more of the latter quality in lesser years, and typically carries an oaky component*

MOUNTAIN VIEW VINTNERS  A négociant brand for a line of table and sparkling wines, Mountain View is owned by Vinformation, a wine-marketing company in San Francisco. The wines first appeared in 80, after which the annual output grew to a peak of 100,000 cases. Chardonnay (50,000 cases) from Monterey County and White Zinfandel (15,000 cases) are the volume leaders. Generic red and white blends account for 25,000 cases. Small batches of other varietals (Sauvignon

Blanc, Cabernet Sauvignon, Pinot Noir) are offered from various regions. Quantities each year depend upon availability. To date, only a vintage or two of Chardonnay has stood out in any special way.

ROBERT MUELLER CELLARS  *Sonoma 1992*  Veteran winemaker Mueller made wines for many brands until building his own small winery. He specializes in small batches of Pinot Noir and Chardonnay from the Russian River Valley. After a slow start, he has achieved great success with Pinot Noir, especially those labeled Emily's Cuvée and Ranch 23. Recent vintages of Chardonnay also have earned up to **. Mueller's winery is located on the outskirts of Healdsburg, and most of his sales are direct from the winery. Annual production is moving toward 2,000 cases.

MUMM NAPA VALLEY  *Napa 1985*  In 83 Mumm of Champagne and Seagram Classic Wine of California started this sparkling wine company as a joint venture. Until 90 the label was Domaine Mumm. In 84 it was producing a range of cuvées in a facility adjacent to Sterling Vineyards, and the first bubbly from Domaine Mumm hit the market in 86. By 88, it was fully ensconced in its present location on the Silverado Trail. From 50 acres in the Carneros and Rutherford areas and another 200 acres available to it through Sterling Vineyards, Mumm produces four styles of sparkling wine. Its most important wine in terms of volume is labeled "Cuvée Napa, Brut Prestige." In presumably exceptional years it makes a Vintage Reserve. The third wine, a vintaged Winery Lake Cuvée, is limited to about 2,000 cases a year and was likely the first vineyard-designated sparkling wine made in California. A Blanc de Noirs, the fourth sparkler, was added in 90.

For its Brut, Mumm has been using about 10% Reserve or older wine, and each year the winery directs more of its production into increasing its supply of older wines. With winemaker Greg Fowler (formerly with Schramsberg Vineyards) directing the operation, the winery harvests its grapes at the 19.5 Brix target, slightly higher than its French parent. In the early going, Mumm performed extremely well, with a wonderful fruity, slightly yeasty Brut displaying the sought-after delicacy of Pinot Noir, and a richer, complex Reserve presenting a creamy, toasty impression. Mumm's annual sales are now close to 165,000 cases. Close to 40% of the total output is sold in the U.K., where its Brut is the top-selling bubbly in its price niche. Across the board, the quality level has been impressive!

MURPHY–GOODE ESTATE VINEYARDS  *Sonoma 1986*  Two of the principals in this winery are longtime, highly regarded vineyardists. Tim Murphy developed vineyards in the Alexander Valley in the mid-60s; his partner Dale Goode is a vineyard manager for several wineries, and a partner in the Alexander Valley Vineyard, for which he serves as vineyard manager. Their combined holdings represent 300 acres of vineyards in the heart of the Alexander Valley. Most wines are made from their estate vineyards. The winery focuses on Chardonnay, Fumé Blanc, Cabernet Sauvignon, Pinot Blanc, and Merlot. The Chardonnays are 100% barrel-fermented and aged *sur lie*. The Fumé Blancs have been extremely varietal, with brisk acidity, and have been awarded °. As part of a general expansion of the line in the 1990s, Zinfandel was added. Murphy-Goode now makes two special Fumé Blancs—a Reserve that is big and intense, and Fume II, an even bigger version barrel-fermented entirely in new French oak. This wine, nicknamed the Deuce, is monstrous and often delicious, earning ** in 95 and *** in 96. The winery now also offers two Reserve Chardonnays. The Alexander Valley Reserve is from the Island Block, and the other is from the Russian River Valley property known as J&K Murphy Vineyard. With a wide array of wines to offer, Murphy-Goode has reached its maximum capacity of 90,000 cases.

### Cabernet Sauvignon

86°  87°  **88°**  **89°°**  **90**  **91**  **92°**  **93**  **94°**  **95**

*Medium-intensity black-cherry fruitiness is combined with sweet oak in a wine of moderate tannins and moderate aging potential; 89 was among the best of the vintage*

### Chardonnay

| 86* | 87 | 88* | 89 | 90 | 91 | 92 | 93 | 94 | 95 | 96 |
|-----|----|----|----|----|----|----|----|----|----|----|

*Straightforward, fairly bright fruit, redolent of apples, pears, and flower blossoms, is enriched by supporting notes of sweet oak in a wine noteworthy for its immediate appeal rather than its aging potential or complexity*

### Merlot

| 86** | 87 | 88** | 89* | 90 | 91** | 92* | 93* | 94 | 95 |
|------|----|------|-----|----|------|-----|-----|----|----|

*Round, open cherry and black cherry fruit, moderately tannic and medium aging*

MURRIETA'S WELL   *Alameda 1990*   Partners Philip Wente (of Wente Brothers) and Sergio Traverso, a Chilean-born winemaker who was once part-owner and the winemaker of Concannon Vineyards, joined forces to produce two upscale Meritage blends, both called by the proprietary name "Vendimia," Spanish for "vintage." The white is made from the historic Louis Mel Vineyard (planted in 1880). This 90-acre vineyard in Livermore Valley was originally established from cuttings taken from Chateau d'Yquem. Early vintages of the high-priced "Vendimia" white consist of barrel-fermented Sauvignon Blanc blended with Semillon and a splash of Muscat Canelli. The red combines Cabernet, Cabernet Franc, and Merlot. Zinfandel made from an old vineyard in the Livermore Valley completes the roster.

ANDREW MURRAY VINEYARDS   *Santa Barbara 1994*   Committed to producing only Rhone-inspired wines, this one has all the makings of a superstar. On steep hillsides that are atypical for Santa Maria Valley, the Murray family (Andrew, the son, is the winemaker) established a total of 34 acres of vineyards. Spread out over 26 separate sites on the estate, the vineyards are planted to Syrah (15 acres), Viognier (10 acres), and Roussanne (5 acres) along with Mourvedre and Grenache. To date the roster of wines made by Andrew Murray is led by Syrah, Les Coteaux (a blend of six hillside Syrah vineyards), Viognier, Roussanne, and Esperance, a red blend of Grenache, Mourvedre, and Syrah. Production has reached 5,000 cases, with 7,500 as the long-term goal.

NALLE WINERY   *Sonoma 1984*   Doug Nalle gained winemaking experience at Jordan and Souverain before going on to become winemaker at Quivira. Like a number of winemakers working within Sonoma County, Nalle came to be fascinated by Zinfandel grown on benchlands in the Dry Creek Valley. To produce wines under his own label, Nalle insists upon Zinfandel from relatively old, low-yielding vines. Using grapes purchased from growers, he has developed a style of Zinfandel that exudes a rich, berrylike fruit but also offers finesse in place of tight tannins. He uses open-top fermenters, and ages his wines in small French oak barrels for close to two years. As a result, his wine has depth of flavor but is ready to enjoy in its youth. His Zinfandel production is steady at 2,000 cases a year. Today Nalle devotes all of his efforts to his own brand.

### Zinfandel

| 84* | 85 | 86** | 87* | 88** | 89** | 90** | 91* | 92* | 93* |
|-----|----|------|-----|------|------|------|-----|-----|-----|
| 94* | 95* | 96 | | | | | | | |

*Sent to market young and presentable, this wine is oriented to berryish fruit, often with a touch of ripeness adding an extra dimension of sweetness to its oak-enriched aspects*

NAPA CREEK WINERY   *Napa 1980*   Renovating a former meat-packing plant located on the Silverado Trail, owner Jack Schulze's winery reached 13,000 cases a year without many successful wines. However, by 86 it was on a much-improved course. In 1994 the trademark and inventory were acquired by Classic Wine Co.

NAPA RIDGE   *(Beringer Vineyards)*   In 85 Wine World, Inc., owners of Beringer Vineyards, established this label to compete in the then-burgeoning low-priced end of the varietal market. Napa Ridge was well received in the marketplace and expanded. It added Sauvignon Blanc, White Zinfandel, and Pinot Noir to its roster. Before long, the blending and bottling operations shifted to the old Colony facility in Asti, acquired by Wine World. Today, Napa Ridge is also offering North Coast Merlot, Pinot Noir, and Gewurztraminer, along with Cabernet Sauvignon. Recent vintages of Pinot Noir and Central Coast Chardonnay have been standouts in their price range. The top-of-the-line wines are Napa Valley Reserve Chardonnay and North Coast Reserve Cabernet Sauvignon which receives 20 months aging in French oak barrels. Annual sales now top 2 million cases.

NAVARRO VINEYARDS *Mendocino 1974* On a 900-acre ranch formerly used as pastureland, Ted Bennett and Deborah Cahn built a beautiful winery which currently enjoys a solid reputation for quality wines. At their Anderson Valley winery, they developed 50 acres of terraced vineyards with Gewurztraminer, Chardonnay, and Pinot Noir predominating. The winery buys Riesling, Zinfandel, and Cabernet Sauvignon from within the county. Navarro's reputation was founded on Gewurztraminer, usually finished with under 1% sugar, and on the occasional and sometimes outstanding *Botrytis*-affected late harvest Gewurztraminer. The winery now produces two versions of Chardonnay. One is a limited-volume, barrel-fermented wine labeled "Premiere Reserve," and the second is a stainless-steel-fermented, oak-aged Chardonnay with a Mendocino appellation. Both have earned * ratings. The bold and assertive Gewurztraminer is often a real knockout.

Since its beginning, Navarro has tried many approaches with Pinot Noir. The estate-bottled Pinot Noir is made by the traditional method of punching down, stem retention, and the addition of whole clusters during fermentation. Among its many small-batch wines, Navarro frequently excels with Sauvignon Blanc in a zesty, brisk style and also to some degree with Zinfandel, Syrah, and Mourvedre. Over one-third of the winery's 12,000 cases are sold direct through the winery's twice-a-year mailings.

NELSON ESTATE *Sonoma 1986* David Nelson, a commercial airline pilot, developed a 20-acre vineyard in the Bennett Valley in the early 80s. Cabernet Franc is the lead variety, but Merlot has been added to the line after the Nelsons converted part of their acreage to Merlot. Its annual output has been holding steady at close to 4,000 cases.

NEVADA CITY WINERY *Nevada 1980* This northernmost winery in the Sierra Foothills produces a variety of wines from local vineyards and from North Coast counties. The owners, avid skiers as well as wine lovers, built a small winery in the center of Nevada City where they sell to locals and the ski crowd. The most popular wine is a proprietary blush, "Alpine Glow." From locally grown grapes they make Syrah, Zinfandel, Chardonnay, Pinot Noir, and Charbono, all bottled with the Nevada County appellation. They also offer Napa Valley Chardonnay, Sonoma County Gewurztraminer, and, when *Botrytis* conditions allow, late harvest Sauvignon Blanc and White Riesling. Both of these late harvest wines have earned * and are exotically rich, but usually limited in production to 200 cases or less. Otherwise, Zinfandel is the most conventional wine made, and the Pinot Noir the most promising. Total production is edging close to the 7,000-case-a-year goal.

NATHANSON CREEK *(Sebastiani Vineyards)* By the end of its first year, Nathanson Creek had sold 1.5 million cases. Chardonnay accounted for more than half of the total. Heavily advertised and sporting an upscale label, this brand was part of Sebastiani's strategy to remove the family name from all low-priced wines.

NEWLAN VINEYARDS & WINERY *Napa 1981* Bruce Newlan was an engineer for Lockheed before deciding to become involved in a vineyard project. In the mid-60s he was both a grape grower and a part-time winemaker in Napa Valley. By 77 he became a partner in the Alaterra Vineyards, which lasted until 80. Relying on his own 30-acre vineyard, he launched his own brand the following year. From his

16-acre Pinot Noir vineyard south of Yountville, Newlan makes 600 to 1,000 cases a year. The wine ferments with 15% whole clusters added at the start. Zinfandel is Newlan's second most important wine today, and has emerged as a critical success. Newlan has also been developing Cabernet Sauvignon, Chardonnay, and a Reserve Pinot Noir. This label has been successful enough to bring the winery total annual production to 10,000 cases. Long-term, Newlan sees 30,000 cases a year as the absolute maximum.

## Cabernet Sauvignon

84° 85° **86° 88° 90°° 91°** 93 **94**

*After a difficult beginning with skimpy, somewhat lean wines, Newlan has delivered deeper, richer, and fuller bottlings more often than not*

## Chardonnay

86 88° 89 90 91 92° 93 **94°**

*Expressively toasty in oak and roasted, nutty qualities, with citrusy and appley fruit in support; angular in structure*

## Pinot Noir

(Napa Valley) 83° 84° 85° 86° **87° 88° 89°°** 91 92 93 94

(Reserve) **91°°** 93

*Generally well-made, this series of wines offers cherryish fruit, a firm but never hard structure, and a dollop of sweet oak; the initial Reserve was deep in fruit and high in creamy oak*

---

NEWTON VINEYARD   *Napa 1979*   After selling his interest in Sterling Vineyards in 77, Peter Newton and his wife, Su Hua, began developing the 650 acres of untamed land they acquired on Spring Mountain. On steep terraces, the Newtons planted 62 acres to Cabernet Sauvignon, Merlot, Cabernet Franc, and Sauvignon Blanc. The early plantings and the first vintages were assisted by Ric Forman, the well-known winemaker whose partnership role in this winery did not work out. In 79 the winery made 2,000 cases of Merlot, and added Cabernet Sauvignon the following year. The winemaking facility is a visual delight, as are the surrounding grounds. A barrel-aging room is housed in an underground cellar. Today, the winery makes Merlot, Cabernet Sauvignon (blended with Merlot), and Chardonnay produced from purchased grapes. It has also offered a "Claret" (a red Meritage), Viognier, and a massive Reserve-type Chardonnay labeled "unfined and unfiltered." The winery's annual production is steady at 25,000 cases.

## Cabernet Sauvignon

80 **81** 82° 83° **84° 85°° 86° 90°° 91°°**

*Moderately rich in oak and exhibiting ripe black-cherry fruit; somewhat coarse tannins; half a decade or more of aging potential, especially in top vintages*

## Chardonnay

86 88 89 90 **91°°** 93 94°° **95° 96°°°**

*Medium-full-bodied wines, usually carrying a nice balance of oak and appley fruit; medium intensity; impressive record of late*

## Merlot

81° 82° 83° 84° **86° 87° 88°** 89° **90° 91 94° 95**

*Ripe cherry and subdued herbal and briary notes are buttressed by a bit of sweet oak in moderately tannic wines*

---

NEYERS WINERY   *Napa 1980*   Bruce Neyers, a research chemist, became interested in wine when he was stationed in San Francisco toward the end of his Army stint. In 71 he started his wine career as a cellar worker at Mayacamas Vineyard. When winemaker Bob Sessions left to become the head winemaker at Hanzell, Neyers found himself wearing many different hats at Mayacamas, including that of winemaker. By 75 he had become acquainted with Joe Phelps, and was hired to establish a marketing program and run the new winery, Joseph Phelps Vineyards. The urge to produce his own wines resurfaced, and with the financial support of Phelps, Neyers began making wines in 80 at the Rombauer facility. He continued to work at Phelps until 1992.

Over his first decade, Neyers was best at making Napa Valley Cabernet Sauvignon. Recently Neyers has teamed up with Ehren Jordan, winemaker for Turley Cellars, and the teamwork has vastly improved the whole line. Rich and silky Chardonnays now come from the Carneros District, as does a powerful Syrah from Hudson Vineyard. An eyedropper amount of Chardonnay from Thierot Vineyard in the Sonoma Coast also has earned high marks. Sauvignon Blanc and Zinfandel (Pato Vineyard, Contra Costa) also have joined the roster as has an impressive Merlot from Neyers' estate vineyard in the Conn Valley region. Annual output will level off at 6,000 cases once the estate vineyard reaches maturity.

NICHELINI WINERY  *(Boeger Winery)*  The original Nichelini Winery began in 1890 and was operated in the Chiles Valley area of Napa Valley until 1986. In 88 four members of the family, one of whom is Greg Boeger, owner of Boeger Winery, revived the label and produced Zinfandel from the old 100-acre Chiles Valley vineyard. The family has gradually been restoring the old winery, and the line has expanded to include Merlot, Cabernet Sauvignon, Petite Sirah, Barbera, and an obscure white, Sauvignon Vert. Of the 2,000 cases made a year, Zinfandel, now labeled Old Vines, remains the pride of the family.

NICHOLS WINERY & CELLARS  *San Luis Obispo 1991*  Chardonnay from the Arroyo Grande district of San Luis Obispo and Pinot Noir from Santa Barbara are the only wines made by Keith Nichols. An advocate of traditional hands-on winemaking, Nichols intends to produce 400–600 cases of each varietal a year.

GUSTAVE NIEBAUM COLLECTION  *Napa 1989*  In desperation, Inglenook introduced this brand for a line of Napa Valley varietals bottled as vineyard-designated wines. Though the quality was good, the label was on the ropes when Francis Ford Coppola acquired it in 1995. He plans to use it for Cabernet Sauvignon and Cabernet Franc as well as other varietals.

NIEBAUM–COPPOLA ESTATE  *Napa 1978*  Francis Ford Coppola, the famous movie director, acquired the historic Niebaum home, built by Gustave Niebaum, Inglenook's founder. He purchased an adjacent vineyard of 10 acres, said to be among the oldest in Napa Valley, and developed an additional property into a total of 120 acres of vines. The primary varieties planted and used to produce a Bordeaux blend are Cabernet Sauvignon (60 acres), Cabernet Franc (20 acres), and Merlot (10 acres). "Rubicon," the proprietary name under which the wine is marketed, is aged at least three years in oak and two or more years in bottle before reaching the market. The initial vintage, the 78, did not appear until 85. The winery, soon settling into a pattern, grew quickly to the 5,000-case level. As of 88 the output of Rubicon was limited to 2,000 cases a year. It has been made in a style that tends to be hard, tannic, and in need of cellaring. In 95 Coppola acquired the remaining pieces of the Inglenook property, including the historic winery, the large barrel aging facility, and 72 acres of prime vineyards from Heublein. This newsworthy sale, estimated to be well over $10 million, also brought Coppola the library of Inglenook wines and the Gustave Niebaum Collection label. As a result Coppola owns a total of 195 acres in the Rutherford region. He also has four labels. Rubicon and Edizione Pennino will grow in volume gradually. The two others, Gustave Niebaum Collection and the Coppola Family Wines (see entry), are likely to be expanded in the years ahead.

### Rubicon

79  80°  81°  82°  **84**  8̶5̶  **86°**  **87°**  **88**  **89**   94°

*This blended wine is always tough in construction and oaky more than fruity; yet it manages in most vintages to be fairly attractive and to promise long-aging improvement*

NOBLE HILL VINEYARDS  *Santa Cruz 1986*  One of many engineers in the computer and software design field jumped ship in 84 to develop a vineyard and prepare for a career in the wine business. On a 24-acre mountain site (1,600-foot elevation) overlooking Los Gatos, owner-winemaker Russ Schildt planted 5 acres to Chardonnay. He also designed his winery, which specializes in white wine production. Barrel-fermented Chardonnay and stainless-steel-fermented Sauvignon Blanc are the only wines produced. Chardonnay from both Sonoma County and the Santa Cruz estate appellation are made on a regular basis. The first efforts displayed more than adequate winemaking ability. With vineyard maturity, the winery will grow to 5,000 cases a year.

NORMAN VINEYARDS  *Paso Robles 1992*  In the Adelaida Hills west of Paso Robles, Art Norman developed his 40-acre vineyard in the early 1970s. A number of local wineries had been buying his Barbera, but Norman decided to showcase his other varieties by getting into winemaking. Though Chardonnay, Cabernet Sauvignon, Merlot, and Sauvignon Blanc are part of his roster, Zinfandel in several styles put Norman Vineyards on the wine map. In most vintages the winery offers "Classic" Zinfandel, "Monster" Zinfandel, and Late Harvest.

OAKFORD VINEYARD  *Napa 1988*  One-time oil explorer Larry Ball decided to slow down and change careers, so he purchased a mature 8-acre vineyard in 86 and moved to Napa Valley. Located on the slope along the Oakville Grade Road, the vineyard is planted entirely to Cabernet Sauvignon. All vintages from 86 to the present have been custom-made. Early production of 800 cases has grown to 1,000 a year. The winery was purchased in 1998 by Floyd and Carol Wilson.

OAKSTONE WINERY  *El Dorado 1996*  A longtime amateur winemaker and analytical chemist by profession, Jim Smith developed a 9-acre vineyard in Somerset. Now a full-time winemaker, he produces Cabernet Sauvignon, Merlot, and red Meritage from his own grapes. He also offers Zinfandel from El Dorado and Chardonnay from Sangiacomo Vineyard in the Carneros District. Annual production is 5,000 cases, and will increase to 7,000 with the addition of Pinot Grigio and Charbono to the roster.

OAKVILLE RANCH VINEYARDS  *Napa 1989*  Cofounded by Bob Miner, who operated Oracle Corporation, and Randy Lewis, now of Lewis Cellars (see entry), Oakville Ranch is now run by the Miner family. Its 50-acre mountainside vineyard sits 1,200 feet above the valley floor. This low-yielding vineyard provides the winery with strongly flavored Chardonnay and Cabernet Sauvignon. So far both wines have been ranked above average, with the Cabernet Sauvignon having potential to move up a notch or two. All wines, including Zinfandel from the Calistoga area, are under the watchful eye of consultant Joe Cafaro. Production is at 3,000 cases a year.

### Cabernet Sauvignon

**89**  **90°°**  **91°°**  **92°°**  **93**  **94°**   95°

*90 and 91 were a mix of bountiful fruit, medium tannins, and creamy oak*

### Chardonnay

(Vista Vineyard)   91   92  **93°°**  **94°**  **95°**  96

(ORV)  **92°°**  **93°°**  **94°**  **96°**

*Deep, ripe, oaky wines in solid, ageworthy stylings*

**OBESTER WINERY**   *Santa Clara 1977*   Sandy Obester is the granddaughter of John Gemello, an historic winemaking figure who founded Gemello Winery in 34. In the same facility she and her husband, Paul, use for Obester wines, she continues the Gemello line of wine, now limited to Cabernet Sauvignon and Zinfandel from purchased fruit. The Obesters operate the tasting room and gift shop in Half Moon Bay, where they produce enough wine to keep their permit active. Total annual production of the Obester line is close to 10,000 cases.

**Chardonnay**

86   87   88   89   90°   91

*Mildly fruity wines with subtle oak, but often exhibiting suggestions of dried brush, and sometimes of ·cardboard, in the background, the 89 and 90 were barrel-fermented and show more oak*

---

**OJAI VINEYARD**   *Ventura 1984*   Adam Tolmach is a vineyardist by training and an adventurer when it comes to making wines. He was once a co-owner of Au Bon Climat, specializing in Chardonnay and Pinot Noir. In 84 he started his own winery, and began developing a 6-acre vineyard. From the beginning, Ojai has made a Syrah and an intriguing blend of Sauvignon Blanc–Semillon. After working with Zinfandel, Tolmach has returned to focus on Syrah and the other Rhone varieties—Viognier and Mourvedre in particular. Annual production is a modest 1,500 cases, with close to half consisting of Syrah. In the 90s, Ojai added a rich, barrel-fermented Chardonnay from the highly regarded Talley Vineyard in Edna Valley, and is also making a lovely fruit-filled Chardonnay from Bien Nacido Vineyard and a medium-intense, crisp version from Sanford & Benedict Vineyard. Recent vintages of Viognier have ranked among our absolute favorites (** in 95 and 96). Ojai is a small town in Ventura County, and this winery is the only important one located there.

**Chardonnay**

(Bien Nacido Vineyard)   91°   92°   94   **95°**   **96°**

(Talley Vineyard)   92   93   **95°**

(Talley Reserve)   92°   **94°°°**   **95°°**

*Relying on two of the finest vineyards in the Central Coast, Ojai has produced a string of impeccably balanced, attractively fruity, richly oaked wines*

**Syrah**

86   **87°**   **89°°**   **90**   **92**   **93°**   **94°**   **96°°**

*Fruit suggestive of cherries and raspberries carries a noticeable herbaceous edge and moderate tannins*

---

**OLIVET LANE ESTATE**   *Sonoma 1986*   On Olivet Road in the Russian River region west of Santa Rosa, the Pellegrini family planted 65 acres to Chardonnay and Pinot Noir in 75. For 20 years after the repeal of Prohibition, the Pellegrinis made wine in Sonoma, only to ease away from it by 56 in order to concentrate on their major business at the time, wine wholesaling. They resumed winemaking on a limited basis primarily to supply house wines to restaurant accounts. By the end of the 80s they were making a line of wines, and Olivet Lane was used for their estate-grown wines. The brand has grown to the 6,000-case-a-year mark, 60% consisting of Chardonnay, which is partially barrel-fermented, and 40% of Pinot Noir. Since the arrival of winemaker Merry Edwards in 91, the quality level has been on the rise. Clovervale Ranch is a brand owned by Pellegrini and applied to its Cabernet Sauvignon and Merlot.

**Chardonnay**

87   88   89   91   92°   94   95   96

*Somewhat understated throughout, with brisk, green appley fruit played off against mild oak, and firm acidity*

OPTIMA    *Sonoma 1984*    This company is a two-man operation that began on a shoe-string budget. Behind it are Mike Duffy, who has been winemaker for Field Stone, and Greg Smith, who gained winemaking experience with Lytton Springs and currently owns the Fitch Mountain Winery. They combined talents to create Optima, with the first wine being a Cabernet Sauvignon–Merlot blend. Starting off with 400 cases, the output has grown to 3,000 cases. In some years the red blend contains Cabernet Franc, Petite Sirah, or Zinfandel. Aged for over three years before its release, Optima tends to be a full-bodied, amply endowed red in need of long cellaring. The owners produce 200 cases of variable-quality Chardonnay from the Carneros region. A similar quantity of often high-quality Russian River Valley Pinot Noir is a new addition. Long-term, the owners hope to expand their total annual output to 6,000 cases.

### Cabernet Sauvignon

84°    85°    86°    87°°°    89    **90°**    **91°**    **92**    **94°**    **95°**

*Ripe and full-bodied, with a mouthful of tannin, these brooding wines barely let their black-cherry fruit show in the first five years and will likely require at least twice that to come into their own*

### Chardonnay

88    89°    90°    91    93    94    95

OPUS ONE    *Napa 1979*    One of the most widely publicized wine projects ever, Opus One is a joint venture between the Robert Mondavi Winery and Château Mouton-Rothschild. In 68 the two respective patriarchs, Robert Mondavi and Baron Philippe de Rothschild (who died in 88), agreed to work together on this project. All grapes are grown in Napa Valley, and the winemaking responsibilities are shared by winemakers from both companies. The release of the first vintage sent shock waves through the wine world for both the fanfare involved and the $50-a-bottle price tag. Though no longer the most expensive California wine, Opus One—a blend of Cabernet Sauvignon, Cabernet Franc, and often Merlot—has been consistently successful. Its annual production grew steadily to reach 12,000 cases by 90. The wines, through 90, have been made and aged in space rented from the Robert Mondavi Winery. Opus One, however, developed its own 110-acre vineyard in Oakville, where a winery has been constructed. Located within a mile of the Robert Mondavi Winery, Opus One's uniquely designed facility is shaped as a hemispherical structure placed in a shallow, specially excavated crater, and the 60,000-square-foot building is not visible from the nearby wine road. In a streak of bad luck, which included a defective cooling system, Opus One was one of the first vineyards to be wiped out by *Phylloxera* in the 90s. When the replanted vineyard reaches full production, the winery will achieve its goal of 30,000 cases a year.

### Red Table Wine

79°°    80°°°    81°°    82°°    83°°    84°°°    85°°    86°°    87°°°
88°°°    89°°    90°°    91°°    92    93°    94°

*Owing most of their character to the substantial Cabernet Sauvignon component, blended with lesser portions of Merlot and Cabernet Franc, these wines are deep in curranty and black-cherry fruit that balances, sometimes somewhat precariously, the generously laid-on creamy oak; bold tannins provide a firm, long-aging quality to this full-bodied wine*

ORFILA VINEYARDS    *San Diego 1993*    Alejandro Orfila, a retired Argentinean diplomat, purchased the former Thomas Jaeger Winery in 1993. Located in the San Pasqual Valley, the winery was expanded and new vineyards planted. The production emphasis falls on Chardonnay, Merlot, and Sauvignon Blanc, with limited amounts of Viognier, Sangiovese, and Syrah. Total annual output is expected to reach 10,000 cases by decade's end.

PACIFIC ECHO   In 1998, the name for Scharffenberger Cellars (see entry) was changed to Pacific Echo. With founder John Scharffenberger no longer involved, the new owners, who are based in France, decided to rename the winery and designed a new label and logo as part of a complete makeover.

PAGE MILL WINERY   *Santa Clara 1976*   Working in a basement in his Los Altos home, owner-winemaker Dick Stark manages to produce a variety of wines in small batches that are almost always noteworthy. Most wines are vineyard-designated, including multiple Chardonnays and Cabernet Sauvignons in most vintages. Most wines are sold directly by the winery, thanks to a well-attended series of preview tastings presented by the owners. What is not sold directly is targeted for the local retail market.

PAHLMEYER WINERY   *Napa 1987*   Jason Pahlmeyer is a trial attorney who confesses to having spent more time reading wine journals than law journals. In the early 80s he began developing a 25-acre parcel planted to the five red Bordeaux varieties. The terraced vineyard, named Caldwell Vineyard after the vineyard manager and partner, John Caldwell, is situated in a cool region to the east of the town of Napa. By mid-93, that partnership abruptly ended, and Pahlmeyer hired consulting winemaker Helen Turley to line up replacement vineyards and to make the wines. She located vineyards north of St. Helena for the red and another in southeastern Napa for the Chardonnay. A proprietary blend primarily of Cabernet Sauvignon and Merlot, the Pahlmeyer red is barrel aged in new oak for two and a half years. It is bottled unfined and unfiltered, as is the barrel-fermented Chardonnay, which may have a harmless enough cloudy appearance as a result. Pahlmeyer has made a majestic Merlot, but the primary emphasis falls upon the red blend and Chardonnay. Annual production is approaching 5,000 cases.

### Cabernet Sauvignon
**86°°  87°  88°  89  90°°  91  92  93°°  95°**

*Ripe, dense, tannic, oaky, deep, long-aging wines*

### Chardonnay
93°°  94°  **95°**

*Despite its occasionally hazy appearance, this wine is clean, fruity, oaky*

### Merlot
**90°  91  92°  94°  95°°**

*Supple at the front, tannic in the finish and nicely fruited in the middle*

PALOMA WINES   *Napa 1995*   Owners Jim and Barbara Richards developed a 15-acre vineyard in 1984, with major emphasis on Merlot and a splash Cabernet. After selling their grapes to many well-known producers, they retained enough of their own 1994 crop to make 600 cases of Merlot. Blended with 20% Cabernet Sauvignon, their first several vintages of Merlot have been among the very best from Spring Mountain. Annual output of 1,200 cases will max out at 3,500, which includes 200 cases of estate-grown Syrah.

GIANNI PAOLETTI   *Napa 1994*   Founded by Los Angeles restaurateur Paoletti, this new winery has produced *** Cabernets in 94 and 95 and a °° Merlot in 95.

PARADIGM WINERY   *Napa 1991*   Ren and Marilyn Harris built a compact redwood winery on their property located just south of Far Niente Winery. Cabernet Sauvignon blended with Merlot and Cabernet Franc is the primary wine produced from their 12-acre vineyard. Early annual production of 1,800 cases is expected to level off at 3,000 cases. The owners bottle a few hundred cases of Merlot and Zinfandel from their estate vineyard.

## Cabernet Sauvignon
**91   92*   93   94**   95****

*Very tasty cherry and cassis-like fruit with an enriching loamy, rooty note; sweet oak and middling tannins*

## Merlot
**94***   95****

*A most impressively fruity debut*

---

PARADISE RIDGE WINERY   *Sonoma 1991*   Located in the hills due north of Santa Rosa near the site of the old Fountain Grove Winery, this small winery was in place by the 1994 harvest. Its first three vintages were produced in a neighboring facility. On his 150-acre estate, owner and physician Walter Byck developed 18 acres to Chardonnay and Sauvignon Blanc. Specializing in Sauvignon Blanc and barrel-fermented Chardonnay, Paradise Ridge markets most of its 1,500-case output through its tasting room and at special events. The winery also makes a few hundred cases of champagne.

---

PARAISO SPRINGS VINEYARDS   *Monterey 1989*   In the early 1970s Rich Smith began developing a 400-acre vineyard west of Soledad. Chardonnay is the oldest and (with 60 acres planted) the largest component; the rest consists of Pinot Noir (55 acres), Johannisberg Riesling (55 acres), Gewurztraminer (25 acres), and Pinot Blanc (10 acres). Smith sells most of the grapes, but he has branched out to bottle Chardonnay, Gewurztraminer, Riesling, Pinot Noir, and Pinot Blanc from his vineyard. The quality is consistent with the generally modest prices. Total production holds steady at 6,000 cases.

---

PARDUCCI WINE ESTATES   *Mendocino 1932*   For many years this was a family-owned and -operated winery. In 1996, after a decade-long power struggle between the Parducci family and its investment partner, Teachers Management Institute, the winery was sold to Hill & Thoma, an investment group that also owns Van Duzer in Oregon and two Napa properties, Clos Fontaine and Carneros Bighorn. In wine circles, Parducci is a highly regarded pioneering name as well as a driving force within Mendocino County viticulture. The winery offers a line of table wines, varietals, and generics. Parducci was the first winery to bottle a varietal French Colombard in the 50s, and was a leader in the evolution of slightly sweet Chenin Blanc. When Petite Sirah came on as a varietal in the 60s, Parducci was in the forefront with its versions.

Like many of his colleagues, winemaster John Parducci, who was forced to retire in 1995, avoided using small oak barrels until recent vintages. In the 70s he made a series of no-oak Chardonnay and Sauvignon Blanc that often were exceptionally attractive. For red wines, he preferred large redwood tanks for aging. Many aspects of the winery have changed over time. The new owners are focusing on red wines, Zinfandel, Merlot, and Petite Sirah. The Reserve wines are labeled "Cellarmaster Selection," which consists of Cabernet Sauvignon, Pinot Noir, and Chardonnay. Although rarely rated above average, Parducci wines are priced moderately and are often good value, particularly the Sauvignon Blanc and Petite Sirah. The winery's production is 400,000 cases per year.

## Cabernet Sauvignon
81   82   83   84   85   86   87   88   89   90   91

*If never getting high marks, this moderately fruity, slightly berry-flavored wine can be a good value in some years when its fruit takes the lead over earthy, woodsy suggestions*

## Chardonnay
83   84*   85   86   87   88   89   90   91   93

*Quietly fruity, somewhat green-appley in character, and showing stiff acidity played against hints of a fresh juicy character*

### Pinot Noir

84   85*   86   87   88   89   90*   92

*Youthful, simple, direct fruit, with little tannin or oak in the way of its immediate quaffability*

### Zinfandel

86   87   88   92   95

*Following a simple, moderate-tannin approach, the wine has average fruit in some years but less than that in others, and is easily ignored*

---

PARKER WINERY   *Santa Barbara 1990*   Long-retired actor Fess Parker (Davey Crockett, Daniel Boone) and his family are slowly venturing into the winemaking world. On the family's diversified 714-acre ranch, the Parkers planted 31 acres to wine varieties, mostly Chardonnay (12.5 acres) and Syrah (12.5 acres). Having built a winery in the Santa Ynez Valley, Parker is now producing Chardonnay, Johannisberg Riesling, Pinot Noir, Syrah, Viognier, Marsanne, Pinot Blanc, Cabernet Franc, and Melange, a blended red wine with a Rhone personality. Recently the Reserves—Syrah, Pinot Noir, and Chardonnay—carry the American Tradition Reserve. With the acquisition of an 80-acre portion of the nearby Sierra Madre Vineyard, Parker Winery is moving close to its maximum annual output of 45,000 cases. As one of the most-visited wineries in the area, Parker sells a lot of wine and many coonskin caps to busloads of tourists. Jed Steele, the highly regarded winemaker, has been acting as a consultant to Parker. From the early vintages Riesling emerged as the quality leader, but recent fine performances have come from Parker's Reserve Chardonnay and Pinot Noir. The Syrah has shown good potential.

### Chardonnay

(Santa Barbara County)   89   90   92   93   94**   95**   96

(Reserve)   92**   93   94*

*Typically firm, sometimes with tropical-toned fruit, these wines can be rich and deep in good vintages*

### Pinot Noir

(Santa Barbara County)   93*   94

(Reserve)   93   95**   96

*Decently fruited wines with potential*

---

PATZ & HALL   *Napa 1988*   James Hall is the winemaker for Honig Cellars and Donald Patz is sales director for Flora Springs Winery. They produce just under 1,500 cases of barrel-fermented Napa Valley Chardonnay. Quality has been consistently high, and encouraged by this and their lofty reviews, Patz & Hall are now offering Chardonnay from Hyde Vineyard, Carr Vineyard, Russian River Valley and Napa Valley. Their foray into Pinot Noir has them bottling two so far, one from Hyde Vineyard and the second from Russian River Valley.

### Chardonnay

(Napa Valley)   88   89*   90**   91*   92   93*   **94***   **95****   96

*This highly regarded wine features ripe, appley fruit and good balance in its best appearances*

---

PAVONA WINES   *Monterey 1994*   Founded by wine marketing veteran Richard Kanakaris, Pavona focuses on three varietals: Pinot Noir, Pinot Blanc, and Zinfandel. The first two are from Paraiso Springs Vineyard in Monterey, and the Zinfandel is from the Twin Hills Vineyard in Paso Robles. Quality is generally in line with the prices. Annual output has reached the optimum 2,500-case level.

**PEACHY CANYON WINERY**   *San Luis Obispo 1988*   Winemaker Doug Beckett founded this winery to make Zinfandel and Cabernet Sauvignon from old vineyards in the Paso Robles region. Merlot was added in 1992. In addition to its primary Paso Robles Estate bottling, the winery bottles Zinfandels labeled "Dusi Ranch," "Westside" "Eastside," "Old Bailey" and "Especial Reserve," all from vineyards within Paso Robles. By clearly demonstrating the different character between wines made from vineyards on the east side and the west side of the Salinas River, the winery planted the idea in the minds of wine geeks that Paso Robles is serious Zinfandel turf. Today Peachy Canyon has 30 acres planted to Zinfandel and is developing a few acres to Sangiovese. It also makes Merlot and Cabernet Sauvignon, but Zinfandel in its numerous guises represents most of the winery's 10,000 cases annual output. Both Westside and Old Bailey have reached ** levels. All Zins share high ripeness as a common trait.

**ROBERT PECOTA WINERY**   *Napa 1978*   Bob Pecota began working for Beringer Vineyards in the early 70s, where he was involved in land acquisitions and later with vineyard management as well as public relations. When the opportunity came up to buy a 35-acre vineyard near Calistoga, Pecota purchased it, and in 78 built a small winery. Originally the vineyard was planted entirely to Petite Sirah. Pecota replanted half to a combination of Cabernet Sauvignon and Sauvignon Blanc. In the early years, in order to stay afloat as the vineyard matured, Pecota produced wines like Gray Riesling and Flora. Eventually his vineyard holdings expanded to 50 acres, led by Sauvignon Blanc (20), Cabernet Sauvignon (18), and Merlot (12). Since 78, he has been buying Gamay to make Gamay Beaujolais by carbonic maceration.

Each year Pecota makes about 3,000 cases of Muscat Blanc, with varying degrees of residual sugar. Named "Sweet Andrea" after his daughter, Pecota's Muscat is on occasion a lush, opulent, dessert-style wine. Of the 20,000 cases produced a year, Sauvignon Blanc represents about 7,000 cases, Cabernet Sauvignon—since 84 made only from the estate (Kara's Vineyard)—is around 3,000 cases. Merlot was added to the line in 89, and accounts for 1,000 cases.

**Cabernet Sauvignon**

(Kara's Vineyard)   84°   **85°°**   **86°**   **87°**   **88°**   **90°**   **91°°**   **93°**
**94°**   **95**

*Ripe, sweet, fairly concentrated cherryish fruit, backed by lots of rich oak, but tending sometimes to be burdened by coarse and drying tannins*

**Merlot**

(Steven Andre Vineyard)   89°   **90°°**   **91°**   **92°°**   **93**   **94°°**   **95°**

*No less big and rich than the Cabernet, this one might be even more long-aging than the Cabernet in recent vinatges*

**PEDRIZZETTI WINERY**   *Santa Clara 1945*   The winery, a pre-Prohibition site located east of Morgan Hill, was originally acquired by the Pedrizzettis in 45, and for years produced a line of generic wines in large bottles. The winery was upgraded in the 60s as the line expanded to include a range of varietals. All grapes crushed are purchased. Among the wines offered, the best-sellers are Barbera made in a rustic style and Chablis. Annual production is steady at the 75,000-case level. Wine quality is adequate at best.

**J. PEDRONCELLI WINERY**   *Sonoma 1904*   This remains a family-run winery and Jim and John Pedroncelli have quietly developed a solid reputation for good value. They currently have 135 acres next to the winery in the Dry Creek Valley. Over the years they have bought grapes from neighboring growers and others in the Alexander Valley to reach a production level of 130,000 cases a year. In the late 60s the winery began to slough off its jug-winery, rustic-wine image and moved into the varietal wine world. For a time Pedroncelli was best known for its reds, Zinfandel and Pinot Noir in particular, but by the 70s it was earning praise, and °on occasion, for Chardonnay, while its other white wines showed signs of improvement. It then settled into a groove where it offered generally straightforward wines that, if a little light in intensity, made up for that by being honestly priced.

Pedroncelli's Chardonnay is its quality leader and has grown in quantity (15,000 cases), but Cabernet Sauvignon remains its volume leader. In some vintages, Zinfandel represents a remarkable value. Both Zinfandel and Cabernet Sauvignon are involved in a modest Reserve program in which the winery will release them some six to seven years after the vintage. In 1995 Pedroncelli introduced a selection of single-vineyard wines such as Morris Fay Vineyard Cabernet Sauvignon aged entirely in French Oak, Pedroni-Bushnell Zinfandel, and two wines—Chardonnay and Pinot Noir—from Frank Johnson Vineyard. As part of this upgrade it also bottles a Zinfandel from the Mother Clone Vineyard, referring to a vineyard propagated and developed from the family's one acre of Zinfandel established in 1905. This Mother Clone Zinfandel achieved ** in the early goings. A fruity and frequently highly rated Fumé Blanc, a floral, slightly sweet–style Gewurztraminer, and an erratic Merlot fill out the line.

### Cabernet Sauvignon

(regular bottling)   83   84   85   **86**   **87**   88   89   90   93   94   95

*Cherry and blackberry fruit is combined with oaky richness and often with an herbal streak*

### Chardonnay

86°   87°   88   89   90   91   92   94   95

*Usually fruity, with hints of pears and blossoms, this light and pretty wine is often one of the true Chardonnay bargains when right*

### Zinfandel

(Sonoma County / Dry Creek Valley)   84°   85   86   87   **88°**   89°   90

(Pedroni-Bushnell)   93   94°   95

(Mother Clone)   94   **95°°**

*Berryish fruit of medium depth is roughened by tannins in a wine that ranges from ripe to shallow, depending on the year*

PEJU PROVINCE   *Napa 1983*   While running his nursery business in Los Angeles, Tony Peju visited the Napa Valley in 79. Not long afterwards, he purchased an established vineyard in the Rutherford region. Retaining the old parts planted to Cabernet Sauvignon, he added new acreage of Chardonnay to bring the total planting to 30 acres. In his first vintage, Peju made a pink wine dubbed "Karma," a blend of Cabernet, Chardonnay, and Colombard. By 85 he was ready to build a winery, but then became involved in a battle with Napa County officials over the right to sell wine from a tasting room, and construction was held up for years. By 89, the winery was completed. Cabernet Sauvignon, Chardonnay, and Merlot are the primary wines offered in its 6,000-case annual output. Merlot and Chardonnay also are made from the HB Vineyard, but this winery remains a Cabernet Sauvignon specialist offering a Reserve and a HB Vineyard bottling.

### Cabernet Sauvignon

(HB Vineyard)   **85°**   **86°**   **87°°**   89°   **90°°**   **91°**   **92°°**   93   **94°°**

*Well-constructed, medium-depth wines, showing black-cherry and cassis fruit, oak, and supporting tannins, and seemingly capable of aging for up to a decade or more*

PELLEGRINI FAMILY VINEYARDS   *(Olivet Lane Estate)*   Zinfandel, Barbera, and Carignane, all produced from some of the oldest vineyards in Sonoma County, are the primary focus of this line. Consulting winemaker Merry Edwards made 400–800 cases of each wine.

ROBERT PEPI WINERY    *Napa 1981*    Robert A. Pepi was in the fur-dressing business in San Francisco when he began looking for a country place for eventual retirement. In 66 he found a 70-acre site in the middle of Oakville, which included 15 acres of Cabernet Sauvignon. Over the next few years, as he expanded the vineyard, he developed a keen personal interest in Sauvignon Blanc, despite the fact that Cabernet Sauvignon was much more in demand at the time. Pepi eventually built a home and a small winery on a knoll overlooking his vineyards. By 81, he had removed all Cabernet Sauvignon, and his 65-acre vineyard consisted of Sauvignon Blanc, Semillon, and Chardonnay.

Made in a consistent style, with 10% to 15% Semillon, the Sauvignon Blancs typically offer spicy, herbal qualities with a touch of oak and a crisp, lively flavor. They often are at the * to ** quality level. After several reconfigurations, the 57-acre vineyard consists of 24 acres of Sauvignon Blanc, 12 acres of Sangiovese, and 12 acres of Merlot. In 88 the winery made the first Sangiovese in the U.S. and labeled it "Colline di Sassi."

In early 95 the winery and vineyards were acquired by Jess Jackson of Kendall-Jackson Winery, which was looking for a Napa Valley base of operations. Under Jackson's ownership, Pepi is making two Sauvignon Blancs (Two Heart Canopy and Reserve), two Sangioveses (Two Heart Canopy and Colline di Sassi), and Pinot Grigio and Malvasia Bianca from the Central Coast. The Oakville winery has been renamed Cardinale and has been expanded to the 500,000-case capacity. It is presently home base for Lokoya, Cardinale, and Pepi. For now Pepi's overall quality level remains good, although the highly regarded Vine Hill Cabernet has disappeared.

### Cabernet Sauvignon

(Vine Hill Ranch)    81**    82*    83*    84    **85***    **86***    **87*****    88 89    **91*****

*Nicely focused curranty fruit—medium-depth in most vintages—quietly enriching oak, moderate tannins, but occasional earthy, mushroomy notes*

PEPPERWOOD GROVE    *(Sebastiani Vineyards)*    Offering a full line of varietals in the competitive low-priced segment, Pepperwood Springs is a new Sebastiani brand of the 90s that earned the distinction of being the volume brand leader for Cabernet Franc. Other varietals offered in the 100,000-case line are Merlot, Zinfandel, Pinot Noir, Cabernet Sauvignon, and Chardonnay.

PEPPERWOOD SPRINGS VINEYARDS    *Mendocino 1981*    This small winery is situated along the beautiful rolling hills at the 1,000-foot level in the Anderson Valley Viticultural Area. At present, its vineyard consists of 4 acres of Pinot Noir and 3 acres of Chardonnay. The vineyard had to be redeveloped following a few years of noncultivation. The present owners, Gary and Phyllis Kaliher, bought the property a few years after the winery's founder and winemaker, Larry Parsons, died in an auto accident. The Kalihers took over in 87, and produced only a few hundred cases of Pinot Noir. With their vineyard back in full production, they are making about 1,000 cases a year, equally divided between Pinot Noir and Chardonnay. Fume Blanc and Zinfandel also are produced.

PER SEMPRE    *Napa 1992*    Cabernet Sauvignon and Sangiovese are the foci of owner/winemaker Dave DiLoreto. From his 5-acre vineyard in the Atlas Peak area he is making a Reserve and regular Napa Valley Cabernet and a Sangiovese. Annually he bottles 800 cases of Cabernet and 200 of Sangiovese.

MARIO PERELLI-MINETTI WINERY    *Napa 1988*    From the Central Valley wine dynasty family, Mario Perelli-Minetti was the manager of his family's once gigantic winery in Delano, the California Wine Association. As the winery and its numerous labels gradually lost their market share in the early 80s, he left to relocate in the Napa Valley. Owning 8 acres planted mostly to Cabernet Sauvignon, Perelli-Minetti had his first few vintages custom-made at Rutherford Hill. In 88 he built a winery on the Silverado Trail and crushed his first vintage there. The wines from 87 were aged and bottled at the new location. Buying Chardonnay from within Napa Valley, the winery makes 5,000 cases, 60% Chardonnay and 40% Cabernet Sauvignon. Long term, the annual production goal is 10,000 cases, following the same 60–40 breakdown.

PERRY CREEK VINEYARDS    *El Dorado 1992*    On a 155-acre ridgetop with great views, Perry Creek began by developing 68 acres of vineyards at the 2,400-foot-elevation site. Another parcel is being developed to 32 acres. As its vineyards were maturing, Perry Creek made Zinfandel, Cabernet, and Merlot. When all the estate vineyards come on-line, the winery will continue making Zinfandel, Cabernet, and Cabernet Franc, but it also has big plans for Italian and Rhone wines. Syrah, Viognier, and Mourvedre top the Rhone roster; Sangiovese and Muscat Canelli are the two Italian additions. As annual production moves toward 30,000 cases, Cabernet, Viognier, and Syrah have shown considerable promise.

PETERSON WINERY    *Sonoma 1992*    Proprietor Fred Peterson owns vineyards in the Dry Creek Valley, and he has access to grapes grown in the Russian River Valley farmed by his partner of many years, Bill Hambrecht, who owns Belvedere Winery. The Peterson label emphasizes red wines, and the current roster includes Zinfandel, Cabernet Sauvignon, Merlot, Barbera, and Syrah. The annual production is steady at 10,000 cases.

PEZZI-KING VINEYARDS    *Sonoma 1993*    The former William Wheeler Winery and its 133- acre estate, 34-acre vineyard, and small winery are now owned by James Rowe of San Francisco. Located on some of the steepest hills along the western slopes of the Dry Creek Valley, the vineyard contains Zinfandel, Cabernet, Merlot, and Cabernet Franc. The winery focuses production on estate-grown Cabernet and Zinfandel along with Chardonnay and Fumé Blanc from bought-in grapes. The new owner got his house in order by the second vintage. Cabernet Sauvignon from the estate Hillside Vineyard is the flagship and volume leader at 5,000 cases, but we have flipped over recent vintages of Fumé Blanc, which is a specialty of winemaker Paul Brasset. Chardonnay has improved with each vintage. Current production of 10,000 cases is expected to double over the next several years.

JOSEPH PHELPS VINEYARDS    *Napa 1973*    As a highly successful contractor-developer in Colorado, Joseph Phelps visited the San Francisco area in 71 to establish an office for his expanding business. There he met the Sangiacomo brothers, who were developing their soon-to-be 700-acre vineyard in Los Carneros. Phelps invested in the vineyard and as a result soon met Bud Mueller, another investor, who was also putting together a partnership to build a winery in Napa Valley to be known as Souverain of Napa and later on as Rutherford Hill Winery. By the time Phelps finished building that facility and also the sister winery, now known as Chateau Souverain in Sonoma County, he owned land in Napa Valley and had decided to build his own winery.

Located in a small indentation known as Spring Valley in the hills east of the Silverado Trail, the Phelps property covered 600 acres. Over the next few years he developed 175 acres to a variety of grapes adjacent to and on the hillsides around the winery. Though it produced some of California's most successful Rieslings in all sweetness categories, as well as successful Gewurztraminers and Sauvignon Blancs, the winery always devoted considerable attention to red wines, and developed what has grown to be a powerful stable of four Cabernet-type bottlings. In 74, Phelps made a Bordeaux blend, marketed under the proprietary name

"Insignia," which has become a genuine collector's item. In 75 the winery produced a limited-volume Cabernet from the Eisele Vineyard in the hills east of Calistoga. In 77, the Backus Vineyard Cabernet, a second vineyard designate, was first produced. Made from a small vineyard now owned by Phelps, just off the Silverado Trail and, the Backus bottling has received as many plaudits as any Cabernet made. Though some earlier vintages (77, 79) of Phelps regular Napa Valley Cabernet Sauvignon aged well, the style was variable until 83, when the winery issued the first of a string of lovely, fruit-highlighted Cabernets. The various Cabernet bottlings represent over 20,000 cases a year.

Among other achievements, Phelps was the first in California to produce a bona fide Syrah—in 74—and also the first to experiment with Scheurebe, a cross variety from Germany. "Vin du Mistral" designates a group of Rhone types now bottled, ranging from Viognier to a Grenache Rosé made from Mourvedre and Grenache, "Le Mistral" (blend of Syrah, Grenache, and Mourvedre), and Syrah. The winery's holdings have been augmented to include 50 acres south of Yountville planted predominantly to Merlot and Chardonnay, 45 acres in Stags Leap planted to Cabernet Sauvignon, 35 acres in Rutherford consisting of Cabernet Sauvignon, Merlot, and Cabernet Franc, and 40 acres of Chardonnay in the Carneros. Phelps also purchases Chardonnay from the Carneros region, and has bottled both a Napa Valley and a Reserve-type Chardonnay named "Ovation."

In 86 Phelps added Merlot to its roster. In the winery's 80,000-case annual output, Cabernet, Chardonnay, and Rhone varieties account for 75% of the total. In the 1990s Phelps has demonstrated a magic touch with all of its Cabernets.

### Cabernet Sauvignon

(Napa Valley)   73   74   75**   76*   77**   78   79   **80**   81*
82   **83**   **84***   **85***   86   87   **88**   **89**   **90***   91   **92****   93
**94**

(Backus Vineyard)   81**   83**   **84\*\*\***   85**   **86\*\***   **87***   **88***
89   **90\*\***   **91***   **92***   **92\*\***

(Eisele Vineyard)   77*   **78\*\***   79*   81*   82   **84\*\***   **85**   **86**
**89***   **91**

*All relatively full-bodied wines, the Napa Valley bottling stresses fruit more than weight and tannin, while the Eisele (no longer made) is loaded with ripe cherry, chocolate, and hints of dried brush to go with its imposing tannins. The Backus melds ripeness and tannin with black-cherry, currant, mint, and herb characteristics*

### Chardonnay

(Napa Valley / Los Carneros)   86*   87   88*   89   **90***   91   92*
**93***   94   95
(Ovation)   **93\*\***   94*   **96***

*Medium-depth wines with appley and slightly citrusy fruit, filled out by moderate oakiness; Ovation is richer, deeper and has the potential to be spectacular*

### Insignia

74**   75*   76**   77*   78**   79**   **80\*\*\***   81*   **82***   **83***
**84\*\*\***   **85\*\*\***   86   87*   88   **89***   90   **91\*\*\***   **92\*\***   **93\*\***
**94\*\*\***   **95\*\***

*Easily the most refined of Phelps's upscale reds, this blend of Cabernet Sauvignon (usually 50–60% but 80% Cabernet Sauvignon in recent vintages), Merlot, and Cabernet Franc typically offers soaring fruit, redolent of cherries and currants, with hints of strawberry, mint, chocolate, and herbs often evident as well. While not as massively tannic as the winery's Eisele or Backus bottlings, this one seems to age equally well on the basis of its livelier fruit and impeccable balance; 91 was a dramatic return to form after half a decade of indifferent results; 94 was one of the finest wines of a very fine vintage*

**Merlot**

87° 89 91° **94°°** **95°**

*Attractive cherryish fruit with suggestions of cassis; midterm aging potential*

**Syrah**

85° 86 **87°** **88°°** 89 **90** 91 **92** **93°** **94°°**

*After mixed results, this Syrah is deeper, spicier and clearly on point in recent vintages*

**Viognier**

88°° 89°° 90°°° 91°° 92° 93° 94° 95°° 96°°

*Wonderfully fruity wines with precise varietal character*

PHILIPPE-LORRAINE  *Napa 1989*  Phil Baxter has been a winemaker (Rutherford Hill, Domaine Michel) and winery manager for more than 20 years, and finally founded his own small brand (3,000 cases annually, to start). Leasing part of the Perelli-Minetti Winery, he makes Cabernet Sauvignon, Chardonnay, Merlot (blended with Cabernet Franc), and, in limited quantity, Cabernet Franc. All bear the Napa Valley appellation. Baxter purchases grapes as well as some ready-made wines from various sources. The initial bottlings of both the Chardonnay and Cabernet Sauvignon have been praised as good values. The long-term production target is 10,000 cases.

R. H. PHILLIPS VINEYARD  *Yolo 1983*  Phillips is an offshoot of a large agricultural venture owned by the Giguiere family. The vineyard project is near Esparto, in the eastern part of Yolo County about 30 miles from Davis. In the late 70s and early 80s this well-known farming family experimented with a few hundred acres of vineyards in an area they referred to as the Dunnigan Hills. With no history of grape growing in this remote area, and as the single pioneers, they needed to create a demand for their grapes. As a result, they made wines in 83 on what they considered would be a one-time-only basis. The varieties they were pushing were mostly whites, led by Chenin Blanc, Colombard, Semillon, and Sauvignon Blanc. The only significant red was Zinfandel. Priced on the low end, the wines sold so well that the owners were encouraged to plunge into winemaking. They built a facility and grew rapidly.

Thanks to low prices and some creative marketing, Phillips has expanded to over 400,000-case production level, with its sights on 750,000. The vineyard holdings have been expanded to 1,600 acres, led by Chardonnay (140), Sauvignon Blanc (115), Chenin Blanc (60), Syrah (208) and Viognier (145). Varietals under the R. H. Phillips label by Sauvignon Blanc (80,000 cases) and Chardonnay (200,000). With 88% of its production in white wines, the winery joined the Rhone Valley varietal brigade and is making Syrah, Mourvedre, and Viognier, as well as Rhone-style blends. The owners' sentimental favorite is Semillon, holding steady at 4,000 cases a year. In order to demonstrate an ability to produce serious wines, Phillips has created a limited line of Exp wines, with emphasis on Viognier and Syrah. Barrel-aged, mid priced Chardonnay and a Cabernet/Syrah blend are labeled Toasted Head. One of California's fastest-growing wineries, Phillips always seems in a constant state of flux. The estate acreage will eventually level off at 2,000 acres, all in the Dunnigan Hills. The winery's current varietal experimental projects are Zinfandel (50 acres are planted) and Tempranillo. From its 14-acre parcel Phillips in 1994 made its first Tempranillo, which may be California's first such varietal. Zinfandel is now sold under the Kempton Clark label. Overall the Chardonnays are good choices in their relative price categories, and Mistura, a blended red, can be a genuine value.

PIGEON CREEK  *Amador 1983*  In the town of Plymouth one finds the largest single vineyard in the county, called Clockspring Cellars. Of the total 350 acres planted to vines, 270 acres contain Zinfandel, with 60 planted to Sauvignon Blanc and the remainder to Muscat and port-type varieties. Most of the crop is sold. The owners have ventured slowly into wine production, but decided to bottle their wines under the Pigeon Creek brand. Three wines are regularly offered—White Zinfandel, Zinfandel, and Sauvignon Blanc. Production now stands at 3,000 cases a year, with 5,000 set as the annual maximum.

PINA CELLARS *Napa 1979* The Pinas—a well-respected Napa Valley family with years of experience as grape growers—decided to make wines from their own small vineyard in the Rutherford region. Most of the wines are sold locally. The original 5-acre vineyard has been expanded to approximately 16 acres of Chardonnay and 4 acres of Cabernet Sauvignon. When the vines reach full maturity, Pina Cellars will level off at 8,500 cases a year, with Chardonnay accounting for 80%.

PINE RIDGE WINERY *Napa 1978* A limited partnership headed by Gary Andrus, Pine Ridge Winery is located on the Silverado Trail in the Stags Leap District. In 78 Andrus purchased a 50-acre site which was partly planted to Chardonnay. After adding Merlot, Cabernet Sauvignon, and more Chardonnay acreage, he built a small winery that by 80 was producing 12,000 cases a year. Over the next decade Pine Ridge expanded, and the winery now owns about 200 acres scattered through several Napa Valley appellations. About one-third of the Pine Ridge output consists of Cabernet Sauvignon, of which there have been as many as five bottlings in a given year. The major bottling is the "Rutherford Cuvée," which is accompanied by the Stags Leap District bottling, Howell Mountain, and by an "Andrus Reserve." A Cabernet labeled "Cuvée Duet" was introduced in 85 but only performed once.

The most expensive wine is the Reserve, made in part from the Cabernet acreage adjacent to the Andrus home in Rutherford. Three Chardonnays are annually bottled—"Knollside Cuvée" (about 8,000 cases), Stags Leap District (2,000 cases) and Carneros (1,000 cases). Merlot blended with small amounts of related Bordeaux varieties now appears under two distinct guises, Carneros District and Crimson Creek, which is a blend of several small Napa vineyards. A new and almost overnight sales sensation is La Petite Vigne, a blend of Chenin Blanc and Viognier. Chenin Blanc remains an important item in the roster; produced in a slightly sweet, fruity style that rises to * , it has been a runaway sales success in some vintages, making it a welcome cash-flow wine. Due to problems with the vintages, Pine Ridge sold most of its 88 Cabernet Sauvignon under its second label, "Silverwood," and only one-third of the 89 vintage was labeled "Pine Ridge." However, today the winery is operating at 85,000 cases a year, with a goal of 100,000. The partnership is also behind Archery Summit (see entry) in Oregon.

### Cabernet Sauvignon

(Andrus Reserve) 80* **83°** **84°** **85°°** **86°** **91°** **94°°** 95°°

(Stags Leap District) 81° 82° **83°°** **84°°** **85°°** **86** 87 89 **91** **92°°** **93°** 94°° **95°**

(Rutherford Cuvée) 78° 79 80 81°° 82° 83° **84°** **85°°** **86** 87 89 **90** **91** **92** **93** **94°** **95°**

*Lavish oak accompanies all of these wines and, in the Andrus Reserve, which is the tightest-structured of the bunch, can sometimes seem the prime focus in lesser vintages; the "Duet" was bottled as the 85 Reserve, and it captured the deepest fruit found under that label to date; Stags Leap Vineyard wines are rich and supple in the style of wines that typify the area; the Rutherford bottling follows the geographic pattern as well in its delivery of rich, curranty flavors supported by moderate tannins*

### Chardonnay

(Knollside Cuvée) 86° 87°° 88 89 90 91° 93° 94 **95°°** 96

(Stags Leap Vineyard) 86 87° 88 89 90 **91°** **93°°** **94°°** 95°

*In years when the grapes ripen enough to give the wine some flesh, the Knollside Cuvée combines deep, firm fruit with toasty oak in a well-knit package; the Stags Leap Vineyard offering is generally more lush and rich, and tends toward riper fruit character than the Knollside Cuvée*

**Merlot**

(Selected Cuvée)   80°   81°   82°   83°   84   85°   86   87°°
88   89   **90**   **91**   **92°**   **93°**   **94°°**

*Ripe cherries, hints of brush and herbs, and rich oak are blended in this medium- to full-bodied series of wines*

---

PIPER SONOMA CELLARS   *Sonoma 1980*   When it began in 80, Piper Sonoma represented a 50–50 venture between Piper Heidsieck and Renfield Imports, but since 88 it is solely owned by Piper Heidsieck. The company has settled on four styles of *méthode champenoise* wines—Brut, Blanc de Noirs, Brut Reserve, and a Tête de Cuvée. All four are vintage-dated and from the Sonoma County appellation. The Brut (75% Pinot Noir, 25% Chardonnay and Pinot Blanc) has improved since 85, and offers refined fruit, subtle yeastiness, and lively, austere character. One of our favorites is the Blanc de Noirs (100% Pinot Noir), a °° performer, noted for its restraint and balanced impression. The Reserve Brut is offered on occasion and is aged for four years *en tirage* and two years on the cork prior to release. The winery's most expensive product is its "Tête de Cuvée" (50% Pinot Noir, 50% Chardonnay). In 1996 the winery and vineyards were sold to Judy Jordan of "J." Since then the Piper Sonoma line has been custom-made by Jordan's sparkling-wine team. Annual output of Piper Sonoma remains at 60,000 cases.

---

PLAM VINEYARDS & WINERY   *Napa 1984*   Ken Plam, an engineer in the Bay Area, frequently worked on projects in the Napa Valley. In the early 80s he purchased an old winery (Hopper Creek Vineyards) in Yountville in southern Napa Valley and began renovating it and expanding the vineyards. Plam's 26-acre vineyard is planted to three varieties—Cabernet Sauvignon, Chardonnay, and Merlot. In its history, the winery experienced erratic quality with Cabernet Sauvignon, but its Chardonnays showed much better.

---

PLUMP JACK WINES   *Napa 1995*   Gordon Getty and his son Bill are well-known San Francisco socialites who operate a number of businesses, including wine shops in San Francisco and Squaw Valley at Lake Tahoe. Using the former Villa Mt. Eden facility and with the services of Nels Venge, former Villa Mt. Eden winemaker, Plump Jack has been bottling two Cabernet Sauvignons from Napa Valley. Both the regular and the Reserve have impressed in the early rounds.

---

PORTER CREEK VINEYARDS   *Sonoma 1982*   Owner and winemaker George Davis began developing a 21-acre vineyard in the early 80s. His first vintage was 87, and since then Davis has been specializing in Pinot Noir and Chardonnay. From the inaugural vintage of 2,000 cases, he plans to grow slowly to a maximum of 8,000 cases.

---

BERNARD PRADEL CELLARS   *Napa 1983*   French-born Pradel was a successful chef in Oregon before settling in the Napa Valley. Though his family is connected with the wine trade in Chablis, he was making Chardonnay over the first few California vintages only while awaiting the maturity of his own vineyard, planted exclusively to Cabernet Sauvignon and Merlot. He has 10 acres and leases another 5. In the late 1990s Pradel sold the trademark and inventory to Goosecross Cellars, which will keep the label alive while there is inventory to sell.

**Cabernet Sauvignon**

84°   85   **86°**   **87**   88   89   **91**

*Somewhat inconsistent from year to year, these wines seem to have exaggerated the differences caused by vintage variation, with the result that they have ranged from*

*underfilled to more ripe than necessary; to their credit, they uniformly contain fo-
cused varietal fruit and attractively rich oak*

PRAGER WINERY & PORT WORKS  *Napa 1979*  Tucked behind the Sutter Home Winery
visitors center just south of St. Helena, the Prager Winery specializes in port. Jim
Prager left a long career in the insurance business to settle in Napa. All of the
ports, often labeled with proprietary names, are 100% varietal in composition.
The three varietals he works with regularly are Cabernet Sauvignon, Petite Sirah,
and Pinot Noir. Most grapes are purchased, but Prager has under 1 acre of Cabernet Sauvignon in his estate vineyard. His first estate-bottled Port was a blend of
82/83. As a rule, the wines are aged in small oak for close to four years, and most
are unfined and unfiltered. The minimal handling approach sometimes allows a
degree of volatile acidity to develop that some find distracting. Maximum production is set at 4,000 cases a year.

PRESTON VINEYARDS  *Sonoma 1975*  In the northern end of the Dry Creek Valley, the
Prestons developed 115 acres in the early 70s. With the intention of selling most
of their crop, they planted 13 varieties. Their first vintage consisted of 1,200 cases
of Zinfandel. Having steadily expanded production since then to the current
18,000-case-a-year level, the winery continues to offer a variety of wines, all from
the estate vineyard. In 84 Lou Preston, trying to tame the aggressiveness of his
Sauvignon Blanc, blended it with Semillon. Labeled "Cuvée de Fumé," this lively,
medium-bodied wine captures well-focused fruit and is capable of ** performance. It has become the best-seller. Other major wines offered by Preston are
Zinfandel and Rhone wines.

Encouraged by the favorable critical reception of its Sirah-Syrah blended red,
Preston stepped up its production of Rhone wines. These currently include "Faux"
(a blend of Syrah, Carignane, and Mourvedre), Viognier, Syrah, Marsanne, and
Mouruedre wine. The early vintages of Viognier and Marsanne were impressive.
Rounding out the line are a Barbera, Sangiovese, Cabernet Sauvignon, Gamay
Beaujolais, Semillon (barrel-fermented), and a lovely dry Rosé named Le Petit
Faux.

**Syrah**

89  **90****  **91****  **92***  93  **94****  **95***

*Deep yet balanced, blackberryish fruit with nicely proportioned tannins*

**Viognier**

91**  92*  93*  94*  95*  96  97*

*Typically fruity with moderate depth*

**Zinfandel**

82  83**  84  85  86*  87*  88*  89  **90***  **91**  **92***  **93***
94  95  **96**

*Centered on berryish, spicy fruit, and quietly enriched by sweet oak, the wine typi-
cally carries light-medium tannins and is capable of several years aging, especially
in its best vintages*

PRIDE MOUNTAIN VINEYARDS  *Napa 1991*  Jim Pride, a dentist who teaches dental
management, acquired a long-abandoned ranch and vineyard site on Spring
Mountain in 1990. New vineyards were developed and Pride Mountain now consists of 50 acres of Cabernet Sauvignon, Merlot, related red varieties along with
lesser amounts of Chardonnay and Viognier. Part of the Pride's vineyard falls on
the Sonoma County side of the mountain, which led to bureaucratic delays in the
construction of a winery. Once a winery is built, the present 10,000 case annual
output will gradually grow to the optimum level of 30,000 cases. Cabernet Sauvignon (blended with Cabernet Franc) and Merlot (blended with Cabernet Sauvignon) are the featured wines. Pride also offers Viognier, which has been one of the

richest, and, in very limited (100–200 cases) quantities, it bottles Reserve Cabernet Sauvignon, Reserve Claret (Meritage blend), and Cabernet Franc.

### Cabernet Sauvignon

(Napa Valley)   **91°**   **92**   94°°   **95°°**

(Reserve)   94°°°

*Dense, moderately to very tight, binary, ageworthy wines*

### Merlot

91   **93°°**   **94°°**   95°

*Consistent with the house style, these wines, while more cherryish in character than the Cabernet, are fairly tight in style*

### Reserve Claret

93°°°

*Deep, concentrated, tannic, good for 15-20 years in bottle*

---

THE PYRAMIDS   *Sonoma 1995*   Greg Graham of Rombauer oversees the winemaking for this small Sonoma winery. From 10 acres planted in 1989, the owners sold their entire crop until reserving a few tons in 1995. Chardonnay in a creamy, barrel-fermented style has been well received by critics for being modestly priced.

---

QUADY WINERY   *Madera 1977*   As head winemaker for a large, now defunct Lodi winery, Andy Quady was encouraged to try his hand at port-making in 75. The request came from Sacramento wine merchant Darrell Corti, who was convinced that Amador County Zinfandel would make quality port. Quady made 600 cases that year, and has been associated with dessert wines ever since. As production grew gradually, Quady expanded the original winemaking facility behind his home. In 81 he decided to devote full time to his own winery. As he worked with port, both vintage and blended, Quady became familiar with many growers in the Central Valley. In 80 he found a few remaining acres of an otherwise abandoned variety, Orange Muscat, which he made into a fortified wine. Since the variety was unknown to consumers, Quady sold the wine as "Essensia," a proprietary name, and presented it in a striking oversized label. Fortified at low levels (14–16% alcohol), Essencia was an immediate sales success and quickly became Quady's flagship wine. In 83 he added a Black Muscat fortified wine which he named "Elysium." It is his second best-selling wine at 4,000 cases a year. "Electra," a low-alcohol Orange Muscat, was added in the 90s.

Amador County continues to supply Zinfandel for his two types of port. Quady uses "Port of the Vintage" for batches in need of only nominal cellaring, and Vintage Port for those with long-aging potential. In 82, a third port was introduced, first identified as "Frank's Vineyard" and now bottled as "Starboard." This Vintage Port is made from a trial planting in Amador of several traditional port varieties— Tinta Cao, Tinta Amerela, Valdepeñas, and Bastardo. Total port production is steady at 3,000 cases a year.

---

QUAIL RIDGE CELLARS & VINEYARD   *Napa 1978*   In the mid-70s founders Elaine Wellesley and her late husband, Jesse Corallo, developed 10 acres of Chardonnay in the Mount Veeder district of the Mayacamas Mountains. The wines were made in an historic aging cellar located on Atlas Peak Road. With expansion of the vineyard to 20 acres of Chardonnay in 83, the winery increased its Chardonnay production, and added Cabernet Sauvignon.

By 88 Quail Ridge needed repairs and improvements, and the Christian Brothers, wanting a limited-volume winery with a hand-crafted image, purchased it. After upgrading the winery, the owners secured 20 additional Chardonnay acres in the Yountville area. Quail Ridge's annual production reached the desired 30,000-case level, with Chardonnay leading the way at 17,000 cases. Acquired by Heublein in 1989, Quail Ridge was sold in 95 to several former Heublein executives who founded Rutherford Benchmarks, a wine-marketing company based in Napa. Quality of late has been inconsistent at best.

QUATRO  *Sonoma 1994*  A separate and limited-edition brand, Quatro wines are made by Bob Broman, a veteran whose track record includes Stag's Leap Wine Cellars and Concannon. Quatro to date offers Pinot Noir from Russian River Valley and Cabernet Sauvignon from vineyards in Sonoma Valley and Russian River Valley. Annual output is fewer than 3,000 cases.

QUINTESSA  *Napa 1993*  In 1990 Franciscan Estates purchased 300 acres in the Rutherford region, and since then they have developed 180 acres to red Bordeaux varieties. This vineyard, said to be Napa's first complete postphylloxera vineyard, contains 60% Cabernet Sauvignon, 30% Merlot, and 10% Cabernet Franc. A blend of all three varieties, Quintessa, much like traditional châteaux in Bordeaux, makes only one wine made from its vineyard. In the early vintages the annual output did not break 1,000 cases, but the vineyard is capable of yielding 20,000 cases. Quality over those early vintages has been exceptionally high—as have prices.

QUIVIRA VINEYARDS  *Sonoma 1981*  Fitting the definition of an estate winery quite literally, Quivira began in 81 with the purchase of an old vineyard site that was expanded into a 75-acre vineyard on the western side of the Dry Creek Valley. An ultra-modern, functional winery was ready for the 87 harvest. Since then, Quivira has moved steadily toward its annual 25,000-case goal, and is on course to produce wines entirely from its own vineyard by the mid-90s. The winery makes three varietals and a blended red. Sauvignon Blanc, Zinfandel, and Cabernet Sauvignon (labeled "Cabernet Cuvée" from 89 onward) are the major varietal offerings, but the vineyard also contains sufficient amounts of Semillon, Petite Sirah, Merlot, and Cabernet Franc. The winery has developed 6 acres to red Rhone varieties. The winery makes two varietals, Zinfandel and Sauvignon Blanc, along with a blend labeled "Dry Creek Cuvee," a Grenache-based wine made with varying amounts of Mourvedre, Syrah, and Zinfandel. Quivira produced a varietal Cabernet Sauvignon until 1988, and replaced it with a blend labeled Cabernet Cuvee. That wine had a run from 89 to 94. Winemaker Grady Wann took over in 1990, and since then he has fine-tuned the winery's brightly fruited style of Sauvignon Blanc and its Zinfandel. Merlot has joined the roster. The Sauvignon Blanc has earned ° for its melon-figgy aroma, forthright oakiness, and well-stuffed flavor impression. A Reserve Sauvignon Blanc, 100% barrel-fermented, is a recent addition.

### Zinfandel

83°°°  84°°  85°  86°  **87°°**  **88°°°**  89  **90°°**  **91**  **92°°**
93  **94**  95  96

*Attractive, well-proportioned wines, carrying bright, ripe-berryish fruit, are enriched by moderate oak; somewhat rough tannins suggest a few years of cellaring, but are not overbearing*

QUPÉ  *Santa Barbara 1982*  Owner Bob Lindquist is part of an innovative trio (which includes the two founders of Au Bon Climat), all of whom once worked together at Zaca Mesa. Each went off to explore different wine types and appellations and ended up creating exciting wines that brought badly needed excitement to Santa Barbara. By the end of the 80s, they all finished up sharing one facility built by the owners of Bien Nacido Vineyard. Initially with Qupé (an American Indian name for a poppy), Lindquist moved in the direction of Rhone Valley wine types. Qupé was among the pioneers of Syrah in California through several vintages made from grapes grown by Estrella River vineyards. It now makes Syrah from the Bien Nacido Vineyard, a source shared with Bonny Doon Vineyards. In addition, Qupé bottles small batches of Syrah from two other appellations—Los Olivos (blended with Mourvedre) and Central Coast. Overall, the winery has regularly earned ° for its Syrahs.

By 90, Qupé was making 2,000 cases of Syrah, and was among the first to bottle Mourvedre, Marsanne, and Viognier. Lindquist has a 1-acre experimental vineyard containing most of the Rhone varieties. Qupé has produced a series of Chardonnays, including on occasion a full-blown Reserve (which earned °° in 93). As the winery grows gradually to the 10,000-case-a-year target, the amount of Chardonnay will level off at 3,000 cases. Qupé's companion label is Vita Nova (see entry).

### Chardonnay

| 86 | 87° | 88°° | 89° | **90°** | 91 | **92°** | 93 | 94 |
|----|-----|------|-----|---------|----|---------|----|----|

| (Reserve) | 90° | 92 | 93°° | 94 |
|-----------|-----|----|------|----|

*Toasty, somewhat buttery notes overlie broad, appley fruit in this series of consistently rich wines*

---

RABBIT RIDGE VINEYARDS   *Sonoma 1985*   Erich Russell began developing a 35-acre vineyard in the early 80s. Erich is a well-known winemaker who was with Belvedere Winery from 1988 to 94. He made small quantities of Rabbit Ridge varietals for a few years, but by 89, from his mature vineyard and from purchased grapes, his winery was offering a full line of wines. From 17 acres planted, Russell bottles a Rabbit Ridge Ranch Chardonnay; a Sonoma County bottling is made in larger quantities. Zinfandel and Rhone wines are the next in importance. Russell has developed "Meadow Glen" as a second label for Sauvignon Blanc and wines that were not used for the Rabbit Ridge line. The Rabbit Ridge Chardonnays become the quality leaders in the winery's initial vintages. By the late 1990s, however, Russell was offering a wide assortment of wines, but it was his Zinfandels, particular the Old Vine (known as OVZ), the Estate Reserve, and single-vineyard versions that gained ** and *** in 95 and 96. Barrel cuvee Zinfandel is popularly priced but not very interesting to date. 95 Cabernet earned **. At times we have praised Russell's Viognier, Reserve Merlot, Syrah, and Sangiovese, but the winery offers many wines from sources that frequently change from one year to the next, making consistency a real problem. Annual production is 30,000 cases.

### Chardonnay

| (Sonoma County) | 86° | 87 | 88°° | 89° | 91 | 92 | 94 | 95 | 96 |
|-----------------|-----|----|------|-----|----|----|----|----|----|

| (Rabbit Ridge Vineyards) | 86 | 87° | 88° | 89 | 93 |
|--------------------------|-----|-----|-----|----|----|

*Both wines are balanced, fairly generous, and full of ripe, bright fruit, seasoned with rich, somewhat toasty oak in a straightforward style*

### Zinfandel

| **89°°** | 90 | **91** | 92° | **93°°** | **94** | **95°°** | **96°** |
|----------|----|--------|-----|----------|--------|----------|---------|

*Filled with bright, ripe, slightly spicy, berryish fruit in top vintages*

---

RADANOVICH WINERY   *Mariposa 1986*   This is a family-owned venture that began with the planting of 7 acres in the early 80s. The varieties planted are Zinfandel and Sauvignon Blanc. With another 15-acre vineyard controlled on a long-term lease, Radanovich is gradually increasing production from the initial annual 2,000-case output. Zinfandel, White and Red, has represented 50% of its production, and Sauvignon Blanc is the second most important wine offered. Production could grow to 10,000 cases a year.

---

A. RAFANELLI WINERY   *Sonoma 1974*   As grape growers, the Rafanelli family have always been held in high esteem by their peers. After selling grapes from their own vineyard and managing vineyards owned by others, the family eased into winemaking in 74. In the early vintages, Cabernet Sauvignon, Zinfandel, and Gamay Beaujolais were offered. By the late 70s the winery was beginning to make a name for itself and helped focus attention on the Dry Creek Valley appellation through a series of magnificent Zinfandels and good, solid Cabernet Sauvignons. Today, Rafanelli has 50 acres, with 22 acres devoted to Zinfandel, 10 acres to Cabernet Sauvignon, and the rest to a mix of varieties. Located midway between Healdsburg and the Warm Springs Dam, the Zinfandel plantings are situated in the hills above the west side of the valley floor. The location is slightly warm, and the non-irrigated hillside vines grow under stress conditions that intensify flavors.

Dave Rafanelli, who now runs the winery, believes, as did his father, Americo, in the special flavors obtained from old, old vines. The Zinfandels made by the winery are characterized by deep, well-defined fruit and berrylike flavors with great substance. Blended with Merlot in some vintages, Rafanelli Cabernet is also intense, sturdy, and imposing. The annual production is at 6,000 cases, with 4,500 of Zinfandel and 1,500 of Cabernet Sauvignon. Both are bottled unfiltered and tend to throw a deposit in the bottle.

### Cabernet Sauvignon
**88°°  89  90°  91°  92°  93°**

*A bit on the rustic side, this one is ripe, brawny, deep, and somewhat coarse in tannins*

### Zinfandel
**78°  79°  80°  81°  82°  83°  84  85°  86°°°  88°°°  89°
90°  91°°  92°°  91°  92°°  93°  94°°  95°**

*Consistently well made, ripe, spicy, fruity, deep, and fairly full in body, this is prototypical Dry Creek Valley Zinfandel*

---

RANCHO SISQUOC WINERY   *Santa Barbara 1977*   The Flood Ranch in the Santa Maria Valley covers 38,000 acres and grows a variety of crops. Rancho Sisquoc is the name for the wine and vineyard sides of this diversified agricultural enterprise. With the oldest parcels established in 68, Rancho Sisquoc is one of the oldest vineyards in the county. Over the first decade it has sold grapes to almost every winery in Santa Barbara, as well as to many outside the region. Its vineyards have been expanded to 211 acres, and the leading varieties planted are Cabernet Sauvignon, Chardonnay, Sylvaner, Merlot, Johannisberg Riesling, and Sauvignon Blanc. Of the 3,000 cases produced by the winery each year, the primary wines are Cabernet Sauvignon, Chardonnay (barrel-fermented), and Riesling, with small quantities of Merlot, Sylvaner, and Sauvignon Blanc. The whites enjoy a much better quality record than the reds. The output remains steady at 6,000 cases.

---

RANDOM RIDGE   *Napa 1981*   The Hawleys began developing their 9 acre vineyard in 1981, and planted Cabernet, Cabernet Franc, Merlot, and Sangiovese on their steep hillsides in the Mt. Veeder appellation. Deliberately crowding some 1200 vines to the acre, which is twice the standard number, the owners hope this system intensifies the flavors in the one wine they bottle, an estate red Meritage wine. Annual production is approaching 1,000 cases.

---

KENT RASMUSSEN WINERY   *Napa 1986*   Kent Rasmussen acquired 10 acres in Los Carneros and planted Pinot Noir, financing the construction of a winery by a system of patronage in which each member-patron would receive wine at cost and/or have the right to custom-make wine at the facility. The scheme worked long enough to get the winery under way, and with the release of the inaugural Pinot Noir and Chardonnay Rasmussen earned enough critical acclaim to keep afloat. His wines are now distributed through traditional channels, except for what is offered to the original patrons. Chardonnay (2,000 cases) and Pinot Noir (1,000 cases) from the Carneros are his primary wines. Small (100–200) case lots of Sauvignon Blanc and are also made. All white wines are fermented and aged in barrels; the reds, in small open-top vats. A self-proclaimed tinkerer, Rasmussen makes small batches of odd wines every year and bottles most of them under his second label, "Ramsey." The Chardonnay has been successful to date; the Pinot Noir is inconsistent.

### Chardonnay

86°°   87   88°   89°   90°   91   92   94°

*Toasty, sometimes buttery, often carrying a citrusy undertone, and usually tight in fruit and structure, the wine is capable of aging for several years after release*

RAVENSWOOD   *Sonoma 1976*   Co-owner and winemaker Joel Peterson was raised by wine-collecting parents, and his father helped form the Vintner's Club (an influential wine-tasting club) in San Francisco. Peterson served as an apprentice with Zinfandel-master Joseph Swan in the early 70s, and in 76 made 500 cases of Zinfandel in a rented corner of Swan's winery. In 81 he formed a partnership and moved into a facility just south of the town of Sonoma. Over the first few vintages Ravenswood made Zinfandel from appellations in Sonoma, Napa, and El Dorado County. The early style of winemaking was a no-holds-barred approach that occasionally went too far. Today's style has been tempered somewhat, though it is still muscular and brawny.

Ravenswood has emerged as a pace-setting producer of Zinfandel, which in recent vintages is represented by 15 bottlings. The volume-leading "Vintner's Blend" (more than 30,000 cases) is the most approachable and the least expensive. The other Zinfandel bottlings are "Sonoma County" and four vineyard-designations—"Old Hill Ranch," "Dickerson Vineyard," "Napa Valley," "Cooke's Vineyard" from Sonoma County, and "Belloni Vineyard" from the Russian River Valley. Merlot is the second most significant varietal, with three separate labels. Again, the "Vintner's Blend" is the volume leader, followed by Merlots labeled "Sonoma County" and "Sangiacomo Vineyard" from the Carneros district. Cabernet Sauvignons originate from Sonoma County and the Gregory Vineyard in the Carneros district. A Merlot–Cabernet red Meritage from the Sonoma Valley is labeled "Pickberry." Only 4% of Ravenswood's annual production is white wine, but there are two separate Chardonnays ("Estate Bottled" and "Sangiacomo Vineyard"). As a red wine specialist, Ravenswood hit paydirt during the recent upswing in the popularity of red wine, and its annual production doubled in five years to its present 150,000 cases. A Rhone-inspired red blend named "Icon" is the first sign of Peterson's newfound interest in red grapes originating in the South of France.

### Cabernet Sauvignon

(Sonoma County)   82°   84°   **85°**   86°   87°   **88°**   89°   90°
**91   92°   93   94   95**

*Sometimes reminding us of Zinfandel in its ripeness and near-berryish fruit, the wine is bold, full, and tannic in structure*

### Chardonnay

86   **87**   88   90   91   92   93   94

*Oaky but shallow in fruit character*

### Pickberry Vineyard Red

86   **87   88   90°   93°   94°°**   95°

*This blend of Cabernet Sauvignon, Merlot, and Cabernet Franc varies in blend from year to year but has consistently followed the Ravenswood style of pert, berryish fruit and rustic tannins*

### Zinfandel

(Dickerson)   83°   84°°   85°   86°   **87°°   88°   89°   90°°°**
**91°   95°**

(Old Hill)   84°°   **85°°°   88°**   89   **90°°   91°   92°°**   95°

(Old Vines)   **88°   89°   90°°   91°   92°**   93   **94°**   95°   96

*Ripe, aromatic, enormously fruity in most years, highly oaked, tannic, bold, and absolutely stamped by the winemaker's hand—and very much in the style of his mentor*

MARTIN RAY VINEYARDS  *(Codera Wine Co.)*  One of California's pioneering names, Martin Ray Vineyards slipped quietly into oblivion in the 1980s. In 1993 the brand was purchased by the Codera Wine Co., which revived the name for its upscale line. The roster includes Cabernet Sauvignon, a Chardonnay labeled "Marriage" and a "California" Pinot Noir. All wines are made in Mendocino County.

**Cabernet Sauvignon**
91**  92  93  94**

*Ripe, blackberryish and well-oaked*

**Chardonnay**
92**  93*  94**  95*

*Very well-made, balanced, somewhat appley wines*

RAYMOND VINEYARD  *Napa Valley 1974*  The Raymond family has been involved in Napa Valley viticulture since Prohibition. Roy Raymond, Sr., married a member of the Beringer family and worked at Beringer Vineyards for over three decades before forming this winery with his two sons, Roy Jr. and Walt Raymond. Together, they began developing their 80-acre vineyard in 71, and made their first wines three years later. Today, Roy Jr. is the vineyardist and Walt the winemaker. After planting a range of varieties and making a wide assortment of wines in the 70s, they decided to concentrate on Chardonnay, Cabernet Sauvignon, and Sauvignon Blanc. In the 90s, they replanted the 75-acre home vineyard and developed 250 acres in the southern part of Napa. This Jameson Canyon Vineyard contains Chardonnay, Merlot, and Pinot Noir. Also, the owners developed 300 acres of Chardonnay in Monterey County.

The roster now consists of four tiers. Raymond Amberhill is the large-volume designation for Chardonnay and Cabernet Sauvignon from the California appellation. It has replaced the La Belle line. The second level is a line of Napa Valley estate wines (Chardonnay, Cabernet Sauvignon, Merlot, Sauvignon Blanc, and Pinot Noir), along with an estate Monterey Chardonnay. The next tier includes Reserve Cabernet Sauvignon, Chardonnay Merlot, Pinot Noir, Sauvignon Blanc and red Meritage. Representing the top of the line is the Generations moniker, consisting of Cabernet Sauvignon (3,000 cases) and Chardonnay (3,000 cases) presented in custom-molded bottles. All Chardonnays are aged in French oak, with the popular-style California given three to four months in barrel, while the Napa Valley and the Reserve are barrel-aged six and nine months respectively. Raymond's Cabernets of the 90s have followed the statewide trend by becoming somewhat softer and less tannic than their brethren of the 70s. The Private Reserve Cabernet is 100% Cabernet, and the Napa Valley Cabernet is usually blended with 10% to 12% Merlot. Over recent vintages, Raymond's Sauvignon Blancs are generally on the fruity, modestly varietal side. All told, Raymond produces 300,000 cases, 65% of that Chardonnay, 20% Cabernet Sauvignon, and 5% Sauvignon Blanc; they added a red Meritage in 89. In early 89, the Raymonds sold the majority interest in their winery and vineyards to Kirin Brewing, Inc., of Japan. The Raymonds retain a minority interest and are the company's managing partners.

**Cabernet Sauvignon**
(Napa Valley Reserve)  78*  79  80  82*  83  84*  **85***  **86***
**87**  88  89*  **90***  **91**  92**  **93**  **94**  95

*Ripe cherry character, with moderate oak, light-medium tannins; usually good in better vintages and somewhat light in lesser years*

**Cabernet Sauvignon**
(Private Reserve)  81**  82**  83*  84**  85**  86*  87  88
90  91**  92*

*Ripe and rich in virtually every vintage, these highly oaked, currant- and cherry-flavored, full-bodied wines earn plaudits for depth, rugged handsomeness, and seeming long-term ageability*

### Chardonnay

| (Reserve) | 86° | 87° | 88° | 89 | 90 | 91 | 92 | 93 | 94 | 96 |
|---|---|---|---|---|---|---|---|---|---|---|
| (Private Reserve) | 84° | 85° | 86° | 87° | 88 | 89° | **90°** | **91°** | 92 | |
| **94°** | | | | | | | | | | |

*Attractive wines in early vintage, the Napa Valley is straightforwardly fruity, while the Reserve is strongly oriented to toasty oak and tends to be fuller-bodied*

REGUSCI WINERY   *Napa Valley 1996*   One of the last independent growers in the Stags Leap District, the Regusci family refurbished the historic Occidental Winery in the area. Cabernet Sauvignon is the primary wine produced from their 30-acre vineyard. In the early 1990s their Chardonnay crop was sold to Venezia and other producers. However, as the family eases into winemaking, Chardonnay, along with Merlot and Zinfandel, will have a place in the lineup.

RENAISSANCE VINEYARD   *Yuba 1978*   With 365 acres of terraced vineyards on the western slopes of the Sierra Nevada Mountains, Renaissance claims to be the largest mountain vineyard in the world. Vineyards and winemaking are just one activity involved in this co-operative venture of arts and crafts lovers. A fine arts museum is adjacent to the winery, and all artifacts made on the premises are sold by the members. A few wines were made in 82, but it was years before Renaissance released substantial quantities. The wines made are Sauvignon Blanc, Chardonnay, White Riesling, Cabernet Sauvignon, and Petite Sirah. With Sauvignon Blanc and Cabernet accounting for 50% of the total, the winery's annual output has climbed to 25,000 cases, which includes wines under Da Vinci, a second label. Long-term plans call for a maximum annual output of 50,000 cases. Cabernet Sauvignon, the most consistent performer to date, will increase in volume as the winery moves closer to full capacity.

RENWOOD   *(Santino Winery)*   After leasing the Santino Winery in Amador County, winemaker Scott Harvey introduced Renwood as his upscale brand for limited volume wines. Zinfandel from the Grandpere Vineyard, Syrah, and Barbera are the main wines made, and vintages to date have all been made in a full-throttle, take-no-prisoners style. Unfortunately, just when the wines were earning high praise, Harvey was forced out of the partnership and eventually landed at Folie-a-Deux (see entry). The current owners continue making Zinfandel, Sangiovese, and other wines from the Sierra Foothills.

RETZLAFF VINEYARDS   *Alameda 1985*   After planting their 10-acre vineyard in the Livermore Valley in 1979, Bob and Gloria Taylor eased slowly into winemaking. He is a research chemist and handles the winemaking chores, while his wife manages the vineyard. The first wine made was Gray Riesling in a medium-sweet style; it remains the backbone of their line, which now also includes Chardonnay and Cabernet Sauvignon, all three from estate-grown grapes. In a copious vintage the annual production approaches 3,000 cases.

REVERIE   *Napa 1993*   Owner Norman Kiken acquired a 27 acre vineyard on Diamond Mountain adjacent to Diamond Creek Vineyard. The vineyard contains Cabernet Sauvignon, Cabernet Franc, and Merlot, and Kiken has added experimental blocks of Barbera and Tempranillo. From a modest production of 250 cases of Cabernet Sauvignon in his first vintage. Kiken, who oversees wine production, plans to gradually take production to 2,000 cases. Cabernet Sauvignon is the primary wine bottled. Barbera and Cabernet Franc are possible future additions to the roster.

REY SOL   *(Mount Palomar Winery)*   With Castelletto for its wines of Italian origins, Mount Palomar is using this label for some Mediterranean-inspired wines. Included in this line are Syrah, Viognier, Mediterrane Blanc (Viognier and Marsanne), and Le Mediterrane (Syrah, Mourvedre). Both the Temecula-grown

Viognier and white blend have been outstanding and sensational values. All told, Rey Sol bottles about 1,000 cases a year.

RICHARDSON VINEYARDS   *Sonoma 1980*   A limited partnership, Richardson is in the Sonoma sector of the Carneros District. Most of its wines originate in the Carneros, and the winery has developed somewhat of a following for its Pinot Noir. Other wines produced in this 2,000-case-capacity winery are Cabernet Sauvignon, Chardonnay, and Merlot. At times its Pinot Noirs (recent vintages have been from the Sangiacomo Vineyard) are a fantastic melange of flavors, with unusual depth and substance. The Chardonnay has rarely enjoyed success; the Zinfandel emerged from its inconsistency to score **°°°** in 90, but has not repeated that success.

### Merlot
(Sangiacomo)   **90   93°   94°   95°   96°**

*Balanced, nicely fruity, consistent wines*

### Pinot Noir
83   84°   85   86°   87°°   88   89   90   **91°   93   94   95**

*Lots of ripe cherry and black-cherry fruit, with nuances of tar and orange rind, en-riched by sweet, creamy oak in wines that are usually fairly full-bodied and youth-fully tannic; less attractive lately*

RIDGE VINEYARDS   *Santa Clara 1962*   In 59 several members of the Stanford Research Institute bought an abandoned hilltop property as an ideal campground and re-treat. When remnants of what was once the famous Monte Bello vineyard were discovered, partner Dave Bennion, who was reluctantly to serve later on as Ridge's first winemaker, convinced the others to preserve that vineyard. The first few harvests were sold, but by 62 Bennion was making 400 gallons of wine and the partners formed Ridge Vineyards. In 67 the partners committed themselves to winemaking by investing money in the property, hired Bennion as full-time winemaker, and began searching for grapes, especially Zinfandel, from old, dry-farmed, mountain vineyards.

Initially, making Zinfandels from Amador County, Paso Robles, Sonoma, and Mendocino, Ridge favored the heavy-duty approach. With the arrival of Paul Draper as winemaker in 69, Ridge continued to ferret out grapes—Zinfandels, Pe-tite Sirah, and Cabernets—from various sources, but turned to more classical re-straint in the winemaking. The adherence to proven traditional procedures such as natural yeast fermentations, small oak aging, and clarification by racking, helped set Ridge Zinfandels apart stylistically from the competition in the early 70s. Among the many vineyard-designated Zinfandels Ridge has offered, the most memorable are the "Geyserville" from the Trentadue Vineyard, first made in 66; the Lytton Springs in Sonoma County, introduced in 72; and the Howell Mountain Beatty Ranch, dating from 79. In retrospect, the success enjoyed by Ridge helped revive Zinfandel, and also may have spared numerous old vineyards likely to have been removed on the basis of simple economics.

Ridge is almost as well known for Cabernet Sauvignon. To some collectors, its limited Monte Bello Cabernet, first produced in 66, ranks among the best any-where. In the 80s Ridge made a Cabernet Sauvignon from York Creek Vineyard lo-cated along Spring Mountain in the Napa Valley region. Starting in 83, Ridge began sorting out the softer, less distinctive lots from Monte Bello and the ad-joining but slightly lower Jimsomare Vineyard to blend a Cabernet with the ap-pellation of Santa Cruz Mountains. In the late 60s a few acres of Merlot were added to the Monte Bello and Jimsomare Vineyards. A varietal Merlot was not made until 85, when Ridge began working with grapes from Bradford Mountain in the Russian River Valley. Finally, Ridge has continued offering Petite Sirah from York Creek Vineyard to help sustain the otherwise neglected varietal. For close to two decades, Ridge has made small amounts of white wine. No more than a barrel or two of Chardonnay was normal until 84, but it is now expanding Chardonnay production, and makes one version from the Santa Cruz Mountains. To prove it is not unaware of fads and trends, Ridge produced a White Zinfandel in the 80s, albeit in a dry, oak-aged style. Otsuka of Japan acquired Ridge in 86. In the 1990s Ridge purchased Lytton Springs Vineyard and the nearby Norton Ranch, known as Lytton West. It also expanded Jimsomare Vineyard to 65 acres, with Chardonnay, Cabernet, and Merlot all being part of this expansion. Its wine lineup has grown to include Mataro (Mourvedre) from Bridgehead Vineyard and Zinfandel from Pagani Ranch. Total output is holding steady at 40,000 cases. Ridge also owns Lytton Springs (see entry).

### Cabernet Sauvignon

(Monte Bello)  68**  70***  71**  72*  73**  74**  75*
76***  77  78*  80  82  83*  84***  85***  86  87  88*
89*  90*  91**  92**  93*  94**  95

*Among the very best Cabernets produced in California, the wine usually is deep in concentrated, curranty fruit, and somehow suggests power and toughness while managing to avoid excesses of alcohol and tannin; the earliest vintages were not so refined but have outlived their rough exteriors and are now among the most desirable of older Cabernets*

### Cabernet Sauvignon

(York Creek)  80*  81  82  84  85*  86  90*

*Although Ridge has made exceptional Zinfandels and Petite Sirahs from this mountainside vineyard, it has had less success with York Creek Cabernet, which seems to display more structure than character*

### Geyserville

78**  79**  80**  81*  82*  83  84*  85**  86**  87**
88*  89**  90***  91**  92*  93*  94**  95***

*Among the longest-lived and most outstanding Zinfandel based wines, this one is loaded with quintessential varietal fruit of great depth, and while usually high in tannin and often approaching late harvest levels of alcohol, maintains its fruit as the foremost element in its large-scaled makeup; 91 is 50% Zinfandel and 50% other reds but most vintages are about 2/3 Zin.*

### Zinfandel

(Lytton Springs)  84*  85***  86*  87**  88*  89*  90***
91***  92  93*  94**  95***
(Howell Mountain)  82  83*  84**  85**  87  88**  89*  90*
(York Creek)  80**  81**  83*  84***  85**  88  91  94**
95*

*As with most wines from Ridge, these vineyard-designated bottlings are long on flavor and full of aging potential; the Lytton Springs is deep and spicy, the other two more straightforwardly fruity and somewhat more tannic*

RITCHIE CREEK VINEYARD  *Napa 1974*  In 64 owner Richard Minor, a dentist in Napa Valley, planted 4 acres to Cabernet Sauvignon and Merlot. Located on Spring Mountain, the low-yielding, extremely steep hillside vineyard did not provide a mature crop until 74. At that time, a small winery was built to produce 600 to 700 cases of Cabernet Sauvignon. Minor added 3 acres of Chardonnay in the early 80s, along with 1 acre of Viognier. Ritchie Creek first offered Viognier from the 86 vintage and shares the pioneer's honor with La Jota Vineyard. However, the site proved too cool to ripen Viognier every year, so despite being one of the Viognier pioneers, Minor replaced it with Pinot Noir and Lemberger. Annual production of 1,200 cases is mostly Cabernet Sauvignon and Chardonnay.

RIVERSIDE VINEYARDS  *(Foppiano Vineyards)*  This second label covers a range of low-priced varietals. All varietals are vintaged and from California. With annual production averaging 150,000 cases, the volume leaders are White Zinfandel and Cabernet Sauvignon. Chardonnay and Zinfandel also are bottled.

ROCHE WINERY  *Sonoma 1988*  In 77, anticipating retirement possibilities, John and Genevieve Roche acquired 2,500 acres of pastureland in the southwestern corner of the Sonoma Carneros region. At the time no vineyard was within 5 miles of the site. By the mid-80s, aware of the reputation of Carneros wine, they established a 25-acre vineyard consisting of Pinot Noir (10 acres) and Chardonnay (15 acres). A winery perched on a knoll overlooking the Sears Point Race Track to the south was operating for the 89 crush. The early annual production of 3,000 cases included a few hundred cases of a Blush Pinot Noir named "Tamarix." Roche Chardonnays are whole-cluster-pressed, barrel-fermented, and aged *sur lie.* The first Estate Pinot Noir was made in 89. The owners would like to expand total production to 25,000 cases a year.

J. ROCHIOLI VINEYARDS  *Sonoma 1979*  The Rochioli family has been in the grape-growing business since the 30 s. They now have 80 acres in the Russian River Valley, planted primarily to Pinot Noir, Sauvignon Blanc, Chardonnay, and Cabernet Sauvignon. In 82 they ventured into winemaking on a modest scale of 1,000 cases. In 85, they hired Gary Farrell (Gary Farrell Vineyards and Davis Bynum Winery) as consulting enologist, and he worked with them through the 86 vintage. Joe Rochioli is the vineyard manager, and his brother Tom now serves as winemaker. The winery's mainstays today are Pinot Noir, Chardonnay, Sauvignon Blanc, and Cabernet Sauvignon. Gewurztraminer is also made, but its availability is restricted to winery sales. Over the years Rochioli has earned a strong reputation for refined, fragrant Pinot Noir and, when bottled, the Reserve Pinot Noir is usually richer, always in great demand. Rochioli is also developing a good record for Sauvignon Blanc in a firm, crisp style that is of ° caliber in most vintages. The reserve wines are usually made from the oldest, low-yielding blocks of the vineyard. Rochioli has also demonstrated a great touch with Zinfandel grown in neighboring vineyards. All told, Rochioli has reached its production of 8,000 cases a year.

### Cabernet Sauvignon

(Neoma's Vineyard Reserve)  85  87  **90°**  91  **92°°**  **93**  **94°**

*Fruity, almost berryish flavors are buttressed by oak in this mildly tannic, mid-term ageworthy offering*

### Chardonnay

(regular bottling)  86°  87°  88°  89°  90  91°  93°  **94°**
**95°  96°**

(Reserve)  89  90°°  91  92°  **93**

*Green appley fruit and toasty oak are featured in these medium-full-bodied, crisp-edged wines that seem to benefit from a year or two in bottle; the Reserve is fuller and richer*

### Pinot Noir

(Russian River)  82°°  83  84°  86°  87°  **89°**  90  **91°°**
**93°°  96°**

(Reserve)  **89°°**  **90°°**  **91°°**  **92°°°**  **94°°°**

*Focused on bright, cherrylike fruit, and enriched by sweet oak, these attractive wines are moderately tannic and geared to enjoyment in their buoyant youth; the Reserve has been nothing short of spectacular in most vintages*

ROCKING HORSE WINERY  *Napa 1989*  Earning their living as furniture dealers in Napa Valley, Jeff Doran and Brian Zealear were home winemakers for a decade before turning pro and founding Rocking Horse Winery. Buying grapes and using Honig Winery for their winemaking, they are producing ripe, oak-enriched Zinfandel and Cabernet Sauvignon. To date, the Zinfandel has been from the Howell Mountain appellation, and the Cabernets from several Napa Valley appellations. Annual output has topped 1,000 cases, with double that set as the maximum level. The quality of the winery's first releases has been impressive.

**Zinfandel**

| (Lamborn Vineyard) | 89 | **90°°** | **91°** | 92 | 93 | **94** | **96°** |
|---|---|---|---|---|---|---|---|

ROEDERER ESTATE  *Mendocino 1982*  At the western edge of the Anderson Valley, the French firm of Louis Roederer found conditions that were felt to best approximate those of Champagne. It purchased over 500 acres, mostly within Philo where cool ocean breezes funnel into the valley. Beginning in the early 80s, Roederer of California developed vineyards on four separate parcels and eventually planted over 400 acres. The vineyards are a roughly 50–50 mix of Chardonnay and Pinot Noir. Though relatively large (40,000 square feet), the winemaking facility was designed to fit snugly into the landscape. Having evaluated numerous experimental cuvées, Roederer assembled a nonvintage cuvée, and after close to two years of aging *en tirage* its first Brut was offered in 88. Firm, crisp, and slightly austere, the Roederer Estate's first offering established a style that is unusual for California. Malolactic fermentation is prevented, and the dosage is low. The quality is very good. Limited-volume non-vintage Rosé and a Vintage Brut have been added to the line. "L'Ermitage," the vintage sparkler, is a full-flavored cuvée of equal parts of Chardonnay and Pinot Noir. It started off on a high °° level, and is a spectacular, rich, complex bubbly. About 5,000 cases of "L'Ermitage" are bottled. Under the direction of winemaker Michel Salgues, formerly a consultant to Roederer of France, California's Roederer Estate plans to grow steadily until leveling off at 90,000 cases. All of its production will originate in vineyards it owns, the same practice followed in Champagne by the parent company.

ROLLING HILLS VINEYARD  *Ventura 1980*  Located in Camarillo just to the north of Los Angeles, Rolling Hills takes its name from the site of its 5-acre vineyard in Temecula. The winery is owned by Ed Pagor, one of many former home winemakers in Southern California taught by John Daume. Renting space in an old warehouse, Pagor makes a few varietals, each in 200-case lots. He buys from several locations, but generally uses grapes from San Luis Obispo and Santa Barbara, as well as from his Temecula holdings. The line includes Chardonnay, Pinot Noir, Cabernet Sauvignon, Merlot, and Zinfandel. All told, Rolling Hills sets 1,000 cases a year as its limit. Quality has been uneven to date.

ROMBAUER VINEYARDS  *Napa 1982*  This winery, hidden behind a knoll at the northern end of the Silverado Trail, is owned and operated by Koerner Rombauer. Former commercial pilot and one-time investor in Conn Creek Winery, Rombauer built his winery in 80 and soon developed a thriving custom-winemaking business. Since opening, the winery has leased space to many labels and has also custom-made wines for many others. As it gradually expanded its own line, Rombauer has focused on Napa Valley Cabernet Sauvignon, Chardonnay (including 200 cases of a Reserve), Merlot, and a red Bordeaux blend, "Le Meilleur de Chai." All grapes are purchased under contract from Napa Valley. A family-owned 23-acre vineyard in Napa Valley grows Zinfandel and Zinfandel joined the roster in the 90s. In 1994 Rombauer bought the Kornell Winery and trademark. He is continuing to produce Kornell Sparkling Wines to be sold primarily at the winery. The large facility is being used for custom storage and winemaking.

Rombauer's Chardonnay is barrel-fermented and aged in small oak for 18 months. The winery's Cabernet Sauvignon is blended with Merlot and occasionally with Cabernet Franc. After a slightly shaky beginning with a few erratic Chardonnay vintages, Rombauer got over the jitters and improved its overall quality. In recent vintages, Rombauer's two red wines, which offer good value, have been outstanding enough to reach °° ratings. A high-priced, limited-edition Cabernet Sauvignon from Diamond Mountain also rates high. In the mid-90s the Rombauers acquired DeMoor Cellars, now operated as Napa Wine Cellars, and are partners in a small winery named Frank Rombauer Larkmead Cellars. Annual output has grown from 3,000 cases in the mid-80s to about 25,000 cases today. Chardonnay and Cabernet Sauvignon account for close to 90% of the total.

## Cabernet Sauvignon

81°   82°   83°   **84°**   **85°°**   **86°°**   **87°**   89   91

*Blended with small amounts of Merlot and Cabernet Franc, this wine combines lavish oak and well-focused, fairly deep curranty fruit, sometimes seasoned with mildly herbal notes, in a tannin-laden, ageworthy setting*

## Chardonnay

(Napa Valley)   86°   87   88   89   90°   91°   **92°°**   93°   94

*From time to time, this wine has suffered from an excess of acidity and more oak than its fruit could comfortably balance*

## Merlot

**86°**   **87°°°**   88   89   **90°**   **91°**   92   **93°**   94   **95°°**

*Nicely focused on cherryish fruit wrapped in oak and tannin*

---

ROSENBLUM CELLARS   *Alameda 1978*   Beginning on an extremely small scale, Rosenblum Cellars eventually outgrew its original facility and moved into a larger one in 87. Veterinarian Kent Rosenblum runs this winery with the help of his brother Roger, and of friends who assist them during the crush period. Zinfandel, Petite Sirah, and Cabernet Sauvignon are the mainstays, and Rosenblum prefers making them from grapes grown in old, unirrigated hillside vineyards in the North Coast. Most red wines are vineyard-identified, and typically the winery, a Zinfandel specialist, now makes upwards of a dozen separate wines of this variety. Often enough, Rosenblum's Zinfandels are intense, ripe, and rich, with plenty of tannin and oak. The most successful Zinfandels reach °° levels when they display persistent berry fruit to see them through the cellaring warranted by their tannin levels. Rosenblum also offers his "Vintner's Cuvée," a user-friendly Zinfandel that is immediately approachable and often a good value. The nonvintaged "Cuvee" is the winery's volume leader by a substantial margin (almost half of the winery's output) and the many special Zinfandel bottlings include those listed below as well as midpriced vintage-dated wines from Napa Valley/Ballentine Vineyard and Contra Costa County. Vetinarian Rosenblum also offers the whimsically named Chateau La Paws, which covers Mourvedre and Carignane. A red Meritage blend of Napa Valley Merlot, Cabernet, and Cabernet Franc is labeled "Holbrook Mitchell Trio." Ranking among the best in recent vintages, Rosenblum's Napa Valley Petite Sirahs offer an unusual level of deep, lively fruit for balance, and have risen to °° levels. Annual production currently stands at 6,500 cases, close to the winery's capacity.

## Zinfandel

(Hendry Vineyard)   81°°   **82°**   83°   84°   **85°°°**   88   **89°°**
**90°°**   **91°**   92

(Hendry Reserve)   **88°°°**   **90°°°**   **91°°**   **92°**   **93°°**   **94°°°**
**95°°°**

(Sonoma County)   83°   **84°°°**   85°   **87°°**   **88°**   **90°**   **91°**
**92°**   **93°**   **94°°**   **95°**

(Brandlin Ranch)   **91°°**   **92°°**   **93°°°**   **94°**   **95°**

(Maggies Reserve)   **90°°**   **92°°°**   93   94   **95°**   **96°**

(Sauret Vineyard)   **90°°°**   91   92   **93°**   **94°**   **95°**   **96°°**

(Coutra Costa County)   **90°°**   91   92   **93°**   **94°**   **95°**   96

(Harris-Kratka)   **93°°**   **94°°°**   **95°°°**   **96°**

*Made in limited quantities, these concentrated, intensely berryish wines are loaded with sweet oak and firmed by medium tannins in Hendry Reserve and Brandlin; the others typically have more open textures*

ROUDON–SMITH VINEYARDS   *Santa Cruz 1972*   In pursuit of a rural lifestyle away from Silicon Valley, two families became partners in this mountainside winery. After making their first vintages in the basement, Bob Roudon and Jim Smith, both electrical engineers, expanded their vision into a full-scale winery in 78. From the 5-acre estate vineyard and purchased varieties, they are edging close to their 10,000-case-a-year target. They focus on three wines from the Santa Cruz Mountain appellation: Chardonnay, the mainstay at 3,000 cases; Cabernet Sauvignon (700 cases); and Pinot Noir (300 cases). A Zinfandel from Sonoma and Merlot and Petite Sirah from San Luis Obispo County are regularly offered. "Claret," their upscale generic red, is the best-seller and represents a third of the total output. The heavy-handed winemaking style evident in the early vintages has given way to some restraint. Overall, most of the wines are well made and true to type.

ROUND HILL VINEYARDS   *Napa 1977*   Beginning as a blender and bottler of bulk wines, sold primarily through a partner's retail chain, Round Hill evolved from a negociant label into a major producer by 87. Having long outgrown its original bottling facility north of St. Helena, Round Hill moved into a new (500,000-case-capacity) home just off the Silverado Trail in Rutherford in 87. As it grew, Round Hill made numerous roster changes. The primary line today is identified by the California appellation, headed by White Zinfandel, and includes Chardonnay, Cabernet Sauvignon, and Zinfandel. Round Hill's mid-priced wines are from the Napa Valley appellation and consist of Cabernet Sauvignon, Chardonnay, Zinfandel, and Merlot. The Napa Valley line is made from grapes purchased from 40 growers throughout the valley and grapes grown by the winery's owners.

Introduced in 82, Round Hill's Reserve Cabernets, especially the 84 and 85, confirmed this winery's ability to hold its own against the competition in the prestige category. By the late 1990s this Reserve Program had spawned a new label, Van Asperen Napa Valley (see entry), which has replaced the Round Hill Reserves as the top of the line. The fourth group of wines produced and bottled by the winery is labeled Rutherford Ranch (see entry). About 60% of the winery's 400,000 cases fall into the "California" line, one that from time to time has produced Chardonnays and Cabernets earning praise for good value.

RUBISSOW–SARGENT WINERY   *Alameda 1988*   After retiring early from the world of biophysics, George Rubissow and Tony Sargent, who had developed a vineyard in the Mount Veeder appellation, branched out into winemaking. Today they have 18 acres planted to Cabernet Sauvignon and Merlot, with enough Cabernet Franc to be used as a blending component in all wines. Early vintages were made at Hess Collection; more recent wines are made in a small winery in Berkeley. Cabernet Sauvignon, Merlot, and "Les Trompettes" (a blend of Cabernet Franc and Merlot) are the only wines offered. The output is 2,300 cases, with "Les Trompettes" accounting for 300 cases. First vintages of Cabernets were impressive enough in a rough-hewn, built-to-last style. The owners plan to expand production slowly to a maximum of 4,500 cases.

RUSTRIDGE VINEYARD & WINERY   *Napa 1984*   In 72 Lu Meyer, a real estate agent from San Francisco, fell in love with a 450-acre ranch located in Chiles Valley. When a buyer backed out, she and her family bought the property, once home to a large thoroughbred horse ranch. In 79 they harvested their first small crop. They continued to sell all or part of their crop, but experimented with winemaking in 82 and 84. In 85 Stan Meyer constructed a winery by renovating an old barn, and made 1,000 cases of Riesling that fall. The vineyard has been expanded to its present 54 acres. After restructuring its vineyard, the winery began directing attention to Chardonnay and two reds, Cabernet Sauvignon and Zinfandel. As Rustridge grows to its 10,000-case goal, Chardonnay and Riesling will account for 60%, with the reds making up 40% of the total.

RUTHERFORD HILL WINERY   *Napa 1976*   Currently owned by Paterno Imports, Rutherford Hill was founded by Pillsbury and was briefly operated as Souverain of Rutherford. In its early vintages, Rutherford Hill gained some recognition for Merlot, and the rest of the line was generally acceptable. In the mid-80s the quality became inexplicably erratic, and a new winemaking team was brought in for the 87 crush. Over the course of time Rutherford Hill has used several different label designations, including a range of Reserve-type names, without any continuity.

In 85 the owners began constructing what turned out at the time to be the biggest man-made aging caves in California, which now hold 8,000 barrels. Total annual production varied in the late 80s. Paterno plans to focus on Merlot, Cabernet, and Chardonnay, with Merlot to account for 75% of the winery's projected annual output of 150,000 cases. The Terlato family, owners of Paterno, plan to gradually bring the winery back to full production. The first vintage reflecting the family's quality commitment was 1996.

**Merlot**

| 82° | 83°° | **84°°** | **85°** | 8̶6̶ | 87 | 88 | 89 | 9̶0̶ | 91 | **92°** | **94** |
|-----|------|----------|---------|-----|----|----|----|-----|----|---------|--------|
| **95** | | | | | | | | | | | |

*Always ripe and generally full-bodied, fleshy, and mouth-filling, this wine tends to be heavier than classic Merlots, but has plenty of richness from oak and deep fruit, and gains a needed firm edge from moderate tannin; recent vintages have lacked the fruit of earlier efforts*

RUTHERFORD RANCH   *(Round Hill Vineyards)*   Once the top-of-the-line label used by its owners for wines made from vineyards they own. The primary vineyard is located in the western hills of Napa Valley. In the early 80s Rutherford Ranch made several vintages of intense, dark, tannic Petite Sirahs and Zinfandels, but those wines were dropped from the line, which now features Chardonnay, Cabernet Sauvignon, and Merlot. With a sturdy constitution derived from their hillside origins, Rutherford Ranch's Cabernets are capable of ° quality and often earn praise for good value.

RUTZ CELLARS   *Sonoma 1993*   In the Sebastopol area of Russian River Valley, Keith Rutz built a winery and aging caves designed to produce Pinot Noir and Chardonnay. Buying grapes from Quail Hill Vineyard, the Dutton Ranch, and other leading local vineyards in the area, he regularly offers Chardonnay from the Russian River Valley and from specific vineyards, including Dutton Ranch, Quail Hill, and Buena Tierra. Small batches of Pinot Noir have been made from Dutton Ranch, Quail Hill, Weir Vineyard, Sleepy Hollow Vineyard, and vineyards in Anderson Valley. Regardless of vineyard source, he tends to shoot from the hip and has hit the target more often with his bold, oak-laced Chardonnays. Still feeling its way toward consistency, Rutz is a name to watch. With a goal of 10,000 cases, annual production has reached 5,000 cases, with the Russian River Valley bottlings accounting for 70% of the total.

SADDLEBACK CELLARS   *Napa 1983*   Nils Venge has been making wines in the Napa Valley since 74 when he started with Villa Mount Eden. In the early 80s he developed a small vineyard near his home in the Oakville area. By 82, when he was hired by the newly formed Groth Vineyard, Venge began thinking about making wines under his own brand as a sideline. The following year he and his father-in-law built a small winery, and made a few hundred cases of wine. The vineyard has since been expanded and includes 8 acres of Cabernet Sauvignon, 5 of Chardonnay, and 2 1/2 of Pinot Blanc. Venge is now making Zinfandel from Napa Valley and has developed a strong following for his rich, deep, stylish Zinfandels. More than 50% of his annual output is Cabernet Sauvignon. Zinfandel and Pinot Blanc (the only such varietal made in Napa Valley) are the two other home-grown wines made. On occasion, Venge buys Sauvignon Blanc and markets it under his second label, Vine Haven.

ST. CLEMENT VINEYARDS *Napa 1976* San Francisco eye surgeon Bill Casey and family bought the site of the original Spring Mountain Vineyards in 76. A few hundred cases of 75 wine remained in the cellars, and represented the first to be sold as St. Clement. In 79 the facility was expanded as a second building was carved into the hills and connected to the original building. Beneath both buildings, a large underground storage facility and barrel-aging room were put into place without changing the appearance of the above-ground structures. The expansion enabled the winery to grow to 10,000 cases a year, with winemaker Dennis Johns in charge of the operation since 80. Johns, a self-taught winemaker, combined numerous small lots drawn from throughout the Napa Valley as he made Cabernet Sauvignon, Chardonnay, Sauvignon Blanc, and in the late 80s, Merlot.

Within a few vintages the winery became well known for its Sauvignon Blancs. The style consistently combined deep, complex fruity character with firming acidity that provided a long life and often earned it **. An even clearer picture of consistency is St. Clement's Cabernet Sauvignons, which are ** caliber and beautifully proportioned. In late 87 Casey sold the winery to the Japanese brewers Sapporo, Inc. One of the changes made was the purchase of the well-established 22-acre Abbott's Vineyard in the Carneros, which is planted to Chardonnay and a small amount of Pinot Noir. This vineyard is used for the winery's Chardonnay, and it is also the source of the winery's Merlot. The new owners retained the services of Dennis Johns. The Abbott's Chardonnay production is steady at 3,500 cases. Merlot now stands at 4,000 cases, and Cabernet is steady at 3,500. The winery's upscale red Meritage is labeled "Oroppas," and about 750 cases of it are made annually. Howell Mountain Cabernet Sauvignon, an exciting newcomer, is made in 200–300-case quantities.

**Cabernet Sauvignon**

78° 79° 80°° 81°° 82° 83° **84°°** **85°°** **86°°** 87°
88 89 **90°** **91°** **92°** 93 **94°** **95°**

*Classically constructed wines that are firm, tight when young, yet show, in many vintages, plenty of curranty fruit underneath and have a fair measure of rich oak; with a bit more stuffing, the best would rate at the top of the list*

**Chardonnay**

(Napa Valley) 86 87° 88 89 90° 91 92
(Abbott's Vineyard) 87° 89° 90°° 91° 92 93 94 95 96

*Tight, somewhat appley fruit, with toasty oak background, but occasionally wanting greater depth*

**Merlot**

85°° **86°°** **87°** 89° **90°** **91°°** **92°** **93°** 94° **95°°**

*Ripe, deep, tannic wines, enriched with creamy oak, appear to possess good aging potential*

**Oroppas**

**92°** 93 **94°°** **95°**

*Typically about 60% Cabernet Sauvignon with equal parts of Merlot and Cabernet Franc, this wine has offered pleasant, somewhat succulent fruit with midterm aging potential*

ST. FRANCIS VINEYARDS *Sonoma 1979* Located in Kenwood directly across the wine road from Chateau St. Jean, St. Francis started out in 73 with the development of 100 acres. The first crush of 79 yielded 5,000 cases total, with the most promise shown by Gewurztraminer and Riesling. As production from its estate vineyard increased, St. Francis lacked a consistent focus until the 83 vintage, in which it produced ** quality Merlot. Now 70 acres are planted to Merlot, with the oldest acres used for the winery's Reserve bottling. Both Merlots are 100% varietal, and they are aged in both American and French oak barrels (the Reserve aging six months longer).

Zinfandel came on like gangbusters in the 90s. St. Francis is now making an intense Old Vines Zinfandel and an equally interesting, to-die-for, deeply fruited Reserve from Pagani Ranch. In the late 1990s the winery purchased the 115-acre Nuns Canyon Vineyard, which was well known for Zinfandel. That acquisition brings its total vineyard holdings to 425 acres. Since the beginning, Chardonnay has come from several appellations and been bottled under several designations. In the mid-80s, the winery removed its Pinot Noir and increased its acreage of Chardonnay. The estate Chardonnay along with a California Chardonnay combine for close to 20,000 cases, with Merlot amounting to 18,000 cases. Cabernet Sauvignon can be exceptional, although only 4,000 cases are made a year. St. Francis makes 50,000 cases a year.

### Cabernet Sauvignon

**85°°  86°°  88°  91  92**  93  94  95

*Ripe black-cherry fruit and lots of rich, vanillin oak are set in a fairly tannic frame*

### Chardonnay

(Estate)  86  87°  88°  90  91  94°  95  96

*Toasty oak, appley, slightly blossomy fruit, crisp acidity*

### Merlot

(regular bottling)  82  83°°  84°°  **85°°  86°°  87°**  88  89
90  91  92°  93°  **94°  95°**

(Reserve)  83°°°  84°°  **85°**  88  **89°  90°**  91°  **92  93°**
**94°°**

*Both wines are ripe, intense, high in sweet, rich oak, and share a tendency to be a little soft in structure and round; appealing on the palate even when tannic*

ST. SUPÉRY VINEYARDS  *Napa 1988*  This winery and adjoining old Victorian home are owned by Skalli Enterprises, a large wine company and distributor in southern France. In the early 80s, the Skallis, like many French vintners, wanted to invest in other regions, and ended up in California. In 82, they acquired a 1,500-acre cattle ranch in the Pope Valley, preparing it and gradually developing it into vineyards. In 86, when the 56-acre Rutherford estate and vineyard was put on the market, Skalli bought it and immediately began building a winemaking facility and office complex. In less than two years, a modern-looking 200,000-case-capacity winery was in place, along with a visitors center. The adjacent 50-acre vineyard was reworked and is now planted primarily to Cabernet Sauvignon.

By 90, the Pope Valley plantings, known as the Dollarhide Ranch, contained 400 acres of vines. The owners are expanding that to 650 acres, the major varieties planted being Sauvignon Blanc, Chardonnay, Cabernet Sauvignon, and Merlot. In 88, the winery began with a first crush of 20,000 cases. With expansion to 100,000 cases, the focus remains on Chardonnay, Sauvignon Blanc, and Cabernet Sauvignon. In early 1994 Bordeaux winemaker Michel Rolland was hired as a consultant, and he had a hand in developing the winery's Meritage wines as well as its Cabernet and Merlot. The first Red Meritage was the 1994; the first White was from 95. A popular tourist destination, St. Supéry added a Zinfandel Rose, which is sold at the winery. Wines not making the first team have been bottled under a second label, Bonverre. Initial efforts have been clean, average quality, and fairly priced. Both the forthright, likable Merlot and sprightly Sauvignon Blanc have been St. Supéry's best values.

### Cabernet Sauvignon

87°  88  89  90°  91  **93  94°°**

*Medium-bodied, straightforward wines with black cherry fruit; 94 captured all the fruit for which the vintage is noted*

### Chardonnay

88  90  91°  92  93  95

*Simple, moderately fruity, often skimpy wines*

### Merlot

89° 90 **91°** 92 93 **94** 95

*Medium-full-bodied, ripish, cherry and sometimes lightly herbal*

SAINT GREGORY *Mendocino 1989* A label owned by Greg Graziano, former wine-maker for Hidden Cellars and La Crema. Working at his own small winery, he buys grapes from several vineyards within Mendocino County to produce Pinot Noir, Pinot Blanc, and a barrel-fermented Chardonnay. Aiming for a big style of Chardonnay, Graziano succeeds in better vintages. With Pinot Noir grown in the Anderson Valley, he uses open-top fermenters and includes whole clusters. The annual output is 1,000 cases of Chardonnay and 400 to 500 of Pinot Noir and Pinot Blanc. Recent vintages of Pinot Blanc offer good value.

SAINTSBURY *Napa 1981* Before starting Saintsbury, longtime friends Dave Graves and Dick Ward worked in the cellars of several wineries both in Napa Valley and Santa Barbara. In 81, they rented space in Pine Ridge Winery, bought Pinot Noir and Chardonnay in Napa and Sonoma Counties, and made 3,000 cases total. They subsequently raised enough money to build a winery in the Carneros where all the grapes for their wines are grown. Saintsbury caught people's attention with a style of Pinot Noir that burst with bright cherry varietal character, enriched by complementary oak. It suffered from no excesses, and was an unusual Pinot Noir in that nothing was out of proportion. In making Pinot Noir, Graves and Ward prefer a lengthy fermentation and employ both punching down and pumping over of the cap. In 83, Saintsbury's Pinot Noir was joined by a lighter version, called "Garnet," made from batches with less intensity and concentration. Their Carneros Chardonnay is barrel-fermented and undergoes malolactic fermentation. Starting in 86, a Reserve Chardonnay has been made from the most intense lots and fermented in new oak. In the 1990s their vineyard was replanted to a wide range of Dijon clones and a variety of rootstocks. By the 1997 crush the owners began to reap some benefits from this new, tightly spaced vineyard. Annual case-production has reached 40,000. Saintsbury's top-of-the-line wines regularly earn high rankings.

### Chardonnay

(regular bottling) 86° 87°° 88° 89° **90°** 91 **92°** **93°** **94°°** 95

(Reserve) 86 87°° 88°°° **90°°°** 91 **92°** **93°** **94°°°** **95°°**

*Firm, solidly fruity wines combine brisk, appley fruit with toasty oak and quiet roasted-grain qualities; the Reserve has joined the elite ranks*

### Pinot Noir

(Garnet) 87° 88° 89° 90° 91 92 93 94 95°

(Carneros) 83° 84°° 85° 86° **87°°** **88°** **89°** **90°°** **91°** **92°** **93°** **94°** **95°** **96°**

(Reserve) **90°** **91°°°** **92°°** **93°** **94°°°** **95°°**

*"Garnet" is the lighter, bouncier wine but, until recent vintages, seemed to lack adequate stuffing; the Carneros bottling is relatively fruity and bright in comparison to most of its competition and has a black-cherry and sweet oak personality; Reserve is among the leading Pinots*

SALAMANDRE WINE CELLARS *Santa Cruz 1986* Owner-winemaker Wells Shoemaker is better known in the town of Aptos as Dr. Shoemaker, pediatrician. A believer in the minimal handling approach to winemaking, he specializes in Chardonnay and makes two versions, one from Arroyo Seco in Monterey and the other from Santa Cruz Mountains. In roughly 100-case quantities, he also makes on occasion Merlot, Sauvignon Blanc, Gewurztraminer, and Pinot Noir. Small-scale cuvées of *méthode champenoise* sparkling wines have been made. The annual output is 1,000 cases (75% Chardonnay). In and around Aptos the long-toed salamander is plentiful and was adopted as the winery's symbol and logo.

SAN SABA VINEYARD   *Monterey 1981*   From vineyards established in 75 in the foothills on the western edge of the Salinas Valley, San Saba makes Cabernet Sauvignon and Chardonnay. The 70-acre vineyard contains 27 acres of Cabernet and 18 of Merlot and Chardonnay. The vineyard is located approximately 2 miles north of the Smith & Hook Winery where the wines are custom-made and aged. Generally, the red wines are aged for two years in French oak barrels, and a further year in bottle before being released. Chardonnay represents about half of the winery's production. San Saba is owned by a physician who lives in Dallas, and the winery's first few vintages were available only in Texas. By 85 the annual production had grown to 5,000 cases and the winery began marketing outside Texas.

SANFORD WINERY   *Santa Barbara 1981*   In 80, by mutual consent, the co-owners of Sanford & Benedict Vineyards decided to dissolve the partnership. Mike Benedict continued operating the original winery as Sanford & Benedict and in 81 Richard Sanford established his own wine company. Sanford's initial vintages were made in leased space—the first two at Edna Valley Vineyards. Through his tasting room in Buellton and through his travels, Sanford developed a strong direct-mail clientele. Although several early vintages of Chardonnay originated in other parts of the Central Coast, all wines made today are from Santa Barbara County, primarily the Santa Ynez Valley.

Sanford is at 50,000 cases a year, with Chardonnay (20,000 cases) and Sauvignon Blanc combining for 70% of the total. Both white wines are complex and full-bodied and, regardless of quality level, they often display a pronounced oak character. Typically, Sanford ferments Chardonnay in new French oak. Even the Sauvignon Blanc is barrel-fermented (in American oak) and often undergoes malolactic fermentation.

Introduced in 82, a Vin Gris from Pinot Noir, barrel-fermented and made in a dry style, remains a regular item in the lineup. Over the years Sanford has earned a reputation for Pinot Noir, and produces about 4,000 cases a year. Fermented in open-top stainless-steel cooperage, Sanford's Pinot Noirs are made in a big, ripe style. In 90, Sanford once again gained control of the 112-acre Benedict Vineyard, which he helped develop in 71. In the mid-90s the Sanfords acquired the 125-acre Santa Rita Vineyard adjacent to their property. Using multiple clones, Sanford has developed 70 acres of Chardonnay and 55 acres of Pinot Noir. When this vineyard hits full stride the winery's annual output will approach 100,000 cases. Sanford uses Barrel Select to designate his limited-edition, Reserve-style Pinot Noir and Chardonnay.

**Chardonnay**

(regular bottling)   86°   87°   88°   89°°   90°   91°   92°   93   **94**   95

(Barrel Select)   87°°°   88°   89°°   90   91°°   92°   93   **94°**   95

*Sanford wines, regardless of nomenclature, are high in oak and carry ripe, often broad and somewhat exotic fruit, with plenty of balancing acidity; the Barrel Select pushes the winery's outgoing style one step further*

**Pinot Noir**

85   86°   87   88°   89   **90°**   **91°**   **92°**   93   **94**   **95**   **96**

*Lacking consistency, this often intense, sometimes too herbal, soft and ripe, tobaccoey wine succeeds in those years when its fruit and structure match up to its intensity level*

SANTA BARBARA WINERY   *Santa Barbara 1972*   One of a handful of wineries located in downtown Santa Barbara, this is also one of the oldest in the county. It began in 62 by making an assortment of table and dessert wines for the local tourist trade.

In 72, it took a more serious turn as its owners began developing what evolved into a 70-acre vineyard in the Santa Ynez Valley. Also under the winery's control is a neighboring 45-acre vineyard. The primary varieties planted include Chardonnay, Chenin Blanc, Sauvignon Blanc, and Riesling among the whites, and Cabernet, Zinfandel, and Pinot Noir among the reds. Among many wines offered, both its Riesling in a medium-sweet, full-fruity style (often ranked as a ° wine) and its Chardonnay have stood out. The barrel-fermented Reserve Chardonnay consists of about 1,000 cases; production of the regular Chardonnay stands at 4,000 cases.

Among the more unusual wines offered, the winery's Chenin Blanc is barrel-fermented to total dryness. Usually blended with Semillon, the Sauvignon Blanc is average in quality, with some fruitiness and character. Also bottled is a Reserve Sauvignon Blanc that is 100% barrel-fermented. On occasion the Reserve Pinot Noir (300 cases) has been exceptional. Today the winery is operating at its optimum production level of 30,000 cases.

**Chardonnay**

| | | | | | | | | |
|---|---|---|---|---|---|---|---|---|
| (regular bottling) | 86° | 88° | 89° | 90° | 94 | 95 | | |
| (Reserve) | 86° | 87°° | 88° | 89° | 90°° | 91 | 92°° | **95°** |

*After a few years of average quality, the winery has begun to produce complex, rich, oaky Chardonnays whose vintage variations derive mostly from the fruit intensity exhibited*

**SANTA CRUZ MOUNTAIN VINEYARDS** *Santa Cruz 1974* The search for an ideal site to plant Pinot Noir ended for Ken Burnap when he bought a long-defunct vineyard high in the Santa Cruz Mountain area. A former Los Angeles restaurateur (The Hobbit), Burnap was seeking a cool climate, relatively poor soils, and a southern exposure in which to develop his vineyard. Pinot Noir now covers 13 acres and Chardonnay 1 acre of his dry-farmed hillside site. Although Pinot Noir was the primary wine in the formative years, the winery currently makes Chardonnay, Merlot, and Cabernet Sauvignon in greater quantities. Recently Burnap has settled on two Cabernets, one from the Santa Cruz Mountains and the second from Cinnabar Vineyard. Only Merlot from the Central Coast appellation is purchased from outside the Santa Cruz Mountain area. The first several vintages of Pinot Noir generated excitement among wine collectors, but met with mixed critical reviews. Burnap insists on allowing his grapes to become very ripe before harvesting them, and he believes in using the native yeasts for fermentation. The resulting wines have been decidedly erratic. After extended bottle aging, the winery's Pinot Noirs are released in their fourth year, the Cabernet Sauvignons in their fifth. For several years, the winery produced and labeled the only Durif made in California. The annual total output of this winery has reached the 4,000-case maximum.

**SANTA YNEZ WINERY** *Santa Barbara 1976* Using a refurbished dairy barn, the original winery, known as Santa Ynez Valley Winery, began in 76 by specializing in white wines. Among its early successes, the winery made Sauvignon Blanc, and both the regular and Reserve offered enticing varietal character balanced by oak. In 88, the facility was purchased by Doug Scott, owner of Sterns Wharf Vintners, who contracts for grapes grown within Santa Barbara County to produce wines for both Sterns Wharf (see entry) and Santa Ynez Winery. The current Santa Ynez Winery lineup features Sauvignon Blanc, Semillon (usually barrel-fermented), Chardonnay, Pinot Blanc, and Riesling for the whites, and Cabernet Sauvignon, Zinfandel, and a Cabernet-Merlot blend among its reds. Also, the winery makes port in limited volume. Production of Santa Ynez Winery is at the 18,000-case-per-year level, close to full capacity.

**SANTINO WINES** *Amador 1979* This winery is located in the middle of the Shenandoah Valley. Unlike many of its neighbors, Santino has always produced a range of wines to balance its interest in Zinfandel. Santino offers an Amador County bottling and an occasional Fiddletown version. All Zinfandels are aged in French oak barrels and bottled-aged for two more years prior to release. All told, Zinfandel combines for about 5,000 cases.

In 88 Santino entered the Rhone-blend division with "Satyricon," a blend of Grenache, Syrah, and Mourvedre.

SARAH'S VINEYARD  *Santa Clara 1978*  One of the few small upscale wineries in the Hecker Pass region, Sarah's is located just west of Gilroy. Owned by Marilyn and John Otteman, the winery is directed by Marilyn, who is also the winemaker. Sarah is a name she dreamed up for the original vineyard, now covering 8 1/2 acres and planted to Chardonnay and Pinot Noir. Chardonnays from both the estate vineyard and from Ventana Vineyards in Monterey represent the major wines offered. First made in 83, the estate Chardonnay has grown to 800 cases a year in quantity. Small amounts of Merlot and a proprietary red, "Cadenza" (made primarily from Grenache), fill out the line of this 2,500-case brand. After several generally successful, often noteworthy early vintages, Sarah's became surprisingly erratic. The prices asked have greatly exceeded the quality offered.

## Chardonnay

| | | | | |
|---|---|---|---|---|
| (Sarah's Vineyard) | 86° | 87 | **88°** | 89 |
| (Ventana Vineyard) | **85°** | 86 | 87 | 88̶ | 89 |

*Initial vintages (early 80s) demonstrated richness and range, but more recent efforts have been overdone in oak while lacking the fruit to make them work—even in the face of sharply escalating prices*

V. SATTUI WINERY  *Napa 1975*  The "V." stands for Vittorio Sattui, great-grandfather of owner Daryl Sattui. With limited experience and financial support, Daryl started his own winery in 75, playing on the family name and winemaking history, even though the original winery was in San Francisco and went out of business in 20. He purchased a well-situated property in the heart of Napa Valley and immediately began courting the tourist trade. A small deli and tasting room along with inviting picnic grounds soon became a popular respite. With increased visitors, Sattui was able to develop a direct sales–marketing approach, and for many years his wines have been available only at the winery or through a mailing list.

In 85, with sales topping 20,000 cases, Sattui built a new winemaking facility and purchased 34 acres of vineyards. That vineyard is now planted to Cabernet Sauvignon, Sauvignon Blanc, and Zinfandel. Buying most of the grapes crushed, Sattui has enjoyed a long and successful arrangement with Preston Vineyard, located in Rutherford and responsible for a vineyard-designated Cabernet Sauvignon. Another dozen wines are produced by the winery. The best-seller, and often among the winery's quality leaders, is Johannisberg Riesling, made in both a Dry and Off-Dry style. In some vintages the Napa Valley Cabernet bottling has been preferred over its Preston Vineyard stablemate. In a typical year close to a quarter million people visit the winery—mostly for the picnic facilities. Annual sales have nudged up to the 50,000-case figure.

## Cabernet Sauvignon

| | | | | | | | |
|---|---|---|---|---|---|---|---|
| (Suzannes Vineyard) | 89 | **90°** | **91°** | **94°** | | | |
| (Preston Vineyards) | 85 | **86°** | **87°** | 88 | 89 | 92 | **94°** |
| (Preston Reserve) | **86** | **87°** | **88°** | **92°** | | | |

*These wines have tended to be high in ripeness and oak, with black cherry fruit holding off moderate to medium tannins; the style is more rustic than refined*

SAUCELITO CANYON VINEYARD  *San Luis Obispo 1982*  In 74 Bill Greenough bought a 100-acre ranch in the Arroyo Grande Valley that included the remains of a winery abandoned in the 40s. He soon discovered 3 acres of Zinfandel planted in the 1880s, and decided to revive both the winery and vineyard. The vineyard has been expanded to 15 acres, 14 of Zinfandel and 1 of Cabernet Sauvignon. In 82 Greenough made his first wine. The annual production is holding steady at 1,500 cases—1,000 cases of Zinfandel and 500 of Cabernet Sauvignon. In general, the Zinfandels are ripe and heavy, and occasionally overdone.

**Zinfandel**

(Arroyo Grande)   89   90   **91°°**   **92°°**   93°   **94°**   95°   **96**

*Very ripe, sometimes overripe, these wines are always full-bodied and brawny in style; they need time for their tannins to calm down but the fruit often wants earlier drinking*

SAUSAL WINERY   *Sonoma 1973*   In 56 the Demostene family acquired the Sausal Ranch in the heart of the Alexander Valley. Inheriting a parcel of red varieties planted in 1890, the family eventually developed 100 acres of vineyards. For over a decade, the Demostene vineyard sold all of its grapes and gradually developed a strong reputation for Zinfandel. Grgich Hills has acquired much of its Zinfandel from this vineyard. In addition to Zinfandel, the vineyard contains Cabernet Sauvignon, Chardonnay, Colombard, and Pinot Noir. In 73, under the leadership of Dave Demostene, the family entered winemaking, first as bulk wine producers and by 74 as producers of bottled wine. Production has been led by its Zinfandel made in a full-bodied but well-aged style. Special lots of longer-aged Zinfandel, made exclusively from non-irrigated 100-year-old vines planted on a knoll overlooking the winery, are bottled as a "Private Reserve." The Zinfandels account for 7,500 cases a year. The rest of the line consists of Cabernet Sauvignon (1,200 cases), Sangiovese, and a blend of Chardonnay and Chenin Blanc labeled "Sausal Blanc." All told, the winery is at its 10,000-case annual goal.

**Zinfandel**

(regular bottling)   81°   82°   83°   84°°   86°   87°   88°   89
90   92°   93°   94   95
(Private Reserve)   87°   **88°**   **91°°°**   **92°°**   **93°°°**   **94°**   **95°**
(Century Vines)   **92°°°**   93   **94°**   **95°°**

*Briary, oaky, full-bodied, usually full of dense and ripe-berryish fruit; occasional hints of tar and raisins*

SCHARFFENBERGER CELLARS   *Mendocino 1981*   John Scharffenberger was raised in Mendocino, and his family owns a highly regarded 75-acre vineyard in the Redwood Valley, growing mainly Zinfandel and Cabernet Sauvignon. After overseeing the family grape-growing business for a time, John decided to produce sparkling wine. Buying all grapes crushed, he slowly increased production to 25,000 cases by 85.

In 89 the French Champagne producer, Pomméry, acquired the majority interest in Scharffenberger Cellars. Pomméry also purchased 640 acres of bare land to be developed into a 180-acre vineyard and a winemaking site for future vintages. In the 90s Pommery merged with Moet Hennessey, and a few years later the brand name was changed from Scharffenberger to Pacific Echo. The parent company plans to take the winery's annual production to 60,000 cases. Recently, the Brut Rosé, much richer than most others, has been our favorite.

SCHERRER VINEYARDS   *Sonoma 1990*   The Scherrer family has a 50-acre vineyard in the midsection of Alexander Valley planted primarily to Zinfandel and Cabernet Sauvignon with a smattering of Chardonnay. Though most grapes are sold, Fred Scherrer, who gained winemaking experience at Dehlinger Winery, makes Zinfandel from the oldest vineyard block established in 1912. True to the old vine scenario, his Zinfandels have been intense and very ripe in style. Once numerous Old Vine Zinfandels came on the market, Scherrer began labeling his as "Old & Mature Vines." He has also added Zinfandel from Shale Terrace and a pinkish wine labeled Vin Gris of Zinfandel. Total annual production is 2,000 cases. Among several wineries using fruit from Scherrer Vineyard, Greenwood Ridge Winery bottles a vineyard-designated Zinfandel.

## Zinfandel
### 91   92°   93°°°   94   95°°   96°

*Lots of berryish fruit and vanillin oakiness combine in wines of uncommon attractiveness and balance*

J. SCHRAM   *(Schramsberg Vineyards)*   This is Schramsberg's label for its top-of-the-line sparkling wine cuvée. Jacob Schram was the 19th-century founder of Schramsberg, which was revived in the 60s by owner Jack Davies. The first bottling of J. Schram (from the 87 vintage) was released in 1992. A blend of Pinot Noir and Chardonnay, J. Schram is barrel-fermented and aged over four years *en tirage* and, for the moment, is the most expensive California sparkling wine. Annual production is 1,000 cases.

SCHRAMSBERG VINEYARDS   *Napa 1966*   In 65 Jack and Jamie Davies purchased the defunct Schramsberg winery, an isolated mountainside estate founded in 1862, and Davies left a successful career in industrial management to specialize in *méthode champenoise* sparkling wines. After renovating the dilapidated winery and estate, he shored up the old aging caves and began developing vineyards, planting the first 5 acres on hillsides near the winery. From grapes purchased, Schramsberg's first offering was a 65 Blanc de Blancs. In 71 Schramsberg was the first in California to bottle a sparkling Blanc de Noirs, and in 72 made California's first Cremant sparkling wine, a style of sparkling wine deliberately low in effervescence.

As its production grew gradually to 25,000 cases a year by the end of the 70s, Schramsberg carved out a fine reputation for both quality and prestige. In the 80s Schramsberg expanded its own vineyard to the present 60 acres and moved toward an annual production goal of 50,000 cases. Today, with the day-to-day operations handled by Jamie Davies after her husband passed away in 1998, it produces five types of sparkling wine. The Blanc de Blancs is primarily Chardonnay with some Pinot Blanc, while the Blanc de Noirs is typically made from Pinot Noir with upwards of 30% Chardonnay. In addition to those two mainstays, the winery offers Brut Rosé, a dry (under 1% sweetness) rosé made from Gamay and Pinot Noir. Its fourth bottling is Cremant, Demi-Sec, a medium-sweet, low-effervescence wine made from Flora and finished with 3% residual sugar. A Reserve bottling, aged at least five years with the yeasts, is offered in most vintages. The other four bottlings of Schramsberg sparklers age on the average for two to three years *en tirage*. A decade ago Schramsberg was arguably California's finest sparkling wine producer; though it is not quite at that level today, it is still among the best. Both its Blanc de Noirs and the late disgorged Blanc de Blancs have been appealing in recent vintages.

SCHUETZ OLES   *Napa 1991*   Rick Schuetz, winemaker at Golden State Vintners, and vineyardist Lore Oles have teamed up to produce Zinfandel and Petite Sirah, both from old vineyards in Napa Valley, along with a barrel-fermented Chardonnay. Zinfandel from Korte Ranch north of St. Helena is the volume leader at 2,000 cases, followed by Chardonnay at 1,000 and Petite Sirah from Rattlesnake Acres Ranch at 400 cases. A special blend of the Petite Sirah and Zinfandel has occasionally been converted into a nonvintage Port. Chardonnay has made an occasional appearance, but the Zinfandels are the wines to check out.

## Zinfandel
### 91°°   92   **93**   94°   95°°   96

*Well-mannered, ripe, blackberryish wines that are typically sturdy, not overly tannic*

SCHUG CELLARS   *Sonoma 1980*   Educated at Geisenheim in Germany, Walter Schug came to California and began his winemaking career in 61. For several years he worked for the Gallo winery, then headed winemaking for Joseph Phelps Vineyards from 73 until 83. By mutual agreement, Schug began developing his own brand in 80. Over the first several vintages, he worked out of a tunnel in Storybook Mountain Vineyards's winery, and later at his own facility in Yountville. Although he earned a good reputation at Joseph Phelps Vineyards for Gewurztraminer and Riesling in a range of styles, and occasionally for Cabernet Sauvignon, Schug prefers to specialize in Chardonnay and Pinot Noir. Until a vineyard was purchased and developed in 90, Schug's Chardonnays came from the Napa Valley–Carneros and were usually vineyard-designated. The Pinot Noirs were made from grapes grown in Los Carneros, along with a separate bottling from Heinemann Vineyard.

With Chardonnay, Schug usually barrel-ferments but prevents the malolactic fermentation in order to make a wine he believes will live a long time. His style of Pinot Noir focuses on the minimal handling, no-filtering approach. In 90, Schug acquired 50 acres in the Sonoma side of Carneros and developed his own 42-acre vineyard. His winery, located next to the vineyard, is designed to produce 15,000 cases a year, a total Schug will achieve when his vineyard reaches full maturity. When that occurs, two-thirds of the total will be Chardonnay, the rest Pinot Noir. The quality has not risen above average levels in recent vintages.

SCHWEIGER VINEYARDS  *Napa 1994*  In 1964 Fred Schweiger purchased acreage in the Spring Mountain District. At first the family developed a Christmas tree forest on the property, but before long they realized the land was better suited for vineyards. Beginning in 1981 they laid out 34 acres and planted Cabernet Sauvignon, Chardonnay, and Merlot. Though still selling about half their tonnage, the Schweigers got off to such a great start as wine producers that eventually they will crush their entire crop. Annual production is now close to 2,000 cases.

SEAVEY VINEYARD  *Napa 1990*  In 1979 Bill Seavey, a San Francisco attorney, bought a pre-Prohibition winery and vineyard site in the Conn Valley area. Over the following years he converted the cattle-grazing land into a 37-acre vineyard. The planting mix is 50% Chardonnay and 50% Cabernet Sauvignon. Walt Raymond, Jr. was the vineyard developer and manager, and every year since the first harvest the majority of Seavey's grapes have been sold to Raymond Vineyards. Seavey converted an old barn into a small winery and in 90 began to produce small amounts of Chardonnay, Merlot and Cabernet Sauvignon. Under the direction of Gary Galleron, consulting winemaker, Seavey now makes about 300 cases of estate-grown Chardonnay, 200 cases of Merlot, and 900 of Cabernet Sauvignon annually.

SEBASTIANI VINEYARDS  *Sonoma 1889*  The Sebastiani family history resembles that of a veritable wine dynasty. A small winery on the outskirts of the town of Sonoma was purchased in 04 by Samuele Sebastiani, the patriarch. Like many early winemakers in California, he was content, both before and after Prohibition, to sell wines to other producers, and often supplied wines to leading Napa Valley producers. In 44 his son August (Gus) Sebastiani took over the reins and the winery's bottled-wine business expanded under his guidance as he gradually developed a line of wines of all kinds under the Sebastiani Vineyard brand. By the early 60s Sebastiani was virtually out of the bulk wine business and was growing so fast with its generic wines that by the end of the 60s it was a major buyer of bulk wines. It began the 70s with a solid reputation, primarily for its red wines in a rustic, long-aged style. The winery was highly regarded for both Barbera and Zinfandel. In the 70s Sebastiani became known as a popular brand of jug wines, both generics such as its Mountain Chablis and Burgundy, and later as a producer of cheap, often thinly constituted varietals such as Cabernet Sauvignon and Chardonnay. The 70s ended with Sebastiani experiencing annual sales of over 4 million cases along with a sagging reputation.

In 80 Sam Sebastiani took over after his father's death. He tried to reverse direction by modernizing the winery, trimming the lengthy line, emphasizing varietals over generics, and crushing grapes only from Sonoma County and Sonoma Valley. The winery production was dramatically reduced, and many other changes occurred. However, the cost was considerable and dissension within the family surfaced. By 86, Sam was voted out, replaced by his younger brother, Don. Today, the winery offers several quality levels, and it is producing well over 6 million cases a year. However, it has gone through numerous changes in direction and its multiple lines have yet to be consistently offered.

The top-of-the-line wines are its vineyard-designated Cabernet Sauvignon, "Cherryblock," Town Merlot and its Dutton Ranch Chardonnay. The next level consists of Sonoma Cask varietals from Sonoma County, headed by Chardonnay (50,000 cases), Cabernet Sauvignon (35,000 cases), Merlot (20,000 cases), and Zinfandel (10,000 cases). This line also includes limited bottlings of Mourvedre, Syrah, Barbera, and Cabernet Franc. Sebastiani owns over 300 acres in Sonoma County, and is a major buyer of locally grown grapes. To produce its three large-volume lines of generics and low-priced varietals—Sebastiani has refurbished a large old facility in Woodbridge, next door to the vast acreage of the Lodi district.

Sebastiani was among the first to produce a blush wine, its "Eye of the Swan," and it was likely the first to make a Nouveau-style red wine. Moreover, it has played a vital role in the evolution of Sonoma County as a rival to Napa Valley. Wine quality at Sebastiani has finally started to show steady improvement and consistency. Some of the individual vineyard-designated bottlings can be quite good. The Cask Merlot delivers real value.

**Merlot**

87    88°    89    90    **93°**    94    **95°**

*Light and fruity, it is among the most priceworthy in good vintages*

SEBASTOPOL VINEYARDS    *Sonoma 1996*    Owned by Joe Dutton, this winery specializes in Chardonnay and Pinot Noir from his family's Dutton Ranch in Sonoma Green Valley. The Dutton Ranch sells grapes to a dozen wineries, including Kistler and Rutz Cellars, and is especially known for Chardonnay. Most of the 2,500 cases made each year by Sebastopol Vineyard are sold from the winery.

SEGHESIO WINERY    *Sonoma 1983*    Here is one of the last of many Sonoma County producers of bulk wine to make the switch to bottling wines under its own name. The Seghesio family bought vineyard land between Asti and Geyserville back in 1894, and by 02 they had finished building their winery. Before and after Prohibition, they supplied wines to Italian Swiss Colony and others. Business was brisk in the 40 s, and in 49 they bought a winery in Healdsburg with 1.2-million-gallon-storage capacity. By the late 70s they began to modernize the facilities for the purpose of offering their own wines. Today, all wines made for their label originate in the family's 362 acres of vineyards, located in Sonoma County.

In 83 Seghesio introduced a line of varietals led in volume by Zinfandel and Cabernet Sauvignon, and White Zinfandel, and including Chardonnay, Pinot Noir, and Sauvignon Blanc. Production, which began at 20,000 cases, grew to a target of 150,000 cases a year. A limited-volume wine called "Chianti Station" is made from a 3-acre block of Sangiovese and other Chianti grapes planted by the Seghesios in 1910. In recent years the family has added 10 acres of Sangiovese and is marketing a Sangiovese varietal. In the 1990s Seghesio replanted much of its vineyards and practically reinvented itself. All wines now have an Italian identity. Zinfandel has emerged as the major wine, with four versions produced. The volume Zinfandel is labeled Sonoma County, which is joined by an Old Vine and two single-vineyard Zinfandels, Home Ranch and San Lorenzo. In addition to Sangiovese, which has grown in importance, Seghesio offers Barbera, Pinot Grigio, and Arneis. As its production expands from 40,000 cases to a long-term goal of 70,000, Seghesio will expand the Sonoma County Zinfandel to almost 50% of its total. Pinot Noir is also made, but under the Keyhole Ranch (see entry) name.

**Cabernet Sauvignon**

86    87    89    90    91    **92°**

**Sangiovese**

(Vitigno Toscano)    91    **92°**    93    94    95

### Zinfandel

| | | | | | | | | | |
|---|---|---|---|---|---|---|---|---|---|
| (Sonoma County) | 87 | 88 | 89 | 90 | 91° | **92°** | 93 | 94 | 95 |
| **96°** | | | | | | | | | |
| (Old Vines) | **93** | **94°°** | **95°°** | **96** | | | | | |

*An improving wine, it is focused on ripe berry fruit in recent vintages; Old Vines is a big, rich Reserve type*

---

SELBY WINERY  *Sonoma 1995*  Winemaker with Rabbit Ridge Vineyards, Sue Selby has offered Sonoma County varietals under her own label. To date she had produced Pinot Noir, Chardonnay, Syrah and an Old Vine Zinfandel. While all have been a bit heavy-handed, the Old Vine Zinfandel responds well to the approach and is a * performer. Combined output, most of which is sold locally, is 500 cases.

---

SELENE WINES  *Napa 1993*  This small winery is operated by Mia Klein, who, along with partner Tony Soter, runs one of the best-known wine consulting businesses in California. Merlot and Sauvignon Blanc from the Carneros District are offered by Selene. The Merlot is rich and balanced but overshadowed by its running mate. Made from the Hyde Vineyard, the Sauvignon Blanc has often been a fascinating mélange of flavors capable of earning ** in many vintages. It is made from the Musque clone of Sauvignon Blanc. On average Selene bottles about 200 cases of each wine.

---

THOMAS SELLARDS  *Sonoma 1980*  Near Sebastopol in southern Sonoma County, Sellards is producing wine out of an expanded shed close to his home. Purchasing most of the grapes crushed from the Alexander Valley, Sellards is currently producing 1,200 cases a year. To date, the line consists of Cabernet Sauvignon, Chardonnay, Zinfandel, and Sauvignon Blanc. The reds ferment in open-top tanks, and the whites follow the more conventional stainless-steel approach.

---

SEQUOIA GROVE VINEYARDS  *Napa 1980*  Jim Allen and his brother Steve are partners in this winery located between Oakville and Rutherford. The property, purchased in 79, was the site of a pre-Prohibition winery whose name is now long forgotten, and the estate contained a few acres of Chardonnay vines. The Allens increased the estate vineyard to its present total of 25 acres. Of the total, 20 acres grow Chardonnay, and the remaining 5 contain Cabernet Sauvignon and related blending varieties. The first estate Cabernet Sauvignon was made in 85. Sequoia Grove buys additional Cabernet to produce a second bottling, usually labeled Napa Valley. The Allens co-own 138 acres in the Carneros, planted primarily to Chardonnay and Pinot Noir. From this vineyard, they produce a Carneros–Napa Valley Chardonnay, and from the Rutherford vineyard they make a Napa Valley Chardonnay. Overall production stands at 20,000 cases, equally divided between Cabernet Sauvignon and Chardonnay. The winery's capacity is 25,000 cases a year. Quality has been quite high for Cabernet Sauvignon, generally good for Chardonnay.

### Cabernet Sauvignon

| | | | | | | | | |
|---|---|---|---|---|---|---|---|---|
| (Napa) | 84° | **85°°°** | **86°** | **87°** | **89°** | 91 | 93 | 94 | 95 |
| (Estate Reserve) | **85°°** | **86°** | **87°** | **89°** | **90°°** | **91°** | **92°** | 93 |
| **94** | | | | | | | | |

*Strong, curranty fruit is surrounded by sweet oak and, in some vintages, hints of herbs and tobacco, and wrapped in medium tannins*

### Chardonnay

| | | | | | | | | | |
|---|---|---|---|---|---|---|---|---|---|
| (Carneros) | 85 | 86 | 87° | 88 | 89° | 90° | 91 | 93 | 94 | 96 |

*Tending a bit toward the pineappley side in both versions, the wines are typically fruity, moderately oaked, and high in brisk acidity*

SEVEN PEAKS WINERY   *Edna Valley 1996*   This is a joint venture between Southcorp Wines, Australia's largest wine producer, and Paragon Vineyard, one of the biggest vineyards on the Central Coast. Paragon, which is co-owner of Edna Valley Vineyard, has 2,000 acres of vineyards that are planted almost entirely to Chardonnay. For Seven Peaks' wines the owners favor the Australian practice of multiregional blending. As a result, most wines carry the Central Coast or California appellation. Chardonnay and Reserve Chardonnay are the two main players in the line up, and both began on a relatively high note. Syrah and Cabernet Sauvignon also are expected to move up in importance in the years ahead.

SHADOW BROOK WINERY   *Napa 1984*   Established grape growers since the 1970s, the Hoffman family is venturing into winemaking for the second time within a decade. With 8 acres near their winery in St. Helena, and 38 acres to the south near the town of Napa, the Hoffmans bottled Shadow Brook wines in 84, 85, and 86. After sitting out the next two vintages by selling grapes and wines in bulk, they resumed producing estate-grown wines in 1989. Chardonnay and Pinot Noir are the only wines they produce, with the oak puncheon–fermented, *sur lie*–aged Chardonnay representing 70% of the annual 7,500-case total.

SHADOW CREEK CHAMPAGNE CELLARS   *(Domaine Chandon)*   In the late 70s when Chateau St. Jean was experimenting with sparkling wine, an entrepreneur named George Vare purchased a considerable quantity for the purpose of marketing sparkling wines under his private label. Vare, former president of Geyser Peak Winery, selected Shadow Creek as his brand name. Priced just below the average retail for *méthode champenoise* wines, Shadow Creek developed a good track record. By the end of 81 it performed well enough to be purchased by Glenmore Distillers, owners of Corbett Canyon, who transferred all production to their Edna Valley facility.

Under Corbett Canyon's direction, Shadow Creek grew to about 30,000 cases a year. Glenmore by mid-87 was losing interest in its wine properties and did not expand production of Shadow Creek. In 88, Glenmore sold its California wine operations to the Wine Group, which in turn sold Shadow Creek shortly thereafter to Domaine Chandon of Napa. Through Shadow Creek, the owners of Chandon have been able to produce sparkling wine from non–Napa Valley sources. In the early 90s Chandon procured an additional 200 acres in Santa Barbara and Sonoma County for its "Shadow Creek" line. So far the roster consists of a Brut and a Blanc de Noirs, with the 25,000-case annual output evenly split between them. The quality in the early rounds was just average. Almost every bottle made is exported.

SHAFER VINEYARDS   *Napa 1979*   In 72, John Schafer purchased a 210-acre estate in the eastern foothills of Napa Valley just beneath the Stags Leap palisades. The abandoned hillside vineyard had to be terraced before it was planted to 42 acres of Cabernet Sauvignon, Merlot, and Cabernet Franc, along with 8 acres of Chardonnay. In 82 the Shafers acquired and developed a 17-acre parcel in the Oak Knoll area near Trefethen Vineyards, and planted it all to Chardonnay. Starting out slowly as producers, Shafer made modest amounts of wine in 78 at another winery. While John's son Doug was finishing the enology program at U.C. Davis, the family was building its own winery. The 79 crush was split between two facilities, and by 80, with their own winery finished, the Shafers, with Doug as winemaker, were ready to focus on barrel-fermented Chardonnay and Cabernet Sauvignon. Zinfandel was made until 87, when it was dropped to make room in the lineup for Merlot, which has come to be an important part of the roster. "Firebreak," Shafer's proprietary blend of Sangiovese and Cabernet Sauvignon, has also earned high marks.

At present two Cabernets are bottled. One is Stags Leap in origin and is usually blended with Merlot; the other is "Hillside Select," a 100% Cabernet aged two years in barrel and two and a half years in bottle by the winery. This Hillside Select was first made in 83, and its production is level at 2,000 cases. Improving over each of its first few vintages, Shafer Merlot, blended with Cabernet Franc and Cabernet Sauvignon, has grown to just under 5,000 cases a year in quantity, and reached ° in quality. In recent years the Shafers have been developing an 83-acre Merlot and Chardonnay vineyard in the Carneros district. The Chardonnay section of this vineyard is known as Red Shoulder. Since the 1994 vintage, Shafer has made about 5,000 cases of Red Shoulder Chardonnay, which has varied in quality but never in its immense size. Syrah is a newcomer to the line. Sangiovese from Firebreak Vineyard has been well made in its first three vintages, earning *** in 94 and * in others. The winery's annual output will remain at 25,000 cases. Sustained quality improvements have placed Shafer among the top echelons of Napa Valley producers.

### Cabernet Sauvignon

(Hillside Select)  83°  84°°  **85°°**  **86°°**  **87°**  88  **89°**  90
**91°°**  **92°**  **93°°°**

(Stags Leap)  78°  79°  **80°**  82  83°  84°  **85°**  **86°**  **87°°**
**88°**  **89°**  **90°°**  91  **92°**  **93°°**  **94°**  95

*Both wines rely on ripe fruit and rich oak as their central themes; the Hillside Select is the bigger, brawnier of the two, and often has a more curranty cast to its fruit than the Stags Leap bottling, which tends more toward the ripe, black-cherry part of the varietal spectrum*

### Chardonnay

86°  87°  88°  89°  90°°  91°  92°  **93°**  **94**  95  **96°°**

*Straightforwardly fruity, in a bright, crisp, appley manner, this one finds its fruit buoyed up by creamy, slightly toasty oak and lots of brisk acidity*

### Merlot

83°  84  85°  86°  **87°°**  **88°°**  89  **90°°**  **91°**  **92°**  **93°**
**94°**  **95°**

*Rich, oaky, accessible, somewhat round fruit with moderate tannins giving a nice sense of supporting structure*

---

SHALE RIDGE  *Monterey 1996*  This is a sister label of Lockwood Vineyard, which owns close to 2,000 acres of vineyards. Shale Ridge aims to offer a light, user-friendly style of moderately priced Chardonnay, Merlot, and Cabernet Sauvignon. Though the prices are indeed moderate, the wines have generally lacked excitement. Annual production has reached 30,000 cases.

SHENANDOAH VINEYARDS  *Amador 1977*  Home winemaker Leon Sobon decided in 77 to turn pro after becoming enthralled by Amador County Zinfandel. He purchased an old vineyard in the Shenandoah Valley and expanded it to 35 acres. From an initial output of 1,200 cases of Zinfandel, the winery grew to 40,000 cases by the end of the 80s, fueled by tremendous demand for its White Zinfandel. Sales of that wine topped 20,000 cases, and today hold steady at 12,000 cases a year. Regular robust Zinfandels (4,000 cases) have often been of ° quality. Since 84 a "Special Reserve" Zinfandel has been offered. This Zinfandel combines grapes from the estate and neighboring vineyards. The winery's third most prominent varietal is a Sauvignon Blanc, made in a consistent forthright, fruity style. Depending on the vintage, the Sauvignon Blanc ranges in quality from acceptable to °. After Shenandoah Vineyards used it as a blender for several years, Sangiovese has blossomed on its own. The winery also has a rich Barbera to make an exciting Italian duo. Sobon has always maintained an interest in fortified wines, first with port and more recently with fortified Orange Muscat and Black Muscat. The three speciality fortified wines have grown in output to 4,000 cases a year. Both the Orange and Black Muscat are very good in their respective categories. Though only 1,000 cases are made, Cabernet Sauvignon originates in the estate vineyard and has been a fixture since 77. In 89, Sobon bought the former D'Agostini Winery in Plymouth and renamed it the Sobon Estate (see entry).

### Zinfandel

86  87  88  89  90  91  92  **93  94**  95  96

*Usually oriented to ripe fruit, with chocolatey and oaky overtones and noticeable tannins*

SIDURI WINES  *Sonoma 1994*  Texans Dianna and Adam Lee became so enamored of Pinot Noir that they moved to California to produce their own wine. Leasing winery space, they made a few hundred cases in 1994. Encouraged by the rave reviews their first vintage generated, they expanded their operation. By 1997 they were making four vineyard-designated Pinot Noirs along with a blend from Oregon. Following traditional, hands-on techniques, the Lees are making Pinot Noirs from the Hirsch Vineyard and Van der Kamp Vineyard in Sonoma County, from Pisoni Vineyard in the Santa Lucia Highlands, and from Archery Summit Vineyard in Oregon. All told, annual production has reached 1,500 cases with 2,500 viewed as optimum. A small winery was in place in late 1998.

SIERRA VISTA WINERY  *El Dorado 1977*  Electrical engineer and home winemaker John MacCready got the wine bug in 72 and purchased 70 acres of bare land next to his sister's home in El Dorado County. Over the next few years he developed a vineyard at the 2,900-foot level on rocky, granitic soils. The varieties favored in his now 43-acre holdings are Cabernet Sauvignon, Zinfandel, Sauvignon Blanc, and Syrah and Chardonnay. Recently, Sierra Vista has developed a Rhone program wit additional plantings of Syrah, Viognier, Grenache, Mourvedre, and Cinsault. This acreage contributes to Rhone blends as well as its Syrah and Viognier. Sierra Vista's Cabernet Sauvignon and Zinfandel are decidedly on the ripe, well-oaked side, but each has earned ° or higher at least once with good value notations. Its Zinfandel bottlings have been among the best from El Dorado County. Though offering juicy fruit and appley character, Sierra Vista's Fumé Blanc is a bit simple and soft. Both the Syrah and barrel-fermented Chardonnay are produced in small volume, but each has shone brightly on occasion, especially the big, ripe Syrah, which has risen to °° quality. Limited-edition, unfined, unfiltered Cabernet and Zinfandel are labeled "Five Star Reserve." Also new to the winery are Merlot and a refreshing pink blend of Grenache and Cinsault named Belle Rosé. The winery makes about 10,000 cases a year.

### Cabernet Sauvignon

87  **88**  92°  93

*Ripe, sometimes weakly focused wines*

### Zinfandel

86°°  87  88°°  **89°  90°**  92

*Good-sized wines, occasionally jammy and usually rich in oak; should age well for half a decade or more*

### Syrah

**87°°**  88  **89°°  91°  92°°  94  95°**

*Spicy, peppery, and ripe blackberry character framed by gruff tannins*

SIGNORELLO VINEYARDS  *Napa 1980*  Ray Signorello, Sr., runs a successful natural resource (gold, silver) development company in Vancouver, Canada. In 77 he bought 100 acres near the Oak Knoll area in the eastern foothills of Napa Valley. The vineyard has been gradually developed and now covers all 100 acres. The major varieties established are Chardonnay (25 acres), Cabernet Sauvignon, Merlot and other Bordeaux reds (15 acres), and Sauvignon Blanc (5 acres). Signorello also has small plantings of Viognier, Syrah, Nebbiolo, Sangiovese, and lesser Italian varieties. Making wines in lots ranging from 100 cases up to 1,000 for Chardonnay, the winery has been bottling a wide array of wines each year, and its roster changes from year to year. By the mid-90s, Ray Signorello, Jr. was running the winery on a daily basis, and had narrowed the wines down to a manageable number. Dropped from the roster were a bold Sauvignon Blanc, a Merlot that earned °°° in 1990, and several others in favor of four varietals: Pinot Noir, Chardonnay, Semillon, and Cabernet Sauvignon. There are currently three bottlings of Pinot Noir— "North Coast" and two vineyard-designated wines, "Martinelli Vineyard" from the Russian River Valley and "Las Amigas" from Carneros. Both an Estate Bottled and a more expensive Reserve bottling of Cabernet Sauvignon are offered. Chardonnay and barrel-fermented Semillon remain volume items as the winery approaches its full production capacity of 7,500 cases annually. By making great quality strides with all wines in the 1990s, Signorello has emerged as a bona fide superstar that merits close watching from now on.

## Cabernet Sauvignon

(Founder's Reserve)  **88°**  **89°**  **90°°°**  **91°**  **92**  **93**  **94°°**

*Blended with small amounts (about 10% of each) of Merlot and Cabernet Franc, this wine is deep, ageworthy, fruity, and very high in rich, vanillin oak.*

## Chardonnay

(Founder's Reserve)  86  87  88  89  90  **91°**  92  **93°**  **94°°°**
**95°°**

(Napa Valley)  **90**  **91°**  **92°**  93  94  **95°**  **96°°**

*Oak and ripe grape character, in need of deeper and richer fruit for balance; recent Reserves have been outstanding*

---

SILVER OAK CELLARS  *Napa 1972*  One-time member of the Christian Brothers Justin Meyer and his wife, Bonny, run this winery in partnership with Raymond Duncan. Meyer and Duncan first joined forces in the early 70s to buy the downtrodden Franciscan Vineyards. As they spruced that property up and improved its overall quality, they started Silver Oak as a sideline. In 79 they sold Franciscan to Eckes of Germany, and began focusing on Silver Oak, which until 79 was making only Cabernet Sauvignon from the Alexander Valley. Cabernet from the Napa Valley and another bottling from Bonny's Vineyard, adjacent to the winery in Oakville, were introduced in 79. After an uneven string of vintages, Silver Oak began to fulfill some of its promise in 78. Throughout the 80s, its Alexander Valley Cabernet has performed consistently well. Aged over two years in American oak, and close to two years in bottle, Silver Oak's Cabernets tend to be relatively mature when they reach the market. Total production has reached 60,000 cases. The Napa Valley Cabernet production is about 20,000 cases a year, and the Alexander Valley bottling has averaged 40,000 cases. Bonny's Vineyard was discontinued after 91. Silver Oak purchased the former Lyeth facility in Geyserville in 1993, and the entire production of the Alexander Valley Cabernet has been shifted to this site.

## Cabernet Sauvignon

(Alexander  Valley)  **75°**  **76°**  **77°**  **78°**  **79°°**  80  **81°°**  **82°°**
**83°°°**  **84°°**  **85°°°**  **86°**  **87°°**  **88°°**  89  **90°**  **91°**  **93°**  **94°°**

(Napa Valley)  79  80  **81°**  **82°°°**  **83°°**  **84°°**  **85°°**  **86°°°**
**87°°**  **88°°**  89  **90°**  **91°**  **93°**

(Bonny's Vineyard)  **79°°**  **82°**  **84°**  85  **86°**

*The wines from the Napa and Alexander valleys have outperformed the pricier offering from Bonny's Vineyard, with the Alexander Valley the fruitiest of the three and the Napa often the richest, while the Bonny's has suffered from ripeness without fully adequate support*

SILVERADO HILL CELLARS   *Napa 1979*   Located along the Silverado Trail a few miles to the north of the town of Napa, this winery has had several incarnations. Founded and operated for a brief period as Pannonia Winery, it failed to generate any interest and was sold to an investor, Louis K. Mihaly. For several years it was known as Louis K. Mihaly Vineyards, and its often strange wines were priced high and targeted exclusively for sale in restaurants and private clubs. That concept was less than totally successful. In 87 Mihaly sold his interest to Minami Kyushu Co. of Japan. The 34-acre vineyard is still planted primarily to Chardonnay and Sauvignon Blanc, with a smattering of Pinot Noir. In 89 the winery decided to make only Chardonnay, and phased out Pinot Noir and Sauvignon Blanc. Its annual production of Chardonnay is reported to be in the 10,000-case range. The winery's capacity is 25,000 cases.

SILVERADO VINEYARDS   *Napa 1981*   In 76 Lilian Disney (Mrs. Walter Disney) purchased vineyards in the Napa Valley. One, located in the Stags Leap District, was highly regarded for Cabernet Sauvignon and was previously owned by the See family, owner of the See's candy company. The second vineyard and ranch, a Chardonnay vineyard situated in the Yountville area, was purchased by her daughter and son-in-law, Mr. and Mrs. Ronald Miller. After selling their grapes for several vintages, the Disney family decided to build a winery on a knoll overlooking the Silverado Trail, and the new winemaking venture was launched. For a time the winery was unofficially known as "Retlaw," which is "Walter" spelled backwards. Since that was dropped, the winery has never played up its association with the Disney family.

In 81 winemaker Jack Stuart, formerly of Durney Vineyards, assumed winemaking chores, and the winery has been a model of consistency and a success story ever since. Sauvignon Blanc and Chardonnay were the first wines offered, and helped establish the winery's style as one of immediate accessibility by combining bright, succulent fruit with moderate complexity. In a similar vein, Silverado's Cabernets usually offer lovely, intense young fruit against a backdrop of tannins and balancing acidity. The winery expanded production smoothly and is approaching 110,000 cases total today, with Chardonnay representing one-third. When its vineyards (two of which were not planted until 89) reach full maturity, the winery plans to level off at 150,000 cases. With vineyards at five locations, including one in Carneros, Silverado Vineyards has 350 acres under vine. Chardonnay acreage stands at 110, Cabernet Sauvignon at 100, and Merlot has been expanded from the original 10 acres to 44. Both Cabernet Sauvignon and Merlot are 100% estate-bottled. Special batches of Chardonnay and Cabernet Sauvignon make up a small-volume, upscale Limited Reserve program. Sangiovese from the winery's 17-acre vineyard has grown in importance. Blended with a dash of Cabernet, the Sangiovese has ranked in the top of its field.

### Cabernet Sauvignon

(Napa Valley/Disney and Mt. George Vineyards)   81*   82   83*   **85***
**86**\*\*   **87***   88   89   **90***   **91**\*\*   **92**\*\*   93   **94***   95
(Limited Reserve)   **86***   **87**\*\*   **90**\*\*\*   **91**\*\*   **93***   94

*Exuberantly fruity, moderately rich, well balanced, softly tannic for moderate aging potential, this one succeeds in a style more suited for near-term enjoyment rather than long-haul cellaring; the Reserve is near classic in depth and age worthiness.*

### Chardonnay

86\*\*   87*   88*   89   90   91*   92*   93   94   95
*Usually amiable in its round, near-juicy, inviting fruit and softly enriching oak*

### Merlot

83   84*   85   **86**\*\*   **87***   **88***   **90***   **91**\*\*   **92**\*\*   93   94   95
*The overriding winery style seems very well suited for Merlot, and results in wines that are fruity, moderately deep, accessible, and inviting*

SILVER HORSE VINEYARDS    *San Luis Obispo 1993*   Thoroughbred horse breeder, Rich and Kristen Simons converted part of their ranch in the eastern side of Paso Robles to a 20-acre vineyard. To date they have made Chardonnay, Zinfandel, White Zinfandel, Cabernet Sauvignon and Pinot Noir. The annual output is 3,000 cases.

SIMI WINERY    *Sonoma 1867*   This historic winery in Healdsburg has gone through several ownership changes since being revived in the late 60s. Each owner enhanced the facility, and the current owner, Moët-Hennessy of France, which also owns Domaine Chandon in Napa and several major wine and Cognac properties in France, has added the finishing touches. Simi is run independently of Domaine Chandon, and since 81 has been under the guidance of Zelma Long, a well-known enologist who came to Simi from the Robert Mondavi Winery. She has strongly influenced the style of Chardonnay, Cabernet Sauvignon, and Sauvignon Blanc, and has brought each wine up to high-quality standards. As the annual output moves closer toward its 190,000-case goal, Simi is near to growing the majority of the grapes needed each year. Between 82 and 84, the winery developed 170 acres in the Alexander Valley, with Cabernet Sauvignon at 99 acres, followed by Chardonnay (29), Sauvignon Blanc (18), and Cabernet Franc (17). Another 120 acres will be developed over the next decade.

Simi's Chardonnay, representing 50% of its total production, is about 50% barrel-fermented. The Cabernet Sauvignon from Sonoma County is 25% of total production. Among other wines offered, the Sauvignon Blanc is partially barrel-fermented and has in some vintages been a °° performer. "Sendal," a barrel-fermented proprietary blend of Sauvignon Blanc and Semillon aged in new oak, has made an impressive °° and °°° run in its first four vintages. A slightly sweet Chenin Blanc from Mendocino County usually earns ° and is often one of the best of its type. On the roster since the mid-70s, a Rosé of Cabernet Sauvignon offers more character than most rosés, but sometimes is overly herbaceous. A Reserve Cabernet Sauvignon and a Chardonnay, 100% barrel-fermented in new oak, are offered regularly. As the winery has reached its optimum level of 200,000 cases, the Reserve Chardonnay has become a single-vineyard wine from Goldfields Vineyard. Also relatively new are Carneros Chardonnay, Carneros Pinot Noir, and a big, brawny Sonoma County Shiraz.

### Cabernet Sauvignon

| (Alexander Valley) | 80 | 81 | 82 | 84° | 85° | 86° | 87 | 8̶8̶ | 89 |
|---|---|---|---|---|---|---|---|---|---|
| **90** | 91 | **92** | **93°** | **94°** | **96°** | | | | |

| (Reserve) | 85°° | 86° | 87° | 88° | 89° | 90° | 91°° | 93° |
|---|---|---|---|---|---|---|---|---|

*Somewhat ripe, but never heavy or bombastic, these wines are enjoyable for their well-focused fruit and their supple, moderately tannic structure; the Reserve shows more oak and is somewhat deeper*

### Chardonnay

| (regular bottling) | 86° | 87° | 88°° | 89 | 90° | 91° | 92 | 93 | 94 |
|---|---|---|---|---|---|---|---|---|---|

| (Reserve) | 86° | 87°° | 88° | 89 | 90° | 92° | 93 | 94 |
|---|---|---|---|---|---|---|---|---|

*Bright, quietly floral fruit is teamed with creamy oak in well-balanced, medium-full-bodied wines; the Reserve is oakier*

SINGLE LEAF VINEYARDS    *El Dorado*   The Miller family purchased a small Zinfandel vineyard in 1988 and decided to start their own winery a few years later. Expanding their vineyard to include Cabernet, Cabernet Franc, Merlot, and Barbera, the Millers offer Cabernet Sauvignon, Zinfandel, and a generic red from their own vineyards along with Chardonnay and Sauvignon Blanc from purchased fruit.

ROBERT SINSKEY VINEYARDS    *Napa 1988*   Eye surgeon Robert Sinskey was a partner in Acacia Winery before founding his own winery, located on the Silverado Trail just south of the Yountville Crossroad. The facility itself was first conceived as the wine center for Acacia's Cabernet and Merlot, wines Sinskey pushed to add to Acacia's roster. The winemaker for the only vintages of Acacia Cabernet and Merlot was Joe Cafaro, who became Sinskey's winemaker. In 83 Sinskey developed a 35-acre vineyard in Carneros, with 15 acres planted to Merlot, and 10 each to Chardonnay and Pinot Noir. 5 acres of Cabernet, Merlot, and Cabernet Franc are situated adjacent to the winery. Another vineyard site in Carneros has 72 acres under development. Once all of its vineyards reach full maturity, the winery will produce only estate-bottled wines.

Four wines are offered: Merlot, Chardonnay, Pinot Noir, "RSV Claret" (a blend of Bordeaux varietals). Partially barrel-fermented, the Chardonnay is aged in French oak for six to eight months. Pinot Noir fermentation occurs in small tanks specially designed to allow the cap to be punched down. With over 5,000 square feet of underground aging caves, the facility was from the start intended to be a highly frequented tourist stop. Chardonnay in a lively, crisp style was the early success story, with Pinot Noir evidencing some ups and downs in quality. The red Meritage is labeled "Carneros Claret," and this limited (1,500 cases) blend relies on Merlot for its appeal. Representing half of Sinskey's production, Merlot is now all from the Carneros region. In addition to its regular bottling, Sinskey uses "Aries" to designate Merlot or Pinot Noir made from young vines. To date, the winery's Reserve program consists of a few hundred cases each year of Carneros Chardonnay labeled "RSV" and an occasional small bottling of "RSV" Carneros Pinot Noir. The annual production has increased to 12,000 cases. The maximum output will be no more than 27,000 cases.

### Chardonnay

86° 87°° 88° 90 92 **93°**

*Brisk but bright appley fruit and toasty oak are supported by plenty of acidity*

### Merlot

86 87° **88°°°** **89°** **90** **91** **92°** 93 **94**

*Generally high in oak, ripe-tasting but often skimpy in fruit; 88 was blended with 22% Cabernet Sauvignon and 19% Cabernet Franc and was labeled as Claret.*

### Pinot Noir

86 87 **88°°** **90°** **91°** 92 **93°** **94°** **95**

*Whether ripe and rich, as in 86, or pinched and lean, as with the 87, the wine comes focused on cherryish varietal fruit*

### RSV Claret

89 **90°°** **91** **92°** **93°**

---

SKY VINEYARDS  *Napa 1979*  On a ridgetop in the Mayacamas Range separating Napa from Sonoma counties, owner-winemaker Lore Olds farms 14 acres of Zinfandel. Planted in 73–74 at the 2,000-foot level, the vineyard is nonirrigated and extremely low-yielding. Total production of Zinfandel is 1,000 to 1,500 cases. Aging takes place in small French oak barrels. The quality ranges far and wide, but the Zinfandels in the better years have been powerful and reasonably balanced. Red House is a second label used occasionally for left-over batches of Zinfandel.

---

SMITH & HOOK WINERY  *Monterey 1980*  On beautiful terraced vineyards along the steep hills west of Soledad, Smith & Hook established 250 acres to red varieties in the mid-70s. Originally, the vineyard consisted of Cabernet Sauvignon (220) and Merlot (30), as the intention was to make only Bordeaux-style red wine. The winery itself is a renovated horse stable and carriage house. From the opening vintage of 79, the production of estate Cabernet Sauvignon has grown gradually and now surpasses 10,000 cases a year. Along the way Merlot was added to the line, and the winery developed 60 acres of Chardonnay. More recently, its Cabernet Franc acreage has been expanded to 10. While reserving the Smith & Hook label for its top-of-the-line red varietal wines, the winery bottles Chardonnay and less ageworthy batches of Cabernet Sauvignon and Merlot under a second label.

Now owned by the Hahn family, the winery is on its way to a maximum production target of 50,000 cases.

## Cabernet Sauvignon

81°    82    83°    85°°    88    90    **92**    **94**    **95**

*Always complex, the wine typically offers brushy, leathery, briary elements, tied to cherryish fruit, which shows vintage variations in depth and richness*

W. H. SMITH WINES   *(La Jota Vineyards)*   La Jota's Bill Smith created this label for Pinot Noir, produced in the cool-climate Sonoma Coast. Beginning in 1993 he has offered two Pinot Noirs, one labeled Sonoma Coast and the other Hellenthal Vineyard, which is found a few miles in from the Pacific Ocean. Among the pioneering producers of Viognier and Cabernet Franc, Smith has always been somewhat adventurous. With his Pinot Noirs he has certainly explored some of the coolest sites and many quality levels to date. On occasion Smith's quality has reached *** with the Hellenthal Pinot. Annually, about 500 cases of each wine are bottled.

SMITH-MADRONE VINEYARDS   *Napa 1977*   Brothers Stu and Charlie Smith bought 200 acres of forested land on Spring Mountain in 71. By the next year they had cleared the land at their hilly, 1,700-foot-elevation property, and planted 20 acres to Cabernet Sauvignon, Chardonnay, Riesling, and Pinot Noir. A graduate of U.C. Davis, Stu serves as vineyardist, and Charlie, a former schoolteacher, serves as winemaker. After focusing on Riesling for close to a decade, the Smiths decided in 85 to alter their vineyards and wine roster, and now emphasize Chardonnay, Cabernet Sauvignon, and Riesling. Pinot Noir was discontinued after 85. Their vineyard covers 41 acres and consists of 18 acres of Chardonnay, 18 of Cabernet, and 5 of Riesling. For blending with future vintages of Cabernet, a few acres of Cabernet Franc and Merlot were planted in 90. Total production has averaged 6,000 cases a year, with 8,000 cases viewed as the absolute maximum. The winery's quality record has been spotty.

SMOTHERS BROTHERS WINES   *Sonoma 1977*   This brother wine act took a few years to get together. In 74 Dick Smothers bought an historic vineyard in the Santa Cruz Mountains named Vine Hill, which was located close to his home. Three years later he produced his first wine, 400 cases of late harvest Gewurztraminer, under the Smothers Winery name. That wine won awards, and the small winery was revived. By 85 it was operating at full capacity of 4,000 cases. Independently, in 71 Tom Smothers had moved to a 110-acre ranch in Glen Ellen, and developed a 35-acre vineyard named Remick Ridge. It was not until 86, when the brothers decided to team up as winemakers, that the brand name changed to Smothers Brothers. They came out with a line of varietals and highly successful blends, "Mom's Favorite White" and "Mom's Favorite Red," both made at another facility. Today Tom Smothers is playing solo again and runs the vineyard operation and a tasting room and gift shop in Kenwood. The best-selling wines are Chardonnay, Merlot, Cabernet Sauvignon, and Mom's Favorite White. Annual output is about 5,000 cases. Recent vintages are labeled Remick Ridge Vineyards.

SNOWDEN WINERY   *Napa Valley 1993*   Owners of a 22-acre vineyard in the foothills of St. Helena, the Snowdens began with a few hundred cases of Cabernet Sauvignon. Modest expansion should take their production to 1,200 cases or so by the year 2001. 94 Cabernet earned *.

SOBON ESTATE   *Amador 1856*   In 89 the D'Agostini Winery in the Shenandoah Valley, the oldest in the county and the third oldest in the state, was bought by the Sobon family, owners of Shenandoah Vineyards. It was run-down and its vineyards were ancient and disease-ridden. Leon Sobon began renovating the old facility and replanting the 113-acre estate to 65 acres of Zinfandel, 11 of Sauvignon Blanc, and 7 acres of Cabernet Sauvignon. Close to 5 acres of Zinfandel remain from the old vineyard. The wines produced by the Sobon Estate are Zinfandel, Viognier, Fumé

Blanc, White Zinfandel, Muscat Canelli, Syrah, Cabernet Franc, and port. The winery aims to produce 20,000 cases a year. Viognier has shown mixed results, as has Syrah. Sobon has also made life exciting for lovers of chunky, full-throttle Zinfandel with its annual release of a trio of Zinfandels: Rocky Top, Cougar Hill, and Lubenko, also known as Fiddletown.

**Zinfandel**

| | | | | |
|---|---|---|---|---|
| (Rocky Top) | 92° | 93 | 94°° | 95°° |
| (Cougar Hill) | 93° | 94° | 95 | 96° |
| (Lubenko) | 92 | 93° | 94°° | 95° |

*Bold, brawny wines favoring ripeness and tannin*

SOLITUDE CELLARS   *Napa 1986*   Richard Litsch, owner-winemaker, was Chalone's assistant winemaker in 1986 and 87. After making limited quantities of Solitude wines during those years, he decided to go off on his own and expanded production to 800 cases. Today as a "one man show," he is focusing on Carneros Chardonnay from the Sangiacomo Vineyard and small batches of "Sonoma County" Pinot Noir. Solitude's barrel-fermented Chardonnays have been extremely attractive and a model of consistency. The annual output is steady at 2,000 cases.

**Chardonnay**

| | | | | | | | |
|---|---|---|---|---|---|---|---|
| (Sangiacomo Vineyard) | 88°° | 89° | 90° | 91°° | 92°° | **93°°** | 95° |
| 96° | | | | | | | |

SOMMER VINEYARDS   *Alexander Valley 1994*   Known until 1994 as the Alexander Valley Trading Company, Sommer is owned by Steve and Candy Sommer, who have been making wines from their 55-acre vineyard since 1975. The lineup is headed by Zinfandel, Chardonnay, and Cabernet Sauvignon. Each year a few hundred cases of Merlot, Shiraz, and Late Harvest Zinfandel are usually made. With an annual production of 10,000 cases, Sommer sells most of its wines at the winery to mailing list customers.

SONOMA CREEK VINEYARDS   *Sonoma 1987*   John Larson and his father, Bob, were independent growers in the Carneros region for several years before starting their own winery. They own 40 acres planted to Chardonnay. A major portion of their crop is still sold, and the winery custom-crushes for various brands. Under its own label, Sonoma Creek is producing about 5,000 cases of estate-grown Chardonnay. Winemaker John Larson favors 100% barrel fermentation in new French oak for Chardonnay. He obtains Cabernet Sauvignon and Zinfandel from the Sonoma Valley, and produces about 1,000 cases of each. The long-term capacity of Sonoma Creek is 20,000 cases. Success has been elusive in early vintages.

**Chardonnay**

| | | | | | |
|---|---|---|---|---|---|
| 88 | 89 | 91 | 92 | 93 | 94 |

*Overoaked and underfilled wines*

**Zinfandel**

| | | | | | |
|---|---|---|---|---|---|
| 88 | 90° | 91° | 92 | 93° | 94° |

*Big, ripe, and rich wines, often high in tannin.*

SONOMA-CUTRER   *Sonoma 1981*   As a winemaking facility, Sonoma-Cutrer is "state of the art" and then some. Located in the cool western corner of the Russian River Valley, the winery was set up by winemaker Bill Bonetti for the exclusive production of Chardonnay. A few vintages of sparkling wine were once made on an experimental basis, but the notion was abandoned, and the winery now focuses all of its energies on its three Chardonnays. Two are vineyard-designated; one from the home Cutrer Vineyard, and the other from Les Pierres Vineyard in the Sonoma Valley. The third Chardonnay is made from several vineyards owned by the winery, and is bottled under the identity of Russian River Ranches. It is by far the volume leader at more than 50,000 cases, as well as the least expensive. The other two, priced substantially higher, fall in the 10,000-case range.

All wines were well received during the early years and the winery has since continued to operate at a fairly high-quality level. In meticulous fashion, all Chardonnays are whole-cluster-pressed, barrel-fermented, and aged *sur lie*. However, the entire vinification process is a study in pampering, with hand-picked grapes transported in small, specially ventilated lug boxes to the winery, where the clusters are sent through a chilling tunnel (40°F.) before each is inspected and any defective grapes culled out. After fermentation and aging, the Russian River Ranches receives one year of bottle age, and the two others are given an additional six to ten months of bottle aging. The wines carry the Sonoma Coast appellation in addition to the individual vineyard names. Annual production reached the 70,000 case optimum level.

### Chardonnay

| | | | | | | | | |
|---|---|---|---|---|---|---|---|---|
| (Les Pierres) | 86° | 87° | 88 | 89 | 9↑ | **92°°** | **93°°** | 94 |
| (Cutrer) | 86 | 87° | 88 | 90 | 91 | 92 | 93° | **94** |
| (Russian River Ranches) | 86° | 87° | 88° | 89° | 90 | 91° | 92° | |
| 93° | 94 | 95 | 96 | | | | | |

*Emphasizing cleanliness and brisk acidity as their hallmarks, these Chardonnays combine a crisp, food-oriented style with varying amounts of oak and richness. The Les Pierres is the deepest in its best vintages, while the Cutrer can be the richest; the popularly priced Russian River Ranches tends to be the most immediately accessible of the trio*

---

SONORA WINERY & PORT WORKS  *Tuolumne 1986*  Winemaker and general partner Richard Matranga features two wines, Zinfandel and Port, both produced from old vineyards. He has offered Zinfandels from two appellations—the "TC" Vineyard in Amador County and Sonoma County. The Amador Zinfandel has been well-focused with typical regional fruit and strength. The limited-volume Port is made from traditional Portuguese varieties grown in the Sierra Foothills. The winery's maximum production capacity is 2,500 cases a year.

---

SOQUEL VINEYARDS  *Santa Cruz 1979*  Soquel was founded under the name of Grover Gulch Winery by home winemakers who tried to maintain two careers, finally giving up in 85. Two years later the small facility was acquired by a partnership headed by Peter and Paul Bargetto of the Bargetto Winery family, who renamed it Soquel Vineyards (though they might revive Grover Gulch in the future). Making wines exclusively from the Santa Cruz Mountains appellation, they obtain grapes from 14 acres under a lease arrangement. As they move toward the ultimate production goal of 2,000 cases, they are making only Cabernet Sauvignon, Chardonnay, Merlot and Pinot Noir. After good starts with each varietal, the wines have become consistently good with Cabernet Sauvignon being the most impressive in recent vintages.

---

SPELLETICH CELLARS  *Cellars Napa 1995*  With their stunning debut Cabernet Sauvignon from 1994, Tim and Barbara Spelletich began their winemaking career on an extremely high note. All of their wines are made in small (100–200 cases) lots from grapes purchased from several sources. Chardonnay from Sonoma County and "Bodog" Red, a Sangiovese blended with Cabernet and other varieties, are also offered each year. Spelletich's Chardonnay also has been well received.

---

SPOTTSWOODE VINEYARD  *Napa 1982*  Moving to Napa Valley in 72 to "retire" and become grape growers, Mary and Jack Novak settled into an old (ca. 1882) Victorian house located on the western edge of St. Helena. The 46-acre estate was the site of a pre-Prohibition vineyard whose last known owner was the Spotts family. Beginning in 73, the vineyard site was planted to 22 acres of Cabernet Sauvignon and a few acres each of Merlot and Cabernet Franc. The next year they planted 8 acres to Sauvignon Blanc and about 2 acres of Semillon. The winery is run today by Mary and her daughter, Beth Novak. In 82 they hired winemaker Tony Soter, who produced extremely attractive vintages of Cabernet Sauvignon and Sauvignon Blanc. In most years the Cabernet is blended with 5% Cabernet Franc or Merlot. Partially barrel-fermented, Spottswoode's Sauvignon Blanc has been blended with as much as 25% Semillon. In better years the Sauvignon Blancs, which earn up to **°°°**, capture ample varietal character to accompany the usually rich-textured, ripe fruit, and oak-enriched style. The winery is producing 6,000 cases a year, with Cabernet Sauvignon tallying 4,000 cases and the remainder consisting of Sauvignon Blanc. During the 80s Spottswoode's Cabernets were consistently among the very best made in California. Today, after being gradually replanted, the organically farmed estate vineyard covers 40 acres, with dense vine planting now being the norm.

### Cabernet Sauvignon

82°°   83°°   **84°°°**   85°°   86°°   87°°   88°°   89°°   90°   91
92°   93°°   94°

*Deep, curranty fruit and rich oak are combined in a wine of substantial proportion, superb balance, and admirable aging potential*

SPRING MOUNTAIN VINEYARDS   *Napa 1968*   In 62, Mike Robbins purchased a run-down Victorian home north of St. Helena with a large wine cellar, which he remodeled with the idea of using it for winemaking. Robbins started producing wines in 68, and within a few years was making Cabernet Sauvignon, Chardonnay, and Sauvignon Blanc. One of the most complex wines he ever made was one of his first—a Cabernet identified as Lot H 68–69, a blend of two vintages aged in oak barrels owned by Heitz Cellars. In the early 70s Spring Mountain's white wines were often leaders in their class. The winemaker (and later consultant) Chuck Ortman helped define an exciting style of oak-aged, moderately grassy, balanced Sauvignon Blanc and barrel-fermented Chardonnay.

In 76, with annual output over 20,000 cases, Robbins sold the property (which was renamed St. Clement) and bought another Victorian house on Spring Mountain Road. This second house was both bigger and more elaborate, with turrets and stained-glass windows throughout, and frequently served as the set for the TV series "Falcon Crest." The winery became a tourist mecca, and Robbins began offering wines under the "Falcon Crest" label. In the mid-80s Robbins appeared to have lost interest in winemaking and put the winery and mansion on the market for an exorbitant price. By 1990, with no takers, he filed for bankruptcy. The winery, 24 acres of vineyards, the mansion, and other assets were finally purchased in 92 by a partnership headed by Tom Ferrell, one-time winemaker for Inglenook and former president of Sterling Vineyards. Not long after, Ferrell's partnership acquired Streblow and Chateau Chevalier, two neighboring wineries with vineyards, and later acquired the Draper Vineyard, also on Spring Mountain. Out of 400 total acres, 150 are planted to vines. Cabernet Sauvignon (blended with Merlot) and Sauvignon Blanc are the leading wines made, but Syrah and Viognier are both likely to increase in importance. Though wines from 1990 were offered, the 93 vintage marks the first wines made entirely under present ownership.

STAGLIN FAMILY VINEYARD   *Napa 1989*   Cabernet Sauvignon, Sangiovese, and Chardonnay are the primary wines from this small family-owned venture. In the mid-80s, the Staglins purchased a mature 47-acre vineyard in Rutherford that had been developed by Beaulieu Vineyard. For many years this vineyard contributed to Beaulieu's Private Reserve Cabernets. Quality began at the ° level in early vintages, and the winery has lately improved its track record.

### Cabernet Sauvignon

89°   90°   91   92°   93°   94°°   95°°

*Rich, ripish, fairly sturdy wines showing attractive currant and black cherry fruit; cellar-aging is necessary*

STAG'S LEAP WINE CELLARS  *Napa 1972*  Former University of Chicago professor of political science Warren Winiarski dabbled as a home winemaker before settling in the Napa Valley in the late 60s. He apprenticed with Lee Stewart of Souverain and worked two harvests at the Robert Mondavi Winery before buying land in 70 and developing vineyards and a winery in the Stags Leap District. The original vineyard consisted of 45 acres planted to Cabernet Sauvignon and Merlot. In 72, Stag's Leap produced 400 cases from its first crop, and though its 73 vintage was only slightly bigger, it became an overnight sensation by winning first place at a famous comparative tasting held in Paris in 76. With vineyard maturity, the winery's production increased, and by the end of the 70s Stag's Leap was offering a full line of varietals.

In 74 it produced its first Reserve-type Cabernet, labeled "Cask 23," made since then only in certain vintages. That same vintage saw the first bottling of Merlot, made on an irregular basis over the following decade. In 86 Stag's Leap acquired a well-known 75-acre Cabernet vineyard from Nathan Fay, and today bottles four Cabernets—""SLV" from the estate vineyards, "Cask 23" from a small parcel of that vineyard, Fay Vinegord and "Napa Valley," made from non-estate-grown grapes. The SLV has been further divided in some vintages into Lots 1 and 2, depending on the vintage. Total production of Cabernet Sauvignon approaches 25,000 cases a year.

Chardonnay ("Napa Valley,""Beckstoffer," and Reserve), Sauvignon Blanc, Merlot, Petite Sirah, and White Riesling from the Birkmyer Vineyard complete the line. Over the last few vintages, Stag's Leap's Cabernets became somewhat erratic in quality. At times the Reserve Chardonnay and the "Napa Valley" bottling have offered more excitement and interest. The winery's total production is 50,000 cases a year. A popularly priced line of wines is also offered under the Hawk Crest (see entry) label.

### Cabernet Sauvignon

(SLV)  78 (Lots 1 & 2)°   79   81°   82   83°   84°   85°°   86
**87**   **88°°**   89   **90**   **93°**   **94°**

(Napa Valley)   83   84   85°   86   **87**   88   **89**   **90°°**   **91**   **92**
**93°**   **95**

*The SLV is capable of rich, round, cherry, and currant fruit, with added notes of loam and occasional hints of truffles and dried violets, the wine has been beset recently by off-putting herbaceousness; the Napa Valley bottling has failed to excite in most vintages*

### Cabernet Sauvignon

(Cask 23)   74°°   77°°   78°°   79°°   83°   **84°**   **85**   **86**   87
**90°**   **91°°°**   **92°°°**   **93**   **94°**

*The winery's most expensive Cabernet, claimed by some to be among the best in California, it has been inconsistent at times. Its still intense and complex character is now often juxtaposed with off-putting, intensely herbaceous, near-vegetal characteristics. Cask 23 is not offered in every year*

### Chardonnay

(Napa Valley)   86°   87°   88   89   90   91   **92°°**   93   94   **95°**   96

*Green appley and quietly floral fruit, usually medium-intense and buttressed by toasty oak and brisk acidity, are the major themes in this generally attractive series of wines*

### Chardonnay

(Reserve)   85°   86°°°   87°°   88°   90°   91°   92°   93°°

*Toasty oak and deep appley fruit combine in this brisk, well-balanced, amply stuffed wine; its typically tight structure seems to demand a few years of bottle aging*

STAGS' LEAP WINERY  *Napa 1972*  This winery is part of an historic 240-acre estate and once prominent guesthouse known as Stags' Leap Manor. Built in 1890, the old mansion was badly damaged by fire and later only partially rebuilt. After being to-tally abandoned in the early 50s, the house and what remained of an old stone winery were bought and returned to life by Carl Doumani and family, who re-stored the winery and began replanting most of the old vineyard, keeping only a 5-acre patch of Petite Sirah planted in the early 1900s. That old parcel was even-tually responsible for many intensely flavored, heavy-bodied red wines labeled "Petite Syrah" by the winery from 72 on. However, the winery became entangled in a long legal battle with its neighbor, Stag's Leap Wine Cellars, over trademark rights. Restoration and expansion plans fell behind schedule because of the legal issues.

It was not until 79 that Doumani first crushed grapes in his own winery. Today the winery is owned by Beringer Estate, which bought it in 1997. Doumani re-tained 30 acres, leaving Stags Leap with 90 acres currently planted. The leading varieties are Cabernet Sauvignon (40), Merlot (28), and Petite Sirah (22). All but 5 acres of Petite Sirah were replanted in the 1990s. Malbec and Petit Verdot are planted as blending varieties. Chardonnay, purchased from vineyards in south-eastern Napa Valley, completes the line. The annual production has grown steadily to the current level of 60,000 cases, the winery's optimum. Merlot at 20,000 cases is the leader by volume followed closely by Cabernet Sauvignon and Chardonnay. Petite Syrah (10,000 cases) remains the pride and joy of the winery, and recent vintages are well received, though not quite as brash and bold as those of a decade ago.

## Cabernet Sauvignon

81   82   83   84   85   **86°**   87   **88**   8̶9̶   **90°**   **91°**   92°
**94°**   95

*Heavyweight efforts are keyed on ripeness and boldness, and have often had the structure for long aging but not the necessary fruit to make the wait a sure thing*

---

P. & M. STAIGER   *Santa Cruz 1973*   Paul Staiger and his wife, Marjorie, acquired a hill-side site that was once home to a pre-1900 vineyard, and by 73 had built a small winery beneath their house in the Santa Cruz Mountains. Facing south, the hill-side estate vineyard consists of 5 acres, half planted to Chardonnay and the other half to Cabernet Sauvignon and Merlot combined. In 79, they harvested their first estate-grown grapes. Now at full maturity, the vineyard yields about 250 cases of Chardonnay and the same of Cabernet Sauvignon. Merlot has been occasionally offered. Working on a small scale, the Staigers follow traditional winemaking practices and rarely filter their wines. Most Cabernet Sauvignon vintages have been unfined as well.

---

PHILIP STALEY WINERY   *Sonoma 1995*   Former founding partner of Alderbrook, Staley developed 14 acres in the Russian River area and buys fruit from Dry Creek Val-ley. Emphasizing Syrah, Sangiovese, Mourvedre, and Grenache among reds and Chardonnay and Viognier among whites, Staly produces several wines in 200–500-case quantities. First vintages of reds were successful, with Zinfandel, Syrah, and Mourvedre showing promise. Annual goal is 3,000 cases.

---

STAR HILL WINERY   *Napa 1988*   Jake Goldenberg, a dentist, was an amateur wine-maker before founding Star Hill. Located on a knoll in Napa, Star Hill is a small stone winery specializing in Pinot Noir and Chardonnay. They have 4 acres of Chardonnay adjacent to the winery and buy grapes from growers in the Carneros and southern Napa regions. Star Hill's Chardonnay is 100% barrel-fermented in new French oak. Fermented by the native yeast, Star Hill's Pinot Noirs are unfined and unfiltered. The roster also includes 200 cases of Cabernet Sauvignon from the Carneros district and a like amount of Zinfandel. Overall production is at 2,000 cases annually, with 3,000 as the maximum goal.

---

STEELE WINES   *Lake 1992*   One of California's most highly regarded winemakers, Jed Steele started out in the 70s at Edmeades Vineyards and became well known during his eight years as Kendall-Jackson's winemaker. After leaving that post during a legal battle, Steele acquired Stuermer, an old Lake County winery, and began offering a line of wines headed by Chardonnay. A few years later he acquired the much-larger Konocti Winery, which enabled him to expand production. Limited-volume, vineyard-designated Chardonnays ("Lolonis," "Sangiacomo," "Du Pratt," "Goodchild," and "Durell"), along with a California blend, are regularly offered. Steele, who developed a cult following for Zinfandel made from old vineyards in Mendocino, offers Zinfandel from DuPratt Vineyard in Anderson Valley, Pacini Vineyard in Redwood Valley, and Catfish Vineyard in Lake County. His work with Pinot Noir now results in two bottlings, Carneros and a Sangiacomo Vineyard. Over recent years Steele has shown strong interest in Syrah and plans to emphasize it in the future. He also has developed Shooting Star into a busy second label offering several lower-priced varietals, including Syrah, Cabernet Franc, Chardonnay, and Cabernet. Overall Steele is best known today for Zinfandel. Of all the Chardonnays we especially like the Lolonis and the DuPratt Vineyard versions.

STELTZNER VINEYARDS   *Napa 1977*   A well-known grower, Dick Steltzner established his own vineyard in 66. Situated at the base of the Stags Leap cliffs, Steltzner's oldest vineyard contains 44 acres of Cabernet Sauvignon, and 5 acres each of Cabernet Franc and Merlot. Steltzner had previously carved out a reputation as a vineyard developer when he planted the vineyards of Diamond Creek, Spring Mountain, and several other producers. He also served as vineyard manager for several wineries. Starting in 77, he made his own wines in other facilities, and in 83 built a functional winery on his Stags Leap property. As a partner in a large vineyard located in the Oak Knoll area near Yountville, Steltzner draws from that source to make Sauvignon Blanc. Both as grower and wine producer, Steltzner has been associated with Cabernet Sauvignon.

The legendary 74 "Insignia" by Joseph Phelps Vineyard was made from Steltzner's grapes. As a wine producer, he has at different times been his own winemaker, although Steltzner's ** achievements were made under the direction of consulting enologists. Nevertheless, in nearly every vintage made, the quality of the Cabernet fruit pushes the final product to some distinction. In 89, the winery made its first varietal Merlot, with the output expected to remain at 500 cases a year. In most vintages, Stelzner produces about 6,000 cases of Cabernet Sauvignon and just over 1,000 of Sauvignon Blanc. The facility has been expanded, with production moving toward a goal of 10,000 cases a year.

### Cabernet Sauvignon

77°°   78°   79°°   80°°   81°°   82   83°   84°   **85°**   **86°**   **87°**
88   89   91   92   **93**   **94**

*Ripe fruit and lots of rich oak are braced by a decade's worth of coarse tannins; some wines will last up to 20 years, but recent wines are of lesser quality in every regard*

ROBERT STEMMLER   *Sonoma 1977*   Born and trained in winemaking in Germany, Robert Stemmler came to California and worked for several wineries, most notably Inglenook and Charles Krug. He became a consulting enologist in the 70s, and it was through his clients that he discovered available readymade wines and sources of grapes. With a partner, he started a winery to make a limited amount of wine through those contacts. However, by 82 he was crushing and fermenting wines, and before long he was making over 10,000 cases a year. Stemmler developed a reputation for rich, often heavy-duty Pinot Noir, in addition to a wide range of wines from Chardonnay to Sauvignon Blanc to Cabernet Sauvignon. In 88 Racke, USA, owner of Buena Vista, bought Stemmler and entered into an unusual arrangement whereby all Stemmler Pinot Noir, produced at the Buena Vista facility in the Carneros, is exclusively marketed by Racke. Pinot Noir production is at 8,000 cases a year.

## Pinot Noir

84   85   86   ~~87~~   90   91   93   94°   **95**

*Ripe, exotic, not always clean, but usually rich and fully stuffed*

STERLING VINEYARDS   *Napa 1967*   Just south of Calistoga on a bluff that disrupts the flat valley floor sits the white, monastic-looking Sterling Vineyards. In 64 four principals of Sterling International Paper Co. planted a 50-acre vineyard in Calistoga and joined forces to start this winery, with the goal of creating a striking facility that would draw thousands of visitors each year. An aerial tram was installed as the primary public approach to the knolltop facility, and a self-guided tour organized that deposited visitors in the tasting and sales room. A fee was charged for the tram ride, however, and in an era when many wineries offered free tours and tastings, Sterling's approach was not a hit. Just about every Napa winery charges a fee for tasting today, and Sterling has become one of the valley's most popular tourist destinations. Sterling began making wines in temporary quarters in 69 under the direction of winemaker Ric Forman, who set out to make Bordeaux wines—Cabernet Sauvignon, Sauvignon Blanc (then labeled Blanc de Fumé), and Merlot (the second one made in California), with Chardonnay, Chenin Blanc, and Gewurztraminer filling out the line. The owners developed close to 400 acres of vineyards in and around the winery and in other generally warm sites, and in 73 completed a winery.

With the exception of a flawed 72 Cabernet Sauvignon, Sterling's quality was above average in most instances. However, the owners were forced to scramble to make ends meet. By the time Coca-Cola of Atlanta came along to purchase the whole package in 77, Sterling was making a wide array of wines. Under Coke, the facility was expanded and additional cask-aging areas built. Forman remained to work with a line trimmed down to Cabernet (regular and Reserve), Merlot, Sauvignon Blanc, and Chardonnay. Having ballooned to well over 100,000 cases a year, the winery's output was also reduced, to 65,000 cases. Coke expanded acreage and purchased the 110-acre Diamond Mountain Ranch, which contains Chardonnay, Cabernet, and a smattering of Merlot to bring the total acreage owned to 750. However, by 83 Coca-Cola had soured on the wine business in general and sold Sterling to Seagram. Since then, more acreage has been added, the well-known Winery Lake Vineyard in the Carneros being the most noteworthy. The winery now draws from its 1,180 total acres planted in 14 sites within Napa Valley.

The Winery Lake acquisition returned Pinot Noir to the lineup. Today, the majority of the production is the estate-bottled line of Sauvignon Blanc, Chardonnay, Cabernet Sauvignon, and Merlot. Vineyard-designated wines have grown to include bottlings of Chardonnay and Cabernet Sauvignon from Diamond Mountain Ranch, Pinot Noir and Chardonnay from Winery Lake Vineyards, and a Cabernet Sauvignon–Merlot blend from the Three Palms Vineyard. The top-of-the-line red is the "Sterling Reserve," a limited-volume (3,000-case average) Bordeaux-style blend.

Sterling's annual output approaches 200,000 cases. After several winemaker changes in the 1990s Sterling appears to be bouncing back from several mediocre vintages. Its current direction is to upgrade Cabernet Sauvignon and Merlot in particular, but also on all of its red wines. Chardonnay and Sauvignon Blanc remain the two primary whites.

## Cabernet Sauvignon

78°   79°   80°   81   82°   83°   85°   **86°**   **87°**   88   89   **90**
**91**   **92**   **93**   95

*A solid performer, this medium-depth wine has cherryish fruit underlaid by a bit of sweet oak, and has a fairly firm, never hard or heavy feel on the palate; the wines of the 70s were a little bigger*

### Cabernet Sauvignon

(Reserve)   73°   74°°   75°°   76   77°   **78°**   **80°°**   82°   83°°°
**84°°**   **85°°**   **86°°**   **87°°**   88°   89°   90°   91°   94

*Ripe yet balanced, full-bodied and fairly intense without becoming ponderous, this rich, always highly oaked, curranty, sometimes minty Cabernet sets its deep, outgoing character against strong tannin; the wines of the 80s are somewhat more refined than their siblings of the previous decade*

### Chardonnay

(Napa Valley)   86°   87°   88°   89   90   91   92   93°   94°
(Diamond Mountain)   86°   87   88   89   90   91   92   93   94
(Winery Lake)   86°°   87   88°   89   90   91   92   93   94

*Mostly average efforts of late from widely varying sources, yet sharing the same penchant for firm, crisp structure and for toasty, slightly creamy oak, these efforts have differed in the slightly broader, more direct fruit of the Napa Valley, in the near hardness of the Diamond Mountain, and in the slight pearlike and citrusy notes of the Winery Lake*

### Merlot

80°   81   82°   83   84°   85°   86°   87   **88°**   89   **90**   **91**
**92**   **93**   **94**   **95**

*Light, sweet oak adds a note of prettiness to the cassis and cherry fruitiness of this moderately rough, fairly ageworthy, medium-intensity wine*

### Pinot Noir

(Winery Lake)   86   87   **88°**   **89°**   **90°**   91   **92**   93   94

*Balanced, moderately rich wines, with surprisingly firm tannins; 91 was earthy; 93 and 94 were thin*

---

STEVENOT VINEYARDS   *Calaveras 1974*   The first winery since Prohibition to open and operate in Calaveras County, Stevenot grew out of an old cattle ranch bought by Bard Stevenot in 69. By 74 he had developed a 27-acre vineyard. His winery opened in 78 and produced 2,200 cases. Within two years it was producing about 10,000 cases as Stevenot bought grapes from vineyardists in El Dorado and Amador to supplement its own. The home vineyard was expanded to 18 acres of Chardonnay, and the first estate-bottled Calaveras Chardonnay was made in 83. Cabernet Sauvignon and Zinfandel are the next most significant varieties planted, both offered as varietals. After backing away from the glutted White Zinfandel market, Stevenot has decided to offer a line of modestly priced California appellation varietals, headed by Chardonnay (9,000 cases), Cabernet Sauvignon (2,000 cases), and Zinfandel (2,000 cases). The top-of-the-line offerings are North Coast varietals led by Merlot (4,000 cases) and Sierra Foothills wines led by Chardonnay and Sangiovese.

### Chardonnay

84   85   86   87   90   91   93   94

*Seemingly a little skimpy in its not-quite-varietal, melonlike fruit, and often on the thin side to boot*

---

STONE CREEK WINES   This négociant label covers a line of varietal and generic wines from various appellations. Stone Creek was launched in 76 when the Bedford Wine Company, a San Francisco bottler and distributor, purchased an array of readymade wines from Souverain. At one time, at its peak level, close to 50,000 cases were bottled by Stone Creek, and at times a few noteworthy limited-volume wines made their way to the marketplace. However, the brand lost ground in the early 80s, and in 87 it was sold to the World Vintage Company, a division of the Simon Levi Company, Ltd. Stone Creek remains a négociant brand, but its owner buys grapes under contract as well as purchasing wines from all regions within

California. It offers a line of vintaged varietals from almost every appellation within California's North Coast. But it has enjoyed enormous sales success with Merlot, and today over half of its total annual output of 200,000 cases is its "Special Selection" Merlot. The leading wines today are Merlot, Cabernet Sauvignon, and Chardonnay, all from the California appellation. With the "Special Selection" wines priced on the low side, Stone Creek added a line of "Chairman Reserve" wines—Merlot, Cabernet, and Pinot Noir—made from Sonoma County. These were a step up in quality as well as in price.

STONEGATE WINERY  *Napa 1973*  Jim Spaulding, a longtime home winemaker in Milwaukee, brought his family to California and purchased a mountainous vineyard in the Mayacamas Range in 69. Situated on the slopes of Diamond Mountain, the vineyard was planted to 35 acres and now contains Cabernet Sauvignon, Chardonnay, and Merlot. In 73, the Spauldings built a small winery in Calistoga, near Sterling Vineyards. A suitable area adjacent to the winery was planted to Sauvignon Blanc and Semillon. Over the first several vintages, as their vineyards were developing, the Spauldings made a wide range of table wines.

In the late 80s, production reached the 17,000-case level, with Chardonnay at 9,000 cases, followed by Cabernet Sauvignon (4,500), Sauvignon Blanc (2,000), and Merlot (1,200). The Cabernets, blended with 10% to 15% Merlot, are aged two years in oak and two years in the bottle prior to being marketed. In 87 Stonegate added a Meritage Reserve (a blend of Cabernet and Merlot), and a few years later introduced a white Meritage blend called "Felicity."

Stonegate's Merlot was such a critical hit that the Spauldings added more acreage and contracted to purchase Merlot from a vineyard contiguous to theirs. Quality has varied from year to year at Stonegate and from variety to variety. Production was scaled down in the 90s to about 8,000 cases. Growing weary of the business, the Spauldings sold it all in 1997 to California Wine Company, owners of Bandiera. Both the varietals and the annual quantity have remained the same. Quality remains less than impressive.

**Cabernet Sauvignon**

84° 85 86 87 88 89 **90 91**

*Suggestions of black-cherry fruit are seasoned with oak in medium- to medium-full-bodied wines*

**Chardonnay**

86 87 88 89 91 92

*Oaky but underfruited and somewhat weakly constituted wines are the rule of late*

STONEHEATH WINERY  *Napa 1995*  Mark Pollock, an attorney in Napa, runs this small winery specializing in wines from Italian varieties. Nebbiolo and Sangiovese were made over the first three vintages, and Dolcetto and Barbera are recent additions. From his 8 1/2-acre vineyard, Pollock is making Barbera and a rare red varietal Aglianico. Combined annual production is fewer than 1,000 cases.

STONESTREET WINERY  . *Sonoma 1989*  Located in the Chalk Hill region of Sonoma County, this facility, originally known as Zellerbach Vineyard, was acquired by Jess Jackson in 89. Jackson, owner as well of Kendall-Jackson and Cambria, bought the winery and its vineyard, but not the Zellerbach brand (see entry). Estate-grown Cabernet Sauvignon, Merlot, and "Legacy," a blended red Meritage are the main items in the Stonestreet line, which also includes Pinot Noir, Gewurztraminer, and Chardonnay. Vineyard holdings have been expanded to 155 acres, mostly Merlot and Cabernet Sauvignon. About 20,000 cases a year were offered in the initial vintages. Early vintages of Pinot Noir rated °°° and Chardonnay rated °° established a tone of high quality. With the 1995 acquisition of the 450-acre Gauer Vineyard in Alexander Valley, Jackson has been able to expand production of Stonestreet's Cabernet and Merlot. Stonestreet has added Sauvignon Blanc from this mountain vineyard, which has merited °° in the early rounds.

With a good supply of many varieties available, a new facility for Stonestreet was planned in Alexander Valley. Capable of handling 500,000 cases, this winery should be up and running by the 1999 harvest.

### Cabernet Sauvignon
**88°**  89  **90°**  **91°**  **92°**  **93°°**  **95°°**

*Very ripe in its black cherryish fruit and fleshy in feel under its nominal tannins, the wine is usually immediately appealing yet capable of bottle age*

### Chardonnay
90°°  91°°  92°°  93°°  94°  **95°°**

*Ripe, open, mouth-filling, deep in juicy fruit and oak, this successful string of wines invites early drinking*

### Pinot Noir
**90°°°**  **91°**  92  ·**94°°**  95

*Inconsistent after its initial success, this wine tries for the open style of its cellar-mates but has lacked the deep fruit more often than not*

STONY HILL VINEYARD  *Napa 1953*  To longtime observers of the California wine scene, Stony Hill merits a special place and special status. In 43 founders Eleanor and Fred McCrea bought an old ranch on a slope of Spring Mountain overlooking St. Helena. They began planting a vineyard consisting of Chardonnay, Riesling, Gewurztraminer, and Semillon. The early crops from their 35-acre vineyard were sold until by 51 a small stone winery was in place. Encouraged to make wines by Lee Stewart of the original Souverain, the McCreas started on a small scale, and even by 75 they were making little more than 1,000 cases total. However, by then Stony Hill was setting quality standards for Chardonnay, and its sales were primarily to those fortunate enough to be on the winery's mailing list.

Stony Hill eventually stopped selling grapes and its annual production expanded to a peak of 3,500 cases. Eleanor McCrea operated the winery after her husband passed away in late 77. A continuity of style and quality has been maintained through winemaker Mike Chelini, at the helm since 72. Peter McCrea and his family have been running the business side of the winery since his mother's death in 1991. Both Riesling and Gewurztraminer are made in a dry style today. Whether it was to do with the special Wente clone used in the vineyard or to the site's microclimate, Stony Hill's Chardonnays had the balance and structure needed for long, graceful aging in most vintages. Even the 76, a not overly successful vintage in general, was fit and attractive in the late 80s. By the mid-80s the winery's estate-grown Chardonnay output was decreased as the old vineyard, troubled by disease and age, was replanted in stages. During this time Stony Hill bought additional Chardonnay from Howell Mountain, which was once separately bottled under the SHV label and has since been blended with Stony Hill's home-grown crop. Generally, Stony Hill Chardonnays are reserved and lean in style, with appley and citrusy fruit played against a subtle oak background. Although they are long-aging, they have been bypassed in favor of newer producers who elevate oak and ripeness over restraint.

STORRS WINERY  *Santa Cruz 1988*  Owners Steve and Pamela Storrs, both enologists from U.C. Davis, started their own winery after working together for a few years at Felton Empire (now Hallcrest) Vineyards. All grapes are purchased, primarily from the Santa Cruz Mountains. Chardonnay from several small vineyards is the main wine produced, followed by Zinfandel and White Riesling. The winery has settled on Merlot from San Ysidro Vineyard, Petite Sirah from Santa Cruz Mountains, Zinfandel from Beauregard Ranch, and Grenache from the Central Coast. As many as four bottlings of Chardonnay have been made in recent years. Cabernet Sauvignon is also made from the Santa Cruz Mountains. The annual production has reached 7,000 cases, with more than half represented by the barrel-fermented Chardonnays, which have achieved °°.

STORY VINEYARDS   *Amador 1973*   With its original 23-acre vineyard among the oldest in the county, Story was a player in the Amador wine renaissance. It has 14 acres of Zinfandel, and 9 of Mission, both planted in the 30 s. For years it made about 3,000 cases of Zinfandel and a blended wine based on the Mission grape. In the early 80s it developed a larger line to include generic wines and blush wines, and at one time was selling 25,000 cases a year. Today, the vineyard has expanded to 40 acres but the winery has returned to its original uncomplicated approach and is offering estate-grown Zinfandel, White Zinfandel, and a small amount of Mission. Annual production is 7,500 cases.

STORYBOOK MOUNTAIN VINEYARD   *Napa 1980*   Former Stanford University history professor Jerry Seps decided to change careers in 76. Two years later, after apprenticing with Joseph Swan, he bought a 90-acre property north of Calistoga that was once the site of the Grimms Brothers Winery, dating to 1888, and named it Storybook Mountain. Building terraces on the moderately steep hillsides, Seps planted 38 acres to Zinfandel. The original aging caves were restored in time for the first crush in 80. Since the opening vintage Storybook has developed a reputation for long-lived, often high-quality Zinfandels that tend to be ripe, intense, and powerful. Through its first decade, the winery has offered three bottlings in most vintages—an estate, a Reserve estate, and Sonoma County (which has now been discontinued). Seps uses a combination of French and American oak for barrel aging. Joining the 90s multiple Zinfandel bottling trend, Seps added Zinfandel from Howell Mountain, from Mayacamas Range, and from Eastern Exposures. The latter was ** quality. Production gradually increased and is approaching the maximum annual goal of 8,500 cases.

**Zinfandel**

(Napa)   81**   82*   83*   84*   85*   **86\*\*\***   **87\*\***   **88\*\***   **89\***
**91\***   **92\*\***   **93\***   **94\*\***

(Napa Reserve)   81*   82**   83**   84**   **86\***   **87\***   **88\***   **89**
**90\*\***   **92\***   **93\***   **94\***

(Howell Mountain)   **91\*\***   **92**   **93**   95

*Intense berryish fruit, lots of sweet oak, and strong tannins and firm acidity add up to some of the most flavorful, long-aging Zinfandels made*

STRATFORD   *Napa 1982*   One of the first upscale négociant brands in California, Stratford was founded by a partnership headed by winemaker Paul Moser and marketing director Tony Cartlidge. The founders focused on buying and blending Chardonnay that could retail for under $10 a bottle throughout the U.S. wine market. Buying Chardonnay from dozens of wineries in both the North and Central Coast regions, Stratford blended wines that often achieved * rankings. The project was so successful that production expanded to include Sauvignon Blanc, Cabernet Sauvignon, and Merlot. Eventually, with production exceeding 75,000 cases a year, Stratford outgrew its original rented space, and the partners looked into the possibility of building a winery. The partners also established Canterbury (a line of lower-priced wines) and Cartlidge & Browne (see entry). In 94 Stratford was sold, and the remaining partners founded the Ehlers Grove (see entry) winery.

STRAUS VINEYARDS   *Napa 1986*   After working in sales and marketing for several companies, including Sebastiani Vineyard, Phillip Toohey decided to make wine. He and his wife, Lisa, set out in 84 to make only Merlot. Their first vintages were made from blends of selected readymade wines from Napa and Sonoma appellations. Recent vintages are from Napa Valley. The style tends toward the full-bodied, with the occasional version having unchecked tannins. Most vintages have been blended with 10% to 15% Cabernet Sauvignon. Overall, given the general shortage of Merlot, the quality attained by Straus has been surprisingly acceptable, with an occasional vintage reaching * quality. The brand was named after Phil Toohey's grandfather. After bottling close to 2,000 cases in each of its first several vintages, Straus is moving gradually toward a goal of 10,000 cases.

**Merlot**

86  **87****  **88***  **89**  91  **95***

*Tending toward ripeness and loaded with sweet oak in best vintages*

RODNEY STRONG VINEYARDS  *Sonoma 1961*  Known until 84 as Sonoma Vineyards, this winery has gone through more changes than most. Originally, it was a tasting-room operation called Tiburon Vintners that expanded and moved to Sonoma County. It then became a wine-by-mail producer known as Windsor Vineyards, which was successful enough by 70 to give birth to a large winery, Sonoma Vineyards. Despite producing close to 500,000 cases in its peak years, the winery always seemed to be struggling. It was taken over in 84 by Renfield Importers, who changed its name to Rodney Strong Vineyards, but the name change did not provide greater stability. Renfield was acquired by Schenley Industries which, in turn, was acquired by Guinness. More recently, the winery has been in the hands of California-based Klein Foods.

Throughout the rapid changes in the 80s, which reduced its sales and annual output to under 200,000 cases, Rodney Strong, one of the founders of Tiburon Vintners, hung on valiantly. Today, Strong is no longer involved, but all winemaking is in the hands of Rick Sayre. Under Klein's ownership, the Strong brand has enjoyed improved sales and completed a major comeback. Today, with 1,200 acres of vineyards in Sonoma County, it produces a line of Sonoma County varietals of more than respectable quality. Three Chardonnays are bottled—""Sonoma County,""Chalk Hill Vineyard," and a Reserve—and each has distinguished itself in the 90s. Cabernet offerings also number three—""Sonoma County,""Alexander's Crown," and a Reserve. The "Alexander's Crown," made from a single vineyard in Alexander Valley, has long been the pride of the winery. Pinot Noir, Sauvignon Blanc, Gewurztraminer, Merlot, and an unusual, brawny "Old Vines" Zinfandel round out the line. The recently added Reserve Chardonnay and Cabernet Sauvignon started on an impressive quality level. The Windsor Vineyards brand, selling through a mailing list and a tasting room in Healdsburg, remains quite active and contributes about one-third of the company's annual 400,000 case output. Any wine buyer faced with few choices or just looking for a safe haven is not likely to be disappointed by a Strong Vineyards wine.

**Cabernet Sauvignon**

(Alexander's Crown)  81  8̶2̶  84*  85*  **87**  **88***  **90***  91  **92**  93  **94***  **95**

*Always ripe and dense, often with a tarry aspect, this wine frequently wants greater fruitiness to keep itself in balance*

**Chardonnay**

(Sonoma County)  86  87  88  89  90*  91  92  93  94  95*  96*

(Chalk Hill)  87  88  90**  91  92*  93  94*  95  96

*Citrusy fruit, somewhat lacking in depth, has often kept the Sonoma County bottling from achieving higher ratings; the 90 showed more fruit, but the 91 reverted to form; the Chalk Hill is deeper and better generally; recent Sonoma County bottlings have been very good values*

**Zinfandel**

(Old Vines / River West)  88*  **90***  **91***  **92***  93*  **94****  95*

SULLIVAN VINEYARDS  *Napa 1972*  Adjacent to Franciscan Vineyards in the area of Rutherford, Sullivan Vineyards began in 72 with the planting of 4 acres of Cabernet Sauvignon. The vineyard has since been expanded to include Merlot, along with small amounts of Chardonnay and Zinfandel. Jim Sullivan, who did the planting, is also the winemaker. During the first several vintages a range of wines were made in 200- to 500-case lots. The winery's annual output has grown to its maximum of 4,000 cases. In addition to Cabernet and Merlot, the winery offers a blend of both, "Coeur de Vigne," which usually favors Cabernet. The Sullivans proudly proclaim themselves as vintners "marching to the beat of a different drummer." We would not dispute that.

SUMMIT LAKE VINEYARDS   *Napa 1986*   In 71 Bob and Sue Brakesman purchased the site of a pre-Prohibition winery on Howell Mountain. With a degree in engineering, Bob began as a cellar worker for Freemark Abbey and later started designing and installing winery equipment. During the same period he was gradually clearing land and planting vineyards at the 2,200-foot level. A few acres of old Zinfandel were revived, and 10 new acres were planted to Zinfandel, Chardonnay, and Cabernet Sauvignon. In 86 their first wines appeared—82 Zinfandel and 84 Chardonnay—with 350 cases of each produced. The winery has also made Sauvignon Blanc. With vineyard maturity, it intends to peak at 2,000 cases a year. The Zinfandel is often worth a special search.

**Zinfandel**

82°   **84°°**   **85°**   **86°**   **88°**   **94°**   **95**

*Tight, somewhat briary, berryish fruit; firm, moderately tannic structure for several years of aging potential*

SUTTER HOME WINERY   *Napa 1960*   Sutter Home Winery has been in existence since 1874, but for many years it produced bulk wines. Owned by the Trinchero family since 47, the winery bottled an assortment of all types of wine until the late 60s. Distressed by soaring prices of Napa Valley grapes, Bob Trinchero eventually found what he wanted in Amador County. In 68 Sutter Home made an Amador County Zinfandel, starting the revival of interest in Amador County wine. By the mid-70s Sutter Home was enjoying enough success with its American oak–aged Amador County Zinfandels to have trimmed its line considerably. In 72, the Trincheros experimented with Zinfandel from Amador County in order to make a small batch of dry, wood-aged Blanc de Noirs. Labeled White Zinfandel, this wine was finished with sweetness for the first time in 75, but that bottling ushered in the blush wine era of the 80s.

In the mid-70s Sutter Home was focused on Amador Zinfandel, a sweet-finished Muscat of Alexandria, and White Zinfandel. Sales grew steadily and by 80 the winery was bottling 100,000 cases a year with well over half consisting of White Zinfandel. The demand for Sutter Home's White Zinfandel continued to grow in the 80s until, by the end of the decade, the winery was making 3 million cases of White Zinfandel a year. After greatly expanding the old winery south of St. Helena, the Trincheros developed a larger facility located on Zinfandel Lane in Napa Valley. Before 80 Sutter Home owned no vineyards, but it began acquiring land and now owns 3,000 acres. In Lake County, the winery has 300 acres planted mostly to Sauvignon Blanc and Chenin Blanc, while its 2,700 acres in the Sacramento Valley region are largely planted to Cabernet Sauvignon, Zinfandel, and Chardonnay.

Amador County is still represented: Sutter Home purchases all Zinfandel grown by the Deaver Ranch. Its Reserve Amador County Zinfandels, which occasionally earn °, continue its series of Amador County bottlings. Cabernet Sauvignon is the second leading wine in terms of volume, with sales close to 240,000 cases. It is followed by Sauvignon Blanc and Chenin Blanc. Chardonnay was first offered from the 89 vintage. Merlot was added in 91. Continuing its innovative streak, Sutter Home has been offering a light, chillable red called "Soleo." With sales of White Zinfandel alone topping 4 million cases a year, Sutter Home is now the fourth-largest wine producer in California. Almost every varietal wine it makes ranks among the top five in sales volume. To appeal to wine collectors it has added a Napa Valley Reserve Cabernet and also developed a high-ticket, designer line of Napa Valley Chardonnay and Cabernet under the M. Trinchero label. Sutter Home also owns Montevina Vineyards in Amador County.

JOSEPH SWAN VINEYARDS  *Sonoma 1969*  Joseph Swan, a soft-spoken, easy-to-like man, made Zinfandels of legendary proportions. In the 70s he and his winery developed something akin to a cult following. The Zinfandels from 68 to 77 and an occasional vintage of Pinot Noir created such excitement that they inspired many new winemakers, and became a galvanizing force for California wine during the 70s. Yet winemaking was Swan's second career. He retired early as an airline pilot, searched for a vineyard site, and in 67 finally selected a small patch in Forestville where he developed a 10-acre vineyard. Like many pioneers, Swan's preference was to make Burgundian wines—Pinot Noir and Chardonnay. As his vines were maturing, he experimented with Zinfandel grown in the Dry Creek Valley by Teldeschi Vineyard. He aged the Zinfandel in French oak and released it to friends and a mailing list in 72. By the time he released the 71, which was given *** in 74, Swan was well on his way to fame.

Typically, his legendary Zins of the 70s were full of ripe, deep fruit, creamy oak, and were indeed long-lived. A few of these early vintages were wonderful two decades later. After 77, Swan lost his favorite source of Zinfandel, so stopped making the varietal until he found an acceptable replacement in 82. However, the Zinfandel magic never fully returned and, in the 80s, it was Swan's Pinot Noir which set the pace. Joe Swan died in 89. The winemaking was turned over to his son-in-law, Rod Berglund, one of many young winemakers to apprentice under him. Over Berglund's first several vintages, the quality was all over the board. But the winemaking seems to have settled down recently. Pinot Noirs are now made from the Estate Vineyard, which is often the best, and from several small vineyards in the Sonoma Mountain appellation. The Zinfandels usually are acceptable. But do not believe anyone who implies that the Swan wines of today continue the tradition established by the wines of Mr. Swan's era.

### Pinot Noir

78**  79*  80**  81*  82  83  84*  85*  **86***  **87**  88  89
92  93

*Varying by vintage according to the depth of fruit delivered by the grapes, these wines are all marked by black-cherry and herb flavors, firm structures, rich oak*

### Zinfandel

**80***  81  82*  83  **85***  **86***  **87**  **88**  89  91  92

*For their first 10 vintages, these were wines of heroic proportion—deep in fruit, high in rich oak, tightly focused on varietal character, solidly structured, long-aging; the wines of the 80s follow in style, but not in level of intensity or in finely focused varietal impressions; latest efforts are off-putting.*

SWANSON WINERY  *Napa 1989*  Heir to Swanson Foods, Clarke Swanson purchased 80 acres in Oakville in 85. A few years later he bought the former Cassayre-Forni winery in Rutherford after a long search. As the old winery was being refurbished, Swanson acquired additional land adjacent to the Silverado Trail, and today Swanson Winery owns about 160 acres of vineyards. Chardonnay, Cabernet Sauvignon, and Merlot are the mainstays. The first offerings, an 87 Cabernet and 88 Chardonnay, added up to 5,000 cases. A Reserve Chardonnay debuted in the 88 vintage. Long-term, the winery is committed to Cabernet and Chardonnay; to supplement the grapes from its own vineyards, it contracts for Chardonnay from the Carneros district and Cabernet from Mount Veeder. These primary varietals and Merlot, Sangiovese, and Syrah will contribute to a total output of 20,000 cases a year. Merlot and Sangiovese have been exceptional, but the entire line has enjoyed critical acclaim. An experimental blend of Cabernet and Syrah made in 1991 has evolved into Alexis, a wonderful red wine made every year since. Even a tiny amount of Late Harvest Semillon, when made, has been highly successful.

## Cabernet Sauvignon

**87°  88°  89  90°  91°°  92°°  93°  94°°  95°**

*Ripe, somewhat curranty flavors achieve a measure of succulence in good vintages, and sweet oak adds a layer of richness*

## Chardonnay

88  89  90  91°  92°°  93°°°  **94°°  95°**  96

*After average results in early vintages, this wine has shown increased levels of appley and citrusy fruitiness to go along with its oak and firm structure*

## Merlot

**90°  91°°°  92°°  93  94°  95°**

*91 was classic; 92 was just about as good; both were deep in succulent, cherryish fruit, exhibited Merlot's supple underbelly, were rich in sweet, vanillin oakiness, and had plenty of tannin and depth for mid- to long-term aging*

## Sangiovese

**91  92°°  93°  95°°**

*Lots of ripe red cherry fruit is buttressed by creamy oak and medium tannins*

## Syrah

**92°°  93°°**  94  95

*Incredibly tannic wines, they do not always contain the fruit needed to balance their muscular structure*

---

TABLAS CREEK VINEYARD   *Paso Robles 1994*   This is a closely-watched, but slow to unfold joint venture between the Perrin family, owners of Chateau Beaucastel in Chateauneuf-du-Pape, and its importers, Robert Haas of Vineyard Brands. After a long search, they purchased 120 acres located 10 miles west of Paso Robles. The vineyard was planted to all 13 Rhone varieties, and the viticultural experiments soon evolved into a vine nursery. The owners decided to cultivate many of the varieties obtained from both French and American sources. The experimental vineyard soon became a Mecca of sorts for winemakers interested in the vines and clones selected and cultivated. Following the Beaucastel practice, all vines are grown organically. With the vineyard under development, the main red varieties grown are Syrah, Grenache, Mourvedre, Cinsault, and Counoise, and the whites planted are Viognier, Marsanne, and Roussanne. Winemaking trials began in 1994, and in 1997 the winery was expanded into a 25,000-case-capacity facility. The early vintages of the white Tablas Creek combine Viognier and Roussanne, and the red Tablas Creek relies heavily on Mourvedre and Syrah.

---

TAFT STREET WINERY   *Sonoma 1982*   What started as a part-time venture among Berkeley-based home winemaking friends and relatives evolved into a full-scale winery. The first vintage made in rented space consisted of 2,000 cases, and after muddling along, making some wines, buying and blending others for a small market, Taft Street settled down in 86. Though still in rented space, it now owns all of the latest equipment and cooperage, including small oak for barrel fermentations of its Chardonnays. After marketing a range of table wines, the winery now emphasizes Chardonnay from two appellations, Sonoma County and Russian River Valley. About 2,000 cases of the Russian River Chardonnay are produced, with the Sonoma County bottling amounting to 10,000 cases. Sauvignon Blanc from Napa Valley and Merlot from Sonoma County are regularly offered. A blended white, "White House White," is the only generic on the roster. The winery's annual production is at 25,000 cases.

---

TALBOTT VINEYARD   *Monterey 1983*   The Talbott family started their winery with the intention of producing only Chardonnay from the Carmel Valley, and midway up the valley developed a hillside vineyard that now covers 32 acres. Knowing that it would mature slowly, the family made their first vintages from grapes obtained from the Gonzales area of the Salinas Valley. In 86, when Robb Talbott took over the winery operation after his father's death, he felt they were outgrowing the original facility. Pleased with the wines produced from the Salinas Valley, the Talbotts decided to build a larger winery near Gonzales and to develop a 60-acre vineyard adjacent to it. Only Chardonnay is produced, but from two separate appellations today. The primary wine labeled Talbott originates in Monterey County; the second, grown exclusively in the family's Carmel Valley holdings, is labeled "Diamond T Estates." Both Chardonnays display ripe fruit character and are barrel-fermented, and French oak-aged for at least 1 year. The Monterey Chardonnay is bottle-aged for one year; the Family Estate is given two years of bottle aging. The long-term production goal for both lines combined is 7,000 cases. In 88, the winery introduced another Chardonnay labeled Logan (see entry). Since 90 all production has taken place in the Gonzales facility.

**Chardonnay**

(Monterey)    86°    87°°°    88°°    89°    90°    91    92°    93

*Potentially among the tops in California, as it was in the 87 vintage, the wine can be rich, appley, buttery, deep, and mouth-filling at its best*

TALLEY VINEYARDS    *San Luis Obispo 1986*    Settling in the Arroyo Grande region, the Talley family began by developing their own 65-acre vineyard. In 86, after expanding the holdings to 85 acres, Talley ventured into winemaking. Chardonnay at 60 acres is the primary variety planted, followed by Pinot Noir (10), Sauvignon Blanc (7), and Riesling (3). When the estate vineyards are mature, Talley has set 15,000 cases as its maximum annual production. All estate-grown wines are identified as originating in the Arroyo Grande Valley, a subregion of San Luis Obispo County. Talley's vintages of Chardonnay and Pinot Noir have been well received, with the Chardonnay earning up to °°, and the Pinot Noir garnering a °° rating in its first appearance and ° after that. Rosemary's Vineyard, a tiny parcel on the estate, yields the winery's finest Pinot Noir. The Talley name also shows up as the source of Chardonnay for several leading Central Coast producers.

**Chardonnay**

89°    90    91°°    92°    93    **94°**    **95°**

*Well-balanced fruity with occasional citrus leanings. This medium-full-bodied wine is capable of one to three years of bottle age in most vintages*

**Pinot Noir**

**89°**    **90°**    **91°°**    92    **93°**    **94°**

*Medium-rich, cherryish wines usually high in oak with midterm potential aging*

IVÁN TAMÁS WINES    This is a brand founded by Iván Tamás Fuezy and Steven Mirassou. In 84 Mirassou left his family winery to join Fuezy, a long time wine-marketing professional. In the first two vintages they offered varietals from both Central and North Coast appellations. For a few years after, most of their wines originated in Mendocino County. The line has remained constant, and features Zinfandel, Chardonnay, Cabernet Sauvignon, and Sauvignon Blanc. In the late 80s, they decided to switch to the Livermore Valley as the primary source of wines. Trebbiano, a seldom-seen varietal, has been added to the lineup. Pinot Grigio is a recent addition. The winery is now solely owned by Steve Mirassou. Overall, the wines are priced on the low end and in some vintages have offered good value. Each year the winery makes about 1,000 cases each of a Reserve Chardonnay and Cabernet Sauvignon which are priced higher. With hoped-for steady growth, the annual output will level off at 85,000 cases.

LANE TANNER    *Santa Barbara 1989*    A chemist by background, Lane Tanner worked in the cellars of Konocti, Zaca Mesa, and Firestone. By 84 she was also making private-label Pinot Noir in Santa Barbara County for a well-known restaurant, the

Hitching Post. By 89 she was on her own, focusing only on Pinot Noir from two appellations. The "Benedict Vineyard" bottling represents about one hundred cases a year, and the Santa Barbara County Pinot Noir bottling is almost 1,000. After her longtime favorite source, the Sierra Madre Vineyard, was sold, she added Pinot Noir from Bien Nacido, which in the early vintages struck us as her best overall performance. Tanner ferments the grapes in open-top tanks and frequently punches down the cap. She ages her wines in French oak for about one year, aiming for a silky-textured, refined style. Tanner sees 1,500 cases as her label's optimum annual output.

TAYLOR CALIFORNIA CELLARS   *Monterey 1978*   Started from scratch in 77 by Coca-Cola of Atlanta's wine division, the Wine Spectrum, Taylor California Cellars brought together the name of the best-known New York State winery, Taylor, and the California identity in what was envisioned as a "can't-miss" brand of wine. With tremendous promotional efforts and generally agreeable wines, Taylor California Cellars quickly became part of the second largest wine empire in the U.S. In the tiny Monterey County town of Soledad, Coke built a large (30-million-gallon-capacity) winemaking facility, and was on a roll. In 80, it bottled over 10 million cases. The only problem was that Taylor California was still second behind Gallo, and it would take a long, tough, and possibly futile effort to try to unseat Gallo as the largest producer. In 83 Coke of Atlanta sold all of its wine properties—Taylor of California and New York, Sterling, and the Monterey Vineyard—to Seagram. Taylor California Cellars continued as one of the biggest wine producers, but its sales were not growing.

In 87, Seagram sold Taylor along with Paul Masson, a brand it owned since the 40 s, to the corporation named Vintners International. Most of the major stockholders were former executives with Seagram and other wine and spirits companies, and Seagram retained 20% of the stock. A few years later the company was acquired by Canandaigua, the giant wine corporation headquartered in New York State. Under this ownership, Taylor California Cellars was positioned as a generic wine brand, offering wines in all sizes from standard-bottled to bag-in-the-box to kegs. A modest line of varietals includes Cabernet Sauvignon, Chardonnay, and the volume item, White Zinfandel. In the 90s, sales have been flat, and the annual production is 2 million cases.

TELDESCHI CELLARS   *Sonoma 1985*   The Teldeschi family has owned vineyards in Dry Creek Valley for three generations. After regularly winning awards as a home winemaker, Dan Teldeschi decided to turn pro and is producing full-flavored Zinfandel from an older block of the family's 80-acre vineyard. Petite Sirah has been added to the line. Teldeschi plans to take production to 2,000 cases a year.

TERRA ROSA   *(Laurel Glen Vineyard)*   Patrick Campbell uses this label for Cabernet Sauvignon made from wines he purchases and blends. The label began in 88 when he was offered a batch of Cabernet too good to pass up. The availability of wine from a given vintage has determined the appellation used for each offering of Terra Rosa. After an initial bottling of 2,000 cases, the quantity bottled has reached 7,500 cases a year. Made in a ready-to-drink style, Terra Rosa has ranged in quality from average to slightly above average.

THE TERRACES   *Napa 1985*   This is a red wine–only brand owned by Wayne Hogue Vineyard of Rutherford. With 5 acres planted in 81 to Zinfandel and Cabernet Sauvignon, Hogue produced his first wine in 85. The terraced vineyard is located in the east Rutherford hills above the Silverado Trail. Originally Hogue intended to use the family name, but the Hogue Winery in Washington owned the trademark and thought otherwise. In general, Wayne Hogue favors fairly long aging, releasing his Zinfandel three years post-harvest, and his Cabernet Sauvignon four. All vintages through 91 were custom-made at Caymus Vineyards, with Hogue's small winery in place for 92. The annual production struggles to hit 1,000 cases, and is averaging 400 cases of Zinfandel, 250 of Cabernet. At times both wines are capable of greatness, though from year to year we give the nod to Zinfandel.

**Cabernet Sauvignon**

86°°  87°°°  88°  89°  90  91  92  93°  94°

**Zinfandel**

85°°°  86  87°°°  88°  89°  90°  92°°  93°  94°°°  95°°°

*Varietal distinctions aside, both of these wines are medium-full-bodied to full-bodied and filled with ripe, juicy fruit, generous amounts of rich oak, and plentiful tannins*

---

TESSERA   *(Seagram)*   Introduced in the mid-90s by Seagram, owners of Sterling and Monterey Vineyard, Tessera consists of modestly (under $10) priced wines sold in a distinctive bottle. In some vintages the Chardonnay has merited good value citations, and the Old Vine Zinfandel is more than adequate for the money. As production moves toward 300,000 cases a year, Chardonnay and Cabernet Sauvignon represent two-thirds of the total.

---

TESTAROSSA VINEYARD   *Monterey 1995*   After making wines at Chalone Vineyards for more than a decade, Michael Michaud tested the market one year and then decided to leave Chalone and devote full time to his own brand. To date Michaud has made Chardonnay Reserve from his own vineyard in Monterey as well as Chardonnay from the Chalone appellation, from Troquato Vineyard, and Santa Barbara County, as well as a small lot of Viognier. Combined annual production is 1,500 cases, with the Santa Barbara version accounting for half of the total.

---

THACKREY & CO.   *Marin 1982*   Owner of Thackrey & Robertson, an art store in San Francisco, Sean Thackrey is a weekend winemaker. Using space next to his home on the Marin Coast, he began dabbling with Pinot Noir before turning his attention to Rhone varietals and proprietary red blends. Favoring proprietary wine names, he first came to our attention with "Aquila," a Merlot–Cabernet Sauvignon blend. The Syrahs, 100% varietal, are marketed under the name "Orion," and Thackrey prefers Syrah from the Rutherford Bench area. Initial vintages of Mourvedre came from the Cline Vineyard in Oakley and were given the name "Taurus." A house red blend following no specific formula each year is dubbed "Pleiades." Thackrey gained modest national recognition through his Syrahs, which became part of the Rhone variety revival in the late 80s. He intends to add a wine made from Viognier. His annual production reached 1,500 cases, with 5,000 set as the maximum.

---

THOMAS–HSI VINEYARD   *Napa 1988*   A small winery specializing in Chardonnay from the Mount Veeder area, Thomas-Hsi made its first wine in 87. Charles Thomas and his wife, Lili Hsi, have worked for many wineries within Napa Valley, and own a small vineyard near their Mount Veeder home. The Thomas-Hsi Chardonnay is 100% barrel-fermented, and about half goes through malolactic fermentation. Aging in small oak barrels is *sur lie* for several months. After the first release of 200 cases, the owners hope to expand to 1,000 cases.

---

THORNTON WINERY   New name for Culbertson Winery (see entry).

---

T.K.C. VINEYARDS   *Amador 1981*   A small winery located east of Plymouth, T.K.C. makes nothing but Zinfandel. Its owner, Harold Nuffer, has 9 acres of Zinfandel. The maximum annual production is slightly over 1,500 cases. While its vineyards were maturing, the winery made Zinfandel from the Bowman Vineyard, a neighbor in the Shenandoah Valley.

TOAD HOLLOW VINEYARD  *Sonoma 1995*  Once you realize that co-owner Todd (Toadie) Williams is the younger brother of comedian Robin Williams, then the Toad Hollow name and a pink wine named Eye of the Toad make better sense. Chardonnay in a simply fruity style represents most of the annual 20,000-case production. Apropos, a delightful, quaffable red, is a blend of Mourvedre and Syrah. Zinfandel and Russian River Valley Pinot Noir complete the line.

PHILIP TOGNI VINEYARD  *Napa 1986*  Journeyman winemaker Philip Togni first came to California to work for Mayacamas Vineyards in 58. Over the ensuing years he made wines at Chalone, Chappellet, and Cuvaison. An extremely meticulous person, even by winemaker standards, Togni developed a reputation for single-mindedness and extreme attention to the smallest detail. After leaving Cuvaison in 81, he began developing his own 10-acre vineyard near his home on Spring Mountain. For several years he was a consultant to several wineries, most notably Chimney Rock. His own winery makes Cabernet Sauvignon. A small amount of Black Muscat is also bottled. From a 300-case first harvest in 83, Togni has expanded production to the 2,000-case mark. Togni's inky-color, massive tannic wines appeal to a small but loyal following.

TOPAZ  *Napa 1988*  When not acting as a consultant, winemaker Jeff Sowells devotes time to his own label, Topaz. Its specialty is a late-harvest, *Botrytis*-affected Sauvignon Blanc/Semillon blend that is 100% barrel-fermented and finished with about 10% residual sugar. Production over the first vintages averaged 600 cases of half-bottles. Sowells has also demonstrated blending skills with his red Meritage, "Rouge de Trois," made from batches of readymade Napa Valley wine that he purchases.

TOPOLOS AT RUSSIAN RIVER  *Sonoma 1978*  South of Forestville, the Topolos family property consists of a winery and a restaurant. Both have gone through many changes in direction over the first decade. Mike Topolos directs the wine operation and owns a 26-acre vineyard in Sonoma, leasing another 37 acres close to the winery. The winery once offered a broad range of table wines—Red, White, and Blanc de Noirs. By 88 the annual production topped 10,000 cases. Unhappy with their lack of focus, the owners decided to trim the line, reduce production, and emphasize red wines only. The current mainstays are Zinfandel, Petite Sirah, Charbono, and Alicante Bouschet. Limited bottlings of vineyard-designated Zinfandel and Petite Sirah from the Rossi Ranch represent the top of the line. Total production is 7,500 cases a year.

MARIMAR TORRES ESTATE  *Sonoma 1989*  A member of the well-known Torres wine family of Spain, Marimar Torres heads the U.S. outpost. In 83 she acquired a 56-acre estate in Sonoma's Green Valley appellation, and since then 30 acres have been planted to Chardonnay, 15 to Pinot Noir, and one to several Spanish varieties. A 15,000-case-capacity winery was completed by 91. Pinot Noir and barrel-fermented Chardonnay are the house specialties. After a mediocre first vintage, the Chardonnays have been rated high in every vintage, and the Pinot Noirs are coming on strong. Torres has planted an additional 10 acres to Pinot Noir. With vineyard maturity, Torres will produce about 12,000 cases of Chardonnay and 5,000 of Pinot Noir.

### Chardonnay

89  90°°  91°  **92°°**  93°  **94°**  95°

*Well-focused, fairly deep and fruity wines with good balancing acidity*

TREANA WINERY  *Paso Robles 1995*  With winemaker Chris Phelps, formerly of Dominus, now part of the team that includes Chuck Wagner of Caymus, Treana produces a red wine from Paso Robles and a white from Monterey. The red Treana is made from Syrah, Cabernet Sauvignon, Mourvedre, and other varieties. Roussanne, Viognier, and Marsanne are components of the white, which is grown in Wagner's vineyard in Monterey. In the early vintages about 6,000 cases of each wine were bottled.

TREFETHEN VINEYARDS  *Napa 1973*  The Trefethen family purchased an old ranch and vineyard named Eshcol Estate in 68. Soon to retire from Kaiser Industries, Gene Trefethen was looking for a rural home site, and with encouragement from his son John and daughter-in-law Janet, he began restoring the century-old wood frame winery and replanting the surrounding vineyard. Located in the cool-growing area between Napa and Yountville, the vineyard was gradually planted to Chardonnay, Pinot Noir, Riesling, and Cabernet Sauvignon. With good timing on their side, the Trefethens were awaiting their first harvests about the time Domaine Chandon was setting up a few miles to the north. Chandon, needing a grape supply while its vineyards were being developed, entered into an arrangement to buy grapes from Trefethen and crush some of the fruit there as well. Other producers purchased Trefethen grapes, including Schramsberg Vineyards in the 70s.

These arrangements allowed Trefethen to expand its vineyard to 600 acres and to move into winemaking at a leisurely pace, which it did with a small first vintage of Chardonnay in 73. Gradually more of the home grapes went into Trefethen wines, and today's lineup consists of Chardonnay, the mainstay, Cabernet Sauvignon, White Riesling, and two wines marketed under the "Eshcol" label—Eshcol Chardonnay and Eshcol Cabernet Sauvignon. Among its varietals, Chardonnay remains the volume leader, usually made in a medium-intense, crisp, balanced style. Its Riesling remains true to the original, holding to a floral, light-bodied, dry style. Merlot is a new addition to the line. Reserve-style Cabernet and Chardonnay appeared in the late 80s, and the popular Eshcol wines remain as important items in the winery's 80,000-case-a-year output. Trefethen wines are typically squeaky clean but lacking in depth and richness.

### Chardonnay

87  88  90°  92  93  94  95

*Crisp, bright, but narrow green appley fruit, with oak appearing only in the background*

TRELLIS VINEYARDS SONOMA  *1991*  Northern California wine distributor Charles Daniels makes a line of Sonoma County varietals under this label. Cabernet Sauvignon, Chardonnay, and Sauvignon Blanc are the primary offerings.

TRENTADUE WINERY  *Sonoma 1969*  Directly east of Chateau Souverain in Geyserville lie a well-manicured vineyard and a small building partially hidden by an oak grove. That property belongs to the Trentadue family, which farms 200 acres planted to a range of varieties, from Zinfandel, which is well suited to the region, to Chardonnay, which is not. For many years it has sold Zinfandel to Ridge Vineyards for separate bottling under the identity "Geyserville" Zinfandel. Still selling much of its crop to others, Trentadue eased into winemaking, and by 80 was making 12,000 cases. A new winemaker in 83, combined with the introduction of a White Zinfandel, increased production to 20,000 cases a year. The winery sells much of its wine out of its tasting room and gift shop. Hearty red wines are still its stronghold. Though no longer made in a rustic, old style, Trentadue's reds are not for the fainthearted. The best, which are often excellent wines these days, are its Sangiovese, Zinfandel, Petite Sirah, and "Old Patch Red," a robust field blend.

TRIA WINERY  *Sonoma 1995*  Winemakers Philip Zorn of Paraiso Springs and Bill Knuttel of Saintsbury are partners in this tiny production label. Favoring vineyard designated wines, they have come up with solid efforts with Syrah* and Zinfandel**–*** from Dry Creek Valley. Labyrinth, their version of a red Meritage, has also been eminently enjoyable. On occasion they have made a Late Harvest Pinot Noir and Sousao Port.

M. TRINCHERO WINERY  *Napa 1995*  Created by the Trinchero family, who own Sutter Home Winery, this upscale label for limited-edition Napa Valley wines is named after founder Mario Trinchero.

TRUCHARD VINEYARDS  *Napa 1989*  Tony Truchard has been growing grapes in the Carneros district since the mid-70s. Situated on gently rolling hillsides, his vineyard covers 167 acres and contains 45 acres of Cabernet Sauvignon, 41 acres of Merlot, and 13 acres of Cabernet Franc. Several memorable bottlings of Cabernet Sauvignon from this vineyard were made in the 70s by neighboring Carneros Creek Winery. Truchard also grows the more typical Carneros varieties, specifically Chardonnay (40 acres) and Pinot Noir (25 acres). Though he continues to sell grapes to almost two dozen producers, in 90 Truchard converted a barn into a small winery. Since then he has been producing Chardonnay, Pinot Noir, Merlot, Zinfandel, Cabernet Sauvignon, and Syrah. Recent vintages of Chardonnay, Merlot, Zinfandel and Pinot Noir have been highly rated. Annual production has reached 10,000 cases.

### Cabernet Sauvignon
89  **90°°**  **91°**  **92°**  **93°**  **94°**  **95°**

*Medium-ripe wines tasting of black cherries and rich oak, capable of mid-term aging*

### Chardonnay
89  90°  91°°  92°°  93  **94°°°**  95°  **96°°**

*Crisp, fruity, often with impressive depth; very consistent results*

### Merlot
89  **90°°**  **91°°**  **92°°**  **93°°**  **94°**  **95°**

*Ripe and supple wines in best vintages, this offering has been among the best Merlots in the 90s*

### Pinot Noir
89°  **90°**  **91°**  92  93  **94**  **95°**

*Medium-ripe cherry fruit is occasionally deep, occasionally thin in fruit*

### Syrah
**92°°**  **93°°**  **94°**  95

*Ripe, blackberry fruit, a bit of spice, rich in oak, fairly tannic*

TURLEY WINE CELLARS  *(Napa) 1994*  Larry Turley, co-founder of Frog's Leap Wine Cellars, started his own brand after he and his partner parted company in 1994. Using the original Frog's Leap facility north of St. Helena, Turley hired his sister, the well-known winemaker Helen Turley. She remained for two vintages to establish a style of in-your-face wines with uncommon ripeness and high alcohol levels. The roster, changing from year to year, features vineyard-designated Zinfandel and Petite Sirah from some of the oldest vineyards grown in Napa, and more recently in other regions. To date the Zinfandel vineyards made over several vintages are Aida, Hayne, Black-Sears, Whitney, and More. Recently Larry Turley has found Zinfandel to his liking from Duarte Vineyard in Contra Costa, Grist Vineyard in Sonoma's Russian River Valley, and an unnamed vineyard in Lodi. The Hayne and Aida Vineyards in Napa also supply Turley with Petite Sirah. Fans of this winery believe that bigger is better. Sauvignon Blanc from the winery's one acre also is made. Total annual output has approached the goal of 4,000 cases.

TURNBULL WINE CELLARS  *Napa 1979*  Longtime friends and associates Bill Turnbull and Reverdy Johnson purchased a dilapidated farmhouse and a neglected 20-acre vineyard in 77. Turnbull had been an architect who helped design the Sea Ranch community on the North Coast, and Johnson served as the project's lawyer. Their plan was to sell grapes and use the remodeled farmhouse as a weekend retreat. The vineyard, originally planted in 67, was in the middle of prime Cabernet Sauvignon turf just north of Oakville. Johnson and Turnbull began replanting, ending up with four separate blocks covering 20 acres (18 1/2 of Cabernet, 1 1/2 of Cabernet Franc). In 78 their neighbor Cakebread Cellars made a Cabernet from their grapes, identifying the wine with a "JT L-1" label. The grapes came from the oldest block, a 5-acre parcel since used by Johnson Turnbull for its occasional "Special Reserve" bottling.

Unfortunately, the vineyards were suffering from phylloxera in the early 90s, and, rather than go through the replanting process, Johnson and Turnbull sold the winery to Patrick O'Dell. He intends to maintain Cabernet Sauvignon as the winery's primary wine. But he will still produce Chardonnay made from the 18-acre Teviot Springs Vineyard situated at the southern end of Knights Valley. Shortly after buying it, O'Dell decided to change the winery's name to Turnbull Wine Cellars. Prior to buying the winery, O'Dell had developed two separate vineyards along the Silverado Trail, and all told, he has 120 acres of vineyards. Cabernet Sauvignon and its four blending varieties represent the lion's share, but Syrah, Zinfandel, and Sangiovese have been planted. Turnbull Cellars will continue to emphasize Cabernet Sauvignon, but the line now includes Merlot, a proprietary red Meritage blend, Syrah, and Zinfandel.

### Cabernet Sauvignon

80°° 81°° 82° 83° **84°** **85** **86** (Lot 67)° **86** (Lot 82) 87 (Lot 67)° 87 90 **91** **92°** **93°°** **94°** **95**

*Always enormously minty, and backed by lots of sweet oak, the wine often delivers satisfactory amounts of fruit to bring itself into balance*

---

TURNING LEAF *(E. & J. Gallo)* When its wines appeared in the early 1990s, Turning Leaf represented a radical departure for Gallo because it was the first label introduced by the family that made no reference to Gallo. Chardonnay and Cabernet Sauvignon are the leading varietals by volume, but the line is rounded out by Zinfandel, Pinot Noir, and Sauvignon Blanc. This primary line uses the California appellation. Made in relatively small quantities, Chardonnay Reserve and Cabernet Sauvignon Reserve carry a Sonoma County identity. Reasonable estimates peg annual sales at two million cases.

---

M. G. VALLEJO WINERY *(Heublein)* In 86 the founders of Glen Ellen Winery (the Benziger family) trotted out this brand to see if it too would catch fire the way the primary brand did in 82. M. G. Vallejo was a general who directed all military affairs in the 1830 s in what is now California. Among many accomplishments, he established the town of Sonoma, and once owned the land upon which Glen Ellen Winery stands. In the beginning the M. G. Vallejo brand donated part of its profits to restoration of the general's home and grounds, a State Historic Park near Sonoma Plaza. After cautiously entering the market with Chardonnay and Cabernet Sauvignon made from purchased wines and sold for below $5 a bottle, the Vallejo brand added White Zinfandel, Fumé Blanc, and Merlot a few years later. All have a California appellation. Although the Vallejo brand didn't repeat the quick success of Glen Ellen, it has grown steadily in volume, first by emphasizing generic wines and more recently by going with modestly priced varietals. Now bottled under the "Harvest Select" label, the leading varietals are Chardonnay, White Zinfandel, and Merlot. Total annual sales have surpassed 500,000 cases. The brand is now owned by Heublein.

---

VALLEY OF THE MOON WINERY *Sonoma 1943* On a peaceful cross street near the town of Glen Ellen, the Valley of the Moon Winery has quietly enjoyed a steady roadside business. It was a major supplier of jug wines to San Francisco restaurants up until the mid-70s. Since then, in order to catch up with the times, the winery has worked to upgrade its varietals. With a 200-acre vineyard, the Parducci family (no relation to the family directing the Parducci Winery of Mendocino) never did make a dent in the fine wine market. By 1997 the family sold to Kenwood Vineyards, which is owned by Gary Heck of Korbel Bros. The old vineyard is being replanted to Zinfandel and other varieties. The winery's new lineup consists of Pinot Blanc, Chardonnay, Syrah, and Merlot from Sonoma County and Zinfandel from Sonoma Valley. Annual production will grow from the present 10,000-case level to 50,000 tops.

**VAN DER KAMP CHAMPAGNE CELLARS** *Sonoma 1981* In 81, using a corner of the St. Francis facility and buying grapes from St. Francis and others in the Sonoma Valley, jeweler Martin Van der Kamp produced 2,000 cases of sparkling wine. Production is now at the optimum 5,500-case level. Of the three sparklers offered, the Brut—which is aged four years on the yeast—is the mainstay at 3,000 cases. Next in importance at 2,000 cases is the Brut Rosé, labeled "Midnight Cuvée" and made mostly from Pinot Noir. The last wine is the "English Cuvée," aged for three years, which when produced amounts to 500 cases. Quality has been on the upswing of late, with both the "Midnight Cuvée" and the "English Cuvée" rated ** or better.

**VENDANGE** *(Sebastiani Vineyard)* Introduced in 1987, Vendange was given a dynamic new label and a big advertising budget in the 1990s. It is now a line of inexpensive varietals led by Chardonnay, Cabernet Sauvignon, Zinfandel, White Zinfandel and Merlot, each bottled in standard and magnum containers. Annual sales are approaching the three-million-case mark, with about half consisting of magnums. Recently Vendange has been expanded to include several imported wines. The leading imports by volume are Merlot from France's Languedoc, Cabernet Sauvignon from Chile, Malbec from Argentina, and Chardonnay from France. Reading the label's fine print is recommended for those curious about what they are drinking.

**VENEZIA** *(Geyser Peak Winery)* Beginning as a label for experimental wines and small lots from unusual vineyards, Venezia evolved into a 20,000-case-a-year standalone brand for upscale wines. The emphasis remains on vineyard-designated Chardonnay, Cabernet, Syrah, and Sangiovese. Bianco Nuovo Mondo, the White Meritage, is one of the better ones available, and an unusual but delicious blend of Sangiovese and Syrah is named Sangiovese Nuovo Mondo. So far the Sangiovese, with as many as three made in a given vintage, often have risen above average.

**VENTANA VINEYARDS** *Monterey 1978* Named after a gigantic wilderness area in Monterey County, Ventana Vineyards has brought considerable recognition to Monterey as a grape source. In the early 70s owner Doug Meador developed what grew to be a 300-acre vineyard on the west side of the Salinas Valley in the Soledad-Greenfield area. A compulsive experimenter with grape varieties and growing techniques, Meador has paved the way for other growers in the county. Chardonnay covers 131 acres, and is easily the greatest success. Numerous producers have made vineyard-designated Ventana Chardonnays, and many are long-term buyers, among them Cronin, Fogarty, Sarah's Vineyard, and Boyer. Johannisberg Riesling at 38 acres is his second most in-demand grape, and Obester Winery, among others, has regularly made a pretty version. Chenin Blanc (38 acres) and Sauvignon Blanc (26 acres) are the other more prominent varieties grown.

As a wine producer, Ventana has offered a dazzling range of wine types in a variety of styles and under several label designations. The winery once produced as many as 30,000 cases a year, but in 85 hit a 5,000-case low. It is now holding steady at 20,000 cases per year. The Gold Stripe Chardonnay (14,000 cases) is followed by White Riesling (4,000) and Sauvignon Blanc (2,000). Under Magnus, a separate label, Meador produces a Cabernet/Merlot/Cabernet Franc blend that has not been impressive to date.

VIADER VINEYARDS *Napa 1989* Owner Delia Viader oversees her 18-acre vineyard planted on the steep rocky slopes of lower Howell Mountain. Situated at an elevation of 1,000 feet, the vineyard is densely planted, with 2,000 vines per acre. Cabernet Sauvignon and Cabernet Franc are the primary varieties grown, and are used to make Viader's only wine, a red table wine. Made by Tony Soter (winemaker at Etude and Spottswoode), Viader Estate wine (usually 60% Cabernet Sauvignon, 40% Cabernet Franc) has maintained the high quality standards it established right from the beginning, with the challenging 1989 vintage. Annual output has leveled off at the optimum 4,500-case level.

**Cabernet Sauvignon/Cabernet Franc**

89°° 90°° 91° 92°° 93°° 94°° 95°

*Blended about 40% Cabernet Franc, this Cabernet Sauvignon–based wine is big, bold, deep, and rich, with abundant black cherry fruit and spicy nuances set against a coarse, astringent frame; the wine calls for a decade or more of cellar aging*

VIANSA WINERY *Sonoma 1988* Within a year after being ousted from the family-run Sebastiani Vineyards, Sam Sebastiani was in business on his own. He rebounded quickly with three varietals under his own label, Sam J. Sebastiani. Though the wines were of decent enough quality, Sam had second thoughts about displaying the family name and having his wines confused with those of his former winery, so by the next vintage the brand name was changed to Viansa. The focus remains on three varietals, all blends of Napa and Sonoma County regions—Sauvignon Blanc, Chardonnay, and Cabernet Sauvignon. A new winery and visitors complex are located in the Sonoma-Carneros District, where a portion of the 85-acre estate is planted to Chardonnay. Production is at 14,000 cases, with Cabernet and Chardonnay combining for 80% of the total. Small amounts of Muscat Canelli and Barbera Blanc are available only at the winery. Viansa is also focusing attention on Nebbiolo, Sangiovese, Trebbiano, and an unusual blended red, "Prindelo." Viansa will produce a maximum of 30,000 cases per year.

VICHON WINERY *Napa 1980* Founded and operated by an association of restaurateurs, Vichon was managed by three partners, winemaker George Vierra, Peter Brucher, and Doug Watson. Each gave two letters from his last name to coin the brand name, Vichon. After making two vintages in rented space, the partners built a winery on the Oakville Grade, to the south of Robert Mondavi Winery.

In early 85 the winery was sold to the three children of Robert Mondavi—Tim, Marcie, and Michael. After the Mondavi Winery went public, the company decided to convert Vichon into an imported brand, and today the name Vichon Mediterranean is seen on Merlot, Cabernet, Chardonnay, Syrah, and Viognier, all made in the Languedoc region of France. The former Vichon winery in Oakville is now home to La Famiglia de Robert Mondavi. A few red wines from Vichon's California era might yet be available at retail.

**Cabernet Sauvignon**

(SLD) 85°° 86° 87°° 88°° 89° 90° 91°° 92°

*Rich, creamy oak is tied to ripe, curranty fruit in a supple, well-proportioned, moderately tannic wine, capable of aging nicely in the cellar*

**Chardonnay**

86°° 87° 88° 89 90° 91° 92° 93 94°

*Firmly structured, tightly balanced, and crisp, oaky, rich*

**Merlot**

85° 86° 87° 88 90 91 92 93 94

*Ripe, supple, somewhat round wines, with lots of rich oak, hints of herbs, and suggestions of cocoa; they are wrapped in a veneer of youthful tannins needing half a decade of aging*

VILLA HELENA WINERY   *Napa 1984*   Located south of St. Helena, Villa Helena is one of Napa's smallest wineries. Owner and winemaker Don McGrath started this weekend winery shortly after retiring as a materials engineer in the early 80s. He specializes in Chardonnay, and also makes Sauvignon Blanc in small quantities. In a typical vintage, about 500 cases of partially barrel-fermented Chardonnay are produced. By the late 80s Villa Helena added an estate Chardonnay from the Mc-Grath vineyard. The winery also grows 4 acres of Viognier.

VILLA MT. EDEN   *Napa 1974*   Ann and James McWilliams revived a pre-Prohibition winery in 70 and used the adjoining home as their part-time residence. Under the direction of winemaker-manager Nils Venge, the vineyard was planted to 80 acres, with Cabernet Sauvignon, Chardonnay, Gewurztraminer, and Pinot Noir predominating. By 80 Villa Mt. Eden was making 15,000 cases a year, 80% of which was Cabernet Sauvignon and Chardonnay.

Over its first decade, Villa Mt. Eden developed a modest reputation for its 100% varietal Cabernet Sauvignon. Save for the 74 Reserve, the Cabernets were generally on the oaky, tannic, and slightly heavy-handed side of the spectrum. In 82 Mike McGrath replaced Venge. In 86 the McWilliamses sold the facility and the name to Stimson Lane, the wine division of the U.S. Tobacco Co. (also owners of Chateau Ste. Michelle and Conn Creek Winery), but they retained the surrounding vineyard, which now occupies 77 acres.

Its new and highly successful owners decided to change production radically at Villa Mt. Eden, which was stuck at 25,000 cases a year, by creating two separate lines. The fast-growing lower-priced line is the California appellation "Cellar Select" program, which includes Cabernet Sauvignon, Chardonnay, Zinfandel, Pinot Noir, and Merlot. Within a few years this line grew to over 200,000 cases a year. The higher-priced "Grand Reserve" line consists of Cabernet, Chardonnay, Syrah, Pinot Blanc, Merlot, Zinfandel, and Pinot Noir, of which only about 10,000 cases have been bottled each year. The transition of Villa Mt. Eden into a dynamic, diversified brand can be attributed to the services of consulting winemaker Jed Steele, who had guided Kendall-Jackson during its historic growth period. However, winemaker Mike McGrath deserves credit for the Cellar Select wines. Both winemakers' names appear on the limited-edition Signature Series Chardonnay and Cabernet Sauvignon. The winery is found today along the Silverado Trail at what once was Conn Creek Winery. To sustain this steady growth, Villa Mt. Eden started developing 400 acres of its own in the late 1990s. Eventually 225 acres in Napa Valley will supply Cabernet Sauvignon and Merlot. In the Greenfield area of Monterey the winery has a 200-acre vineyard planted primarily to Chardonnay and Pinot Noir. The vineyard also contains Pinot Blanc and Pinot Gris.

### Cabernet Sauvignon

74°°   75°   76   77°°   78°   79°   80°   81°   83   85   **86°**
87°   **88°**   89   **90°°**   **91°**   **92°°**   **93°**

*Curranty, oaky, fairly deep wines with good aging potential*

### Chardonnay

(Napa Valley Reserve)   90   91   92°   93°   **94°°**   95°
(Signature Series)   **93°°°**   94   **95°°**   **96°°**

*Both wines are oaky, fairly rich, balanced; Signature Series has been spectacular*

VINE CLIFF CELLARS   *Napa 1990*   Charles Sweeney acquired a pre-Prohibition winery site and vineyard in the hills just southeast of Oakville. After replanting the hillside vineyard to Cabernet Sauvignon, Merlot, and Cabernet Franc, Sweeney quickly established a quality image for Vine Cliff with impressive Cabernets over the first few vintages. As his Cabernet production has crept up to 2,500 cases, the quality and the style have been remarkably consistent. The winery also ventured into the Chardonnay world with a Napa Valley and Proprietess Reserve bottling. About 1,500 cases of Chardonnay are made each year, with the Reserve steady at 300.

### Cabernet Sauvignon
**90°   91°°   92   93°   94°°   95°°**

*Sturdy, briary, ripe black cherry, fairly tannic, cellarable*

VINEYARD 29   *Napa 1992*   Located north of St. Helena at 2929 Highway 29, this winery is owned by Tom Paine and Teresa Norton, who planted 3 1/2 acres to Cabernet Sauvignon. The densely planted vineyard is managed by Dave Abreu, and it will yield 750 cases of Cabernet Sauvignon when fully productive. Available mainly by mailing list, the Cabernet developed cult status by its third vintage. Overseeing winemaking is consultant Heidi Peterson-Barrett.

VINO NOCETO   *Amador County 1992*   Despite following winemaker Scott Harvey as he moved from one winery to another, Suzy and Jim Gullett have been able to maintain high quality and develop a strong following for their Sangiovese. Made from their 12 1/2-acre vineyard, which they planted to several clones, their 100% Sangiovese displays forthright fruit and plenty of depth to improve with some age. In the near future the Gulletts intend to build their own winery and expand acreage in Amador. Annual output is steady at 2,200 cases.

VITA NOVA   *Santa Barbara 1986*   The co-owners, Jim Clendenen of Au Bon Climat and Bob Lindquist of Qupé, originally joined forces to make a Bordeaux-style Cabernet Sauvignon blend. The components used in each vintage have varied since the release of their 86 bottling. Generally, the red has been a combination from Santa Barbara and other Central Coast regions emphasizing, in order of importance, Cabernet Franc, Merlot, and Cabernet Sauvignon. A Chardonnay from the Rancho Vinedo Vineyard is now also made. About 3,000 cases are produced annually under this label, with Chardonnay representing 60% of the total. Today, the label includes a barrel-fermented Sauvignon Blanc–Semillon blend from the Santa Ynez Valley. "Reservatum" is the proprietary name now used for the Bordeaux red and white blends.

### Chardonnay
**87°°   88°°   89°°   90°   91**

*Simply loaded with rich, toasty, and buttery components, presented in league with deep, broad, appley fruit and brisk balancing acidity*

VON STRASSER VINEYARDS   *Napa 1990*   After acquiring an 8-acre vineyard and winery that was operated as Roddis Cellars from 1970–80, the Von Strassers immediately began improving the neglected property. The steep terraced mountainside vineyard, neighboring Diamond Creek Vineyards, is planted entirely to Cabernet Sauvignon. Chardonnay is obtained from a neighbor's 2 1/2 acre block, and Von Strasser is making 400–500 cases of barrel-fermented Chardonnay. Using a remodeled barn as its winery, Von Strasser produces between 750 and 1,400 cases of Cabernet Sauvignon annually. Early vintages were deep in fruit and fairly tannic; 90 and 91 earned ° while 92 was °°. Freestone is a second label for Cabernet Sauvignon and Sauvignon Blanc.

### Cabernet Sauvignon
**90°   91°   92°°   93°°   94°°   95**

*Deep, ripe, brawny wines, loaded with tannin and concentrated, closed-in fruit; cellar aging is required*

VOSS VINEYARDS   *Napa 1991*   This brand is owned by Australian wine importer Robert Hill Smith, and his winemaker is fellow Aussie Simon Adams of the down-under Yalumba Winery. Chardonnay from Napa Valley, Merlot from the Oakville region, and Zinfandel from Alexander Valley comprise the line. Chardonnay accounts for more than one-third of the output, which is projected to grow to 10,000 cases. Initial vintages of barrel-fermented Chardonnay met with modest critical success.

In 1996 Voss acquired a 48-acre vineyard in Rutherford that contained Cabernet, Merlot, and Sauvignon Blanc. The following year Voss began planting a portion of this vineyard to Shiraz and Zinfandel.

WATTLE CREEK WINERY   *Sonoma 1994*   Australians Chris and Kris Williams purchased the former Pat Paulsen property in northern Alexander Valley and immediately began redeveloping its 56 acres. The winery is producing Sauvignon Blanc, Chardonnay, Cabernet Sauvignon, and Shiraz. The style of Sauvignon Blanc is decidedly racy and vibrant, with herbal and grassy notes. Powerful and loaded with oak and ripe fruit flavors, the Shiraz has the makings of becoming a real hit. The combined annual output will remain at about 4,000 cases. For the curious, wattle is the Australian version of an acacia tree.

WEIBEL VINEYARDS   *Mendocino 1945*   One of the largest and oldest family-run wineries in California, Weibel is probably best known for its Green Hungarian. It began operations in Fremont, near San Jose, where it produced large quantities of sparkling wines. For many years, Weibel was remarkable for its private-label business; at one time it was bottling wines for close to 700 brands.

Its emphasis is now back on the sparkling wines—Stanford Champagne, Frediana Spumante—along with private labels and the omnipresent Green Hungarian, which is said to sell at the rate of 45,000 cases a year.

WELLINGTON VINEYARDS   *Sonoma 1989*   The Wellingtons, father and son, acquired an old 11-acre vineyard in Glen Ellen and built a new winery in 89. The old vineyard is a field blend of reds, including Zinfandel, Petite Sirah, Mourvedre, and Criolla (aka Mission). An additional 11 acres of newly planted hillside vineyards contain Cabernet Sauvignon, Cabernet Franc, Merlot, and Chardonnay. Buying about half its grapes from Sonoma Valley neighbors, Wellington offers a lengthy list of wines, headed by a rare, oak-aged Criolla, and more mundane wines such as Cabernet Sauvignon, Chardonnay, Merlot, Syrah, and Zinfandel. "Cote de Sonoma" is the winery's name for a red Rhone blend. Total production, currently at 3,000 cases per year, will peak at 6,000 cases.

### Cabernet Sauvignon

(Mohrhardt Ridge)   **89°**   **90°**   **91°°**   **92**   93

(Random Ridge)   **90**   **91**   **92**   93   **94**

*The Mohrhardt Ridge wine is ripe, deep, and tannic while; the Random Ridge, although grown on Mount Veeder, has been somewhat understuffed*

### Merlot

**91°**   **92**   **93°**   **94°**

*Ripe cherry/black cherry flavors are framed by oak and moderate tannins*

### Zinfandel

(Old Vines)   89   **90°°**   **94**   **95°°**   96

(Casa Santinamaria)   **92**   **93°**   **94°**   **95°°**   **96°**

*Nicely filled, spicy and berryish style, well-mannered ripeness and tannins*

WENTE BROS.   *Alameda 1883*   A veritable pioneer and family wine dynasty, Wente Bros. is now in the hands of the fourth generation. From a modest 50-acre vineyard developed in 1883 in the heart of the Livermore Valley, Wente Bros. made a range of wines that were highly regarded before Prohibition, especially its sweet white wines produced from Semillon and Sauvignon Blanc. Though still known today as a name synonymous with Gray Riesling, Wente has been a pioneer and quality leader in many areas. In 36 Wente released a varietal Chardonnay, the first in California to be varietally labeled. In 60, a decade before Chardonnay became popular, Wente was the leading proponent and grower with 70 acres planted to Chardonnay—about one-third of the state's total. In 33 Wente also offered the first California wine labeled Sauvignon Blanc. In the mid-60s the family, needing to develop new vineyards to meet the anticipated demand for its white wines, became one of the pioneers in Monterey County viticulture. Today, Wente has 650 acres of vineyards in northern Monterey County.

The winery was the first to market a late harvest Riesling made from *Botrytis cinerea* when it released its 69 Monterey County Johannisberg Riesling, "Spatlese." In 70, it added a sweet-finished Blanc de Blancs to accompany its ever popular Gray Riesling, Chenin Blanc, and Sauvignon Blanc. By the end of the 70s, popularity was forcing the winery to market some of its wine too early, and even its true-to-type Sauvignon Blanc and no-oak-aged Chardonnays were becoming erratic. Today, back on a steady course, Wente Bros. owns 1,200 acres in Livermore Valley, with 527 acres devoted to Chardonnay. Its Livermore Valley holdings emphasize Sauvignon Blanc and Chardonnay, along with a dozen other varieties. From the Arroyo Seco holdings in Monterey, Wente bottles Riesling, Gewurztraminer, and Chardonnay.

In the 90s Wente consolidated its numerous wines into two categories, estate-grown varietals and estate Reserve, a line of limited-volume varietals. It also restored the neighboring historic Cresta Blanca Winery, and turned it and the surrounding land into a champagne-making facility and restaurant. Produced here now is a Brut from Monterey County–grown Chardonnay and Pinot Noir, along with a Blanc de Blancs, Blanc de Noirs, and Reserve Brut, all made by the *méthode champenoise*. After several attempts to upgrade quality, Wente now seems to have figured out how to do it. The quality improvements are most evident in its Reserve Chardonnay and its Riva Ranch Chardonnay. Of course, its Sauvignon Blanc remains ever reliable. Annual production at Wente Bros. is just in excess of 600,000 cases.

**Chardonnay**

(Arroyo Seco)   86   87   88   89   90   91   92   93   95°

*Medium-intensity wines, often exhibiting suggestions of tropical fruits and flowers as adjuncts to the straightforward fruit, are structured on the round and accessible side*

WERMUTH WINERY   *Napa 1982*   What began as a hobby with home winemaker Ralph Wermuth developed into a small wine business. The Wermuth winery is located on the Silverado Trail, just south of Calistoga. A small tasting room was built to sell the winery's first, and at the time only, wine, a Dry Colombard. The winery has since developed its direct sales program, and now produces several varietals, led by Colombard, Gamay, Cabernet Sauvignon, and Sauvignon Blanc. By 97 it reached its production goal of 3,000 cases.

MARK WEST VINEYARDS   *Sonoma 1976*   A scenic pastoral property bordering the Mark West Creek, the Mark West Winery and Vineyards were started by Joan and Bob Ellis. Located in the cool lower portion of the Russian River Valley, the vineyards were planted in 74 predominantly to early-ripening varieties—Gewurztraminer, Riesling, Chardonnay, and Pinot Noir—and now has 60 acres under vine. Chardonnay, produced in two styles, accounts for 10,000 cases per year of the total. One of the winery's specialties has been Gewurztraminer finished with under 1% sugar; in some vintages, that wine achieves ° status. In the early 80s the winery began producing Zinfandel from the Robert Rue Vineyard, and the quality has been up and down. The winery experienced several ownership changes in the early 90s and is now owned by a custom winemaking company, Associated Vintage Group, headquartered in Mendocino County. The owners produce Chardonnay, Gewurztraminer, Late Harvest Gewurztraminer, and Pinot Noir from the estate vineyard. All of the estate vineyards are organically grown. Sauvignon Blanc from a vineyard in Occidental joined the roster in 1994. Mark West has been averaging about 25,000 cases a year. All of the estate vineyards are organically grown. Sauvignon Blanc from a vineyard in Occidental joined the roster in 1994.

## Chardonnay

(Russian River Valley)   86°   87   89°   90   91°   92°   95

*Well balanced and nicely fruity; oak adds a bit of richness to fill out the firm under-pinnings*

---

WHALER VINEYARD   *Mendocino 1981*   On a 35-acre ranch south of Ukiah, owners Russ and Ann Nyborg developed a 24-acre vineyard. Planted in 72, the vineyard consisted of Zinfandel which over the first several harvests was sold to other producers. In 81, the Nyborgs began making Zinfandel from their own vineyard. The style of the first few vintages was light and simple, emphasizing berry fruitiness. The 85 vintage showed more depth in a medium-bodied style. The owners made an attractive White Zinfandel in the mid-80s, but now are making only an estate Zinfandel. Each year 500–700 cases from the best barrels are bottled as Flagship Zinfandel. Recent vintages of this Zinfandel have occasionally risen to ° quality.

---

WILLIAM WHEELER WINERY   *Sonoma 1981*   The William Wheeler family ran this winery until 1992, when they sold their interest to Parabas, a French banking company. The French banking company soon bailed out, selling to another French firm which within a year sold the winemaking facility and the beautiful Dry Creek Valley vineyards, retaining only inventory and the Wheeler Winery name. William Wheeler's current vintages are produced from wines purchased on the bulk market.

---

WHITCRAFT WINES   *Santa Barbara 1985*   After a stint as a wine retailer and wholesaler, Chris Whitcraft produced private-label wines for restaurants and retail outlets for several years, an experience that encouraged him to start his own brand. Whitcraft specializes in Chardonnay and Pinot Noir. For both, he adheres to a non-interventionist approach throughout by, among other techniques, using a gravity-flow system to avoid pumping the wine. He produces several Pinot Noirs, all unfined and unfiltered, which have been well-oaked but erratic in quality. The primary one is from the Bien Nacido Vineyard in the Santa Maria Valley, while the second is a limited-volume Pinot Noir from Sonoma County's Russian River Valley. Overall annual output has reached 1,200 cases, with 2,000 as Whitcraft's eventual target.

---

WHITE COTTAGE WINERY   *Napa 1994*   Dennis Johns, winemaker for St. Clement, has 22 acres of vineyards in the Howell Mountain district. In 1994 he produced 150 cases of intensely flavored Merlot that was sold through a mail list. The Merlot output today is 400 cases. Growing a few acres of Sangiovese, Johns intends to offer a varietal Sangiovese in the near future.

---

WHITE OAK VINEYARDS   *Sonoma 1981*   The original White Oak facility was built by owner Bill Myers in 80, just a few blocks away from the Healdsburg town plaza. He owns 6 acres planted to Chardonnay and Cabernet in the Alexander Valley, and buys from growers throughout Sonoma County. Chardonnay and Sauvignon Blanc account for 70% of the 10,000 cases produced annually. In 1998, after outgrowing its old facility, White Oak moved into a new winery in the heart of Alexander Valley. Its current roster features three Chardonnays (Sonoma County, Poplar Ranch, and Reserve) as well as Zinfandel, Cabernet Sauvignon, and Merlot. A series of "Limited Reserve" Chardonnays (100% barrel-fermented) and Cabernet Sauvignons have been offered, with the majority of the grapes for each originating in Myers's own vineyard.

## Chardonnay

(Sonoma County)   86°   87°   88°   89   90   91   94

(Reserve)   88°   89   90   91   94°

*Direct, bright citrus and fresh appley fruit, with just enough background oak to add breadth to the crisp flavors*

WHITE ROCK VINEYARDS   *Napa 1987*   In the southern foothills of the Stags Leap District, Claire and Henri Vandendriessche purchased vineyard land and a pre-Prohibition winery site in 77. In 79 they began developing 35 acres, planting Chardonnay and Cabernet Sauvignon, and including 5 acres of Cabernet Franc, Merlot, and Petit Verdot. Situated on steep terraces, the vines are planted closely together in European fashion, and the owners are proud of the fact that they use neither insecticides nor herbicides in vineyard cultivation. White Rock's first few harvests of red grapes were sold. In 86, to test the waters, they had their own Bordeaux blend of red wine made, which they labeled "Claret." That first bottling consisted of 600 cases, and the quality level encouraged the owners to go commercial. In 88 the Vandendriessches built an underground winery and aging caves, with the expectation of eventually producing 2,000 cases a year. Their Chardonnay is entirely fermented in new French oak barrels, and all of its barrel aging is *sur lie.*

### Chardonnay

88** 89* 90 91 92* 95 96

*Relies on oak and ripe grapes when it succeeds; it started well, but failed to come up to the quality of generally top-notch 90 vintage*

### Claret

86 **87*** 88 89 **91*** **92*** 93 **94**

*This blend of Cabernet Sauvignon (70–80%) with Merlot, Cabernet Franc, and Petit Verdot can be very rich and is always high in oak but has tended to lack balance in early vintages*

---

WHITEHALL LANE   *Napa 1980*   After vacationing in Napa Valley with their wives for several years, architect Art Finkelstein was ready to design a winery, while his brother, Alan Steen, a plastic surgeon, was prepared to take charge of a vineyard. In 79 they bought an old vineyard site on the main wine road south of St. Helena. The 26-acre vineyard was planted to Chardonnay, Sauvignon Blanc, and Merlot. Forced to buy grapes until 85, Whitehall Lane experienced a few rough times, but also discovered some excellent fruit and developed definite notions on winemaking.

In 84, choosing Merlot from a grower in the Knight's Valley, the winery began building an impressive record for Merlot. In 88 the winery was sold to Hideaki Ando of Japan. Art Finkelstein left to start his own winery, Judd's Hill (see entry), and Whitehall Lane was soon back on the market. It was sold in 93 to Tom Leonardini, a San Francisco Bay Area entrepreneur and wine retailer. He has put it back on a course to produce 20,000 cases a year. Through his direction, Whitehall Lane has become a highly regarded red wine producer. Its top-of-the-line wines are Reserve Merlot from Leonardini Vineyard and Reserve Cabernet from Morisoli Vineyard. Merlot from the Knights Valley remains in the lineup, accompanied by a Napa Valley Merlot, Napa Cabernet, and Napa Zinfandel. Chardonnay, Sauvignon Blanc, and Johannisberg Riesling are the whites regularly offered.

### Cabernet Sauvignon

(regular bottling) 81* 82* 83* 84** **85** **86** **87** 88
**90** 91 92 **93*** **94*** **95**

(Reserve) 84** **85** **86** 87 88* **89*** **90*** **91*** **92***
**93*** **94***

*Made in similar styles, these wines feature very ripe, open fruit, plenty of depth, and lots of sweet oak, and carry abundant tannins that assure good aging capability*

### Merlot

82 83 84** 85** 86 87 **88** **89*** 90* 91 **92***
**93*** 94 **95*** 96

(Reserve) **93** **94***** **95*****

*Like the Cabernet, these are ripe, rich, tasty wines, with oak adding to its sweet, forward character; tannins are a bit lighter and the wine is a little softer, but it too can age; recent Reserves have topped the list*

WILD HOG VINEYARD   *Sonoma 1990*   Located in the cool-climate Sonoma Coast town of Cazadera, this winery specializes in red wines, primarily Pinot Noir and Zinfandel. The former is made from the winery's 4 1/2 acre vineyard, and the latter is made from the neighboring "Porter Bass Vineyard." A few hundred cases of Cabernet Sauvignon round out the roster. Annual production is close to the 1,500 case optimum. This winery should not be confused with Wild Hog Hill Winery, which began in 1988 but appears to have gone quietly out of business.

WILD HORSE WINERY   *San Luis Obispo 1982*   Owner-winemaker Ken Volk built a solid reputation surprisingly fast, but he earned it the old-fashioned way—by making outstanding wines. He first rose to prominence on the strength of small batches of vineyard-designated (Sierra Madre Vineyard, Bien Nacido) Pinot Noir from Santa Barbara County. He has added Chardonnay, Merlot, and Cabernet Sauvignon to the line, and has expanded the volume of Pinot Noir. Volk's winery is located in Templeton and his 33-acre vineyard is adjacent. The vineyard contains 20 acres of Chardonnay, 5 of Cabernet Sauvignon, and 8 combined of Merlot and Cabernet Franc. By 90 the winery was producing 25,000 cases, with Chardonnay as the leader, followed by Pinot Noir, Cabernet Sauvignon, Pinot Blanc, and Merlot. The primary bottling of Pinot Noir is labeled Santa Barbara County. Reserve-type Pinot Noir is bottled under the "Cheval Sauvage" (see entry) label. Volk, who started in 83 with one tank and an old barn, intends to level off production at 90,000 cases a year.

### Chardonnay

86° 87°° 88 89° 90° 91 **94°** **95°**

*Full of ripe and luscious fruit to balance its imposing oaky, toasty seasonings*

### Pinot Noir

85 86°° 87° 88° 89° 90 91 92 93° 94 95

*Bright, cherryish fruit and moderate tannins combine for wines capable of improving for a few years at best*

WILLIAMS SELYEM WINERY   *Sonoma 1981*   Founded by Ed Selyem and Burt Williams, this brand started out making wine, primarily Zinfandel, under the name of Hacienda del Rio, a name never officially registered. However, when its use was challenged by Hacienda Winery, the name was quickly changed. The original winery was actually a converted garage behind a house on River Road in the southern corner of the Russian River Valley. In 83 the partners began to specialize in Pinot Noir purchased from several vineyards within Sonoma County. They have made small batches (300–600 cases) of Pinot Noir from the Howard Allen Vineyard, Olivet Lane, the Rochioli Vineyard, and the Sonoma Coast and Sonoma County appellations. In 90, they moved the winemaking operation to a larger building owned by vineyardist Howard Allen. The winemaking style is quite traditional, with open-top fermenters used and warm fermentations that include stem retention. The wines are aged for an average of 18 months in heavily toasted barrels. Typically, this winery's Pinot Noirs have been full-blown without much restraint in evidence, and have varied in their degree of fruitiness and in their degree of success. Zinfandel from the Martinelli Vineyard in the Russian River Valley is also made. Total production is 3,000 cases a year maximum. In 1998 the brand, inventory, and goodwill were acquired by John Dyson, owner of Millbrook Winery in New York, for a rumored $9 million.

WINDEMERE WINES   *San Luis Obispo 1985*   Cathy MacGregor worked in the enology department of several Sonoma County wineries before founding her own winery in 85. Only Chardonnay from the Edna Valley is made, and the production is limited to 1,000 cases a year. The grapes are grown at the MacGregor Vineyard, a well-known 90-acre vineyard in the Edna Valley owned by her parents. Windemere's wine is 100% barrel-fermented, and half undergoes malolactic fermentation. Early vintages were capable of earning ° . The 95 vintage, however, was one of the top Chardonnays from the Central Coast.

### Chardonnay

86   87°   88   89   91   92   94   **95°°**   96

*Capable of offering bright, appley, and quietly tropical fruit, backed by rich oak; medium intensity*

---

WINDWARD VINEYARD   *Paso Robles 1993*   A rare Pinot Noir specialist in Paso Robles, Windward is owned by Marc Goldberg, who developed 10 acres in the early 1990s. With winemaking assistance from Ken Volk of Wild Horse Winery, Windward is now producing about 1,200 cases a year. The style in mind is big and highly extracted, and Windward's Pinot Noirs are bottled unfined and unfiltered. Experiencing some bumps in the road over its first few vintages, the winery began to come on strong with its 1996 release.

---

WING CANYON VINEYARD   *Napa 1986*   Bill and Kathy Dennert have devoted 12 acres on their Mount Veeder property to red Bordeaux varieties. In 1986 they began planting on the steepest hillside sites. It 1991 they celebrated their first commercial bottling of a Meritage red blend. A few hundred cases of Chardonnay made from purchased grapes brings Wing Canyon's annual production to 1,000 cases.

---

CHRISTINE WOODS VINEYARDS   *Mendocino 1982*   Longtime growers in the Anderson Valley, the Vernon Rose family owns two vineyards, both located opposite the Roederer Estate in Navarro. The main vineyard is planted on the valley floor and is devoted to Chardonnay and Pinot Noir; most of the crop from this vineyard is sold. The other parcel is situated at higher elevations to the south and contains Cabernet Sauvignon and Gamay Beaujolais. Fewer than 2,000 cases a year were made during the first several years. The only offering creating some interest was a barrel-fermented Chardonnay. Christine Woods is the name of one of the early settlers in the Anderson Valley. The winery's total plantings amount to 20 acres.

---

YORK CREEK VINEYARDS   *Napa 1994*   One of the best-known independent vineyards in Napa Valley, York Creek is owned by Fritz Maytag, who also owns the Anchor Steam Brewery in San Francisco and the Maytag Cheese Company in Wisconsin. Located in the Spring Mountain District, his vineyard contains 125 acres, and for more than twenty vintages Ridge has produced Petite Sirah, Zinfandel, and Merlot from York Creek. With Cathy Corison overseeing winemaking at York Creek, Maytag is focusing on a red Meritage. The first vintage consisted of 800 cases, but annual output is likely to grow to 2,500 cases by 2001.

---

YORK MOUNTAIN WINERY   *San Luis Obispo 1882*   The old stone winery was built in 1882 by the York family, which also planted the mountainside vineyard to the west of Templeton. In 70 the Goldman family purchased the property and set about refurbishing both winery and vineyard. 5 acres have been replanted to a mix of varieties—Pinot Noir, Cabernet Sauvignon, Zinfandel, and Chardonnay. The winery has an old and honorable association with Zinfandel, and it is the leading variety planted. Augmented by grapes purchased from the Central Coast, York Mountain currently offers Zinfandel, Pinot Noir, Merlot, and Cabernet Sauvignon, with Chardonnay as its only white. Total output is at 6,000 cases a year. Quality levels have too often been ordinary.

---

YORKVILLE CELLARS   *Mendocino 1993*   On the highlands east of the Anderson Valley sits the little town of Yorkville. In the late 1980s, Edward Wallo acquired a small vineyard. He expanded the vineyard to its current total of 30 acres and converted it to organic farming methods. Now in a small winery Yorkville is producing Merlot, Cabernet Sauvignon, Cabernet Franc, Sauvignon Blanc, Chardonnay, and Semillon. Eleanor of Aquitaine, a blend of barrel-fermented Sauvignon Blanc and Semillon, has been far and away the winery's finest effort to date. Annual production will gradually increase to the 5,000-case level.

ZABACO VINTNERS    *(Gallo of Sonoma)*    Zabaco is a midpriced line of Sonoma County varietals made by Gallo at its large winery in Dry Creek Valley. Chardonnay, Sauvignon Blanc, Pinot Noir, and Zinfandel have been offered to date.

ZACA MESA WINERY    *Santa Barbara 1976*    Second only to Firestone Vineyards in terms of production in Santa Barbara, Zaca Mesa has had a rather tumultuous early history. It was founded by oil executive Louis Ream, and at one time the winery owned or controlled 340 acres of vineyards in the county. In the early 80s it was cranking out a range of wines for an annual production of close to 100,000 cases. By 86 Ream had sold his interests, and Zaca Mesa was reorganized into a corporation while the winery also underwent changes. Resurfacing with 212 acres in the Santa Ynez Valley, Zaca Mesa produced a range of table wines from the Santa Barbara appellation. A rather extensive line of wines was trimmed down in the early 90s. Since then Zaca Mesa has reduced the line to Chardonnay, Pinot Noir, Syrah, and several limited-volume Rhone-style wines. The winery has had success with its Syrah, which in some vintages has contained up to 20% Viognier. It is also increasing its production of Roussanne and its special red Rhone blend, Z Cuvée. An exciting but small-volume "Alumni Series" of wines made by well-known ex-winemakers have yielded some outstanding Chardonnays to date. Overall, about 75% of the Zaca Mesa's total annual production today is Chardonnay. Of late the Chardonnays have represented excellent value.

ZD WINES    *Napa 1969*    Originally located in Sonoma Valley, ZD was founded by Gino Zepponi and Norman de Leuze, aerospace engineers who worked in Sacramento. After outgrowing the first facility, they relocated in Napa Valley in 79, building a winery about midway along the Silverado Trail. To the west of the winery, they planted 3.2 acres to Cabernet. As their production expanded, de Leuze served as winemaker while Zepponi became active with Domaine Chandon, serving as plant engineer there until his death in 85. Now owned and operated by the de Leuze family, the winery continues to produce Chardonnay with a California appellation and Pinot Noir from Napa Valley or Carneros. The third most important wine, Cabernet Sauvignon, is labeled Napa Valley.

ZD's first estate-bottled Cabernet was made in 87. Entirely barrel-fermented, ZD's Chardonnays are a blend derived from Napa, Sonoma, and the Central Coast regions. ZD was one of the first Napa Valley wineries to buy Chardonnay from Santa Barbara County. Aged in barrel for close to a year, ZD's Chardonnays are noted for a ripe, viscous texture and a rich, tropical fruit aroma. The winery has developed such a strong reputation for Chardonnay that more than 15,000 cases are being produced per year. However, ZD also has been offering Carneros Pinot Noir for more than twenty years, and it, too, has a solid track record for quality and ageability. An early-bottled, fruity style of Pinot Noir is labeled Rosa Lee. In the 1990s a Reserve Cabernet program sets aside 500–800 cases each year, and Merlot is the most recent newcomer to the line. ZD has 3 1/2 acres of Cabernet adjacent to the winery. In the Carneros District, it has developed 35 acres containing Chardonnay and Pinot Noir. The winery's total output is 30,000 cases.

### Cabernet Sauvignon

(Napa Valley)    83°    84°    85    **86**    **87**    **88°°**    89    **90°**    **91°**    **92°°**    **93°**    **94°**    **95°**

*Often showing more tannin than fruit, the wine is always long-aging; very consistent in the 90s*

### Chardonnay

86°°   87°°   88   89°   90°   91°   92°   **93**°°   **94**°   **95**°   **96**°

*Among the top Chardonnays in most years, the wine typically combines ripe and broad appley fruit with toasty oak and roasted-grain flavor complexities*

### Pinot Noir

82°   83°   84   85   86   **87**°   **88**°°   89°   **90**°°   **91**°°   **92**°°
**93**°°   **94**°   **95**°°

*Cherryish fruit, moderate oak, light-medium tannins, and good depth in most years*

ZELLERBACH VINEYARD   *Mendocino 1978*   In the Chalk Hill area of the Alexander Valley, Stephen Zellerbach completed a winery in 78 to process his first harvest. His estate vineyard was planted in 72 to Cabernet Sauvignon and Merlot, and he produced Chardonnay from a vineyard under contract. It was business as usual for Zellerbach until 86 when with a production of 20,000 cases he found he was gaining neither inner peace nor financial bliss. He leased the winery along with his brand to William Baccala, who had just sold his own winery in Mendocino County to Robert Jepson. Baccala hired a winemaker and marketing team. Within a year, they were selling existing inventory at reduced prices and had built a strong following for Zellerbach Chardonnay. The next year they added a Sauvignon Blanc. In 88 entrepreneur Jess Jackson of Kendall-Jackson picked up the lease/option to buy from Baccala and bought the whole shebang—winery, 165-acre estate, and what was by then a 65-acre vineyard. The trademark name Zellerbach was retained by the Baccala family, which continues to offer Chardonnay, and Cabernet Sauvignon. In 93, Baccala purchased the Tijsseling winery in Mendocino, where Zellerbach wines are now bottled.

# The Northwest

ADELSHEIM VINEYARDS   *Willamette Valley, Oregon 1978*   In 72 Dave Adelsheim began developing a vineyard that now covers 47 acres. As his vineyard was maturing, he studied winemaking and learned the practical side by working in the cellars at Eyrie Vineyards. On a hill overlooking the vineyards, Adelsheim built a winery and crushed in it for the first time in 82. The winery's vineyard contains Pinot Noir, Chardonnay, and Riesling. Adelsheim also makes a Pinot Gris and on occasion a Minlot. Cold-fermented to dryness, and not oak-aged, Adelsheim Pinot Gris usually captures both fruit and some depth of flavor. Best known for its Pinot Noir, the winery makes Reserve and Willamette Valley bottlings, each of which has earned good ratings. The winery's annual production has reached 15,000 cases.

### Pinot Noir

(Willamette Valley)   82   83   84°   85°   86°   87°   **88**°°   89°
90   **91**   **93**°°   **94**°°°   95

(Reserve/Seven Springs)   87°°   88   **89**°   **90**   **92**°°   **93**   **95**

*Straightforwardly fruity wines are, in the latest vintages, showing greater range of character*

AIRLIE WINERY   *Willamette Valley, Oregon 1986*   Located in the Salem area in the small town of Monmouth, Airlie is owned by Larry Preedy, who settled in Oregon originally to grow Christmas trees. In small stages he developed a 15-acre vineyard that now consists of Pinot Noir, Müller-Thurgau, Riesling, Pinot Gris, and Gewurztraminer. The first vintages of Pinot Noir leaned toward the simple, fruity style. With maturity of the estate vineyard, the owner anticipates that production will gradually grow to a maximum of 3,500 cases.

ALEXIA   *Woodinville 1996*   Longtime cellarmaster at Columbia Crest, Gordy Rawson is the owner and winemaker behind this upscale brand of sparkling wine. From Pinot Noir and Chardonnay grown in southwestern Washington, near LaCenter, he follows the classic *méthode champenoise* to produce Brut and Blanc de Noir sparklers. To showcase his products he built a cozy tasting room in the highly touristed Woodinville area.

**AMITY VINEYARDS** *Willamette Valley, Oregon 1976* In 74, owner Myron Redford purchased the 70-acre site in the town of Amity, just in the southern part of the Eola Hills. His vineyard now covers 15 acres supplying just under half of the grapes crushed. He has 7 acres of Pinot Noir and 3 acres of Pinot Blanc. Amity began by making 350 cases in 76; production has grown steadily to the present 7,500-case level. It is currently producing Pinot Noir, White Riesling, Gewurztraminer, and Pinot Blanc. The Pinot Noir is made in two styles—a Nouveau and a traditionally fermented version. The conventional Pinot Noirs are fermented in small vats, punched down by hand, and aged in French oak barrels. In some vintages, Amity bottles four conventional Pinot Noirs—""Oregon,""Willamette Valley,""Estate," and "Winemakers Reserve." Typically, the Willamette Valley Pinot Noir is the volume leader at 2,000 cases and is made every vintage. In general, we have found Amity's Willamette Valley Pinot to display more fruit than the Reserve. Amity has been making a Nouveau by carbonic maceration since 76, longer than any other U.S. winery. It is also working with the true Gamay Noir of Beaujolais, making its first batch of 200 cases in 88. In most years, Amity's Gewurztraminer is one of Oregon's best.

**APEX** *(Washington Hills Cellars)* A label used for Reserve-caliber Cabernet Sauvignon, Merlot, and Chardonnay. In some vintages a Dry Gewurztraminer, Pinot Noir, and Late Harvest Riesling also have appeared. Although the entire line has improved in quality, Merlot,* richly flavored with ripeness aplenty, now receives high marks. In an average year about 8,000 cases of Apex will be bottled.

**ARBOR CREST WINERY** *Spokane, Washington 1982* Among Washington's first quality-minded producers, Arbor Crest was also among the first with an aggressive out-of-state marketing program. Located on a bluff 450 feet above the Spokane River, the current winery was built in 87. The adjacent historic mansion has been converted into a tasting room. Owned by the Mielke family, longtime growers and orchard owners, Arbor Crest has specialized in white wines from its first harvest, and today three-fourths of its 30,000-case production consists of Sauvignon Blanc and Chardonnay. Cabernet Sauvignon and Merlot complete the lineup. The winery has enjoyed moderate success with an oak-aged Chardonnay and a full-bodied, tannic-style Cabernet Sauvignon. Arbor Crest owns 80 acres of vineyards in the Columbia River appellation, over 100 miles to the south. Annual production will level off at 40,000 cases.

**ARCHERY SUMMIT** *Willamette Valley, Oregon 1993* Gary Andrus and other partners in Napa Valley's Pine Ridge Winery began looking for vineyard sites in the Dundee Hills, and by 1990 they had acquired 77 acres located adjacent to Domaine Drouhin. The first two vintages of Pinot Noir, which were critical successes, were crushed and fermented at Pine Ridge. A new facility and aging caves in the Dundee Hills were completed by 1995, and the winery was designed to move wine only by gravity flow. The winery will take its annual production to 2,500 cases which includes a few hundred cases of Pinot Gris. Both 93 Pinots earned°°. With more than 70 acres developed at four locations, Archery Summit currently produces two vineyard-designated Pinot Noirs—Arcus Estate and Red Hills Estate—and will add others as new vineyards come into productivity. Vireton, a delicious white blend of Pinot Gris, Chardonnay, and Pinot Blanc, also is a key player on the roster.

**ARGYLE** *Willamette Valley, Oregon 1987* Australian winemaker Brian Croser teams up with local grower and investor Cal Knudsen in this joint venture. They operate the business as the Dundee Wine Company, but use Argyle as their wine label. A winemaking facility is located in the industrial section of Dundee, and all grapes crushed are purchased under long-term contract. Sparkling wine made by the *méthode champenoise* is the main thrust, and the line consists of Brut, the volume leader, along with a Rosé and a Blanc de Blanc. Four varietal wines—a barrel-fermented Chardonnay, Pinot Gris, Pinot Noir, and a dry Riesling—are offered under the Argyle label. Croser is the winemaker and manager for Petaluma Wines in Australia, and produces sparkling wine under the Croser label along with Petaluma table wines. He plans to take Argyle's sparkling wine to an annual production level of 25,000 cases. The output for Chardonnay and Riesling will remain at 3,000 cases each. Argyle's Reserve Pinot Gris often is one of Oregon's most complex.

ASHLAND VINEYARDS   *Rogue Valley, Oregon 1988*   Located in the beautiful and popular tourist destination of Ashland, home to the annual Shakespeare Festival, this winery is able to sell much of its production at its cellar doors. After a long and rather bumpy early history it is now under the quality-minded ownership of Phil Kodak. Though the Pinot Gris and Mueller-Thurgau are both pleasant, the wines receiving the most attention recently are Cabernet Sauvignon and Merlot. About 3,500 cases are made each year.

AUTUMN WIND VINEYARD   *Willamette Valley, Oregon 1987*   Situated about 7 miles west of Newberg, Autumn Wind sits on a hilltop surrounded by tall oak trees. Escaping from Los Angeles, owner and winemaker Tom Kreutner purchased a 50-acre neglected cherry orchard in 82. About 10 acres have been planted to vines, with Pinot Noir predominating. Over the first few vintages Autumn Wind has made Pinot Noir, Müller-Thurgau, and Sauvignon Blanc. When the estate vineyard is fully mature, Autumn Wind will focus on Pinot Noir, Pinot Gris, and Chardonnay. Optimum capacity is 4,000 cases a year.

BADGER MOUNTAIN   *Kennewick, Washington 1992*   As Washington's first certified organic vineyard, Badger Mountain needed a few years to get the hang of working with organically grown fruit. But winemaker Bill Powers, who owns a 75-acre vineyard situated on a south-facing slope in Columbia Valley, has recently been turning out good wines. Currently Badger makes Cabernet Sauvignon, Riesling, and Chardonnay. The Cabernet Sauvignon is the most noteworthy.

BALCOM & MOE WINERY   *Pasco, Washington, 1994*   This winery made wines for several years under the Quarry Lake label. It was renamed by owner Maury Balcom, who operates Moe Farms, a large, diversified farm in Columbia Valley. About 100 acres are given over to wine grapes, with Cabernet Sauvignon, Merlot, Chardonnay, and Sauvignon Blanc as leaders. Wine quality has been steadily improving. Merlot has recently emerged as the winery's best.

BARNARD GRIFFIN WINERY   *Kennewick, Washington 1983*   Rob Griffin, winemaker for Hogue, and Deborah Barnard, his wife, operate this winemaking business. About 75% of their efforts are devoted to making Fumé Blanc and Chardonnay, with 400-case batches each of Merlot and Cabernet Sauvignon. Both Sauvignon Blanc and Chardonnay are barrel-fermented and aged *sur lie* in a no-holds-barred approach. In 1997 the Griffins moved into their new winery in the Tri-Cities Area, and the winery was quickly operating at its full capacity of 20,000 cases. About half of the total is Fumé Blanc. In recent vintages Cabernet Sauvignon has improved, and the Reserve Cabernet is well worth a special search. The Reserve Merlot also is much improved recently. The whites are acceptable.

BEAUX FRÈRES   *Willamette Valley 1992*   Owned by Michael Etzel and his brother-in-law, wine journalist Robert Parker, Beaux Frères specializes in Pinot Noir from the family's own 30-acre vineyard. With vines deliberately planted close together, the vineyard yields on average about two tons per acre. The quality has been generally high. Production has reached 3,000 cases, a few hundred cases shy of the projected annual maximum.

**BENTON LANE WINERY**  *Benton County, Oregon 1992*  Two former California winery owners, Steve Girard (Girard Winery) and Carl Doumani (Stags' Leap Winery), are partners in this Pinot Noir venture. They have developed 125 acres to Pinot Noir in western Oregon midway between Eugene and Corvallis. The first vintages yielded 3,500 cases per year. The quality has been above average. This is an up-and-coming winery. Annual production is closing in on the winery's 25,000-case capacity.

**BETHEL HEIGHTS VINEYARD**  *Willamette Valley, Oregon 1984*  Twin brothers Terry and Ted Casteel began developing a vineyard on property located in the Eola Hills region, northwest of Salem, in 77. They planted 51 acres on a south-facing slope on typically thin volcanic soils. Pinot Noir is the primary variety, with 29 acres planted, followed by Chardonnay at 14.5 acres. The Casteels sold their entire crop until 84, when they made their first wine. Ted is the vineyard manager and Terry is winemaker. As growers, they became quickly respected for the quality of their grapes by selling to producers within Oregon and a few in California, most notably Bonny Doon. Bethel Heights still sells grapes under contract. Today the winery makes Pinot Noir, Chardonnay, Pinot Gris, Pinot Blanc, and Gewurztraminer. Presently four Pinot Noirs are made—Estate, Southeast Block Reserve, Wadenswil Block Reserve, and Eola Hills Cuvée. An Estate Chardonnay is joined by two limited bottlings, Reserve and Eola Hills Cuvée. Winemaker Terry Casteel believes in using about 25% new French oak for Pinot Noir aging. Also, his Pinot Noirs are given minimal handling and are only lightly filtered, if at all. The winery's Chardonnays are 100% barrel-fermented, and aged entirely *sur lie*. An average of 3,500 cases of Chardonnay is made each year. The winery's total annual production is 10,000 cases.

### Chardonnay

86°   87   89   91   92

*In early vintages, the wine was fruity, with citrus blossom notes and restrained oak adding extra interest, but two recent vintages have been clunkers*

### Pinot Noir

(Willamette Valley)   84°°   86°   87   **88°**   **89°**   91   **92°**   93   **94°**   95

(Reserve)   86°   88°   **89°°**   91°   **93°°**   95

*Direct, slightly narrow, cherrylike fruit, occasionally displays the depth and suppleness needed to earn high ratings*

**BLACKWOOD CANYON VINTNERS**  *Benton, Washington 1982*  At the eastern corner of the Yakima Valley, owner Mike Moore and his family planted grapes on the 100-acre ranch and eased into winemaking. In 85, just when the winery was beginning to make a name for itself, it was destroyed by a fire. After rebuilding, Moore resumed a range of wines in a highly individualistic mode. His whites (Chardonnay and Semillon) display considerable evidence of extended oak and *sur lie* aging. Blackwood Canyon has produced several unusual sweet dessert wines from *Botrytis*-affected grapes, including Semillon, Riesling, and a most unusual wine labeled "Penultimate Gewurztraminer. Ice Wine." The winery's total production had reached the optimum level of 15,000 cases.

**BONAIR WINERY**  *Zillah, Washington 1985*  Aiming to please its many winery visitors, Bonair offers wines in many different styles. "Sunset," a pink wine made from Riesling with a splash of Cabernet, is medium sweet and a best-seller. A similar style of red wine named Bonnie Bonair is a close second in sales. Owners Gail and Shirley Puryear have a 5-acre vineyard and buy fruit from throughout Yakima Valley area to produce 6,500 cases a year. For traditionalists they make a Reserve Chardonnay, Merlot, and Cabernet Sauvignon. Their Yakima Valley Merlot is the quality leader, and the barrel-fermented dry Riesling can be almost as good. However, one of the rare specialties here is an authentic and delicious Mead.

BOOKWALTER WINERY   *Pasco, Washington 1984*   Owner/winemaker Jerry Bookwalter runs his small winery on a part-time basis; the rest of his time is given over to a vineyard management service. Formerly manager for Sagemoor Farms, the Northwest's largest vineyard, Bookwalter prefers to select grapes from growers for his own wines. He offers Chardonnay and Riesling regularly, and in most vintages he has bottled Merlot, Cabernet Sauvignon, Chenin Blanc, and Muscat. Production has varied, but on average about 3,000 cases are made per year. An occasional small batch (100–300 cases) of Vintners Select Cabernet Sauvignon displays uncommon intensity and depth. As the winery moves toward the 10,000-case mark, Cabernet will become more prominent.

BRICK HOUSE VINEYARDS   *Willamette 1992*   One of Oregon's first vineyards to expound the organic farming approach, Brick House grows Chardonnay, Pinot Noir, and Gamay. All wines made are estate-grown in the 26-acre vineyard overlooking the Chehalem Valley. A take-no-prisoners-style is evident in all three wines—Chardonnay, Pinot Noir, and Gamay. With production level at 1,000 cases, the Pinot Noir responds best to this approach and can be awesome.

W. B. BRIDGEMAN   *Sunnyside, Washington 1993*   Part of the same winery-producing Washington Hills and Apex, Bridgeman began as a label for the local market, but it has evolved into a separate label of generally low-priced varietals. Its best-sellers are Cabernet Sauvignon, Chardonnay, Merlot, and Lemberger. All are priced modestly and deliver lots of honest flavor. A Cabernet Franc and Syrah, both produced in 400-case lots, are priced higher but still appeal to the bargain hunters of the world. Combined annual output is 6,000 cases.

BRIDGEVIEW VINEYARDS   *Illinois Valley, Oregon 1986*   Situated in this southern Oregon valley, Bridgeview began in 80 with the development of a 75-acre vineyard. Reflecting their German heritage, owners Robert and Lelo Kerivan planted Gewurztraminer, Müller-Thurgau, and Pinot Gris, along with Chardonnay and Pinot Noir. The owners are proud of the fact that their vines are planted in the European tradition of close spacing. Recently the winery developed a 35-acre vineyard to Merlot and Syrah. Now operating at full capacity, Bridgeview offers a full line of varietals. The volume leaders are Chardonnay, Riesling, and Sem-Chard, all offering good value. Merlot is also more than adequate for the price tag. In 86 they built their large (45,000-case-capacity) winery.

BROADLEY VINEYARDS   *Willamette Valley, Oregon 1986*   Leaving California in pursuit of the lifestyle of small winery owners, Claudia and Craig Broadley ended up in the southern Willamette Valley. Starting from scratch, they cleared the land along the eastern slopes above the small town of Monroe and planted 18 acres of Pinot Noir and Chardonnay, along with 2 acres of Pinot Gris. The Broadleys are producing a regular and Reserve Pinot Noir and Chardonnay. The first vintages of Reserve Pinot Noir showed considerable promise. When its vineyards are fully productive, the winery is expected to reach its capacity of 3,000 cases a year.

CALLAHAN RIDGE WINERY   *Umpqua Valley, Oregon 1993*   A popular tourist spot, Callahan Ridge offers a dozen wines, most of which are styled for popular appeal. From its own 4-acre parcel and local vineyards, the winery offers the usual mix of Oregon wines along with Merlot, Cabernet, and Zinfandel. The best-seller is Riesling made in both a dry and slightly sweet style. Annual output is 5,000 cases.

CAMERON WINERY   *Willamette Valley, Oregon 1984*   This winery is a three-way partnership of winemaker John Paul, vineyardist Bill Wayne, and builder Marc Douchez. They have taken it from a small operation in a rented warehouse to a modern facility located just above the town of Dundee. Winemaker John Paul gained experience in California with Konocti and Carneros Creek Winery. With 20 acres of vineyards to rely on, the winery focuses on Pinot Noir and Chardonnay, making a regular and Reserve version of each in most years. The winery also bottles a Pinot Blanc that is aged in oak and a Pinot Bianco that is not. John Paul, one of Oregon's more outspoken winemakers, has developed a strong following for his heavy-duty Reserve Pinot Noirs.

CANOE RIDGE VINEYARD  *Walla Walla, Washington 1990*  On 200 acres of land overlooking the Columbia River, Canoe Ridge first began to take shape with the development of 44 acres in the late 80s. The initial planting consisted of Cabernet Sauvignon and Merlot. In 90, Chalone, Inc., of California (owners of Acacia, Carmenet, Chalone, and other wine properties) acquired a 50% interest in Canoe Ridge. Shortly thereafter, 50 additional acres were planted to Merlot and Chardonnay, and a 25,000-case-capacity winery was under construction. Merlot is the main item at Canoe Ridge, with Chardonnay increasing in importance and Cabernet Sauvignon rounding out the line. Operating at full capacity today, Canoe Ridge is beginning to make supple, smooth Merlot at the * level.

CAROWAY VINEYARDS  *Kennewick, Washington 1984*  Vineyard owner Wayne Miller established 40 acres to several varieties in the early 80s. Located 5 miles from the Columbia River, the vineyard came into bearing in 83, a time when there was a grape surplus in Washington. As a result, the Millers made wines from their own grapes that year. Every year since, if and when some of the crop is not purchased, Miller produces Caroway wines. Riesling, Chardonnay, and Chenin Blanc are the major grapes planted.

CATERINA WINERY  *Spokane, Washington 1991*  Winemaker Mike Scott heads a partnership that acquired the former Steven Thomas Livingstone Winery after it went out of business in 1990. Purchasing the majority of the grapes he crushes from the Waluke slope in the Columbia Valley, Scott is making Cabernet Sauvignon, Sauvignon Blanc, Merlot, and Chardonnay. When the quality is there, Caterina makes a barrel-fermented Reserve Chardonnay. Generally well made, Caterina wines are priced modestly and sell out quickly.

CAVATAPPI WINERY  *Kirkland, Washington 1984*  In Seattle, owner-winemaker Peter Dow is better known for his restaurant, Café Juanita, than for his wines. The restaurant in suburban Kirkland features northern Italian fare, and Dow wanted to offer his own house wine to go with it. After a long battle with local officials, he got the go-ahead. Cavatappi (the name means "corkscrew" in Italian) makes Sangiovese, Sauvignon Blanc, Cabernet Sauvignon, and Nebbiolo. From a small planting in the Red Willow Vineyard, Dow produced Washington's first Nebbiolo in 87. A minuscule amount of Syrah from Red Willow Vineyard has become a hot wine in the Northwest. Total production remains under 1,000 cases.

CHAMPOEG WINE CELLARS  *Willamette Valley, Oregon 1992*  From 20 acres established in 1974, Champoeg specializes in estate-grown Chardonnay, Riesling, and Pinot Noir. However, it also offers Mueller-Thurgau, Pinot Gris, and Gewurztraminer that are popular in its tasting room. In vintages with hard-to-ripen fruit, it also produces Pinot Noir Blanc.

CHATEAU BENOIT  *Willamette Valley, Oregon 1979*  Situated on a hilltop, Chateau Benoit affords visitors a wonderful view of Oregon farmlands and the Willamette Valley. Back in 72 the Benoit family built their first winery in the south, due west of Eugene. But when owner and then-winemaker Fred Benoit decided to devote all his time to winemaking, he also decided to move closer to the winemaking center near McMinnville. While still farming 10 acres of Pinot Noir in the south, the Benoits have planted 22 acres to vines on their 65-acre estate. For a few years the winery was known for its balanced, fruity Müller-Thurgau and Riesling. However, in the mid-80 s it began focusing more on Pinot Noir and Chardonnay. The quality of those two wines has been erratic. The winery is now at the 7,000-case-a-year production mark, about halfway to its goal.

---

CHATEAU BIANCA   *Willamette Valley, Oregon 1991*   Owned by the Wetzel family, which developed vineyards in Forest Grove in the 1970 s, Chateau Bianca produces a wide array of varietal, proprietary blends, and sparkling wines. The family's 15-acre vineyard is planted to Chardonnay, Pinot Noir, and a smattering of other varieties. Annual production of 6,000 cases is led by Chardonnay and Riesling. Most sales are direct at the winery.

---

CHATEAU STE. MICHELLE   *Woodinville, Washington 1934*   This winery, which was originally located in the industrial sector of Seattle, produced fruit and berry wines for many years. In 67, it made a few thousand cases of vinifera varietals from an experimental vineyard in the Yakima Valley. Then in 74, the U.S. Tobacco Company purchased Chateau Ste. Michelle and invested several million dollars in vineyard development and winemaking facilities. A new winery/visitors center was built in 76 in the woodsy area of Woodinville, just outside Seattle. In the 70 s, the winery developed a reputation for varietally correct Riesling, Gewurztraminer, Semillon, and Grenache. Its early efforts with red wines, especially Pinot Noir, led to disapointment. Most of its wines were made in an old facility located in the Yakima Valley town of Grandview; but as production grew in the 80s, the owners constructed a third facility, known as River Ridge, along the Columbia River and closer to the company's 3,000 acres of vineyards. However, Ste. Michelle has shifted its entire red winemaking program to a fabulous new facility also within view of the Columbia River. Known as Canoe Ridge Estate Vineyard, this winery, which has replaced the old Grandview facility, was ready for the 94 crush. It is focusing on Merlot, Cabernet Sauvignon, Ste. Michelle's Reserve Meritage blend, and one limited production white, a Canoe Ridge Estate Chardonnay. Most of the grapes crushed are grown in the newly developed 420 acre vineyards planted on the slopes of Canoe Ridge.

From these three facilities, Ste. Michelle enjoyed solid growth, and as the wine market evolved into different segments, Ste. Michelle created new brands to keep pace. Out of the River Ridge facility, the winery introduced the Columbia Crest label, originally for low-end-priced white wines, but now a complete line (see entry). Under the Ste. Michelle label, the focus falls on a line of varietals led by Chardonnay, Cabernet Sauvignon, and Merlot. In the late 80 s Ste. Michelle released a series of vineyard-designated Chardonnays, Merlots, and Cabernet Sauvignons. This exciting single-vineyard program has expanded to include Chardonnay from Cold Creek Vineyard, Indian Wells Vineyard (a relatively warm site located at the base of the Wahluke Slope), as well as Canoe Ridge. Located directly across the river from Indian Wells, Cold Creek is one of the oldest vineyards in Columbia Valley. Merlot is now offered from three vineyards—Canoe Ridge, Indian Wells, and Cold Creek Vineyard. There is also a Cold Creek Vineyard Cabernet Sauvignon, and in cooler vintages such as 92, 93, and 95, the winery bottles Cabernet Franc from Cold Creek. In some vintages Cabernet Sauvignon is separately bottled from Horse Haven Vineyard, another major vineyard that is also the source of Ste. Michelle's lively Sauvignon Blanc.* In addition to the single-vineyard, limited-edition wines, Ste. Michelle offers Reserve Chardonnay, Reserve Merlot, an Estate Red, and, when the vintage cooperates, Late Harvest Riesling, Late Harvest Semillon, and an Ice Wine Reserve. An Artist Series red Meritage, a collector's item, sits at the top of this extensive roster. Its sparkling wines, for years the object of considerable research, are now labeled "Domaine Ste. Michelle." Made by the *méthode champenoise,* this line has grown to 200,000 cases. Overall, Ste. Michelle table wine production (excluding Columbia Crest) is moving toward 750,000 cases a year.

**Cabernet Sauvignon**

83°   85   86°   87   88   **89°**   **90°**   **91**   **92°**   **93°**   94

*Medium-intensity fruit suggesting currants and cherries is quietly supported by sweet oak and firmed by moderate tannins; the wines seem to age well for several years*

### Cabernet Sauvignon

(Cold Creek Vineyard)   78°   80   **85°**   **87°**   **91**   93

*Bold tannins but only medium fruit; ages longer than the winery's regular bottling*

### Chardonnay

(Columbia Valley)   86   87   88   90   91   92   93   94   95   96

(Cold Creek Vineyard)   90°   91   92°   93°   94°   **95°**   .96

*Mild fruit, slightly citrusy in cast, is filled out partially by oak in these brisk, firm, sometimes too lean wines; the Cold Creek is riper, deeper and oakier*

### Merlot

81   82   84   86°   87°   **88°**   92   **93°**   **94**   95

*A medium-bodied wine with cherryish and herbal flavors, it has been unable to sustain its fruit in earlier vintages but has done better lately*

---

CHEHALEM   *Willamette Valley, Oregon 1995*   After buying the "going nowhere fast" Veritas Winery and its vineyards, a partnership headed by Harry Peterson-Nedry set this winery on a fast and quality-minded track. The partners have access to 127 acres spread over three sites: Ridgecrest, Stoller, and Corral Creek. Ridgecrest contains the winery's oldest Pinot Noir, and Corral Creek is a favored site for Pinot Gris and Riesling. Stoller now has 62 acres, but it has another 300 acres of prime land that could be developed. After enlisting the consulting services of Patrice Rion from Burgundy's Domaine Daniel Rion, the owners settled down to produce Pinot Noir, Pinot Gris, Chardonnay, a dry Riesling, and Cerise, a fruit-forward blend of Pinot Noir and Gamay. The two Reserve Pinot Noirs (Ridgecrest and Rion Reserve) have clearly stood out in the early vintages, but the Reserve Chardonnay, produced entirely from a selection of Dijon clones, also has attracted considerable attention. Annual output has moved up to 7,500 cases and will increase to 12,000 once all the replanted vineyards return to production.

---

CHINOOK WINES   *Prosser, Washington 1983*   Owners Kay Simon and Clay Mackey both worked for Chateau Ste. Michelle before starting Chinook. Simon was a winemaker, and Mackay was in charge of vineyard operations. Both left to start independent consulting businesses, but a short time later they married and decided to run their own winery. All grapes are purchased for the winery's line of Chardonnay, Semillon, Sauvignon Blanc (blended with Semillon), Merlot, and occasionally a Cabernet Franc. Showing tremendous depth and complexity, Chinook's Semillon may well be one of the finest made in the United States today. Also selling out days after its release, the Merlot usually is full of juicy, berry flavors. Production has been steady at 4,000 cases per year. The goal is about 6,000 cases.

---

CLAAR CELLARS   *Pasco, Washington 1996*   One of many diversified farms in the area, Claar carved out 70 acres of vineyards in the midst of 300 acres of apples and asparagus. With its south-facing exposure, the vineyard site bodes well for high-quality grapes. After selling the first 15 harvests, the Whitelatch family hired winemaker Tom DiBello, who had been with Stag's Leap Wine Cellars, and eased into winemaking. In the early vintages Riesling in a dry and Late Harvest style was the main wine offered, but the winery is now making Cabernet Sauvignon, Merlot, Chardonnay, and experimental lots of Sangiovese and Syrah. Growing quickly to 20,000 cases, Claar is an up-and-coming winery.

---

COLUMBIA CREST   *Paterson, Washington 1984*   This brand developed almost by chance. In the early 80s Chateau Ste. Michelle bought a huge processing plant and surrounding corn fields and turned them into a winemaking facility and vineyards covering about 2,000 acres. In 84, with a grape surplus on its hands, the owners used this winery at River Ridge to process the excess grapes and divert them toward a stopgap generic wine program. Under the name "Columbia Crest," they bottled a blended-white Table Wine and a Blush. Experiencing strong demand, Columbia Crest was converted into its own brand by 87, offering a line of low-priced varietals. The mainstays are Chardonnay and Sauvignon Blanc among whites, and Merlot and Cabernet Sauvignon for reds. A Semillon-Chardonnay blend is among its best sellers.

With strong advertising support and good value in the bottle, Columbia Crest grew to sales of over 750,000 cases by 95. The $26 million winery has become the showcase of the area and is in effect run today as a separate but equal sister brand of Chateau Ste. Michelle. Recent additions to the Columbia Crest line include an "Estate Series" group of varietals (once labeled "Barrel Select"), with a little more depth and complexity than the popular-priced Columbia Valley varietals. The Estate Series wines are Cabernet, Chardonnay, Merlot, and Sauvignon Blanc. A Reserve program includes rare and unusual wines such as the Ice Wine and Late Harvest Semillon made in some vintages. Also part of the Reserve line are Chardonnay, Syrah, Reserve Red, and Willamette Valley Pinot Noir. To date all Reserve wines have merited the special designation, and the Red Reserve, a Bordeaux blend, is definite major-league material.

COLUMBIA WINERY    *Bellevue, Washington 1962*    This brand evolved over time from a winery known as Associated Vintners. Started in 62 as an association of amateur vintners, many of them working for the University of Washington, Associated Vintners acquired acreage in the Yakima Valley. Its commercial wines made in 67 were of high enough quality to gain the attention of winemakers in Washington and elsewhere. The first well-publicized Washington vinifera wine was this winery's Gewurztraminer. After moving to a larger facility in 76, the partners increased production to close to 10,000 cases a year. By 84 the winery was suffering financially and sold its vineyards. At that time David Lake, winemaker since 79, was put in charge of the entire operation, and the brand name was changed to Columbia Winery.

In 88, with production at the 100,000-case mark, Lake moved the winemaking operation to Woodinville. Though presently offering a large line of varietals, Columbia is focusing attention on Chardonnay, Semillon, Cabernet Sauvignon, and Merlot. Two vineyard-designated Cabernets—Red Willow Vineyard and Otis Vineyard—have been especially noteworthy. Two Merlots are offered, including one from Red Willow Vineyard. Lake has added Cabernet Franc, Syrah, Pinot Gris, and Sangiovese to the roster. From the Red Willow Vineyard, the Syrah shows tremendous promise. Production is steady at 110,000 cases a year.

COOPER MOUNTAIN VINEYARDS    *Willamette Valley, Oregon 1987*    About 15 miles southwest of Portland, Cooper Mountain is an extinct volcano that overlooks the Tualatin Valley. In 78 vineyardist Bob Gross purchased a 125-acre estate on the mountainside and began developing a vineyard. He now has 75 acres planted to Pinot Noir, Chardonnay, and Pinot Gris. Most of the crop from his vineyard is sold to others. However, in 87 Gross hired a winemaking consultant and has since been producing 2,000 cases of estate-grown Pinot Noir, Pinot Gris, and Chardonnay. Its record for Pinot Noir shows steady improvement, and its Pinot Gris is one of the best made in Oregon.

COVENTRY VALE WINERY    *Grandview, Washington 1983*    From its inception until 86, this 1-million-gallon winemaking facility was a custom-crush outfit. Several rapidly expanding wineries in the 80 s, especially Columbia Winery, used it to handle the bulk of their crush. In 86 owners David Wyckoff and Donald Toci decided to bottle some of their own wine. The first bottling was something less than 1,000 cases of an estate-grown Cabernet Sauvignon. A modest line of *méthode champenoise* sparkling wines also is available under the Coventry Vale label. With over 600 acres of vineyards established, the owners may move into the bottled-wine business in a significant way.

COVEY RUN VINTNERS   *Zillah, Washington 1980*   Known as Quail Run until 86, Covey Run changed its name in order to avoid legal battles with Quail Ridge, a California winery. The vineyards are planted to Riesling (70 acres), Chardonnay (30 acres), Cabernet Sauvignon (30 acres), Merlot (20 acres), and Chenin Blanc (25 acres). Producing 65,000 to 70,000 cases a year, Covey Run purchases Sauvignon Blanc as well as additional tonnage of Merlot and Chardonnay. Offering one of the largest lines of table wines in the state, Covey Run devotes 50% of its attention to Riesling and Chardonnay; the other half is given over to Fumé Blanc, Merlot, and Lemberger. A red grape developed in Germany, Lemberger has been made in a variety of styles by Covey Run. Acquired by Associated Vintners (Columbia Winery, Paul Thomas) in 1996, Covey Run has improved its Reserve Program, which includes Cabernet, Merlot, and Chardonnay.

**Chardonnay**

| (Yakima Valley) | 84° | 7̶2̶ | 87 | 89 | 90° | 92 | 93° |
|---|---|---|---|---|---|---|---|
| (Reserve) | 89 | 90°° | 91 | 92 | | | |

*Inconsistent to date, these wines are simple, straightforward, fruity, low in oak, and sometimes a little on the earthy side; the Reserve is oakier but rarely deeper or much more interesting*

CRISTOM VINEYARDS   *Salem, Oregon 1992*   After Pellier Cellars closed its doors, the property was purchased in 92 by Paul Gerrie, a wine lover who runs an oil-exploration company in Pennsylvania. He immediately began replanting the old 90-acre vineyard, concentrating on Pinot Noir and Chardonnay. Pinot Gris also has been planted and is now in the lineup. Pinot Noir and Chardonnay, each with a regular and a Reserve bottling, receive most of winemaker Steve Doerner's attention these days. Cristom's annual production will grow to 7,000 cases.

CUNEO CELLARS   *Willamette Valley, Oregon 1993*   Located in the Eola Hills, Cuneo specializes in red wines from its 5-acre vineyard. Cabernet Sauvignon, Merlot, and Pinot Noir top the list. "Cana's Feast" is the proprietary name given to the Cabernet Sauvignon.

DELILLE CELLARS   *Washington 1992*   This family-owned winery is a small but spare-no-expense facility near Chateau Ste. Michelle's headquarters in Woodinville. Only two wines are produced, both made from Cabernet Sauvignon, Merlot, and Cabernet Franc. The top of the line is named "Chaleur Estate" and is made from several vineyard sources. Wines that do not make it into that bottling are sold under the name of "D2." In either case, aging takes place for approximately 20 months in new French oak. The quality level is extremely high. The winery also makes minuscule amounts of Estate Blanc (barrel-fermented Semillon and Sauvignon Blanc) as well as a single-vineyard Cabernet Sauvignon from Harrison Hills. Most of the 3,000-case annual production consists of Chaleur Estate and D2.

DENINO ESTATE WINERY   *Umpqua Valley, Oregon 1988*   On the outskirts of Roseburg, Dino DeNino established 24 acres to a variety of wine grapes. The majority are planted to Cabernet and Merlot, along with Sauvignon Blanc and Semillon. He also has half-acre blocks of Sangiovese, Dolcetto, and Malbec. Annual output of 2,000 cases is mainly Cabernet, Merlot, and Papa's Legacy, a Meritage blend.

DiSTEFANO WINERY   *Seattle, Washington 1993*   After trying to produce world-class sparkling wine for several years under the Domaine Whittlesey Mark label, the owners created the DiStefano brand for Cabernet Sauvignon and Fumé Blanc. These two wines were so well received that the name now covers the bubbly as well. Because owner Mark Newton is a high-profile Microsoft executive, the activity of this wine producer tends to get noticed in the Northwest and also by slick wine magazines, which feed on any kind of celebrity status. However, though definitely displaying lavish amounts of new oak, the first vintages of Cabernet hit the * level. Annual output will stay level at 2,000 cases.

DOMAINE DROUHIN    *Willamette Valley, Oregon 1988*    In 87, Maison Joseph Drouhin, the highly respected wine firm in France's Burgundy, purchased 100 acres in the Red Hills of Dundee for the purpose of producing Oregon Pinot Noir. Today, the Drouhins own 180 acres in the area, where they have built a 15,000-case-capacity facility. The eight-floor-high winery is designed to allow all wine to be moved by gravity only. Over its first three vintages, Domaine Drouhin made about 2,000 cases a year, all from purchased grapes. As of 91, its wines are made entirely from grapes from the Drouhin vineyards adjacent to the winery. The first four vintages, 88 to 91, garnered °° or °°°, and turned Drouhin into a much-followed producer. Since 1992 the winery has bottled a special estate Pinot Noir labeled "Laurene," and Drouhin also has been offering a few hundred cases of Chardonnay from its own 5-acre parcel. Annual production has reached 12,000 cases.

### Pinot Noir
**88°°°   89°°   90°°   91°°°   92°°   93°°   94°°°   95°**

*The leading Pinot Noir of Oregon and among the best on the entire West Coast, the wine is loaded with ripe, layered fruit buttressed by creamy yet spicey oak and firmed by medium tannins*

DOMAINE SERENE    *Willamette Valley 1990*    In 89 the Evenstad family purchased 42 acres of vineyard land in the Dundee Hills area for the purpose of producing only Pinot Noir. The following year Ken Evenstad produced two versions, a "Reserve" and an "Evenstad Reserve." For a few vintages, a Carter Vineyard Pinot has been offered. As production moves toward 2,500 cases a year, the Evenstad Vineyard Pinot has emerged as the quality leader. Made by traditional techniques, the Pinot Noirs are bottled unfiltered.

DUCK POND CELLARS    *Willamette Valley, Oregon 1989*    In 1986 the Fries family developed 13 acres to Chardonnay and Pinot Noir southwest of Dundee, and the family made its first vintage in 1989. An additional 30 acres, half Chardonnay and half Pinot Noir, were planted in 1988. Chardonnay and Pinot Noir top the line, which also includes Riesling, Pinot Gris and Gewurztraminer. After moving into a new winemaking facility in 1993, the owners were on a course to take annual production up to 30,000 cases. Most of the wines are made in a no-nonsense, drink-now style, and they have been priced fairly. Cabernet from Washington State soon will be coming from the winery's vineyard on Wahluke Slope.

ELK COVE VINEYARDS    *Willamette Valley, Oregon 1977*    After outgrowing their original winery, a converted barn, Joe and Pat Campbell moved into a new winery in 81 which enjoys a spectacular setting on a ridgetop separating Yamhill from Washington County. The initial 22-acre vineyard has been expanded to 45 acres. The Campbells grow Pinot Noir, Chardonnay, Riesling, and lesser amounts of Gewurztraminer and Pinot Gris. Theirs was among the first vineyards on the West Coast to adopt the French system of close vine spacing. Among the wines offered, Elk Cove routinely produces Cabernet Sauvignon and a late-harvest Riesling. In most years, Elk Cove bottles one or two vineyard-designated Pinot Noirs in addition to its own estate-bottled and Reserve Pinot Noir. The winery's style of Pinot Noir captures enough depth to place some wines in the ° category.

Usually Elk Cove ferments Pinot Noir in 200-gallon bins for maximum extraction and to allow for frequent punching down of the cap. Its barrel-fermented, *sur lie*–aged Chardonnays have not appealed as much, lacking real focus in some vintages. A new 100-acre vineyard planted to Dijon clones should help improve the Chardonnay picture once the vines reach maturity. However, Elk Cove's Rieslings are among the best made in Oregon, and the winery's Pinot Gris are also noteworthy. All told, Elk Cove has earned its stripes for good winemaking, and it is one of the more reliable names in the Northwest. It is making about 7,000 cases a year. With vineyard maturity, the winery could be at its full capacity of 40,000 cases a year within a decade.

EOLA HILLS WINE CELLARS  *Willamette Valley, Oregon 1986*  Eola Hills Wine Cellars is owned by Tom Huggins, a well-known vineyardist who worked with Elk Cove for several years. Huggins built his own winery in 86. The vineyard, located in the emerging Eola Hills region, now has 66 acres under vine. The primary varieties planted are Chardonnay, Pinot Noir, Sauvignon Blanc, and Cabernet Sauvignon. Winemaker Ken Wright, formerly with Ventana Vineyards and Talbott in Monterey County, arrived in 86 and made the Eola Hills wines for three vintages before giving way to another winemaker. The early vintages of Eola Hills Pinot Noirs have been acceptable in quality, and its Cabernet Sauvignons showed some promise, especially when compared to other Oregon Cabernets. Today, with an emphasis on single-vineyard Chardonnay and Pinot Noir, the roster is a lengthy one. Heading the list from a quality standpoint are Pinot Noir from Temperance Hill Vineyard and the Estate bottling. Perhaps if the winery made fewer wines, the list of above-average wines would be longer. Annual production is 10,000 cases.

ERATH VINEYARDS  *Willamette Valley, Oregon 1968*  One of the oldest producers and one of the largest, Erath is located high in the Red Hills area of Dundee. In 68, on the advice of Dick Sommer of Hillcrest Vineyards, Dick Erath came to Dundee from California to develop a vineyard. The spot he picked in the Red Hills area ranks among the more picturesque vineyards today. In 72 he became partners with Cal Knudsen, who also owned a vineyard, and their first crush, made in a basement, yielded 400 cases. Currently Erath is once again the sole owner, and Knudsen is a partner in Argyle. The winery owns a total of 103 acres, and contracts with local growers for more grapes or leases. Erath believes in fermenting Pinot Noir in small, closed, stainless-steel tanks, but at high (90–95°F.) temperatures. The malolactic fermentation is encouraged to occur simultaneously with the alcoholic fermentation. Erath also insists on an extended maceration period after fermentation.

Chardonnay, 100% barrel-fermented with extended *sur lie* aging, Pinot Gris, Pinot Blanc, and Riesling (as a rule made slightly sweet), are the other major varietals offered. Occasionally when the Riesling develops *Botrytis*, Erath offers a "Vintage Select" dessert-style Riesling. Made in modest quantities, Gewurztraminer and Cabernet Sauvignon fill out the varietal lineup. A small-volume line of *méthode champenoise* wines is only available locally. The winery's total production now stands at 50,000 cases a year, with Pinot Noir accounting for about 40% in a typical vintage.

EVESHAM WOOD VINEYARDS  *Polk County, Oregon 1986*  Relying on their 10-acre vineyards located just outside of Salem, Russell and Mary Raney make Chardonnay, Pinot Noir, and Pinot Gris under this brand. Their annual production is steady at 2,000 cases. Overall, the quality level is high. The winery's Tête de Cuvée Chardonnay is one of Oregon's best, and the Pinots in their many manifestations show skillful winemaking.

EYRIE VINEYARD  *Willamette Valley, Oregon 1970*  The indisputable champion for Pinot Noir in Oregon, owner-winemaker David Lett arrived in 66 and selected the Red Hills of Dundee as the site for his vineyard. Lett, a graduate of U.C. Davis, was the first to plant vinifera grapes in the northern Willamette Valley, and ended up with 26 acres planted to Pinot Noir and Chardonnay. In the late 70s a few acres of Riesling were replaced by Pinot Gris. Today, Eyrie has close to 50 acres. Unlike most Oregon winemakers, Lett never supported the Riesling variety. However, beginning in the early 80s he began campaigning in favor of Pinot Gris as Oregon's second best white wine after Chardonnay. In the town of McMinnville, Lett converted a turkey-processing plant into an efficient winery, with a production capacity of 15,000 cases.

Eyrie's lineup today consists of Pinot Noir, occasionally a Reserve Pinot Noir, Chardonnay, Pinot Gris, and Muscat Ottonel, made in a dry style. Pinot Gris has emerged as the volume leader. Pinot Noir remains the flagship, though. In its history, Eyrie has produced some of Oregon's finest Pinot Noirs. Eyrie's Chardonnays are generally well made and typical of the respective vintages. On occasion, they have enough depth to merit °. Despite the attention devoted to Pinot Gris, Eyrie was surprisingly erratic with this wine, but from the mid-1990s on, its Pinot Gris has displayed deeper flavors and better balance.

**Pinot Noir**

83°   84   86   87   88°   89°   92   94

*Exhibiting more range than depth, this set of fruity, sometimes thin wines can capture elusive hints of spices and herbs to go along with medium body and oaky richness in better vintages*

**FACELLI WINERY**   *Redmond, Washington 1984*   Louis Facelli, the owner and winemaker, started making wines under this label in Idaho. It was there that he made a noteworthy vintage of Chardonnay from Washington grapes and first developed a modest following. However, in an attempt to raise capital, he sold controlling interest in that business venture and was ultimately edged out. He moved to the present location, taking his name with him, and started over. In 88 Facelli was back in business with a line of Washington varietals. The mainstays in this 5,000-case-capacity winery are Chardonnay, Semillon, Riesling, and Merlot.

**FIRESTEED**   *Seattle, Washington 1992*   A virtual winery in the sense of being a marketing company without vineyards and winery, Firesteed set out to offer Oregon Pinot Noir priced under ten bucks. The company contracts for grapes and then has them custom-crushed and fermented. Within a few vintages, sales of the Oregon Pinot Noir had reached 10,000 cases a year. The niche marketing concept has been successful enough for Firesteed to reach out to Italy in 1995 to import a Barbera from Asti under the Firesteed label.

**FLYNN VINEYARDS**   *Willamette, Oregon 1990*   By Oregon standards, Flynn became an overnight success and is now one of the big-volume producers. Its original vineyards were developed in 1982 and have been expanded to 123 acres. Owner Bob Flynn, like others before him, set out to make great sparkling wine by the traditional champagne method. Like most others who learn the capital-intensive reality of that product, he subsequently branched out into a line of Pinot Noir, Chardonnay, and Pinot Gris. Now representing 20% of the winery's 85,000-case production, the bubbly consists of a Brut and a vintage Blanc de Blanc aged for 5 years *en tirage*.

**E. B. FOOTE WINERY**   *Seattle, Washington 1978*   Gene Foote, an engineer with Boeing Aerospace, was a home winemaker for years before turning pro. In 1996 he sold the winery to Rich Higginbotham, who continues making about 1,000 cases a year. Chardonnay and Cabernet Sauvignon from Columbia Valley are the main items. Most sales are direct from the winery, located in Seattle's Southpark area.

**FORIS VINEYARDS**   *Cave Junction, Oregon 1987*   Founders Ted and Meri Gerber planted 24 acres of grapes in the remote wilderness area near Cave Junction in 1974. Since then, in partnership with the neighboring Berard family, they have planted 42 more acres to wine varieties. As producers, they are concentrating on Cabernet, Merlot, Pinot Noir, Chardonnay, and Gewurztraminer. Included in the line are Pinot Blanc, Pinot Gris, and Gewurztraminer. One of the first to cultivate all available Dijon clones of Chardonnay and Pinot Noir, Foris has come on strong in the 1990s with Pinot Noir from the Rogue Valley. Its deluxe Maple Ranch Pinot Noir can be exceptional. The winery also has made great quality improvements in its barrel-fermented Chardonnay. Merlot from both the Rogue Valley and from Klipsun Vineyards in Washington place Foris at the top of producers of Northwest Merlot. Expanding in the 1990s to 30,000 cases a year, Foris also has managed to upgrade quality by several levels and demonstrate to some degree that Rogue Valley is a bona fide, distinctive appellation.

GIRARDET WINE CELLARS   *Umpqua Valley, Oregon 1983*   In 72 Bonnie and Philippe Girardet, with limited experience in grape growing, deciding to quit the academic profession and move to Oregon to start a vineyard. They bought 55 acres in the foothills west of Roseburg, and planted 18 acres to Pinot Noir, Chardonnay, Riesling, Sauvignon Blanc, and a range of hybrids on an experimental basis. Girardet's first crush was in 83, but it was not until 86 that the winery began making Pinot Noir and Chardonnay in significant quantities. In addition, it now offers blended red and white table wines from the hybrids and vinifera, labeled "Vin Blanc" and "Vin Rouge." These blends represent over one-third of the winery's annual output, which is close to the maximum level of 9,000 cases.

GLEN FIONA WINERY   *Walla Walla 1995*   Owned by Berle Figgins, brother of Gary Figgins of Leonetti Cellars, Glen Fiona is an emerging and closely watched Rhone wine specialist. After its 1995 Syrah was judged best overall wine in the Northwest, Figgins, who studied winemaking in Australia, began developing a small Syrah vineyard in Walla Walla. At present he offers three bottlings of Syrah—Reserve, Walla Walla, and Columbia Valley. Small amounts of Viognier and a Grenache-Cinsault blend have been added to the lineup. Current production of 2,200 will level off at 4,000 cases in a few years.

GORDON BROTHERS CELLARS   *Pasco, Washington 1983*   Potato farmers for many years, Bill and Jeff Gordon decided to try their hand with wine grapes. On family property located 10 miles northeast of Pasco above the Snake River, they began vineyard development in 80 and now have over 80 acres of vineyards. Their primary varieties are Chardonnay, Sauvignon Blanc, Cabernet Sauvignon, and Merlot. Occupying a beautiful, protective site, Gordon's vineyards have been under contract to Hogue and are known to be among Washington's finest for red grapes. In the mid-90s Jeff Gordon, who had dabbled as a wine producer, decided it was time to get serious. Holding back a certain percentage for his own label, he turned winemaking over to a professional staff that now oversees the production of Merlot, Cabernet Sauvignon, Chardonnay and Tradition, a red Meritage. The reds, especially the Merlot, stood out in the early vintages of Gordon Brothers' comeback. Annual output is steady at 5,500 cases.

HEDGES CELLARS   *Benton City, Washington 1990*   Owners Tom and Anne-Marie Hedges began making wines in 88, and built their own cellars by 90. The family's 40-acre vineyard is located in the southeastern corner of the Yakima Valley. In a prime red wine area now known as Red Mountain, the 40-acre vineyard is half Cabernet and half Merlot. Whether lucky or clever, Hedges had an inside track in the export market, so the winery was able to expand production quickly. Secondly, Hedges opted to price its volume wines, and up-front fruity Cabernet-Merlot blend and a Fumé-Chardonnay, at attractive price levels. It was sailing along selling about 75,000 cases, and the sailing was so smooth the Hedges built a showcase winery in the Red Mountain area. As it moves toward the optimum production level of 100,000 cases a year, Hedges makes 1,000–1,500 cases of Red Mountain Reserve Red and 3,000 cases of Three Vineyard Cabernet. Both are major-league wines capable of competing with the finest Cabernets from California.

HENRY ESTATE WINERY   *Umpqua Valley, Oregon 1978*   After working for several years in the aerospace industry in California, Scott Henry returned to Oregon to begin running the family ranch and to explore the possibility of developing a vineyard. Started in 72, the now 31-acre vineyard beside the Umpqua River contains Pinot

Noir, Chardonnay, and Gewurztraminer. Henry also produces Müller-Thurgau and Riesling, the latter occasionally in an award-winning *Botrytis*-affected dessert-wine style. The winery is expanding steadily, and its annual output, led by Pinot Noir and Chardonnay, has increased from 4,000 cases in 85 to 14,000 cases today.

HILLCREST VINEYARD   *Umpqua Valley, Oregon 1963*   As indicated by the founding date, Hillcrest was the true pioneer in the state, especially with vinifera wines. After graduating from U.C. Davis, Dick Sommer went north in search of a vineyard site and settled on a farm about 10 miles west of Roseburg. This was the first post-Prohibition vinifera vineyard to be established in Oregon, and today it covers 35 acres. Sommer has always devoted most of his attention to viticulture, leaving the winemaking to others for most of the winery's history. Hillcrest's specialty is Riesling, usually in a dry style, but a late harvest version is produced whenever possible. It is one of Sommer's beliefs that Riesling improves with bottle aging, and to prove his point he releases his Riesling a year or more after the vintage. In 78 Hillcrest produced a rare Ice Wine from Riesling. Chardonnay, Pinot Noir, and Cabernet Sauvignon are the other key wines offered. Hillcrest is one of the few Oregon wineries to grow and produce Zinfandel. The winery's annual production has reached the peak level of 8,000 cases.

HINMAN VINEYARDS   *Willamette Valley, Oregon 1979*   Located about 10 miles southwest of Eugene, Hinman emerged in the 80 s as the renegade Oregon winery. Its production, with a strong emphasis on Washington State grapes, approached 40,000 cases a year, and in the late 80 s the facility was custom-crushing for several brands. Hinman also made a point in its marketing to offer wines priced below the norm for Oregon. Most of its grapes come from the large Bordman Farms in Washington; the winery itself is surrounded by 27 acres of vineyards. The primary varietals offered today are Pinot Noir, Chardonnay, Riesling, Gewurztraminer, and Pinot Gris. A line of Charmat sparkling wine is also made. Silvan Ridge (see entry) is its Reserve line of higher-priced varietals.

HINZERLING VINEYARDS   *Prosser, Washington 1976*   Mike Wallace, owner and winemaker, was one of the pioneer grape growers in the Yakima Valley. His first vineyard was planted in 72, and when it was reaching maturity, he built a winery in the valley, the first to be established there. The 30-acre vineyard contained Cabernet Sauvignon, Chardonnay, Gewurztraminer, and Riesling. Over the winery's first decade, Wallace produced several acceptable Cabernets, and a host of late harvest, *Botrytis*-affected Gewurztraminers (labeled "Die Sonne") and Rieslings. In 87 Wallace sold the winery to pursue other interests, then bought it back in 89. Today it is making about 3,500 cases a year.

HOGUE CELLARS   *Prosser, Washington 1982*   The Hogue family own a 1,500-acre ranch and farm, and for many years were the most important hop growers in the state. Gradually, they became diversified farmers, adding potatoes, mint, asparagus, Concord grapes, and row crops, and moved into cattle farming. In 74–75, they established a small vinifera vineyard, and by 82, when the vines were producing, they began making wines. Hogue's first vintages of Riesling and Chenin Blanc emphasized fruitiness in a refreshing, slightly sweet style. Both became quite popular, and Hogue began to augment its vineyard holdings. In 84, Rob Griffin came to Hogue from Preston Vineyards and served as winemaker, guiding the winery through the next growth phase.

Today, Hogue's vineyard covers 500 acres, with Chardonnay (60 acres) and Riesling (50 acres) as the leaders, followed by Sauvignon Blanc, Chenin Blanc, Cabernet, and Merlot, each in the 20–25-acre range. In 85, the winery produced 45,000 cases; in 89, it made 175,000, with plans to grow to 350,000. It grows about 40% of the grapes now crushed. Recently, Hogue has produced ° caliber zesty Fumé Blanc, and a Semillon of some interest. These two are its most consistent successes. Its red wines are led by a solid-quality Cabernet Sauvignon, and some of the most attractive Merlot from the Northwest. In better vintages, its Reserve Cabernet

Sauvignons and Merlots are especially rich and ageworthy. An upscale line of limited-volume wines is grouped under the Genesis logo. To date Genesis consists of Syrah, Cabernet Franc, Barrel Fermented Semillon, Blue Franc (Lemberger), Cabernet Sauvignon, and Crawford Vineyard Chardonnay.

### Cabernet Sauvignon

84°   85   86°   87   89°   90   91   92   93   94

*Early success has not been repeated in the 90s*

### Chardonnay

(regular bottling)   86   88   89   90°   92   93   94   95   96

*Less than ambitious in approach, these wines offer medium fruit, somewhat brisk acidity and a background of oak*

### Merlot

(regular bottling)   85°°   86°   87°   88°   89°   90   91°   92°
**94°**   95

*Ripe, round, cherrylike wines of supple texture and moderate tannins*

---

HONEYWOOD WINERY   *Salem, Oregon 1934*   The state's oldest wine producer, Honeywood offered only fruit and berry wines for many years. In the late 70 s it began developing a line of vinifera varietals. Today it produces the typical range—Chardonnay, Pinot Noir, Riesling, and Gewurztraminer. In the 80 s, as sales continued to increase, Honeywood began making what it calls "Twin Harvest" wines that combine vinifera wine with fruit juice. With two tasting rooms, a gift shop, and a full lineup, Honeywood is one of Oregon's biggest producers, making more than 70,000 cases of assorted products.

---

HOOD RIVER VINEYARD   *Hood River, Oregon 1981*   East of Portland in an area where few vines grow, owner and home winemaker Cliff Blanchette started his own winery. After making fruit wines for a few years, in 74 he began planting a vineyard at the intersection of the Columbia River and the Cascades. From this 12-acre vineyard in an area known as the Hood River, he produces Chardonnay, Pinot Noir, Zinfandel, Cabernet Sauvignon, Riesling, and Gewurztraminer. The winery also makes wines from locally grown pears and raspberries. The grape wine line has grown to about 3,000 cases a year.

---

HOODSPORT WINERY   *Hoodsport, Washington 1980*   One of the few wineries on the western Olympic Peninsula, Hoodsport is best known for a line of fruit wines, but in the mid-80 s it branched out with a line of vinifera. Although most of the winery's 15,000-case output continues to consist of fruit and berry wines, it started upgrading its grape wine production in 87. Chardonnay, Riesling, Gewurztraminer, and Merlot have become regular items.

---

HORIZON'S EDGE WINERY   *Zillah, Washington 1985*   Aptly named, Horizon's Edge is perched on a ridgetop overlooking the Yakima Valley. Founded by Tom Campbell, one-time winemaker for Jekel Vineyards and Chateau Ste. Michelle, Horizon's Edge has a 20-acre vineyard planted half to Chardonnay, with the remaining acreage planted to Muscat and Pinot Noir. Favoring ripe grapes and barrel fermentation for Chardonnay, Campbell has enjoyed some success with the early vintages. Cabernet Sauvignon and Muscat are also part of this 3,000-case winery's line.

---

HUNTER HILL VINEYARDS   *Othello, Washington 1984*   In the northern sector of the Columbia Valley appellation, Hunter Hill is part of a 200-acre farm owned by airline pilot Arthur Byron. In 81 he began developing 28 acres of Riesling, Gewurztraminer, and Merlot. The first few vintages were produced in leased space by a succession of consultants. Annual production has averaged 2,000 cases.

**HYATT VINEYARDS**   *Zillah, Washington 1987*   With their vineyard located in the foothills of the Rattlesnake Mountains north of Zillah, the Hyatts have been grape-growers for many years. However, they were basically growing Concord until, in the early 80s, they converted 73 acres to vinifera. Chardonnay, Cabernet Sauvignon, Sauvignon Blanc, Riesling, and Merlot are the primary varieties planted. The first crush in 87 doubled in 88 to 5,000 cases. The Hyatts built a winery with a capacity of 25,000 cases. With recent planting of Cabernet Sauvignon, Merlot, and Syrah, Hyatt now has 97 acres developed and is close to its 25,000-case production goal. Merlot, Cabernet, Chardonnay, and Fumé Blanc are the major wines offered, with lesser amounts of Syrah, Riesling, and Muscat rounding out the primary line. The most impressive wines are the Reserve Cabernet* and Merlot* produced in most vintages, the occasional Late Harvest Riesling, and rare but gorgeous Sauvignon Blanc Ice Wine, which was last made in 1995. First produced in 1995, Syrah looks like a rising star.

**INDIAN CREEK WINERY**   *Kuna, Idaho 1987*   Owner William Stowe is a native of Idaho who returned after retiring from the Air Force. In 82 he began developing 15 acres of vineyards, and a few years later converted a mule barn into a small winery. With a production capacity of 4,000 cases a year, Stowe is producing White Riesling, Pinot Noir, Chardonnay, and Chenin Blanc. The Riesling, labeled "Almost bone dry," is the best-selling wine.

**KING ESTATE WINES**   *Eugene, Oregon 1992*   In the southern end of the Willamette Valley, the King family acquired a 550-acre estate in 90. Plans were immediately under way to develop 400 acres to vineyards, and a winery with a capacity of 150,000 cases was ready in time for the 92 harvest. King's first few vintages were made from purchased grapes, and the early offerings consisted of Chardonnay, Pinot Noir, Pinot Gris, and Cabernet. The winery makes a rare but good Zinfandel from Oregon. King Estate could be the largest winery in Oregon in ten years.

**KINGS RIDGE**   *(Rex Hill Vineyards)*   This second label is used for lower-priced Chardonnays and other wines from the estate vineyard.

**KIONA VINEYARDS**   *Benton City, Washington 1980*   On the eastern side of the Yakima Valley in a subregion known locally as Red Mountain, the owners of Kiona planted 30 acres in 75. On otherwise barren land growing little save sagebrush, they drilled their own well, a rarity in the area, and began planting Chardonnay, Chenin Blanc, Riesling, Cabernet Sauvignon, Merlot, and Lemberger. A partnership of two families—Pat and Jim Holms, and Ann and John Williams—Kiona has continued to sell grapes as it eased into winemaking. After moving into a new facility in 83, annual production increased to 15,000 cases. At various times, Kiona has been successful with barrel-fermented Chardonnay, the slightly sweet Riesling, and Chenin Blanc. The owners prefer making Lemberger in a ripe, oak-aged style. Reasonably priced, Kiona's red wines are made in an easygoing, user-friendly style, and the Merlot and Lemberger are reliable wines for everyday enjoyment.

**KRAMER VINEYARDS**   *Willamette Valley 1989*   From 12 acres planted in 84, the Kramers eased into winemaking in 89. Having been successful amateur winemakers, they built a small winery in 88 where they now make Pinot Noir, Chardonnay, Pinot Gris, and a Dry Riesling. Annual production is gradually expanding from 1,000 cases to the winery's capacity of 4,000 cases. The limited edition Reserve Chardonnay and Reserve Pinot Noirs are Kramer's top-quality wines.

**KRISTIN HILL WINERY**   *Willamette Valley, Oregon 1990*   Located just north of Amity, this winery sells a wide assortment of wines in its popular tasting room. Its roster includes Chardonnay, Pinot Noir, Gewurztraminer, and *méthode champenoise* sparkling wine. Annual production approaches 1,000 cases.

**LANGE WINERY**   *Willamette Valley, Oregon 1987*   Don Lange was teaching school in Santa Barbara when he first became interested in wine. In his spare time, he began working for Ballard Canyon and the Santa Barbara Winery, and became intrigued by Pinot Noir. He and his wife first visited Oregon in March 87, returned to buy 27 acres in the Dundee area in May, and moved in by June. In September, the Lange Winery made its first commercial wine. The roster focuses on Chardonnay, Pinot Noir, and Pinot Gris. Lange's estate vineyard consists of 6 acres of Pinot Noir and 2 acres of Pinot Gris. Traditional winemaking practices are followed, even for the Pinot Gris, which is barrel-fermented and aged *sur lie.* Production is expected to grow gradually to an annual level of 5,000 cases.

**LA BOHEME VINEYARD**   *(Elk Cove Vineyards)*   Introduced in 89, this is a special label for wines made from the 14-acre La Boheme Vineyard. Situated on steep, south-facing slopes adjacent to the winery's primary estate vineyard, this vineyard was planted in 85 to Pinot Noir and Chardonnay. Elk Cove is using "La Boheme" as a label for a few hundred cases each of Pinot Noir and barrel-fermented Chardonnay. So far, the Pinot has been the more successful of the two, often earning °.

**LATAH CREEK WINE CELLARS**   *Spokane, Washington 1982*   Owner Mike Conray gained experience by working four years at Hogue Cellars before establishing his own winery in Spokane. In the first few vintages, Latah Creek developed a following in the Northwest for Riesling and Chenin Blanc. However, Merlot is the wine Conray set out to focus on. Owning no vineyards, he has bought Merlot from Hogue as well as other growers. Chardonnay, Cabernet Sauvignon, and Semillon are other wines in his lineup. Latah Creek's annual production has grown to 14,000 cases, close to full capacity. One of the most consistent wineries in the Northwest, Latah Creek has developed a loyal following for Merlot and Lemberger; the latter is often considered the best of the breed.

**LAUREL RIDGE WINERY**   *Tualatin Valley, Oregon 1986*   On one of the oldest vineyard sites in Oregon, Laurel Ridge is the latest and probably the last winery to operate there. Located on a knoll just west of Forest Grove, the winery has been involved in several ownership changes. One of the first to commence here in the modern era was the Charles Coury Winery, making wines that ranged from acceptable to below average. After Coury left the business, the same facility was soon making wines under the name of Reuter's Hill Vineyard. When it too went out of business, three couples in the Portland area formed a partnership and rescued the facility in 86, giving it a fresh start under the Laurel Ridge name. The 24-acre vineyard adjacent to the winery has been brought back to life, and the owners also have another 50 acres under vine in Yamhill County. The primary varieties planted are Pinot Noir, Gewurztraminer, Sauvignon Blanc, Sylvaner, and Riesling. White varietal wines and blends top the list of table wines, and *méthode champenoise* sparkling wines, headed by a Brut, represent about 30% of the total output. The winery's maximum capacity is 10,000 cases.

**LAVELLE WINERY**   *Willamette Valley, Oregon 1977*   In 71–72 Lee Smith began developing his 17-acre vineyard in a then-untried wine region west of Eugene in the southern Willamette Valley. Acting from instinct, Smith planted the typical varieties for Oregon, Pinot Noir, Chardonnay, Riesling, and Pinot Gris, but added a few acres of Cabernet Sauvignon. The Smiths celebrated their first crush in 77. As time went by, their production came to focus more and more on Pinot Noir, Riesling, and Pinot Gris. In 1995 Smith sold Forgeron Vineyard to Doug LaVelle, who now operates it under the LaVelle Winery name.

**L'ÉCOLE NO. 41**   *Lowden, Washington 1983*   In a building that once housed classrooms for School District 41, Jean and Baker Ferguson once occupied one floor as their home, and used the two others for a winery and tasting room. Located 12 miles west of Walla Walla, it is the only building of any size in the area. Merlot and Semillon are the major wines offered. Now in the capable hands of winemaker Marty Clubb, the winery has blossomed in the 1990s. A new and much larger facility now sits behind the old schoolhouse. Its barrel-fermented Semillon is one of the finest made, and Clubb has gained considerable fame for Merlot. In addition to its Columbia Valley Merlot, which Clubb blends from as many as eight vineyards, L'École added Merlot from Seven Hills Vineyard, which started off with a real bang. Now Clubb is showing a fine hand with Cabernet Sauvignon from Windrow Vineyard in Walla Walla and from Columbia Valley. Apogee, a proprietary blend of Merlot and Cabernet, is produced from Pepper Bridge Vineyard, a source L'École shares with neighbors Leonetti and Woodward Canyon. Cabernet will increase in importance as the winery grows from the present 12,000 cases to 15,000 cases a year level.

LEONETTI CELLAR   *Walla Walla, Washington 1977*   A red-wine-only winery, Leonetti specializes in Merlot and Cabernet Sauvignon, offering regular and Reserve bottlings in most years. Owner-winemaker Gary Figgins started out in a makeshift building behind his home and by the early 80 s was producing 500 cases a year. However, several early vintages gained awards and distinctions, and along the way Leonetti became something of a cult winery. A new winery on the property has allowed production to expand to 4,500 cases. Generally, we find Leonetti's style of winemaking to be in need of some restraint. However, the Merlot and Cabernet have earned high ratings at times. In the late 1990s Figgins began developing his own Cabernet and Merlot vineyard adjacent to Seven Hills. He also is making Sangiovese, which is as big and powerful as the variety allows. In recent years Leonetti sells every bottle available during its once-a-year open house.

MARQUAM HILLS VINEYARD   *Willamette Valley 1988*   From 20 acres established on the remote eastern edge of Willamette Valley, Marquam offers a typical full arsenal of Oregon wines. The roster includes Chardonnay, Pinot Noir, Pinot Gris, Gewurztraminer, Riesling (in several sweetness levels), and Mueller-Thurgau. Annual output is moving in on 4,000 cases.

MATTHEWS CELLARS   *Woodinville, Washington 1994*   Moving into the high-rent district occupied by Ste. Michelle, Columbia Winery, and DeLille Estate, Matthew Loso is hoping to make a name for himself as a red wine specialist. A Bordeaux blend is his primary interest, with Cabernet Sauvignon and Merlot offered in tiny quantities. As annual production edges toward 3,000 cases, Matthews still is almost all potential, but it remains a winery to watch.

MCCREA CELLARS   *Lake Stevens 1988*   A family-owned winery, McCrea Cellars divides its winemaking attention between Chardonnay and a group of Rhone-inspired wines. Two Chardonnays are bottled, one from Columbia Valley and the second from the Elerding Vineyard in Yakima Valley. Attracting considerable interest today is Doug McCrea's Rhone program, which includes Syrah, Viognier, Grenache, and a blend of Syrah and Grenache, "Tierra del Sol." Recent vintages of Tierra del Sol, Syrah, and Elerding Chardonnay have impressed. As annual production edges toward 3,000 cases a year, Syrah will represent about one-third.

MCKINLAY VINEYARDS   *Willamette, Oregon 1987*   McKinlay made its first wines in 87. Its owners, the Kinne family, are making only Pinot Noir and Chardonnay in their small winery. The maximum combined output is about 800 cases.

MONT ELISE VINEYARDS   *Bingen, Washington 1975*   After experimenting with almost every available grape variety, owner Charles Henderson selected Gewurztraminer, Pinot Noir, and Gamay as the most suitable for the Bingen area. He developed 50 acres in a subregion known as the Columbia River Gorge, and built a winery to the east of Bingen. At one time Henderson had several partners, and his winery was known as Bingen Wine Cellars. In 78 he bought out the partners, and the winery's name was changed to Mont Elise, after his daughter Elise. The winery specializes in Gewurztraminer, Gamay, and sparkling wine made from Pinot Noir. It has a production capacity of 7,500 cases.

MONTINORE VINEYARDS    *Tualatin Valley, Oregon 1987*    On a 600-acre estate, the Graham family began developing vineyards in 82. Located just south of Forest Grove, the vineyards covered 450 acres by the late 80 s, and the winery—which resembles a grand old manor house—stood out in the middle of them. The major varieties planted are Pinot Noir (150 acres), Chardonnay (108 acres), White Riesling (45 acres), and Pinot Gris (35 acres). From its beginning, this winery wanted to become Oregon's biggest and most ambitious. It is geared to making a line of varietal wines and for sparkling wines that will be aged in specially built caves. In 87 it began by making limited amounts of varietals, and by 90 it was making close to 50,000 cases. The lineup of varietals is led by Pinot Noir and Chardonnay, and includes Riesling, Pinot Gris, and Gewurztraminer. The winemaking facility was built to handle a maximum of 150,000 cases. To date both the crisp Pinot Gris and the Reserve Pinot Noir have frequently earned best values citations.

MOUNT BAKER VINEYARDS    *Everson, Washington 1982*    One of the first wineries trying to grow grapes successfully in western Washington, Mount Baker is in the northwest corner of the state about 11 miles east of Bellingham. It has two vineyards totaling 25 acres, with the older planting started in 77. It grows conventional cool-climate varieties, such as Gewurztraminer, Müller-Thurgau, and Chardonnay, but plantings also contain some obscure grapes, such as Madeline Angevine (from the Loire Valley) and Okanogan Riesling (a Canadian variety). Enjoying some success with whites in a slightly sweet style, the winery began to show improvements with oak-aged Chardonnays. Production overall has averaged between 10,000 and 12,000 cases per year.

NORTHSTAR    *Grandview, Washington 1994*    A collaborative effort between winemaker Jed Steele of California and Gordy Hill of Washington's Columbia Crest, Northstar is a brand backed by Stimson Lane to showcase Columbia Valley Merlot. Allowed to use some of the finest vineyards, the winemakers make wine in a full-throttle style, and later cherry-pick the best barrels for Northstar. Blended with Cabernet and aged in French oak for 16 months, Northstar Merlot has been impressive from the get-go. Initial production of 1,000 cases has expanded to 2,500.

OAK KNOLL WINERY    *Tualatin Valley, Oregon 1970*    West of Portland in the northern Tualatin Valley, Oak Knoll has a history which mirrors that of the Oregon wine industry. Founded in 70 by the Vuylsteke family, who converted their hobby, homemade fruit and berry wine, into a part-time business, it was within a few years turning out some of the best fruit and berry wines made anywhere. Beginning in 75, the winery started making vinifera wines and gradually over the years shifted its emphasis more and more to varietals. Now producing about 32,000 cases of vinifera wines, over 80% of its output, Oak Knoll buys all grapes from several Oregon growing regions. Heading its list are Pinot Noir, Chardonnay, Riesling, Cabernet Sauvignon, Gewurztraminer, and generic blends, and it still makes a highly enjoyable Loganberry and Raspberry wine. On occasion, Oak Knoll's Pinot Noirs rise above the crowd.

PANTHER CREEK CELLARS    *Willamette Valley, Oregon 1986*    After making wines in California from 79 to 85, winemaker Ken Wright moved to Oregon in 86 primarily because he wanted to work with Pinot Noir. Before joining in the start-up of Panther Creek, he moonlighted to raise money and finally found a site in an industrial part of McMinnville. Panther Creek makes about 3,000 cases of Pinot Noir. Buying grapes from the Eola Hills area, the owner believes in a long fermentation and maceration period of over three weeks for Pinot Noir. The first vintages were among the most intense and tannic produced in Oregon. The winery also produces a Melon varietal. Wright sold out his interest in 1994 to start his own winery. Owners Ron and Linda Kaplan have continued producing Melon and the standout Chardonnay from Celilo Vineyard, and have expanded the single-vineyard Pinot Noir offerings. Today Panther Creek bottles Pinots from Freedom Hill, Shea Vineyard, and Bednarik, along with a Reserve. The maximum production target is 7,500 cases a year.

PATRICK M. PAUL VINEYARDS   *Walla Walla, Washington 1988*   In the early 1980s Patrick Paul planted several wine varieties in his 4.5 acre vineyard. To date he has achieved modest success as a winemaker with his Cabernet Franc and Merlot. Cabernet Sauvignon and Chardonnay are also planted. The winery's annual production is close to the 1,000 case optimum level.

PINTLER WINERY   *Nampa, Idaho 1988*   Longtime agriculturists in the Snake River area, the Pintler family started growing grapes in 83. In 87 the buyer for their first full crop backed out at the last minute, so the Pintlers custom-crushed it themselves at another facility. After making their first vintage under the Desert Sun name, they built a winery and changed their brand to the present name in 88. Pintler now has 12 acres under vine. The wine roster consists of Riesling, Semillon, Chardonnay, Merlot and Pinot Noir. Currently, annual production is close to the winery's 4,500-case capacity.

PONTIN DEL ROZA   *Prosser, Washington 1984*   With both vineyard and winery situated beside the Roza Canal, the Pontin family have been farming in the Yakima Valley since the early 50s. They began developing their 15-acre vineyard in 79, and planted Riesling, Chenin Blanc, Merlot, Cabernet, and Chardonnay. Using the Coventry Vale facility, they started making wines in 84. To date, Riesling in a slightly sweet style has been the most consistent wine.

PONZI VINEYARDS   *Willamette Valley, Oregon 1974*   One of the pillars of Oregon wine-making, Ponzi is jointly managed by Dick and Nancy Ponzi. The winery is located in Beaverton, about 15 miles southwest of Portland, tucked away in the middle of rolling farmlands. From its initial 10 acres planted in 70, Ponzi now has 95 acres near the winery and contracts with two local growers within a close radius. On the estate Ponzi grows Pinot Noir (two distinct clones), Chardonnay, Pinot Gris, and Riesling. The winery was among the first in Oregon to make a Pinot Gris, and Ponzi was among the first to produce a "white" Pinot Noir; it is now proud of being among the first to quit making it. In the 1990s, the winery became Oregon's first producer of Arneis, a rare Italian white wine, and recently it has made Vino Gelato, Ponzi's Italian version of a Riesling ice wine.

Producing a truly dry Riesling since 75, Ponzi manages to be successful with this wine the majority of the time. Chardonnays are 100% barrel-fermented in a combination of Allier and Limousin oak, and the quality level is usually average. Ponzi's Pinot Noirs often display a minty, earthy, and tobacco leaf combination that is unusual, but not always easy to appreciate. In making Pinot Noir, Ponzi ferments in 300-gallon open vats and at temperatures in the mid-80s (F). Aging takes place in French oak with about 30% new barrels each year; the Reserve Pinot Noir is aged longer in barrel. The winery's total production is 15,000 cases a year. The Ponzis also own Bridgeport Brewing Co., a small brewery.

PORTTEUS VINEYARDS   *Zillah, Washington 1987*   The Portteus family purchased property in the Yakima Valley and developed a 50-acre vineyard. Cabernet Sauvignon and Chardonnay dominate the planting, with a few acres devoted to Semillon. Barrel-fermented Chardonnays have not been as impressive as the early Cabernet Sauvignon vintages. Merlot and Syrah are newcomers to the roster. Long-term, the winery will expand to about 10,000 cases.

POWERS WINERY   *Kennewick, Washington 1992*   A sister label to Badger Mountain (see entry), Powers is a line of attractively priced varietals from Bill Powers' 75-acre vineyard. Offering the standard lineup of Cabernet, Merlot, Chardonnay, and

Fumé Blanc, Powers has recently been performing admirably with a velvety smooth yet intensely flavored Cabernet Sauvignon from Mercer Ranch and a rich Chardonnay that is a real bargain. Also good but priced up there with the big boys is the Powers Merlot. Not to be overlooked, the Cabernet-Merlot blend is made for quality everyday enjoyment.

PRESTON WINE CELLARS  *Pasco, Washington 1976*  By 80 this family-owned winery was earning critical praise and winning many awards on the strength of its Fumé Blancs and Chardonnays. Then the winery seemingly lost its winning ways and faded into the background. Since 84 it has had a succession of winemakers. The quality became inconsistent and even the Fumé Blancs have not been as successful as in the early vintages. The Merlot has been dreadful and the Cabernet Sauvignon (in both regular and Reserve bottlings) has been average. By the mid-1990s Preston finally showed signs of coming out of its tailspin, and both Merlot and Cabernet Sauvignon have been back on a pleasant course. The winery owns 180 acres of vineyards in the southern part of the Columbia River Valley. Annual output has averaged 60,000 cases.

QUILCEDA CREEK VINTNERS  *Snohomish, Washington 1979*  Cabernet Sauvignon is the primary wine of this small winery located just 25 miles north of Seattle. Owner-winemaker Alex Golitzin graduated from U.C. Berkeley with a degree in chemistry and moved to the Northwest, where he has been working for a paper company. Making wines in his spare time, Golitzin buys Cabernet from the Yakima Valley, Kiona Vineyards being a frequent supplier. He was encouraged to pursue winemaking commercially by his uncle, the famous winemaker André Tchelistcheff. In each of the first two vintages he made 200 cases of Cabernet. Today, he keeps production under 2,500 cases. The wine is aged for two years in French and American oak barrels, most of which are new each year. Rarely seen beyond Washington's borders, Quilcada Creek Cabernet enjoys a very favorable local reputation. Also high-priced, Merlot from the Ciel du Cheval Vineyard has joined the roster.

RANDALL HARRIS WINES  *Seattle 1994*  The entrepreneurial spirit hit Randy Leitman, who operates Randall Harris. Rather than build his own winery, he buys grapes from the Columbia Valley and arranges to have his wines custom-made at Washington Hills Cellars. His line is headed by Cabernet and Merlot, with a Reserve Red and Chardonnay also adding to the 6,000-case annual production.

REDHAWK VINEYARD  *Salem, Oregon 1988*  Owner Tom Robertson was a Portland businessman who developed a passion for wine in the late 70 s. Redhawk Vineyard began with 5 acres planted in 79, and today the total planted is 17 acres. Early on, Robertson earned a reputation as a maverick who does not hold back in his approach to winemaking. His regular and Reserve Pinot Noirs are neither fined nor filtered, and the quality has been extremely erratic. Several of Redhawk's lesser wines sport humorous labels, and its most popular is a blended Pinot Noir labeled "Grateful Red." Chardonnay is the winery's second most important wine. Production at Redhawk is moving toward an annual goal of 6,000 cases.

REX HILL VINEYARDS  *Willamette Valley, Oregon 1983*  Situated on a hilltop overlooking the town of Newberg, Rex Hill is by Oregon standards a fairly ornate winery. Although its large tasting room has a few more gold fixtures than might be necessary, it occupies a building that was formerly a fruit and nut drying shed. Founded in 83 by Paul Hart, who now is chairman of the corporation, Rex Hill has a knack for gaining attention. It was the first Oregon winery to price its wines at over $20 a bottle, and it changes prices each year based on the perceived quality. The winery occupies a 22-acre site, with 11 acres planted to Pinot Noir and 4 acres to Chardonnay. All wines were produced from purchased fruit through 88. Today Rex Hill owns or manages 225 acres of vineyards.

Crushing grapes from as many as 12 suppliers within the Willamette Valley, Rex Hill developed a reputation for vineyard-designated Pinot Noirs; about 60% of its total production is Pinot Noir. Its white wines consist of Chardonnay, Pinot Gris, Riesling, and Sauvignon Blanc. However, Pinot Noir is the mainstay, and in some vintages Rex Hill has bottled five vineyard-designated and two blended Pinot Noirs. Many of its Pinot Noirs have been firmly structured, medium-bodied wines, often earning ° ratings.

ROGUE RIVER VINEYARDS   *Illinois Valley, Oregon 1984*   Situated in southwestern Oregon, Rogue River Vineyards is owned by four families who pooled their resources and talents in 81 and began working on weekends to build the winery over the next three years. From its 5-acre vineyard and purchased fruit, it produces a line of popular-styled table wines such as slightly sweet blush wines and Nouveaux reds. Its two conventionally made wines are Chardonnay and Cabernet Sauvignon. Most of the winery's efforts are focused on the wine types that sell in its tasting room in Portland as well as at the winery. Rogue River is currently operating at its full capacity of 8,000 cases a year.

NICOLAS ROLIN WINERY   *Willamette Valley, Oregon 1990*   A family-owned winery emphasizing Pinot Noir made by traditional winemaking practices. Purchasing grapes from vineyards within the Willamette Valley, owners Trent and Robin Bush ferment the must in open-top fermenters and add about 30% whole berries. After being aged one year in small oak barrels, the wine is bottled unfiltered. A few cases of Chardonnay are now made each year, to bring total production to 1,000 cases.

ROSE CREEK VINEYARDS   *Hagerman, Idaho 1984*   Having at one time been involved in potato and wheat growing, Jamie Martin became interested in vineyards in 80. With both winery and vineyards located southeast of Boise and just a few miles east of the Snake River, the Martin family has the only winery in the area and sold most of its first few vintages directly to visitors. Riesling and Chardonnay are the two primary varieties planted in the 30-acre vineyard. As production grew to the 5,000-case per year level, Rose Creek has settled on Riesling, Cabernet Sauvignon, and Chardonnay from Idaho. A popular Blush, "Rose Creek Mist," has been the best-seller in the tasting room.

SETH RYAN WINERY   *Yakima Valley 1984*   Trying its best to outboutique California's boutiques, Seth Ryan is developing an 80-acre vineyard site in the Red Mountain District adjacent to Kiona. Until that vineyard comes on-line, the owners will continue purchasing grapes from most of the best-known vineyards in Columbia Valley. Based on its performance to date, Merlot and Cabernet Sauvignon are the potential superstars. Cabernet Sauvignon from Klipsun Vineyard, oak-aged for more than 3 years, is deep and unfathomable, but the regular Cabernet Sauvignon and Merlot are made in an accessible style. Gewurztraminer, Riesling, and Rapture, a pink wine, fill out the line of this 4,000-case producer.

STE. CHAPELLE VINEYARDS   *Caldwell, Idaho 1976*   The winery to first put Idaho on the wine map, Ste. Chapelle is among the largest in the Northwest today. Founded in 76, Ste. Chapelle was originally located in Emmett, where its founder, Bill Broich, built a small winery. Grapes were purchased primarily from the Symms Ranch, a large 200-acre vineyard located in the warmest viticultural region of Idaho, known as Sunny Slope. In 76 the Symms family became a partner in the business, and by 79 the Symms were controlling owners and immediately built a large (175,000-case-capacity) winery in Sunny Slope. Broich stayed as winemaker until 85.

From the winery's 180-acre vineyard, Ste. Chapelle produces Riesling, Chardonnay, Gewurztraminer, and several sparkling wines, the majority of which are made by the Charmat process. It also produces Cabernet Sauvignon and Merlot grown in Washington, along with Chenin Blanc, sometimes from Idaho, sometimes from Washington. But Riesling is the primary wine produced, and in copious years the amount bottled exceeds 40,000 cases. In most vintages Ste. Chapelle's Rieslings retain about 2.5% residual sugar. An experiment with a drier version (1% sugar) resulted in the regular production of a Dry Johannisberg Riesling. Two Chardonnays are in the line: the inexpensive, no-oak "Canyon Chardonnay," and the oak-aged "Idaho Chardonnay." Although the winery is experimenting with *méthode champenoise* sparkling wine, it turns out close to 30,000 cases a year of Charmat-produced Riesling, Chardonnay, and Blanc de Noirs sparklers. Annual production has edged up to 150,000 cases. Ste. Chapelle's wines rarely receive ratings higher than average.

ST. INNOCENT WINERY *Salem, Oregon 1988* A limited partnership made up of local wine lovers, this winery began by making 400 cases in 88. Its current production is 5,200 cases. Owning no vineyards, St. Innocent makes vineyard-designated Pinot Noir and Chardonnay and a sparkling wine by the *méthode champenoise.* All are from the Willamette Valley appellation. In the early rounds, its Chardonnay was from the O'Connor Vineyard, and the Pinot Noir from the Seven Springs Vineyard. With winemaker Mark Vlossak now in charge and making full-blown wines, the winery offers Pinot Noir from O'Connor Vineyard, Seven Springs Vineyard, Brickhouse Vineyard, and a Willamette Valley blend. Chardonnays are made from Seven Springs, O'Connor, and Freedom Hill Vineyard. A newcomer to the line is Pinot Gris, and soon it will be accompanied by a fruity-style Tocai. Annual output has reached 5,000 cases, about half being Pinot Noir. Our favorite has been the Seven Springs Pinot Noir, which in ripe vintages can be noteworthy.

SALISHAN VINEYARDS *La Center, Washington 1976* In southwestern Washington about 30 miles north of Portland, Linc and Joan Wolverton planted 11 acres to wine grapes. Beginning the vineyard in 71 when they were both amateur winemakers, they moved the family close to the vineyard and started this commercial venture in 76, though until 82 they actually made wine at other wineries. In their own 4,000-case-capacity winery, they are emphasizing Pinot Noir and Chardonnay (partially barrel-fermented), along with Cabernet.

SECRET HOUSE VINEYARDS *Willamette Valley 1989* Balancing production of sparkling wine and table wine much better than most wineries of its size, Secret House owns a 15-acre vineyard planted to Pinot Noir, Chardonnay, and Riesling. Northern Silk and Red Silk are the names of its two well-made sparkling wines produced by the classic Champagne method. Of the table wines, Secret House has a knack for making lively Riesling, and occasionally its Reserve Pinot Noir rises above average.

SERENDIPITY CELLARS *Monmouth, Oregon 1981* After an apprenticeship at Amity Vineyards, owner Glen Longshore began developing a vineyard and winery in the Eola Hills region. The 3-acre vineyard is adjacent to his home and contains two varieties atypical for the region, Maréchal Foch and Chenin Blanc. Regularly produced in quantities of 200 cases each are Pinot Noir, Chardonnay, Müller-Thurgau, and Zinfandel. In light or cool seasons, the red varieties are made into blush wines. All told, the annual output is holding steady at 2,000 cases.

SEVEN HILLS WINERY *Walla Walla 1988* While its winery is located in the Oregon part of Walla Walla, Seven Hills makes most of its wines from the appellation's Washington side. To make sure wine lovers are paying really close attention, the winery's owners buy Cabernet Sauvignon and Merlot from a vineyard they developed but no longer own, Seven Hills Vineyard. After a few overdone early vintages, the winery has settled down and is making several noteworthy wines. Topping the list are its Merlots from three appellations: Columbia Valley, Klipsun Vineyard, and Seven Hills Vineyard in Walla Walla. Both single-vineyard Merlots are often immense, powerful, mouth-filling wines. Cabernet Sauvignon also are made from the same three appellations, and again both the Klipsun Vineyard and Seven Hills Vineyard tend toward the powerful, well-oaked side of the spectrum. As its annual output zeros in on 5,000 cases, the winery also makes small batches of Pinot Gris and Pinot Blanc from Oregon and Syrah from Walla Walla.

SHAFER VINEYARD CELLARS   *Willamette Valley, Oregon 1981*   After developing a 30-acre vineyard in 73, owner Harvey Shafer sold his crop until his own winery was constructed in time for the 81 crush. Located in the Tualatin Valley area, unlike most of its neighbors the winery both outside and inside resembles a small modern California facility. The estate vineyard provides most of the Pinot Noir, Chardonnay, and Riesling grapes needed to produce the three primary varietals. Lesser amounts of Sauvignon Blanc are also grown and made as a varietal that in some warm years has the depth to soften its pungent nature. Barrel fermentations have been the norm for Shafer's Chardonnays, while for Pinot Noir the winery uses small-scale bins to facilitate punching down of the cap by hand. With Chardonnay and Pinot Noir leading the way, the winery's annual production is at the maximum 8,000-case level.

SILVAN RIDGE   *(Hinman Vineyards)*   This name belongs to Hinman Vineyards, which in the early 90 s considered using it in place of Hinman. Recently, however, Hinman wines have won several medals at wine competitions, and the owners decided to stay the course with Hinman.

SILVER LAKE WINERY   *Woodinville 1988*   Having been reinvented several times, Silver Lake is now headquartered in Woodinville, where it also has created a visitor's center. Silver Lake produces sparkling wine by the traditional Champagne method, along with a line of varietals and a few Hard Fruit Ciders for nonwine drinkers. The latest developments at Silver Lake were made possible by a public stock offering. Today, with many shareholders, the winery intends to expand its sparkling wine production.

SISKIYOU   VINEYARDS   *Illinois Valley, Oregon 1978*   One of the pioneer wineries in southern Oregon, Siskiyou began developing its 12-acre vineyard in 74. Located at 1,800 feet above sea level, the vineyard site is hospitable to late-ripening varieties, and the two primary grapes planted are Cabernet Sauvignon and Semillon. The winery has been operated by Suzi David since 83, and produces Cabernet Sauvignon, Pinot Noir, Müller-Thurgau, and Chardonnay. Annual production tops 7,000 cases.

SNOQUALMIE WINERY   *Snoqualmie, Washington 1983*   What began as an exciting, dynamic new wine venture ran into many problems in the first few years. This winery was started by well-known winemaker Joel Klein along with several investors. The business went well enough until 87, when Klein and his partners became involved in the Langguth Winery. Before the year was done, Klein was out of both wineries. The brand stumbled along until 91, when Stimson Lane acquired it. Today it is offering a line of varietals including Cabernet Sauvignon, Chardonnay, Chenin Blanc, Riesling, and Fumé Blanc. Most of the grapes come from the Columbia Valley. Production is holding steady at 30,000 cases a year. Part of the facility is given over to a line of low-priced varietals widely distributed within Washington State, marketed under a second label, "Saddle Mountain." The winery's setting, in the hills east of Seattle, is among the most attractive in all of winedom.

SOKOL BLOSSER WINERY   *Willamette Valley, Oregon 1977*   In 71 Bill Blosser and Susan Sokol purchased 125 acres of bare land in Dundee, close to a vineyard owned by Eyrie Vineyard. By 74 they were selling the first crop from their 45-acre vineyard and raising capital to build a winery. Both the winery and tasting room were completed by 77, and the 30,000-case-capacity winery was one of the biggest in Oregon for a decade. In 78 it made what is believed to be the first varietal Müller-Thurgau in the U.S. Over the next few years the owners gradually increased production and were operating at peak capacity by 85.

The home vineyard contains Riesling, Pinot Noir, Chardonnay, and Gewurztraminer. In addition to a Sokol Blosser bottling, Pinot Noir is made from the Hyland Vineyards and the Durant Vineyards, whose owners became shareholders in the winery in 87. These two grape-growing partners combine to bring the total acreage controlled by the winery to 135. A fourth Pinot Noir, the most interesting and successful of this group—usually receiving ° ratings—is a blend of the estate vineyard and the Durant Vineyard labeled "Redland." A fifth Pinot Noir bottling, and the lightest in style, is identified as Yamhill County. Both its Chardonnays and Pinot Noirs tend to be medium- to medium-full-bodied wines, with moderate oak, and they rise to ° rankings on occasion.

---

SOOS CREEK WINE CELLARS    *Renton, Washington 1989*    Owner-winemaker Dave Larson specializes in Cabernet Sauvignon which is usually blended with Merlot. He has been buying all grapes crushed from the Columbia Valley. The few hundred cases produced each year are aged 4 years in French oak prior to bottling. The tiny winery is located behind the Larsons' residence.

---

SPRINGHILL CELLARS WINERY    *Willamette Valley, Oregon 1988*    In the remote farmland area of mid-Willamette Valley, Springhill's owner, Mike McLain, tends to his 10-acre vineyard, half planted to Pinot Noir. Making Pinot Noir and Pinot Gris from the estate and Riesling from purchased fruit, McLain has moved close to the winery's capacity of 2,000 cases a year. His Estate Reserve Pinot Noir, made in 200-case lots, has recently attracted rave reviews.

---

STARR WINERY    *Willamette Valley, Oregon 1991*    Owning a Portland wineshop, Rachel Starr made fewer than 100 cases in her first vintage. Encouraged by the results, she and Eric Brown, now partner and winemaker, decided to expand the operation. Making Pinot Noir and Chardonnay from purchased fruit, the winery is now bottling 1,500 cases a year, divided equally between the two wines. To date the unfiltered Chardonnay has earned favorable reviews.

---

STATON HILLS VINEYARD & WINERY    *Wapato, Washington 1984*    An attorney by training, David Staton moved to San Francisco to head a new company and promptly got bitten by the wine bug. Unhappy with California's real estate prices, he purchased an apple orchard in the Yakima Valley, just a few miles outside of Yakima. After several experiments, he planted 16 acres to wine varieties and began making wine in 84. Today, Staton's winery, modeled after a country-style château, is one of the few genuine tourist attractions in the area. The winery makes Chardonnay (barrel-fermented), Sauvignon Blanc, Cabernet Sauvignon, Merlot, and Phoenix. Staton Hills became famous (or notorious) for being the first in Washington to make a "Pink Riesling," a blush wine made by adding a splash of red wine to the overproduced Riesling. In 1992 new owners came along to trim the line and get rid of the oddball pink wines and other weird things, including sparkling wines. Today's emphasis is on Cabernet and Merlot, and Phoenix, a red blend of the two. All reds are aged for close to three years in barrel, and the quality level has taken a giant leap up. Both whites—the Fumé Blanc and Chardonnay—are good wines for the price, and the Fumé Blanc is crisp and flavorful and definite * material. Annual output of 12,000 cases will gradually grow to 30,000.

---

STEWART VINEYARDS    *Sunnyside, Washington 1983*    Dr. George Stewart established his medical practice in Sunnyside in the early 60 s. He purchased an old estate where grapes once grew, and his interest in grape growing commenced. In the late 60 s he purchased 160 acres along the Wahluke Slope, and started planting what turned out to be 70 acres of vinifera. A winery was constructed, and has since been expanded to its current 14,000-case capacity. Though producing a large line of wines for its size, Stewart has been able to handle them all with moderate success. Chardonnay Reserve, Gewurztraminer, and Riesling (ranging from dry to late harvest) are highlights. Cabernet Sauvignon and Merlot are now the main wines.

TAGARIS WINERY   *Snoqualmie, Washington 1987*   Making their first vintages in rented space, vineyardist Mike Taggares and winemaker Peter Bos plan to locate in the town of Snoqualmie. Taggares (who altered the spelling of his name for the brand) owns 120 acres of vines in the Columbia Valley. The major varieties established are Riesling, Chardonnay, Sauvignon Blanc, Cabernet Sauvignon, and Pinot Noir.

TEFFT CELLARS   *Yakima Valley, Washington 1991*   Though still remembered in the Northwest for his early vintages of off-the-wall wines and oddball varietals, winemaker Joel Tefft now directs most of his attention to classic styled Cabernet, Merlot, and a Proprietor's Reserve Red, a Meritage blend. Apparently the delightfully wacky side was never totally repressed as the winemaker still offers Black Ice, an ice wine from Black Muscat, and a pink wine named "Rosey Outlook." Cabernets, especially the Cabernet Reserve, show Tefft at his best. From a 12-acre vineyard and purchased grapes, the winery makes about 3,000 cases annually.

TEMPEST VINEYARDS   *Willamette Valley, Oregon 1988*   Located in the vicinity of Amity, Tempest purchases grapes from several growers to produce Pinot Noir, Chardonnay, and Pinot Gris. That will eventually change once the 20-acre vineyard planted by owner Keith Orr reaches full production. All wines demonstrate excellent winemaking skills, and in some vintages the Winemaker's Reserve Pinot Noir rises above the crowd. The winery's annual output is steady at 2,000 cases.

TERRA BIANCA VINTNERS   *Yakima Valley, Washington 1993*   Located high on the slopes of Red Mountain, Terra Bianca is the first Washington winery to build underground aging caves. Owner Keith Pilgrim also developed 48 acres of vineyards in this prime region. Most of the acreage is devoted to Cabernet, Merlot, and Syrah. As winemaker, Pilgrim is offering Cabernet, Merlot, and Onyx, a red blend of the two. For white wines he is focusing on barrel-fermented Chardonnay, and Aria, a blend of Semillon and Sauvignon Blanc. When the climate permits, he plans to produce Late Harvest Riesling and Gewurztraminer. Long-term plans call for the winery's annual production to level off at 20,000 cases.

PAUL THOMAS WINERY   *Bellevue, Washington 1979*   Paul Thomas first became known in the Northwest for his "Crimson Rhubarb" wine and fruit wines. In 79, Thomas set up a modest winery in an industrial sector of Bellevue, just outside Seattle. For a few years he specialized in fruit wines and raspberry wine before branching out to offer a line of vinifera wines. Buying all grapes, Thomas offers Chenin Blanc, Chardonnay, Riesling, Cabernet Sauvignon, and Merlot. A Reserve Chardonnay, entirely barrel-fermented, was added in 87. Accentuating forthright fruitiness in his wines, Thomas has been consistent with its light-style Chenin Blanc and Riesling. Cabernet Sauvignon and Merlot have both been good values.

TORII MOR WINERY   *Willamette Valley, Oregon 1988*   Proprietors Don and Trish Olsen established their vineyard in 1972, making it one of Yamhill County's oldest. Today they produce limited quantities of Pinot Noir, Chardonnay and Pinot Gris. The vineyard has been expanded to 7.5 acres, and the owners also lease a 26-acre vineyard in the Red Hills area of Dundee. Quality began to improve dramatically in 1993 with the arrival of veteran winemaker Patty Green. Both Pinot Gris and Pinot Noir reached well-above-average quality in Green's first few vintages. The top wines are the Pinots from the appellations of Yamhill and Willamette Valley.

TROON VINEYARD   *Rogue Valley, Oregon 1992*   In an area of the Rogue Valley known as the Missouri Flats, Troon is a small winery surrounded by its 10-acre vineyard. Dick Troon planted Chardonnay, Cabernet, and Zinfandel, and produces wines from each variety. With annual production at 2,000 cases, Troon is developing a modest track record for his Reserve Cabernet Sauvignon.

TUALATIN VINEYARDS *Willamette Valley, Oregon 1973* Near the town of Forest Grove some 30 miles west of Portland, owners Bill Fuller and Bill Malkmus founded their winery in the middle of the Tualatin Valley. Fuller is a winemaker from California who worked for the Louis Martini Winery for nine years before moving north to join Malkmus, the marketing director, who is a graduate of Harvard Business School. After a long search for a site, they bought land and planted 85 acres to several cool-climate varieties with Riesling, Chardonnay, and Pinot Noir predominating. Also grown are Gewurztraminer and Müller-Thurgau. Best known for its Pinot Noir Reserve, Tualatin has also earned * for its Chardonnay Reserve in several vintages.

TUCKER CELLARS *Sunnyside, Washington 1981* One of the longtime growers in the Yakima Valley, the Tucker family have grown almost everything on their 500-acre farm. In the early 80 s when the market for sugar beets turned sour, the family looked around for another crop. Under the supervision of Dean Tucker, they planted 22 acres of vinifera varieties. Today, the vineyard covers 60 acres. Randy Tucker, Dean's son, manages the vineyard and winery operation. Cabernet Sauvignon, Chardonnay, Riesling, Gewurztraminer, and Muscat Canelli top the list of varietals produced. About 8,000 cases are made annually.

TYEE WINE CELLARS *Corvallis, Oregon 1985* This small winery is a partnership led by Barney Watson, the head of Oregon State University's Enology Department. So far 6 acres have been developed to several varieties, including Pinot Noir, Chardonnay, Pinot Blanc, Pinot Gris, and Gewurztraminer. The winery has a capacity of 2,000 cases a year.

UMPQUA RIVER VINEYARDS *Umpqua Valley, Oregon 1988* Within the Roseburg area, the DeNino family have developed a 20-acre vineyard. The plantings were oriented toward warm-weather varieties such as Cabernet Sauvignon and Sauvignon Blanc. By 88 the winery was making about 1,000 cases of table wine, with Cabernet Sauvignon the volume leader.

VALLEY VIEW VINEYARDS *Rogue Valley, Oregon 1978* The southernmost winery in all of Oregon, Valley View's 26-acre vineyard is at the 1,500-foot level of the Applegate Valley, a region that is the sunniest and warmest in the state. Developed in 72, the vineyard contains Cabernet Sauvignon, Merlot, and Chardonnay. From purchased grapes the winery produces Pinot Noir and Gewurztraminer. In terms of emphasis, this winery is trying to make a name for itself for Merlot and Cabernet Sauvignon. Anna Maria is the winery's Reserve moniker seen on small batches of Merlot, Cabernet Sauvignon, Reserve Red (Merlot, Cabernet blend), and Fumé Blanc. In the late 1990s the owners began developing 30 acres to Merlot, Chardonnay, Syrah, and Zinfandel. To date the winery is best known for Merlot, which tends toward a big, mouth-filling, and somewhat rough style. Total production is closing in on the target of 20,000 cases.

VAN DUZER *(William Hill Winery)* Napa Valley vintner and vineyard developer William Hill and his partners own a 500-acre vineyard site in the Eola Hills area. Hill developed the Van Duzer brand before planting the first vine. He has been purchasing grapes and leases space in several nearby wineries to produce Riesling, Chardonnay, and Pinot Noir, along with experimental batches of sparkling wine. As of now, wines have been marketed under two label designations, Reserve and Eola Selections. Most of the wines have displayed correct varietal personality, but the Pinots could benefit from a little more stuffing. Our favorite over the winery's history has been its brisk, bracing, and very varietal Riesling*. Annual total production is 30,000 cases.

WALLA WALLA VINTNERS  *Walla Walla 1993*  A partnership of three local wine lovers and amateur winemakers who could not resist going pro, this winery specializes in red wines, Cabernet, Merlot, and Cabernet Franc. Purchasing grapes from within Columbia Valley, the winery established fine winemaking credentials over its first vintages. As production moves toward the 3,000-cases-a-year goal, Cabernet and Merlot will be the primary wines, with about 500–600 cases of Cabernet Franc made each year.

WASHINGTON HILLS CELLARS  *Sunnyside, Washington 1988*  Going beyond plain to homely, this winery is actually a converted creamery plant. But looks aside, the winery has everything needed to function properly, and its line of wines, which extends beyond a dozen, contains a few hidden gems. For the price, you cannot go wrong with the Chardonnay, Merlot, and the Semillon-Chardonnay, which is made in a quaffable style. Lemberger is the quaffable red wine counterpart. The best bargain of them all often is the Cabernet-Merlot. With annual output steady at 100,000 cases, this winery is turning out nicely made, honest wines. It also owns W. B. Bridgeman (see entry) and Apex (see entry).

WATERBROOK WINERY  *Lowden, Washington 1984*  This family-owned winery is located in the Walla Walla region. Buying grapes from the Columbia Valley and elsewhere, Waterbrook concentrates on Sauvignon Blanc and Chardonnay for whites, and Cabernet Sauvignon and Merlot for reds. Owners Janet and Eric Rindal are among a small group of local vintners who have never made a Washington Riesling. In the 1990s Waterbrook developed 32 acres to Chardonnay and a smattering of other varieties. With Chardonnay representing half of its production, the winery is moving toward 40,000 cases as its maximum. Made from Klipsun Vineyard, Waterbrook's Merlot also has grown in importance and now includes a few hundred cases of a Reserve. For several years Waterbrook was touted as a good-value winery for Chardonnay and Cabernet, but once price increases took it out of that category, the winery now rests its laurels on Merlot. In recent vintages its Columbia Valley Merlots have been most attractive.

WESTON WINERY  *Caldwell, Idaho 1982*  One-time filmmaker and river guide Cheyne Weston decided to settle down and become a winery owner. To learn the trade, he apprenticed at Chateau Ste. Chapelle. He also developed 20 acres of vineyards in the Sunny Slope area above the Snake River. Riesling and Chardonnay are the major grapes planted, but Weston grows Gewurztraminer and Pinot Noir as well. He experimented with Zinfandel for several years, and continues to buy Cabernet Sauvignon from Washington State. With a capacity of 4,000 cases a year, Weston Winery devotes about 50% of its production to Riesling, with a barrel-fermented Chardonnay in second place. In recent years the winery has been producing a few hundred cases of sparkling wine by the *méthode champenoise*.

WESTRY WINES  *Willamette Valley 1993*  After working at Cameron, Adelsheim, Rex Hill, and other stops, Amy Wesselman and Dave Autry rented a building in McMinnville and began making their own wine. Buying all grapes, they have a roster made up of the popular trio of Pinot Noir, Chardonnay, and Pinot Gris. Sharing winemaking chores, the couple is moving the winery toward a maximum annual production of 5,000 cases. So far, the overall quality is solid and the prices are more than fair.

WHITE HERON CELLARS  *George, Washington 1986*  Veteran winemaker (ex–Worden Winery and Champs de Brione) Cameron Freis founded his own winery in George, midway between Seattle and Spokane. He refurbished a former service station, and puts up with jokes about getting good mileage from his wines. Three wines are produced—Pinot Noir, Dry Riesling, and a red Meritage, "Chantpierre." Annual production will level off at 2,000 cases.

**WILLAKENZIE ESTATE** *Willamette Valley 1995* Willakenzie is the name of a prevailing type of soil found in this winery's 80-acre vineyard. Developed by Bernard Lacroute of Burgundy, the vineyard, which will grow to 110 acres, is laid out on a series of noncontiguous slopes. Winemaker Laurent Montalieu, who apprenticed at Bridgeview, is overseeing production of Pinot Noir, Chardonnay, Pinot Gris, and Pinot Blanc. This winery's success with its beautiful early vintages of Pinot Blanc is partly responsible for the surge of interest in Pinot Blanc throughout Oregon today. The three-level winery was designed to move wine only by gravity, and the bottom level houses the barrel aging room. The present annual output of 12,000 cases is expected to double when the vineyard is fully productive. A quality name to watch closely.

**WILLAMETTE VALLEY VINEYARDS** *Willamette Valley 1989* After bumbling along for its first few years, Willamette Valley Vineyards decided to raise money through public stock offerings. After being successful at fund-raising, the company expanded its vineyard acreage and begin increasing production. Today with 65 acres planted, the winery is among the top five sellers in Oregon. Among its rather large menu of wines, the Riesling and Pinot Gris win lots of medals, and the Founder's Reserve Pinot Noir, Chardonnay, and Cabernet Sauvignon are its most successful. Annual sales of 60,000 is expected to expand to 75,000 over the next few years.

**ANDREW WILL WINERY** *Vashon Island, Washington 1989* Merlot and Cabernet Sauvignon are the specialties of this small winery located on Vashon Island, near Seattle. Owner and former restaurateur Chris Camarda is particular when it comes to grapes: he buys only from low-yielding vineyards. He follows traditional winemaking procedures (barrel to barrel racking) and ages both wines close to two years in new and one-year-old French oak barrels. A limited-volume barrel-fermented Chenin Blanc, "Cuvee LuLu," is produced occasionally. Total production is approaching 3,000 cases, with 4,000 cases per year envisioned as the maximum. Will's Merlots have ranked among the state's best. Today Will offers an array of single-vineyard Merlot—Klipsun, Ciel du Cheval, and Pepper Bridge—along with a Washington State and a Reserve bottling. As part of a small consortium of winemakers, Camarda purchased the well-known Mercer Ranch, since renamed Champoux Vineyard. This 130-acre vineyard, home to some of Washington's finest Cabernet and Merlot, had supplied fruit to Camarda before the sale. In addition to a Reserve Cabernet, he bottles Cabernets from Pepper Bridge and Ciel du Cheval. A Sangiovese also has broken into the lineup.

**WILRIDGE WINERY** *Seattle 1993* Located in the heart of Seattle, the winery is actually part of an old house with an improvised tasting and sales room. Specializing in single-vineyard wines, Wilridge makes Cabernet Sauvignon from Klipsun Vineyard, and to date has made Merlot from Klipsun and also from The Crawford Vineyard. Made in 100–200-case lots, both wines from Klipsun Vineyard have been well above average in quality.

**WITNESS TREE VINEYARD** *Willamette Valley, Oregon 1987* In the Eola Hills area 9 miles northwest of Salem, owner Doug Gentzkow developed 35 acres of vineyards in 80. After making wines as a hobby for a few years as well as selling grapes, he built a winery and hired a consulting enologist, Rick Nunes from Erath Vineyards, to help out. The winery was sold in 1993 to a local partnership consisting of two families, who now have a total of 45 acres of vineyards. Witness Tree is specializing in Pinot Noir and Chardonnay, and plans to grow to an annual output of 4,000 cases.

**WOODWARD CANYON WINERY** *Lowden, Washington 1981* Rick Small, owner-winemaker of this winery, had been involved in his family's agricultural endeavors (wheat, cattle raising) for years before planting a vineyard in the late 70s. Small is a strong promoter of the Walla Walla Valley appellation, but in his first decade of winemaking he made wines from several sources. Using a renovated machine-shop building as his winery, Small emphasizes two varietal wines: a likable Chardonnay, barrel-fermented in new oak, and an average Cabernet Sauvignon. In recent years he has added two proprietary wines, Charbonneau Red (Cabernet Sauvignon, Merlot) and "Charbonneau White" (Semillon, Sauvignon Blanc). Merlot from the Columbia Valley, Pinot Noir from the Oregon side of Walla Walla, and Chardonnay from Celilo Vineyard are relatively new members on the roster. The winery's reputation rests on its massive, oak-laced Chardonnay, which begs for aging. However, based on recent vintages, Merlot seems destined to prove to be even more exciting. The winery is operating at its peak capacity of 5,000 cases per year.

### Cabernet Sauvignon

86   87°   88   89   90°°   91   92°   93°   95°

*Cherrylike fruit comes with sweet oak in medium-full-bodied wines that can reach high rankings in best vintages*

### Chardonnay

88   89°   90°   91°   92   93°   94°

*Oak-oriented, with typically ripe and bright flavors*

---

**WORDEN WASHINGTON WINERY**   *Spokane, Washington 1980*   Opening the first winery in Spokane in the modern era, owner Jack Worden started using a shed as his winery and an old log cabin as his tasting room. Making wines primarily from Columbia River Valley grapes, he has emphasized the popular, slightly sweet style of Riesling, along with Chenin Blanc, Rosé of Gamay Beaujolais, and Gewurztraminer. In the late 80 s he began working with a Cabernet Sauvignon–Merlot blend, a dry-style Fumé Blanc, and oak-aged Chardonnay. Production is 30,000 cases a year.

---

**KEN WRIGHT CELLARS**   *Willamette Valley, Oregon 1994*   After selling his interest in Panther Creek in 94, Wright established his own winery in a facility in Forest Grove. He shares space with Domaine Serene, and continues to serve as Serene's winemaker. Having earned a good reputation for Pinot Noir at Panther Creek, Wright is now making about 2,000 cases of Pinot Noir. Additionally, he buys Chardonnay from Washington State to produce 600 cases of barrel-fermented Chardonnay. Enjoying a near-fanatic following for his single-vineyard Pinot Noirs, Wright currently is offering Pinot Noir from the following vineyards: Freedom Hill, Shea Vineyard, Carter Vineyard, Guadalupe Vineyard, Kircher, and Canary Hill Vineyard.

---

**YAKIMA RIVER WINERY**   *Prosser, Washington 1979*   Among the first five wineries in the region, Yakima River Winery was founded by John and Louise Rauner, both involved in home winemaking prior to moving from New York. Over its history, the winery has purchased grapes from many sources, the Ciel du Cheval Vineyard being its favorite. Though better known for its late harvest–style white wines, Yakima River Winery produces much more red wine than white. Cabernet Sauvignon and Merlot are the major reds, with small amounts of Lemberger also produced. Among the sweet, dessert wines, an 88 Riesling Ice Wine remains its greatest accomplishment. The winery's production has been averaging 25,000 cases a year.

---

**YAMHILL VALLEY VINEYARDS**   *Willamette Valley, Oregon 1985*   In 1982 several partners, including the present managing director, Dennis Burger, purchased a 200-acre site in the foothills west of McMinnville. Over the following few years the partners developed their 100-acre vineyard, which today is planted to Pinot Noir, Chardonnay, Pinot Gris, and Pinot Blanc. After several vintages of erratic quality, the winery steadied itself in the 1990s. Producing 10,000–12,000 cases a year, Yamhill Valley has risen to * levels with its Estate Reserve Pinot Noir and Chardonnay. Made in a user-friendly, tank-fermented style, Pinot Gris sells out quickly. Riesling also is made. Though new to the line, Pinot Blanc has shown tremendous promise.

ZILAH OAKES VINTNERS    *Zillah, Washington 1987*    The grape-growing partners behind Covey Run responded to the surplus of grapes in 87 by building a second facility and launching this brand. With a capacity of 8,000 cases, its initial efforts went into table wines headed by Riesling, Muscat, Chardonnay, and Semillon.

# The Producers Rated
## The Top Producers of the Leading Wines

The continuing expansion in West Coast wine production has brought us to the point at which there are now more than 1,000 bonded wineries operating in California, Washington, and Oregon. Setting aside those who make wines of little or no interest and those whose output is so tiny as to make them invisible to all but the most inveterate and peripatetic collectors, we have focused in the following pages on the leading producers of the most important varieties. Because these listings of the best comprise substantially less than half of all the wines we have tasted, every wine that appears in the following pages is worthy of special notice.

These ratings are based on the extensive tastings conducted by *Connoisseurs' Guide to California Wine,* a monthly newsletter edited and published by Charles Olken and Earl Singer. For subscription information, please see page xiii at the front of the book. In general, the ratings that follow are more heavily oriented to recent performance (generally three to five years), but they also recognize the long-term performance of those producers with extended track records. As regards newer wineries, please recognize, dear readers, that their fortunes often change over time as production levels grow and vineyards mature.

In the listings that follow, we have divided the leading wineries, and their wines, into three categories: World Class, Outstanding, and Admirable. Regardless of rating, any winery listed must have shown substantial success with its wines to earn its place in these pages. Thus, many wineries whose products are entirely acceptable and wholly enjoyable do not appear here. But whether a winery is listed or not, you need only look to its entry in the WINERIES AND WINES chapter to find detailed information about its performance. When a winery is listed with an additional notation after its name (e.g., "ROBERT MONDAVI Reserve"), it signifies that we are referring to one specific bottling from a winery which produces more than one of that variety.

WORLD CLASS — Wines in this category regularly earn two or three stars from *Connoisseurs' Guide* in good vintages. They represent the top 1 to 2% of all wines we review, and, depending on vintage, each represents the very pinnacle of vinous excellence.

OUTSTANDING — These wines typically earn one to two stars in the better vintages and occasionally rise into the world class range of three stars. Each is an excellent example of its variety and is surpassed in quality by only a handful of wines.

ADMIRABLE — Most wines in this category merit one star or better in a majority of vintages. A few wineries fall into this category because of variable performance (see their individual entries for more detail), but most of those so listed make thoroughly enjoyable, often collectible wines on a regular basis.

---

# Ratings of Cabernet Sauvignon Producers

Arguably the single best wine produced in California, and second to Merlot in Washington, Cabernet easily achieves World Class status with its best examples. It is bigger in personality than its French counterparts and has proved that top examples can age for 20 years and more. It tends to follow vintage patterns more closely than other varietals and produces scores of very fine wines in the leading vintages. The best are usually expensive, ranging from $25 to $100.

## World Class

CORNERSTONE Beatty Ranch
DUNN Howell Mountain
DUNN Napa Valley
LA JOTA Anniversary Bottling
ROBERT MONDAVI Reserve
JOSEPH PHELPS Insignia
RIDGE Monte Bello
STAGS LEAP WINE CELLARS Cask 23

## Outstanding

ALTAMURA
S. ANDERSON Chambers Vineyard
ANDRUS Reserve (Pine Ridge)
BEAULIEU Private Reserve
BRYANT FAMILY
CARDINALE
CAYMUS Special Selection
CHÂTEAU ST. JEAN Cinq Cepages
CHÂTEAU SOUVERAIN Winemakers
  Reserve
CHATEAU SOUVERAIN Alexander Valley

CLOS DU VAL Reserve
ROBERT CRAIG Mount Veeder
DALLA VALLE
ETUDE
FAR NIENTE
FLORA SPRINGS Trilogy
GALLO Northern Sonoma
GEYSER PEAK Alexandre's Reserve
GIRARD Reserve
JUDD'S HILL
KARL LAWRENCE
KENDALL-JACKSON Grand Reserve
KATHRYN KENNEDY
LAUREL GLEN Sonoma Mountain
LEWIS Reserve
LIPARITA Howell Mountain
MAYA (Dalla Valle)
MERRYVALE
MOUNT VEEDER
OPUS ONE
PAHLMEYER
PARADIGM

PEJU PROVINCE HB Vineyard

JOSEPH PHELPS Backus Vineyard

PRIDE MOUNTAIN

SHAFER Hillside Select

SHAFER Stags Leap District

SIGNORELLO Founders Rèserve

SIMI Reserve

SPOTTSWOODE

STAGLIN

STONESTREET Alexander Valley

SWANSON

VIADER

VINE CLIFF

VON STRASSER

WHITEHALL LANE Reserve

ZD

**Admirable** (wines identified with an asterisk * are more likely than their like-rated peers to achieve higher ratings in good vintages)

ANDERSON'S CONN VALLEY

ARAUJO

ARROWOOD★

DAVID ARTHUR Meritagio

BARNETT★

BENZIGER Tribute

BENZIGER Sonoma County

BERINGER Private Reserve★

BERINGER Knights Valley

BERNARDUS Marinus

BUEHLER

CAFARO★

CARMENET Meritage

CAYMUS

CHAPPELLET

CHATEAU MONTELENA★

CHATEAU STE. MICHELLE

CLOS DU BOIS Marlstone

CLOS DU VAL

CLOS PEGASE

B. R. COHN Olive Hill

CONN CREEK Limited Release

CORISON★

ROBERT CRAIG Affinity★

ROBERT CRAIG Howell Mountain

CRONIN Concerto

DE LILLE

DE LOACH OFS

DE LOACH Russian River Valley

DIAMOND CREEK Volcanic Hill★

DIAMOND CREEK Red Rock Terrace

DIAMOND CREEK Gravelly Meadow

DOMINUS★

DRY CREEK Reserve

DUCKHORN

DUNCAN PEAK★

TOM EDDY★

ESTANCIA Meritage

GARY FARRELL

FERRARI–CARANO Sonoma County

FETZER Barrel Select

FISHER Coach Insignia★

FORMAN

FRANCISCAN Magnificat★

FREEMARK ABBEY

FROGS LEAP★

GALANTE Red Rose Hill★

GALANTE Blackjack

GALLO Frei Ranch★

GEYSER PEAK Reserve

GIRARD Napa Valley

GRACELAND

GRGICH HILLS

HANNA

HARRISON★

HEITZ Martha's Vineyard

HEITZ Bella Oaks

HESS COLLECTION

IRON HORSE

JARVIS★

JUSTIN Isosceles

KENWOOD Artist Series

KENWOOD Jack London Ranch

LA JOTA Howell Mountain★

LAVA CAP

L'ECOLE No. 41

PETER MICHAEL Les Pavots★

ROBERT MONDAVI Napa Valley

MOUNT EDEN Old Vines

NEWLAN

NIEBAUM–COPPOLA Rubicon

OAKVILLE RANCH★

OPTIMA

ROBERT PECOTA Kara's Vineyard★

PINE RIDGE Stags Leap District★

PINE RIDGE Rutherford Cuvee

QUILCEDA CREEK

RAFANELLI

RAVENSWOOD Pickberry

RAVENSWOOD Gregory

MARTIN RAY★

RAYMOND Private Reserve

ROCHIOLI Reserve Neoma's Vineyard

ROCKING HORSE

ROSENBLUM Holbrook-Mitchell

ST. CLEMENT Orropas★

ST. SUPERY Dollarhide Ranch

SATTUI Suzanne's Vineyard

SEQUOIA GROVE Estate Reserve

SILVERADO Limited Release★

SILVERADO Disney/Mt. George★

SILVER OAK Alexander Valley

SILVER OAK Napa Valley

SPRING MOUNTAIN

STAGS LEAP WINE CELLARS Fay Vineyard

STAGS LEAP WINERY

RODNEY STRONG Alexander's Crown

TRUCHARD★

TURNBULL★

T VINE★

VENEZIA Meola Vineyard★

WHITEHALL LANE Napa Valley

WOODWARD CANYON

# Ratings of Merlot Producers

Gaining in popularity for its open, supple, and inviting character, Merlot is capable of producing highly prized wine in vintages that are also favorable for Cabernet Sauvignon and even in those which are somewhat too cool for Cabernet. Most leading Merlots are enjoyable from five to ten years of age, but the sturdier wines, especially those with some Cabernet Sauvignon or Cabernet Franc adding a bit of tannic spine, can age well into their second decades. Highly rated Merlots typically cost $15 to $40, but the rare wine can run into the same stratospheric price range attached to the priciest Cabernets.

## World Class

BERINGER Bancroft Ranch

LEWIS CELLARS Reserve

MATANZAS CREEK

WHITEHALL LANE Reserve Leonardini Vineyard

PARADIGM

ROBERT PECOTA Steven André Vineyard.

PINE RIDGE Carneros

PRIDE MOUNTAIN

ST. CLEMENT Napa Valley

ST. FRANCIS Reserve

TRUCHARD

## Outstanding

CAFARO

CHATEAU STE. MICHELLE Reserve

FRANCIS COPPOLA FAMILY

GARY FARRELL Ladi's Vineyard

HAVENS Reserve

MAC ROSTIE

MERRYVALE

**Admirable** (wines identified with an asterisk * are more likely than their like-rated peers to achieve higher ratings in good vintages)

APEX

ARROWOOD★

BENZIGER

| | |
|---|---|
| CHAPPELLET | LOLONIS Private Reserve |
| CHATEAU ST. JEAN★ | LONGORIA |
| CHATEAU SOUVERAIN | MARKHAM |
| CLOS DU VAL | MEITZ |
| CLOS PEGASE | ROBERT MONDAVI Napa Valley |
| CUVAISON | OAKVILLE RANCH |
| DUCKHORN Three Palms Vineyard★ | PAHLMEYER★ |
| DUCKHORN Howell Mountain★ | JOSEPH PHELPS |
| DUCKHORN Napa Valley | PINE RIDGE Select Cuvee |
| ESTANCIA | RABBIT RIDGE Grand Reserve★ |
| FERRARI–CARANO | RAVENSWOOD Pickberry★ |
| FORIS | RAVENSWOOD Sonoma County |
| FRANCISCAN | RICHARDSON Sangiacomo |
| FREEMARK ABBEY | RIDGE Montebello★ |
| FROG'S LEAP | ROMBAUER★ |
| GEYSER PEAK | ST. FRANCIS Sonoma County |
| GREENWOOD RIDGE★ | SEBASTIANI |
| HOGUE | SELENE★ |
| JUDD'S HILL★ | SHAFER★ |
| KEENAN★ | SILVERADO |
| KENDALL–JACKSON Grand Reserve | SINSKY RSV |
| KENWOOD Jack London Ranch★ | STELTZNER |
| L'ECOLE No. 41★ | SWANSON |
| LEONETTI★ | WATERBROOK★ |
| LIPARITA Howell Mountain | WELLINGTON |

# Ratings of Pinot Noir Producers

An enigma in California, an enigma in Oregon, an enigma everywhere it is grown except on a few fabled slopes in its native Burgundy, Pinot Noir tantalizes wine-lovers and winemakers alike with its supple, rich nature. When it succeeds, Pinot makes thoroughly exciting red wine. But the grape is less reliable from vintage to vintage and from site to site than other reds, and is accordingly less amenable to easy categorization. The ratings below reflect its vagaries in the smaller number of high-rated producers relative to the other leading reds. At its best, Pinot Noir ages comfortably for a decade, and some of the sturdier examples last twice that long. And while not as pricey as Cabernet, top-quality Pinots typically sell for $18 to $50.

## World Class

DEHLINGER Octagon House
DEHLINGER Reserve
DOMAINE DROUHIN
ROCHIOLI Reserve West Block
SAINTSBURY Reserve

## Outstanding

ACACIA Reserve
ADELSHEIM Oregon
ANCIEN
DAVID BRUCE Chalone
CARNEROS CREEK Signature Series

DEHLINGER Goldridge
DEHLINGER Russian River Valley
GARY FARRELL Rochioli Vineyard
GARY FARRELL Allen Vineyard
GREENWOOD RIDGE
ROCHIOLI Russian River Valley
TALLEY Rosemary's Vineyard
ZD

**Admirable** (wines identified with an asterisk * are more likely than their like-rated peers to achieve higher ratings in good vintages)
ACACIA Carneros
ARCHERY SUMMIT
AU BON CLIMAT La Bauge
BABCOCK Estate
BEAULIEU Reserve
BEAUX FRERES
BENTON LANE
BENZIGER
BETHEL HEIGHTS Southeast Block
BOUCHAINE Carneros
DAVID BRUCE Russian River Valley
BUENA VISTA Grande Reserve
BYRON Reserve
CALERA Jensen
CARNEROS CREEK Carneros
CASTALIA Rochioli Vineyard*

CHATEAU SOUVERAIN Winemaker's Reserve
CHAUFFE–EAU
CHEVAL SAUVAGE★
CRICHTON HALL★
DE LOACH OFS
ELKHORN PEAK Fagan Creek★
EL MOLINO
ETUDE★
GARY FARRELL Bien Nacido Vineyard★
GARY FARRELL Russian River Valley
FIDDLEHEAD Willamette Valley★
FORIS Rogue Valley
GREGORY GRAHAM Carneros
IRON HORSE
LA CREMA VINERA
LAURIER
MAC ROSTIE Reserve
MAHONEY Las Piedras
ROBERT MONDAVI Reserve★
ROBERT MONDAVI Carneros
OAK KNOLL Vintage Reserve
SAINTSBURY Carneros
STEELE Carneros
STONESTREET Russian River Valley
TALLEY Arroyo Grande
LANE TANNER Bien Nacido Vineyard
VILLA MT. EDEN Bien Nacido Vineyard
WHITCRAFT Bien Nacido Vineyard
YAMHILL VALLEY★

# Ratings of Zinfandel Producers

Relying for the most part on their berryish, zesty fruit for appeal, the current Zinfandel bottlings are somewhat riper and richer in style than was their wont for vintages prior to those of the mid-90s. Indeed, some wines are now so ripe and heavy that they challenge use with all but the heartiest of foods. But, change in style or not, Zinfandel is a wine to be drunk in its youth or to be aged up to a decade at most. It is only the rare wine, regardless of rating, which keeps improving beyond its tenth birthday. Zinfandel is often the last variety picked by a producer, and it fares better in warm seasons, thereby making it somewhat less reliable from vintage to vintage than, for instance, Cabernet Sauvignon. Zinfandel has become so popular that many Zinfandels now garner prices of up to $30.

## World Class

RIDGE Geyserville
RIDGE Lytton Springs
ROSENBLUM Hendry Vineyard Reserve
THE TERRACES

## Outstanding

BENZIGER Old Vines
BIALE Monte Rosso Vineyard
DE LOACH OFS
EDIZIONE PENNINO
EDMEADES Mendocino
FERRARI-CARANO
HARTFORD COURT Hartford Vineyard
LIMERICK LANE Collins Vineyard
LOLONIS Private Reserve
NEWLAN
RAFANELLI
RIDGE Sonoma Station
ROSENBLUM Harris-Kratka
ROSENBLUM Sauret Vineyard
ROSENBLUM Brandlin Ranch
SAUSAL Century Vines
SCHERRER Old Vines
SCHEUTZ OLES Korte Ranch
SEGHESIO San Lorenzo
STORYBOOK MOUNTAIN Eastern Exposures
TRIA Dry Creek Valley
VILLA MT. EDEN Grand Reserve Monte
   Rosso Vineyard
WHITEHALL LANE

## Admirable (wines identified with an asterisk * are more likely than their like-rated peers to achieve higher ratings in good vintages)

BANNISTER
BEAULIEU Napa Valley
BELVEDERE
BUEHLER
CHATEAU POTELLE VGS*
CHATEAU SOUVERAIN
CLINE Big Break Vineyard*
CLINE Bridgehead Vineyard
DE LOACH Barbieri*
DE LOACH Papera
DE LOACH Pelletti
DE LOACH Gambogi
DEUX AMIS
DRY CREEK Reserve*
DRY CREEK Old Vines
ELYSE Howell Mountain
FIFE Old Vines
FRITZ Old Vine
GALLO Frei Ranch
GREEN & RED Chiles Valley Vineyard
GRGICH HILLS*
GUNDLACH-BUNDSCHU Rhinefarm
   Vineyard
HAYWOOD Rocky Terraces
HENDRY Block 7
HENDRY Brandlin Ranch
KARLY Warrior Fires
KENWOOD Mazzoni Vineyard

LAMBORN FAMILY

LAVA CAP★

MADRONA

MARIETTA Sonoma County

MURPHY-GOODE Sonoma County

NALLE

PEACHY CANYON Westside

RABBIT RIDGE OVZ Reserve★

RAVENSWOOD Old Hill★

RAVENSWOOD Dickerson★

RAVENSWOOD Old Vine

RENWOOD Grandpère

RENWOOD Old Vine

RIDGE York Creek Vineyard★

RIDGE Pagani Vineyard★

RIDGE Dusi Ranch

ROCHIOLI Sodini Vineyard

ROCKING HORSE Lamborn Vineyard

ROSENBLUM Maggie's Reserve

SAUCELITO CANYON

SAUSAL Private Reserve★

SEGHESIO Old Vine

STORYBOOK MOUNTAIN Estate Reserve★

STORYBOOK MOUNTAIN Napa Valley

RODNEY STRONG Old Vines

SUMMIT LAKE

TRIA Napa Valley

TRUCHARD

TURLEY Hayne Vineyard★

WELLINGTON Casa Santinamaria★

WELLINGTON 100-Year-Old Vines★

# Ratings of Chardonnay Producers

California's best and most popular white varietal, Chardonnay is greatly influenced by vintage variation, yet still manages to succeed in most years because it is "early-ripening" and can reach ripeness in all but the most inhospitable harvests. Chardonnays are usually enjoyable when released, but many of the top bottlings seem to hold up well in bottle for as long as a decade. Chardonnay's popularity has pushed its price range upward in recent years, albeit not at the same pace as Cabernet Sauvignon; the leading Chardonnays now typically fetch $20 to $40.

## World Class

KISTLER McCrea Vineyard

KISTLER Kistler Vineyard

OJAI Reserve Talley Vineyard

SAINTSBURY Reserve

TRUCHARD

## Outstanding

BERINGER Private Reserve

BYRON Reserve

CAMBRIA Reserve

CHASSEUR

CRONIN Santa Cruz Mountains

CRONIN Stuhlmuller Vineyard

EL MOLINO

GARY FARRELL Allen Vineyard

THOMAS FOGARTY Estate Reserve

FRANCISCAN Cuvee Sauvage

GALLO Northern Sonoma

GUENOC Estate Reserve

PAUL HOBBS Dinner Vineyard

KENDALL-JACKSON Grand Reserve

KISTLER Durell Vineyard

KISTLER Vine Hill Vineyard

LEWIS Reserve

MATANZAS CREEK

MER SOLEIL

MIRASSOU Showcase Selection

ROBERT MONDAVI Reserve

MORGAN Reserve

MURPHY-GOODE Reserve Murphy Vineyard

NEWTON

OAKVILLE RANCH "ORV"

PAHLMEYER

PATZ & HALL

PINE RIDGE Stags Leap District

MARTIN RAY Mariage

RUTZ Dutton Ranch

SIGNORELLO Founder's Reserve

SOLITUDE Sangiacomo Vineyard

STONESTREET Sonoma County

SWANSON Carneros

TORRES Don Miguel Vineyard

VILLA MT. EDEN Signature Series

**Admirable** (wines identified with an asterisk * are more likely than their like-rated peers to achieve higher ratings in good vintages)

ACACIA Reserve

ACACIA Carneros

ARROWOOD Cuvee Michel Berthoud

AU BON CLIMAT (various Reserves)

BABCOCK Mt. Carmel Vineyard

BEAULIEU Reserve

BOUCHAINE Estate Reserve

BOYER

BUEHLER Reserve

BYRON Santa Maria Valley

CALE Sangiacomo Vineyard★

CALERA Central Coast

CAMELOT Santa Barbara

CARNEROS CREEK

CHALK HILL★

CHALONE

CHAPPELLET

CHATEAU STE. MICHELLE Canoe Ridge

CHATEAU STE. MICHELLE Cold Creek

CHATEAU SOUVERAIN Winemaker's
   Reserve

CHAUFFE-EAU Sangiacomo Vineyard

CHIMNEY ROCK Carneros

CINNABAR Saratoga Vineyards

CRONIN Nancy's Cuvée

DELHLINGER Russian River Valley★

DE LOACH OFS★

DE LOACH Russian River Valley

EDNA VALLEY VINEYARDS

GARY FARRELL Bien Nacido Vineyard

GLORIA FERRER

FERRARI–CARANO Reserve★

FERRARI–CARANO

FREEMARK ABBEY

GEYSER PEAK Reserve

GREENWOOD RIDGE Du Pratt Vineyard

GRGICH HILLS

HANNA Russian River Valley

HARRISON

KUNDE Reserve★

KUNDE Kinneybrook Vineyard★

LAMBERT BRIDGE

LANDMARK Damaris Reserve★

LAVA CAP Reserve

LONG

MAC ROSTIE★

MARKHAM

MERIDIAN Reserve

PETER MICHAEL★

ROBERT MONDAVI Carneros

MORGAN Monterey

MOUNT EDEN Santa Cruz Mountains

MUELLER Gauer Ranch

NICHOLS Talley Ranch

OAKVILLE RANCH Vista Vineyard

PHELPS Ovation

PINE RIDGE Knollside Cuvee

ROCHIOLI Russian River Valley

ROMBAUER★

SAINTSBURY Carneros

SANTA BARBARA Reserve

SHAFER Red Shoulder Ranch★

SONOMA–CUTRER Les Pierres

STEELE DuPratt★

STEELE Goodchild Vineyard★

STEELE Lolonis Vineyard

TALBOTT Sleepy Hollow Vineyard

TALLEY

VILLA MT. EDEN Grand Reserve

VINE CLIFF★

WILD HORSE

WOODWARD CANYON

ZD★

# Ratings of Sauvignon Blanc Producers

Virtually unchallenged as the number-two white wine in California, Sauvignon Blanc has retained its perky, bright personality and its endearing priceworthiness even as the cost of the other leading varieties has continued an upward spiral. While some of the sturdiest and best-stuffed wines can age well for a half decade or more, most Sauvignon Blancs seem not to benefit appreciably from extended cellaring. And even though the prices of some wines now reach upwards of $20, the available majority still fall in the $10 to $15 range.

## World Class

FRITZ

GAINEY Limited Selection

MATANZAS CREEK

ROBERT MONDAVI Reserve To-Kalon
   Vineyard

SIMI Sendahl

## Outstanding

BABCOCK Eleven Oaks

BERINGER Alluvium

CAYMUS

DUCKHORN

FERRARI-CARANO Fumé

MERRYVALE Vignette

MURPHY-GOODE The Deuce

ROBERT PEPI Two-Heart Canopy

QUIVIRA Reserve

SELENE Hyde Vineyard

SPOTTSWOODE

**Admirable** (wines identified with an asterisk * are more likely than their like-rated peers to achieve higher ratings in good vintages)

BENZIGER Fumé

BERINGER Napa Valley

BYRON★

CAIN Musqué

CARMENET Meritage

CHATEAU POTELLE

CHATEAU SOUVERAIN

DE LOACH Fumé★

DRY CREEK Reserve

DRY CREEK Sonoma County

ESTANCIA Pinnacles Fumé

FIDDLEHEAD

FLORA SPRINGS Soliloquy

HONIG

HUSCH La Ribera

IRON HORSE Fumé T-bar-T

KENWOOD

KUNDE Magnolia Lane

LAMBERT BRIDGE

MERRYVALE Napa Valley

ROBERT MONDAVI Stags Leap District

MURPHY-GOODE Fumé

ROCHIOLI Russian River Valley

ST. CLEMENT

SEGHESIO

STONESTREET Pinnacle Block

# Ratings of Sparkling Wine Producers

The ratings in this section have been the most subject to fluctuation from year to year. Many producers are new to the scene and have experienced changing production levels and grape sources. In addition, even those wineries with fairly evolved "house" styles continue to experiment with production techniques. That said, there are observable patterns of success which have emerged for many of the established producers, and we have been instructed by those patterns in formulating the ratings which follow. Prices for sparkling wines have remained more or less steady for many years, and while the number of expensive, reserve-type bottlings is growing, the price of the typical Brut or Blanc de Noirs has remained in the $12 to $18 range. A handful of wines, probably no more than a dozen overall, carry price tags of $30 to $60.

## World Class

CHANDON Reserve
J (Jordan Sparkling Wine Company)
J (in magnum)

## Outstanding

CHANDON Etoile
DOMAINE CARNEROS Brut
IRON HORSE Vrais Amis
MUMM NAPA Blanc de Noirs (in magnum)
MUMM NAPA DVX
ROEDERER L'Hermitage
SCHRAMSBERG Cuvée de Pinot

## Admirable (wines identified with an asterisk * are more likely than their like-rated peers to achieve higher ratings in good vintages)

CHANDON Blanc de Noirs (in magnum)
CHANDON Blanc de Noirs
CHANDON Brut
CHANDON Brut (in magnum)
GLORIA FERRER Brut
GLORIA FERRER Royal Cuvée
IRON HORSE Brut
IRON HORSE Wedding Cuvée★
KRISTON Rosé
MUMM NAPA Blanc de Noirs
MUMM NAPA Brut
MUMM NAPA Brut (in magnum)
ROEDERER Brut
ROEDERER Rosé
SCHARFFENBERGER Rosé
J SCHRAM
SCHRAMSBERG Blanc de Blancs
VAN DER KAMP Midnight Rosé

# Wine Language

ACETIC   All wines contain acetic acid—vinegar. Usually the amount is quite small, being less than 0.06% and ranging as low as 0.03%. When table wines reach 0.07% or above, tasters begin to notice a sweet, slightly sour and vinegary smell and taste in the wine. Such wines are acetic and are also said to have ascescence. At low levels, ascescence often enhances the attractiveness of a well-made wine. At higher levels (over 0.10%), the acetic qualities can become the dominant character of the wine and are considered a major fault. A related substance, ethyl acetate, contributes the smell associated with the presence of acetic acid.

ACIDIC   Describes wines whose total acid is so high that they taste tart or sour and have a sharp feel in the mouth.

ACIDITY   Labels mentioning acidity express it in terms of total acid, a measure of the several most common acids. These are tartaric, malic, lactic, and citric. The acidity of balanced dry table wine falls in the range between 0.6% and 0.75% of the wine's volume. However, for sweet wines, 0.70% total acidity or less is considered low because the wine usually tastes flat or unbalanced. For balance, generally, the sweeter the wine, the higher the acidity should be. It is legal in California to correct deficient acidity by adding malic, tartaric, or citric acid to achieve a balanced wine.

AFTERTASTE   The taste left in the mouth after the wine is swallowed. Both the character and the length of the aftertaste are considered. Finish is a related term.

ALCOHOL BY VOLUME   Wineries are required by law to state the alcohol level on their labels—usually expressed as a numerical percentage of the volume. For table wines the law allows a 1.5% variation in either direction from the stated percentage as long as the alcohol does not exceed 14%. An alternative taken by a few producers is to describe the wine as a table wine or light wine, omitting the percentage notation. By definition, sherry ranges from 17% to 20% alcohol by volume; other dessert wines fall into the 18–21% range.

ANGULAR   The combination of hard, often tart-edged flavors and tactile impressions given by many young dry wines. Angular wines are the opposite of round, soft, or supple.

APERITIF   A legal classification for wines having not less than 15% alcohol by volume; vermouth is the best example. However, current fashion also uses the term generically to describe any wine likely to be enjoyed before a meal, regardless of alcohol level.

APPLEY   This term often carries additional modifiers. "Ripe apples" suggests a full, fruity, open smell characteristic of some Chardonnays. "Fresh apple" aromas are occasionally associated with Rieslings, whereas "green apple" aromas come from wines made from barely ripe or underripe grapes. And, should you encounter a wine with the aroma of "stale apples," you are probably smelling a flawed wine exhibiting the first stages of oxidation.

AROMA   Traditionally defined as the smell that wine acquires from the grapes and from fermentation, now it more commonly means the wine's smell, including changes that occurred in the bottle. One assesses the intensity of aroma and also describes its character with virtually any adjective that fits, ranging, for example, from appley to raisiny and from fresh to tired. Bouquet has a similar meaning in common usage.

ASCESCENCE   The sweet and sour, sometimes vinegary smell and taste that, along with a sharp feeling in the mouth, mark the presence of acetic acid and ethyl acetate.

ASTRINGENT   Many red wines and a few whites have a rough, harsh, puckery feel in the mouth, usually from tannin. When the harshness stands out, the wine is astringent. Tannic astringency is reduced with age, but sometimes a wine will fail to outlive the tannin.

AUSTERE   Said of wines that are low in fruit and firm, sometimes hard, in texture. Sparkling wine is often meant to be austere, in the sense that "fruit" is intentionally kept in the background so that the wine can show the richness it acquires in its aging process.

BALANCE   A wine has balance when its elements are harmonious—no one part dominates. Acid balances against sweetness; fruit balances against oak and tannin; alcohol balances against acid and flavor. Wine not in balance may be acidic, cloying, flat, or harsh, among other things.

BARREL-FERMENTED   Some wines are fermented in small casks (usually 55-gallon oak barrels) rather than in large tanks. Advocates believe that barrel fermentation contributes better harmony between the oak and the wine and increases body. Its liabilities are that more labor is required and greater risks involved. It is being used increasingly with California Chardonnay and for a few Sauvignon Blancs and Viogniers.

BERRYLIKE   The expected aroma and taste of Zinfandel. "Berrylike" is equated with the ripe, sweet, fruity qualities of blackberries, raspberries, cranberries, and cherries. Other red grapes may also produce wines with berrylike character.

BIG   A wine, either red or white, possessing rich, full flavors and fairly full body. Big red wines are usually tannic. Big whites often are high in alcohol and glycerine. For some tasters, "bigger is better," especially for bold wines like Zinfandel, Syrah, and Petite Sirah.

BITTER   One of the four basic tastes (along with sour, salty, and sweet). Some grapes—notably Gewurztraminer and Muscat—often have noticeable bitterness in their flavors. Another major source of bitterness is tannin. If the bitter quality dominates the wine's flavor or aftertaste, it is considered a fault. In sweet wines a trace of bitterness may complement the flavors and make the wine more enjoyable.

BODY   The tactile impression of weight or fullness on the palate usually experienced from a combination of glycerine, alcohol, and sugar.

BOTRYTIS CINEREA   A mold or fungus that attacks grapes under certain climatic conditions, *Botrytis* requires high humidity and/or some moisture. When it commences just before the grapes reach maturity, it causes them to shrivel, concentrating both sugar and acid. It is beneficial and highly desirable for some white varieties, especially Johannisberg Riesling. The resulting wines are uniquely aromatic and flavored, sweet and luscious, if the *Botrytis* is widespread. Lacking official definition, wines said to have *Botrytis* vary both in flavor intensity and in sweetness.

BOTTLE-FERMENTED   Generally indicates the champagne was not produced by the bulk process. It could apply to either the *méthode champenoise* or the transfer process. However, since producers following the former method usually say so on their labels, champagne bearing this description is more likely made by the transfer method.

BOTTLED BY   When it appears by itself without the designation "produced by" or "made by," the indication is that the named winery played a very minor role in the wine's production. The wine could have been purchased readymade and simply bottled; or it could have been made under contract by another winery only to be transferred, aged, and then bottled by the designated producer.

BOUQUET   Technically, that part of a wine's smell that develops after it is put in the bottle. Since most of the smell develops before bottling and bouquet comes mostly with years of cellar aging, the term "aroma" is almost always more appropriate when discussing a wine's smell.

BRAWNY   Term used for wines that are full of muscle and low on elegance. The term is used mainly for younger reds with high tannin and alcohol levels—thus referring both to body and to texture. Petite Sirahs with Napa, Sonoma, and Mendocino appellations are more likely than not to be brawny. Most reds from Amador are brawny.

BREED   Used for the loveliest, most harmonious, and refined wines, those whose charms reach classical expectations of varietal character, balance, and structure. The term is usually reserved for wines from the best varieties and is rarely associated with common grapes like French Colombard or Ruby Cabernet.

BRIARY   Like the thicket of thorns from which the wine term is derived, a briary wine gives a prickly, aggressive tactile impression on the palate not unlike flecks of black pepper. The term is most often applied to young, dry red wines with noticeable tannin and alcohol.

BRIGHT   Wines with fresh, zesty, fruity qualities are said to be bright, or to have brightness. It is a characteristic expected in most younger wines, especially whites and rosés, and can be a pleasant surprise in older bottlings. The bright aspects of a wine are part of its overall balance, and of the interplay between acidity, body, oakiness, alcohol, and sweetness in determining how the wine smells and tastes.

BRILLIANT   Term describing the appearance of very clear wines: absolutely no visible suspended or particulate matter in evidence. Brilliant wines are often the product of heavy filtration, a process that may remove the flavor along with the solids. See also Unfiltered, Cloudy, and Hazy.

BRIX   Name of a system used by American winemakers to measure the sugar content of grapes, must, and wine. On labels Brix normally refers to the degree of ripeness (meaning the sugar level at harvest) and occasionally is used to indicate the sugar in the finished wine. For most table wines the usual range at the harvest is 20° to 25° Brix. By multiplying the stated Brix at harvest by .55, one obtains the approximate alcohol by volume possible if the wine were fermented to dryness.

BROWNING   The normal tints of young table wines contain no brown. Browning is a sure sign that wine is beginning to age. Wines with good depth and character can be quite enjoyable even though a good deal of browning shows. For lesser wines the onset of browning usually signals the downside of the hill.

BRUT   An exclusive champagne modifier widely used to designate a relatively dry-finished wine, often the driest champagne made by the producer. In the absence of a legal definition, however, Brut does not guarantee that the champagne will be dry. Wineries in the U.S. use the term as they see fit, but you can count on "Brut" being near dry in virtually all sparklers produced by the *méthode champenoise* technique.

BULK PROCESS   A speedy, large-volume, and inexpensive method of making champagnes. The secondary fermentation that provides the bubbles takes place in a large, closed container, as opposed to a bottle. Wineries have the option of putting either "bulk process" or "Charmat" (a synonymous term) on their labels.

CANDYLIKE   Modern technology enables winemakers to capture the perfumed fresh fruit aromas and flavors of the grape. This candylike fruitiness can be attractive in wines intended for early consumption, such as *Nouveau*-style wines and slightly sweet whites and rosés. It is out of place in longer-aging reds and in the better white varieties.

CARBONIC MACERATION   A technical procedure in which grapes are placed whole into a fermenter. Their weight breaks the skins, beginning an intracellular fermentation. The resulting wines (usually red) are intensely fruity, light-bodied, and meant for early consumption. Some wines labeled "Nouveau" are made this way. Occasionally a winery may blend some carbonic maceration wine with conventionally fermented wine for added fruitiness and freshness.

CASK #   Sometimes attached to very special wines; sometimes used as a gimmick. It is meant to imply that the wine spent its entire cellar life in one cask and that it was produced in small amounts. Neither condition need be met for the term to be used.

CELLARED BY   Technically means the wine was not produced at the winery where it was bottled. Usually indicates that the wine was purchased from someone else and aged or cellar-treated by the bottling winery, but there is no minimum time requirement for aging. This lack of precision makes "cellared by" highly suspect, even though it occasionally appears on wines that received long aging and personal attention from the bottling winery.

CHARMAT   Same as the bulk process of champagne making. The second fermentation occurs in large tanks, not individual bottles. It is a large-volume method involving fewer hand procedures. Since the champagne can be made quickly and the costs are lower, it is the usual method for all inexpensive champagnes. Many wineries prefer this label term since it sounds better than "bulk process."

CHEWY   Rich, heavy, tannic wines are said to be chewy because, figuratively, one could not swallow them without chewing first.

CITRUSY   Term describing a wine with aroma and flavor constituents reminiscent of citrus fruits. Such wines need not be high in acid, since citrusy refers to taste sensations that go beyond the basic qualities of sour, sweet, salty, and bitter. Many white wines from colder climates, especially Monterey County, have a citrusy quality that recalls grapefruit.

CLASSIC   A meaningless term when used on wine labels (e.g., Classic Chardonnay), its appearance there derives from its use by wine tasters to describe a wine that conforms to expected norms of character for a certain type or style. In that latter context, "breed" is a similar term.

CLONE   A group of vines originating from a single, individual plant whose descendants have been propagated asexually, usually by means of cuttings or grafts. A clone is selected for its special viticultural and wine merits (productivity, adaptability to particular growing conditions, and wine quality). Clonal selection studies have improved West Coast Chardonnay and Pinot Noir, and increasingly are playing significant roles in other varieties as well.

CLOSED-IN   Term for wines that are presently low in intensity, but high in concentrated, correct character, and that are expected to develop greater intensity with age.

CLOUDY   An obvious lack of clarity in wines is undesirable. With the exception of old wines not decanted properly, cloudy wines are usually the result of winemaking error. They are caused by a variety of unwanted occurrences, such as protein instability, yeast spoilage, and refermentation in the bottle. Cloudy wines usually taste unpleasant.

CLOYING   When the sweetness annoys by dominating flavors and aftertaste, a wine is said to be cloying. Such excessively sugary wines lack the balance provided by acid, alcohol, bitterness, or intense flavor.

COLD STABILIZATION   A clarification technique involving lowering the temperature to 32° F. for one to three weeks. The cold encourages the tartrates and other insoluble solids to precipitate, rendering the wine clear. The tartrates cast by the wine are actually tasteless and harmless and are removed for appearance only.

COMPLEX   A wine of beauty and balance harmoniously combining many aroma and flavor elements is considered complex. This is the elusive quality that separates a great wine from a very good one.

COOPERAGE   Those who build wooden barrels are called coopers. In present usage cooperage refers to any container for holding or aging wine. Collectively, it covers containers of all sizes and of all materials, from oak to stainless steel.

CORKED   Some corks are flawed by the presence of a chemical in their makeup which makes the wine in the bottle taste and smell musty and dank. For reasons not well understood by the wine industry or the cork producers, this phenomenon is increasing; according to some studies, corked wines (that is, wines destroyed in attractiveness by diseased corks) are appearing in as many as 1 bottle in 30. Unfortunately, there is no way to test every cork before it goes into the bottle, so wineries and producers can only sample each batch of corks in the hope of detecting an unusually high percentage of bad ones.

CREAM   Loosely used term for a style of sherry that is very sweet and is intended for enjoyment with desserts.

CRISP   A tactile sensation somewhat akin to hardness but less imposing, crispness is generally the result of a high level of acidity relative to other balancing aspects. Dry and slightly sweet white and rosé wines are often crisp, and when they are bright as well, are likely to be attractive.

CROSS   A grape created by mating 2 members of the same vine species. For example, the mating of two *Vitis vinifera* grapes, Cabernet Sauvignon and Carignane, produced Ruby Cabernet. Other notable crosses are Emerald Riesling, Flora, and Carnelian.

CRUSH   Popularly used in the U.S. for the harvest season or the vintage. It also refers more specifically to the breaking (or crushing) of grape skins, which begins the winemaking process.

CUVEÉ   Commonly used in the U.S. to identify a specific batch or lot of wine (as in Cuvée 8). In general, it refers to a blend of wines. Seen on both champagnes and table wines as a substitute for a vintage date.

DECANTING   Procedure by which wine is poured slowly and carefully from the bottle into another container before serving. The purpose is to leave the sediment behind. Many old red wines and a few young ones made with a minimum of clarification tend to throw a deposit or sediment in the bottle.

DELICATE   Any wine of light to medium-light body and of lower-intensity flavors can be described as delicate. The term is usually, but not always, applied to attractive wines.

DEMI-SEC   For reasons now forgotten, the language of champagne relating to sweetness is misleading when interpreted literally. Although this word means half-dry, *demi-sec* champagnes are usually slightly sweet to medium sweet. The term is occasionally applied also to still wines.

DEPTH   A wine with flavors of good intensity that seem to fill the mouth from front to back is said to have depth. It is a characteristic that one should expect of most premium wines, save for youthful, lighter-bodied whites. See also LINGERING.

DESSERT WINE   A term with two meanings. The first is a legal classification of wines whose alcohol content is at least 17% but not higher than 24% by volume, and whose higher alcohol was obtained by adding either brandy or neutral spirits. Such wines are also known legally as fortified wines. The second use is general, covering sweet and very sweet wines of any alcohol level that are customarily enjoyed with dessert or by themselves at the end of a meal.

DIRTY   This term covers a multitude of vinous sins. All of the foul, rank smells that can show up in wine—from the musty cachet of unclean barrels to the cabbage and garlic odors of undesirable fermentation by-products—render a wine dirty.

DOSAGE   In bottle-fermented champagne, the yeast sediment collected is eventually removed. Along with it a little wine is lost. To replace the wine and to adjust the sweetness level of the final product, winemakers add a dosage, usually a mixture of sweet syrup and wine.

DRY   A wine with no perceptible taste of sugar in its makeup is dry. Wines fermented to dryness have 0.2% residual sugar or less. Most wine tasters begin to perceive the presence of sugar at levels of 0.5% to 0.7%. For our purposes, we use "dry" for any wine with residual sugar up to 0.5%. The term is used more loosely on wine labels.

DUMB   A young wine with undeveloped aromas and flavors is often called dumb because it seems unable to speak. "Closed-in" is a similar term. Both words are reserved for wines expected to improve.

EARTHY   Wine tasters use this term to cover characteristics that range from the pleasant, rich earthiness of loamy topsoil to the unpleasant, rotting-grass earthiness of the compost heap. Earth may be dirt, but an earthy wine is not necessarily dirty.

ELEGANT   Wines of grace, balance, and beauty are called elegant. The term is applied more often to white wines than to reds, although a few medium-bodied Cabernet Sauvignons of breed and complexity may also be called elegant.

EN TIRAGE   Sparkling wines are aged in the bottle during the secondary fermentation stage. This time spent *en tirage* (the French term means literally "in drawing" and refers to the fact that the wine has been drawn from the barrel) keeps the wine in contact with the dead yeast cells and adds a rich, toasty, sometimes creamy aspect. This is often regarded as a key component in the character of the best sparklers.

ESSENCE   Used for a time by wineries to describe a late harvest, sweet red wine. It appeared on several Zinfandels made from grapes picked at 35° Brix or higher.

ESTATE BOTTLED   Once used by producers for those wines made from vineyards that they owned and could see from the winery. Until recently, its definition had been stretched beyond recognition. New regulations have now tightened its definition and restricted its application.

ETHYL ACETATE   The sweet, vinegary smell that often accompanies acetic acid is ethyl acetate. It exists to some degree in all wines and can complement other elements in the aroma and taste, especially those of sweet, rich wines. In most wines, however, noticeable ethyl acetate is considered a flaw.

EXTRA DRY   In keeping with the French Champagne tradition, wines labeled extra dry are not. They usually possess residual sugar in the 2–6% range and bridge the gap between the drier *Brut*-styled wines and those still sweeter.

FAT   The combination of medium to full body and slightly low acid gives wine a fat impression on the palate. The wine feels and tastes a bit more obvious and often lacks a touch of elegance. In fuller-flavored wines the fat quality is highly prized by some tasters. A fat, oily Riesling would be less so, unless made in a late harvest style. "Fleshy" and "mouth-filling" are related terms.

FERMENTATION   A complex chemical reaction by which yeasts through their enzymes transform the grapes' sugar into equal parts of alcohol and carbon dioxide. The process generates heat, so most winemakers control the temperature nowadays by circulating cooling agents within the jackets of their stainless-steel fermentation tanks.

FIELD BLEND   This was once a widespread practice in California. Vineyards were planted to several different varieties, and the grapes were harvested together to produce a single wine. Thus, the wine was blended in the field. A few such vineyards, mainly of red varieties, remain in California. Ridge Geyserville is a classic example of a wine made from an old vineyard containing a "field blend" of varieties.

FIELD CRUSHING   Generally used in concert with mechanical harvesters. The grapes are picked and immediately crushed in the vineyards or field; the fresh juice (called "must") being ultimately transferred to the winery for fermentation. The advantages are that the juice avoids oxidation and, since a blanket of carbon dioxide surrounds it, the juice will not ferment too early. Still experimental and somewhat controversial with regard to wine character.

FILTERING   A mechanical process of removing yeast cells and other particles from wine after fermentation. Sometimes used before fermentation to clarify press juice. Most wines (except those labeled unfiltered) are filtered for both clarity and stability.

FINING   Technique of clarifying wine by introducing various agents. The most common fining agents are bentonite (powdered clay) and gelatin; the most traditional is egg whites. Such agents precipitate to the bottom of the tank or barrel, carrying suspended particles with them.

FINISH   The tactile and flavor impressions left in the mouth when wine is swallowed. The tactile sensations of the finish may be hot, harsh, tannic, smooth, or soft, and lingering, short, or nonexistent.

FLAT  Term for wine suffering a lack of balance or lack of flavor. Flatness means the absence of vigor and liveliness and is caused by very low acidity. Flat flavors are insipid or old.

FLOR  A specific yeast that imbues *flor* or Fino sherries from Spain with their unique aroma and flavor. This *flor* yeast (*Saccharomyces fermentati*) does not occur naturally in the U.S. or in other wine regions outside Spain. However, several Canadian and California researchers have developed a *flor* yeast culture that can be introduced to the would-be sherry and imparts a similar character. The technique is called the submerged flor or cultured flor process.

FLORAL  (also FLOWERY) Literally, having the characteristic aromas of flowers. Floral is employed without modifier to describe pleasant, often delicate aromas found in white wines. In particular, Johannisberg Riesling often displays such attributes, as do Chenin Blanc, Muscat, and Gewurztraminer to a lesser degree. Very few red wines are floral.

FORTIFIED  A wine whose alcohol content has been increased by the addition of brandy or neutral spirits is said to be fortified. In the U.S. sherries are fortified to a minimum of 17% alcohol by volume; other fortified wines have an 18% alcohol minimum. Dessert wine is a synonymous term when used to describe a wine that has been fortified.

FOXY  Poorly chosen word traditionally used to describe the unique musky and grapey characters of many native American labrusca varieties and many French-American hybrids.

FREE-RUN JUICE  The juice that flows freely after the grape skins are crushed and before the stems and pulp are pressed for the remaining yield. About 60–70% of the total juice yield is free-run; it is generally smoother, less bitter, and less tannic than press wine. A few special bottling wines are fermented entirely from free run. However, most winemakers choose to blend the two in some proportion.

FRESH  Having the lively, youthful, uncomplicated qualities sought in lighter reds, rosés, and most whites. Such wines are usually fruity and clean and have ample acidity.

FRUITY  Having the distinctive aroma and taste of fruit, a quality found mostly in young wines. A fruity wine usually has intensity, freshness, and distinctive character; for example, it is berrylike, appley, or herbaceous. Young wines lacking fruitiness, especially whites, are often sweetened to fill the holes in their flavor profiles.

GASSY  Said of table wines containing carbonation (gas) usually from unwanted fermentation in the bottle. The term "spritzy" also describes carbonation in wine, but does not carry the negative connotation of gassy.

GENERIC WINE  Any wine whose name is part of a general category or type, as opposed both to varietal wines (which are derived from a grape variety such as Cabernet Sauvignon) and to specially coined proprietary names (Caymus' Conundrum, Phelps's Insignia). The best-known generic designations are those with European place names (Burgundy, Chablis, Chianti, Champagne, and Rhine) as well as the type categories (Blanc de Blancs, Blanc de Noirs, Claret, Rosé, Sherry, and Table Wine).

GLYCERINE  This by-product of fermentation is found to some extent in all wines. It is most noticeable in higher-alcohol and late harvest wines, in which high levels of glycerine give the wine a slippery, smooth tactile impression and contribute fullness to the wine's body. Glycerine has a sweet taste on the tip of the tongue.

**GRAPEFRUITY**   Cold-climate white wines often exhibit a distinct grapefruity character. Such wines also may contain floral qualities that blend nicely with the more citrusy grapefruit notes. The young white wines of Monterey County frequently possess this intriguing, fresh quality.

**GRAPEY**   Simple flavors and aromas more like fresh table grapes than fine wine are called grapey. Many of the native American varieties and French-American hybrids produce grapey wines.

**GRASSY**   A light fresh grassiness can enhance some wines (especially Sauvignon Blanc). However, the more grassy a wine is, the more likely it is to be unappealing. In the extreme, grassiness can take over a wine and render it unattractive.

**GREEN**   Wines made from unripe fruit have a green taste. The flavors are usually monochromatic, somewhat sour and angular, and often grassy. The color green (light tints in a straw/pale yellow color) is not unusual in many young white wines, especially Johannisberg Riesling, and does not necessarily signal a green wine.

**GROWN, PRODUCED, AND BOTTLED BY**   Used by a few producers to declare explicitly that they performed all functions, from growing the grapes to bottling the wine. Much more precise and reliable than "estate bottled."

**HARD**   Tactile firmness taken one step further by high acidity or tannin yields a hard wine. The quality is appropriate in young red wines suitable for aging and can also enhance dry white wines that are served with shellfish.

**HARSH**   Highly astringent wines, often relatively high in alcohol, may give this nasty, rough tactile sensation. With age, some of the nastiness goes away, but the relevant question is whether the wine is worth the wait. "Rough" and "hard" are related terms.

**HAZY**   Term for wines with moderate amounts of visible particulate matter. If you see a slight haze in wine, especially if it carries the words "unfined" or "unfiltered," there is probably no cause for alarm. But if the wine is so hazy that the suspended matter causes it to lose clarity, it may be flawed.

**HEARTY**   Generally used to describe the full, warm qualities found in red wines with high alcohol, especially those made in straightforward styles such as the heavier red jugs, some Zinfandels, and Petite Sirahs.

**HERBACEOUS**   Literally, having the taste and smells of herbs (undefined as to species). Herbaceousness is often said to be a varietal character of Cabernet Sauvignon and, to a lesser extent, of Merlot and Sauvignon Blanc.

**HOT**   Wines high in alcohol that tend to burn or prickle the palate and nose are called hot. This character is accepted in dessert offerings like port, sherry, and late harvest Zinfandel. It is noticeable but less appreciated in Cabernet Sauvignon and Chardonnay and actually undesirable in light, fruity wines like Johannisberg Riesling.

**HYBRIDS**   Varieties developed by geneticists through crossing (and often recrossing) grapes from two or more different species. Full-scale efforts began in the search for resistance to the *Phylloxera* disease. Grapes resulting from the cross-pollination experiments of vinifera with a native American variety became known as French hybrids or as French-American hybrids. Those hybrids presently cultivated in the U.S. were chosen for their ability to survive cold winters and to yield balanced wines in short growing seasons. Among the best known hybrids are Baco Noir, De Chaunac, Foch, Seyval Blanc, and Vidal Blanc.

**JAMMY, JAMLIKE**  The combination of ripe, concentrated fruitiness and the natural grapey or berrylike character of certain red varieties yields wines that have jam-like aromas and flavors. Zinfandel from Amador County is frequently jammy.

**JUG WINES**  Inexpensive wines generally sold in large containers. The term originates in the tradition of consumers' bringing their own containers, jug bottles, to wineries for their purchases. Most wines so described are generics, but a few varietals also appear in jug containers. "Jug-wine quality" describes wines low in character and palatable at best.

**LABRUSCA**  Shorthand for the native American grape species, *Vitis labrusca,* whose wines have a heavy, grapey character of the sort typified by Concord grape juice.

**LATE HARVEST**  On labels, a signal that the wine was made from grapes picked at a higher Brix than normal. The term describes the condition of the fruit, not the calendar date. It is possible, though not requisite, that the high sugar levels were achieved through the influence of *Botrytis cinerea.* The general implication for late harvest white wines is that the wine is finished sweet to some degree; for red wines it means they may be either high in alcohol or finished sweet. Most late harvest wines are enjoyed after the main course as unfortified dessert wines.

**LEAFY**  Some wines, including attractive wines, exhibit a slightly herbaceous, vegetative quality analogous to the smell of leaves. When a wine is leafy, it is not necessarily flawed and may actually be more interesting if the leafy quality adds a note of complexity.

**LEES**  The sediment falling to the bottom of a wine container. When mentioned on labels, it usually refers to the sediment precipitated during fermentation, most of which consists of dead yeast cells. Most wines are removed from the lees as soon as possible, since they are thought to contribute inappropriate, and sometimes unappealing, odors and flavors. However, some Chardonnays are left in contact with the lees for several months (see *sur lies*) and sparkling wines gain much of their character by being kept in contact with the lees aging *en tirage* (see entry).

**LEES STIRRING**  is an option whenever wines are aging on the lees. While lees contact contributes viscosity and enhances "mouthfeel," winemakers believe that by stirring the lees on a regular basis they can increase what is often called the "toasted bread" character in the aroma, sometimes described as a "roasted grain" aroma. Stirring also seems to better integrate the oak and lees components. Lees stirring is labor-intensive since a simple whisk-like device is inserted into a barrel and the lees that have fallen to the bottom are agitated and mixed. As a rule, winemakers stir the lees once a month; some prefer twice a month, and we suspect some compulsive types stir weekly.

**LEESY**  A leesy wine is one having the toasty, roasted-grain character that is typically acquired by wines aged on the lees.

**LEMONY**  White wine with fairly high acid often takes on a lemony quality. Such wines are not necessarily tart or sour; the acid may be balanced by intense flavors or sweetness.

**LIGHT WINE**  Through the confluence of high technology and Madison Avenue marketing techniques, Light Wine was spawned in 1981. By legal definition, a Light Wine should contain fewer calories per comparable serving than a regular glass of table wine. In order to make a claim of "fewer calories" on the label, the producer must authenticate and document that statement. Wines can be made Light by decreasing either one or both sources of calories—alcohol and sugar. Most commonly, the calories are reduced by picking the grapes very early, before full maturity, or by removing the alcohol in a finished wine through a vacuum distillation process. Used as a tasting term, "light" indicates that the wine's viscosity is hard to distinguish from that of water.

LIMITED BOTTLING   In the absence of legal definition, this high-sounding phrase is used on bottlings that run the gamut from small lots of special wine to every drop of the designated wine that the producer has to offer.

LINGERING   Both flavor and tactile impressions may remain in the mouth after the wine is swallowed. When the aftertaste or finish remains in the mouth for more than a few seconds, it is said to be lingering. One would hope that the character is also clean, balanced, and attractive.

LIVELY   Wines that are fruity and fresh in character, usually with ample acidity, are called lively because of their vigor. Such wines may occasionally be spritzy and usually are relatively low in sweetness and alcohol. The term is applied more often to white wines, but sometimes to reds.

LOT #   Used in several different ways. The most legitimate is to differentiate wines of the same type from the same vintage that were bottled at different times. It also can suggest that the wine is a blend of two or more different vintages or different growing regions. A very few use it to indicate that the same wine was aged in different kinds of barrels. However, the term has no legal definition and therefore means as little or as much as the winery wishes it to mean.

LUSH   Wines with the soft, viscous tactile impression created by high levels of residual sugar (usually in the sweet and very sweet ranges) are called lush.

MADE AND BOTTLED BY   Though sounding the same as "produced and bottled by," this term has an entirely different meaning. The only requirement is that the named producer fermented a minimum of 10% of the wine in the bottle. That is hardly an intimate personal involvement with the wine.

MADERIZED   This term originates in the brownish color and slightly sweet, slightly appley, sometimes nutty character found in the wines of Madeira. However, it is not intended as a compliment when used in conjunction with table wines. Maderized wines have been exposed to air and have lost their freshness. Sherrified is a similar term, but oxidized is the most common synonym.

MALOLACTIC FERMENTATION   A secondary fermentation occurring in some wines, this natural process converts malic acid into softer lactic acid and carbon dioxide, thus reducing the wine's total acidity. It is also accompanied by fairly unpleasant odors that blow off as the gas escapes into the air. If it is not complete before bottling, the gas and undesirable odors remain trapped in the wine, usually spoiling its appeal. Malolactic fermentation is said to add complexity as well as softness to red wines, but, with the exception of high-acid Chardonnay, is considered undesirable in whites.

MATCHSTICK   An unpleasant smell coming from high levels of sulfur dioxide (a widely used chemical preservative); similar to the smell of burnt matches. A cardboard or chemically grassy note often comes across as well. Fairly common in newly bottled white wines, it should dissipate with airing.

MEDIUM SWEET   We use medium sweet to describe wines with residual sugar levels in the range of 1.5–2.9%. Such wines are perceptibly sweet to the taste, yet are not so sweet as to be limited to use with dessert. However, wines labeled medium sweet may be much sweeter than our range, because there is no industry agreement on how the term should be applied. See also Sweet.

MERITAGE   California wineries have adopted this made-up term ("merit" plus "heritage") as the name under which to bottle wines that are blends which mimic the proportions of some wines produced in France's Bordeaux region. For red wines, the grapes allowed are Cabernet Sauvignon, Merlot, Cabernet Franc, Petite Verdot, and Malbec. For whites, it is Sauvignon Blanc and Semillon. The need for a special term has been brought about by government labeling regulations, which (for consumer protection) require wines with varietal names to contain at least 75% of the named variety. Heretofore, when California wineries bottled blends of wines in proportions that did not fit the 75% requirement, they were forced to use a generic name for the wine (Red Table Wine, Claret, etc.) or to make up their own proprietary name (such as Phelps's "Insignia" and Flora Springs'"Trilogy"). Now, many wineries making Bordeaux-style blends, red and white, will label their wines Meritage, often in conjunction with their own proprietary names.

MÉTHODE CHAMPENOISE   The most labor-intensive and costly way to make champagne. Once the wine is placed in the bottle to begin its second fermentation, it never leaves that bottle until it is poured into a glass for drinking. When expertly done, the champagne achieves a persistent effervescence of extremely tiny bubbles. It is the only permitted method for all French Champagnes. On U.S. labels, producers normally state that their wine was made by the *méthode champenoise* and often add "fermented in this bottle." However, if the label reads "fermented in the bottle" or "bottle fermented," chances are that the wine was made by the transfer process.

MOUNTAIN   Labels carrying this term are often attached to wines of lowly jug-wine quality. Most come from grapes grown in the flattest and hottest areas of California, where the mountains are seen only on clear days.

MOUTH-FILLING   Wines with intense round flavors, often in combination with glycerine or slightly low acidity, are said to be mouth-filling. They seem to have character and tactile presence everywhere in the mouth.

MUSCATTY   The character of muscat grapes shows up from time to time in the wines of other varieties—most notably Flora and Gewurztraminer. (See Muscat Blanc in the GRAPES AND WINE TYPES chapter for a more complete description of muscatty character.)

MUST   The unfermented juice of grapes produced by crushing or pressing.

MUSTY   Term for a wine with dank, moldy, or mildewy smells, the result of being stored in improperly cleaned tanks and barrels, being made from moldy grapes, or victimized by a poor cork.

NATURAL   A champagne term indicating that the wine is either totally dry or the driest made by the producer. Variants occasionally seen are *naturel, natur,* and *au naturel.* The term lacks strict definition.

NOSE   The character of a wine ascertained through the olfactory senses is called its nose. This can also be called the aroma and includes the bouquet.

NOUVEAU   A style of light, fruity, youthful red wine often presented as harbinger of the new vintage. In the U.S. some are produced by carbonic maceration, and others are simply bottled as soon as possible. *Nuevo* and *premier* are synonyms. All indicate a wine that is best when young.

NUTTY   Table wines exposed to air will often take on a nutty smell similar to some sherries. The wine is usually oxidized and, thus, flawed.

OAKY   Having aroma or taste elements contributed by the oak barrels or casks in which the wine was aged. Both vanillin, which comes from the oak itself, and toasty or roasted qualities, derived from the char contributed by the open flame used to heat the staves during barrelmaking, are common characteristics of oaky wines.

OFF–DRY   On our scale of describing and measuring sweetness in wine, we equate off-dry with slightly sweet and mean that the residual sugar in the wine is barely perceptible (0.6–1.4% residual sugar). In wine labeling the term has no agreed-on definition and is used by wineries indiscriminately to indicate levels of sweetness from slight to overbearing. (See Sweet for a more complete discussion.)

OILY   The fat, round, slightly slippery tactile impression on the palate created by the combination of high glycerine and slightly low acid. It is a characteristic found and enjoyed in many of the best Chardonnays and also in other big wines, as well as in sweet, late harvest wines.

OLD VINES   This undefined designation originally appeared on wines which were produced entirely from vines planted in the pre-Prohibition era. It is meant to suggest that old vines yield better wines and thus the wine bearing this moniker is *ipso facto* a better wine. But, like other terms without legal definition (see "Reserve," etc.), "Old Vines" can mean whatever the producers want it to mean. Some wineries now use the designation for wines coming from vines as young as 20 years old. As with so many "label-enhancing" terms, this one is only as useful as the reputation of the winery allows it to be.

OVERRIPE   Grapes left on the vine beyond normal maturity develop a concentrated, often dried-out, sometimes raisiny character. Zinfandel can yield very attractive overripe-tasting wines; Chardonnay and Cabernet are generally not enhanced by overripe qualities.

OXIDIZED   Wine exposed too long to air takes on a brownish color, loses its freshness, and often begins to smell and taste like sherry or old apples. Oxidized wines are also called maderized or sherrified.

PERFUMED   Refers to the strong, usually sweet and floral aromas of some white wines, notably Johannisberg Riesling, Gewurztraminer, and Muscat.

PH   A chemical measurement (hydrogen ions in solution) used by wineries—along with grape ripeness and acidity levels—as a possible determinant of grape and wine quality. pH generally affects a wine's color, taste, texture, and long-term stability. The desirable pH range for white table wines is 3.0 to 3.4, and for red table wines 3.3 to 3.6. However, in varieties that mature with a high degree of ripeness, the pH levels of the finished wines can be somewhat higher.

PHYLLOXERA   A vine disease brought about by tiny aphids or root lice that attack *Vitis vinifera* roots. It was widespread in both Europe and California during the late 19th century. Eventually, growers discovered a solution, which entailed grafting vinifera onto native American rootstocks that were naturally resistant to *Phylloxera*. Some were more resistant than others. Unfortunately, one widely used rootstock, AXR1, was chosen more for its adaptability and productivity. By the late 1980s this rootstock began to fail as vineyards in the North Coast and several other regions showed unmistakable signs of phylloxera. Anywhere from 30% to 50% of all coastal vineyards will have been systematically replanted by the year 2000. Several phylloxera-resistant rootstocks are available. Most vines today are grafted, except in the new vineyards of California's Central and South coasts and the Pacific Northwest.

POMACE   The mass of grape skins, seeds, and stems left after a wine has been pressed.

PONDEROUS   Wines that are full in body and low in acid or tannin are ponderous. They have weight on the palate, but nothing to give them balance and structure.

Wine Language

**POWERFUL** Wines high in alcohol (and tannin for reds), often with big flavors, are said to have power. Brawny is a similar concept. The term is applied most often to red wines, but may also be useful to describe big, dry white wines.

**PRESS WINE** Juice extracted under pressure after pressing for white wines and after fermenting for reds. It is the opposite of free-run juice. Press wine has more flavor and aroma, deeper color, and often more tannins—all resulting from longer contact with grape skins. Wineries usually handle it separately and later blend all or part back into the free run and bottle what is left under second labels, using generic or proprietary names; some may sell it off in bulk to other producers.

**PRIVATE RESERVE** This high-minded phrase may once have had meaning for special, long-aged wines. Lacking external regulation, it is now used inconsistently. It should apply to wines deemed worthy of special attention. Sometimes it does so, but not often enough to serve as a reliable guide.

**PRODUCED AND BOTTLED BY** Indicates that the named winery crushed, fermented, and bottled at least 75% of the wine in the bottle. Quite different from the similar-sounding "made and bottled by."

**PROPRIETOR S RESERVE** A variant of "Private Reserve."

**PRUNEY** Very overripe, dried-out grapes give a pruney, pungent quality that is undesirable in fine wines.

**PUCKERY** Used to describe wines high in tannin, which tend to dry out the mouth and cause one's teeth and cheeks to feel as though they were stuck together.

**RACKING** The most traditional way of clarifying a wine: transferring it from one container to another, leaving the precipitated matter behind. This labor-intensive practice has been augmented (and often replaced) by filtration, fining, and centrifugation.

**RAISINY** Somewhat rich, almost caramel, concentrated, dried-grape taste. Some wines, such as late harvest Zinfandel and port, can be pleasant with a little raisiny character, but most other wines are not. Some wines made from Central Valley–grown grapes taste raisiny because the excessive heat of the area dries out the grapes even as they are ripening on the vine.

**REFINED** Said of wines that are in balance, have distinct varietal character, and are not brawny or out of proportion. The term is almost always used in a highly favorable context with varieties that tend to be powerful if left unchecked.

**REGIONS I–V** A classification of grape-growing regions according to the amount of heat to which the vines are exposed during the growing season. Its basis is the "degree day" system, using 50° F. as the base line. (There is almost no shoot growth below 50° F.) The mean temperature above 50° F. each day during the period of vine growth is multiplied by the number of days in the period, giving the total of degree days.

Using the degree-day system California is divided into five climatic categories. Region I is the coolest (fewer than 2,500 degree days) and is comparable to European areas where Johannisberg Riesling and Gewurztraminer thrive. Region II is warmer (2,501–3,000 degree days) and is comparable to Bordeaux. Region III (3,001–3,500) is comparable to the Rhone region in France and to Tuscany in Italy. Region IV (3,501–4,000) compares with the Midi of France, and Region V (4,000+) experiences conditions comparable to Mediterranean growing areas.

**RESIDUAL SUGAR** A statement of the unfermented grape sugar in a finished wine expressed either as the percentage by volume or the percentage by weight. Thus, residual sugar either of 2.6% or of 2.6gm/100ml is exactly the same. Such information helps determine how the wine should be enjoyed and is most often found on sweet-finished white wines. For a detailed breakdown, see Sweet.

RICH  Wines with generous, full, pleasant flavors, usually sweet and round in nature, are described as rich. In dry wines, richness may be supplied by high alcohol and glycerine, by complex flavors, and by vanilla, oaky character. Decidedly sweet wines are also described as rich when the sweetness is backed up by fruity, often ripe flavors.

RIPE  The desirable elements within each grape's own special varietal character come out when the grapes reach optimum maturity in the vineyard. Ripe-tasting wine usually has round flavors, tends toward being rich, and is more sweetly fruity than other wines possessing the same levels of scientifically measurable sweetness.

ROTTEN EGG  The smell of hydrogen sulfide ($H_2S$) in wine, a flaw that ranges from mildly bothersome at low levels to vile at very high levels.

ROUGH  Used for the grainy, somewhat puckery, tactile sensation of young, tannic red wines. A related term, astringent, refers to more noticeable levels of harsh tannins.

ROUND  Used to describe both flavors and tactile sensations. In both contexts, round connotes completeness, the absence of angularity or any dominating characteristic. Round flavors are balanced and tend toward richness and ripeness. On the palate, round wines usually are slightly low in acid, often have glycerine or residual sugar to fill in the angles or cover any roughness, and are low in tannin.

SEC  Literally means "dry." However, tradition is that a champagne labeled *sec* falls in the sweet-to-very-sweet range.

SELECT  Implies that the wine has special qualities. Lacking legal definition and consistent application, it most often means nothing.

SELECT HARVEST  Absolutely inconsistent usage and, therefore, meaningless.

SELECTED LATE HARVEST  Seen on white wines, primarily Johannisberg Rieslings, but lacking consistent usage. A few producers use it to indicate that the grapes were riper and the wine finished sweeter than a late harvest style. However, the phrase has different meanings from winery to winery.

SHARP  The slightly biting tactile sensation of excess acidity, or high acetic acid, and the accompanying bite in the taste.

SHERRIFIED  When table wines are exposed to air over long periods, they become oxidized. One of the signs of oxidation is a nutty aroma and taste reminiscent of sherry. Maderized is a comparable term.

SIMPLE  Wines with very straightforward character—immediately accessible with no nuances or complex notes. Most of the world's wines are simple when compared to the highly praised château and estate bottlings, yet can be delightful if clean, fruity, and fairly well balanced.

SLIGHTLY SWEET  Most appropriately used to describe the levels of sweetness lying just above the threshold of perception (in the range of 0.6–1.4% sugar). Off-dry is a similar term. See Sweet.

SOFT  Describes wines low in acid or tannin (sometimes both) that are, therefore, not firm and hard on the palate. Also used for wines with reduced alcohol levels and less of the consequent hot impact of higher alcohol.

SOLERA  A blending system used for both sherries and ports. A *solera* consists of barrels stacked in tiers with the oldest wine on the bottom tier and the youngest on top. As wine is drawn from the oldest barrel for bottling, younger wine from each tier is moved forward a stage. The objective is to blend for uniformity and consistency. About 10 California wineries and several in New York and Michigan maintain *soleras*.

SOUR  When wine is so high in acid that it is out of balance, it tastes sour or very tart. As a tasting term, it is used for a wine high in acetic acid and volatile acidity.

SPICY  Denotes somewhat pungent, often attractive aromas and flavors suggestive of cloves, cinnamon, anise, caraway, and similar substances. The most typically spicy grape is Gewurztraminer; other varieties that may show lesser degrees of spiciness are Zinfandel and Chardonnay.

SPRITZY  Wines with fairly modest degrees of pinpoint carbonation are described as spritzy. In slightly sweet and medium-sweet white wines, a little spritz can give a lively impression that enhances the wine's balance. Most dry wines are not enhanced by spritziness.

STALE  Refers to wines that have lost their fresh, youthful qualities and have taken on dull, tired, sometimes stagnant qualities—often from being stored too long at the winery in large containers before bottling. Tanky is a related term.

STRUCTURE  A wine's structure is determined by the interplay of those elements that create tactile impressions in the mouth: acid, tannin, glycerine, alcohol, body. It is a term that needs a modifier like firm, sturdy, or weak to be meaningful.

SUPPLE  Used most often to describe the tactile impression of red wines possessing general amiability and underlying softness in spite of fairly firm structure, ample acid, and noticeable tannin. Young, hard wines are often allowed to age until they achieve more agreeable, supple qualities.

SUR LIES  Wines aged *sur lies* are kept in contact with the dead yeast cells and other sedimentary matter that remain when the fermentation is completed. In the last decade, this practice has become fairly commonplace in the making of Chardonnay and is followed also on occasion for Sauvignon Blanc. The hope is that *sur lies* aging will add complex quality to the wine—often akin to a toasty, roasted-grain character.

SWEET  One of the four basic tastes perceived by the tongue, as opposed to the hundreds of flavors that we actually experience with our olfactory senses. The presence of sugar (or occasionally of glycerine) is required to taste sweetness, according to the wine scientist.

A few wine writers, ourselves included, have attempted to define sweetness levels in terms that can be applied consistently. The gradations of sweetness appearing in *Connoisseurs' Guide to California Wine* and adopted in this book are:

| | |
|---|---|
| Less than 0.5% residual sugar | Dry |
| 0.6–1.4% residual sugar | Slightly Sweet |
| 1.5–2.9% residual sugar | Medium Sweet |
| 3.0–5.9% residual sugar | Sweet |
| More than 5.9% residual sugar | Very Sweet |

The scents of intense fruitiness, of ripe or overripe grapes, and of vanilla oakiness often seem to be sweet, especially when found in conjunction with each other. For that reason, when we use sweet to describe a wine's aroma, we add other descriptive terms to indicate the probable source of the sweet scents. The sweet taste of wine may be similarly modified when describing a nonsugary sweetness. Varying levels of acid, alcohol, and tannin and the inherent bitterness of some grape varieties balance against sugar and affect the level of sweetness that is perceived in wine.

TANKY   Used for the tired, somewhat dank qualities that show up in wines aged too long in large tanks.

TANNIN   The puckery substance in red wines and a few whites is tannin. It is derived primarily from grape skins, grape seeds and stems, and the barrels in which wine is aged. Brawny, young red wines usually have substantial tannin that requires years of cellar aging to soften. Tannin serves as a natural preservative that helps the wine develop, but must be kept in balance with depth and potential. Excessively tannic wines can remain tannic long after the flavors have peaked. Tannin can dry out the aftertaste and can taste bitter if not kept in balance. Astringent is a related term.

TART   The sharp taste of acidity in wine is described as tart or sour.

THIN   Wines lacking body and depth are known as thin. Such wines tend to feel and taste watery. The French describe such wines as meager—a very apt word.

TIGHT   Young wines with angular flavors and a hard tactile impression in the mouth are called tight. "Closed-in" and "dumb" are related terms.

TOASTY   Toasty smells and flavors in wines are derived from the oak barrels in which the wines are aged, and from contact with dead yeast cells and other sedimentary matter following the completion of fermentation. This character is thought by some to be particularly attractive in Chardonnay and sparkling wine, and may also be observed in other varieties when the winemaker is seeking an extra measure of character and complexity.

TOPPING   Winery practice of adding wine to barrels and tanks to replace what was lost by evaporation. It minimizes contact with air and, thus, oxidation.

TRANSFER PROCESS   A modern method of making bottle-fermented champagne. At the end of its second fermentation, the wine is poured out of the bottle into pressurized tanks where it is filtered to remove the sediment prior to being rebottled. Such champagnes may be labeled "bottle fermented" or "transfer process," often accompanied by "fermented in the bottle."

UNDERRIPE   When grapes fail to reach maturity on the vine, their wines usually lack round flavors and tactile impressions. Typically, their varietal character remains undeveloped, they possess high acidity, and they display green flavors.

UNFILTERED   Indicates that the wine achieved its state of clarification and stabilization without being filtered. However, this does not mean that other cellar treatments, such as fining, centrifugation, and cold stabilization, were necessarily also avoided. The trend today is for more and more small-volume producers to bottle their wines unfiltered.

UNFINED   Seen on many Cabernets and Zinfandels to suggest the wine received minimal treatment. It means the wine was not fined, though it could well have been filtered or clarified by other methods.

VARIETAL   A wine named after the predominant grape variety in its composition. Regulations enacted in the mid-80s require a wine to have a minimum of 75% of the given grape in its makeup to qualify as a varietal. Until the 80s, varietal wines needed only to contain at least 51% of the named variety.

VARIETAL CHARACTER   The unique combination of smells, tastes, and tactile impressions typically offered by a grape when ripened to maturity. The most highly prized wine grapes have distinctive and attractive varietal character. Lesser grapes have less distinct varietal character. And some grapes, including such familiar names as Green Hungarian and Grey Riesling, have virtually no uniquely identifiable character. In Zinfandel the berrylike taste is the typical varietal character; in Cabernet it is black currants; and in Chardonnay it is a round, oily texture and generous, round, fruity flavors. Breed is a related concept.

VEGETAL   The smell and taste of some wines contain elements reminiscent of plants and vegetables. In Cabernet Sauvignon a small amount of this vegetal quality is said to be part of varietal character. However, when the vegetal element takes over the wine or when it shows up in wines in which it does not belong, those wines are considered to be flawed. Wine scientists have been able to identify the chemical constituent that makes wines smell like asparagus and bell peppers, but are not sure why it occurs more often in Central Coast vineyards than in others.

VERY SWEET   In our system of differentiation, wines that possess 6.0% or more residual sugar are described as very sweet. Their obvious, inescapable sweetness leads generally to enjoyment with dessert or by themselves after the meal. Some of California's most exciting (and expensive) wines fall into this category, including late harvest Rieslings and Gewurztraminers.

VINOUS   Literally meaning "winelike," vinous is usually applied to dull wines lacking enough character to be described in more vivid terms. Vinous and its noun, vinosity, are used with relatively clean wines.

VINTAGE DATE   To give a wine a vintage date, the winery must have made at least 95% of the wine from grapes harvested in the stated calendar year. Such dates provide useful information about a wine's freshness or its aging requirements. However, a vintage-dated wine is not necessarily a "vintage" wine, even though most high-quality wines carry vintage dates.

VINTED BY   A pleasant-sounding but meaningless phrase that may be used on wine labels even when the named winery had no more involvement with the wine than purchasing it in bulk from another winery and bottling it upon arrival.

VITICULTURAL AREA   This is now an official legal designation, also known as "American Viticultural Area" (AVA), representing an effort by the federal government to upgrade the use of place names and grape-growing regions on wine labels when the area is smaller than a state and does not conform to county boundaries. Interested parties must petition the government and make a case for the uniqueness of the particular region on the basis of climate, soil, elevation, history, and definable boundaries. Beginning in 1983, only those areas approved and established may be used on labels and in advertising. The federal requirement is that 85% of the wine in question be made from grapes grown within that specified Viticultural Area. If the wine is a varietal bottling, a minimum of 75% of that wine must be made from the designated grape variety.

VITIS LABRUSCA   A species of wild grapevine believed to be native to North America. Few of the grapes used to make wine are pure labrusca because most have been accidentally cross-pollinated with other species, including vinifera. All labrusca-type wines share, to varying degrees, a characteristic aroma and flavor traditionally and inexplicably described as foxy. This is another way of saying that they smell like Concord grape juice and have a strong grapey personality. The best-known wine varieties are Concord, Catawba, Delaware, and Niagara.

VITIS VINIFERA   The species of grapevine responsible for the world's best wines. It probably originated in the Mediterranean basin and subsequently was cultivated throughout Europe. Today, the species is often referred to as the Old World or European vine. The vinifera (wine-bearer) family may have close to 5,000 members, but fewer than 100 are considered important as wine grapes. As a family, vinifera vines require sufficient heat to bring the grapes to ripeness and are not at all hardy to freezing winter spells. They are also vulnerable to numerous parasites and to many fungus diseases. Vinifera vines also interbreed easily and do not breed true when propagated from seeds.

Freezing winter temperatures have stymied their cultivation in many parts of the U.S.; high summer humidity encouraging various molds has eliminated their cultivation in many Southern states as well. With its mild, rainy winter and long, dry, warm summer, California offers a climate generally favorable to vinifera vines. Parts of Washington, Oregon, Michigan, and New York, and several Mid-Atlantic states have also been successful in cultivating the European vine.

VOLATILE    Denotes aromas that come out of the glass aggressively, almost fiercely. They are usually caused by high levels of volatile acidity and alcohol or by chemical faults.

VOLATILE ACID    The smell of ethyl acetate and the palate sharpness of acetic acid (they almost always occur simultaneously) are often referenced collectively as volatile acid or volatile acidity. Occasionally wine labels will tell the level of volatile acidity (VA) in the wine. In general, the lower the better. The threshold at which most tasters notice VA in wine is just under 0.1%—more than most wines contain. The legal limit of volatile acidity is just over 0.1%.

WARM    Some red wines—Cabernet, Merlot, Petite Sirah, and Zinfandel—possess both flavor intensity and balance to offset their high alcohol. Such wines are described as warm. This is a positive attribute, unlike the term hot, which refers to excessive alcohol.

WEIGHTY    Term for wines with a heavy, full-bodied sense of presence on the palate.

WOODY    The smell or taste of the wooden containers in which wines are aged—usually strongest for wines aged in new barrels. The aromas and flavors of some wines are substantially benefited by the extra dimension garnered from the wood. However, wines that stay too long in the barrel become excessively woody and lose their interest. Oaky is a closely related term.

YEASTY    Occasionally a very young wine will be so fresh from the fermenter when released to market that its character is affected by the taste of the fermentation yeast, reminiscent of freshly baked bread. In sparkling wines, the term refers to the toasty, vaguely soylike character imparted to the wine by the dead (autolyzed) yeast during its secondary fermentation and bottle-aging *(en tirage)* phase.

A NOTE ON THE TYPE

The text of this book was set in Palatino, a typeface designed between 1948 and 1952 by the noted German typographer Hermann Zapf. Named after Giovanbattista Palatino, a writing master of Renaissance Italy, Palatino was the first of Zapf's typefaces to be introduced in America. The display and numerals in the text were set in Bembo, cut by Francesco Griffo, one of the most celebrated goldsmiths of the mid-fifteenth century. Both of these faces are admired for their balance, proportion, and great legibility.

Composed by ComCom, an RR Donnelley & Sons Company,
Allentown, Pennsylvania.
Printed and bound by Quebecor Printing,
Martinsburg, West Virginia.